797,885 Books

are available to read at

Forgotten Books

www.ForgottenBooks.com

Forgotten Books' App
Available for mobile, tablet & eReader

ISBN 978-0-331-06704-0
PIBN 11100439

This book is a reproduction of an important historical work. Forgotten Books uses state-of-the-art technology to digitally reconstruct the work, preserving the original format whilst repairing imperfections present in the aged copy. In rare cases, an imperfection in the original, such as a blemish or missing page, may be replicated in our edition. We do, however, repair the vast majority of imperfections successfully; any imperfections that remain are intentionally left to preserve the state of such historical works.

Forgotten Books is a registered trademark of FB &c Ltd.
Copyright © 2017 FB &c Ltd.
FB &c Ltd, Dalton House, 60 Windsor Avenue, London, SW19 2RR.
Company number 08720141. Registered in England and Wales.

For support please visit www.forgottenbooks.com

1 MONTH OF FREE READING

at

www.ForgottenBooks.com

By purchasing this book you are eligible for one month membership to ForgottenBooks.com, giving you unlimited access to our entire collection of over 700,000 titles via our web site and mobile apps.

To claim your free month visit:
www.forgottenbooks.com/free1100439

* Offer is valid for 45 days from date of purchase. Terms and conditions apply.

English
Français
Deutsche
Italiano
Español
Português

www.forgottenbooks.com

Mythology Photography **Fiction** Fishing Christianity **Art** Cooking Essays Buddhism Freemasonry Medicine **Biology** Music **Ancient Egypt** Evolution Carpentry Physics Dance Geology **Mathematics** Fitness Shakespeare **Folklore** Yoga Marketing **Confidence** Immortality Biographies Poetry **Psychology** Witchcraft Electronics Chemistry History **Law** Accounting **Philosophy** Anthropology Alchemy Drama Quantum Mechanics Atheism Sexual Health **Ancient History Entrepreneurship** Languages Sport Paleontology Needlework Islam **Metaphysics** Investment Archaeology Parenting Statistics Criminology **Motivational**

A TOPOGRAPHICAL DICTIONARY OF YORKSHIRE;

CONTAINING THE NAMES OF ALL THE
TOWNS, VILLAGES, HAMLETS, GENTLEMEN'S SEATS, &c.

IN THE

County of York,

Alphabetically arranged under the Heads of the

NORTH, EAST, AND WEST-RIDINGS,
AND THE AINSTY;

THE RESPECTIVE DISTANCES

From two, three, or more Market or Post-Towns,

ALSO IN WHAT

Parish, Wapentake, Division, and Liberty
They are situate;

THE NAMES OF ALL THE
ACTING MAGISTRATES,
LORDS AND CHIEF BAILIFFS OF LIBERTIES,
With Directions for Warrants;

The Clerks of Peace, and their Deputies,
Treasurers, Coroners, Chief Constables, Clerks of General
And Subdivision Meetings of Lieutenantcy, Bailiffs, &c.
With their respective Residences;

The Markets and Fairs,

AND THE DAYS ON WHICH THEY ARE HELD;

THE NAMES OF ALL THE

BANKERS, and the PRINCIPAL INNS;

POPULATION of every TOWNSHIP, according to Returns made to
Parliament in 1801;

RISE AND COURSE OF RIVERS AND CANALS;
ASSIZES AND SESSIONS.

BY THOMAS LANGDALE.

NORTHALLERTON:
PRINTED AND SOLD BY J. LANGDALE;
BY WILKIE AND ROBINSON, PATERNOSTER-ROW, LONDON,
And by the principal Booksellers in the County of York.

1809.

Entered at Stationers' Hall.

PREFACE.

IN offering this Work to the Public, the first NOMINA VILLARUM, on this plan, ever yet attempted, it may seem proper, and indeed necessary, briefly to state from what sources the intelligence for the present work has been derived, and to furnish introductory explanations of the method observed, and of the information to be expected by the reader.

The Population Abstracts, and Returns relating to the Poor have furnished the names of places, far more correctly than could be obtained by former compilers; but that in a work comprising so many thousand names, errors should not be found, particularly relative to distances, which in the remote parts of the county were found extremely difficult to ascertain, is more than the compiler will venture to assert. He can, however, assure the reader, that his utmost endeavours have been to render it as correct as possible, that various sources of information have been explored, and that he travelled over the greatest part of the West, and various parts of the North and East-Ridings for that purpose, and from his correspondence with the Chief Constables and others, in the different Ridings, fully competent to give such information as was required, to

PREFACE.

whom he is much indebted for Returns made, according to Schedules sent to them, he flatters himself, that it will be found as correct, as the nature of the subject will admit. For the Markets and Fairs, and names of Bankers, he is indebted to many respectable Tradesmen in the different Market-Towns in the County.—The names of Acting Magistrates, Lords and Chief Bailiffs, Clerks of the Peace, Coroners, Chief Constables, Bailiffs, Sessions, &c. are taken from the Orders printed for the use of Magistrates for each Riding, and corrected to the present time.

The Orthography of every name is given according to the present use and mode of spelling; and where any doubt has arisen, the other names in use have been added. After the name of the Place, the Parish, Wapentake, and Liberty, if any, in which it is situate, the Gentlemen's Seats, the Distances from two, three, or more Market or Post Towns, the City and Boroughs, which send Members to Parliament, the Population of each Township, according to returns made to Parliament, in 1801.*

The expence and labour attending the completion of the work, have far exceeded any calculation that could be made; but the latter has been considerably lessened by the ready communication of several Gentlemen, who have favoured the Compiler with complete and ample information, and to whom he takes this opportunity of returning his sincere thanks; and solicits further communications, if any errors should appear, that nothing may be wanting to render a future Impression more correct, which he may venture to anticipate, will, ere long, be called for.

* Places having no Population annexed, are not of themselves Townships, but included in those which are.

YORKSHIRE.

YORKSHIRE,* in the times of the Ancient Britains, was inhabited by the Brigantes, whose territories included our present Counties of Cumberland, Durham, Lancashire, Westmoreland, and Yorkshire.

When the Emperor Constantine divided Britain into three parts, viz. *Britannia Prima*, *Britannia Secunda*, and *Maxima Cæsariensis*, this County was included in the last, and York was the Capital City of it.

When the Saxons had settled themselves in this part of the Island, and divided it amongst their leaders into Seven Kingdoms, this County was part of the Kingdom of Northumberland; which being divided into two parts, *Deira*, and *Bernicia*, this County was under the Government of the King of *Deira*, who, after a Succession of Six Kings of Bernicia, in the space of twenty-seven Years, became master of the whole; and continued until the West Saxons subdued the other Six Kingdoms of the Saxons, and made the whole a Monarchy.

Yorkshire is by far the largest County in the Kingdom, containing about 3,698,380 Acres of Land, with a Population of 858,892 Persons.

It is 130 miles long from East to West, and 90 broad from north to South, and 460 in circumference. It is bounded on the East by the German Ocean, on the South by Derby, Nottingham, and Lincolnshires; on the West by Lancashire, and a small part of Cheshire; and on the North by the Counties of Durham and Westmoreland.

The North-Riding† is bounded by the River Tees on the

* Called EOFORWICSCIRE by the Saxons.

† In the Division of England by the Saxons, for the better Government of it, there were Tythings, Hundreds or Wapentakes, and Trithings or Ridings.

YORKSHIRE.

North, which separates it from the County of Durham; the German Ocean on the East; the East-Riding on the South-East; and by the Ainsty, and the West-Riding on the South; and the County of Westmoreland on the West. It is divided into 12 Wapentakes, containing 5 boroughs, viz. Richmond, Scarborough, Northallerton, Malton, and Thirsk, 31,512 Houses, and 155,506 Inhabitants.

The East-Riding is bounded on the East by the German Ocean; on the South by the Humber; on the West by the Rivers Ouse and Derwent; and on the North by the latter and the little River Hertford. It is divided into 6 Wapentakes, containing 3 Boroughs, viz. Beverley, Hedon, and Hull, 25,781 Houses, and 139,433 Inhabitants.

The West-Riding is bounded on the East by the Ainsty and the River Ouse, which separates it from the East-Riding; on the South by parts of Nottinghamshire and Derbyshire; on the West by parts of Cheshire, Lancashire, and Westmoreland; and on the North by the North-Riding. It is divided into 10 Wapentakes, containing 5 Boroughs, viz. Ripon, Pontefract, Boroughbridge, Aldborough, and Knaresborough, containing 111,146 Houses, and 563,953 Inhabitants. The whole County contains thirteen Boroughs and one City, which sends thirty Members to Parliament.

The Ainsty,* accounted a twentieth part of the County at large, is now a District on the West-side of York, under the jurisdiction of the Lord-Mayor, Aldermen, and Sheriffs of the City, to which it was annexed the 27th of Henry the 6th, though before it was a Wapentake of the West-Riding, and has ever since been called the County of the City of York. The whole District was anciently a forest, but dis-forested by Charters of King Richard the 1st, and King John.

A Tything consisted of Ten Families, subject to the care of the Overseer or Tything-man, who was to be answerable for the behaviour of the Masters of those Families, as they were of their Children or Servants. Ten of these Tythings made a Hundred or Wapentake, from the Saxon word Wæpon, i e arms, and tac, a touch. For it appears by the Laws of King Edward, that when any one came to take the Government of a Wapentake, upon a day appointed, all that owed suit and service of that Hundred, came to meet their new Governor, at the usual place of Rendezvous. He, upon his arrival, set up his Spear, and took fealty of them; the ceremony of which was, that all who were present, touched the Governor's Lance, with their own, in token of confirmation, in as much, as by the touch of each others arms, they had entered into an agreement to stand by one another. A similar custom prevailed among the Romans at the meeting of the Centumviri. Ridings or Trithings, were the third part of a County, and to them appeals were made in cases not determinable in the wapentakes.

*Ainsty, from Ancientcy, to denote its Antiquity; or more probably from the German Word, Antossen, implying a bound, or limit. CAMDEN.

NAMES OF WAPENTAKES.

NORTH-RIDING.

ALLERTONSHIRE,
BIRDFORTH,
BULMER,
GILLING-EAST,
GILLING-WEST,
HALIKELD,
HANG-EAST,
HANG-WEST,
LANGBARUGH,
PICKERING-LYTHE,
RYDALE,
WHITBY-STRAND.

EAST-RIDING.

BUCKROSE,
DICKERING,
HARTHILL,
HOLDERNESS,
HOWDENSHIRE,
OUSE-AND-DERWENT,
TOWN AND COUNTY OF KINGSTON UPON HULL.

WEST-RIDING.

AGBRIGG AND MORLEY,
BARKSTON-ASH,
CLARO,
EWCROSS,
OSGOLDCROSS,
SKIRACK,
STAINCLIFFE,*
STAINCROSS,
STRAFFORTH AND TICKHILL,
AND AINSTY.

* Staincliffe and Ewcross are treated in this work, as two distinct wapentakes; and though only two Chief Constables are at present appointed, yet it seems that there were formerly three, viz. two for Staincliffe, and one for Ewcross, as appears by the Estreat Book, of the year, 1776.

A TOPOGRAPHICAL DICTIONARY OF YORKSHIRE.

NORTH-RIDING.

ABBOTSIDE, HIGH, *(a Vale)* in the parish of Aysgarth, wapentake of Hang-West, liberty of Richmondshire; 1 mile from Hawes, 6 from Askrigg.—Population 559.

ABBOTSIDE, LOW, *(a Vale)* in the parish of Aysgarth, wapentake of Hang-West, liberty of Richmondshire; 1 mile from Hawes, 6 from Askrigg.—Population 235.

ACKLAM, in the parish of Acklam, west-division of the wapentake and liberty of Langbargh, *(the seat of Thomas Hustler, Esq.)* 7 miles from Yarm, 7 from Stokesley, 10 from Guisbrough.—Population 98.

ACRE-INGS, in the parish of Lythe, east-division of the wapentake and liberty of Langbargh; 8 miles from Whitby, 14 from Stokesley.

ADDLEBOROUGH, *(a Hill)* in the parish of Aysgarth, wapentake of Hang West, liberty of Richmondshire; 2 miles from Askrigg, 9 from Leyburn.

AGGLETHORPE, in the parish of Coverham, wapentake of Hang-West, liberty of Richmondshire; 3 miles from Middleham, 4 from Leyburn, 11¼ from Richmond.—Population 156.

AIKBER, in the parish of Fingall, wapentake of Hang-West, liberty of Richmondshire; 4 miles from Leyburn, 5 from Middleham, 6 from Richmond.—Population 29.

AINDERBY-MYERS, in the parish of Hornby, wapentake of Hang-East, liberty of Richmondshire; 3 miles from Catterick, 4 from Bedale, 9 from Richmond.—Pop. 69.

AINDERBY-STEEPLE, in the parish of Ainderby-Steeple, wapentake of Gilling-East, liberty of Richmondshire; 3 miles from Northallerton, 5 from Bedale.—Population 207.

AINDERBY-QUERNHOW, in the parish of Pickhill, wa-

A

pentake of Halikeld, liberty of Richmondshire; 6 miles from Thirsk, 8 from Ripon, 8 from Bedale.—Population 78.

AINTHORP, in the parish of Danby, east-division of the wapentake and liberty of Langbaugh; 9 miles from Guisbrough, 13 from Stokesley.

AIRSHOLME, in the parish of Stainton, west-division of the wapentake and liberty of Langbaugh; 4 miles from Stockton, *(Durham)* 8 from Yarm.

AIRYHOLME, in the parish of Hovingham, wapentake of Rydale; 7 miles from Malton, 8 from Helmsley, 8½ from Kirby-Moorside.—Population 31.

AISENBY, in the parish of Topcliffe, wapentake of Halikeld, liberty of Allertonshire; 5¼ miles from Boroughbridge, 6 from Thirsk, 12¼ from Northallerton.—Population 215.

AISKEW, in the parish of Bedale, wapentake of Hang-East, liberty of Richmondshire; ¼ mile from Bedale, 7¼ from Northallerton, 11¼ from Richmond.—Population 500.

AISLABY, in the parish of Middleton, wapentake and liberty of Pickering-Lythe; *(the seat of Thomas Hayes, Esq.)* 1¼ miles from Pickering, 6¼ from Kirby-Moorside, 10¼ from Malton.—Population 163.

AISLABY, in the parish of Whitby, east-division of the wapentake and liberty of Langbaugh; *(the Seats of Mark Noble, and J. Benson, Esqrs.)* 3 miles from Whitby, 19 from Guisbrough, 19 from Pickering.—Population 211.

ALDBY, in the parish of Bossall, wapentake of Bulmer; *(Aldby Park, the seat of Henry Darley, Esq.)* 10 miles from Malton, 10 from York, 15 from Easingwold.

ALDBROUGH, in the parish of St. John, Stanwick, wapentake of Gilling-West, liberty of Richmondshire; 7 miles from Richmond, 7 from Darlington, *(Durham.)*—Pop. 461.

ALDBROUGH, in the parish of Masham, wapentake of Hang-East; 2 miles from Masham, 6 from Bedale.

ALDWARK, in the parish of Alne, wapentake of Bulmer, a part in the liberty of St. Peter; 5 miles from Boroughbridge, 6 from Easingwold, 13 from York.—Population 173.

ALLERSTON, in the parish of Allerston, wapentake and liberty of Pickering-Lythe; 5¼ miles from Pickering, 13¼ from Scarborough, 12 from Malton.—Population 319.

ALLERTHORPE, in the parish of Burniston, wapentake of Halikeld, liberty of Allertonshire; 5 miles from Bedale, 8 from Thirsk, 8 from Northallerton, 12 from Ripon.

ALLERTON-NORTH, see *Northallerton.*

ALLOWTHORNE, in the parishes of Hornby and Patrick-Brompton, wapentake of Hang-West, liberty of Richmondshire; 5 miles from Richmond, 5½ from Leyburn, 7 from

NORTH-RIDING.

Middleham.—Population 67.

ALNE, in the parish of Alne, wapentake of Bulmer, a part in the liberty of St. Peter; *(the seat of E. S. Strangeway, Esq.)* 4 miles from Easingwold, 6 from Boroughbridge, 11 from York.—Population 342.

AMOTHERBY, in the parish of Appleton-le-street, wapentake of Rydale; 2½ miles from Malton, 11 from Kirby-Moorside, 15 from Helmsley.—Population 285.

AMPLEFORTH, in the parishes of Ampleforth and Oswaldkirk, wapentakes of Rydale and Birdforth, a part in the liberty of St. Peter; 4 miles from Helmsley, 9 from Kirby-Moorside, 16 from Malton.—Population 405.

AMPLEFORTH OUT-HOUSES, in the parish of Oswaldkirk, wapentake of Rydale; 3½ miles from Helmsley, 8¼ from Kirby-Moorside, 15 from Malton.

ANGRAM, in the parish of Grinton, wapentake of Gilling-West, liberty of Richmondshire; 6 miles from Askrigg, 12 from Reeth, 22 from Richmond.

ANGRAM, in the parish of Coxwold, wapentake of Birdforth, liberty of Ripon; 5 miles from Easingwold, 8 from Thirsk.—Population 22.

ANNGROVE, in the parish of Ayton, west-division of the wapentake and liberty of Langbarugh; 2 miles from Stokesley, 6 from Yarm, 6¼ from Guisbrough.

APPLEGARTH, in the parish of Marske, wapentake of Gilling-West, liberty of Richmondshire; 6 miles from Richmond, 7 from Reeth.

APPLETON-LE-MOOR, in the parish of Lastingham, wapentake of Rydale; 4 miles from Kirby-Moorside, 10 from Helmsley, 14 from Malton.—Population 254.

APPLETON, EAST, in the parish of Catterick, wapentake of Hang-East, liberty of Richmondshire; 5 miles from Bedale, 7 from Richmond.—Population 95.

APPLETON-LE-STREET, in the parish of Appleton-le-street, wapentake of Rydale; 4 miles from Malton, 9 from Kirby-Moorside, 14 from Helmsley.—Population 151.

APPLETON, WEST, in the parish of Catterick, wapentake of Hang-East, liberty of Richmondshire; 6 miles from Bedale, 6 from Richmond.

APPLETON-WISKE, in the parish of Great-Smeaton, west-division of the wapentake and liberty of Langbarugh; 7 miles from Yarm, 7½ from Northallerton.—Population 451.

ARDEN, in the parish of Hawnby, wapentake of Birdforth, *(Arden Hall, the seat of Charles Tancred, Esq.)* 7¼ miles from Thirsk, 10 from Helmsley, 10 from Northallerton.—Population 126.

ARDEN-SIDE, in the parish of Hawnby, wapentake of Birdforth; 8 miles from Thirsk, 10 from Helmsley, 10 from Northallerton.

ARKENGARTHDALE, in the parish of Arkengarthdale, wapentake of Gilling-West, liberty of Richmondshire; 3 miles from Reeth, 13 from Askrigg, 13 from Richmond.—Population 1,186.

ARNCLIFFE, in the parish of Arncliffe, west-division of the wapentake and liberty of Langbarugh; (*the seat of Mrs Mauleverer,*) 8 miles from Northallerton, 8 from Stokesley, 13 from Thirsk.—Population 253.

ARNGILL, in the parish of Romaldkirk, wapentake of Gilling-West, liberty of Richmondshire; 5 miles from Barnardcastle, (*Durham*) 8 from Greta-bridge, 20 from Richmond.

ASHGILL, in the parish of Coverham, wapentake of Hang-West; 2 miles from Middleham, 4 from Leyburn, 12¼ from Richmond.

ASKE, in the parish of Easby, wapentake of Gilling-West, liberty of Richmondshire; (*the seat of Lord Dundas,*) 2 miles from Richmond, 5 from Catterick.—Population 73.

ASKRIGG, in the parish of Aysgarth, wapentake of Hang-West, liberty of Richmondshire; 5 miles from Hawes, 11 from Reeth, 12 from Leyburn, 18 from Richmond, 19 from Sedberg, 246 from London.—*Market*, Thursday.—*Fairs*, May 11, and first Thursday in June, for Woollen-Cloth, &c. October 28 and 29, for Horned Cattle, Sheep, &c —*Principal Inn*, Red Lion.—Population 751.

AYSDALE, in the parish of Guisbrough, east-division of the wapentake and of liberty of Langbarugh; 3 miles from Guisbrough, 11 from Stokesley, 18 from Whitby.

AYSGARTH, in the parish of Aysgarth, wapentake of Hang-West, liberty of Richmondshire; 4 miles from Askrigg, 7 from Leyburn.—Population 268.

AYTON, in the parish of Ayton, west-division of the wapentake and liberty of Langbarugh; 3 miles from Stokesley, 5 from Guisbrough.—Population 865.

AYTON, LITTLE, in the parish of Ayton, west-division of the wapentake and liberty of Langbarugh; 3¼ miles from Stokesley, 6 from Guisbrough, 12 from Yarm.—Pop. 69.

AYTON, EAST, in the parish of Seamor, wapentake and liberty of Pickering-Lythe; 5 miles from Scarborough, 13 from Pickering, 17 from Malton.—Population 290.

AYTON, WEST, in the parish of Hutton-Bushell, wapentake and liberty of Pickering-Lythe; 5 miles from Scarborough, 13 from Pickering, 17 from Malton.—Population 102.

NORTH-RIDING.

B.

BAGBY, in the parish of Kirby-Knowle, wapentake of Birdforth; 4 miles from Thirsk, 7 from Easingwold.—Pop. 213.

BAINBRIDGE, in the parish of Aysgarth, wapentake of Hang-West, liberty of Richmondshire; 1¼ miles from Askrigg, 4 from Hawes, 19½ from Richmond.—Population 785.

BALDERSBY, in the parish of Topcliffe, wapentake of Halikeld, liberty of Richmondshire; 5¼ miles from Thirsk, 5¾ from Ripon, 9 from Bedale.—Population 247.

BALKE, in the parish of Kirby-Knowle, wapentake of Birdforth, 4¼ Miles from Thirsk, 8 from Easingwold.—Pop. 106.

BARDEN, and BARDEN DYKES, in the parish of Hawkswell, wapentake of Hang-West, liberty of Richmondshire; 3 miles from Leyburn, 4½ from Middleham, 5 from Richmond.—Population 91.

BARFORTH, in the parish of Gilling, wapentake of Gilling-West, liberty of Richmondshire; 7 miles from Greta-bridge, 10 from Richmond.—Population 142.

BARNABY-HOUSE, in the parish of Guisbrough, east-division of the wapentake and liberty of Langbarugh; 2¼ miles from Guisbrough, 10¼ from Stokesley.

BARNBY, in the parish of Bossall, wapentake of Bulmer; 9 miles from Malton, 10 from York, 13 from Easingwold.

BARNBY, EAST, in the parish of Lythe, east-division of the wapentake and liberty of Langbarugh; 6 miles from Whitby, 16 from Guisbrough.—Population 254.

BARNBY, WEST, in the parish of Lythe, east-division of the wapentake and liberty of Langbarugh; 6¼ miles from Whitby, 15¼ from Guisbrough.

BARNINGHAM, in the parish of Barningham, wapentake of Gilling-West, liberty of Richmondshire; *(the seat of William Milbank, Esq.)* 2 miles from Greta-bridge, 6 from Barnardcastle, *(Durham)* 10 from Richmond.—Population 325.

BARTON, in the parishes of St. John Stanwick, and Gilling, wapentake of Gilling-East, liberty of Richmondshire; 7 miles from Darlington, *(Durham)* 8 from Richmond.—Pop. 461.

BARTON, in the parish of Barton, wapentake of Rydale; *(the seat of Isaac Leatham, Esq.)* 5¼ miles from Malton, 9 from Kirby-Moorside, 12 from Helmsley.—Pop. 168.

BARTON-LE-WILLOWS, in the parish of Cramb, wapentake of Bulmer; 8 miles from Malton, 10¼ from York, 14 from Easingwold.—Population 149.

BARUGH, GREAT, in the parish of Kirby-Misperton, wapentake and liberty of Pickering-Lythe; 7 miles from

Malton, 7 from Pickering, 7 from Kirby-Moorside.—Population 188.

BARUGH, LITTLE, in the parish of Kirby-Misperton, wapentake and liberty of Pickering-Lythe; 5 miles from Pickering, 7 from Malton, 7 from Kirby-Moorside

BARUGH ROOK, in the parish of Normanton, wapentake of Rydale; 4 miles from Kirby-Moorside, 10 from Malton, 10 from Helmsley.

BATTERSBY, in the parish of Ingleby-Greenhow, west-division of the wapentake and liberty of Langbarugh; 5 miles from Stokesley, 6 from Guisbrough, 13 from Yarm.—Population 78.

BAXTER-HOWE, in the parish of Hovingham, wapentake of Rydale; 7¼ miles from Kirby-Moorside, 8 from Malton, 8¼ from Helmsley.

BAYSDALE, in the parish of Stokesley, west-division of the wapentake and liberty of Langbarugh; 7 miles from Guisbrough, 8 from Stokesley.

BEADLAM, in the parish of Kirkdale, wapentake of Rydale; 3 miles from Kirby-Moorside, 3 from Helmsley, 17 from Malton.—Population 93.

BEDALE, in the parish of Bedale, wapentake of Hang-East, liberty of Richmondshire; *(the seat of Henry Peirse, Esq.)* 6 miles from Masham, 7 from Catterick, 8 from Northallerton, 12 from Ripon, 12 from Middleham, 222 from London.—*Market*, Tuesday.—*Fairs*, Easter and Whit Tuesdays, for Horned Cattle and Sheep; July 6 and 7, October 11 and 12, for Horned Cattle, Sheep, and Leather; Monday se'night before Christmas Day, for Horned Cattle, Sheep, and Pigs.—*Principal Inn*, Black Swan.—Population 1,005.

BELLERBY, in the parish of Spennithorne, wapentake of Hang-West, liberty of Richmondshire; 1 mile from Leyburn, 3¼ from Middleham, 7½ from Richmond.—Pop. 309.

BENINGBROUGH, in the parish of Newton-upon-Ouse, wapentake of Bulmer; 7 miles from York, 7 from Easingwold, 11 from Boroughbridge.—Population 84.

BENINGBROUGH-HALL, in the parish of Newton-upon-Ouse, wapentake of Bulmer; *(the seat of Giles Earle, Esq.)* 7 miles from Easingwold, 8 from York.

BENKIL-GRANGE, in the parish of Bedale, wapentake of Hang-East; *(the seat of Mrs. Brooke;)* ¼ mile from Bedale, 6 from Masham, 7 from Catterick.

BERWICK, in the parish of Stainton, west-division of the wapentake and liberty of Langbarugh; 3 miles from Yarm, 6½ from Stokesley, 14½ from Guisbrough.—Population 162.

BILSDALE, EAST-SIDE, in the parish of Helmsley,

— wapentakes of Birdforth and Rydale; 8 miles from Helmsley, 8 from Stokesley, 14 from Thirsk.—Population 644.

BILSDALE, WEST-SIDE, in the parish of Hawnby, wapentake of Birdforth; 8 miles from Helmsley, 8 from Stokesley, 14 from Thirsk.—Population 115.

BINCOE, in the parish of West-Tanfield, wapentake of Halikeld; 4 miles from Masham, 6 from Bedale, 8 from Ripon.

BIRCH, in the parish of Stonegrave, wapentake of Rydale; 3¼ miles from Helmsley, 7¼ from Kirby-Moorside.

BIRDFORTH, *(which gives name to the wapentake)* in the parish of Coxwold, wapentake of Birdforth; 5 miles from Thirsk, 5 from Easingwold.—Population 32.

BIRKBY, in the parish of Birkby, wapentake and liberty of Allertonshire; 6 miles from Northallerton, 11 from Darlington, *(Durham.)*—Population 91.

BIRKDALE, in the parish of Grinton, wapentake of Gilling West, liberty of Richmondshire; 1 mile from Reeth, 9 from Richmond.

BIRK RIGGS, in the parish of Aysgarth, wapentake of Hang-West, liberty of Richmondshire; 2½ miles from Hawes, 7 from Askrigg, 10 from Leyburn.

BIRKS, in the parish of East-Witton, wapentake of Hang-West; 5 miles from Masham, 7 from Middleham, 9 from Leyburn.

BISHOP'S DALE, in the parish of Aysgarth, wapentake of Hang-West; 3 miles from Hawes, 5 from Askrigg.—Pop. 84.

BLADES, in the parish of Grinton, wapentake of Gilling-West, liberty of Richmondshire; 4 miles from Reeth, 14 from Richmond.

BLAKEHOW HOUSE, in the parish of Lastingham, wapentake of Rydale; 10¼ miles from Kirby-Moorside, 15 from Stokesley.

BLAKEHOW TOPPING, in the parish of Allerston, wapentake and liberty of Pickering-Lythe; 9 miles from Pickering, 12 from Whitby, 17 from Scarborough.

BLANSBY PARK, in the parish of Pickering, wapentake and liberty of Pickering-Lythe; 2 miles from Pickering, 10 from Kirby-Moorside, 11 from Malton.

BLEAN, HIGH, in the parish of Aysgarth, wapentake of Hang-West; 4 miles from Askrigg, 5 from Hawes, 15 from Leyburn.

BLEAN, LOW, in the parish of Aysgarth, wapentake of Hang-West; 4 miles from Askrigg, 5 from Hawes, 15 from Leyburn.

BOLDRON, in the parish of Bowes, wapentake of Gilling-West, liberty of Richmondshire; 3 miles from Greta-bridge,

3 from Barnardcastle, (*Durham*) 15 from Richmond.—Population, 128.

BOLTBY, in the parish of Feliskirk, wapentake of Birdforth; 6 miles from Thirsk, 8 from Helmsley.—Pop. 344.

BOLTON, CASTLE, in the parish of Wensley, wapentake of Hang-West, liberty of Richmondshire; 5 miles from Leyburn, 6¼ from Middleham, 11 from Richmond.—Pop. 242.

BOLTON HALL, in the parish of Wensley, wapentake of Hang-West, liberty of Richmondshire; *(the seat of Lord Bolton,)* 2¼ miles from Leyburn, 4½ from Middleham.

BOLTON-UPON-SWALE, in the parish of Catterick, wapentake of Gilling-East, liberty of Richmondshire; 3 miles from Catterick, 6 from Richmond, 10 from Northallerton.—Population 93.

BOOZE, in the parish of Arkengarthdale, wapentake of Gilling-West, liberty of Richmondshire, 3 miles from Reeth, 13 from Richmond.

BORNESSES, in the parish of Croft, wapentake of Gilling-East; 6¼ miles from Darlington, (*Durham*) 7 from Richmond.

BORROWBY, in the parish of Lythe, east-division of the wapentake and liberty of Langbarugh; 9 miles from Whitby, 12 from Guisbrough, 19¼ from Stokesley.—Population 81.

BORROWBY, in the parish of Leak, wapentakes of Allertonshire and Birdforth; 5 miles from Northallerton, 5 from Thirsk.—Population 251.

BOSSALL, in the parish of Bossall, wapentake of Bulmer; *(the seat of Robert Belt, Esq.)* 9 miles from York, 11 from Malton, 13 from Easingwold.

BOULBY, in the parish of Easington, east-division of the wapentake and liberty of Langbarugh; 11 miles from Whitby, 11 from Guisbrough.

BOW-BANK, in the parish of Romaldkirk, wapentake of Gilling-West, liberty of Richmondshire; 9 miles from Barnardcastle, (*Durham,*) 11 from Greta-bridge.

BOW-BRIDGE-HALL, in the parish of Aysgarth, wapentake of Hang-West, liberty of Richmondshire; 1 mile from Askrigg, 4 from Hawes, 19 from Richmond.

BOWES, in the parish of Bowes, wapentake of Gilling-West, liberty of Richmondshire; 4 miles from Barnardcastle, (*Durham,*) 6 from Greta-bridge, 16 from Richmond.—Pop. 670.

BOWFORTH, in the parish of Kirkdale, wapentake of Rydale; 2¼ miles from Kirby-Moorside, 6 from Helmsley.

BRACKENBROUGH, in the parish of Kirby-Wiske, wapentake of Birdforth; 4 miles from Thirsk, 6 from Northallerton, 10 from Ripon.

Middleham.—Population 67.

ALNE, in the parish of Alne, wapentake of Bulmer, a part in the liberty of St. Peter; *(the seat of E. S. Strangeway, Esq.)* 4 miles from Easingwold, 6 from Boroughbridge, 11 from York.—Population 342.

AMOTHERBY, in the parish of Appleton-le-street, wapentake of Rydale; 2¼ miles from Malton, 11 from Kirby-Moorside, 15 from Helmsley.—Population 285.

AMPLEFORTH, in the parishes of Ampleforth and Oswaldkirk, wapentakes of Rydale and Birdforth, a part in the liberty of St. Peter; 4 miles from Helmsley, 9 from Kirby-Moorside, 16 from Malton.—Population 405.

AMPLEFORTH OUT-HOUSES, in the parish of Oswaldkirk, wapentake of Rydale; 3¼ miles from Helmsley, 8½ from Kirby-Moorside, 15 from Malton.

ANGRAM, in the parish of Grinton, wapentake of Gilling-West, liberty of Richmondshire; 6 miles from Askrigg, 12 from Reeth, 22 from Richmond.

ANGRAM, in the parish of Coxwold, wapentake of Birdforth, liberty of Ripon; 5 miles from Easingwold, 8 from Thirsk.—Population 22.

ANNGROVE, in the parish of Ayton, west-division of the wapentake and liberty of Langbarugh; 2 miles from Stokesley, 6 from Yarm, 6¼ from Guisbrough.

APPLEGARTH, in the parish of Marske, wapentake of Gilling-West, liberty of Richmondshire; 6 miles from Richmond, 7 from Reeth.

APPLETON-LE-MOOR, in the parish of Lastingham, wapentake of Rydale; 4 miles from Kirby-Moorside, 10 from Helmsley, 14 from Malton.—Population 254.

APPLETON, EAST, in the parish of Catterick, wapentake of Hang-East, liberty of Richmondshire; 5 miles from Bedale, 7 from Richmond.—Population 95.

APPLETON-LE-STREET, in the parish of Appleton-le-street, wapentake of Rydale; 4 miles from Malton, 9 from Kirby-Moorside, 14 from Helmsley.—Population 151.

APPLETON, WEST, in the parish of Catterick, wapentake of Hang-East, liberty of Richmondshire; 6 miles from Bedale, 6 from Richmond.

APPLETON-WISKE, in the parish of Great-Smeaton, west-division of the wapentake and liberty of Langbarugh; 7 miles from Yarm, 7½ from Northallerton.—Population 451.

ARDEN, in the parish of Hawnby, wapentake of Birdforth, *(Arden Hall, the seat of Charles Tancred, Esq.)* 7¼ miles from Thirsk, 10 from Helmsley, 10 from Northallerton.—Population 128.

by-Moorside, 11 from Malton.

BROMPTON, in the parish of Northallerton, wapentake and liberty of Allertonshire; 1¼ mile from Northallerton, 13¼ from Yarm, 14¼ from Stokesley.—Population 994.

BROMPTON, in the parish of Brompton, wapentake and liberty of Pickering-Lythe; *(the seat of Sir George Cayley, Bart.)* 8 miles from Scarborough, 10 from Pickering, 14 from Malton.—Population 370.

BROMPTON-UPON-SWALE, in the parish of Easby, wapentake of Gilling-East, liberty of Richmondshire; 2 miles from Catterick, 3 from Richmond.—Population 401.

BROTTON, in the parish of Skelton, east-division of the wapentake and liberty of Langbarugh; 6 miles from Guisbrough, 14 from Stokesley, 15 from Whitby.—Population 373.

BROUGH, in the parish of Catterick, wapentake of Hang-East, liberty of Richmondshire; *(Brough-Hall, the seat of Sir John Lawson, Bart.)* 5 miles from Richmond, 7 from Bedale.—Population 86.

BROUGTON, in the parish of Appleton-le-street, wapentake of Rydale; 1½ miles from Malton, 12½ from Kirby-Moorside. —Population 71.

BROUGHTON, GREAT, in the parish of Kirkby, west-division of the wapentake and liberty of Langbarugh; 2 miles from Stokesley, 9 from Guisbrough, 10 from Yarm.—Population 460.

BROUGHTON, LITTLE, in the parish of Kirkby, west-division of the wapentake and liberty of Langbarugh, 2 miles from Stokesley, 8 from Guisbrough, 10 from Yarm.

BROXA, in the parish of Hackness, in the wapentake and liberty of Whitby-Strand, 7 miles from Scarborough, 15½ from Whitby, 18 from Pickering.—Population 49.

BULLAMOOR-HOUSES, in the parish of Northallerton, wapentake and liberty of Allertonshire; 1¼ miles from Northallerton, 9 from Thirsk, 15 from Stokesley.

BULMER, *(which gives name to the wapentake,)* in the parish and wapentake of Bulmer; *(the seat of the Rev. William Preston,)* 6 miles from Malton, 13 from Easingwold, 14 from York.—Population 295.

BURNISTON, in the parish of Burniston, wapentake of Halikeld, liberty of Richmondshire; 3¼ miles from Bedale, 9 from Ripon, 9 from Masham.—Population 280.

BURNISTON, in the parish of Scalby, wapentake and liberty of Pickering-Lythe; 4 miles from Scarborough, 17 from Whitby.—Population 246.

BURNIKILL-GRANGE, in the parish of Burniston, wapentake of Halikeld, liberty of Richmondshire; 2 miles

from Bedale, 8 from Northallerton, 15¼ from Boroughbridge.
BURRELL, in the parish of Bedale, wapentake of Hang-East, liberty of Richmondshire; 2 miles from Bedale, 7 from Masham.—Population 104.
BURTERSETT, in the parish of Aysgarth, wapentake of Hang-West, liberty of Richmondshire; 1 mile from Hawes, 4 from Askrigg, 17 from Leyburn.
BURTON, in the parish of Aysgarth, wapentake of Hang-West, liberty of Richmondshire; *(the seat of William Purchase, Esq.)* 5¼ miles from Askrigg, 6½ from Leyburn. —Pop. 446.
BURTON, CONSTABLE, in the parish of Fingall, wapentake of Hang-West, liberty of Richmondshire; *(the seat of the Rev. Christopher Wyville)* 5 miles from Leyburn, 5 from Middleham, 5½ from Richmond.—Population 217.
BURTON, HIGH, in the parish of Masham, wapentake of Hang-East, liberty of Richmondshire; 1 mile from Masham, 5 from Bedale.
BURTON, LOW, in the parish of Masham, wapentake of Hang-East, liberty of Richmondshire; ½ mile from Masham, 5¼ from Bedale.
BURTON, HUM, in the parish of Kirby-on-the-Moor, wapentake of Halikeld; 3 miles from Boroughbridge, 7 from Ripon, 9 from Thirsk.
BURTON-UPON-URE, in the parish of Masham, wapentake of Hang-East, liberty of Richmondshire; 2 miles from Masham, 5¼ from Bedale.—Population 217.
BUSBY, GREAT, in the parish of Stokesley, west-division of the wapentake and liberty of Langbarugh; 2 miles from Stokesley, 10 from Guisbrough, 14 from Northallerton.— Population 121.
BUSBY, LITTLE, in the parish of Stokesley, west-division of the wapentake and liberty of Langbarugh; *(Busby-Hall, the seat of William Marwood, Esq.)* 2 miles from Stokesley, 10 from Yarm, 14 from Northallerton.
BUSBY-STOOP, in the parish of Topcliffe, wapentake of Birdforth; 3 miles from Thirsk, 8 from Ripon, 9 from Northallerton, 10 from Boroughbridge.
BUSCO, in the parih of Lythe, East division of the wapentake and liberty of Langbarugh; 6 miles from Whitby, 16 from Guisbrough.
BUTCHER-HOUSES, in the parish of Pickhill, wapentake of Halikeld, liberty of Richmondshire; 7 miles from Ripon, 7¼ from Thirsk, 8 from Bedale.
BUTTERCRAMBE, in the parish of Bossall, wapentake of Bulmer; 10 miles from York, 10 from Malton, 15 from Easingwold.—Population 74.

BUTTERWICK, in the parish of Barton-in-the-Street, wapentake of Rydale; 7 miles from Kirby-Moorside, 8 from Malton, 10 from Helmsley.—Population 73.
BYLAND, in the parish of Byland, wapentake of Birdforth; 5 miles from Helmsley, 9 from Thirsk.
BYLAND-ABBEY, in the parish of Coxwold, wapentake of Birdforth; 6 miles from Helmsley, 7 from Easingwold, 9 from Thirsk.—Population 133.
BYLAND, OLD, in the parish of Old Byland, wapentake of Birdforth; 4 miles from Helmsley, 9 from Thirsk.—Population 118.

C.

CALDBERG, in the parish of Coverham, wapentake of Hang-West; 2¼ miles from Middleham, 4 from Leyburn, 11 from Masham.—Population 73.
CALVERT-HOUSE, in the parish of Grinton, wapentake of Gilling-West, liberty of Richmondshire; 8 miles from Reeth, 18 from Richmond.
CALDWLLL, or COLDWELL, in the parish of St. John, Stanwick, wapentake of Gilling-West; 6 miles from Barnardcastle, *(Durham)* 8 from Richmond.—Population 181.
CAMP-HALL, in the parish of Burneston, wapentake of Halikeld; *(the seat of W. R. L. Serjeantson, Esq.)* 5 miles from Bedale, 7 from Masham, 7½ from Ripon.
CAMS-HOUSE, in the parish of Aysgarth, wapentake of Hang-West, liberty of Richmondshire; 2¼ miles from Hawes, 2¼ from Askrigg, 20½ from Richmond.
CARR-BRIDGE, in the parish of West-Rounton, west-division of the wapentake and liberty of Langbarugh; 7 miles from Yarm, 8 from Northallerton.
CARKEN, in the parish of Gilling, wapentake of Gilling-West, liberty of Richmondshire; 7 miles from Richmond, 8 from Darlington, *(Durham.)*—Population 55.
CARLTON, in the parish of Coverham, wapentake of Hang-West, liberty of Richmondshire; 4 miles from Middleham, 5 from Leyburn.—Population 236.
CARLETON, in the parish of Carleton, west-division of the wapentake and liberty of Langbarugh; 3 miles from Stokesley, 13¼ from Northallerton.—Population 275.
CARLETON, in the parish of Helmsley, wapentake of Rydale; 2 miles from Helmsley, 7 from Kirby-Moorside.
CARLETON-HUSTHWAITE, in the parish of Husthwaite,

wapentake of Birdforth; 6 miles from Easingwold, 7 from Thirsk.—Population 159.

CARLETON-HALL, in the parish of St. John, Stanwick, wapentake of Gilling-West, liberty of Richmondshire; *(the seat of H. R. Pulleine, Esq.)* 8 miles from Richmond, 7 from Darlington, *(Durham.)*

CARLETON-MINIOTT, in the parish of Thirsk, wapentake of Birdforth, liberty of St. Peter; 2 miles from Thirsk, 9 from Ripon.—Population 185.

CARPERBY, in the parish of Aysgarth, wapentake of Hang-West, liberty of Richmondshire; 4 miles from Askrigg, 7 from Leyburn.

CARR-END, in the parish Aysgarth, wapentake of Hang-West, liberty of Richmondshire; 3 miles from Askrigg, 2 from Hawes.

CARR-HALL, in the parish of Whitby, wapentake and liberty of Whitby-Strand; *(the seat of Christopher Preston, Esq.)* 3 miles from Whitby, 18 from Pickering.

CARTHORPE, in the parish of Burneston, wapentake of Halikeld, liberty of Richmondshire; 4¼ miles from Bedale, 7 from Masham, 8 from Ripon.—Population 350.

CASTLE-HOWARD, in the parish of Bulmer, wapentake of Bulmer; *(the seat of the Earl of Carlisle,)* 6 miles from Malton, 15 from York, 15 from Easingwold.

CASTLETON, in the parish of Danby, east-division of the wapentake and liberty of Langbargh; 9 miles from Guisbrough, 12 from Stokesley, 14 from Whitby.

CATTERICK, in the parish of Catterick, wapentake of Hang-East, liberty of Richmondshire; 5 miles from Richmond, 7 from Bedale, 13 from Northallerton, 13 from Darlington, *(Durham)* 14¼ from Greta-bridge, 30 from York, 228 from London.—*Principal Inn*, Angel.—Pop. 641.

CATTERICK-BRIDGE INN, in the parish of Catterick; wapentake of Hang-East, liberty of Richmondshire; 1 mile from Catterick, 4 from Richmond, 12 from Northallerton, 12 from Darlington, *(Durham)* 13¼ from Greta-bridge.

CATTO, in the parish of Leak, wapentake and liberty of Allertonshire; 4 miles from Northallerton, 6¼ from Thirsk.

CATTON, in the parish of Topcliffe, wapentake of Birdforth; 5 miles from Thirsk, 8 from Ripon.—Population 116.

CAWTHORNE, in the parish of Middleton, wapentake and liberty of Pickering-Lythe; 4 miles from Pickering, 6 from Kirby-Moorside, 13 from Malton.

CAWTON, in the parish of Gilling, wapentake of Rydale; *(the seat of William Garforth, Esq)* 6 miles from Helmsley, 9 from Kirby-Moorside, 14 from Malton.—Population 92.

CAYTON, in the parish of Cayton, wapentake and liberty of Pickering-Lythe: 4 miles from Scarborough, 19 from Pickering, 21 from Malton.—Population 354.

CITTADILLA, in the parish of Easby, wapentake of Gilling-East, liberty of Richmondshire; 2 miles from Catterick, 4 from Richmond, 12 from Northallerton.

CLAXTON, in the parish of Bossall, wapentake of Bulmer; 8 miles from York, 11 from Malton, 13 from Easingwold.—Population 127.

CLEASBY, in the parish of Cleasby, wapentake of Gilling-East; 5 miles from Darlington, (*Durham*) 13 from Northallerton.—Population 123.

CLEVELAND-PORT, in the parish of Ormesby, west-division of the wapentake and liberty of Langbarugh; 8¼ miles from Guisbrough, 9 from Stokesley.

CLIFFE, in the parish of Manfield, wapentake of Gilling-West, liberty of Richmondshire; *(the seat of Henry Witham, Esq.)* 5 from Darlington, 10 miles from Richmond, 11 from Barnardcastle, *(Durham.)*—Population 46.

CLIFTON, in the parishes of St. Michael-le-Belfrey, and St. Olave, York, wapentake of Bulmer, liberty of St. Peter; 1 mile from York, 12 from Easingwold, 19 from Malton.—Population 383.

CLIFTON-CASTLE, in the parish of Thornton-Watlass, wapentake of Hang-East; *(the seat of Timothy Hutton, Esq.)* 3 miles from Masham, 5 from Bedale.

CLIFTON-LODGE, in the parish of Thornton-Watlass, wapentake of Hang-East, liberty of Richmondshire; 3 miles from Masham, 4 from Bedale, 8 from Middleham.

CLINTS, in the parish of Maske, wapentake of Gilling-West, liberty of Richmondshire, *(the seat of Thomas Errington, Esq.)* 5 miles from Reeth, 6½ from Richmond.

CLOUGHTON, in the parish of Scalby, wapentake and liberty of Pickering-Lythe; 5 miles from Scarborough, 16 from Whitby.—Population 291.

CLOWBECK, in the parish of Cleasby, wapentake of Gilling-East, liberty of Richmondshire; 6 miles from Darlington, *(Durham)* 8 from Richmond.

COATHAM, EAST and WEST, in the parish of Kirkleatham, east-division of the wapentake and liberty of Langbarugh; 6 miles from Guisbrough, 14 from Stokesley, 14 from Stockton, *(Durham)* 27 from Whitby.

COCK-BUSH, in the parish of Arncliffe, west-division of the wapentake and liberty of Langbarugh; 8 miles from Northallerton, 8 from Stokesley.

NORTH-RIDING. 15

COBSHAW, in the parish of Bedale, wapentake of Halfkeld, liberty of Richmondshire; 2 miles from Bedale, 9 from Northallerton, 10 from Richmond.

COCK-MILL, in the parish of Sneaton, wapentake and liberty of Whitby-Strand; 1½ miles from Whitby, 19½ from Scarborough.

COGDEN-HALL, in the parish of Grinton, wapentake of Hang-West, liberty of Richmondshire; 1¼ miles from Reeth, 10¼ from Leyburn, 11 from Richmond.

COLBURN or COWBURN, in the parish of Catterick, wapentake of Hang-East, liberty of Richmondshire; 3 miles from Richmond, 3 from Catterick, 9 from Bedale.—Pop. 138.

COLD-CAM, in the parish of Scawton, wapentake of Rylale; 6 miles from Helmsley, 10 from Thirsk.

COLDWELL, *see Caldwell.*

COMBOOTS, in the parish of Scalby, wapentake and liberty of Pickering-Lythe; 5 miles from Scarborough, 15 from Pickering, 15 from Whitby.

COMMON-DALE, in the parish of Guisbrough, east-division of the wapentake and liberty of Langbarugh; 4½ miles from Guisbrough, 9 from Stokesley, 16 from Whitby.—Pop. 68.

CONEYSTHORPE, in the parish of Barton, wapentake of Bulmer, 4 miles from Malton, 13 from Pickering.—Pop. 120.

CORNBROUGH, in the parish of Sheriff-hutton, wapentake of Bulmer; 7 miles from Easingwold, 9½ from York, 13 from Malton.—Population 61.

COTCLIFFE, (extraparochial,) wapentake and liberty of Allertonshire; 4¼ miles from Northallerton, 6 from Thirsk.

COTEGARTH-HOUSE, in the parish of Burneston, wapentake of Halikeld, liberty of Richmondshire; 3 miles from Bedale, 8 from Masham, 9 from Northallerton.

COTESCUE, in the parish of Coverham, wapentake of Hang-West; 1 mile from Middleham, 2½ from Leyburn, 12 from Richmond.

COTHERSTON, in the parish of Romaldkirk, wapentake of Gilling-West, liberty of Richmondshire; 3 miles from Barnardcastle, *(Durham)* 6 from Greta-bridge, 18 from Richmond.—Population 103.

COTTERDALE, in the parish of Aysgarth, wapentake of Hang-West, liberty of Richmondshire; 4 miles from Hawes, 9 from Askrigg, 21 from Leyburn.

COULTON or COLTON, in the parish of Hovingham, wapentake of Rydale; 7 miles from Helmsley, 9 from Kirby-Moorside, 12 from Malton.—Population 98.

COUNTERSIDE, in the parish of Aysgarth, wapentake of Hang-West, liberty of Richmondshire; 3 miles from Askrigg, 4 from Hawes, 15 from Leyburn.

COVERBRIDGE, in the parish of Coverham, wapentake of Hang-West; 3 miles from Leyburn, 9 from Richmond.

COVERHAM-ABBEY, in the parish of Coverham, wapentake of Hang-West, liberty of Richmondshire; *(the seat of Edward Lister, Esq.)* 1¼ miles from Middleham, 3 from Leyburn.—Population 328.

COWFOLD-HOUSE, in the parish of Burneston, wapentake of Halikeld, liberty of Richmondshire; 2¼ miles from Bedale, 7¼ from Northallerton, 13 from Richmond.

COWLING, in the parish of Bedale, wapentake of Hang-East, liberty of Richmondshire; 2 miles from Bedale, 5 from Masham, 10 from Richmond.

COWSBY, in the parish of Cowsby, wapentake of Birdforth; 8 miles from Thirsk, 9 from Northallerton.—Population 67.

COWTON, EAST or LONG, in the parish of East-Cowton, wapentake of Gilling-East, liberty of Richmondshire; 8 miles from Northallerton, 9 from Darlington, *(Durham.)*—Population 323.

COWTON-GRANGE, in the parish of East-Cowton, wapentake of Gilling-East, liberty of Richmondshire; 8 miles from Northallerton, 9 from Darlington. *(Durham.)*

COWTON, NORTH, in the parish of Gilling, wapentake of Gilling-East, liberty of Richmondshire; 7 miles from Northallerton, 10 from Darlington.—Population 282.

COWTON, SOUTH, in the parish of Gilling, wapentake of Gilling-East, liberty of Richmondshire; 6 miles from Northallerton, 11 from Darlington, *(Durham.)*—Population 142.

COXWOLD, in the parish of Coxwold, wapentake of Birdforth; 2 miles from Thirsk, 5 from Easingwold, 8 from Helmsley.—Population 289.

CRACKPOTT, in the parish of Grinton, wapentake of Gilling-West, liberty of Richmondshire; 5 miles from Reeth, 15 from Richmond.

CRAGG, in the parish of Romaldkirk, wapentake of Gilling-West, liberty of Richmondshire; 5 miles from Barnardcastle, *(Durham)* 6 from Greta-bridge, 17 from Richmond.

CRAKE and CRAKE-CASTLE, *(a part of the Bishoprick of Durham)* in the parish of Crake, wapentake of Bulmer; 2¼ from Easingwold, 12 from York.—Population 404.

CRAKEHALL, in the parish of Topcliffe, wapentake of Birdforth; 6 miles from Thirsk, 8 from Ripon.

CRAKEHALL, in the parish of Bedale, wapentake of Hang-East, liberty of Richmondshire; *(the seat of — Hudson Esq.)* 2 miles from Bedale, 10 from Richmond.—Pop. 460.

CRAKEHALL, LITTLE, in the parish of Bedale, wapen-

NORTH-RIDING. 17

take of Hang-East, liberty of Richmondshire; 2 miles from Bedale, 10 from Richmond.

CRAMBE, in the parish of Crambe, wapentake of Bulmer; 6¼ miles from Malton, 11¼ from York, 15 from Easingwold.—Population 139.

CRATHORNE, in the parish of Crathorne, west-division of the wapentake and liberty of Langbarugh; *(the seat of Thomas Crathorne, Esq.)* 4 miles from Yarm, 6 from Stokesley, 12 from Northallerton.—Population 307.

CROFT, in the parish of Croft, wapentake of Gilling-East, liberty of Richmondshire; *(Croft-Hall, the seat of William Chaytor, Esq.)* 3¼ miles from Darlington, *(Durham)* 12¼ from Northallerton.—Population 330.

CRONKLEY, in the parish of Romaldkirk, wapentake of Gilling-West; 13 miles from Barnardcastle, *(Durham)* 27 from Richmond.

CROPTON, in the parish of Middleton, wapentake and liberty of Pickering-Lythe; 4 miles from Pickering, 5 from Kirby-Moorside, 13 from Malton.—Population 269.

CROSBY, in the parish of Leak, wapentake and liberty of Allertonshire; 3 miles from Northallerton, 6¼ from Thirsk.—Population 39.

CROSBY-COTE, in the parish of Leak, wapentake and liberty of Allertonshire; 3 miles from Northallerton, 7 from Thirsk.

CROSETT, in the parish of Helmsley, wapentake of Rydale; 8 miles from Helmsley, 12 from Stokesley.

CROSS-BUTTS, in the parish of Whitby, wapentake and liberty of Whitby-Strand; 2 miles from Whitby, 19 from Guisbrough.

CROSSWICK, in the parish of Romaldkirk, wapentake of Gilling-West; 11 miles from Barnardcastle, *(Durham)* 26 from Richmond.

CUNDALL, in the parish of Cundall, wapentake of Halikeld, liberty of Richmondshire; 4 miles from Boroughbridge, 7 from Thirsk, 10 from Ripon.—Population 204.

D.

DALBY, in the parish of Dalby, wapentake of Bulmer; 9 miles from Easingwold, 13 from Malton, 15 from York.—Population 125.

DALBY, in the parish of Thornton, wapentake and liberty

C

of Pickering-Lythe; 5 miles from Pickering, 12 from Malton, 16 from Whitby.

DALE-HOUSE, in the parish of Lythe, east-division of the wapentake and liberty of Langbargh; 13 miles from Whitby, 13 from Guisbrough.

DALE-TOWN, in the parish of Hawnby, wapentake of Birdforth; 6 miles from Helmsley, 9 from Thirsk.—Pop. 47.

DALTON, in the parish of Topcliffe, wapentake of Birdforth; 5 miles from Thirsk, 7 from Ripon, 7½ from Boroughbridge. —Population 86.

DALTON, in the parish of Kirkby-Ravensworth, wapentake of Gilling-West, liberty of Richmondshire; 6 miles from Richmond, 6 from Greta-bridge, 9 from Barnardcastle, *(Durham.)*—Population 230.

DALTON-UPON-TEES, in the parish of Croft, wapentake of Gilling-East, liberty of St. Peter; 5 miles from Darlington, *(Durham)* 10 from Richmond, 11 from Northallerton. —Population 124.

DANBY, in the parish of Danby, east-division of the wapentake and liberty of Langbarugh; 9 miles from Guisbrough, 12 from Whitby, 14 from Stokesley.—Pop. 990.

DANBY, in the parish of Thornton-Steward, wapentake of Hang-East, liberty of Richmondshire; *(the seat of Simon Thomas Scroope, Esq.)* 2 miles from Middleham, 3 from Leyburn.

DANBY-BEACON, in the parish of Danby, east-division of the wapentake and liberty of Langbarugh; 10¼ miles from Guisbrough, 10¼ from Whitby.

DANBY-LODGE, in the parish of Danby, east-division of the wapentake and liberty of Langbarugh; *(the seat of Lord Downe)* 10 miles from Guisbrough, 12 from Whitby, 18 from Kirby-Moorside.

DANBY-HILL, in the parish of Danby, wapentake of Gilling-East, liberty of Richmondshire; *(the seat of the Rev. William Cust)* 3¼ miles from Northallerton, 7½ from Bedale, 13¼ from Richmond.

DANBY, LITTLE, in the parish of Danby-Wiske, wapentake of Gilling-East, liberty of Richmondshire; 3 miles from Northallerton, 7 from Bedale, 13¼ from Richmond.

DANBY-WISKE, in the parish of Danby-Wiske, wapentake of Gilling-East, liberty of Richmondshire; 4 miles from Northallerton, 8 from Bedale, 13½ from Richmond.—Population 302.

DEEPDALE, in the parish of Romaldkirk, wapentake of Gilling-West, liberty of Richmondshire; 1 mile from Barnardcastle, *(Durham)* 4½ from Greta-bridge.

NORTH-RIDING.

DEEPDALE, in the parish of Hackness, wapentake and liberty of Pickering-Lythe; 6 miles from Scarborough, 10 from Pickering, 14 from Whitby.

DEIGHTON, in in the parish of Northallerton, wapentake and liberty of Allertonshire; 5 miles from Northallerton, 10 from Yarm, 11¼ from Darlington, *(Durham.)*—Pop. 146.

DIDDERTON-GRANGE, in the parish of Melsonby, wapentake of Gilling-West, liberty of Richmondshire; 5 miles from Richmond, 7 from Darlington, *(Durham.)*

DINSDALE, OVER, in the parish of Sockburn, *(Durham)* wapentake and liberty of Allertonshire; 6 miles from Darlington, *(Durham)* 7 from Yarm, 9 from Northallerton.—Population 237.

DISHFORTH, in the parish of Topcliffe, wapentake of Halikeld, liberty of Richmondshire; 4 miles from Boroughbridge, 5 from Ripon, 8 from Thirsk.—Population 291.

DOE-PARK-HALL, in the parish of Romaldkirk, wapentake of Gilling-West; *(the seat of Timothy Hutchinson, Esq.)* 4 miles from Barnardcastle, *(Durham)* 7 from Gretabridge, 19 from Richmond.

DOWNHOLME, in the parish of Downholme, wapentake of Hang-West, liberty of Richmondshire; 4 miles from Reeth, 4¼ from Leyburn, 6 from Middleham.—Population 114.

DOWTHWAITE-DALE, in the parish of Lastingham, wapentake of Rydale; *(the seat of Richard Shepherd, Esq.)* 3 miles from Kirby-Moorside, 10 from Helmsley.

DROMANBY, GREAT or HALL, in the parish of Kirkby, west-division of the wapentake and liberty of Langbarugh; 2 miles from Stokesley, 10½ from Yarm, 9¼ from Guisbrough.

DROMANBY, LITTLE, in the parish of Kirkby, west-division of the wapentake and liberty of Langbarugh; 2 miles from Stokesley, 10 from Yarm.

DRUID'S TEMPLE, in the parish of Masham, wapentake of Hang-East; 2 miles from Masham, 9 from Bedale, 9 from Ripon.

DUNBOGS, in the parish of Lythe, east-division of the wapentake and liberty of Langbarugh; 6 miles from Whitby, 16 from Guisbrough.

DUNCOMBE-PARK, in the parish of Helmsley, wapentake of Rydale; *(the seat of Charles Duncombe, Esq.)* ½ a mile from Helmsley, 6½ from Kirby-Moorside, 14 from Thirsk, 23 from York.

DUNSLEY, in the parish of Whitby, wapentake and liberty of Whitby-Strand; 3½ miles from Whitby, 19 from Guisbrough, 20 from Pickering.

E.

EARBY, in the parish of West-Rounton, wapentake and liberty of Allertonshire; 6¼ miles from Yarm, 8¼ from Northallerton.

EARSWICK, in the parishes of Strensall and Huntington, wapentake of Bulmer, a part in the liberty of St. Peter; 3 miles from York, 12 from Easingwold, 14 from Malton.—Population 48.

EASBY, in the parish of Easby, wapentake of Gilling-West, liberty of Richmondshire; 1 mile from Richmond, 4 from Catterick.—Population 85.

EASBY, in the parish of Stokesley, west-division of the wapentake and liberty of Langbarugh; 3½ miles from Stokesley, 7 from Guisbrough, 11 from Yarm.—Population 138.

EASINGTON, in the parish of Easington, east-division of the wapentake and liberty of Langbarugh; 10 miles from Guisbrough, 12 from Whitby, 18 from Stokesley.—Population 500.

EASINGWOLD, in the parish of Easingwold, wapentake of Bulmer, liberty of Pickering-Lythe; 10 miles from Thirsk, 11 from Boroughbridge, 13 from York, 13 from Helmsley, 16 from Malton, 213 from London.—*Market*, Saturday.—*Fairs*, July 6, September 26, for Cattle and Sheep.—*Principal Inns*, Rose and Crown, and Post-Boy.—Population 1,467.

EASTERSIDE, in the parish of Hawnby, wapentake of Birdforth; 7 miles from Helmsley, 11 from Thirsk.

EAST-MOORS, in the parish of Helmsley, wapentake of Rydale; 4 miles from Helmsley, 8 from Kirby-Moorside, 20 from Malton.

EAST-ROW, in the parish of Whitby, wapentake and liberty of Whitby-Strand; 2¼ miles from Whitby, 18¼ from Guisbrough.

EAST-THORPE, in the parish of Appleton-le-street, wapentake of Rydale; *(East-Thorpe Park, the seat of Robert Roydes, Esq.)* 2¼ miles from Malton, 11 from Kirby-Moorside, 13 from Helmsley.

EASTWOOD, in the parish of Barningham, wapentake of Gilling-West, liberty of Richmondshire, *(the seat of John Hanby, Esq.)* 1 mile from Greta-bridge, 4 from Barnard-castle, *(Durham)* 12 from Richmond.

EBBERSTON, in the parish of Ebberston, wapentake and liberty of Pickering-Lythe; 6 miles from Pickering, 10¼ from Scarborough, 13 from Malton.—Population 365.

NORTH-RIDING.

EDSTONE, in the parish of Edstone, wapentake of Rydale; 3 miles from Kirby-Moorside, 8 from Helmsley, 10 from Malton.—Population 144.

EDSTONE, LITTLE, in the parish of Sinnington, wapentake of Rydale; 3 miles from Kirby-Moorside, 8 from Helmsley, 10 from Malton.

EGGLESTON-ABBEY, in the parish of Startforth, wapentake of Gilling-West, liberty of Richmondshire; 2 miles from Greta-bridge, 2 from Barnardcastle, *(Durham)* 14 from Richmond.

EGTON, in the parish of Lythe, east-division of the wapentake and liberty of Langbarugh; 7 miles from Whitby, 14 from Pickering, 15 from Guisbrough.—*No Market.*—*Fairs,* Tuesday before Palm-Sunday, Tuesday before Old May-day, September 4, Tuesday before Old Martinmas-day, for horned Cattle, Sheep, &c. every Tuesday from May-day, till July 1, for Cattle.—Population 971.

EGTON-BANKS, in the parish of Lythe, east-division of the wapentake and liberty of Langbarugh; 8 miles from Whitby, 15 from Guisbrough.

EGTON-BRIDGE, in the parish of Lythe, east-division of the wapentake and liberty of Langbarugh; *(the seat of Thomas Smith, Esq.)* 8 miles from Whitby, 16 from Guisbrough.

ELLERBECK, in the parish of Osmotherley, wapentake and liberty of Allertonshire; 5 miles from Northallerton, 9 from Thirsk, 11 from Yarm, 11 from Stokesley.—Population 78.

ELLERBURN, in the parish of Ellerburn, wapentake and liberty of Pickering-Lythe; 3¼ miles from Pickering, 10¼ from Malton, 19 from Whitby.

ELLERBY, in the parish of Lythe, east-division of the wapentake and liberty of Langbarugh; 7 miles from Whitby, 15 from Guisbrough, 23 from Stokesley.—Population 74.

ELLERTON, in the parish of Downholme, wapentake of Hang-West, liberty of Richmondshire; 3 miles from Reeth, 8 from Richmond.—Population 79.

ELLERTON-UPON-SWALE, in the parish of Catterick, wapentake of Gilling-East, liberty of Richmondshire; 1 mile from Catterick, 6 from Richmond, 10 from Northallerton.—Population 116.

ELLINGSTRING, in the parish of Masham, wapentake of Hang-East, liberty of St. Peter; 4 miles from Masham, 9 from Richmond.—Population 123.

ELLINGTON, HIGH, in the parish of Masham, wapentake of Hang-East; 5 miles from Masham, 9 from Richmond.—Population 111.

NORTH-RIDING.

ELLINGTON, LOW, in the parish of Masham, wapentake of Hang-East, a part in the liberty of St. Peter; 4 miles from Masham, 9 from Richmond.

ELMER, in the parish of Topcliffe, wapentake of Birdforth; 5 miles from Thirsk, 7 from Ripon.—Population 85.

ENTERCOMMON, in the parish of Great-Smeaton, wapentake of Gilling-East; 8 miles from Northallerton, 8 from Darlington, *(Durham)* 10½ from Richmond.

ENTERPEN, in the parish of Rudby, west-division of the wapentake and liberty of Langbarugh; 4½ miles from Stokesley, 6 from Yarm, 11¼ from Northallerton.

EPPLEBY, in the parish of Gilling, wapentake of Gilling-West, liberty of Richmondshire; 8 miles from Richmond, 8 from Darlington, 10 from Barnardcastle, *(Durham.)*—Population 168.

ERYHOLME, in the parish of Gilling, wapentake of Gilling-East, liberty of Richmondshire; 4¼ miles from Darlington, *(Durham)* 11 from Richmond, 12 from Northallerton.—Population 163.

ESKDALESIDE, in the parish of Whitby, wapentake and liberty of Whitby-Strand; 5¼ miles from Whitby, 17 from Pickering, 18 from Scarborough.—Population 344.

ESKLITH, in the parish of Arkengarthdale, wapentake of Gilling-West, liberty of Richmondshire; 4 miles from Reeth, 14 from Richmond.

ESKLITTS, in the parish of Stokesley, west-division of the wapentake and liberty of Langbarugh; 11 miles from Guisbrough, 11 from Kirby-Moorside, 12 from Stokesley.

ESTON, in the parish of Ormesby, east-division of the wapentake and liberty of Langbarugh; 4 miles from Guisbrough, 8 from Stokesley, 8½ from Stockton, *(Durham)* —Population 288.

EVERLEY, in the parish of Hackness, wapentake and liberty of Whitby-Strand; 4½ miles from Scarborough, 18 from Whitby.

EWE, or WETHER-COTE, in the parish of Kirkdale, wapentake of Rydale; 4 miles from Kirby-Moorside, 5 from Helmsley, 17 from Malton.

EXILBY, in the parish of Burneston, wapentake of Halikeld, liberty of Richmondshire; 2 miles from Bedale, 8 from Masham, 9 from Northallerton.—Population 532.

EXILBY, or HUTTON-GRANGE, in the parish of Burneston, wapentake of Halikeld, liberty of Allertonshire; 2½ miles from Bedale, 9¼ from Northallerton, 10½ from Ripon.

F.

FACEBY, in the parishes of Faceby and Whorlton, west division of the wapentake and liberty of Langbarugh; *(Faceby-Lodge, the seat of James Favell, Esq.)* 4 miles from Stokesley, 9 from Yarm, 12 from Northallerton.—Pop. 127.

FADMOOR, in the parish of Kirby-Moorside, wapentake of Rydale; 2 miles from Kirby-Moorside, 7 from Helmsley, 16 from Malton.—Population 133.

FAGGER-GILL, in the parish of Arkengarthdale, wapentake of Gilling-West, liberty of Richmondshire; 6 miles from Reeth, 16 from Richmond.

FALLING-FOSS, in the parish of Whitby, wapentake and liberty of Whitby-Strand; 7 miles from Whitby, 13 from Pickering, 14 from Scarborough.

FAREHOLME, in the parish of Ainderby-Steeple, wapentake of Gilling-East, liberty of Richmondshire; 5 miles from Northallerton, 5 from Bedale.

FARLINGTON, in the parish of Farlington, wapentake of Bulmer; 6 miles from Easingwold, 10 from York, 13 from Malton.—Population 174.

FARMANBY, in the parishes of Ellerburn and Thornton, wapentake and liberty of Pickering-Lythe; $2\frac{1}{2}$ miles from Pickering, 9 from Malton, 12 from Whitby.—Pop. 310.

FARNDALE-EAST-SIDE, in the parish of Lastingham, wapentake of Rydale; 4 miles from Kirby-Moorside, 10 from Helmsley, 18 from Malton.—Population 381.

FARNDALE-WEST-SIDE, in the parish of Kirby-Moorside, wapentake of Rydale; 4 miles from Kirby-Moorside, 10 from Helmsley, 18 from Malton.—Population 356.

FAWDINGTON, in the parish of Cundall, wapentake o Birdforth; 5 miles from Boroughbridge, 6 from Easingwold.

FEARBY, in the parish of Masham, wapentake of Hang-East, liberty of Richmondshire; 2 miles from Masham, 8 from Richmond.—Population 205.

FEETHAM, in the parish of Grinton, wapentake of Gilling-West, liberty of Richmondshire; 3 miles from Reeth, 9 from Askrigg, 13 from Richmond.

FEETHAM-HOLME, in the parish of Grinton, wapentake of Hang-West, liberty of Richmondshire; 3 miles from Reeth, 9 from Askrigg, 13 from Richmond.

FELDOM, in the parish of Marske, wapentake of Gilling-West, liberty of Richmondshire; 5 miles from Richmond, 8 from Reeth.

FELISKIRK, in the parish of Feliskirk, wapentake of Birdforth; 3 miles from Thirsk, 11 from Helmsley, 13 from Easingwold.—Population 113.

FENCOTE, GREAT, in the parish of Kirkby-Fleatham, wapentake of Hang-East, liberty of Richmondshire; 4 miles from Bedale, 8 from Richmond.

FENCOTE, LITTLE, in the parish of Kirkby-Fleatham, wapentake of Hang-East, liberty of Richmondshire; 4 miles from Bedale, 8 from Richmond.

FIELD, LOW, in the parish of Kirkby-Fleatham, wapentake of Hang-East, liberty of Richmondshire; 3 miles from Catterick, 6 from Bedale, 8 from Richmond.

FIELD-HOUSES, in the parish of Gilling, wapentake of Gilling-West, liberty of Richmondshire; 7 miles from Richmond, 7 from Barnardcastle, *(Durham.)*

FILEY, in the parish of Filey, wapentakes of Pickering-Lythe and Dickering, *(East-Riding)* liberty of Pickering-Lythe; 8 miles from Scarborough, 9 from Bridlington, 18 from Driffield.—Population 505.

FINGAL, in the parish of Fingal, wapentake of Hang-West, liberty of Richmondshire; 5 miles from Leyburn, 5 from Middleham, 7 from Bedale.—Population 114.

FIRBY, in the parish of Bedale, wapentake of Hang-East, liberty of Richmondshire; 1 mile from Bedale, 6 from Masham, 9 from Northallerton.—Population 73.

FIRBY-GRANGE, in the parish of Bedale, wapentake of Hang-East, liberty of Richmondshire; *(the seat of Thomas Core, Esq.)* 1 mile from Bedale, 6 from Masham, 8 from Catterick.

FLAWITH, in the parish of Alne, wapentake of Bulmer, liberty of St. Peter; 5 miles from Easingwold, 5 from Boroughbridge, 12 from York.—Population 87.

FLAXTON, in the parishes of Bossall and Foston, wapentake of Bulmer, a part in the liberty of St Peter; 9 miles from York, 9¼ from Malton, 11 from Easingwold.—Pop: 227.

FLEATHAM, in the parish of Kirkby-Fleatham, wapentake of Hang-East, liberty of Richmondshire; 5 miles from Bedale, 7 from Richmond.

FLEATHAM, KIRKBY, in the parish of Kirkby-Fleatham, wapentake of Hang-East, liberty of Richmondshire; *(the seat of Miss Lawrence)* 6 miles from Bedale, 6 from Richmond.—Population 443.

FOOLRICE, in the parishes of Brunsby and Whenby, wapentake of Bulmer; 7 miles from Easingwold, 12 from Malton, 14 from York.

FORCETT, in the parish of Gilling, wapentake of Gilling-West; liberty of Richmondshire; *(Forcett-Hall the seat of Charles Mitchell, Esq.)* 7 miles from Richmond, 8 from Darlington, 10 from Barnardcastle, *(Durham.)*—Pop. 201.

FOSSDALE, in the parish of Aysgarth, wapentake of Hang-West, liberty of Richmondshire; 1¼ miles from Hawes, 6 from Askrigg, 18 from Leyburn.

FOSTON, in the parish of Foston, wapentake of Bulmer; 7¼ miles from Malton, 11 from York, 13 from Easingwold.—Population 75.

FOWGILL, in the parish of Arncliffe, west-division of the wapentake and liberty of Langbarugh; 8 miles from Stokesley, 8 from Northallerton.

FOXBERRY, in the parish of St. John, Stanwick, wapentake of Gilling-West, liberty of Richmondshire; 7 miles from Catterick, 7 from Richmond.

FOX-HALL, in the parish of Kirkby-Ravensworth, wapentake of Gilling-West, liberty of Richmondshire; 6 miles from Richmond, 7 from Catterick.—Population 150.

FOXTON, in the parish of Sigston, wapentake and liberty of Allertonshire; 5 miles from Northallerton, 9 from Thirsk.

FREMINGTON, in the parish of Grinton, wapentake of Gilling-West, liberty of Richmondshire; *(the seat of P. Dennis, Esq.)* 1 mile from Reeth, 9 from Richmond—Pop. 879.

FRITH, in the parish of Grinton, wapentake of Gilling-West, liberty of Richmondshire; 7 miles from Askrigg, 14 from Reeth, 17 from Greta-bridge, 24 from Richmond.

FRYOP, GREAT and LITTLE, in the parish of Danby, east-division of the wapentake and liberty of Langbarugh; 11 miles from Guisbrough, 15 from Stokesley.

FRYTON, in the parish of Hovingham, wapentake of Rydale; 7¼ miles from Malton, 9 from Helmsley, 9 from Kirby-Moorside.—Population 72.

FYLINGDALE, in the parish of Fylingdale wapentake and liberty of Whitby-Strand; 7 miles from Whitby, 14 from Scarborough, 16 from Pickering.—Population 1,568.

FYLING-HALL, in the parish of Fylingdale, wapentake and liberty of Whitby-Strand; 7 miles from Whitby, 13 from Scarborough.

G.

GAILES, in the parish of Kirkby-Ravensworth, wapentake of Gilling-West; liberty of Richmondshire, 5 miles from Richmond, 7 from Greta-bridge, 10 from Barnardcastle, *(Durham.)*

GALLOW-GREEN, in the parish of Sneaton, wapentake and liberty of Whitby-Strand; 2 miles from Whitby, 19 from Pickering.

GAMMERSGILL, in the parish of Coverham, wapentake of Hang-West, liberty of Richmondshire; 6 miles from Middleham, 7 from Leyburn, 7 from Kettlewell.

GANTHORPE, in the parish and wapentake of Bulmer; *(the seat of the Rev. John Forth)* 5 miles from Malton, 13 from Easingwold, 15¼ from York.—Population 101.

GARRISTON, in the parish of East-Hawkswell, wapentake of Hang-West, liberty of Richmondshire; 3 miles from Leyburn, 6 from Richmond, 5 from Middleham.—Pop. 63.

GATERLEY, HIGH and LOW, in the parish of Catterick, wapentake of Gilling-East; 4 miles from Catterick, 5 from Richmond.

GATENBY, in the parish of Burneston, wapentake of Halikeld, liberty of Richmondshire; 4¼ miles from Bedale, 9 from Northallerton, 12 from Ripon.—Population 67.

GAYLE, in the parish of Aysgarth, wapentake of Hang-West; ¼ a mile from Hawes, 5½ from Askrigg, 17 from Leyburn. —Population 190.

GEBDYKE, in the parish of Masham, wapentake of Hang-East; 1 mile from Masham, 6 from Bedale.

GELDABLE, in the parish of Leak, wapentake of Birdforth; 5 miles from Thirsk, 6 from Northallerton.—Pop. 115.

GERSHAM, or GRASSHOLME, in the parish of Romaldkirk, wapentake of Gilling-West, liberty of Richmondshire; *(the seat of the Earl of Darlington)* 16 miles from Barnardcastle, *(Durham)* 20 from Greta-bridge, 23 from Richmond.

GILLAMOOR, in the parish of Kirby-Moorside, wapentake of Rydale; 2 miles from Kirby-Moorside, 8 from Helmsley, 16 from Malton.—Population 228.

GILES, ST. in the parish of Catterick, wapentake of Hang-East, liberty of Richmondshire; 3 miles from Catterick, 8 from Richmond.

GILLING, *(which gives name to the wapentake)* in the parish of Gilling, wapentake of Gilling-West, liberty of Richmondshire; *(the seat of the Rev. William Wharton)* 3 miles from Richmond, 5 from Catterick, 8¼ from Greta-bridge.—Population 809.

GILLING, in the parish of Gilling, wapentake of Rydale; 5 miles from Helmsley, 8¼ from Easingwold, 10 from Kirby-Moorside, 18 from York.—Population 197.

GILLING-CASTLE, in the parish of Gilling, wapentake of Rydale; *(the seat of Charles Fairfax, Esq.)* 5 miles from

Helmsley, 8 from Easingwold, 10 from Kirby-Moorside, 18 from York.

GILMONBY, in the parish of Bowes, wapentake of Gilling-West, liberty of Richmondshire; 4 miles from Barnardcastle, *(Durham)* 5 from Greta-bridge, 17 from Richmond.--Pop. 145.

GIRLINGTON, in the parish of Wycliffe, wapentake of Gilling-West, liberty of Richmondshire; 6 miles from Barnardcastle, *(Durham)* 9 from Richmond.

GIRSBY, in the parish of Dinsdale, *(Durham)* wapentake and liberty of Allertonshire; 6 miles from Yarm, 7 from Darlington, *(Durham)* 10 from Northallerton.—Pop. 80.

GLAZEDALE, in the parish of Danby, east-division of the wapentake and liberty of Langbarugh; 9 miles from Whitby, 15 from Guisbrough, 19 from Stokesley.—Population 763.

GOLDSBROUGH, in the parish of Lythe, east-division of the wapentake and liberty of Langbarugh; 6 miles from Whitby, 16 from Guisbrough.

GOADLAND, in the parish of Pickering, wapentake and liberty of Pickering-Lythe; 10 miles from Whitby, 11 from Pickering, 20 from Malton.

GRANGE, in the parish of Aysgarth, wapentake of Hang-West, liberty of Richmondshire; 1 mile from Askrigg, 4 from Hawes.

GRANGE, in the parish of Oswaldkirk, wapentake of Rydale; 2½ miles from Helmsley, 8 from Kirby-Moorside, 15 from Malton.

GRAYSTONES, in the parish of St. John, Stanwick, wapentake of Gilling-West, liberty of Richmondshire; 5 miles from Darlington, *(Durham)* 9 from Richmond.

GREENHOW, in the parish of Ingleby-Greenhow, west-division of the wapentake and liberty of Langbarugh; 5 miles from Stokesley, 11 from Guisbrough, 13 from Yarm. —Population 118.

GRETA-BRIDGE, in the parish of Brignall, wapentake of Gilling-West, liberty of Richmondshire; 3 miles from Barnardcastle, *(Durham,)* 12 from Richmond, 15 from Catterick, 11 from Reeth, 19 from Brough, *(Westmoreland.)*

GRIMESCAR, in the parish of Scruton, wapentake of Hang-East, liberty of Richmondshire; 3 miles from Bedale, 6 from Northallerton, 11 from Richmond.

GRIMESTONE, in the parish of Gilling, wapentake of Rydale; 6 miles from Helmsley, 10 from Kirby-Moorside, 14 from Malton.—Population 47.

GRINKLE-PARK, in the parish of Easington, east-division of the wapentake and liberty of Langbarugh; *(the seat of R. W. Middleton, Esq.)* 11 miles from Guisbrough, 14 from Whitby.

GRINTON, in the parish of Grinton, wapentake of Hang-West, liberty of Richmondshire; 1 mile from Reeth, 10 from Richmond, 11 from Leyburn.—Population 518.

GRISTHORPE, in the parish of Filey, wapentake and liberty of Pickering-Lythe; 6 miles from Scarborough, 10 from Bridlington, 18 from Pickering.—Population 129.

GRISTHWAITE, in the parish of Topcliffe, wapentake of Birdforth; 2½ miles from Thirsk, 9 from Ripon, 9 from Boroughbridge.

GROWMOND-ABBEY, in the parish of Lythe, east-division of the wapentake and liberty of Langbarugh; 8 miles from Whitby, 19 from Guisbrough, 21 from Stokesley.

GUISBROUGH, in the parish of Guisbrough, east-division of the wapentake and liberty of Langbarugh; 8 miles from Stokesley, 14 from Yarm, 12 from Stockton, *(Durham,)* 21 from Whitby, 24 from Kirby-Moorside, 51 from York, 248 from London.—*Market*, Friday.—*Fairs*, Third Monday and Tuesday after April 11, for Horned Cattle, Horses, Linen Cloth, &c. Whit-Tuesday for Pedlary Ware; August 26 and 27, September 19 and 20, Monday after November 11, for Horned Cattle, Horses, &c.—*Principal Inn*, the Cock.—Population 1,719.

GUNNERSET, or GUNNERSIDE, in the parish of Grinton, wapentake of Gilling-West, liberty of Richmondshire; 6 miles from Reeth, 8 from Askrigg, 16 from Richmond.

H.

HABTON, GREAT, in the parish of Kirby-Misperton, wapentake and liberty of Pickering-Lythe; 4 miles from Malton 6 from Pickering, 9 from Kirby-Moorside.—Population 85.

HABTON, LITTLE, in the parish of Kirby-Misperton, wapentake and liberty of Pickering-Lythe; 4 miles from Malton, 6 from Pickering, 9 from Kirby-Moorside.—Population 46.

HACKFORTH, in the parish of Hornby, wapentake of Hang-East, liberties of St. Peter and Richmondshire; 3 miles from Bedale, 8 from Richmond.—Population 135.

HACKNESS, in the parish of Hackness, wapentake and liberty of Whitby-Strand; *(the seat of Lady Johnstone,)* 4 miles from Scarborough, 17 from Whitby.—Population 170.

HAGG, in the parish of Kirkdale, wapentake of Rydale; 2½ miles from Kirby-Moorside, 6 from Helmsley, 10⅝ from Malton.

NORTH-RIDING. 29

HAGG, in the parish of Whitby, wapentake and liberty of Whitby-Strand; 2¼ miles from Whitby, 18¼ from Pickering.

HAGWORTH-HALL, in the parish of Romaldkirk, wapentake of Gilling-West, liberty of Richmondshire; 8 miles from Barnardcastle, *(Durham)* 11 from Greta-bridge, 22 from Richmond.

HALFPENNY-HOUSE, in the parish of Downholme, wapentake of Hang-West, liberty of Richmondshire; 3 miles from Leyburn, 5 from Richmond, 5 from Middleham.

HALFPENNY-HOUSE, in the parish of Thornton-Watlass, wapentake of Hang-East, liberty of Richmondshire; 4 miles from Bedale, 8 from Masham.

HALIKELD, in the parish of Sigston, wapentake and liberty of Allertonshire; 2¼ miles from Northallerton, 13¼ from Stokesley.

HALL-GATE, in the parish of Kirkby-Ravensworth, wapentake of Gilling-West, liberty of Richmondshire; 5 miles from Richmond, 8 from Leyburn.

HALL-GATE-HOW, in the parish of Kirkby-Ravensworth, wapentake of Gilling-West, liberty of Richmondshire; 5 miles from Richmond, 8 from Leyburn.

HALNABY-HALL, in the parish of Croft, wapentake of Gilling-East, liberty of Richmondshire; *(the seat of Sir. Ralph Milbank, Bart.)* 6¼ miles from Richmond, 6¼ from Catterick, 6½ from Darlington, *(Durham.)*

HAMBLETON-HOUSE, in the parish of Cold-Kirby, wapentake of Birdforth; 7 miles from Helmsley, 7 from Thirsk, 14 from Northallerton.

HAMERS, in the parish of Middleton, wapentake and liberty of Pickering-Lythe; 9 miles from Kirby-Moorside, 10 from Pickering, 14 from Whitby.

HAMMER, in the parish of East-Witton, wapentake of Hang-West, liberty of Richmondshire; 3 miles from Middleham, 5 from Leyburn, 6 from Masham.

HANDALL, in the parish of Loftus, east-division of the wapentake and liberty of Langbarugh; 9 miles from Guisbrough, 12 from Whitby.

HANG-BANK, in the parish of Melsonby, wapentake of Gilling-West, liberty of Richmondshire; 5 miles from Darlington, *(Durham)* 6 from Richmond.

HANGERSKILL, in the parish of Romaldkirk, wapentake of Gilling-West, liberty of Richmondshire; 7 miles from Richmond, 13 from Barnardcastle, *(Durham.)*

HARAM-GRANGE, in the parish of Topcliffe, wapentake of Halikeld, liberty of Richmondshire; 5 miles from Ripon, 5½ from Thirsk, 6 from Boroughbridge.

HARDRAW, in the parish of Aysgarth, wapentake of Hang-West, liberty of Richmondshire; 1¼ miles from Hawes, 5¼ from Askrigg.

HARKERSIDE, in the parish of Grinton, wapentake of Hang-West, liberty of Richmondshire; 2¼ miles from Reeth, 7 from Askrigg, 8 from Leyburn.

HARLSEY, EAST, in the parish of East-Harlsey, wapentake of Birdforth; *(the seat of Col. Burnett)* 6¼ miles from Northallerton, 10 from Stokesley, 12 from Thirsk.—Population 361.

HARLSEY, WEST, in the parish of Osmotherley, wapentake and liberty of Allertonshire; 5 miles from Northallerton, 11 from Thirsk, 11¼ from Stokesley.—Population 79.

HARNBY, in the parish of Spennithorne, wapentake of Hang-West, liberty of Richmondshire; 1 mile from Leyburn, 1 from Middleham.—Population 176.

HARTFORTH, in the parish of Gilling, wapentake of Gilling-West, liberty of Richmondshire; *(the seat of Sheldon Craddock, Esq.)* 4 miles from Richmond, 8 from Catterick, 8 from Greta-bridge.

HARTOFT, in the parish of Middleton, wapentake and liberty of Pickering-Lythe; 7 miles from Pickering, from Kirby-Moorside, 15 from Whitby.—Population 89.

HARTON, in the parish of Bossall, wapentake of Bulmer; 9 miles from York, 9¼ from Malton, 13 from Easingwold. —Population 154.

HARUM, in the parish of Helmsley, wapentake of Rydale; 3 miles from Helmsley, 4¼ from Kirby-Moorside, 15¼ from Malton.—Population 373.

HARWOOD-DALE, in the parish of Hackness, wapentake and liberty of Whitby-Strand; 7 miles from Scarborough, 14 from Whitby.—Population 185.

HARRIOT-AIR, in the parish of Helmsley, wapentake of Rydale; 2¼ miles from Helmsley, 8 from Kirby-Moorside.

HAWES, in the parish of Aysgarth, wapentake of Hang-West, liberty of Richmondshire; 6 miles from Askrigg, 14 from Kettlewell, 14¼ from Sedberg, 17 from Leyburn, 47 from York, 253 from London.—*Market*, Tuesday.— *Fairs*, Whit-Tuesday, for Woollen Goods, &c. September 28, for Horned Cattle, Horses, Sheep, Woollen Cloth, &c.—*Principal Inn*, Goat.—Population 1,223.

HAWKNEST, in the parish of East-Harlsey, wapentake of Birdforth; 6 miles from Northallerton, 10 from Yarm.

HAWKSWELL, EAST, in the parish of East-Hawkswell, wapentake of Hang-West, liberty of Richmondshire; *(the seat of Henry Gale, Esq.)* 4¼ miles from Leyburn, 5 from

Richmond, 6 from Middleham.—Population 115.

HAWKSWELL, WEST, in the parish of East-Hawkswell, wapentake of Hang-West, liberty of Richmondshire; 4¼ miles from Leyburn, 5 from Richmond, 6 from Middleham,—Population 31.

HAWKHILL-FARM, in the parish of Easingwold, wapentake of Bulmer; 1 mile from Easingwold, 12 from York.

HAWNBY, in the parish of Hawnby, wapentake of Birdforth; 6 miles from Helmsley, 10 from Thirsk, 14 from Northallerton.—Population 274.

HAWSKER, in the parish of Catterick, wapentake of Hang-East, liberty of Richmondshire; 3 miles from Catterick, 6 from Bedale, 6 from Richmond.

HAWSKER, in the parish of Whitby, wapentake and liberty of Whitby-Strand; 3 miles from Whitby, 18 from Scarborough.

HAXBY, in the parish of Strensall, wapentake of Bulmer, liberty of St. Peter; 4 miles from York, 10 from Easingwold, 15 from Malton.—Population 325.

HEALAUGH, in the parish of Grinton, wapentake of Gilling-West, liberty of Richmondshire; 1 mile from Reeth, 11 from Richmond.

HEALEY, in the parish of Masham, in the wapentakes of Hang-East and West, liberty of Richmondshire; 4 miles from Masham, 9 from Middleham, 11 from Leyburn.—Pop. 354.

HEALY-COTE, in the parish of Masham, wapentake of Hang-East, liberty of Richmondshire; 8 miles from Bedale, 18 from Richmond.

HEANING, in the parish of Aysgarth, wapentake of Hang-West, liberty of Richmondshire; 4½ miles from Askrigg, 6 from Leyburn, 6 from Middleham.

HEANING-HOUSE, in the parish of Aysgarth, wapentake of Hang-West, liberty of Richmondshire; 5¼ miles from Askrigg, 8 from Leyburn.

HELLBECK-LANDS, in the parish of Aysgarth, wapentake of Hang-West, liberty of Richmondshire; 6 miles from Hawes, 10¼ from Askrigg.

HELPERBY, in the parish of Brafferton, wapentake of Bulmer, liberty of St. Peter; 5 miles from Boroughbridge, 5 from Easingwold, 16 from York.—Population 548.

HELMSLEY, in the parish of Helmsley, wapentake of Rydale; 6 miles from Kirby-Moorside, 13 from Easingwold, 14 from Thirsk, 16 from Stokesley, 16 from Malton, 20 from Northallerton, 23 from York, 221 from London.—*Market*, Saturday.—*Fairs*, May 19, July 16, October 1 and 2, November 5 and 6, for Horned Cattle, Sheep, Linen and Woollen

Cloth, &c. if the Fairs for Horned Cattle, fall on a Monday, the Sheep Fairs will be held on Saturday preceeding.—*Principal Inn*, Black Swan.—Population 1,449.

HELMSLEY, GATE, in the parish of Gate-Helmsley, wapentake of Bulmer, liberty of St. Peter; 6 miles from York, 13 from Easingwold, 14 from Malton.—Pop. 151.

HELMSLEY-OVER, or UPPER, in the parish of Over-Helmsley, wapentake of Bulmer; *(the seat of E. I. Whittell, Esq.)* 7 miles from York, 12 from Malton, 14 from Easingwold, 14 from Malton.—Population 47.

HELWITH, in the parish of Kirkby-Ravensworth, wapentake of Gilling-West, liberty of Richmondshire; 8 miles from Richmond, 13 from Barnardcastle, *(Durham.)*

HEMLINGTON, in the parish of Stainton, wapentake and liberty of Langbargh; *(Hemlington-Hall, the seat of General Hall,)* 6 miles from Stokesley, 7 from Yarm, 9 from Guisbrough.—Population 58.

HENDERSKELFE, in the parish and wapentake of Bulmer; 6 miles from Malton, 15 from York, 15 from Easingwold.—Population 137.

HERBY, in the parish of Barningham, wapentake of Gilling-West, liberty of Richmondshire; 7 miles from Barnardcastle, *(Durham,)* 8 from Richmond.

HEWORTH, in the parishes of St. Cuthbert, St. Saviour, St Giles, York, wapentake of Bulmer; 1 mile from York, 14 from Easingwold, 17 from Malton.—Population 82.

HEWTHWAITE, in the parish of Whorlton, wapentake and liberty of Langbargh; 6 miles from Stokesley, 11 from Northallerton, 14 from Guisbrough.

HIELDENLEY, in the parish and wapentake of Bulmer; *(the seat of Lady Strickland,)* 3 miles from Malton, 15¼ from York, 18 from Easingwold.

HIGH-CLOSE-HOUSE, in the parish of St. John, Stanwick, wapentake of Gilling-West, liberty of Richmondshire; 6 miles from Richmond, 7 from Darlington, *(Durham.)*

HIGHTHORNE, in the parish of Husthwaite, wapentake of Birdforth; *(the seat of C. Goulton, Esq.)* 4 miles from Easingwold, 8 from Thirsk.

HILLER-GREEN, in the parish of Hackness, wapentake and liberty of Pickering-Lythe; 7 miles from Scarborough, 11 from Pickering, 16 from Whitby.

HILTON, in the parish of Rudby, wapentake and liberty of Langbargh; 4 miles from Yarm, 4 from Stokesley.—Population 136.

HINDERWELL, or HILDERWELL, in the parish of Hinderwell, east-division of the wapentake and liberty of Lang-

NORTH-RIDING.

barugh; 8 miles from Whitby, 14 from Guisbrough, 21¼ from Stokesley.—Population 1,224.

HINLETHWAITE, in the parish of Coverham, wapentake of Hang-West, 6 miles from Middleham 7 from Leyburn.

HIPSWELL, in the parish of Catterick, wapentake of Hang-East, liberty of Richmondshire; 3 miles from Richmond, 8 from Leyburn.—Population 240.

HIPSWELL-LODGE, in the parish of Catterick, wapentake of Hang-East, liberty of Richmondshire; *(the seat of Thomas Hutchinson, Esq.)* 2¼ miles from Richmond, 7¼ from Leyburn.

HIRST, in the parish of Marrick, wapentake of Gilling-West, liberty of Richmondshire; 3 miles from Reeth, 7 from Richmond.

HOLE OF HERCUM, in the parish of Leavisham, wapentake and liberty of Pickering-Lythe; 8 miles from Pickering, 13 from Whitby, 17 from Malton.

HOLLIN-HILL, in the parish of Coxwold, wapentake of Birdforth; 3 miles from Easingwold, 9 from Helmsley, 13 from Thirsk.

HOLME, in the parish of Aysgarth, wapentake of Hang-West, liberty of Richmondshire; 1¼ miles from Askrigg, 4¼ from Hawes.

HOLME, in the parish of Pickhill, wapentake and liberty of Allertonshire; 6 miles from Bedale, 8 from Northallerton, 9 from Ripon.—Population 72.

HOLME, NORTH, in the parish of Kirkdale, wapentake of Rydale; 3 miles from Kirby-Moorside, 5¼ from Helmsley, 9 from Malton.—Population 16.

HOLME, SOUTH, in the parish of Hovingham, wapentake of Rydale; 7 miles from Kirby-Moorside, 8 from Helmsley, 10 from Malton.—Population 53.

HOLTBY, in the parish of Holtby, wapentake of Bulmer; *(the seat of the Rev. R. Warbottom)* 5 miles from York, 15¼ from Malton.— Population 117.

HOLTBY, in the parish of Hornby, wapentake of Hang-East, liberty of Richmondshire; 3¼ miles from Bedale, 4 from Catterick, 9 from Richmond.

HOLWICK, in the parish of Romaldkirk, wapentake of Gilling-West, liberty of Richmondshire; 11 miles from Barnardcastle, *(Durham)* 13 from Greta-bridge, 25 from Richmond.—Population 196.

HOOD-GRANGE, in the parish of Kilburn, wapentake of Birdforth, liberty of Ripon; 7 miles from Thirsk, 8 from Easingwold, 9 from Helmsley.—Population 21.

E

HOPE, in the parish of Barningham, wapentake of Gilling-West, liberty of Richmondshire; 3 miles from Greta-bridge, 4 from Barnardcastle, *(Durham)* 13 from Richmond.

HORNBY, in the parish of Hornby, wapentake of Hang-East, liberties of St. Peter and Richmondshire; 5 miles from Bedale, 7 from Richmond.—Population 111.

HORNBY, in the parish of Great-Smeaton, wapentake and liberty of Allertonshire; 7 miles from Yarm, 8 from Northallerton, 10 from Darlington, *(Durham.)*—Population 228.

HORNBY-CASTLE, in the parish of Hornby, wapentake of Hang-East, liberty of Richmondshire; *(the seat of the Duke of Leeds)* 5 miles from Bedale, 7 from Richmond.

HORNBY-GRANGE, in the parish of Great-Smeaton, wapentake and liberty of Allertonshire; *(the seat of Major General Hewgill,)* 7 miles from Northallerton, 8 from Yarm, 9 from Darlington, *(Durham.)*

HORSEHOUSE, in the parish of Coverham, wapentake of Hang-West, liberty of Richmondshire; 6 miles from Middleham, 7 from Leyburn.

HOULTBY, HIGH, in the parish of Hornby, wapentake of Hang-East, liberty of Richmondshire; 3 miles from Bedale, 9 from Richmond.

HOULTBY, LOW, in the parish of Bedale, wapentake of Hang-East, liberty of Richmondshire; 4 miles from Bedale, 8 from Richmond.

HOVINGHAM, in the parish of Hovingham, wapentake of Rydale *(the seat of Edward Worsley, Esq.)* 7 miles from Kirby-Moorside, 7¼ from Helmsley, 9 from Malton.—Population 495.

HOWE, in the parish of Pickhill, wapentake of Halikeld; 5 miles from Thirsk, 6 from Ripon, 7 from Boroughbridge. —Population 24.

HOWGRAVE, in the parish of Kirklington, wapentake of Halikeld; 7 miles from Bedale, 7 from Ripon.

HOWGRAVE, in the parish of Pickhill, wapentake and liberty of Allertonshire; 5¼ miles from Bedale, 8½ from Northallerton.

HOWLSIKE, in the parish of Danby, east-division of the wapentake and liberty of Langbarugh; 10 miles from Guisbrough, 10¼ from Whitby.

HOWS, in the parish of West-Rounton, wapentake and liberty of Allertonshire; 6 miles from Yarm, 9 from Northallerton.

HOWTHORPE, in the parish of Hovingham, wapentake of Rydale; 7 miles from Malton, 8¼ from Kirby-Moorside, 8¼ from Helmsley.

HUBY, in the parish of Sutton-on-the-Forest, wapentake of Bulmer, liberty of Pickering-Lythe; 4 miles from Easingwold, 9 from York, 16 from Malton.—Population 393.

HUDSWELL, in the parish of Catterick, wapentake of Hang-West, liberty of Richmondshire; 2 miles from Richmond, 9 from Leyburn.—Population 227.

HULANDS, in the parish of Marrick, wapentake of Gilling-West, liberty of Richmondshire; 3 miles from Reeth, 7 from Richmond.

HUM-BURTON, see Burton, Hum.

HUNDERTHWAITE, in the parish of Romaldkirk, wapentake of Gilling-West, liberty of Richmondshire; 6 miles from Barnardcastle, *(Durham)* 9 from Greta-bridge, 21 from Richmond.—Population 334.

HUNTERS-HALL, in the parish of Coverham, wapentake of Hang-West, liberty of Richmondshire; *(the seat of — Smith, Esq.)* 8 miles from Middleham, 8½ from Leyburn.

HUNT-HOUSE, in the parish of Pickering, wapentake and liberty of Pickering-Lythe; 10 miles from Pickering, 13 from Whitby, 17 from Kirby-Moorside.

HUNTINGTON, in the parish of Huntington, wapentake of Bulmer, a part in the liberty of St. Peter; 3 miles from York, 13 from Easingwold, 16 from Malton.—Pop. 312.

HUNTON, in the parishes of Hornby and Patrick-Brompton, wapentake of Hang-West, liberties of St. Peter and Richmondshire; 6 miles from Leyburn, 6 from Richmond, 6½ from Middleham.—Population 388.

HURRY, in the parish of Romaldkirk, wapentake of Gilling-West, liberty of Richmondshire; 7 miles from Barnardcastle, *(Durham)* 21 from Richmond.

HUSTHWAITE, in the parish of Husthwaite, wapentake of Birdforth, liberty of St. Peter; 4 miles from Easingwold, 5 from Thirsk.—Population 288.

HUTTON, in the parish of Rudby, west-division of the wapentake and liberty of Langbarugh; 4¼ miles from Stokesley, 6 from Yarm, 12 from Northallerton.—Population 707.

HUTTON, in the parish of Sessay, wapentake and liberty of Allertonshire; 5 miles from Easingwold, 6 from Thirsk.—Population 85.

HUTTON, in the parish of Hutton, wapentake of Gilling-West; 3 miles from Greta-bridge, 6 from Barnardcastle, *(Durham)* 9 from Richmond.—Population 200.

HUTTON-BONVILLE, in the parish of Birkby, wapentake and liberty of Allertonshire; *(the seat of Anthony Hammond, Esq.)* 5 miles from Northallerton, 11¼ from Darlington, *(Durham.)*—Population 150.

HUTTON-BUSHELL, in the parish of Hutton-Bushell, wapentake and liberty of Pickering-Lythe; *(the seat of Mrs. Osbaldeston,)* 6 miles from Scarborough, 12 from Pickering, 16 from Malton.—Population 410.

HUTTON-CONYERS, in the parish of North-Otterington, wapentake and liberty of Allertonshire; 1 mile from Ripon, 6 from Boroughbridge.—Population 133.

HUTTON-HANG, HIGH, in the parish of Bedale, wapentake of Hang-West, liberty of Richmondshire; 5 miles from Bedale, 6 from Leyburn, 8 from Richmond.—Pop. 34.

HUTTON-HANG, LOW, in the parish of Bedale, wapentake of Hang-West, liberty of Richmondshire; 3 miles from Middleham, 4¼ from Leyburn, 8 from Bedale.

HUTTON-IN-THE-HOLE, in the parish of Lastingham, wapentake of Rydale; 3 miles from Kirby-Moorside, 7 from Pickering.—Population 238.

HUTTON-LODGE, in the parish of Sheriff-hutton, wapentake of Bulmer; *(the seat of Leonard Thompson, Esq.)* 8 miles from Easingwold, 10 from York, 12½ from Malton.

HUTTON-LONGVILLERS, or MAGNA, in the parish of Gilling, wapentake of Gilling-West, liberty of Richmondshire; 3 miles from Greta-bridge, 8 from Richmond. —Population 278.

HUTTON, LOW, in the parish of Huttons Ambo, wapentake of Bulmer; 3¼ miles from Malton, 16 from York, 19 from Easingwold.—Population 286.

HUTTON-LOWCROSS, in the parish of Guisbrough, east-division of the wapentake and liberty of Langbarugh; 2 miles from Guisbrough, 8½ from Stokesley, 22 from Whitby. —Population 59.

HUTTON-MULGRAVE, in the parish of Lythe, east-division of the wapentake and liberty of Langbarugh; 6 miles from Whitby, 16 from Guisbrough, 22 from Stokesley.— Population 93.

HUTTONS AMBO, in the parish of Huttons Ambo, wapentake of Bulmer: *(the seat of R. J. Stainforth, Esq.)* 8½ miles from Malton, 15 from York, 18 from Easingwold.—Pop. 139

HUTTON, SAND, in the parish of Thirsk, wapentake of Birdforth; 3 miles from Thirsk, 8 from Northallerton, 11 from Boroughbridge.—Population 240.

HUTTON, SAND, in the parish of Bossall, wapentake of Bulmer; *(the seat of the Rev. T. C. R. Read)* 7 miles from York, 12 from Malton, 13 from Easingwold.— Population 170.

HUTTON, SHERIFF, in the parish of Sheriff-Hutton, wapentake of Bulmer; 8 miles from Easingwold, 10 from York, 12 from Malton.—Population 597.

HUTTON-UPON-DERWENT, in the parish of Huttons Ambo, wapentake of Bulmer; 3 miles from Malton, 16 from York, 19 from Easingwold.

I.

IBORN-DALE, in the parish of Whitby, wapentake and and liberty of Whitby-Strand; 4 miles from Whitby, 17 from Pickering.

ILTON, or HILTON, in the parish of Masham, wapentake of Hang-East, liberty of Richmondshire; 4 miles from Masham, 13 from Richmond.—Population 224

ING-HEAD, in the parish of Marrick, wapentake of Gilling-West, liberty of Richmondshire; 7 miles from Richmond, 8 from Leyburn.

INGLEBY, in the parish of Arncliffe, west-division of the wapentake and liberty of Langbarugh; 8 miles from Northallerton, 8 from Stokesley, 8 from Yarm, 14 from Thirsk. —Population 253.

INGLEBY-CROSS, in the parish of Arncliffe, west-division of the wapentake and liberty of Langbarugh; 8 miles from Northallerton, 8 from Stokesley, 8 from Yarm, 14 from Thirsk.

INGLEBY, or INGLEBY-GREENHOW, in the parish of Ingleby, west-division of the wapentake and liberty of Langbarugh; 4¼ miles from Stokesley, 8 from Guisbrough.— Population 180.

INGLEBY-MANOR, in the parish of Ingleby, west-division of the wapentake and liberty of Langbarugh; *(the seat of Sir William Foulis, Bart.)* 5 miles from Stokesley, 8½ from Guisbrough.

IRTON, or URTON, in the parish of Seamor, wapentake and liberty of Pickering-Lythe; 4 miles from Scarborough, 15 from Pickering, 19 from Malton.

ISLEBECK, in the parish of Thirsk, wapentake of Birdforth; 4 miles from Thirsk, 7 from Easingwold.

IVELET, in the parish of Grinton, wapentake of Gilling-West, liberty of Richmondshire; 5 miles from Askrigg, 7 from Reeth, 17 from Richmond.

JEATOR-HOUSES, in the parish of Sigston, wapentake and liberty of Allertonshire, 5 miles from Northallerton, 7¼ from Thirsk, 12¼ from Yarm.

JERVEAUX-ABBEY, in the parish of East-Witton, wapentake of Hang-West, liberty of Richmondshire; 3 miles from Middleham, 4¼ from Leyburn, 7 from Bedale.

JOHN, ST. in the parish of St. John, Stanwick, wapentake of Gilling-West, liberty of Richmondshire; 7 miles from Richmond, 8 from Darlington, *(Durham.)*

JOLBY, in the parish of Croft, wapentake of Gilling-East, liberty of Richmondshire; 3 miles from Darlington, *(Durham)* 8 from Richmond.

JELLY-PARK, *formerly* JULIAN-PARK-HOUSES, in the parish of Lythe, east-division of the wapentake and liberty of Langbarugh; 8 miles from Whitby, 15 from Pickering, 16 from Kirby-Moorside.

K.

KEARTON, in the parish of Grinton, wapentake of Gilling-West, liberty of Richmondshire; 3 miles from Reeth, 7 from Askrigg, 13 from Richmond.

KEEPWICK, or CUBECK, in the parish of Aysgarth, wapentake of Hang-West, liberty of Richmondshire; 1¼ miles from Askrigg, 6 from Hawes, 11 from Leyburn.

KELD, in the parish of Grinton, wapentake of Gilling-West, liberty of Richmondshire; 7 miles from Askrigg, 12 from Reeth, 22 from Richmond.

KELDHOME, in the parish of Kirby-Moorside, wapentake of Rydale; 1 mile from Kirby-Moorside, 7 from Helmsley, 13 from Malton.

KELLERBY-HALL, in the parish of Cayton, wapentake and liberty of Pickering-Lythe; 4 miles from Scarborough, 19 from Pickering, 21 from Malton.

KELTON, in the parish of Romaldkirk, wapentake of Gilling-West, liberty of Richmondshire; 10 miles from Barnardcastle, *(Durham)* 22 from Richmond.—Pop. 135.

KEMPSWIDDEN, in the parish of Kildale, west-division of the wapentake and liberty of Langbarugh; 7 miles from Guisbrough, 15 from Stokesley.

KEPWICK, in the parishes of Leak and Cowsby, wapentake of Birdforth; 8 miles from Northallerton, 9 from Thirsk, 11 from Helmsley.—Population 167.

KETTLENESS, in the parish of Lythe, east-division of the wapentake and liberty of Langbarugh; 7 miles from Whitby, 15 from Guisbrough.

KIDSTONE, in the parish of Aysgarth, wapentake of Hang-West; 5 miles from Askrigg, 10¼ from Middleham, 12¼ from Leyburn.

KILBURN, HIGH, in the parish of Low-Kilburn, wapentake of Birdforth, liberties of Ripon and Pickering-Lythe; 8 miles from Thirsk, 8 from Easingwold, 8 from Helmsley.

KILBURN, LOW, in the parish of Low-Kilburn, wapentake of Birdforth, liberties of Ripon and Pickering-Lythe; 8 miles from Thirsk, 8 from Easingwold, 8 from Helmsley.—Population 468.

KILDALE, in the parish of Kildale, west-division of the wapentake and liberty of Langbarugh, *(the seat of Robert Bell Livesey, Esq.)* 6 miles from Stokesley, 6 from Guisbrough, 14 from Yarm.—Population 201.

KILGRAM-BRIDGE, in the parish of West-Witton, wapentake of Hang-West, liberty of Richmondshire; 3 miles from Masham, 5 from Bedale.

KILLERBY, in the parish of Catterick, wapentake of Hang-East, liberty of Richmondshire; *(the seat of Thomas Booth, Esq.)* 1¼ miles from Catterick, 6 from Richmond, 6 from Bedale.—Population 86.

KILMONT-SCAR, in the parish of Bowes, wapentake of Gilling-West, liberty of Richmondshire; 3 miles from Greta-bridge, 4 from Barnardcastle, *(Durham)* 16 from Richmond.

KILTON, in the parish of Skelton, east-division of the wapentake and liberty of Langbarugh; 7 miles from Guisbrough, 15 from Stokesley, 16 from Whitby.—Pop. 129.

KILTON-THORPE, in the parish of Skelton, east-division of the wapentake and liberty of Langbarugh; 6 miles from Guisbrough, 14 from Stokesley.

KILVINGTON, NORTH, in the parish of Thornton-le-street, wapentake and liberty, of Allertonshire; 2¼ miles from Thirsk, 6¼ from Northallerton.—Population 57.

KILVINGTON, SOUTH, in the parish of South Kilvington, wapentake of Birdforth; 1¼ miles from Thirsk, 8 from Northallerton.—Population 229.

KINGTHORPE, in the parish of Pickering, wapentake and liberty of Pickering-Lythe; *(the seat of John Fothergill, Esq.)* 3 miles from Pickering, 12 from Malton, 18 from Whitby.—Population 37.

KIPLIN, in the parish Catterick, wapentake of Gilling-East, liberty of Richmondshire; *(the seat of Robert Croxc, Esq.)* 6 miles from Catterick, 7 from Northallerton, 8 from Richmond.—Population 95.

KIRBY, COLD, in the parish of Cold-Kirby, wapentake of Birdforth; 5 miles from Helmsley, 8 from Thirsk.—Population 158.

KIRBY-ON-THE-MOOR, or KIRBY-HILL, in the parish of Kirby-on-the-Moor, wapentake of Halikeld, liberty of Allertonshire ; 1 mile from Boroughbridge, 5 from Ripon, 8 from Knaresborough.—Population 140.

KIRBY-KNOWLE, in the parish of Kirby-Knowle, wapentake of Birdforth ; 6 miles from Thirsk, 9 from Northallerton.—Population 129.

KIRBY-MILLS, in the parish of Kirby-Moorside, wapentake of Rydale; 1 mile from Kirby-Moorside, 6¼ from Helmsley, 12¼ from Malton.

KIRBY-MISPERTON, ir the parish of Kirby-Misperton, wapentake and liberty of Pickering-Lythe; 4 miles from Pickering, 6 from Malton, 7 from Kirby-Moorside.— Population 129.

KIRBY-MOORSIDE, in the parish of Kirby-Moorside, wapentake of Rydale; 6 miles from Helmsley, 8 from Pickering, 14 from Malton, 24 from Guisbrough, 28½ from York, 228 from London.—*Market*, Wednesday.—*Fairs*, Wednesday in Whitsun-week, and September 18, for Horned Cattle, Sheep, and Linen.—*Principal Inn.*—White Horse. —Population 1,396.

KIRBY-WISKE, in the parish of Kirby-Wiske, wapentake of Gilling-East, liberty of Richmondshire ; 4 miles from Thirsk, 7 from Northallerton, 12 from Boroughbridge.— Population 150.

KIRKBY, in the parish of Kirkby, west-division of the wapentake and liberty of Langbarugh ; 2¼ miles from Stokesley, 10 from Guisbrough, 10 from Yarm.—Population 165.

KIRKBY-BRIGGS, in the parish of Bedale, wapentake of Hang-West, liberty of Richmondshire; 2 miles from Bedale, 5 from Catterick, 9 from Leyburn.

KIRKBY-RAVENSWORTH, or KIRKBY-HILL, in the parish of Kirkby-Ravensworth, wapentake of Gilling-West, liberty of Richmondshire ; 4½ miles from Richmond, 7 from Catterick, 8 from Greta-bridge.—Population 143.

KIRKDALE, in the parish of Kirkdale, wapentake of Rydale ; 2 miles from Kirby-Moorside, 9 from Pickering.

KIRKLEATHAM, in the parish of Kirkleatham, east-division of the wapentake and liberty of Langbarugh ; *(the seat of Sir Charles Turner, Bart.)* 4½ miles from Guisbrough, 12 from Yarm, 12 from Stockton, *(Durham)* 12½ from Stokesley.—Population 680.

KIRKLEVINGTON, in the parish of Kirklevington, west-division of the wapentake and liberty of Langbarugh ; 2 miles, from Yarm, 6 from Stokesley, 6 from Stockton, 14 from Guisbrough.—Population 239.

KIRKLINGTON, in the parish of Kirklington, wapentake

of Halikeld, liberty of Richmondshire; 6 miles from Bedale, 7 from Ripon, 7½ from Masham.—Population 273.

KNAYTON, in the parish of Leak, wapentake and liberty of Allertonshire; 3¼ miles from Thirsk, 6 from Northallerton, 17 from Stokesley.—Population 321.

KNEETON-HALL, in the parish of Middleton-Tyas, wapentake of Gilling-East, liberty of Richmondshire; 5 miles from Richmond, 7 from Darlington, *(Durham.)*

KNEETON-UNDER, in the parish of Middleton-Tyas, wapentake of Gilling-East, liberty of Richmondshire; 5 miles from Richmond, 7 from Darlington, *(Durham.)*

L.

LACKENBY, in the parish of Wilton, east-division of the wapentake and liberty of Langbarugh; 4½ miles from Guisbrough, 9 from Stokesley, 10¼ from Yarm.

LAITH, in the parish of Romaldkirk, wapentake of Gilling-West, liberty of Richmondshire; 9 miles from Barnardcastle, *(Durham)* 13 from Greta-bridge.

LAMBHILL, in the parish of Masham, wapentake of Hang-West, liberty of Richmondshire; 2 miles from Masham, 6 from Bedale.

LAMBHILL, in the parish of Bowes, wapentake of Gilling-West; 4 miles from Greta-bridge, 4 from Barnardcastle, *(Durham.)*

LANDMOTH, in the parish of Leak, wapentake and liberty of Allertonshire; 4 miles from Northallerton, 6½ from Thirsk.—Population 46.

LANE-END, in the parish of St. John, Stanwick, wapentake of Gilling-West, liberty of Richmondshire; 5 miles from Darlington, 9 from Barnardcastle, *(Durham)* 9 from Richmond.

LANE-HEAD, in the parish of Gilling, wapentake of Gilling-West, liberty of Richmondshire; 3 miles from Greta-bridge, 9 from Richmond.

LANGBARUGH, *(which gives name to the wapentake)* in the parish of Ayton, west-division of the wapentake and liberty of Langbarugh; 3 miles from Stokesley, 5 from Guisbrough.

LANGTHORNE, in the parish of Bedale, wapentake of Halikeld; 3 miles from Bedale, 9 from Masham, 10 from Richmond.—Population 104.

LANGTHORPE, in the parish of Kirby-on-the-Moor, wapentake of Halikeld; ¼ a mile from Boroughbridge, 5¼ from Ripon, 7¼ from Knaresborough.—Population 114.

LANGTON, GREAT, in the parish of Great-Langton, wapentake of Gilling-East, liberty of Richmondshire; 6 miles from Northallerton, 9 from Richmond.—Population 101.

LANGTON, LITTLE, in the parish of Great-Langton, wapentake of Gilling-East, liberty of Richmondshire; *(Langton-Lodge, the seat of Francis Redfearn, Esq.)* 5 miles from Northallerton, 10 from Richmond.—Population 67.

LANGWITH, or LONGWITH, in the parish of Well, wapentake of Hang-East, liberty of Richmondshire; 3 miles from Bedale, 5 from Masham.—Population 124.

LARTINGTON, in the parish of Romaldkirk, wapentake of Gilling-West, liberty of Richmondshire; *(the seat of Henry Mair, Esq.)* 2 miles from Barnardcastle, *(Durham)* 6 from Greta-bridge, 17 from Richmond.—Population 223.

LASKILL, in the parish of Helmsley, wapentake of Rydale; 6¼ miles from Helmsley, 12 from Kirby-Moorside.—Pop. 79.

LASTINGHAM, in the parish of Lastingham, wapentake of Rydale; 4 miles from Kirby-Moorside, 10 from Helmsley, 16 from Malton.—Population 222.

LAYSTHORPE, in the parish of Stonegrave, wapentake of Rydale; 4 miles from Helmsley, 7 from Kirby-Moorside, 13½ from Malton.

LAYTON, EAST, in the parishes of Melsonby and St. John, Stanwick, wapentake of Gilling-West, liberty of Richmondshire; *(the seat of Thomas Barker, Esq.)* 6 miles from Richmond, 7 from Greta-bridge, 8 from Catterick.—Pop. 95.

LAYTON, WEST, in the parish of Hutton, wapentake of Gilling-West, liberty of Richmondshire; *(the seat of Lord Rokeby)* 6 miles from Richmond, 6 from Greta-bridge, 9 from Catterick.—Population 56.

LAZENBY, in the parish of Wilton, east-division of the wapentake and liberty of Langbarugh; 5 miles from Guisbrough, 10 from Stokesley, 10½ from Yarm.

LAZENBY-HALL, in the parish of Northallerton, wapentake and liberty of Allertonshire; 4 miles from Northallerton, 12 from Yarm, 12½ from Darlington, *(Durham.)*

LEAK, in the parish of Leak, wapentake and liberty of Allertonshire; 5 miles from Northallerton, 6 from Thirsk.—Population 7.

LEALHOLM, and LEALHOLM-BRIDGE, in the parish of Danby, east-division of the wapentake and liberty of Langbarugh; 9 miles from Whitby, 13 from Guisbrough, 18 from Stokesley.

LEALHOLM-HALL, in the parish of Lythe, east-division

of the wapentake and liberty of Langbarugh; 8½ miles from Whitby, 12 from Guisbrough.

LEASES, in the parish of Bedale, wapentake of Hang-East, liberty of Richmondshire; *(the seat of Mrs. Arden)* 2¼ miles from Bedale, 4¼ from Catterick, 6¼ from Northallerton.

LEASHEAD, in the parish of Whitby, wapentake and liberty of Whitby-Strand; 7 miles from Whitby, 14 from Pickering.

LEBBERSTON, in the parish of Filey, wapentake and liberty of Pickering-Lythe; 4 miles from Hunmanby, 6½ from Scarborough.—Population 120.

LECKBY, in the parish of Cundall, wapentake of Halikeld, liberty of Richmondshire; 5 miles from Boroughbridge, 8 from Thirsk, 9 from Easingwold.

LEEMING, in the parish of Burneston, wapentake of Halikeld, liberty of Richmondshire; 2 miles from Bedale, 6¼ from Catterick, 7 from Northallerton, 8 from Masham.

LEEMING, LITTLE, in the parish of Bedale, wapentake of Hang-East, liberty of Richmondshire, 2 miles from Bedale, 6½ from Catterick, 7 from Northallerton, 8 from Masham.

LEIGHTON, in the parish of Masham, wapentake of Hang-East; 5 miles from Masham, 10 from Middleham, 11 from Bedale.

LEVEN-BRIDGE, in the parish of Rudby, west-division of the wapentake and liberty of Langbarugh; 2 miles from Yarm, 4 from Stockton, *(Durham)* 6 from Stokesley.

LEVEN-GROVE, in the parish of Rudby, west-division of the wapentake and liberty of Langbarugh; *(the seat of Lady Amhurst)* 2 miles from Stokesley, 6 from Yarm.

LEVINGTON-CASTLE, in the parish of Kirk-Levington, west-division of the wapentake and liberty of Langbarugh; 3¼ miles from Yarm, 5 from Stokesley.—Population 47.

LEVINGTON, KIRK, in the parish of Kirk-Levington, west-division of the wapentake and liberty of Langbarugh; 2 miles from Yarm, 6 from Stokesley.—Population 239.

LEVISHAM, in the parish of Levisham, wapentake and liberty of Pickering-Lythe; 6 miles from Pickering, 15 from Malton, 16 from Whitby.—Population 123.

LEYBURN, in the parish of Wensley, wapentake of Hang-West, liberty of Richmondshire; 2 miles from Middleham, 8 from Richmond, 10 from Reeth, 12 from Askrigg, 12 from Bedale, 120 from Ripon, 38 from York, 235 from London.—*Market* Friday.—*Fairs,* second Friday in February, second Friday in May, second Friday in October, second Friday in December, for Horned Cattle, Sheep, &c.—*Bankers,* Messrs. Hutton, Wood, Simpson, Other, Robson, and

Ellis, draw on Messrs. Down, and Co. Bartholomew-lane.— *Principal Inns*, Bolton's Arms, and King's Arms.—Pop. 1446.

LILLING, EAST, in the parish of Sheriff-Hutton, wapentake of Bulmer; 9 miles from York, 10 from Easingwold, 10 from Malton.—Population 142.

LILLING, WEST, in the parish of Sheriff-Hutton, wapentake of Bulmer; 9 miles from Malton, 9 from Easingwold, 10 from York.

LIMBER-HILL, in the parish of Lythe, east-division of the wapentake and liberty of Langbarugh; 8 miles from Whitby, 15 from Guisbrough.—Population 345.

LINGY-MOOR, in the parish of Middleton-Tyas, wapentake of Gilling-East; 5 miles from Catterick, 5 from Richmond, 9¼ from Darlington, *(Durham.)*

LINTHORPE, or LEVENTHORPE, in the parish of Acklam, west-division of the wapentake and liberty of Langbarugh; 4 miles from Stockton, *(Durham)* 7 from Stokesley.—Population 214.

LINTON, in the parish of Newton-upon-Ouse, wapentake of Bulmer; 6 miles from Easingwold, 8 from Boroughbridge, 10 from York.—Population 246.

LITHERSKEW, in the parish of Aysgarth, wapentake of Hang-West; liberty of Richmondshire; 1 mile from Hawes, 4 from Askrigg, 16 from Leyburn.

LITTLE-BECK, in the parish of Whitby, wapentake and liberty of Whitby-Strand; 6 miles from Whitby, 15 from Pickering, 16 from Scarborough.

LIVERTON, in the parish of Easington, east-division of the wapentake and liberty of Langbarugh; 9 miles from Guisbrough, 15 from Stokesley, 16 from Whitby.—Pop. 230.

LOBSTER-HOUSE, in the parish of Bossall, wapentake of Bulmer; 7¼ miles from York, 10¼ from Malton, 12 from Easingwold.

LOCKTON, in the parish of Middleton, wapentake and liberty of Pickering-Lythe; 6 miles from Pickering, 15 from Malton, 15 from Whitby.—Poplation 245.

LODGE-GREEN, in the parish of Grinton, wapentake of Gilling-West, liberty of Richmondshire; 6 miles from Askrigg, 6 from Reeth, 16 from Richmond.

LOFTUS, in the parish of Loftus, east-division of the wapentake and liberty of Langbarugh; 8 miles from Guisbrough, 14 from Whitby, 16 from Stokesley.—Population 1,186.

LONDONDERRY, in the parish of Burneston, wapentake of Halikeld, liberty of Richmondshire; *(the seat of Timothy Hunton, Esq.)* 3 miles from Bedale, 8 from Northallerton, 9 from Masham, 12 from Ripon.

NORTH-RIDING.

LONGTHWAITE, in the parish of Arkengarthdale, wapentake of Gilling-West, liberty of Richmondshire; 3 miles from Reeth, 13 from Richmond.

LONTON, in the parish of Romaldkirk, wapentake of Gilling-West, liberty of Richmondshire; 8 miles from Barnardcastle, *(Durham)* 11 from Greta-bridge.

LOUP-SIDE, in the parish of Romaldkirk, wapentake of Gilling-West; 4 miles from Barnardcastle, *(Durham)* 7 from Greta-bridge, 22 from Richmond.

LOUSEY-CROSS, in the parish of St. John, Stanwick, wapentake of Gilling-West, liberty of Richmondshire; 7 miles from Richmond, 7 from Darlington, *(Durham.)*

LOVESOME-HILL, in the parish of Birkby, wapentake and liberty of Allertonshire; 3¼ miles from Northallerton, 12¼ from Darlington, *(Durham.)*

LOW-FIELDS, see Fields, Low.

LOW-FIELDS, in the parish of Bowes, wapentake of Gilling-West, liberty of Richmondshire; 4 miles from Greta-bridge, 5 from Barnardcastle, *(Durham.)*

LOW-MOORS, in the parish of Kirby-Misperton, wapentake and liberty of Pickering-Lythe; 5 miles from Pickering, 5 from Malton, 10 from Kirby-Moorside.

LOW-NESS, in the parish of Pickhill, wapentake of Halikeld, liberty of Richmondshire; 5¼ miles from Bedale, 8 from Thirsk, 9½ from Ripon.

LOW-ROW, n the parish of Grinton, wapentake of Gilling-West, liberty of Richmondshire; *(the seat of — Parke, Esq.)* 5 miles from Reeth, 9 from Askrigg, 15 from Richmond.

LUNE-DALE, in the parish of Romaldkirk, wapentake of Gilling-West, liberty of Richmondshire; 7 miles from Barnardcastle, *(Durham)* 10 from Greta-bridge, 22 from Richmond.—Population 307.

LYTHE, in the parish of Lythe, east-division of the wapentake and liberty of Langbarugh; 4 miles from Whitby, 17 from Guisbrough.—Population 1,037.

M.

MAINS, HIGH, in the parish of Masham, wapentake of Hang-East; 2 miles from Masham, 8 from Bedale.

MAINS, LOW, in the parish of Masham, wapentake of Hang-East; 1 mile from Masham, 7 from Bedale.

MALTBY, in the parish of Stainton, west-division of the

wapentake and liberty of Langbarugh; 4 miles from Yarm, 6 from Stokesley, 11 from Guisbrough.—Population 141.

MALTON, NEW, in the parishes of St. Leonard and St. Michael, Malton, wapentake of Rydale, a part in the liberty of St. Peter; 9 miles from Pickering, 11¼ from Sledmere, 14¼ from Kirby-Moorside, 16 from Helmsley, 18 from York, 19 from Easingwold, 22¼ from Scarborough, 27 from Thirsk, 28¼ from Beverley, 217 from London.—*Market*, Saturday. —*Fairs*, Saturday before Palm-Sunday, for Horned Cattle, and that day, and the week preceeding, for Horses; Saturday before Whit-Sunday, October 11 and 12, for Sheep, Hardware, &c.—*Bankers*, Messrs. Hayes and Co. draw on Messrs. Bond and Co. Change-Alley; Messrs. Raikes and Co. draw on Messrs. Denison and Co. St. Mary-Axe; Messrs. Pease and Co. draw on Messrs. Harrisons and Co. Mansion-house Street.—Sends two Members to Parliament. —*Principal Inns*, Talbot, and White Horse.—Pop. 3,047.

MALTON, OLD, in the parish of Old-Malton, wapentake of Rydale, a part in the liberty of St. Peter; 9 miles from Pickering, 11¼ from Sledmere, 14¼ from Kirby-Moorside, 16 from Helmsley.—Population 741.

MANFIELD, in the parish of Manfield, wapentake of Gilling-East, liberty of Richmondshire; 5 miles from Darlington, *(Durham)* 9 from Richmond,—Population 229.

MANLESS-GREEN, in the parish of Skelton, east division of the wapentake and liberty of Langbarugh; 4 miles from Guisbrough, 12 from Stokesley, 18 from Whitby.

MARDERBY, in the parish of Feliskirk, wapentake of Birdforth, liberty of Ripon; 2¼ miles from Thirsk, 11¼ from Helmsley.

MARRICK, or MARWICK, in the parish of Marrick, wapentake of Gilling-West, liberty of Richmondshire; 3 miles from Reeth, 7 from Richmond.—Population 474.

MARRIFIRTH, in the parish of Thornton-Watlass, wapentake of Hang-East, liberty of Richmondshire; 5 miles from Bedale, 5 from Masham, 5 from Middleham.

MARSETT, in the parish of Aysgarth, wapentake of Hang-West; 4 miles from Hawes, 4¼ from Askrigg, 15 from Leyburn.

MARSHES, or MARISHES, EAST and WEST, in the parishes of Pickering and Thornton, wapentake and liberty of Pickering Lythe; 4 miles from Pickering, 5 from Malton, 12 from Kirby-Moorside.—Population 200.

MARSKE, in the parish of Marske, east division of the wapentake and liberty of Langbarugh; *(Marske-Hall, the seat of the Hon. Lawrence Dundas,)* 6 miles from Guisbrough, 14 from Stokesley, 20 from Whitby.—Pop. 505.

MARSKE, in the parish of Marske, wapentake of Gilling-West, liberty of Richmondshire; *(the seat of John Hutton, Esq.)* 6 miles from Richmond, 7 from Leyburn, 6 from Catterick.—Population 239.

MARTIN'S St. ABBEY, in the parish of Catterick, wapentake of Hang-East, liberty of Richmondshire; 1½ mile from Richmond, 5 from Catterick.—Population 16.

MARTON, in the parish of Sinnington, wapentakes of Rydale and Pickering-Lythe, a part in the liberty of St. Peter, 4 miles from Pickering, 5 from Kirby-Moorside, 9½ from Helmsley.—Population 192.

MARTON, in the parish of Marton, west division of the wapentake and liberty of Langbarugh; *(the seat of Bartholomew Rudd, Esq.)* 5 miles from Stockton, *(Durham.)* 7 from Stokesley, 7 from Guisbrough, 8 from Yarm.—Population 342.

MARTON, in the parish of Marton, wapentake of Bulmer, liberty of Ripon; 5 miles from Easingwold, 11 from York, 14 from Malton.—Population 208.

MARTON-LE-MOOR, in the parish of Topcliffe, wapentake of Halikeld, 2½ miles from Boroughbridge, 4 from Ripon, 9½ from Knaresborough.—Population 166.

MARTON-LORDSHIP, in the parish of Marton, wapentake of Bulmer, liberty of Ripon; 5 miles from Easingwold, 8 from York.

MASHAM, in the parish of Masham, wapentake of Hang-East, liberties of St. Peter and Richmondshire; 6 miles from Bedale, 8¼ from Middleham, 10 from Ripon, 10 from Leyburn, 14 from Richmond, 26 from York, 223 from London.—*Market*, Wednesday.—*Fairs*, September 17, 18, and 19, for Horned Cattle, Sheep, Pedlary Ware, &c.—*Principal Inn*, King's Head.—Population 1,022.

MAUNBY, in the parish of Kirby-Wiske, wapentake of Gilling-East, liberty of Richmondshire; *(the seat of Thomas Walker, Esq.)* 6 miles from Northallerton, 6 from Thirsk.—Population 244.

MELMERBY, in the parish of Wath, wapentake of Halikeld, liberty of Richmondshire; *(the seat of William Priestley, Esq.)* 4½ miles from Ripon, 7 from Thirsk, 7 from Boroughbridge.—Population 229.

MELMERBY, in the parish of Coverham, wapentake of Hang-West, liberty of Richmondshire; 3½ miles from Middleham, 4 from Leyburn.—Population 106.

MELSONBY, in the parish of Melsonby, wapentake of Gilling-West, liberty of Richmondshire; 6 miles from Richmond, 6 from Greta-bridge.—Population 338.

MELWATER, in the parish of Bowes, wapentake of Gilling-West, liberty of Richmondshire; 6¼ miles from Barnardcastle, *(Durham)* 7 from Greta-bridge, 16 from Richmond.

MICKLEBY, in the parish of Lythe, east-division of the wapentake and liberty of Langbargh; 7 miles from Whitby, 15 from Guisbrough, 21 from Stokesley.

MICKLETON, in the parish of Romaldkirk, wapentake of Gilling-West, liberty of Richmondshire; 7 miles from Barnardcastle, *(Durham)* 22 from Richmond.—Pop. 330.

MIDDLEHAM, in the parish of Middleham, wapentake of Hang-West, liberty of Richmondshire; 2 miles from Leyburn, 8¼ from Masham, 10 from Bedale, 10 from Richmond, 13¼ from Askrigg, 15 from Kettlewell, 36 from York, 232 from London.—*Market,* Monday.—*Fairs,* November 5 and 6 for Horned Cattle and Sheep.—*Principal Inn,* White Swan. —Population 728.

MIDDLESBROUGH, in the parish of Acklam, west division of the wapentake and liberty of Langbargh; 5 miles from Stockton, *(Durham)* 10 from Stokesley, 12 from Guisbrough.—Population 25.

MIDDLETON-UPON-LEVEN, in the parish of Rudby, west-division of the wapentake and liberty of Langbargh; 4 miles from Yarm, 5 from Stokesley.—Population 110.

MIDDLETON, in the parish of Middleton, wapentake and liberty of Pickering-Lythe; 1 mile from Pickering, 7 from Kirby-Moorside, 10 from Malton.—Population 235.

MIDDLETON-LODGE, in the parish of Middleton-Tyas, wapentake of Gilling-East, liberty of Richmondshire; *(the seat of Francis Hartley, Esq.)* 6 miles from Richmond, 6 from Catterick, 10 from Greta-bridge.

MIDDLETON-QUERNHOW, in the parish of Wath, wapentake of Halikeld, liberty of Richmondshire; 5 miles from Ripon, 7¼ from Boroughbridge, 7¼ from Thirsk.—Pop. 87.

MIDDLETON-TYAS, in the parish of Middleton-Tyas, wapentake of Gilling-East, liberty of Richmondshire; 4¼ miles from Catterick, 6 from Richmond, 10 from Greta-bridge. —Population 526.

MIDDLETON, WEST, in the parish of Gilling, wapentake of Gilling-West, liberty of Richmondshire; 7 miles from Richmond, 7 from Barnardcastle, *(Durham.)*

MILBY, in the parish of Kirby-on-the-Moor, wapentake of Halikeld, liberty of Richmondshire; 1 mile from Boroughbidge, 7 from Ripon, 8 from Knaresbrough.

MITTON-HILL, in the parish of Whitby, wapentake and

liberty of Whitby-Strand; 4 miles from Whitby, 16 from Scarborough.

MOOR-COTE, in the parish of East-Witton, wapentake of Hang-West; 4 miles from Middleham, 5 from Masham, 6 from Leyburn.

MOOR-HOUSE, in the parish of Brignall, wapentake of Gilling-West, liberty of Richmondshire; 2 miles from Greta-bridge, 4 from Barnardcastle, (Durham) 12 from Richmond.

MOOR-HOUSES, in the parish of Helmsley, wapentake of Rydale; 4 miles from Helmsley, 7 from Kirby-Moorside.

MOOR-HOUSE, LITTLE, in the parish of Thornton-Steward, wapentake of Hang-West, liberty of Richmondshire; 2 miles from Middleham, 8 from Bedale.

MOOR-ROW, in the parish of St. John, Stanwick, wapentake of Gilling-West, liberty of Richmondshire; 9 miles from Richmond, 9 from Barnardcastle, (Durham.)

MOORSOME, GREAT, in the parish of Skelton, east division of the wapentake and liberty of Langbarugh; 5 miles from Guisbrough, 12 from Stokesley, 17 from Whitby.—Population 302.

MOORSOME, LITTLE, in the parish of Skelton, east division of the wapentake and liberty of Langbarugh; 4½ miles from Guisbrough, 12½ from Stokesley, 17½ from Whitby.

MORTHAN-ABBEY, in the parish of Rokeby, wapentake of Gilling-West, liberty of Richmondshire; 1 mile from Greta-bridge, 3 from Barnardcastle, (Durham) 12 from Richmond.

MORTON, in the parish of Ormesby, east-division of the wapentake and liberty of Langbarugh; 3½ miles from Guisbrough, 4 from Stokesley.—Population 27.

MORTON, (extraparochial) wapentake of Birdforth, 5¼ miles from Helmsley, 8½ from Thirsk, 10 from Easingwold.—Population 40.

MORTON-UPON-SWALE, in the parish of Ainderby-Steeple, wapentake of Gilling-East, liberty of Richmondshire; 4 miles from Northallerton, 4 from Bedale, 8 from Catterick.—Population 184.

MOSS-DALE, in the parish of Aysgarth, wapentake of Hang-West, liberty of Richmondshire; 4 miles from Hawes, 9 from Askrigg.

MOULTON, in the parish of Middleton-Tyas, wapentake of Gilling-East, liberty of Richmondshire; 3 miles from Catterick, 6 from Richmond.—Population 174.

MOUNT-GRACE, in the parish of East-Harlsey, wapen-

G

take of Birdforth; 7 miles from Northallerton, 9 from Stokesley, 11 from Thirsk.

MOUNT ST. JOHN, in the parish of Feliskirk, wapentake of Birdforth, liberty of Ripon; *(the seat of the Rev. H. Ellsley)* 4¼ miles from Thirsk, 10 from Helmsley, 14 from Ripon.

MOWTHORPE, in the parish of Terrington, wapentake of Bulmer; 8 miles from Malton, 9 from Easingwold, 14 from York.

MOXBY, in the parish of Marton, wapentake of Bulmer, liberty of Ripon; 5 miles from Easingwold, 11 from York, 14 from Malton.

MUKER, in the parish of Grinton, wapentake of Gilling-West, liberty of Richmondshire; 6 miles from Askrigg, 9 from Reeth, 19 from Richmond.—Population 1,119.

MULGRAVE-CASTLE, in the parish of Lythe, east division of the wapentake and liberty of Langbarugh; *(the seat of Lord Mulgrave)* 4 miles from Whitby, 17 from Guisbrough, 25 from Stokesley.

MURTON, in the parish of Osbaldwick, wapentake of Bulmer, liberty of St. Peter; 3 miles from York, 15 from Easingwold, 17 from Malton.—Population 110.

MUSCOATES, in the parish of Kirkdale, wapentake of Rydale; 4 miles from Kirby-Moorside, 7 from Helmsley, 8 from Malton.—Population 70.

MYTON, in the parish of Myton, wapentake of Bulmer; *(Myton-Hall, the seat of Sir Martin Stapleton, Bart.)* 3 miles from Boroughbridge, 7 from Easingwold, 15 from York.—Population 126.

N.

NABY, in the parish of Romaldkirk, wapentake of Gilling-West, liberty of Richmondshire; 3 miles from Barnardcastle, *(Durham)* 6 from Greta-bridge, 18 from Richmond.

NAPPA, in the parish of Aysgarth, wapentake of Hang-West, liberty of Richmondshire; 1½ miles from Askrigg, 6¼ from Hawes, 10¼ from Leyburn, 11 from Middleham.—Population 32.

NAPPA-HALL, in the parish of Aysgarth, wapentake of Hang-West, liberty of Richmondshire; *(the seat of Lord Grantham,)* 1½ miles from Askrigg, 6¼ from Hawes, 11 from Leyburn.

NAPPA-SCAR, in the parish of Aysgarth, wapentake of

liberty of Whitby-Strand; 4 miles from Whitby, 16 from Scarborough.

MOOR-COTE, in the parish of East-Witton, wapentake of Hang-West; 4 miles from Middleham, 5 from Masham, 6 from Leyburn.

MOOR-HOUSE, in the parish of Brignall, wapentake of Gilling-West, liberty of Richmondshire; 10 miles from Greta-bridge, 4 from Barnardcastle, (Durham) 12 from Richmond.

MOOR-HOUSES, in the parish of Helmsley, wapentake of Rydale; 4 miles from Helmsley, 7 from Kirby-Moorside.

MOOR-HOUSE, LITTLE, in the parish of Thornton-Steward, wapentake of Hang-West, liberty of Richmondshire; 2 miles from Middleham, 9 from Bedale.

MOOR-ROW, in the parish of St. John, Stadwick, wapentake of Gilling-West, liberty of Richmondshire; 9 miles from Richmond, 9 from Barnardcastle, (Durham.)

MOORSOME, GREAT, in the parish of Skelton, east-division of the wapentake and liberty of Langbarugh; 5 miles from Guisbrough, 12 from Stokesley, 17 from Whitby.—Population 302.

MOORSOME, LITTLE, in the parish of Skelton, east-division of the wapentake and liberty of Langbarugh; 4¼ miles from Guisbrough, 12¼ from Stokesley, 17¼ from Whitby.

MORTHAN-ABBEY, in the parish of Rokeby, wapentake of Gilling-West, liberty of Richmondshire; 1 mile from Greta-bridge, 3 from Barnardcastle, (Durham) 12 from Richmond.

MORTON, in the parish of Ormesby, east-division of the wapentake and liberty of Langbarugh; 3½ miles from Guisbrough, 4 from Stokesley.—Population 27.

MORTON, (extraparochial) wapentake of Birdforth, 5¼ miles from Helmsley, 8½ from Thirsk, 10 from Easingwold.—Population 40.

MORTON-UPON-SWALE, in the parish of Ainderby-Steeple, wapentake of Gilling-East, liberty of Richmondshire; 4 miles from Northallerton, 4 from Bedale, 8 from Catterick.—Population 184.

MOSS-DALE, in the parish of Aysgarth, wapentake of Hang-West, liberty of Richmondshire; 4 miles from Hawes, 9 from Askrigg.

MOULTON, in the parish of Middleton-Tyas, wapentake of Gilling-East, liberty of Richmondshire; 3 miles from Catterick, 6 from Richmond.—Population 174.

MOUNT-GRACE, in the parish of East-Harlsey, wapen-

G

take of Birdforth; 7 miles from Northallerton, 9 from Stokesley, 11 from Thirsk.

MOUNT ST. JOHN, in the parish of Feliskirk, wapentake of Birdforth, liberty of Ripon; *(the seat of the Rev. H. Ellsley)* 4¼ miles from Thirsk, 10 from Helmsley, 14 from Ripon.

MOWTHORPE, in the parish of Terrington, wapentake of Bulmer; 8 miles from Malton, 9 from Easingwold, 14 from York.

MOXBY, in the parish of Marton, wapentake of Bulmer, liberty of Ripon; 5 miles from Easingwold, 11 from York, 14 from Malton.

MUKER, in the parish of Grinton, wapentake of Gilling-West, liberty of Richmondshire; 6 miles from Askrigg, 9 from Reeth, 19 from Richmond.—Population 1,119.

MULGRAVE-CASTLE, in the parish of Lythe, east-division of the wapentake and liberty of Langbarugh; *(the seat of Lord Mulgrave)* 4 miles from Whitby, 17 from Guisbrough, 25 from Stokesley.

MURTON, in the parish of Osbaldwick, wapentake of Bulmer, liberty of St. Peter; 3 miles from York, 15 from Easingwold, 17 from Malton.—Population 110.

MUSCOATES, in the parish of Kirkdale, wapentake of Rydale; 4 miles from Kirby-Moorside, 7 from Helmsley, 8 from Malton.—Population 70.

MYTON, in the parish of Myton, wapentake of Bulmer; *(Myton-Hall, the seat of Sir Martin Stapleton, Bart.)* 3 miles from Boroughbridge, 7 from Easingwold, 15 from York.—Population 126.

N.

NABY, in the parish of Romaldkirk, wapentake of Gilling-West, liberty of Richmondshire; 3 miles from Barnardcastle, *(Durham)* 6 from Greta-bridge, 18 from Richmond.

NAPPA, in the parish of Aysgarth, wapentake of Hang-West, liberty of Richmondshire; 1¼ miles from Askrigg, 6¼ from Hawes, 10¼ from Leyburn, 11 from Middleham.—Population 32.

NAPPA-HALL, in the parish of Aysgarth, wapentake of Hang-West, liberty of Richmondshire; *(the seat of Lord Grantham,)* 1¼ miles from Askrigg, 6¼ from Hawes, 11 from Leyburn.

NAPPA-SCAR, in the parish of Aysgarth, wapentake of

Hang-West, liberty of Richmondshire ; 1½ miles from Ask-rigg, 6¼ from Hawes, 11 from Leyburn.

NAWTON, in the parish of Kirkdale, wapentake of Rydale, liberty of St. Peter; 3 miles from Helmsley, 3 from Kirby-Moorside, 17¼ from Malton.—Population 197.

NAWTON-LODGE, in the parish of Kirkdale, wapentake of Rydale, liberty of St. Peter ; *(the seat of Thomas Dun-combe, Esq.)* 4 miles from Helmsley, 4 from Kirby-Moorside, 17 from Malton.

NESS, EAST, in the parish of Hovingham, wapentake of Rydale ; *(the seat of Thomas Kendall, Esq.)* 6 miles from Kirby-Moorside, 7 from Helmsley, 11 from Malton.—Population 74.

NESS, HIGH, in the parish of Pickhill, wapentake of Halikeld, liberty of Richmondshire ; 5 miles from Bedale, 8 from Thirsk, 9 from Ripon, 11 from Boroughbridge.

NESS, LOW, *see Low-Ness.*

NESS, WEST, in the parish of Stonegrave, wapentake of Rydale ; 6 miles from Kirby-Moorside, 7 from Helmsley, 11 from Malton.—Population 49.

NETTLEPOTT, in the parish of Romaldkirk, wapentake of Gilling-West, liberty of Richmondshire ; 7 miles from Barnardcastle, *(Durham)* 11 from Greta-bridge.

NEWBIGGIN, in the parish of Aysgarth, wapentake of Hang-West, liberty of Richmondshire ; 5 miles from Askrigg, 6 from Middleham, 6 from Leyburn.—Pop. 121.

NEWBIGGIN, in the parish of Lythe, east-division of the wapentake and liberty of Langbarugh ; *(the seat of Henry Yeoman, Esq.)* 5 miles from Whitby, 17 from Guisbrough.

NEWBROUGH, in the parish of Coxwold, wapentake of Birdforth; *(Newbrough-Hall, the seat of Thomas Edward Winn Bellasyse, Esq.)* 5 miles from Easingwold, 10 from Thirsk.—Population 148.

NEWBY, in the parish of Scalby, wapentake and liberty of Pickering-Lythe ; 3 miles from Scarborough, 17 from Pickering, 18 from Whitby.—Population 44.

NEWBY, in the parishes of Seamer and Stokesley, west-division of the wapentake and liberty of Langbarugh ; 3 miles from Stokesley, 8 from Yarm, 11 from Guisbrough.—Population 127.

NEWBY-PARK, in the parish of Topcliffe, wapentake of Halikeld, liberty of Richmondshire ; *(the seat of Lord Grantham,)* 4 miles from Boroughbridge, 5 from Ripon, 11 from Knaresborough.

NEWBY-WISKE, in the parish of Kirby-Wiske, wapentake of Gilling-East, liberty of Richmondshire; *(the seat of William Mitford, Esq.)* 5 miles from Northallerton, 6 from Thirsk, 14½ from Boroughbridge.—Population 241.

NEW-BUILDING, in the parish of Kirby-Knowle, wapentake of Birdforth; *(the seat of Francis Smyth, Esq.)* 6 miles from Thirsk, 9 from Northallerton.

NEW-FOREST, in the parish of Arkengarthdale, wapentake of Gilling-West; 4 miles from Reeth, 8 from Richmond.—Population 68.

NEWHAM, in the parish of Marton, west-division of the wapentake and liberty of Langbargh; 4 miles from Stokesley, 5 from Guisbrough, 6 from Stockton, *(Durham.)*

NEW-INN, Leeming-Lane, in the parish of Burneston, wapentake of Halikeld, liberty of Richmondshire; 5 miles from Bedale, 9 from Thirsk, 9½ from Ripon, 10¼ from Catterick, 10½ from Northallerton, 11¼ from Boroughbridge.

NEWHOLME, in the parish of Whitby, wapentake and liberty of Whitby-Strand; 2½ miles from Whitby, 18½ from Guisbrough, 24 from Stokesley.—Population 346.

NEWPORT, in the parish of Acklam, west-division of the wapentake and liberty of Langbargh; 4¼ miles from Stockton, *(Durham)* 8½ from Stokesley.

NEWSAM, in the parish of Appleton-le-Street, wapentake of Rydale; 2½ miles from Malton, 11 from Kirby-Moorside.

NEWSHAM, in the parishes of Kirkby-Ravensworth and Barningham, wapentake of Gilling-West, liberty of Richmondshire; 4 miles from Greta-bridge, 8 from Richmond, 11 from Catterick.—Population 491.

NEWSHAM, in the parish of Kirby-Wiske, wapentake of Birdforth; 3¼ miles from Thirsk, 6¼ from Northallerton, 12¼ from Boroughbridge.—Population 117.

NEWSTEAD, in the parish of East-Witton, wapentake of Hang-West, liberty of Richmondshire; 3¼ miles from Middleham, 5½ from Leyburn, 6 from Masham.

NEWSTEAD-GRANGE, in the parish of Thornton, wapentake and liberty of Pickering-Lythe; 5 miles from Malton, 5 from Pickering, 13 from Kirby-Moorside.

NEWTON, in the parish of Newton, west-division of the wapentake and liberty of Langbargh; 4 miles from Stokesley, 4 from Guisbrough, 12 from Yarm.—Population 149.

NEWTON, in the parish of Pickering, wapentake and liberty of Pickering-Lythe; 4 miles from Pickering, 13 from Malton, 15 from Whitby.—Population 151.

NEWTON, in the parish of Stonegrave, wapentake of Rydale, liberty of St. Peter; *(the seat of Sir George Wombwell, Bart.)* 4 miles from Helmsley, 6½ from Kirby-Moorside, 13 from Malton.—Population 69.

NEWTON-DALE, in the parishes of Pickering and Levisham, wapentake and liberty of Pickering-Lythe; 7 miles from Pickering, 14 from Whitby, 16 from Malton.—Population 151.

NEWTON-GRANGE, in the parish of Oswaldkirk, wapentake of Rydale; 3 miles from Helmsley, 7½ from Kirby-Moorside, 14 from Malton.

NEWTON-HOUSE, in the parish of Burneston, wapentake of Halikeld, liberty of Richmondshire; *(the seat of Mrs. Harrison)* 3 miles from Bedale, 5 from Catterick, 8 from Northallerton, 14 from Boroughbridge.

NEWTON-LE-WILLOWS, in the parish of Patrick-Brompton, wapentake of Hang-East, liberty of Richmondshire; 3 miles from Bedale, 9 from Richmond.—Population 216.

NEWTON-MURRELL, in the parish of St. John, Stanwick, wapentake of Gilling-East, liberty of Richmondshire; 6 miles from Darlington, *(Durham)* 9 from Richmond.—Population 40.

NEWTON-MULGRAVE, in the parish of Lythe; east division of the wapentake and liberty of Langbarugh; 8 miles from Whitby, 14 from Guisbrough, 21 from Stokesley.—Population 133.

NEWTON, SCAB, in the parish of Burneston, wapentake of Halikeld, liberty of Richmondshire; 4 miles from Bedale, 8 from Northallerton, 13 from Ripon, 13 from Richmond.

NEWTON-UPON-OUSE, in the parish of Newton, wapentake of Bulmer, 6 miles from Easingwold, 9 from York, 9 from Boroughbridge.—Population 338.

NEW-TOWN, in the parish of Rudby, east-division of the wapentake and liberty of Langbarugh; 2¼ miles from Yarm, 5¼ from Stokesley.

NICHOLAS, ST. in the parish of Richmond, wapentake of Gilling-West, liberty of Richmondshire; 1 mile from Richmond, 5 from Catterick.

NORMANBY, in the parish of Normanby, wapentake of Rydale; 4 miles from Kirby-Moorside, 9 from Malton, 10 from Helmsley.—Population 148.

NORMANBY, in the parish of Ormesby, east-division of the wapentake and liberty of Langbarugh; *(the seat of William Ward Jackson, Esq.)* 4¼ miles from Guisbrough, 7 from Stokesley.—Population 99.

NORMANBY, in the parish of Fylingdale, wapentake and liberty of Whitby-Strand; 4 miles from Whitby, 17 from Scarborough.

NORTHALLERTON, *(which gives name to the wapentake)* in the parish of Northallerton, wapentake and liberty of Allertonshire; 9 miles from Bedale, 9 from Thirsk,

10 from Catterick, 15 from Richmond, 16 from Darlington, *(Durham)* 16 from Yarm, 16 from Stokesley, 17 from Ripon, 19 from Boroughbridge, 20 from Helmsley, 32 from York, 226 from London by *Boroughbridge*, 231 by *York*. —*Market*, Wednesday.—*Fairs*, February 14 for Horses, Horned Cattle, &c. and a week preceeding, for Horses only; May 5 and 6, for Horses, Horned Cattle, Sheep, Leather, Woollen-Cloth, &c. September 5 and 6, for Horned Cattle, Sheep, Leather, &c. October 3, and 4, for Horned Cattle, Sheep, &c. second Wednesday in October, for Cheeses.—*Bankers*, North-Riding Bank, Messrs. Hammond, Hirst, and Close draw on Willis, Wood, and Co. 76, Lombard-Street, London.—Sends two Members to Parliament.—*Principal Inns*, Golden Lion and King's Head.—Population 2,138.

NORTH-COTE, in the parish of Masham, wapentake of Hang-East; 6 miles from Bedale, 15 from Richmond.

NORTH-FIELDS, in the parish of Bowes, wapentake of Gilling-West, liberty of Richmondshire; 2 miles from Barnardcastle, *(Durham)* 6 from Greta-bidge, 14 from Richmond.

NORTH-INGS, in the parish of Sheriff-Hutton, wapentake of Bulmer; 8 miles from Easingwold, 11 from York, 14 from Malton.

NORTON-CONYERS, in the parish of Wath, wapentake and liberty of Allertonshire; *(the seat of Sir. Bellingham Graham, Bart.)* 2 miles from Ripon, 9 from Boroughbridge, 9 from Bedale.—Population 56.

NORTON-LE-CLAY, in the parish of Cundall, wapentake of Halikeld, liberty of Richmondshire; 3 miles from Boroughbridge, 6 from Ripon, 6 from Thirsk.—Pop. 110.

NOSTERFIELD, in the parish of West-Tanfield, wapentake of Hang-East, liberty of Richmondshire; 3¼ miles from Masham, 6 from Bedale, 6 from Ripon.

NUN-HOUSE, in the parish of Osmotherley, wapentake and liberty of Allertonshire; 8 miles from Northallerton, 9 from Thirsk.

NUNNINGTON, in the parishes of Nunnington and Stonegrave, wapentake of Rydale; *(the seat of Sir Bellingham Graham)* 5¼ miles from Kirby-Moorside, 5¼ from Helmsley, 12 from Malton.—Population 291.

NUNTHORPE, in the parish of Ayton, west-division of the wapentake and liberty of Langbarugh; 3¼ miles from Stokesley, 6 from Guisbrough, 10 from Yarm.—Pop. 132.

NUTWITH-COTE, in the parish of Masham, wapentake of Hang-East, liberty of Richmondshire; 1 mile from Masham, 7 from Bedale, 9 from Ripon.

O.

OAK-TREE INN, *Leeming-Lane*, in the parish of Burneston, wapentake of Hallikeld, liberty of Richmondshire; 5 miles from Bedale, 10 from Thirsk, 10 from Northallerton, 10 from Ripon, 10 from Catterick, 12 from Boroughbridge.

OLAVE, St. in the parish of St. Olave, wapentake of Bulmer; ¼ a mile from York, 12¼ from Easingwold.—Population 606.

OLDBROUGH, *see Aldbrough*.

OLDSTEAD, in the parish of Kilburn, wapentake of Birdforth; 7 miles from Easingwold, 7 from Helmsley, 10 from Thirsk.—Population 114.

OLLIVER, in the parish of Easby, wapentake of Gilling-West, liberty of Richmondshire; 1 mile from Richmond, 12 from Darlington, *(Durham.)*

ORGATE, in the parish of Marske, wapentake of Gilling-West, liberty of Richmondshire; 5 miles from Reeth, 7 from Richmond.

ORMESBY, in the parish of Ormesby, west-division of the wapentake and liberty of Langbarugh; *(Ormesby-Hall, the seat of Sir William Pennyman, Bart.)* 6 miles from Guisbrough, 7 from Stokesley, 7 from Stockton, *(Durham.)* —Population 357.

OSBALDWICK, in the parishes of Osbaldwick and Gate-Helmsley, wapentake of Bulmer, liberty of St. Peter; 2 miles from York, 15 from Easingwold, 18 from Malton.— Population 123.

OSGOODBY, in the parish of Kilburn, wapentake of Birdforth, liberty of Ripon; 5 miles from Thirsk, 8 from Easingwold.

OSGOODBY, in the parish of Cayton, wapentake and liberty of Pickering-Lythe; 3 miles from Scarborough, 20 from Pickering, 22 from Whitby.

OSMOTHERLEY, in the parish of Osmotherley, wapentake and liberty of Allertonshire; 7 miles from Northallerton, 10 from Stokesley, 11¼ from Thirsk.—Population 534.

OSWALDKIRK, in the parish of Oswaldkirk, wapentake of Rydale; *(the seat of T. P. Banner, Esq.)* 3¼ miles from Helmsley, 7½ from Kirby-Moorside, 13 from Malton. —Population 193.

OTTERINGTON, NORTH, in the parish of North-Otterington, wapentake and liberty of Allertonshire; 3 miles from Northallerton, 14 from Ripon, 16 from Boroughbridge. —Population 42.

OTTERINGTON, SOUTH, in the parish of South-Otterington, wapentake of Birdforth, liberties of Allertonshire and Ripon; 5 miles from Northallerton, 6 from Thirsk, 14 from Boroughbridge.—Population 144.

OULSTON, in the parish of Coxwold, wapentake of Birdforth; 3¼ miles from Easingwold, 11 from Thirsk.—Population 212.

OVERTON, in the parish of Overton, wapentake of Bulmer; 5 miles from York, 8 from Easingwold, 20 from Malton.—Population 44.

OVINGTON, in the parish of Wycliffe, wapentake of Gilling-West, liberty of Richmondshire; 4 miles from Gretabridge, 6 from Barnardcastle, *(Durham)* 10 from Richmond.—Population 157.

OXCLOSE-HOUSE, in the parish of West-Rounton, wapentake and liberty of Allertonshire; 6 miles from Yarm, 9 from Northallerton.

OXGUE, in the parish of Marrick, wapentake of Gilling-West, liberty of Richmondshire; 5 miles from Reeth, 7 from Richmond.

P.

PARADISE, in the parish of Grinton, wapentake of Gilling-West; 4 miles from Reeth, 9 from Askrigg, 14 from Richmond.

PARK-GATE, in the parish of Whitby, wapentake and liberty of Whitby-Strand; 5 miles from Whitby, 16 from Scarborough.

PARK-HALL, in the parish of Grinton, wapentake of Gilling-West, liberty of Richmondshire; 2 miles from Reeth, 9 from Askrigg, 12 from Richmond.

PARK-HALL, in the parish of Guisbrough, east-division of the wapentake and liberty of Langbarugh; *(the seat of Robert Chaloner, Esq.)* 2 miles from Guisbrough, 9 from Stokesley.

PASTURE-HOUSE, in the parish of Bedale, wapentake of Hang-East, liberty of Richmondshire; 3 miles from Bedale, 13 from Richmond.

PATRICK-BROMPTON, in the parishes of Patrick-Brompton and Bedale, wapentake of Hang-East, liberty of Richmondshire; 3 miles from Bedale, 9 from Richmond.—Population 163.

PEAK, in the parish of Scalby, wapentake and liberty of Whitby-Strand; *(the seat of Sunderland Cook, Esq.)* 8 miles from Whitby, 12 from Scarborough.

PEN-HILL, in the parish of Aysgarth, wapentake of Hang-West, liberty of Richmondshire; 4 miles from Middleham; 4 from Leyburn.

PEEP-O'DAY, in the parish of Husthwaite, wapentake of Birdforth; 1¼ miles from Easingwold, 11 from Thirsk.

PEPPER-HALL, in the parish of South-Cowton, wapentake of Gilling-East, liberty of Richmondshire; *(the seat of John Arden, Esq.)* 6 miles from Northallerton, 7 from Richmond, 11 from Darlington, *(Durham.)*

PICKERING, in the parish of Pickering, wapentake and liberty of Pickering-Lythe; 8 miles from Kirby-Moorside, 9 from Malton, 18¼ from Scarborough, 21 from Whitby, 27 from York, 226 from London.—*Market*, Monday.—*Fairs*, first Monday before May-day, September 14, Holy Rood-day, first Monday before Martinmas-day, for Horned Cattle, Horses and Sheep.—*Principal Inns*, White Swan, and Black Swan.—Population 1,994.

PICKHILL, in the parish of Pickhill, wapentake of Halikeld, liberty of Richmondshire; 7 miles from Bedale, 7 from Thirsk, 8 from Northallerton, 9 from Ripon.—Pop. 875.

PICKTON, in the parish of Kirk-Levington, west-division of the wapentake and liberty of Langbargh; 4 miles from Yarm, 8 from Stokesley, 9 from Northallerton.—Pop. 91.

PINCHINTHORPE, in the parish of Guisbrough, east-division of the wapentake and liberty of Langbargh; *(the seat of James Lee, Esq.)* 3 miles from Guisbrough, 5 from Stokesley.—Population 92.

PLANTATION, or TOCKETS, in the parish of Guisbrough, east-division of the wapentake and liberty of Langbargh; *(the seat of Gen. Hale)* 1 mile from Guisbrough, 9 from Stokesley.—Population 65.

PLANTATION, in the parish of Smeaton, wapentake of Gilling-East, liberty of Richmondshire; 6 miles from Darlington *(Durham)* 10 from Northallerton, 12 from Richmond.

POCKLEY, in the parish of Helmsley, wapentake of Rydale; 2 miles from Helmsley, 5¼ from Kirby-Moorside.—Pop. 228.

POLLING, in the parish of Grinton, wapentake of Hang-West, liberty of Richmondshire; 5 miles from Reeth, 6 from Leyburn.

POND-HOUSE, in the parish of Thornton-Watlass, wapentake of Hang-East, liberty of Richmondshire; 4 miles from Bedale, 5 from Masham, 7 from Middleham.

POST-GRANGE, or HALL, in the parish of Masham, wa-

H

pentake of Hang-East; 6 miles from Masham, 8 from Middleham, 10 from Bedale.

POTTO, in the parish of Whorlton, west-division of the wapentake and liberty of Langbarugh; 6 miles from Stokesley, 8 from Yarm, 10 from Northallerton.—Population 174.

PRESTON-UNDERSCAR, in the parish of Wensley, wapentake of Hang-West; liberty of Richmondshire; 3 miles from Leyburn, 4½ from Middleham, 10 from Richmond.—Population 260.

R

RAINSDALE-GRAVEN, in the parish of Hawnby, wapentake of Birdforth; 8 miles from Helmsley, 8 from Stokesley.

RAINTON, in the parish of Topcliffe, wapentake of Halikeld, liberty of Richmondshire; 4¼ miles from Ripon, 4 from Boroughbridge, 6 from Thirsk.—Population 331.

RALPH'S-CROSS, or WESTERDALE-BEACON, in the parish of Stokesley, west-division of the wapentake and liberty of Langbarugh; 11¼ miles from Kirby-Moorside, 12¼ from Guisbrough.

RAND-GRANGE, in the parish of Bedale, wapentake of Hang-East, liberty of Richmondshire; ¼ a mile from Bedale, 6 from Catterick, 9¼ from Middleham.—Pop. 13.

RASH, in the parish of Grinton, wapentake of Gilling-West, liberty of Richmondshire; 7 miles from Askrigg, 9 from Reeth, 19 from Richmond.

RASKELF, in the parish of Easingwold, wapentake of Bulmer; 2 miles from Easingwold, 9 from Boroughbridge, 14 from York.—Population 338.

RATHWAITHE, in the parish of Whitby, wapentake and liberty of Whitby-Strand; 3 miles from Whitby, 18 from Guisbrough.

RAVENS' SEAT, in the parish of Grinton, wapentake of Gilling-West, liberty of Richmondshire, 13 miles from Askrigg, 15 from Reeth, 25 from Richmond.

RAVENSWORTH, in the parish of Kirkby-Ravensworth, wapentake of Gilling-West, liberty of Richmondshire, 5 miles from Richmond, 7 from Greta-bridge, 10 from Barnardcastle, *(Durham.)*—Population 269.

RAVENTHORPE-MILL, in the parish of Feliskirk, wapentake of Birdforth; *(the Seat of Captain Manners)* 4 miles from Thirsk, 9 from Helmsley.

RAWCLIFFE, in the parishes of St. Michael-le-Belfrey,

and St. Olave, York, wapentake of Bulmer, liberty of St. Peter; 2¼ miles from York, 11 from Easingwold, 18 from Malton.—Population 73.

RAWMER, in the parish of Masham, wapentake of Hang-East; 2 miles from Masham, 8 from Ripon.

RAYDALE, in the parish of Aysgarth, wapentake of Hang-West, liberty of Richmondshire; *(the seat of Henry Peirse Esq.)* 4 miles from Askrigg, 4 from Hawes, 15 from Leyburn.

REDCAR, in the parish of Marske, east-division of the wapentake and liberty of Langbarugh; 7 miles from Guisbrough, 15 from Stockton, *(Durham)* 16 from Yarm, 22 from Whitby.—Population 431.

READINGS, or REDDINGS, in the parish of Grinton, wapentake of Gilling-West, liberty of Richmondshire; 1 mile from Reeth, 10 from Askrigg, 11 from Richmond.

RED-HALL, in the parish of Catterick, wapentake of Hang-East; *(the seat of John Fall, Esq.)* 2 miles from Catterick, 4 from Bedale, 7 from Richmond.

REDHIRST, in the parish of Arkengarthdale, wapentake of Gilling-West; 4 miles from Reeth, 9 from Richmond.

REDMIRE, in the parish of Wensley, wapentake of Hang-West, liberty of Richmondshire; 4¼ miles from Leyburn, 5¼ from Middleham, 10 from Richmond.—Population 320.

REETH, in the parish of Grinton, wapentake of Gilling-West, liberty of Richmondshire; 10 miles from Leyburn, 10 from Richmond, 11 from Askrigg, 11 from Greta-bridge, 14 from Barnardcastle, *(Durham)* 17 from Brough, *(Westmoreland)* 48 from York, 245 from London.—*Market*, Friday.—*Fairs*, Good-Friday, Friday before old May-day, Friday before old Midsummer-day, Friday before St. Bartholomew, Friday before old Martinmas-day, Friday before St. Thomas's day, for Woollen Cloth, Hawkers' and Pedlary Ware, &c.—*Principal Inn*, White-Hart.—Population 1,128.

RICHMOND, in the parish of Richmond, wapentake of Gilling-West, liberty of Richmondshire; *(the seat of John Yorke, Esq.)* 5 miles from Catterick, 8 from Leyburn, 10 from Reeth, 12 from Darlington, *(Durham)* 12 from Greta-bridge, 15 from Northallerton, 18 from Askrigg, 21 from Yarm, 44 from York, 234 from London.—*Market*, —Saturday.—*Fairs*, Saturday before Palm-Sunday, first Saturday in July, September 14, Holy Rood-day, for Horned Cattle, Sheep, Horses, Woollen Cloth, &c.—*Bankers*, Richmond-Bank, Messrs. Sir John Lawson, Stapleton, and Co. draw on Messrs. Moffatt, Kensington and Co. 20, Lombard-Street; Richmond and Swaledale-Bank, Messrs.

Hutton, Wood, Simpson, Other, Robson, and Ellis draw on Messrs Down, Thornton, and Co. Bartholomew-lane.—Sends two Members to Parliament.—*Principal Inns*, King's Head and King's Arms.—Population 2,861.

RIVALX, or RIEVAULX, in the parish of Helmsley, wapentake of Rydale; 2 miles from Helmsley, 8 from Kirby-Moorside, 12 from Thirsk, 19 from Malton.—Pop. 223.

RISEBROUGH, see *Thornton-Risebrough.*

ROAKSBY, in the parish of Pickhill, wapentake of Halikeld, liberty of Richmondshire; 7 miles from Thirsk, 8 from Northallerton, 9 from Ripon.

ROBIN-HOOD'S BAY, in the parish of Fylingdale, wapentake and liberty of Whitby-Strand; 6 miles from Whitby, 14 from Scarborough.

ROKEBY, in the parish of Rokeby, wapentake of Gilling-West, liberty of Richmondshire; *(Rokeby-Park, the seat of John Bacon Sawrey Morritt, Esq.)* 1 mile from Greta-bridge, 3 from Barnardcastle, 13 from Richmond.—Population 185.

ROMALDKIRK, in the parish of Romaldkirk, wapentake of Gilling-West, liberty of Richmondshire; 6 miles from Barnardcastle, *(Durham)* 9 from Greta-bridge, 21 from Richmond.—Population 276.

ROMANBY, in the parish of Northallerton, wapentake and liberty of Allertonshire; ¼ a mile from Northallerton, 7¼ from Bedale, 9¼ from Thirsk.—Population 250.

ROOK-BARGH, see *Bargh Rook.*

ROOKWITH, in the parish of Thornton-Watlass, wapentake of Hang-East, liberty of Richmondshire; 4 miles from Bedale, 12 from Richmond.—Population 92.

ROSEBERRY-TOPPING, *(a Hill)* in the parish of Newton, east-division of the wapentake and liberty of Langbarugh; 3 miles from Guisbrough, 5 from Stokesley.

ROSEDALE, EAST-SIDE, in the parish of Middleton, wapentake and liberty of Pickering-Lythe; 7 miles from Kirby-Moorside, 9 from Pickering, 18 from Whitby.—Population 287.

ROSEDALE, WEST-SIDE, in the parish of Lastingham, wapentake of Rydale; 6 miles from Kirby-Moorside, 12 from Helmsley.—Population 117.

ROSKEL-HOUSE, in the parish of Well, wapentake of Hang-East; 2 miles from Masham, 3 from Bedale, 9 from Middleham.

ROTHERFORTH-BRIDGE, in the parish of Barningham, wapentake of Gilling-West, 4 miles from Greta-bridge, 4½ Barnardcastle, *(Durham)* 14 from Richmond.

ROUNDFIELD-HILL, in the parish of Hornby, wapentake of Hang-East, liberty of Richmondshire; 3 miles from Bedale, 9 from Catterick.

ROUNTON, EAST, in the parish of Rudby, west-division of the wapentake and liberty of Langbarugh; *(Rounton-Grange, the seat of John Wailes, Esq.)* 7 miles from Northallerton, 8 from Yarm, 9 from Stokesley.—Pop. 109.

ROUNTON, WEST, in the parish of West-Rounton, wapentake and liberty of Allertonshire; 7 miles from Northallerton, 7¼ from Yarm, 9 from Stokesley.—Population 226.

ROUSBY, or ROXBY, in the parish of Hinderwell, east-division of the wapentake and liberty of Langbarugh; 11 miles from Guisbrough, 11½ from Whitby.—Population 190.

ROW, in the parish of Grinton, wapentake of Gilling-West, liberty of Richmondshire; 1 mile from Reeth, 9¼ from Richmond.

ROW, in the parish of Whitby, wapentake and liberty of Whitby-Strand; 5 miles from Whitby, 16 from Guisbrough.

RUCKCROFT, in the parish of Grinton, wapentake of Gilling-West, liberty of Richmondshire; 2 miles from Reeth, 9 from Askrigg, 12 from Richmond.

RUDBY, in the parish of Rudby, west-division of the wapentake and liberty of Langbarugh; 4 miles from Stokesley, 6 from Yarm, 11½ from Northallerton.—Population 80.

RUNSWICK, in the parish of Hinderwell, east-division of the wapentake and liberty of Langbarugh; 7 miles from Whitby, 10 from Guisbrough, 22 from Stokesley.

RUSTON, in the parish of Wykeham, wapentake and liberty of Pickering-Lythe; 7 miles from Scarborough, 11 from Pickering, 15 from Malton.

RUSWARP, in the parish of Whitby, wapentake and liberty of Whitby-Strand; *(the seats of John Marshall and Henry Askew, Esqrs.)* 2 miles from Whitby, 18¼ from Pickering, 19 from Guisbrough.—Population 1,565.

RUSWICK, in the parish of Fingall, wapentake of Hang-East, liberty of Richmondshire; 4½ miles from Middleham, 5 from Leyburn, 5 from Bedale.

RYTON, in the parish of Kirby-Misperton, wapentake and liberty of Pickering-Lythe; 3 miles from Malton, 7 from Pickering, 11 from Kirby-Moorside.—Population 192.

ton, wapentake of Hang-East, liberty of Richmondshire; 4 miles from Catterick, 8 from Bedale.—Population 70.

SCRAFTON, LITTLE, in the parish of Coverham, wapentake of Hang-West, liberty of Richmondshire; 3¼ miles from Middleham, 5 from Leyburn, 15 from Richmond.

SCRAFTON, WEST, in the parish of Coverham, wapentake of Hang-West, liberty of Richmondshire; 3¼ miles from Middleham, 5 from Leyburn, 15 from Richmond.—Population 107.

SCRUTON, in the parish of Scruton, wapentake of Hang-East, liberty of Richmondshire; *(the seat of Henry Gale, Esq.)* 4 miles from Bedale, 4½ from Northallerton, 6 from Catterick.—Population 379.

SCUGDALE, in the parish of Whorlton, west division of the wapentake and liberty of Langbarugh; 5 miles from Stokesley, 11¼ from Northallerton, 14 from Guisbrough.

SEAMER, in the parish of Seamer, west division of the wapentake and liberty of Langbarugh; 2 miles from Stokesley, 6 from Yarm, 10 from Guisbrough.—Population 240.

SEAMOR, or SEAMOOR, in the parish of Seamor, wapentake and liberty of Pickering-Lythe; 4 miles from Scarborough, 15 from Pickering, 18 from Bridlington.—*No Market.—Fair,* July 15, for Horses, Boots, Shoes, &c.

SEAL-HOUSES, in the parish of Arkengarthdale, wapentake of Gilling-West, liberty of Richmondshire; 5 miles from Reeth, 15 from Richmond.

SEDBURY-HALL, in the parish of Gilling, wapentake of Gilling-East, liberty of Richmondshire; *(the seat of Sir Robert D'Arcy Hildyard, Bart.)* 4 miles from Richmond, 6 from Catterick, 10 from Greta-bridge.

SEDBUSK, in the parish of Aysgarth, wapentake of Hang-West; 1 mile from Hawes, 4 from Askrigg, 16 from Leyburn.

SEMERDALE, in the parish of Aysgarth, wapentake of Hang-West, liberty of Richmondshire; 2 miles from Hawes, 3¼ from Askrigg.

SESSAY, in the parish of Sessay, wapentake and liberty of Allertonshire; *(Sessay-Hall, the seat of the Hon. and Rev. William Henry Dawnay)* 5 miles from Easingwold, 6 from Thirsk.—Population 292.

SEXHOW, in the parish of Rudby, west division of the wapentake and liberty of Langbarugh; 4¼ miles from Stokesley, 6 from Yarm, 12¼ from Guisbrough.—Population 44.

SHAW, in the parish of Marrick, wapentake of Gilling-West, liberty of Richmondshire; 3 miles from Reeth, 7 from Richmond.

NORTH RIDING.

SHAW, and SHAW-COTE, in the parish of Aysgarth, wapentake of Hang-West, liberty of Richmondshire; 2¼ miles from Hawes, 3 from Askrigg.

SHEPHERDS' HILL, in the parish of Whorlton, west division of the wapentake and liberty of Langbarugh; 7 miles from Stokesley, 9 from Northallerton, 9 from Yarm.

SHERFITT-HALL, in the parish of Grinton, wapentake of Gilling-West, liberty of Richmondshire; 3 miles from Reeth, 10 from Askrigg, 13 from Richmond.

SHIPTON, in the parish of Overton, wapentake of Bulmer, a part in the liberty of St. Peter; 6 miles from York, 7 from Easingwold, 19 from Malton.—Population 341.

SHIPTON-SMITHY, in the parish of Overton, wapentake of Bulmer; 6 miles from York, 7 from Easingwold, 19 from Malton.

SIGSTON, in the parish of Sigston, wapentake and liberty of Allertonshire; 3 miles from Northallerton, 8 from Thirsk, 13 from Yarm.—Population 115.

SIGSTON-SMITHY, in the parish of Sigston, wapentake and liberty of Allertonshire; 3¼ miles from Northallerton, 7¼ from Thirsk, 12¼ from Yarm.

*SILTON, HIGH, or OVER, in the parish of Cowsby, wapentake of Birdforth; 8 miles from Northallerton, 9 from Thirsk.—Population 74.

SILTON, LOW, or NETHER, in the parish of Leak, wapentake of Birdforth; 7 miles from Northallerton, 8 from Thirsk, 13 from Stokesley.—Population 326.

SIMONSTONE, in the parish of Aysgarth, wapentake of Hang-West, liberty of Richmondshire; 1¼ mile from Hawes, 5¼ from Askrigg.

SINDERBY, in the parish of Pickhill, wapentake of Halikeld, liberty of Richmondshire; 6 miles from Thirsk, 7 from Ripon, 8 from Bedale.—Population 43.

SINNINGTON, in the parish of Sinnington, wapentake and liberty of Pickering-Lythe; 4 miles from Pickering, 10 from Helmsley.—Population 274.

SION-HILL, in the parish of Kirby-Wiske, wapentake of Gilling East, liberty of Richmondshire; *(the seat of Edward D'Oyly, Esq.)* 4 miles from Thirsk, 7½ from Northallerton, 13 from Boroughbridge.

SKEEBY, in the parish of Easby, wapentake of Gilling-West, liberty of Richmondshire; *(the seat of E. Johnson, Esq.)* 2 miles from Richmond, 4 from Catterick, 10 from Darlington. *(Durham.)*—Population 134.

SKELTON-COTE, and SKELGILL, in the parish of Ays-

---
* SILTON, OVER, a ch. to Cowsby or Kilburn.—BACON'S THESAURUS.

I

garth, wapentake of Hang-West, liberty of Richmondshire; 1¼ miles from Askrigg, 4 from Hawes.

SKELDERSKEW-GRANGE, in the parish of Guisbrough, east-division of the wapentake and liberty of Langbarugh; 4 miles from Guisbrough, 10 from Stokesley, 18 from Yarm.

SKELTON, in the parishes of Skelton and Overton, wapentake of Bulmer, a part in the liberty of St. Peter; 4 miles from York, 9 from Easingwold, 18 from Malton.—Pop. 203.

SKELTON, in the parish of Marske, wapentake of Gilling-West, liberty of Richmondshire; 6 miles from Richmond, 6 from Reeth.

SKELTON, in the parish of Skelton, east-division of the wapentake and liberty of Langbarugh; *(Skelton-Castle, the seat of John Wharton, Esq.)* 3¼ miles from Guisbrough, 11¼ from Stokesley, 16 from Stockton, *(Durham.)*—Population 700.

SKELTON-SMITHY, in the parish of Skelton, wapentake of Bulmer, 3 miles from York, 10 from Easingwold, 18 from Malton.

SKEWSBY, in the parish of Dalby, wapentake of Bulmer; 9 miles from Easingwold, 13 from Malton, 15 from York.

SKINNINGRAVE, in the parish of Skelton, east-division of the wapentake and liberty of Langbarugh; *(the seat of John Easterby, Esq.)* 7 miles from Guisbrough, 14 from Whitby, 15 from Stokesley.—Population 67.

SKIPLAM, in the parish of Kirkdale, wapentake of Rydale; 3 miles from Kirby-Moorside, 4 from Helmsley, 17 from Malton.—Population 70.

SKIPTON, and SKIPTON-BRIDGE, in the parish of Topcliffe, wapentake of Birdforth; 4 miles from Thirsk, 7 from Ripon, 10 from Northallerton.—Population 103.

SKUTTERSKELFE, in the parish of Rudby, west division of the wapentake and liberty of Langbarugh; 2 miles from Stokesley, 6 from Yarm.—Population 42.

SLAPE-WATH, in the parish of Guisbrough, east-division of the wapentake and liberty of Langbarugh; 2¼ miles from Guisbrough, 10 from Stokesley, 19 from Whitby.

SLEDDALE, in the parish of Guisbrough, east-division of the wapentake and liberty of Langbarugh; 3 miles from Guisbrough, 11 from Stokesley.

SLEDSHOE, in the parish of Lastingham, wapentake of Rydale; 12 miles from Kirby-Moorside, 17 from Helmsley.

SLEETHOLME, in the parish of Bowes, wapentake of Gilling-West, liberty of Richmondshire; 7 miles from Barnardcastle, *(Durham)* 8 from Greta-bridge, 16 from Richmond.

SLEIGHTS, in the parish of Whitby, wapentake and liberty

of Whitby-Strand; *(Sleights-Hall, the seat of Mrs. Bateman, and Eske-Hall, the seat of J. C. Coates. Esq.)* 4 miles from Whitby, 17 from Pickering.

SLINGSBY, in the parish of Slingsby, wapentake of Rydale; 7 miles from Malton, 9 from Kirby-Moorside, 9 from Helmsley.—Population 434.

SMALLWAYS, in the parish of Kirkby-Ravensworth, wapentake of Gilling-West; 2 miles from Greta-bridge, 8 from Richmond.

SMARBER, in the parish of Grinton, wapentake of Gilling-West, liberty of Richmondshire; 5 miles from Reeth, 9 from Askrigg, 15 from Richmond.

SMEARHOLMES, in the parish of Burneston, wapentake of Halikeld, liberty of Richmondshire; 4 miles from Bedale, 9 from Masham, 10 from Northallerton, 11 from Ripon.

SMEATON, GREAT, in the parish of Great-Smeaton, wapentake of Gilling-East, liberty of Richmondshire; 7 miles from Northallerton, 9 from Darlington, *(Durham)* 9 from Yarm, 13 from Richmond.—Population 230.

SMEATON, LITTLE, in the parish of Birkby, wapentake and liberty of Allertonshire; 6 miles from Northallerton, 9 from Yarm, 10 from Darlington, *(Durham.)*—Pop. 72.

SNAINTON, in the parishes of Brompton and Ebberston, wapentake and liberty of Pickering-Lythe; *(the seat of James Lister, Esq.)* 7¼ miles from Pickering, 10 from Scarborough, 12 from Malton.—Population 450.

SNAPE, in the parish of Well, wapentake of Hang-East, liberty of Richmondshire; *(Snape-Hall, the seat of William Milbank, Esq.)* 3 miles from Masham, 3¼ from Bedale.—Population 679.

SNAYSHOLME, in the parish of Aysgarth, wapentake of Hang-West, liberty of Richmondshire; 2¼ miles from Hawes, 7¼ from Askrigg.

SNEATON, in the parish of Sneaton, wapentake and liberty of Whitby-Strand; *(Sneaton-Hall, the seat of Sir Jonathan Miles, Bart.)* 3 miles from Whitby, 18 from Pickering, 18 from Scarborough.—Population 173.

SNEATON-THORPE, in the parish of Sneaton, wapentake and liberty of Whitby-Strand; 4 miles from Whitby, 17 from Scarborough.

SNILESWORTH, in the parish of Hawnby, wapentake of Birdforth; 10 miles from Helmsley, 12 from Northallerton, 14 from Thirsk.

SOBER-GATE, in the parish of Kirby-Wiske, wapentake of Gilling-East; 4 miles from Northallerton, 7 from Thirsk, 7 from Bedale.

SOBER-HILL, in the parish of Ainderby-Steeple, wapentake of Gilling-East, liberty of Richmondshire; 4 miles from Northallerton, 6 from Bedale.

SOBER-LOW, in the parish of Ainderby-Steeple, wapentake of Gilling-East, liberty of Richmondshire; 4 miles from Northallerton, 6 from Bedale.

SOUR-LEYS, in the parish of Helmsley, wapentake of Rydale; 3¼ miles from Helmsley, 9¼ from Kirby-Moorside, 20¼ from Malton.

SOUTH-FIELD, in the parish of Kirkdale, wapentake of Rydale; 3 miles from Kirby-Moorside, 6 from Helmsley, 13 from Malton.

SOWERBY, in the parish of Thirsk, wapentake of Birdforth; 1 mile from Thirsk, 10 from Northallerton, 11½ from Ripon. Population 639.

SOWERBY-UNDER-COTCLIFFE, in the parish of Sigston, wapentake and liberty of Allertonshire; 3 miles from Northallerton, 7 from Thirsk.—Population 38.

SOWERSETT, in the parish of Coverham, wapentake of Hang-West; 6¼ miles from Middleham, 7½ from Leyburn.

SPANHAM, in the parish of Barningham, wapentake of Gilling-West; 4 miles from Greta-bridge, 5 from Barnardcastle, *(Durham)* 12 from Richmond.

SPANTON, in the parish of Lastingham, wapentake of Rydale; 4 miles from Kirby-Moorside, 9½ from Helmsley, 13 from Malton.—Population 107.

SPANTON-LODGE, in the parish of Lastingham, wapentake of Rydale; *(the seat of R. Darley, Esq.)* 4 miles from Kirby-Moorside, 10 from Helmsley, 14 from Malton.

SPENNYTHORNE, in the parish of Spennythorne, wapentake of Hang-West, liberty of Richmondshire, *(the seats of William Chaytor, and Turner Strawbenzie, Esqrs.)* 1 mile from Middleham, 2 from Leyburn, 9 from Richmond.—Population 170.

SPITTAL-BRIDGE-INN, in the parish of Cramb, wapentake of Bulmer; 7¼ miles from Malton, 10¼ from York, 14 from Easingwold.

SPITTAL-HOUSE, in the parish of Bowes, wapentake of Gilling-West, liberty of Richmondshire; 7¼ miles from Brough, *(Westmoreland)* 9¼ from Barnardcastle, *(Durham)* 11¼ from Greta-bridge.

SPRING-END, in the parish of Grinton, wapentake of Gilling-West, liberty of Richmondshire; 6 miles from Reeth, 9 from Askrigg, 16 from Richmond.

SPROXTON, in the parish of Helmsley, wapentake of Rydale; 1 mile from Helmsley, 7 from Kirby-Moorside, 16 from Malton.—Population 213.

SPROXTON-COURT, in the parish of Helmsley, wapentake of Rydale; 2 miles from Helmsley, 7 from Kirby-Moorside, 16 from Malton.

STADDLE-BRIDGE, in the parish of East-Harlsey, wapentake and liberty of Allertonshire; 7 miles from Northallerton, 9 from Stokesley, 10 from Yarm.

STAINSACRE, in the parish of Whitby, wapentake and liberty of Whitby-Strand; *(the seat of J. Sanders, Esq.)* 2 miles from Whitby, 19 from Scarborough.—Pop. 144.

STAINSBY, in the parish of Stainton, west-division of the wapentake and liberty of Langbarugh; 3 miles from Stockton, *(Durham)* 4½ from Yarm.

STAINTON, in the parish of Stainton, west division of the wapentake and liberty of Langbarugh; *(the seat of The Rev. Archdeacon Baillie)* 4 miles from Stokesley, 4 from Stockton, *(Durham)* 5 from Yarm.—Population 272.

STAINTON, in the parish of Downholme, wapentake of Hang-West, liberty of Richmondshire; 5 miles from Leyburn, 7 from Middleham, 7 from Richmond.

STAINTON-DALE. in the parish of Scalby, wapentake and liberty of Pickering-Lythe; 8 miles from Scarborough, 10 from Whitby.—Population 271.

STAINTON-GRANGE, in the parish of Stainton, west-division of the wapentake and liberty of Langbarugh; 4 miles from Stokesley, 5 from Yarm.

STAITHES, in the parish of Hinderwell, east-division of the wapentake and liberty of Langbarugh; 11 miles from Whitby, 13 from Guisbrough.

STAKESLEY, HIGH, in the parish of Whitby, wapentake and liberty of Whitby-Strand; *(the seats of Joseph Barker, and John Blackburn, Esqrs.)* 1 mile from Whitby, 20 from Pickering, 20 from Guisbrough.

STAKESLEY, LOW, in the parish of Whitby, wapentake and liberty of Whitby-Strand; *(the seat of Abel Chapman, Esq.)* ½ a mile from Whitby, 20¼ from Pickering.

STALLING-BUSK, in the parish of Aysgarth, wapentake of Hang-West; 5 miles from Askrigg, 17 from Middleham.

STANDARD-HILL, in the parish of Northallerton, wapen. and liberty of Allertonshire; 3 miles from Northallerton, 13 from Darlington.

STANGHOW, in the parish of Skelton, east-division of the wapentake and liberty of Langbarugh; *(the seat of Richard Scarth, Esq.)* 4¼ miles from Guisbrough, 12¼ from Stokesley, 17 from Whitby.—Population 118.

STANK, in the parish of Sigston, wapentake and liberty of Allertonshire; 2¼ miles from Northallerton, 10¼ from Thirsk.

STANWICK, in the parish of St. John, Stanwick, wapentake of Gilling-West, liberty of Richmondshire; *(the seat of the Duke of Northumberland)* 8 miles from Richmond, 9 from Darlington, *(Durham.)*—Population 80.

STAPLETON, in the parishes of St. John, Stanwick, and Croft, wapentake of Gilling-East; 2¼ miles from Darlington, *(Durham)* 11 from Richmond.—Population 89.

STARTFORTH, HIGH, in the parish of High Startforth, wapentake of Gilling-West, liberty of Richmondshire; 1 mile from Barnardcastle, *(Durham)* 3 from Greta-bridge, 15 from Richmond.—Population 336.

STEARSBY, in the parish of Bransby, wapentake of Bulmer; 6 miles from Easingwold, 13 from Malton.

STEPNEY, in the parish of Whitby, wapentake and liberty of Whitby-Strand; ¼ of a mile from Whitby, 19¼ from Guisbrough.

STILLINGTON, in the parish of Stillington, wapentake of Bulmer, liberty of St. Peter; *(the seat of Stephen Croft, Esq.)* 4 miles from Easingwold, 10 from York, 16 from Malton.—Population 531.

STITTENHAM, in the parish of Sheriff-Hutton, wapentake of Bulmer; 9 miles from Malton, 9 from Easingwold, 12 from York.—Population 77.

STOCKTON-ON-THE-FOREST, in the parish of Stockton-on-the-Forest, wapentake of Bulmer, a part in the liberty of St. Peter; *(the seat of Benjamin Agar, Esq.)* 4 miles from York, 11 from Easingwold, 14 from Malton.—Population 255.

STOKESLEY, in the parish of Stokesley, west division of the wapentake and liberty of Langbarugh; 8 miles from Guisbrough, 8 from Yarm, 10 from Stockton, *(Durham)* 16 from Northallerton, 16 from Helmsley, 20 from Thirsk, 44 from York, 237 from London.—*Market*, Saturday.—*Fairs*, Palm-sun-eve, Trinity Saturday, for Horses, Horned Cattle, Sheep, Linen Cloth, &c. first Saturday after old Lammas-day, for Linen Cloth.—*Principal Inn*, Black Swan.—Population 1,369.

STONEGILL-GATE, in the parish of Danby, east-division of the wapentake and liberty of Langbarugh; 8 miles from Whitby, 13 from Guisbrough.

STONEGRAVE, in the parish of Stonegrave, wapentake of Rydale; 5 miles from Helmsley, 7½ from Kirby-Moorside, 10¼ from Malton.—Population 126.

STONESDALE, EAST, in the parish of Grinton, wapentake of Gilling-West, liberty of Richmondshire; 11 miles from Askrigg, 13¼ from Reeth.

STONESDALE, WEST, in the parish of Grinton, wapentake of Gilling-West, liberty of Richmondshire; 12 miles from Askrigg, 13 from Reeth.

STONEY-CLOSE-HOUSE, in the parish of Thornton-Watlass, wapentake of Hang-East; 3 miles from Masham, 4 from Bedale, 8 from Middleham.

STONEYKELD, in the parish of Bowes, wapentake of Gilling-West, liberty of Richmondshire; 5¼ miles from Barnardcastle, *(Durham)* 6 from Greta-bridge.

STORTHWAITE-HALL, in the parish of Arkengarthdale, wapentake of Gilling-West, liberty of Richmondshire; 3 miles from Reeth, 13 from Richmond.

STOW-BROW, in the parish of Whitby, wapentake and liberty of Whitby-Strand; 8 miles from Whitby, 12 from Scarborough.

STRANDMIRE, in the parish of Hovingham, wapentake of Rydale; 8 miles from Helmsley, 8½ from Kirby-Moorside.

STRENSALL, in the parish of Strensall, wapentake of Bulmer, liberty of St. Peter; 6 miles from York, 9 from Easingwold, 13 from Malton.—Population 297.

STUDDOW, in the parish of Fingall, wapentake of Hang-West, liberty of Richmondshire; 2¼ miles from Leyburn, 3 from Middleham, 7 from Richmond.

SUFFIELD, in the parish of Hackness, wapentake and liberty of Whitby-Strand; 4 miles from Scarborough, 18 from Whitby.—Population 110.

SUMMER-LODGE, in the parish of Grinton, wapentake of Hang-West, liberty of Richmondshire; ¼ miles from Reeth, 6 from Askrigg, 9 from Leyburn.

SUNLEY-HILL, in the parish of Kirkdale, wapentake of Rydale; *(the seat of Arthur Cayley, Esq.)* 3 miles from Kirby-Moorside, 6 from Helmsley, 11 from Malton.

SUNNY-CROSS, in the parish of Ayton, west-division of the wapentake and liberty of Langbarugh; 4 miles from Stokesley, 7 from Guisbrough, 9 from Yarm.

SUTTON, in the parish of Kirklington, wapentake of Halikeld; 5 miles from Ripon, 7 from Bedale, 8 from Thirsk, 8 from Masham.—Population 110.

SUTTON-ON-THE-FOREST, in the parish of Sutton-on-the-Forest, wapentake of Bulmer; *(the seat of Sir Charles Hoare Harland, Bart.)* 5 miles from Easingwold, 8 from York, 15 from Malton.—Population 449.

SUTTON-UNDER-WHITESTONECLIFFE, in the parish of Feliskirk, wapentake of Birdforth, liberty of Ripon; 4 miles from Thirsk, 10 from Helmsley, 15 from Ripon.—Population 281.

SUTTON-PEN, in the parish of Masham, wapentake of Hang-East; 3 miles from Bedale, 15 from Richmond.

SWAINBY, in the parish of Whorlton, west-division of the wapentake and liberty of Langbarugh; 6 miles from Stokesley, 10 from Northallerton, 10 from Yarm.

SWAINBY, in the parish of Pickhill. wapentake of Halikeld, 6¼ miles from Bedale, 8 from Northallerton.—Pop. 40.

SWALE-HALL, in the parish of Grinton, wapentake of Hang-West, liberty of Richmondshire; 1½ miles from Reeth, 7 from Leyburn, 11 from Richmond.

SWINESIDE, in the parish of Coverham, wapentake of Hang West, liberty of Richmondshire; 7 miles from Middleham, 8½ from Leyburn;

SWINETHWAITE, in the parish of Wensley, wapentake of Hang-West, liberty of Richmondshire; 5 miles from Leyburn, 5¼ from Middleham.

SWINTON, in the parish of Masham, wapentake of Hang-East, liberty of Richmondshire; *(the seat of William Danby, Esq.)* 1 mile from Masham, 7 from Bedale.—Pop. 174.

SWINTON, in the parish of Appleton-le-street, wapentake of Rydale; 2¼ miles from Malton, 11¼ from Kirby-Moorside.—Population 217.

SYLPHO, in the parish of Hackness, wapentake and liberty of Whitby Strand; 5 miles from Scarborough, 16 from Whitby.

T

TANFIELD, EAST, in the parish of West-Tanfield, wapentake of Halikeld; 6 miles from Ripon, 7 from Bedale.—Population 26.

TANFIELD-HALL, in the parish of West-Tanfield, wapentake of Halikeld; 6¼ miles from Ripon, 6¼ from Bedale.

TANFIELD, WEST, in the parish of West-Tanfield; wapentake of Halikeld, 6¼ miles from Ripon, 6½ from Bedale,—Population 639.

TANTON, in the parish of Stokesley, west-division of the wapentake and liberty of Langbarugh; 3 miles from Stokesley, 7 from Stockton, *(Durham.)*

TELPHIT, in the parish of Marske, wapentake of Gilling-West, liberty of Richmondshire; 7 miles from Richmond, 9 from Leyburn.

TEMPLE, in the parish of South-Cowton, wapentake of Gilling-East; 7 miles from Northallerton, 8 from Darlington, *(Durham)* 9 from Richmond.

NORTH-RIDING. 73

TEMPLE-HOUSE, in the parish of Wensley, wapentake of Hang-West, liberty of Richmondshire; 5¼ miles from Leyburn, 5½ from Middleham, 14¼ from Richmond.

TERRINGTON, in the parish of Terrington, wapentake of Bulmer; 8 miles from Malton, 8 from Easingwold, 15 from York.—Population 463.

THEAKSTON, in the parish of Burneston, wapentake of Halikeld, liberty of Richmondshire, *(the seat of Edward Carter, Esq.)* 3 miles from Bedale, 8 from Masham, 9 from Ripon.—Population 73.

THIMBLEBY, in the parish of Osmotherley, wapentake and liberty of Allertonshire; 6 miles from Northallerton, 9 from Thirsk, 11 from Stokesley.—Population 163.

THIMBLEBY-LODGE, in the parish of Osmotherley, wapentake and liberty of Allertonshire; *(the seat of Richard William Christopher Peirse, Esq.)* 6¼ miles from Northallerton, 9¼ from Thirsk, 10¼ from Stokesley.

THIRKLEBY, HIGH, in the parish of High Thirkleby, wapentake of Birdforth; *(Thirkleby-Hall, the seat of Sir Thomas Frankland, Bart.)* 4 miles from Thirsk, 7 from Easingwold.—Population 281.

THIRKLEBY, LOW, in the parish of High-Thirkleby, wapentake of Birdforth; 4 miles from Thirsk, 7 from Easingwold.

THIRLBY, in the parish of Feliskirk, wapentake of Birdforth; 5¼ miles from Thirsk, 10 from Helmsley.—Pop. 168.

THIRN, in the parish of Thornton-Watlass, wapentake of Hang-East; 3 miles from Masham, 4½ from Bedale, 7 from Middleham.—Population 131.

THIRSK, in the parish of Tkirsk, wapentake of Birdforth; 9 miles from Northallerton, 10 from Easingwold, 11 from Boroughbridge, 11 from Ripon, 14 from Bedale, 14 from Helmsley, 19 from Yarm, 20 from Stokesley, 23 from York, 222 from London.—*Market*, Monday.—*Fairs*, Shrove-Monday, April 4 and 5, for Horned Cattle, Sheep, Leather, &c. Easter-Monday, and Whit-Monday, for Woollen Cloth, Toys, &c. August 4 and 5, October 28 and 29, for Sheep, Horned Cattle, and Leather; first Tuesday after December 11, for Horned Cattle, Leather, &c.—*Bankers*, Messrs. Scott, Nicholson, and Smith draw on Messrs. Boldero, Lushington, and Co. 30, Cornhill.—Sends two Members to Parliament.—*Principal Inns*, Three Tuns and King's Arms.—Pop. 2,092.

THOLTHORPE, in the parish of Alne, wapentake of Bulmer, liberty of St. Peter: 5 miles from Easingwold, 5 from Boroughbridge, 13 from York.—Population 188.

K

garth, wapentake of Hang-West, liberty of Richmondshire; 1¼ miles from Askrigg, 4 from Hawes.

SKELDERSKEW-GRANGE, in the parish of Guisbrough, east-division of the wapentake and liberty of Langbarugh; 4 miles from Guisbrough, 10 from Stokesley, 18 from Yarm.

SKELTON, in the parishes of Skelton and Overton, wapentake of Bulmer, a part in the liberty of St. Peter; 4 miles from York, 9 from Easingwold, 18 from Malton.—Pop. 203.

SKELTON, in the parish of Marske, wapentake of Gilling-West, liberty of Richmondshire; 6 miles from Richmond, 6 from Reeth.

SKELTON, in the parish of Skelton, east-division of the wapentake and liberty of Langbarugh; *(Skelton-Castle, the seat of John Wharton, Esq.)* 3¾ miles from Guisbrough, 11¼ from Stokesley, 16 from Stockton, *(Durham.)*—Population 700.

SKELTON-SMITHY, in the parish of Skelton, wapentake of Bulmer, 3 miles from York, 10 from Easingwold, 18 from Malton.

SKEWSBY, in the parish of Dalby, wapentake of Bulmer; 9 miles from Easingwold, 13 from Malton, 15 from York.

SKINNINGRAVE, in the parish of Skelton, east-division of the wapentake and liberty of Langbarugh; *(the seat of John Easterby, Esq.)* 7 miles from Guisbrough, 14 from Whitby, 15 from Stokesley.—Population 67.

SKIPLAM, in the parish of Kirkdale, wapentake of Rydale; 3 miles from Kirby-Moorside, 4 from Helmsley, 17 from Malton.—Population 70.

SKIPTON, and SKIPTON-BRIDGE, in the parish of Topcliffe, wapentake of Birdforth; 4 miles from Thirsk, 7 from Ripon, 10 from Northallerton.—Population 103.

SKUTTERSKELFE, in the parish of Rudby, west division of the wapentake and liberty of Langbarugh; 2 miles from Stokesley, 6 from Yarm.—Population 42.

SLAPE-WATH, in the parish of Guisbrough, east-division of the wapentake and liberty of Langbarugh; 2¼ miles from Guisbrough, 10 from Stokesley, 19 from Whitby.

SLEDDALE, in the parish of Guisbrough, east-division of the wapentake and liberty of Langbarugh; 3 miles from Guisbrough, 11 from Stokesley.

SLEDSHOE, in the parish of Lastingham, wapentake of Rydale; 12 miles from Kirby-Moorside, 17 from Helmsley.

SLEETHOLME, in the parish of Bowes, wapentake of Gilling-West, liberty of Richmondshire; 7 miles from Barnard-castle, *(Durham)* 8 from Greta-bridge, 16 from Richmond.

SLEIGHTS, in the parish of Whitby, wapentake and liberty

of Whitby-Strand; *(Sleights-Hall, the seat of Mrs. Bateman, and Eske-Hall, the seat of J. C. Coates. Esq.)* 4 miles from Whitby, 17 from Pickering.

SLINGSBY, in the parish of Slingsby, wapentake of Rydale; 7 miles from Malton, 9 from Kirby-Moorside, 9 from Helmsley.—Population 434.

SMALLWAYS, in the parish of Kirkby-Ravensworth, wapentake of Gilling-West; 2 miles from Greta-bridge, 8 from Richmond.

SMARBER, in the parish of Grinton, wapentake of Gilling-West, liberty of Richmondshire; 5 miles from Reeth, 9 from Askrigg, 15 from Richmond.

SMEARHOLMES, in the parish of Burneston, wapentake of Halikeld, liberty of Richmondshire; 4 miles from Bedale, 9 from Masham, 10 from Northallerton, 11 from Ripon.

SMEATON, GREAT, in the parish of Great-Smeaton, wapentake of Gilling-East, liberty of Richmondshire; 7 miles from Northallerton, 9 from Darlington, *(Durham)* 9 from Yarm, 13 from Richmond.—Population 230.

SMEATON, LITTLE, in the parish of Birkby, wapentake and liberty of Allertonshire; 6 miles from Northallerton, 9 from Yarm, 10 from Darlington, *(Durham.)*—Pop. 72.

SNAINTON, in the parishes of Brompton and Ebberston, wapentake and liberty of Pickering-Lythe; *(the seat of James Lister, Esq.)* 7¼ miles from Pickering, 10 from Scarborough, 12 from Malton.—Population 450.

SNAPE, in the parish of Well, wapentake of Hang-East, liberty of Richmondshire; *(Snape-Hall, the seat of William Milbank, Esq.)* 3 miles from Masham, 3¼ from Bedale.—Population 679.

SNAYSHOLME, in the parish of Aysgarth, wapentake of Hang-West, liberty of Richmondshire; 2¼ miles from Hawes, 7½ from Askrigg.

SNEATON, in the parish of Sneaton, wapentake and liberty of Whitby-Strand; *(Sneaton-Hall, the seat of Sir Jonathan Miles, Bart.)* 3 miles from Whitby, 18 from Pickering, 18 from Scarborough.—Population 173.

SNEATON-THORPE, in the parish of Sneaton, wapentake and liberty of Whitby-Strand; 4 miles from Whitby, 17 from Scarborough.

SNILESWORTH, in the parish of Hawnby, wapentake of Birdforth; 10 miles from Helmsley, 12 from Northallerton, 14 from Thirsk.

SOBER-GATE, in the parish of Kirby-Wiske, wapentake of Gilling-East; 4 miles from Northallerton, 7 from Thirsk, 7 from Bedale.

SOBER-HILL, in the parish of Ainderby-Steeple, wapentake of Gilling-East, liberty of Richmondshire; 4 miles from Northallerton, 6 from Bedale.

SOBER. LOW, in the parish of Ainderby-Steeple, wapentake of Gilling-East, liberty of Richmondshire; 4 miles from Northallerton, 6 from Bedale.

SOUR-LEYS, in the parish of Helmsley, wapentake of Rydale; 3½ miles from Helmsley, 9½ from Kirby-Moorside, 20¼ from Malton.

SOUTH-FIELD, in the parish of Kirkdale, wapentake of Rydale; 3 miles from Kirby-Moorside, 6 from Helmsley, 13 from Malton.

SOWERBY, in the parish of Thirsk, wapentake of Birdforth; 1 mile from Thirsk, 10 from Northallerton, 11½ from Ripon. Population 639.

SOWERBY-UNDER-COTCLIFFE, in the parish of Sigston, wapentake and liberty of Allertonshire; 3 miles from Northallerton, 7 from Thirsk.—Population 38.

SOWERSETT, in the parish of Coverham, wapentake of Hang-West; 6¼ miles from Middleham, 7¼ from Leyburn.

SPANHAM, in the parish of Barningham, wapentake of Gilling-West; 4 miles from Greta-bridge, 5 from Barnardcastle, *(Durham)* 12 from Richmond.

SPANTON, in the parish of Lastingham, wapentake of Rydale; 4 miles from Kirby-Moorside, 9¼ from Helmsley, 13 from Malton.—Population 107.

SPANTON-LODGE, in the parish of Lastingham, wapentake of Rydale; *(the seat of R. Darley, Esq.)* 4 miles from Kirby-Moorside, 10 from Helmsley, 14 from Malton.

SPENNYTHORNE, in the parish of Spennythorne, wapentake of Hang-West, liberty of Richmondshire, *(the seats of William Chaytor, and Turner Strawbenzie, Esqrs.)* 1 mile from Middleham, 2 from Leyburn, 9 from Richmond.—Population 170.

SPITTAL-BRIDGE-INN, in the parish of Cramb, wapentake of Bulmer; 7¼ miles from Malton, 10¼ from York, 14 from Easingwold.

SPITTAL-HOUSE, in the parish of Bowes, wapentake of Gilling-West, liberty of Richmondshire; 7¼ miles from Brough,*(Westmoreland)* 9¼ from Barnardcastle, *(Durham)* 11¼ from Greta-bridge.

SPRING-END, in the parish of Grinton, wapentake of Gilling-West, liberty of Richmondshire; 6 miles from Reeth, 9 from Askrigg, 16 from Richmond.

SPROXTON, in the parish of Helmsley, wapentake of Rydale; 1 mile from Helmsley, 7 from Kirby-Moorside, 16 from Malton.—Population 213.

SPROXTON-COURT, in the parish of Helmsley, wapentake of Rydale; 2 miles from Helmsley, 7 from Kirby-Moorside, 16 from Malton.

STADDLE-BRIDGE, in the parish of East-Harlsey, wapentake and liberty of Allertonshire; 7 miles from Northallerton, 9 from Stokesley, 10 from Yarm.

STAINSACRE, in the parish of Whitby, wapentake and liberty of Whitby-Strand; *(the seat of J. Sanders, Esq.)* 2 miles from Whitby, 19 from Scarborough.—Pop. 144.

STAINSBY, in the parish of Stainton, west-division of the wapentake and liberty of Langbarugh; 3 miles from Stockton, *(Durham)* 4½ from Yarm.

STAINTON, in the parish of Stainton, west division of the wapentake and liberty of Langbarugh; *(the seat of The Rev. Archdeacon Baillie)* 4 miles from Stokesley, 4 from Stockton, *(Durham)* 5 from Yarm.—Population 272.

STAINTON, in the parish of Downholme, wapentake of Hang-West, liberty of Richmondshire; 5 miles from Leyburn, 7 from Middleham, 7 from Richmond.

STAINTON-DALE, in the parish of Scalby, wapentake and liberty of Pickering-Lythe; 8 miles from Scarborough, 10 from Whitby.—Population 271.

STAINTON-GRANGE, in the parish of Stainton, west-division of the wapentake and liberty of Langbarugh; 4 miles from Stokesley, 5 from Yarm.

STAITHES, in the parish of Hinderwell, east-division of the wapentake and liberty of Langbarugh; 11 miles from Whitby, 13 from Guisbrough.

STAKESLEY, HIGH, in the parish of Whitby, wapentake and liberty of Whitby-Strand; *(the seats of Joseph Barker, and John Blackburn, Esqrs.)* 1 mile from Whitby, 20 from Pickering, 20 from Guisbrough.

STAKESLEY, LOW, in the parish of Whitby, wapentake and liberty of Whitby-Strand; *(the seat of Abel Chapman, Esq.)* ½ a mile from Whitby, 20½ from Pickering.

STALLING-BUSK, in the parish of Aysgarth, wapentake of Hang-West; 5 miles from Askrigg, 17 from Middleham.

STANDARD-HILL, in the parish of Northallerton, wapen. and liberty of Allertonshire; 3 miles from Northallerton, 13 from Darlington.

STANGHOW, in the parish of Skelton, east-division of the wapentake and liberty of Langbarugh; *(the seat of Richard Scarth, Esq.)* 4½ miles from Guisbrough, 12½ from Stokesley, 17 from Whitby.—Population 118.

STANK, in the parish of Sigston, wapentake and liberty of Allertonshire; 2½ miles from Northallerton, 10¼ from Thirsk.

SOBER-HILL, in the parish of Ainderby-Steeple, wapentake of Gilling-East, liberty of Richmondshire; 4 miles from Northallerton, 6 from Bedale.

SOBER-LOW, in the parish of Ainderby-Steeple, wapentake of Gilling-East, liberty of Richmondshire; 4 miles from Northallerton, 6 from Bedale.

SOUR-LEYS, in the parish of Helmsley, wapentake of Rydale; 3¼ miles from Helmsley, 9¼ from Kirby-Moorside, 20¼ from Malton.

SOUTH-FIELD, in the parish of Kirkdale, wapentake of Rydale; 3 miles from Kirby-Moorside, 6 from Helmsley, 13 from Malton.

SOWERBY, in the parish of Thirsk, wapentake of Birdforth; 1 mile from Thirsk, 10 from Northallerton, 11¼ from Ripon. Population 639.

SOWERBY-UNDER-COTCLIFFE, in the parish of Sigston, wapentake and liberty of Allertonshire; 3 miles from Northallerton, 7 from Thirsk.—Population 38.

SOWERSETT, in the parish of Coverham, wapentake of Hang-West; 6¼ miles from Middleham, 7¼ from Leyburn.

SPANHAM, in the parish of Barningham, wapentake of Gilling-West; 4 miles from Greta-bridge, 5 from Barnardcastle, *(Durham)* 12 from Richmond.

SPANTON, in the parish of Lastingham, wapentake of Rydale; 4 miles from Kirby-Moorside, 9¼ from Helmsley, 13 from Malton.—Population 107.

SPANTON-LODGE, in the parish of Lastingham, wapentake of Rydale; *(the seat of R. Darley, Esq.)* 4 miles from Kirby-Moorside, 10 from Helmsley, 14 from Malton.

SPENNYTHORNE, in the parish of Spennythorne, wapentake of Hang-West, liberty of Richmondshire, *(the seats of William Chaytor, and Turner Strawbenzie, Esqrs.)* 1 mile from Middleham, 2 from Leyburn, 9 from Richmond.—Population 170.

SPITTAL-BRIDGE-INN, in the parish of Cramb, wapentake of Bulmer; 7¼ miles from Malton, 10¼ from York, 14 from Easingwold.

SPITTAL-HOUSE, in the parish of Bowes, wapentake of Gilling-West, liberty of Richmondshire; 7¼ miles from Brough, *(Westmoreland)* 9¼ from Barnardcastle, *(Durham)* 11¼ from Greta-bridge.

SPRING-END, in the parish of Grinton, wapentake of Gilling-West, liberty of Richmondshire; 6 miles from Reeth, 9 from Askrigg, 16 from Richmond.

SPROXTON, in the parish of Helmsley, wapentake of Rydale; 1 mile from Helmsley, 7 from Kirby-Moorside, 16 from Malton.—Population 213.

SPROXTON-COURT, in the parish of Helmsley, wapentake of Rydale; 2 miles from Helmsley, 7 from Kirby-Moorside, 16 from Malton.

STADDLE-BRIDGE, in the parish of East-Harlsey, wapentake and liberty of Allertonshire; 7 miles from North-allerton, 9 from Stokesley, 10 from Yarm.

STAINSACRE, in the parish of Whitby, wapentake and liberty of Whitby-Strand; *(the seat of J. Sanders, Esq.)* 2 miles from Whitby, 19 from Scarborough.—Pop. 144.

STAINSBY, in the parish of Stainton, west-division of the wapentake and liberty of Langbarugh; 3 miles from Stockton, *(Durham)* 4½ from Yarm.

STAINTON, in the parish of Stainton, west division of the wapentake and liberty of Langbarugh; *(the seat of The Rev. Archdeacon Baillie)* 4 miles from Stokesley, 4 from Stockton, *(Durham)* 5 from Yarm.—Population 272.

STAINTON, in the parish of Downholme, wapentake of Hang-West, liberty of Richmondshire; 5 miles from Leyburn, 7 from Middleham, 7 from Richmond.

STAINTON-DALE- in the parish of Scalby, wapentake and liberty of Pickering-Lythe; 8 miles from Scarborough, 10 from Whitby.—Population 271.

STAINTON-GRANGE, in the parish of Stainton, west-division of the wapentake and liberty of Langbarugh; 4 miles from Stokesley, 5 from Yarm.

STAITHES, in the parish of Hinderwell, east-division of the wapentake and liberty of Langbarugh; 11 miles from Whitby, 13 from Guisbrough.

STAKESLEY, HIGH, in the parish of Whitby, wapentake and liberty of Whitby-Strand; *(the seats of Joseph Barker, and John Blackburn, Esqrs.)* 1 mile from Whitby, 20 from Pickering, 20 from Guisbrough.

STAKESLEY, LOW, in the parish of Whitby, wapentake and liberty of Whitby-Strand; *(the seat of Abel Chapman, Esq.)* ½ a mile from Whitby, 20¼ from Pickering.

STALLING-BUSK, in the parish of Aysgarth, wapentake of Hang-West; 5 miles from Askrigg, 17 from Middleham.

STANDARD-HILL, in the parish of Northallerton, wapen- and liberty of Allertonshire; 3 miles from Northallerton, 13 from Darlington.

STANGHOW, in the parish of Skelton, east-division of the wapentake and liberty of Langbarugh; *(the seat of Richard Scarth, Esq.)* 4½ miles from Guisbrough, 12½ from Stokesley, 17 from Whitby.—Population 118.

STANK, in the parish of Sigston, wapentake and liberty of Allertonshire; 2½ miles from Northallerton, 10¼ from Thirsk.

STANWICK, in the parish of St. John, Stanwick, wapentake of Gilling-West, liberty of Richmondshire; *(the seat of the Duke of Northumberland)* 8 miles from Richmond, 9 from Darlington, *(Durham.)*—Population 80.

STAPLETON, in the parishes of St. John, Stanwick, and Croft, wapentake of Gilling-East; 2¼ miles from Darlington, *(Durham)* 11 from Richmond.—Population 89.

STARTFORTH, HIGH, in the parish of High Startforth, wapentake of Gilling-West, liberty of Richmondshire; 1 mile from Barnardcastle, *(Durham)* 3 from Greta-bridge, 15 from Richmond.—Population 336.

STEARSBY, in the parish of Bransby, wapentake of Bulmer; 6 miles from Easingwold, 13 from Malton.

STEPNEY, in the parish of Whitby, wapentake and liberty of Whitby-Strand; ¼ of a mile from Whitby, 19¼ from Guisbrough.

STILLINGTON, in the parish of Stillington, wapentake of Bulmer, liberty of St. Peter; *(the seat of Stephen Croft, Esq.)* 4 miles from Easingwold, 10 from York, 16 from Malton.—Population 531.

STITTENHAM, in the parish of Sheriff-Hutton, wapentake of Bulmer; 9 miles from Malton, 9 from Easingwold, 12 from York.—Population 77.

STOCKTON-ON-THE-FOREST, in the parish of Stockton-on-the-Forest, wapentake of Bulmer, a part in the liberty of St. Peter; *(the seat of Benjamin Agar, Esq.)* 4 miles from York, 11 from Easingwold, 14 from Malton.—Population 255.

STOKESLEY, in the parish of Stokesley, west division of the wapentake and liberty of Langbarugh; 8 miles from Guisbrough, 8 from Yarm, 10 from Stockton, *(Durham)* 16 from Northallerton, 16 from Helmsley, 20 from Thirsk, 44 from York, 237 from London.—*Market*, Saturday.—*Fairs*, Palm-sun-eve, Trinity Saturday, for Horses, Horned Cattle, Sheep, Linen Cloth, &c. first Saturday after old Lammas-day, for Linen Cloth.—*Principal Inn*, Black Swan.—Population 1,369.

STONEGILL-GATE, in the parish of Danby, east-division of the wapentake and liberty of Langbarugh; 8 miles from Whitby, 13 from Guisbrough.

STONEGRAVE, in the parish of Stonegrave, wapentake of Rydale; 5 miles from Helmsley, 7½ from Kirby-Moorside, 10¼ from Malton.—Population 126.

STONESDALE, EAST, in the parish of Grinton, wapentake of Gilling-West, liberty of Richmondshire; 11 miles from Askrigg, 13¼ from Reeth.

STONESDALE, WEST, in the parish of Grinton, wapentake of Gilling-West, liberty of Richmondshire; 12 miles from Askrigg, 13 from Reeth.

STONEY-CLOSE-HOUSE, in the parish of Thornton-Watlass, wapentake of Hang-East; 3 miles from Masham, 4 from Bedale, 8 from Middleham.

STONEYKELD, in the parish of Bowes, wapentake of Gilling-West, liberty of Richmondshire; 5½ miles from Barnardcastle, *(Durham)* 6 from Greta-bridge.

STORTHWAITE-HALL, in the parish of Arkengarthdale, wapentake of Gilling-West, liberty of Richmondshire; 3 miles from Reeth, 13 from Richmond.

STOW-BROW, in the parish of Whitby, wapentake and liberty of Whitby-Strand; 8 miles from Whitby, 12 from Scarborough.

STRANDMIRE, in the parish of Hovingham, wapentake of Rydale; 8 miles from Helmsley, 8½ from Kirby-Moorside.

STRENSALL, in the parish of Strensall, wapentake of Bulmer, liberty of St. Peter; 6 miles from York, 9 from Easingwold, 13 from Malton.—Population 297.

STUDDOW, in the parish of Fingall, wapentake of Hang-West, liberty of Richmondshire; 2¼ miles from Leyburn, 3 from Middleham, 7 from Richmond.

SUFFIELD, in the parish of Hackness, wapentake and liberty of Whitby-Strand; 4 miles from Scarborough, 18 from Whitby.—Population 110.

SUMMER-LODGE, in the parish of Grinton, wapentake of Hang-West, liberty of Richmondshire; ¼ miles from Reeth, 6 from Askrigg. 9 from Leyburn.

SUNLEY-HILL, in the parish of Kirkdale, wapentake of Rydale; *(the seat of Arthur Cayley, Esq.)* 3 miles from Kirby-Moorside, 6 from Helmsley, 11 from Malton.

SUNNY-CROSS, in the parish of Ayton, west-division of the wapentake and liberty of Langbarugh; 4 miles from Stokesley, 7 from Guisbrough, 9 from Yarm.

SUTTON, in the parish of Kirklington, wapentake of Halikeld; 5 miles from Ripon, 7 from Bedale, 8 from Thirsk, 8 from Masham.—Population 110.

SUTTON-ON-THE-FOREST, in the parish of Sutton-on-the-Forest, wapentake of Bulmer; *(the seat of Sir Charles Hoare Harland, Bart.)* 5 miles from Easingwold, 8 from York, 15 from Malton.—Population 449.

SUTTON-UNDER-WHITESTONECLIFFE, in the parish of Feliskirk, wapentake of Birdforth, liberty of Ripon; 4 miles from Thirsk, 10 from Helmsley, 15 from Ripon.—Population 281.

SUTTON-PEN, in the parish of Masham, wapentake of Hang-East; 3 miles from Bedale, 15 from Richmond.

SWAINBY, in the parish of Whorlton, west-division of the wapentake and liberty of Langbarugh; 6 miles from Stokesley, 10 from Northallerton, 10 from Yarm.

SWAINBY, in the parish of Pickhill, wapentake of Halikeld, 6¼ miles from Bedale, 8 from Northallerton.—Pop. 40.

SWALE-HALL, in the parish of Grinton, wapentake of Hang-West, liberty of Richmondshire; 1¼ miles from Reeth, 7 from Leyburn, 11 from Richmond.

SWINESIDE, in the parish of Coverham, wapentake of Hang West, liberty of Richmondshire; 7 miles from Middleham, 8¼ from Leyburn;.

SWINETHWAITE, in the parish of Wensley, wapentake of Hang-West, liberty of Richmondshire; 5 miles from Leyburn, 5¼ from Middleham.

SWINTON, in the parish of Masham, wapentake of Hang-East, liberty of Richmondshire; *(the seat of William Danby, Esq.)* 1 mile from Masham, 7 from Bedale.—Pop. 174.

SWINTON, in the parish of Appleton-le-street, wapentake of Rydale; 2¼ miles from Malton, 11¼ from Kirby-Moorside.—Population 217.

SYLPHO, in the parish of Hackness, wapentake and liberty of Whitby Strand; 5 miles from Scarborough, 16 from Whitby.

T

TANFIELD, EAST, in the parish of West-Tanfield, wapentake of Halikeld; 6 miles from Ripon, 7 from Bedale.—Population 26.

TANFIELD-HALL, in the parish of West-Tanfield, wapentake of Halikeld; 6¼ miles from Ripon, 6¼ from Bedale.

TANFIELD, WEST, in the parish of West-Tanfield, wapentake of Halikeld, 6¼ miles from Ripon, 6¼ from Bedale, —Population 639.

TANTON, in the parish of Stokesley, west-division of the wapentake and liberty of Langbarugh; 3 miles from Stokesley, 7 from Stockton, *(Durham.)*

TELPHIT, in the parish of Marske, wapentake of Gilling-West, liberty of Richmondshire; 7 miles from Richmond, 9 from Leyburn.

TEMPLE, in the parish of South-Cowton, wapentake of Gilling-East; 7 miles from Northallerton, 8 from Darlington, *(Durham)* 9 from Richmond.

TEMPLE-HOUSE, in the parish of Wensley, wapentake of Hang-West, liberty of Richmondshire; 5¼ miles from Leyburn, 5½ from Middleham, 14½ from Richmond.

TERRINGTON, in the parish of Terrington, wapentake of Bulmer; 8 miles from Malton, 8 from Easingwold, 15 from York.—Population 463.

THEAKSTON, in the parish of Burneston, wapentake of Halikeld, liberty of Richmondshire, *(the seat of Edward Carter, Esq.)* 3 miles from Bedale, 8 from Masham, 9 from Ripon.—Population 73.

THIMBLEBY, in the parish of Osmotherley, wapentake and liberty of Allertonshire; 6 miles from Northallerton, 9 from Thirsk, 11 from Stokesley.—Population 163.

THIMBLEBY-LODGE, in the parish of Osmotherley, wapentake and liberty of Allertonshire; *(the seat of Richard William Christopher Peirse, Esq.)* 6¼ miles from Northallerton, 9¼ from Thirsk, 10¼ from Stokesley.

THIRKLEBY, HIGH, in the parish of High Thirkleby, wapentake of Birdforth; *(Thirkleby-Hall, the seat of Sir Thomas Frankland, Bart.)* 4 miles from Thirsk, 7 from Easingwold.—Population 281.

THIRKLEBY, LOW, in the parish of High-Thirkleby, wapentake of Birdforth; 4 miles from Thirsk, 7 from Easingwold.

THIRLBY, in the parish of Feliskirk, wapentake of Birdforth; 5½ miles from Thirsk, 10 from Helmsley.—Pop. 168.

THIRN, in the parish of Thornton-Watlass, wapentake of Hang-East; 3 miles from Masham, 4½ from Bedale, 7 from Middleham.—Population 131.

THIRSK, in the parish of Tkirsk, wapentake of Birdforth; 9 miles from Northallerton, 10 from Easingwold, 11 from Boroughbridge, 11 from Ripon, 14 from Bedale, 14 from Helmsley, 19 from Yarm, 20 from Stokesley, 23 from York, 222 from London.—*Market*, Monday.—*Fairs*, Shrove-Monday, April 4 and 5, for Horned Cattle, Sheep, Leather, &c. Easter-Monday, and Whit-Monday, for Woollen Cloth, Toys, &c. August 4 and 5, October 28 and 29, for Sheep, Horned Cattle, and Leather; first Tuesday after December 11, for Horned Cattle, Leather, &c.—*Bankers*, Messrs. Scott, Nicholson, and Smith draw on Messrs. Boldero, Lushington, and Co. 30, Cornhill.—Sends two Members to Parliament.—*Principal Inns*, Three Tuns and King's Arms.—Pop. 2,092.

THOLTHORPE, in the parish of Alne, wapentake of Bulmer, liberty of St. Peter: 5 miles from Easingwold, 5 from Boroughbridge, 13 from York.—Population 188.

K

THORALBY, in the parish of Aysgarth, wapentake of Hang-West, liberty of Richmondshire; 4¼ miles from Askrigg, 7½ from Leyburn.—Population 313.

THORESBY, in the parish of Aysgarth, wapentake of Hang-West, liberty of Richmondshire; 5¼ miles from Leyburn, 6 from Middleham, 11¼ from Richmond.

THORMANBY, in the parish of Thormanby, wapentake of Bulmer, liberty of Ripon; 4 miles from Easingwold, 6 from Thirsk.—Population 131.

THORNABY, in the parish of Stainton, west-division of the wapentake and liberty of Langbarugh; 4 miles from Yarm, 7¼ from Stokesley, 12 from Guisbrough.—Population 167.

THORNBROUGH, in the parish of West-Tanfield, wapentake of Halikeld, liberty of Richmondshire; 6 miles from Masham, 6 from Ripon, 7 from Bedale.

THORNBROUGH, in the parish of South-Kilvington, wapentake of Birdforth; 3 miles from Thirsk, 8 from Northallerton.—Population 39.

THORNEY-BROW, in the parish of Scalby, wapentake and liberty of Whitby-Strand; 8 miles from Whitby, 12 from Scarborough.

THORN-PARK, in the parish of Seamor, wapentake and liberty of Pickering-Lythe; 5 miles from Scarborough, 15 from Pickering, 19 from Malton.

THORNS, in the parish of Grinton, wapentake of Gilling-West, liberty of Richmondshire; 7 miles from Askrigg, 12 from Reeth, 19 from Leyburn.

THORNTON, in the parish of Thornton, wapentake and liberty of Pickering-Lythe; 2½ miles from Pickering, 9 from Malton, 16¼ from Scarborough.—Population 731.

THORNTON, in the parish of Stainton, west-division of the wapentake and liberty of Langbarugh; 4 miles from Stockton, *(Durham)* 4¼ from Yarm, 5¼ from Stokesley.

THORNTON-BRIDGE, in the parish of Cundall, wapentake of Halikeld, liberty of Richmondshire; 5 miles from Boroughbridge, 5 from Easingwold, 10 from Thirsk.—Population 33.

THORNTON-LE-BEANS, in the parish of North-Otterington, wapentake and liberty of Allertonshire; 3½ miles from Northallerton, 5¾ from Thirsk.—Population 189.

THORNTON-LE-MOOR, in the parish of North-Otterington, wapentake of Birdforth; *(the seat of Thomas Beckett, Esq.)* 5 miles from Thirsk, 5 from Northallerton, 8¼ from Bedale.—Population 261.

THORNTON-LE-STREET, in the parish of Thornton-le-street, wapentake and liberty of Allertonshire; 3 miles from Thirsk, 6 from Northallerton.—Population 112.

NORTH-RIDING.

THORNTON-ON-THE-HILL, in the parish of Coxwold, wapentake of Birdforth; 5 miles from Easingwold, 10 from Thirsk.

THORNTON-RISEBROUGH, in the parish of Normanby, wapentake of Rydale; *(the seat of Luke Robinson, Esq.)* 4 miles from Pickering, 5 from Kirby-Moorside, 10 from Helmsley.—Population 33.

THORNTON-RUST, in the parish of Aysgarth, wapentake of Hang-West, liberty of Richmondshire; 2 miles from Askrigg, 7 from Hawes.—Population 130.

THORNTON-STEWARD, in the parish of Thornton-Steward, wapentake of Hang-West, liberty of Richmondshire; 6 miles from Leyburn, 7 from Bedale.—Population 222.

THORNTON-UPON-CLAY, in the parish of Foston, wapentake of Bulmer; 8 miles from Malton, 11 from York, 12 from Easingwold.—Population 146.

THORNTON-WATLASS, in the parish of Thornton-Watlass, wapentake of Hang-East; *(the seat of the Rev. F. Dodsworth, D. D.)* 3 miles from Bedale, 3 from Masham.—Population 184.

THOROBY, in the parish of Stainton, west-division of the wapentake and liberty of Langbarugh; 2 miles from Stokesley, 10 from Guisbrough.

THORPE, in the parish of Fylingdale, wapentake and liberty of Whitby-Strand; 6 miles from Whitby, 15 from Scarborough.

THORPE, in the parish of Wycliffe, wapentake of Gilling-West, liberty of Richmondshire; *(the seat of Sheldon Craddock, Esq.)* 2 miles from Greta-bridge, 4 from Barnardcastle, *(Durham)* 9 from Reeth, 11 from Richmond.

THORPE-FIELD-HOUSES, in the parish of Topcliffe, wapentake of Birdforth; 1¾ miles from Thirsk, 9½ from Boroughbridge, 9¼ from Ripon.

THORPE-PERROW, in the parish of Well, wapentake of Hang-East; liberty of Richmondshire; *(the seat of William Milbank, Esq.)* 2 miles from Bedale, 5 from Masham.

THORPE-UNDER-STONE, in the parish of Catterick, wapentake of Hang-West, liberty of Richmondshire; 4 miles from Richmond, 8¼ from Leyburn, 10¼ from Middleham.

THRINTOFT, in the parish of Ainderby-Steeple, wapentake of Gilling-East, liberty of Richmondshire; 3 miles from Northallerton, 5¼ from Bedale, 14 from Richmond.—Population 136.

THROSTENBY, or **THROXENBY**, in the parish of Scalby, wapentake and liberty of Pickering-Lythe; 2 miles from Scarborough, 19 from Whitby.—Population 48.

THUNDERBUSH, in the parish of Kildale, west-division of the wapentake and liberty of Langbarugh; 4 miles from Guisbrough, 10¼ from Stokesley, 17 from Stockton.

THWAITE, in the parish of Grinton, wapentake of Gilling-West, liberty of Richmondshire; 6 miles from Askrigg, 9 from Reeth.

THWAITE-BRIDGE, in the parish of Aysgarth, wapentake of Hang-West, liberty of Richmondshire; 4 miles from Hawes, 8 from Askrigg, 11 from Sedberg.

THWING-GARTH, in the parish of Romaldkirk, wapentake of Gilling-West, liberty of Richmondshire; 10 miles from Barnardcastle, *(Durham)* 13 from Greta-bridge.

TOCKETTS, see *Pluntation*.

TOLESBY, in the parish of Marton, west-division of the wapentake and liberty of Langbarugh; 6 miles from Stokesley, 6 from Yarm.

TOLLERTON, in the parish of Alne, wapentake of Bulmer, liberty of St. Peter; 4 miles from Easingwold, 7 from Boroughbridge, 10 from York.—*No Market*.—*Fair*, August 15, for Horned Cattle and Sheep.—Pop. 396.

TONTINE-INN, *(New-Road)* in the parish of Arncliffe, west-division of the wapentake and liberty of Langbarugh; 8 miles from Northallerton, 8 from Stokesley, 8 from Yarm, 14 from Thirsk.

TOPCLIFFE, in the parish of Topcliffe, wapentake of Birdforth, a part in the liberty of St. Peter; 4 miles from Thirsk, 7 from Boroughbridge, 12 from Northallerton.—*No Market*.—*Fair*, July 17 and 18, for Sheep, Horses, Horned Cattle, &c.—Population 589.

TOWTHORPE, in the parishes of Strensall and Huntington, wapentake of Bulmer; a part in the liberty of St. Peter; 4 miles from York, 10 from Easingwold, 14 from Malton.—Population 68.

TRENHOLME, or TRAINHOLME, in the parish of Whorlton, west-division of the wapentake and liberty of Langbarugh; 8 miles from Stokesley, 10 from Yarm.

TRINIAN, ST. in the parish of Richmond, wapentake of Gilling-West, liberty of Richmondshire; *(the seat of —— l'anson, Esq.)* 1 mile from Richmond, 4 from Catterick.

TROUTS' DALE, in the parish of Brompton, wapentake and liberty of Pickering-Lythe; 10 miles from Pickering, 10 from Scarborough, 17 from Whitby.—Population 53.

TUNSTALL, in the parish of Catterick, wapentake of Hang-East, liberty of Richmondshire; 6 miles from Richmond, 5 from Catterick.—Population 214.

NORTH-RIDING.

U.

UCKERBY, in the parish of Catterick, wapentake of Gilling-East, liberty of Richmondshire; 4¼ miles from Catterick, 6 from Richmond.—Population 75.

UGGLEBARNBY, in the parish of Whitby; wapentake and liberty of Whitby-Strand; 3¼ miles from Whitby, 17¼ from Pickering, 18½ from Scarborough.—Population 476.

UGTHORPE, in the parish of Lythe, east-division of the wapentake and liberty of Langbarugh; 7 miles from Whitby, 13 from Guisbrough, 18 from Stokesley.—Population 245.

UGTHORPE-RAILS, in the parish of Lythe, east-division of the wapentake and liberty of Langbarugh; 8 miles from Whitby, 14 from Guisbrough.

ULSHAW-BRIDGE, in the parish of East-Witton, wapentake of Hang-West; 1 mile from Middleham, 3 from Leyburn, 9 from Bedale.

ULVELANDS, in the parish of Marrick, wapentake of Gilling-West, liberty of Richmondshire; 3 miles from Reeth, 7 from Richmond.

UNION-HOUSE, in the parish of Pickhill, wapentake of Halikeld, liberty of Richmondshire; 7 miles from Ripon, 7 from Bedale, 8 from Masham.

UNTHANK, in the parish of Romaldkirk, wapentake of Gilling-West; 11 miles from Barnardcastle, *(Durham)* 21 from Richmond.

UPLEATHAM, in the parish of Guisbrough, east-division of the wapentake and liberty of Langbarugh; *(Upleatham-Hall, the seat of Lord Dundas)* 3 miles from Guisbrough, 11 from Stokesley, 14 from Stockton, *(Durham.)* Population 237.

UPSALL, in the parish of Ormesby, west-division of the wapentake and liberty of Langbarugh; 4 miles from Guisbrough, 6 from Stokesley, 7 from Stockton, *(Durham.)*

UPSALL, and UPSALL-CASTLE, in the parish of South-Kilvington, wapentake of Birdforth; 4 miles from Thirsk, 8 from Northallerton.—Population 102.

UPSLAND, in the parish of Kirklington, wapentake of Halikeld, liberty of Richmondshire; 7 miles from Ripon, 7 from Bedale, 7½ from Masham.

UPTON, in the parish of Easington, east-division of the wapentake and liberty of Langbarugh; 8¼ miles from Guisbrough, 16½ from Stokesley.

URE, or YOREHEAD, *(a River)* in the parish of Aysgarth, wapentake of Hang-West; 10 miles from Hawes, 15 from Askrigg, 16 from Sedbergh.

VIEWLEY-HALL, in the parish of St. John, Stanwick, wapentake of Gilling-West, liberty of Richmondshire; 7 miles from Richmond, 9 from Darlington, *(Durham.)*

VIEWLEY HILL, in the parish of Thornton-le-street, wapentake of Allertonshire; 4 miles from Thirsk, 5¼ from Northallerton.

W.

WAITWITH, in the parish of Catterick, wapentake of Hang-East, liberty of Richmondshire; 2 miles from Richmond, 7¼ from Leyburn, 8 from Middleham.

WALBURN, in the parish of Downholme, wapentake of Hang-West, liberty of Richmondshire; 3¼ miles from Leyburn, 5¼ from Middleham, 6 from Richmond.—Pop. 40.

WALDEN, or WELDEN, in the parish of Aysgarth, wapentake of Hang-West, liberty of Richmondshire; 7 miles from Askrigg, 11 from Leyburn.

WALLSGRAVE, or FALSGRAVE, in the parish of Scarborough, wapentake of Pickering-Lythe, liberty of Scarborough; 1 mile from Scarborough, 17 from Pickering, 20 from Whitby.—Population 279.

WANLASS, in the parish of West-Witton, wapentake of Hang-West, liberty of Richmondshire; 3½ miles from Leyburn, 4½ from Middleham, 15½ from Bedale.

WAPLEY, in the parish of Loftus, east-division of the wapentake and liberty of Langbarugh; 10½ miles from Guisbrough, 18½ Stokesley.

WAPLEY-NEW-INN, in the parish of Loftus, east-division of the wapentake and liberty of Langbarugh; 9 miles from Guisbrough, 12 from Whitby.

WARDERMASK, in the parish of Masham, wapentake of Hang-East, liberties of St. Peter and Richmondshire; 2 miles from Masham, 4 from Bedale.

WARLABY, in the parsh of Ainderby-Steeple, wapentake of Gilling-East, liberty of Richmondshire; 2¼ miles from Northallerton, 6½ from Bedale.—Population 60.

WARREN-HOUSE, in the parish of Masham, wapentake of Hang-East; 3 miles from Masham, 9 from Bedale.

WARTHILL, in the parish of Warthill, wapentake of Bulmer, a part in the liberty of St. Peter; 5 miles from York, 12 from Easingwold, 14½ from Malton.—Population 115.

WASHFORTH, in the parish of Marrick, wapentake of

Gilling-West, liberty of Richmondshire; 7 miles from Leyburn, 8 from Richmond.

WASS, in the parish of Kilburn, wapentake of Birdforth ; 6 miles from Helmsley, 12 from Kirby-Moorside.—Pop. 131.

WATH, in the parish of Wath, wapentake of Halikeld, liberty of Richmondshire ; 4¼ miles from Ripon, 8 from Thirsk, 9 from Masham.—Population 168.

WATH, in the parish of Hovingham, wapentake of Rydale; 8 miles from Malton, 8 from Helmsley, 8½ from Kirby-Moorside.—Population 19.

WATLASS-MOOR-HOUSE, in the parish of Well, wapentake of Hang-East; 2 miles from Masham, 4 from Bedale, 8 from Middleham.

WATSON-HOUSES, in the parish of Grinton, wapentake of Gilling-West, liberty of Richmondshire ; 1 mile from Reeth, 11 from Richmond.

WAYBILL, in the parish of Romalkirk, wapentake of Gilling-West ; 7 miles from Barnardcastle, *(Durham)* 10½ from Greta-bridge.

WEEDALE, in the parish of Brompton, wapentake and liberty of Pickering-Lythe ; 10 miles from Pickering, 10 from Scarborough, 14 from Malton.

WELBURN, in the parish and wapentake of Bulmer; 5½ miles from Malton, 14 from Easingwold, 14 from York.— Population 322.

WELBURN, in the parish of Kirkdale, wapentake of Rydale; *(the seat of Arthur Cayley, Esq.)* 1¼ miles from Kirby-Moorside, 4¼ from Helmsley.—Population 103.

WELBURY, in the parish of Welbury, wapentake of Birdforth; 7 miles from Northallerton, 9 from Yarm.--Pop. 249.

WELDALE, in the parish of Ebberston, wapentake and liberty of Pickering-Lythe; 7 miles from Pickering, 11 from Scarborough, 13 from Malton.

WELL, in the parish of Well, wapentake of Hang-East, liberty of Richmondshire; *(the seat of Richard Strangways, Esq.)* 4 miles from Bedale, 4 from Masham.—Pop. 368.

WENSLEY, in the parish of Wensley, wapentake of Hang-West, liberty of Richmondshire ; *(the seat of Thomas Maude, Esq.)* 1¼ miles from Leyburn, 3½ from Middleham, 10½ from Richmond.—Population 237.

WESTERDALE, in the parish of Stokesley, west-division of the wapentake and liberty of Langbarugh; *(the seat of A. Paris, Esq.)* 10 miles from Guisbrough, 11 from Stokesley, 16 from Whitby.—Population 257.

WEST-HOUSE, in the parish of Kildale, west-division of

the wapentake and liberty of Langbarugh; 4½ miles from Guisbrough, 7½ from Stokesley.

WHALE, in the parish of Barningham, wapentake of Gilling-West; 5 miles from Barnardcastle, *(Durham)* 12 from Richmond.

WHASHTON, in the parish of Kirkby-Ravensworth, wapentake of Gilling-West, liberty of Richmondshire; 4 miles from Richmond, 8 from Greta-bridge, 12 from Barnardcastle, *(Durham.)*—Population 113.

WHASHTON-SPRINGS, in the parish of Kirkby-Ravensworth, wapentake of Gilling-West, liberty of Richmondshire; 3 miles from Richmond, 8 from Catterick, 10 from Darlington.—*(Durham.)*

WHEAT-CROFT, in the parish of Scarborough, wapentake and liberty of Pickering-Lythe; 1 mile from Scarborough, 18 from Pickering.

WHENBY, in the parish of Whenby, wapentake of Bulmer; 7 miles from Easingwold, 12 from Malton, 13 from York. —Population 87.

WHITBY, in the parish of Whitby, wapentake and liberty of Whitby-Strand; *(Whitby-Abbey, the seat of Henry Cholmley, Esq.)* within ½ a mile of Whitby, are the following seats; *Airy-Hill, Richard Moorsome, Esq. Meadow-Field, Henry Simpson, Esq. Field-House, Christopher Richardson, Esq. Prospect-Hill, Miss Boulby; The Mount, William Reynolds, Esq.* 21 miles from Guisbrough, 20 from Scarborough, 21 from Pickering, 28 from Stokesley, 48 from York, 246 from London.—*Market,* Saturday.—*Fairs,* August 25, 26, and 27, Martinmas-Day, for Pedlary, &c.—*Bankers,* Messrs. Richardson, Pease, and Co. draw on Messrs. Harrison, Pricket and Broome, 1, Mansion-House-Street; Messrs. Simpson and Co. draw on Messrs. Elton, Hammond and Co. 21 Milk-Street.— *Principal Inns,* Angel, Golden Lion, King's Head, and White-Horse.—Population 7,483.

WHITAL, HIGH, and LOW, in the parish of Grinton, wapentake of Hang-West, liberty of Richmondshire; 2½ miles from Reeth, 12 from Richmond.

WHITAL SIDE, in the parish of Grinton, wapentake of Hang-West, liberty of Richmondshire; 3½ miles from Reeth, 6 from Askrigg, 9 from Leyburn.

WHITWELL, in the parish of Catterick, wapentake of Gilling-East, liberty of Richmondshire; 5 miles from Catterick, 8 from Richmond, 9 from Northallerton.—Pop. 77.

WHITWELL, in the parish of Cramb, wapentake of Bulmer;

5 miles from New-Malton, 12 from York, 15 from Easingwold.—Population 166.

WHORLTON, and CASTLE, in the parish of Whorlton, west-division of the wapentake and liberty of Langbarugh; 5 miles from Stokesley, 11 from Northallerton, 11 from Yarm.—Population 544.

WIDDALEFOOT, in the parish of Aysgarth, wapentake of Hang-West; 2 miles from Hawes, 7 from Askrigg.

WIGGINTHORPE, in the parish of Terrington, wapentake of Bulmer; *(the seat of William Garforth, Esq.)* 8 miles from Easingwold, 10 from New-Malton, 15 from York.

WIGGINTON, in the parish of Wigginton, wapentake of Bulmer, liberty of St. Peter; 4 miles from York, 9 from Easingwold, 18 from Malton.—Population 260.

WILDEN, in the parish of Coxwold, wapentake of Birdforth, liberty of Ripon; 7 miles from Thirsk, 7 from Easingwold, 8 from Helmsley.—Population 28.

WILTON, in the parish of Wilton, wapentake and liberty of Pickering-Lythe; 4 miles from Pickering, 10 from Malton, 22 from Whitby.—Population 186.

WILTON, in the parish of Wilton, east-division of the wapentake and liberty of Langbarugh; *(the seat of John Lowther, Esq.)* 3 miles from Guisbrough, 11 from Stokesley, 13¼ from Yarm, 24 from Whitby.—Population 328.

WIMBLETON, in the parish of Kirkdale, wapentake of Rydale; 2 miles from Kirby-Moorside, 4 from Helmsley, 14 from Malton.—Population 220.

WINTERING-GARTHS, in the parish of Grinton, wapentake of Gilling-West, liberty of Richmondshire; 6 miles from Reeth, 8 from Askrigg, 16 from Richmond.

WINTON, in the parish of Sigston, wapentake and liberty of Allertonshire; 3 miles from Northallerton, 12 from Thirsk, 13 from Stokesley.—Population 132.

WISE-HILL, in the parish of Romaldkirk, wapentake of Gilling-West, liberty of Richmondshire; 5 miles from Gretabridge, 12 from Barnardcastle, *(Durham.)*

WITTON, EAST, in the parish of East-Witton, wapentake of Hang-West, liberty of Richmondshire; 2 miles from Middleham, 4 from Leyburn, 8 from Masham.—Pop. 682.

WITTON, WEST, in the parish of Wensley, wapentake of Hang-West, liberty of Richmondshire, 4 miles from Leyburn, 4¼ from Middleham, 12 from Richmond.—Pop. 446.

WOODALE, or WOOD-DALE, in the parish of Aysgarth, wapentake of Hang-West, liberty of Richmondshire; 7 miles from Middleham, 8 from Leyburn, 17 from Bedale.

WOODALE-HOUSES, in the parish of Lythe, east-division

L

of the wapentake and liberty of Langbarugh; 9 miles from Whitby, 12 from Guisbrough, 25 from Stockton, *(Durham.)*

WOOD-END, in the parish of Thornton-le-street, wapentake and liberty of Allertonshire; *(the seat of Samuel Crompton, Esq.)* 4 miles from Thirsk, 6 from Northallerton.

WOODLANDS, in the parish of Whitby, east-division of the wapentake and liberty of Langbarugh; *(the seat of Henry W. Yeoman, Esq.)* 4 miles from Whitby, 17½ from Pickering, 17½ from Guisbrough.

WOOL-KNOWLE, in the parish of Hovingham, wapentake of Rydale; 8 miles from Helmsley, 9 from Kirby-Moorside, 10 from Malton.

WORMERGILL, in the parish of Romaldkirk, wapentake of Gilling-West; *(the seat of the Earl of Strathmore)* 14 miles from Barnardcastle, *(Durham)* 17 from Greta-bridge.

WORSALL, HIGH, in the parish of Northallerton, wapentake and liberty of Allertonshire; 4 miles from Yarm, 12 from Northallerton.—Population 105.

WORSALL, LOW, or PEIRSEBURGH, in the parish of Kirklevington, west-division of the wapentake and liberty of Langbarugh; *(Worsall-Hall, the seat of James Ward, Esq.)* 3 miles from Yarm, 13 from Northallerton.—Population 165.

WORTON, in the parish of Aysgarsh, wapentake of Hang-West; 1 mile from Askrigg, 6 from Hawes, 11 from Leyburn.

WRELTON, in the parish of Middleton, wapentake and liberty of Pickering-Lythe; 3 miles from Pickering, 5 from Kirby-Moorside, 12 from Malton.—Population 166.

WYCLIFFE, in the parish of Wycliffe, wapentake of Gilling-West, liberty of Richmondshire; *(Wycliffe-Hall, the seat of F. Constable, Esq.)* 2½ miles from Greta-bridge, 5 from Barnardcastle, *(Durham)* 10 from Richmond.—Pop. 138.

WYCOMB, in the parish of Old-Malton, wapentake of Rydale; 2¼ miles from Malton, 14 from Kirby-Moorside, 17 from Helmsley, 31 from Whitby.

WYKEHAM, in the parish of Wykeham, wapentake and liberty of Pickering-Lythe, 7 miles from Scarborough, 11 from Pickering 15 from Malton.—Population 382.

WYKEHAM-ABBEY, in the parish of Wykeham, wapentake and liberty of Pickering-Lythe; *(the seat of Richard Langley, Esq.)* 8 miles from Scarborough, 12 from Pickering, 16 from Malton.

WYKEHAM-GRANGE, in the parish of Wykeham, wapentake and liberty of Pickering-Lythe, 8 miles from Scarborough, 11 foom Pickering, 17 from Malton.

Y.

YAFFORTH, in the parish of Danby-Wiske, wapentake of Gilling-East, liberty of Richmondshire; 1¼ miles from Northallerton, 7 from Bedale, 13½ from Richmond.—Population 125.

YARM, in the parish of Yarm, west-division of the wapentake and liberty of Langbarugh; *(the seat of Thomas Meynell, Esq.)* 4 miles from Stockton, *(Durham)* 8 from Stokesley, 10 from Darlington, *(Durham)* 14 from Guisbrough, 16 from Northallerton, 19 from Thirsk, 21 from Richmond, 42 from York, 237½ from London.—*Market*, Thursday.—*Fairs*, Thursday before April 5, Holy-Thursday, August 2, for Horned Cattle, Horses, Sheep and Cheeses; October 19, for Horned Cattle and Horses, 20 for Sheep and Cheeses.—*Principal Inn*, George and Dragon.—Population 1,300.

YEARSLEY, in the parish of Coxwold, wapentake of Birdforth; 4 miles from Easingwold, 8 from Helmsley, 14 from Thirsk.—Population 164.

YEARSLEY-BURTON, in the parish of Coxwold, wapentake of Birdforth; 5 miles from Helmsley, 8 from Easingwold, 14 from Thirsk.

YERBY, in the parish of Kirkleatham, wapentake and liberty of Langbarugh; 4½ miles from Guisbrough, 12¼ from Stokesley.

YORE-COTTON-MILL, in the parish of Aysgarth, wapentake of Hang-West, liberty of Richmondshire; 4 miles from Askrigg, 7 from Leyburn, 19 from Bedale.

YORK-GATE, in the parish of Wath, wapentake of Halikeld, liberty of Richmondshire; 5 miles from Ripon, 6 from Thirsk, 6¼ from Boroughbridge, 9 from Bedale.

YOULTON, in the parish of Alne, wapentake of Bulmer; 5 miles from Easingwold, 5 from Boroughbridge, 12 from York.—Population 50.

NORTH-RIDING.

LORD LIEUTENANT.

HIS GRACE THE DUKE OF LEEDS, *Hornby-Castle.*

NAMES OF ACTING MAGISTRATES.

ALDERSON, JONATHAN,	Clerk,	*Hornby.*
BAILIE, CHARLES, ...	Clerk,	*Stainton.*
BELL, JOHN, ...	Esq.	*Thirsk.*
BELLASYSE, T. E. W.	Esq.	*Newbrough-Hall.*
BRAND, THOMAS, ...	Clerk.	*Wath.*
CAYLEY, SIR GEORGE,	Bart.	*Brompton.*
CAYLEY, ARTHUR, ...	Esq.	*Welburn.*
CHALONER, ROBERT, ...	Esq.	*Guisbrough.*
CHAYTOR, WILLIAM, ...	Esq.	*Spennythorne.*
CHAYTOR, WILLIAM, Jun.	Esq.	*Croft.*
CHAYTOR, M. W.	Esq.	*Spennythorne.*
COMBER, WILLIAM, ...	Clerk,	*Kirby-Moorside.*
CONSETT, WARCOP, ...	Esq.	*Brawith.*
CRADOCK, SHELDON, ...	Esq.	*Hartforth.*
CROWE, ROBERT, ...	Esq.	*Kiplin.*
CUST, WILLIAM, ...	Clerk,	*Danby-Hill.*
DEALTRY, WILLIAM, ...	Clerk,	*Wigginton,*
DENT, WILLIAM, ...	Esq.	*Thirsk.*
DENT, WILLIAM, ...	Clerk,	*East-Harlsey.*
DODSWORTH, FREDERICK,	D. D.	*Thornton-Watlass*
D'OYLY, EDWARD, ...	Esq.	*Sion-Hill.*
DUNCOMBE, CHARLES, ..	Esq.	*Duncombe-Park.*
DUNCOMBE, THOMAS, ..	Esq.	*Grimston.*
DUNDAS, RT. HON. LORD,		*Upleatham.*
DUNDAS, HON. LAWRENCE,		*Marske.*
DUNDAS, HON. THOMAS,		*Aske.*
ELLLIS, JOHN, ...	Clerk,	*Strensall.*
FENDALL, WILLIAM, ...	Esq.	*Tanfield-Hall.*
FOULIS, JOHN ROBINSON,	Esq.	*Heslerton.*
FOWLER, DAVID BURTON,	Esq.	*Yarm.*
GILBY, JOHN, ...	Clerk,	*Thornton.*
HARLAND, SIR C. H.	Bart.	*Sutton-on-Forest.*
HARRISON, JOHN, ...	Esq.	*Guisbrough.*
HAYES, THOMAS, ...	Esq.	*Aislaby.*
HEADLAM, JOHN, ...	Clerk,	*Wycliffe.*
HILDYARD, SIR R. D. ...	Bart.	*Sedbury-Hall.*

NORTH-RIDING.

HEWGILL, EDWIN,	Esq.	*Hornby-Grange.*
HUSTLER, THOMAS,	Esq.	*Acklam.*
HUTCHINSON, TIMOTHY,	Esq.	*Eggleston-Abbey.*
HUTCHINSON, WILLIAM,	Esq.	
JACKSON, W. WARD,	Esq.	*Normanby.*
LISTER, JAMES,	Esq.	*Snainton.*
MARKHAM, GEORGE,	D. D.	*York.*
MATTHEWS, JOHN,	Esq.	*North-Shields.*
MIDDLETON, R. W.	Esq.	*Grinkle-Park.*
MOORSOM, RICHARD,	Esq.	*Whitby.*
MOORSOM, RICHARD, Jun.	Esq.	*Ditto.*
MORLEY, T. W.	Clerk,	*Easby.*
MORRITT, J. B. S.	Esq.	*Rokeby-Park.*
NEWTON, THOMAS, Jun.	Clerk,	*Coxwold.*
NORCLIFFE, THOMAS,	Esq.	*York.*
OSBALDESTON, GEORGE,	Esq.	*Hutton-Bushell.*
PEIRSE, R. W. C.	Esq.	*Thimbleby-Lodge:*
PLACE, THOMAS,	Clerk,	*Kirklington.*
PRESTON, THOMAS,	Clerk,	*Moreby.*
READ, T. C. R.	Clerk,	*Sandhutton.*
RICE, HON. EDWARD,	Clerk,	*Sutton.*
RICHARDSON, C.	Esq.	*Whitby.*
RUDD, BARTHOLOMEW,	Esq.	*Marton.*
SAYER, GEORGE,	Clerk,	*Eaglescliffe.*
SEDGWICK, LEONARD,	Clerk,	*Brafferton.*
SLEIGH, WILLIAM,	Esq.	*Stockton-on-Tees.*
STRAWBENZEE, T.	Esq.	*Spennythorne.*
STRICKLAND, SIR W.	Bart.	*Boynton.*
SUTTON, GEORGE,	Esq.	*Stockton-on-Tees,*
SYKES, SIR M. M.	Bart.	*Sledmere.*
SYKES, CHRISTOPHER,	Clerk,	*Westow.*
TINDALL, JAMES,	Esq.	*Scarborough.*
TOPHAM, EDWARD,	Esq.	*Wold-Cottage.*
TROTTER, JOHN,	Esq.	*Croft.*
WADDILOVE, R. D	D. D.	*Ripon,*
WALKER, BENJAMIN,	Clerk,	*Northallerton.*
WHARTON, JOHN,	Esq.	*Skelton-Castle.*
WHARTON, WILLIAM,	Clerk,	*Gilling,*
WILLIAMSON, T. PYM.	Clerk,	*Guisbrough,*
WOLLEY, GODFREY,	Clerk,	*Hutton-Bushell.*
WOODALL, JOHN,	Esq.	*Scarborough,*
WYVILLE, CHRISTOPHER,	Clerk,	*Constable-Burton.*

M

NORTH-RIDING.

LORDS AND CHIEF BAILIFFS.

HIS GRACE THE DUKE OF LEEDS, *Hornby-Castle.* } RICHMONDSHIRE.
THE RIGHT REV. THE LORD BISHOP OF DURHAM. } ALLERTONSHIRE.
REV. G. MARWOOD, *Busby-Hall,* LANGBARUGH.
RICHARD HILL, Esq. *Thornton,* PICKERING-LYTHE.
HENRY CHOLMLEY, Esq. *Housham,* WHITBY-STRAND.

CLERK OF THE PEACE.

ROBERT STOCKDALE, Esq. *Knaresborough.*
THOMAS PAUL, Esq. *Malton,* his Deputy.

TREASURER.

VAL. KITCHINGMAN, Esq. *Carlton-Husthwaite.*

CORONERS.

HENRY BREARY, ——— *York.*
JOHN WRIGHTSON, ——— *Thirsk.*
THOMAS HARRISON, ——— *Kirby-Moorside.*
JOHN MARSHALL, ——— *Whitby.*
THOMAS SMITH, ——— *Stokesley.*

CHIEF CONSTABLES.

T. DOWSON, *Northallerton,* ——— } ALLERTONSHIRE.
J. LANGDALE, *Ditto.* ———
J. BRIGNALL, *Sowerby,* ——— } BIRDFORTH.
J. SHEPPARD, *Newbrough,* ———
JOHN GRAY, *Skirpenbeck,* ——— } BULMER.
W. WARE, *Newton-upon-Derwent,*

NORTH-RIDING. 87

G. READMAN, *Kiplin*, ... } GILLING-EAST.
THOMAS MEEK, *Kirby-Wiske*...

JOHN NEWBY, *West-Thorpe*, ... } GILLING-WEST.
THOMAS LAX, *Ravensworth*,....

HENRY PLEWS, *Bedale*, ... } HANG-EAST.
JOHN PLEWS, *Low-Street*, ...

THOMAS PLACE, *Spennythorne*, } HANG-WEST.
W. SADLER, *Bolton-Hall*, ...

JOHN I'ANSON, *Melmerby*, ... } HALIKELD.
WILLIAM FALL, *Thornbrough*,

J. HICKSON, uisbrough, ... LANGBARUGH-EAST.
R. BRIGHᴬ Hutton-Rudby, ... LANGBARUGH-WEST.

T. SEAᵀ *Pickering*, ... } PICKERING-LYTHE.
J. W GIIBY, *Wykeham*, ...

Y, *Thornton-Risebrough*, } RYDALE.
ER, *Oswaldkirk*, ...

..., YOUNG, *Whitby*, ... WHITBY-STRAND.

CLERK OF GENERAL MEETINGS OF LIEUTENANTCY.

HENRY HIRST, Esq. *Northallerton.*

CLERKS OF SUBDIVISION MEETINGS OF LIEUTENANTCY.

J. LANGDALE, *Northallerton*, ..ALLERTONSHIRE.
J. WRIGHTSON, *Thirsk*, ...BIRDFORTH.
J. PLOWMAN, *Haxby*, ...BULMER.
C. FRYER, *Scorton*, ...GILLING-EAST.
T. BOWMAN, *Richmond*, ...GILLING-WEST.
W. DINSDALE, *Bedale*, ...HANG-EAST.
P. GREATHEAD, *Spennythorne*,..HANG-WEST.
R. STEWARDSON, *Theakston*, ..HALIKELD,
H. NEWTON, *Guisbrough*, ...LANGBARUGH-EAST.
W. POWELL, *Stokesley*, ...LANGBARUGH-WEST.
TRAVIS & WOODALL, *Scarbro'*PICKERING-LYTHE, EAST
T. SEAVERS, *Pickering*, ...PICKERING-LYTHE, WEST
J. BAILEY, *Thornton-Risebrough*,RYDALE.
J. MARSHALL, *Whitby*, ...WHITBY-STRAND.

NORTH-RIDING.

BAILIFFS.

JAMES MONKMAN, *York*, ... BULMER.
JEROM NARES, *Pickering*, ... RYDALE.
HENRY MASTERMAN, *Thirsk*, ... BIRDFORTH.

BAILIFFS AT LARGE WHO RESIDE IN THIS RIDING.

WILLIAM SLATER, ... *Bedale*.
THOMAS MASTERMAN, ... *Northallerton*.
JOHN BOULTON, ... *Malton*.

DEPUTY BAILIFFS.

W. FLOWER, *Northallerton*, ... ALLERTONSHIRE.
THOMAS SMITH, *Stokesley*, ... LANGBARUGH.
R. THOMPSON, *Richmond*, ... RICHMONDSHIRE.
WILLIAM RIDLEY, *Middleham*, DITTO.
JEROM NARES, *Pickering*, ... PICKERING-LYTHE.
WHITBY-STRAND.

DIRECTIONS FOR WARRANTS, ON WRITS, TO LIBERTIES.

ALLERTONSHIRE. ... To the Chief Bailiff of Allerton and Allertonshire, and his Deputies.
LANGBARUGH. ...... To the Chief Bailiff of the Liberty of Langbarugh and his Deputies.
PICKERING-LYTHE. ... To the Chief Bailiff of the Liberty of Pickering-Lythe, and his Deputies.
RICHMONDSHIRE. .... To the Chief Bailiff of the Liberty of Richmond and Richmondshire, and his Deputies.
SCARBOROUGH. .... To the Bailiffs of the Town of Scarborough, and their Serjeants at Mace.
WHITBY-STRAND. ... To the Chief Bailiff of the Liberty of Whitby and Whitby-Strand, and his Deputies.

SESSIONS.

The *Christmas* General-Quarter Sessions of the Peace are held at Richmond, on Tuesday in the first week after the Epiphany, where all Vagrants, confined in the House of Correction at Northallerton, are discharged, or otherwise disposed of.—And all Felons committed from within the several wapentakes of *Allertonshire, Gilling-East, Gilling-West, Hang-East, Hang-West*, and *Halikeld* are tried; and all Appeals, Traverses, and other business from within the same, there heard and determined. And the same Sessions are held, by adjournment, at New-Malton, on the Friday following, when and where all Felons committed from the several wapentakes of *Birdforth, Bulmer, Langbarugh, Pickering-Lythe, Rydale*, and *Whitby-Strand* are tried; and all Appeals, Traverses, and other business from within the same, are there held and determined.—The *Easter-Sessions* are held at Northallerton, on Tuesday in the first whole week after Easter.—The *Midsummer-Sessions* are held at the same place, on Tuesday in the first whole week after St. Thomas the Martyr; and *Michaelmas-Sessions*, at the same place, on Tuesday in the first whole week after St. Michael the Archangel.

POSTSCRIPTUM

EAST-RIDING.

ACKLAM, in the parish of Acklam, wapentake of Buckrose, liberty of St. Peter; 6¼ miles from Malton, 9 from Pocklington.—Population 255.

ADDLETHORPE, or EDDLETHORPE, in the parish of Westow, wapentake of Buckrose; *(the seat of Joseph Field, Esq.)* 5 miles from Malton, 13¼ from Pocklington, 14 from York.—Population 93.

ALDBROUGH, in the parish of Aldbrough, middle division of the wapentake and liberty of Holderness; *(the seat of the late Christopher Scott, Esq.)* 8 miles from Hedon, 14 from Hull, 17 from Beverley.—Population 555.

ALLERTHORPE, in the parish of Thornton, Wilton-Beacon division of the wapentake of Harthill, liberty of St. Peter; *(the seat of John Dyesberry, Esq.)* 2 miles from Pocklington, 8 from Market-Weighton, 12 from York.—Population 125.

ANLABY, in the parish of Hessle, in the County of the Town of Kingston-upon-Hull; 4¼ miles from Hull, 8¼ from South-Cave, 01 from Beverley.—Population 226.

ARGAM, *(extraparochial)* wapentake of Dickering; 4 miles from Hunmanby, 5 from Bridlington.—Population 21.

ARGLAM, in the parish of Holme-on-Spalding-Moor, Holme-Beacon division of the wapentake of Harthill; 7 miles from Market-Weighton, 7 from Howden.

ARNOLD, in the parish of Swine, north-division of the wapentake and liberty of Holderness; 7 miles from Beverley, 11¼ from Hull, 14¼ from Great-Driffield.

ARRAM, in the parish of Leckenfield, Hunsley-Beacon division of the wapentake of Harthill; 4¼ miles from Beverley, 13 from Driffield.

ARRAM-HALL, in the parish of Atwicke, north-division of the wapentake and liberty of Holderness; 11 miles from Bridlington, 11 from Driffield, 13 from Beverley.

ARRAS, in the parish of Market-Weighton, Holme-Beacon division of the wapentake of Harthill; 2¼ miles from Market-Weighton, 7 from Beverley.

ASSELBY, in the parish of Howden, wapentake and liberty of Howdenshire; 2 miles from Howden, 8 from Selby, 14 from South-Cave.—Population 259.

ATWICK, in the parish of Atwick, north-division of the wapentake and liberty of Holderness; 2¼ miles from Hornsea, 13 from Driffield, 13¾ from Bridlington, 14 from Beverley.—Population 368.

AUBURN, in the parish of Fraisthorpe, wapentake of Dickering; 3½ miles from Bridlington, 12 from Hornsea, 20¼ from Beverley.

AUGHTON, in the parish of Aughton, Holme-Beacon division of the wapentake of Harthill; 8 miles from Howden, 10 from Pocklington, 13 from York.—Population 187.

AUGHTON-RUDDINGS, in the parish of Aughton, Holme-Beacon division of the wapentake of Harthill; 8 miles from Howden, 8 from Pocklington.

AYKE, in the parishes of St. John, Beverley, and Lockington, Bainton-Beacon division of the wapentake of Harthill; 6 miles from Beverley, 8 from Driffield.—Population 47.

B.

BABTHORPE, in the parish of Hemingbrough, wapentake of Ouse and Derwent, liberty of Howdenshire; 5 miles from Selby, 6½ from Howden, 13½ from York.

BAFFAM, in the parish of Kirby-Underdale, wapentake of Buckrose, 8 miles from Pocklington, 10 from Malton, 14 from York.

BAINTON, *(which gives name to the division)* in the parish of Bainton, Bainton-Beacon division of the wapentake of Harthill; 6 miles from Great-Driffield, 8 from Sledmere, 10 from Beverley, 10 from Pocklington.— Population 220.

BALKHOLME, in the parish of Howden, wapentake and liberty of Howdenshire; 2¼ miles from Howden, 12 from South-Cave, 12¼ from Selby.—Population 120.

BARLBY, in the parish of Hemingbrough, wapentake of Ouse and Derwent, liberty of Howdenshire; 2¼ miles from Selby, 8 from Howden, 12 from York.—Population 241.

BARMBY, in the parish of Howden, wapentake and liberty of Howdenshire; 3¾ miles from Howden, 7 from Selby.—Population 364.

BARMBY-MOOR-INN, in the parish of Barmby-on-the-Moor, Wilton-Beacon division of the wapentake of Harthill; 2 miles from Pocklington, 7½ from Market-Weighton, 11 from York.

BARMBY-ON-THE-MOOR, in the parish of Barmby-on-the-Moor, Wilton-Beacon division of the wapentake of Harthill, liberty of St. Peter; 2 miles from Pocklington, 9 from Market-Weighton, 11 from York.—Population 321.

BARMSTON, in the parish of Barmston, north-division of the wapentake and liberty of Holderness; 6¼ miles from Bridlington, 11 from Driffield, 17 from Beverley.—Pop 163.

BARROW-HILL, in the parish of Lockington, Bainton-Beacon division of the wapentake of Harthill; 8 miles from Beverley, 9 from Driffield.

BARTHORPE-BOTTOMS, in the parish of Acklam, wapentake of Buckrose, liberty of St. Peter; 8 miles from Malton, 10 from Pocklington, 13 from York.

BARTON-DALE, in the parish of Hunmanby, wapentake of Dickering; 3 miles from Hunmanby, 5 from Bridlington.

BASWICKE, HIGH, in the parish of Brandesburton, north-division of the wapentake and liberty of Holderness; 6 miles from Driffield, 9 from Beverley, 14 from Bridlington.

BASWICKE, LOW, in the parish of Brandesburton, north-division of the wapentake and liberty of Holderness; 6 miles from Driffield, 9 from Beverley, 14 from Bridlington.

BATTLEBURN, in the parish of Kirkburn, Bainton-Beacon division of the wapentake of Harthill; 3½ miles from Driffield, 11 from Beverley, 13 from Pocklington.

BEEFORD, in the parish of Beeford, north-division of the wapentake and liberty of Holderness; 8 miles from Driffield, 10 from Bridlington, 13 from Beverley, 19 from Hull.—Population 378.

BEILBY, in the parish of Hayton, Holme-Beacon division of the wapentake of Harthill; liberty of St. Peter; 4 miles from Pocklington, 5 from Market-Weighton, 15 from York.—Population 178.

BELBY, in the parish of Howden, wapentake and liberty of Howdenshire; 1¼ mile from Howden, 10¼ from South-Cave, 11¼ from Selby, 11½ from Snaith.—Population 38.

BELLASIZE, in the parish of Eastrington, wapentake and liberty of Howdenshire; 5 miles from Howden, 7 from South-Cave.—Population 153.

BELL-HALL, in the parish of St. Dennis, York, wapentake of Ouse and Derwent; *(the seat of Hewby John Baines, Esq.)* 5 miles from York, 9¼ from Selby, 14 from Pocklington.

BELTHORPE, in the parish of Bishop-Wilton, Wilton-Beacon division of the wapentake of Harthill, liberty of St. Peter; 5 miles from Pocklington, 12 from York, 13 from Malton.—Population 15.

BEMPTON, in the parish of Bridlington, wapentake of Dickering; 4¼ miles from Bridlington, 7 from Hunmanby.—Population 222.

BENNETLAND, in the parish of Eastrington, wapentake and liberty of Howdenshire; 5½ miles from Howden, 6¼ from South-Cave.

BENNINGHOLME, in the parish of Swine, middle-division of the wapentake of Holderness; 8 miles from Beverley, 9 from Hedon, 9 from Hull.—Population 78.

BENNINGHOLME-GRANGE, in the parish of Swine, middle-division of the wapentake and liberty of Holderness; *(the seat of John Harrison, Esq.)* 7 miles from Beverley, 10 from Hedon, 10 from Hull.

BENTLEY, in the parish of Rowley, Hunsley-Beacon division of the wapentake of Harthill; 2¼ miles from Beverley, 7 from South-Cave, 8 from Hull.

BESSINGBY, in the parish of Bridlington, wapentake of Dickering; *(the seat of Harrington Hudson, Esq.)* 1½ mile from Bridlington, 10 from Driffield.—Pop. 87.

BESWICKE, in the parish of Kilnwick, Bainton-Beacon division of the wapentake of Harthill; 6½ miles from Beverley, 6¼ from Driffield.—Population 136.

BEVERLEY, in the parishes of St. John, St. Mary, St. Nicholas, and St. Martin, Beverley, Hunsley-Beacon division of the wapentake of Harthill, liberty of Beverley; 9 miles from Hull, 9¼ from South-Cave, 10 from Market-Weighton, 13 from Driffield, 14 from Hornsea, 24 from Bridlington, 28½ from Malton, 29 from York, from London by Lincoln 183, by York 227.—*Market*, Saturday.—*Fairs*, Thursday before Old Valentine-day, Holy Thursday, July 5, Wednesday before September 25, November 5, for Horned Cattle, Sheep, Horses, &c. every other Wednesday for Horned Cattle and Sheep.—*Bankers*, East-Riding Bank, Messrs Raikes and Curries draw on Messrs. Lefevre and Co. 29, Cornhill; Beverley-Bank, Messrs. Machell and Co. draw on Messrs. Boldero, Lushington and Co. 3o, Cornhill.—Sends two Members to Parliament.—*Principal Inns*, Beverley-Arms, Cross-Keys, Rose and Crown.—Population 5,401.

BEVERLEY-PARKS, in the parish of St. John, Beverley, Hunsley-Beacon division of the wapentake of Harthill, liberty of Beverley; 1½ mile from Beverley, 7¼ from Hull.

BEWHOLME, in the parish of Nunkilling, north-division of the wapentake and liberty of Holderness; 10 miles from Driffield, 10¼ from Beverley, 10½ from Bridlington.

BEWICK, in the parish of Aldbrough, middle-division of the

wapentake and liberty of Holderness; 8¼ miles from Hedon, 13 from Hull, 16 from Beverley,

BILTON, in the parish of Swine, middle-division of the wapentake and liberty of Holderness; 4 miles from Hedon, 4 from Hull, 13 from Beverley.—Population 101.

BINNINGTON, iu the parish of Willerby, wapentake of Dickering; 6 miles from Hunmanby, 10 from Scarborough, 14 from Bridlington.—Population 38.

BIRDSALL, in the parish of Birdsall, wepentake of Buckrose; *(the seat of Lord Middleton)* 4 miles from Malton, 8 from Sledmere.—Population 234.

BISHOP-WILTON, see *Wilton, Bishop.*

BLACKDALE-HOUSE, in the parish of Norton, wapentake of Buckrose; 2¼ miles from Malton, 12 from Sledmere, 12 from Pickering.

BLACKTOFT, in the parish of Brantingham, wapentake and liberty of Howdenshire; 8 miles from Howden, 9 from South-Cave.—Popnlation 238.

BLANCH, in the parish of North-Dalton, Bainton-Beacon division of the wapentake of Harthill; 7 miles from Pocklington, 9 from Driffield, 12 from Beverley.

BOLTON, in the parish of Pocklington, Wilton-Beacon division of the wapentake of Harthill, liberty of St. Peter; *(Bolton-Hall, the seat of the Rev. John Menithorpe)* 3¼ miles from Pocklington, 10 from York, 10 from Market-Weighton.—Population 92.

BONWICK, in the parish of Skipsea, north-division of the wapentake and liberty of Holderness; 9 miles from Beverley, 9 from Driffield, 9 from Bridlington.—Population 31.

BOOTH, in the parish of Howden, wapentake and liberty of Howdenshire; 2 miles from Howden, 8 from Snaith, 10 from Selby, 12 from Thorne.

BOREAS-HILL, in the parish of Paul, south-division of the wapentake and liberty of Holderness; 2 miles from Hedon, 10 from Hull.

BORSEA, in the parish of Holme-on-Spaldingmoor, Holme-Beacon division of the wapentake of Harthill; 7 miles from Market-Weighton, 8 from Howden.

BOURNE, or BRIND, in the parish of Wressle, Holme-Beacon division of the wapentake of Harthill; 2¼ miles from Howden, 9 from Selby, 12 from Market-Weighton.

BOURNE, or BRIND-LEYS, in the parish of Wressle, Holme-Beacon division of the wapentake of Harthill; 3¼ miles from Howden, 9 from Selby, 12 from Market Weighton.

BOWTHORPE, or BOLTHORPE, in the parish of Hemmingbrongh, wapentake of Ouse and Derwent; 5 miles from Selby, 6 from Howden, 14 from Pocklington.

BOYNTON, in the parish of Boynton, wapentake of Dickering; *(the seat of Sir William Strickland, Bart.)* 3 miles from Bridlington, 14 from Sledmere, 17 from Driffield.—Population 66.

BOYTHORPE, in the parish of Foxholes, wapentake of Dickering; 10 miles from Bridlington, 12 from Scarborough.

BRACKENDALE, in the parish of Carnaby, wapentake of Dickering; 4¼ miles from Bridlington, 11¼ from Hornsea.

BRACKENHILL, in the parishes of Garton and Rooss, middle-division of the wapentake and liberty of Holderness; 9 miles from Hedon, 16 from Hull, 21 from Beverley.

BRACKENS, in the parish of Kilnwick, Bainton-Beacon division of the wapentake of Harthill; 7¼ miles from Driffield, 8 from Beverley.—Population 14.

BRACKENHOLME, in the parish of Hemingbrough, wapentake of Ouse and Derwent; 5 miles from Selby, 6 from Howden, 14 from York.—Population 65.

BRANDESBURTON, in the parish of Brandesburton, north-division of the wapentake and liberty of Holderness; 8¼ miles from Beverley, 11 from Driffield, 15 from Bridlington.—*No Market.*—*Fairs*, May 14, for Horses, Horned Cattle, and Sheep; every other Wednesday for Horned Cattle and Sheep.—Population 432.

BRANTINGHAM, in the parish of Brantingham, wapentake and liberty of Howdenshire; *(the seat of Isaac Broadley, Esq.)* 2 miles from South-Cave, 9 from Beverley, 12 from Hull.—Population 173.

BRIDLINGTON, in the parish of Bridlington, wapentake of Dickering; 10 miles from Hunmanby, 11¼ from Driffield, 16 from Hornsea, 17 from Sledmere, 20 from Scarborough, 24 from Beverley, 41 from York, from London *by Lincoln*, 208, *by York* 238¼.—*Market*, Saturday. —*Fairs*, Monday before Whitsuntide, October 21, for Horned Cattle, Linen, &c.—*Bankers*, Messrs. Thompson and Co. draw on Messrs. Forster, Lubbocks and Co. 11, Mansion house-Street.—*Principal Inn*, Scarborough-Castle. —Population 3,130.

BRIDLINGTON-QUAY, in the parish of Bridlington, wapentake of Dickering; 1 mile from Bridlington, 11 from Hunmanby, 12¼ from Driffield.—*Principal Inn*, Ship.

BRIGHAM, in the parish of Foston, wapentake of Dickering; 5 miles from Driffield, 12 from Bridlington.—Population 80.

BRIGHTON, or BREIGHTON, in the parish of Bubwith, Holme-Beacon division of the wapentake of Harthill; 4 miles from Howden, 7 from Selby, 14½ from York.—Population 157.

BROMFLEET, in the parish of South-Cave, Hunsley-Beacon division of the wapentake of Harthill, liberty of St. Peter; 3 miles from South-Cave, 10 from Market-Weighton, 12 from Beverley.—Population 126.

BROMPTON, POTTER, in the parish of Ganton, wapentake of Dickering; 8 miles from Hunmanby, 9 from Scarborough.

BROUGH, in the parish of Skipsea, north-division of the wapentake and liberty of Holderness; 10 miles from Driffield, 11 from Bridlington, 15 from Beverley.

BROUGH-FERRY, in the parish of Elloughton, Hunsley-Beacon division of the wapentake of Harthill; 3¼ miles from South-Cave, 11 from Beverley, 12 from Hull.

BUBWITH, in the parish of Bubwith, Holme-Beacon-division of the wapentake of Harthill, a part in the liberty of St. Peter; 6 miles from Howden, 7 from Selby, 11 from Market-Weighton.—Population 424.

BUCKTON, in the parish of Bridlington, wapentake of Dickering; 3¼ miles from Bridlington, 6¼ from Hunmanby.—Population 111.

BUCKTON-HALL, in the parish of Bridlington, wapentake of Dickering; *(the seat of Sir William Foulis, Bart.)* 4¼ miles from Bridlington, 5 from Hunmanby.

BUGTHORPE, in the parish of Bugthorpe, wapentake of Buckrose, liberty of St. Peter; 6¼ miles from Pocklington, 12 from York.—Population 244.

BURDALE, in the parish of Wharam-Percy, wapentake of Buckrose; 10 miles from Malton, 10 from Driffield.

BURLAND, in the parish of Eastrington, wapentake and liberty of Howdenshire; 2 miles from Howden, 10½ from Market-Weighton, 12 from South-Cave.

BURNBUTTS, in the parish of Watton, Bainton-Beacon division of the wapentake of Harthill; 6 miles from Driffield, 9 from Beverley, 12 from Pocklington.

BURNBY, in the parish of Hayton, Wilton-Beacon division of the wapentake of Harthill; 3 miles from Pocklington, 5 from Market-Weighton, 16 from York.—Population 111.

BURSALL, or BURSHILL, in the parish of Brandesburton, north-division of the wapentake and liberty of Holderness; 8 miles from Beverley, 10 from Driffield, 11 from Pocklington

BURSTWICK, and BURSTWICK-GARTH, in the parish of Skeckling, south-division of the wapentake and liberty of Holderness; 4 miles from Hedon, 8 from Pattrington, 11 from Hull.—Population 335.

BURTON, in the parish of Hornsea, north-division of the

wapentake and liberty of Holderness ; 2½ miles from Hornsea, 14 from Beverley, 16 from Driffield.

BURTON-AGNES, in the parish of Burton-Agnes, wapentake of Dickering ; *(the seat of Sir Francis Boynton, Bart.)* 5¼ miles from Bridlington, 6¼ from Driffield.—Population 283.

BURTON, BISHOP, in the parish of Bishop-Burton, Hunsley-Beacon division of the wapentake of Harthill; *(Bishop-Burton-Hall, the seat of Richard Watts, Esq.)* 2½ miles from Beverley, 6½ from South-Cave, 7½ from Market-Weighton.—Population 412.

BURTON, CONSTABLE, in the parish of Swine, middle-division of the wapentake and liberty of Holderness ; *(the seat of Francis Constable, Esq.)* 5 miles from Hedon, 9 from Hull, 14 from Beverley.

BURTON, CHERRY, in the parish of Cherry-Burton, Hunsley-Beacon division of the wapentake of Harthill; *(the seat of Burton Fowler, Esq.)* 2¼ miles from Beverley, 9 from Market-Weighton, 11 from Driffield.—Pop. 299.

BURTON-FLEMING, in the parish of Burton-Fleming, wapentake of Dickering ; 3 miles from Hunmanby, 7½ from Bridlington.—Population 237.

BURTON-HOUSE, in the parish of Full-Sutton, Wilton-Beacon division of the wapentake of Harthill ; 5 miles from Pocklington, 10 from York, 12 from Malton.

BURTON-PIDSEA, in the parish of Burton-Pidsea, middle-division of the wapentake of Holderness, liberty of St. Peter ; 4 miles from Hedon, 11 from Hull, 16 from Bridlington.—Population 272.

BURYTHORPE, in the parish of Burythorpe, wapentake of Buckrose ; 4 miles from Malton, 9½ from Sledmere.—Population 135.

BUTTERWICK, in the parish of Foxholes, wapentake of Dickering ; 5 miles from Sledmere, 10 from Bridlington, 11 from Driffield, 12 from Scarborough.—Pop. 85.

C.

CAMERTON, in the parish of Paul, south-division of the wapentake and liberty of Holderness ; *(the seat of Edward Ombler, Esq.)* 3 miles from Hedon, 7 from Pattrington, 11 from Hull.

CARLTON, in the parish of Aldbrough, middle-division of

the wapentake and liberty of Holderness; 8 miles from Hedon, 13 from Hull, 16 from Beverley.

CARNABY, in the parish of Carnaby, wapentake of Dickering; 2¼ miles from Rridlington, 9¼ from Driffield.—
Population 129.

CASTLE-HILL, in the parish of Sutton, middle-division of
the wapentake and liberty of Holderness; 4 miles from Hull,
8 from Hedon, 9 from Beverley.

CASTLEHOLMES, in the parish of Lowthorpe, wapentake
of Dickering; 5 miles from Great-Driffield, 11 from Bridlington.

CATFOSS, in the parish of Sigglesthorne, north-division of
of the wapentake and liberty of Holderness; 9½ miles from
Beverley, 12¼ from Driffield, 15 from Bridlington, 15½
from Hull.—Population 46.

CATFOSS-HALL, in the parish of Sigglesthorne, north-division of the wapentake and liberty of Holderness; *(the
seat of Mrs. Bethell)* 9 miles from Beverley, 12¼ miles from
Driffield, 15 from Bridlington.

CATTON, HIGH, or UPPER, in the parish of Low-Catton, Wilton-Beacon division of the wapentake of Harthill;
7 miles from Pocklington, 7 from York, 14 from Malton.
—Population 181.

CATTON, LOW, or NETHER, in the parish of Low-Catton, Wilton-Beacon division of the wapentake of Harthill;
7 miles from Pocklington, 7¼ from York, 15 from Malton.
—Population 147.

CATWICK, in the parish of Catwick, north-division of the
wapentake and liberty of Holderness; 7¾ miles from Beverley, 12¼ from Driffield, 14 from Hull, 17 from Bridlington.—Population 132.

CAVE, NORTH, in the parish of North-Cave, Hunsley-
Beacon division of the wapentake of Harthill, a part in the
liberty of St. Peter; 2 miles from South-Cave, 7 miles from
Market-Weighton, 10 from Beverley, 11½ from Howden,
14 from Hull, 25¼ from York, from London *by Lincoln* 188,
by York, 224.—*Principal Inn*, White-Hart.—Pop. 639.

CAVE, SOUTH, in the parish of South-Cave, Hunsley-Beacon division of the wapentake of Harthill, a part in the liberty of St. Peter; *(Cave-Castle, the seat of H. B. Barnard, Esq.)* 2 miles from North-Cave, 8 from Market-
Weighton, 9½ from Beverley, 11½ from Howden, 12½ from
Hull, 27¼ from York, from London, *by Lincoln*, 186,
by York, 226.—*Market*, Monday.—*Fair*, Trinity-Mon-
day, for Horses and Sheep.—*Principal Inn*, Fox.—Pop 707.

CAVIL, in the parish of Eastrington, wapentake and liberty

of Howdenshire; 2 miles from Howden, 12 from Selby, 12 from South-Cave.

CAWKILL, in the parish of Watton, Bainton-Beacon division of the wapentake of Harthill; 6¼ miles from Driffield, 8¼ from Beverley, 13 from Pocklington.

CAYTHORPE, in the parishes of Boynton and Rudston, wapentake of Dickering; 3¼ miles from Bridlington, 8¼ from Hunmanby, 10 from Driffield.

CHEAPSIDES, in the parish of Eastrington, wapentake and liberty of Howdenshire; 5½ miles from South-Cave, 6¼ from Howden.

CLIFFE, LONG, in the parish of Hemingbrough, wapentake of Ouse and Derwent; 3 miles from Selby, 7½ from Howden, 14 from York, 16 from Pocklington.—Pop. 424.

CLIFFE, NORTH, in the parish of Sancton, Hunsley-Beacon division of the wapentake of Harthill; 3 miles from Market-Weighton, 5 from South-Cave, 10 from Beverley. —Population 89.

CLIFFE, SOUTH, in the parish of North-Cave, Hunsley-Beacon division of the wapentake of Harthill; 3 miles from Market-Weighton, 5 from South-Cave, 10 from Beverley. —Population 106.

COWDEN, or COLDEN-GREAT, in the parish of Mappleton, north-division of the wapentake and liberty of Holderness; 10 miles from Hedon, 14 from Hull, 15 from Beverley, 17¼ from Driffield.—Population 115.

COWDEN, or COLDEN, LITTLE, in the parish of Mappleton, north-division of the wapentake and liberty of Holderness; 9 miles from Hedon, 13 from Hull, 16 from Beverley, 18 from Driffield.

CONISTON, in the parish of Swine, middle-division of the wapentake and liberty of Holderness; 6 miles from Hedon, 7 from Hull, 9 from Beverley.—Population 106.

CORPS-LANDING, in the parish of Hutton-Cranswick, Bainton-Beacon division of the wapentake of Harthill; 6 miles from Driffield, 12 from Beverley.

COTHAM, in the parish of Langtoft, wapentake of Dickering liberty of St. Peter; *(the seat of Robert Knowsley, Esq.)* 5 miles from Driffield, 11 from Bridlington.—Population 16.

COTTINGHAM, in the parish of Cottingham, Hunsley-Beacon division of the wapentake of Harthill; *(the seat of George Knowsley. Esq.)* 5 miles from Hull, 6 from Beverley, 9 from South-Cave.—Population 1,927.

COTTINGWITH, EAST, in the parish of Aughton, Holme-Beacon division of the wapentake of Harthill; 8½ miles from Pocklington, 9 from Selby, 10 from Howden.—Pop. 250.

COTTINGWITH, WEST, in the parish of Thorganby, wapentake of Ouse and Derwent; 8 miles from Selby, 10 from Howden, 12 from York.

COTTNESS, in the parish of Howden, wapentake and liberty of Howdenshire; 4 miles from Howden, 14 from Selby, 12 from South-Cave.—Population 27.

COURTGARTH-WATH, in the parish of South Dalton, Bainton-Beacon division of the wapentake of Harthill; 4 miles from Market-Weighton, 7 from Beverley, 10 from Pocklington.

COURTHOUSES, in the parish of Yeddingham, wapentake of Buckrose; 9 miles from Sledmere, 11 from Malton, 14 from Scarborough.

COWLAM, in the parish of Cowlam, wapentake of Buckrose; 2¼ miles from Sledmere, 6¼ from Driffield.—Pop. 17.

CRANSWICK, in the parish of Hutton-Cranswick, Bainton-Beacon division of the wapentake of Harthill; 4 miles from Driffield, 9½ from Beverley.

CROAM, or CROOM, in the parish of Sledmere, wapentake of Buckrose; ¼ a mile from Sledmere, 8½ from Driffield.

CROWGARTH, in the parish of Beeford, north-division of the wapentake and liberty of Holderness; 7 miles from Driffield, 9 from Bridlington, 14 from Beverley.

D.

DALTON, NORTH, in the parish of North-Dalton, Bainton-Beacon division of the wapentake of Harthill; 7¼ miles from Driffield, 9 from Pocklington, 10¼ from Beverley.—Population 272.

DALTON, SOUTH, in the parish of South-Dalton, Hunsley-Beacon division of the wapentake of Harthill; *(the seat of Sir Charles Hotham, Bart.)* 6 miles from Beverley, 6 from Market-Weighton, 10 from Driffield.—Pop. 190.

DANES-DALE, in the parish of Great Driffield, Bainton-Beacon division of the wapentake of Harthill; 3 miles from Driffield, 10¼ from Bridlington, 15 from Beverley.

DANTHORPE, in the parish of Humbleton, middle-division of the wapentake and liberty of Holderness; 6 miles from Hedon, 12 from Hull, 19 from Beverley.—Population 51.

DEEPDALE, in the parish of Kirby-Underdale, wapentake of Buckrose; 9 miles from Malton, 9 from Sledmere, 9 from Pocklington.

DEIGHTON, in the parish of Escrick, wapentake of Ouse

and Derwent; 5¼ miles from York, 10 from Selby, 12 from Pocklington.—Population 172.

DEIGHTON-HILL, in the parish of Escrick, wapentake of Ouse and Derwent; 4¼ miles from York, 10¼ from Selby, 11¼ from Pocklington.

DEMMING, in the parish of Carnaby, wapentake of Dickering; 4 miles from Bridlington, 8 from Driffield.

DIMLINGTON, in the parish of Easington, south-division of the wapentake and liberty of Holderness; 6 miles from Pattrington, 16 from Hedon, 24 from Hull.

DOWTHORPE, in the parish of Swine, middle-division of the wapentake and liberty of Holderness; 7 miles from Hedon, 7 from Hull, 9 from Beverley.

DREWTON, in the parish of North-Cave, Hunsley-Beacon division of the wapentake of Harthill; 1 mile from South-Cave, 8 from Beverley, 15 from Hull.—Population 129.

DRIFFIELD, GREAT, in the parish of Great Driffield, Bainton-Beacon division of the wapentake of Harthill, a part in the liberty of St. Peter; 8 miles from Sledmere, 13 from Beverley, 11½ from Bridlington, 15 from Pocklington, 23 from Scarborough, 29 from York, from London *by Lincoln* 196, *by York* 227¼.—*Market*, Thursday.—*Principal Inn*, Red Lion.—Population 1,411.

DRIFFIELD, LITTLE, in the parish of Great-Driffield, Bainton-Beacon division of the wapentake of Harthill; a part in the liberty of St. Peter; 1 mile from Great Driffield, 7 from Sledmere, 14 from Beverley, 16 from Pocklington. —*No Market.*—*Fairs*, Easter-Monday, Whit-Monday, August 26, September 19, for Horses, Horned Cattle, and Sheep.

DRINGHOW, in the parish of Skipsea, north-division of the wapentake and liberty of Holderness; 9 miles from Driffield, 10 from Bridlington, 14 from Beverley, 20 from Hull.—Population 122.

DRYPOOL, in the parish of Drypool, middle-division of the wapentake and liberty of Holderness; ½ a mile from Hull, 8 from Hedon, 10 from Beverley.—Population 436.

DUFFIELD, NORTH, in the parish of Skipwith, wapentake of Ouse and Derwent, liberty of Howdenshire; 5 miles from Selby, 7½ from Howden, 11 from York, 13 from Market-Weighton.—*No Market.*—*Fair*, May 4, for Horned Cattle and Sheep.--Population 313.

DUFFIELD, SOUTH, in the parish of Hemingbrough, wapentake of Ouse and Derwent, liberty of Howdenshire; 4½ miles from Selby, 8 from Howden, 13 from Pocklington.— Population 160.

EAST-RIDING. 103

- DUGGLEBY, in the parish of Kirby-Grindalyth, wapentake of Buckrose; 4 miles from Sledmere, 8 from Malton.—Population 93.
- DUNCOATES, in the parish of Howden, wapentake and liberty of Howdenshire; 2¼ miles from Howden, 10 from South-Cave.
- DUNNINGTON, in the parish of Beeford, north-division of the wapentake and liberty of Holderness; 7 miles from Hornsea, 10 from Driffield, 10½ from Bridlington, 13½ from Beverley.—Population 67.
- DUNNINGTON, in the parish of Dunnington, wapentake of Ouse and Derwent, liberty of St. Peter; 4 miles from York, 9 from Pocklington, 16 from Selby.—Pop. 430.
- DUNSWELL, or BEER-HOUSES, in the parish of Cottingham, Hunsley-Beacon division of the wapentake of Harthill; 4½ miles from Hull, 4½ from Beverley.

E.

EASINGTON, in the parish of Easington, south-division of the wapentake and liberty of Holderness; 5¼ miles from Pattrington, 15¼ from Hedon, 24 from Hull.—Pop. 306.
EASTBURN, in the parish of Kirkburn, Bainton-Beacon division of the wapentake of Harthill; 3 miles from Driffield, 12 from Beverley.—Population 11.
EASTON, in the parish of Bridlington, wapentake of Dickering; 1 mile from Bridlington, 9 from Hunmanby.—Population 21.
EASTRINGTON, in the parish of Eastrington, wapentake and liberty of Howdenshire; 3¼ miles from Howden, 10 from South-Cave, 14 from Market-Weighton.—Pop. 330.
EASTHORPE, in the parish of Londesbrough, Holme-Beacon division of the wapentake of Harthill; 2 miles from Market-Weighton, 6 from Pocklington, 9 from Beverley.—Population 17.
EASTWOOD, in the parish of Thornton, Holme-Beacon division of the wapentake of Harthill; 6 miles from Pocklington, 9 from Market-Weighton, 10 from York.
EDDLETHORP, in the parish of Weston, wapentake of Buckrose; 4 miles from Malton, 11 from Sledmere.—Population 93.
EIGHT-AND-FORTY-HOUSE, in the parish of Eastrington, Holme-Beacon division of the wapentake of Harthill 5 miles from South-Cave, 7 from Howden.

ELLA, KIRK, in the parish of Kirk-Ella, County of the Town of Kingston-upon-Hull; *(the seats of R. C. Pease, and John Sykes, Esqs.)* 5¼ miles from Hull, 7 from South-Cave.—Population 212.

ELLA, WEST, in the parish of Kirk-Ella, County of the Town of Kingston-upon-Hull; *(the seat of the Rev. John Sykes,)* 5¼ miles from Hull, 7½ from South-Cave.—Pop. 79.

ELLERBY, in the parish of Swine, middle-division of the wapentake and liberty of Holderness; 6 miles from Hedon, 8 from Hull, 8 from Beverley.—Population 151.

ELLERKER, in the parish of Brantingham, wapentake and liberty of Howdenshire; 10 miles from Beverley, 13 from Hull.—Population 181.

ELLERTON, in the parish of Ellerton, Holme-Beacon division of the wapentake of Harthill; 8¼ miles from Pocklington, 9 from Howden.—Population 243.

ELLOUGHTON, in the parish of Elloughton, Hunsley-Beacon division of the wapentake of Harthill; a part in the liberty of St. Peter; 2 miles from South-Cave, 11 from Beverley, 11 from Hull.—Population 332.

ELMOTLANDS, in the parish of Frodingham, north-division of the wapentake and liberty of Holderness; 5 miles from Driffield, 10 from Beverley, 18 from Hull.

ELSTERNWICK, or ELSTRONWICK, in the parish of Humbleton, middle-division of the wapentake and liberty of Holderness; 5 miles from Hedon, 11 from Hull, 19 from Beverley.—Population 126.

ELVINGTON, in the parish of Elvington, wapentake of Ouse and Derwent; *(the seat of Charles Blois, Esq.)* 7 miles from York, 7¼ from Pocklington, 15 from Selby.—Population 225.

EMSWELL, in the parish of Great-Driffield, Bainton-Beacon division of the wapentake of Harthill; 2 miles from Driffield, 14 from Beverley.—Population 72.

ENTHORPE, in the parish of Lund, Bainton-Beacon division of the wapentake of Harthill; 4 miles from Market-Weighton, 8½ from Beverley, 9 from Pocklington.

EPPLEWITH, in the parish of Skidby, Hunsley-Beacon division of the wapentake of Harthill; 4¼ miles from Beverley, 6 from Hull.

ESCRICK, in the parish of Escrick, wapentake of Ouse and Derwent; *(Escrick-Hall, the seat of Richard Thompson, Esq.)* 6 miles from York, 8 from Selby, 12 from Pocklington.—Population 406.

ESKE, in the parish of St. John, Beverley, north-division of the wapentake and liberty of Holderness; 4 miles from

Beverley, 13 from Hull, 17 from Driffield.—Population 321.

ETHERDWICK, in the parish of Aldbrough, middle-division of the wapentake and liberty of Holderness; 7 miles from Hedon, 11 from Hull, 16 from Beverley.

ETTON, in the parish of Etton, Hunsley-Beacon division of the wapentake of Harthill; *(the seats of Lady Legard, and Henry Grimston, Esq.)* 4 miles from Beverley, 7 from Market-Weighton, 10 from Driffield.—Pop. 321.

EVERINGHAM, in the parish of Everingham, Holme-Beacon division of the wapentake of Harthill; *(the seat of Maxwell Constable Esq.)* 5 miles from Market-Weighton, 5 from Pocklington.—Population 229.

EVERTHORPE, in the parish of North-Cave, Hunsley-Beacon division of the wapentake of Harthill; 2 miles from South-Cave, 6 from Market-Weighton, 11¼ from Beverley.

F.

FAIRHOLME, in the parish of Swine, middle-division of the wapentake and liberty of Holderness; 7 miles from Hedon, 7 from Beverley, 8 from Hull.

FALCONER'S HALL, in the parish of Foxholes, wapentake of Dickering; *(the seat of Col. Thornton)* 10 miles from Bridlington, 12 from Scarborough.

FANGFOSS, in the parish of Barmby-on-the-Moor, Wilton-Beacon division of the wapentake of Harthill; *(the seat of Mrs. Overend)* 4 miles from Pocklington, 9 from York, 11 from Market-Weighton.—Population 131.

FAXFLEET, in the parish of South-Cave, Hunsley-Beacon division of the wapentake of Harthill, liberty of St. Peter; 3 miles from South-Cave, 8 from Market-Weighton.—Population 139.

FERRIBY, in the parish of Ferriby, County of the Town of Kingston-upon-Hull; *(the seats of J. C. Broadley, Esq. and Sir Henry Etherington, Bart.)* 4¼ miles from South-Cave, 8 from Hull.—Population 250.

FILEY, in the parish of Filey, wapentakes of Dickering and Pickering-Lythe; *(North-Riding)* 4 miles from Hunmanby, 7 from Scarborough, 11 from Bridlington.—Pop. 505.

FIMBER, in the parish Wetwang, wapentake of Buckrose, liberty of St. Peter; 4 miles from Sledmere, 7 from Driffield.—Population 81.

FIRBY, in the parish of Westow, wapentake of Buckrose; 6 miles from Malton, 14 from York, 14 from Sledmere.

FITLING, in the parish of Humbleton, middle-division of the wapentake and liberty of Holderness, 8 miles from Hedon, 12 from Hull, 20 from Beverley.—Population 127.

FIVELIN-NOOK, in the parish of Nunkilling, north-division of the wapentake and liberty of Holderness; 7 miles from Hornsea, 10 from Driffield, 12 from Beverley.

FLAMBOROUGH, in the parish of Flamborough, wapentake of Dickering; 3½ miles from Bridlington, 10 from Hunmanby.—Population 731.

FLAMBOROUGH-HEAD, *(a Promontory)* in the parish of Flamborough, wapentake of Dickering; 5¼ miles from Bridlington.

FLINTON, in the parish of Humbleton, middle-division of the wapentake and liberty of Holderness; 6 miles from Hedon, 10 from Hull, 16 from Beverley.—Population 105.

FLIXTON, in the parish of Folkton, wapentake of Dickering; 4 miles from Hunmanby, 7½ from Scarborough, 13¼ from Bridlington.—Population 154.

FLOTMANBY, EAST, in the parish of Folkton, wapentake of Dickering; 2¼ miles from Hunmanby, 7 from Scarborough, 10¼ from Bridlington.

FLOTMANBY, WEST, in the parish of Folkton, wapentake of Dickering; 3¼ miles from Hunmanby, 6½ from Scarborough, 11¼ from Bridlington.

FOGGATHORPE, in the parish of Bubwith, Holme-Beacon division of the wapentake of Harthill; 6 miles from Howden, 7 from Market-Weighton, 11 from Selby.—Population 78.

FOLKTON, in the parish of Folkton, wapentake of Dickering; 3 miles from Hunmanby, 8¼ from Scarborough, 12¼ from Bridlington.—Population 112.

FORDON, in the parish of Hunmanby, wapentake of Dickering; 4 miles from Hunmanby, 9 from Bridlington, 12 from Scarborough.

FOSHAM, or FOSHOLME, in the parish of Aldbrough, middle-division of the wapentake and liberty of Holderness; 6 miles from Hedon, 10 from Hull, 14 from Beverley.

FOSTON, in the parish of Foston, wapentake of Dickering; 6 miles from Driffield, 11 from Bridlington.—Pop. 175.

FOXHOLES, in the parish of Foxholes, wapentake of Dickering, *(the seat of the Rev. Christopher Sykes)* 6 miles from Hunmanby, 10 from Driffield, 11¼ from Scarborough.—Population 130.

FRAISTHORPE, ia the parish of Carnaby, wapentake of Dickering; 4½ miles from Bridlington, 9½ from Driffield, 11¼ from Hornsea,—Population 87.

FRIDAYTHORPE, in the parish of Fridaythorpe, wapentake of Buckrose, a part in the liberty of St. Peter; 5¼ miles from Sledmere, 9 from Pocklington, 10 from Driffield, 18¼ from York.—Population 112.

FRODINGHAM, NORTH, in the parish of North-Frodingham, north-division of the wapentake and liberty of Holderness; 6 miles from Driffield, 12 from Bridlington, 13 from Beverley, 35 from York.—*Market*, Thursday.—*Fairs*, July 10, and October 2. for Toys, Pedlary-Ware, &c.— Population 365.

FRODINGHAM, SOUTH, in the parish of Owthorn, south-division of the wapentake and liberty of Holderness; 4 miles from Pattrington, 10 from Hedon, 18 from Hull.—Pop. 50.

FULFORD, GATE, in the parish of Gate-Fulford, wapentake of Ouse and Derwent; *(the seat of Thomas Wilson, Esq.)* 1¼ mile from York, 12¼ from Selby, 12¼ from Pocklington.—Population 642.

FULFORD, WATER, in the parish of Gate-Fulford, wapentake of Ouse and Derwent, a part in the liberty of St. Peter; *(the seat of John Kay, Esq.)* 2½ miles from York, 11¼ from Selby, 13 from Pocklington.

G.

GALLY-GAP, in the parish of Scrayingham, wapentake of Buckrose; 6 miles from Malton, 12 from Pocklington, 13 from York.

GANSTEAD, in the parish of Swine, middle division of the wapentake and liberty of Holderness; 4¼ miles from Hedon, 4¼ from Hull, 12 from Beverley.—Population 58.

GANTON, in the parish of Ganton, wapentake of Dickering; *(the seat of Digby Legard, Esq.)* 1 mile from Hunmanby, 10 from Scarborough, 16 from Bridlington.—Pop. 223.

GANTON-DALE-INN, in the parish of Ganton, wapentake of Dickering; 10¼ miles from Driffield, 10¼ from Scarborough, 14 from Bridlington.

GANWICK, in the parish of Hutton-Cranswick, Bainton-Beacon division of the wapentake of Harthill; 3¼ miles from Driffield, 9¼ from Beverley, 14 from Pocklington.

GARRABY, in the parish of Kirby-Underdale, wapentake of Buckrose; 6 miles from Pocklington, 10 from Driffield, 11¼ from Sledmere, 13 from York.

GARTON, in the parish of Garton, wapentake of Dickering, a part in the liberty of St. Peter; 3 miles from Driffield, 15 from Bridlington, 16¼ from Malton.—Pop. 288.

GARTON, in the parish of Garton, middle division of the wapentake and liberty of Holderness; 9 miles from Hedon, 9¼ from Hornsea, 13 from Hull, 20 from Beverley.—Population 105.

GEMBLING, in the parish of Foston, wapentake of Dickering; 6 miles from Driffield, 11 from Bridlington.—Population 61.

GILBERDIKE, in the parish of Eastrington, wapentake and liberty of Howdenshire; 5¼ miles from Howden, 6¼ from South-Cave.—Population 337.

GILRIDDING, in the parish of St. Dennis, York, wapentake of Ouse and Derwent; 4 miles from York, 9¼ from Pocklington, 12 from Selby.

GIVENDALE, GREAT, in the parish of Great-Givendale, Wilton-Beacon division of the wapentake of Harthill; liberty of St. Peter; 3 miles from Pocklington, 10 from Market-Weighton, 14 from York.—Population 54.

GIVENDALE, LITTLE, in the parish of Great Givendale, Wilton-Beacon division of the wapentake of Harthill; 2¼ miles from Pocklington, 9½ from Market-Weighton, 14½ from York.

GOODMANHAM, in the parish of Goodmanham, Holme-Beacon division of the wapentake of Harthill, a part in the liberty of St. Peter; 1½ mile from Market-Weighton, 6 from Pocklington.—Population 149.

GOWTHORPE, in the parish of Bishop-Wilton, Wilton-Beacon division of the wapentake of Harthill, liberty of St. Peter; 5 miles from Pocklington, 9 from York, 13 from Malton.

GOWTHORPE, in the parish of Brantingham, wapentake and liberty of Howdenshire; 8 miles from Howden, 9 from South-Cave.

GOXHILL, in the parish of Goxhill, north-division of the wapentake and liberty of Holderness; 6 miles from Pocklington, 12 from Beverley, 14 from Driffield, 15 from Hull.—Population 54.

GRANGE-HOUSE, in the parish of Humbleton, middle-division of the wapentake and liberty of Holderness; 4 miles from Hedon, 9 from Hull, 16 from Beverley.

GRANSMOOR, or GRANSMERE, in the parish of Burton-Agnes, wapentake of Dickering; 7 miles from Driffield, 8 from Bridlington.—Population 49.

GREEN-OAK, in the parish of Eastrington, wapentake and liberty of Howdenshire; 4 miles from Howden, 8¼ from South-Cave.

GREENWICK, in the parish of Bishop-Wilton, Wilton-

Beacon division of the wapentake of Harthill; 5 miles from Pocklington, 14 from York, 14 from Malton.

GRIBTHORPE, in the parish of Bubwith, Holme-Beacon division of the wapentake of Harthill; 5 miles from Howden, 9 from Market-Weighton.—Population 120.

GRIMSTON, in the parish of Dunnington, wapentake of Ouse and Derwent, a part in the liberty of St. Peter; 2¼ miles from York, 10 from Pocklington, 15 from Selby, 15¼ from Market-Weighton.—Population 51.

GRIMSTON, in the parishes of Garton and Roose, middle division of the wapentake and liberty of Holderness; *(the seat of Thomas Grimston, Esq.)* 10 miles from Hedon, 14 from Hull, 21 from Beverley.

GRIMSTON-HANGING, in the parish of Kirby-Underdale, wapentake of Buckrose; 8 miles from Pocklington, 9 from Sledmere.

GRIMSTON, NORTH, in the parish of North-Grimston, wapentake of Buckrose, a part in the liberty of St. Peter; 4 miles from Malton, 8 from Sledmere, 15¼ from Driffield.—Population 131.

GRIMTHORPE, in the parish of Great-Givendale, Wilton-Beacon division of the wapentake of Harthill, liberty of St. Peter; 4 miles from Pocklington, 9 from Market-Weighton, 15 from York.—Population 16.

GRINDALE, in the parish of Bridlington, wapentake of Dickering, liberty of St. Peter; 4 miles from Bridlington, 6 from Hunmanby.—Population 88.

GROVE-HILL, in the parish of St. Nicholas, Beverley, Hunsley-Beacon division of the wapentake of Harthill, liberty of Beverley; 1 mile from Beverley, 9 from Hull, 14 from Driffield.

GUNBY, in the parish of Bubwith, Holme-Beacon division of the wapentake of Harthill; 7 miles from Selby, 7 from Howden.

GARTON, in the parish of Garton, middle-division of the wapentake and liberty of Holderness; 9 miles from Hedon, 9¼ from Hornsea, 13 from Hull, 20 from Beverley.—Population 105.

H.

HAGTHORPE, in the parish of Hemingbrough, wapentake of Ouse and Derwent; 5¼ miles from Selby, 6½ from Howden.

HALLITREE-HOLME, in the parish of Leven, north-division of the wapentake and liberty of Holderness; 6 miles from Driffield, 10 from Beverley, 18 from Hull.

HALSHAM, in the parish of Halsham, south-division of the wapentake and liberty of Holderness; 3¼ miles from Pattrington, 7 from Hedon, 15 from Hull.—Population 266.

HALTEMPRICE, in the parish of Cottingham, Hunsley-Beacon division of the wapentake of Harthill; 4¼ miles from Hull, 4½ from Beverley.

HARLETHORPE, in the parish of Bubwith, Holme-Beacon division of the wapentake of Harthill; 7 miles from Howden, 9 from Selby, 9 from Market-Weighton.—Pop. 62.

HARPHAM, in the parish of Burton-Agnes, wapentake of Dickering; 6 miles from Driffield, 7½ from Bridlington.—Population 172.

HARSWELL, in the parish of Harswell, Holme-Beacon division of the wapentake of Harthill; 5 miles from Market-Weighton, 6 from Pocklington.—Population 73.

HASHOLME, in the parish of Holme-on-Spalding-Moor, Holme-Beacon division of the wapentake of Harthill; 7 miles from Howden, 8 from Market-Weighton.

HATFIELD, GREAT, in the parishes of Mappleton and Sigglesthorne, north-division of the wapentake and liberty of Holderness; 3¼ miles from Hornsea, 11 from Beverley, 12 from Hull, 15 from Driffield.—Population 127.

HATFIELD, LITTLE, in the parish of Sigglesthorne, north-division of the wapentake and liberty of Holderness; 3 miles from Hornsea, 10 from Beverley, 13½ from Hull, 16 from Driffield.—Population 24.

HAY-HOLME, in the parish of Leven, north-division of the wapentake and liberty of Holderness; 7 miles from Driffield, 9 from Beverley, 18 from Hull.

HAYSTHORPE, in the parish of Burton-Agnes, wapentake of Dickering; 3½ miles from Bridlington, 8 from Driffield.—Population 89.

HAYTON, in the parish of Hayton, Holme-Beacon division of the wapentake of Harthill; *(the seat of Rudston Coverdale, Esq.)* 2¼ miles from Pocklington, 4½ from Market-Weighton, 13 from York.—Population 135.

HEDON, in the parish of Hedon, middle-division of the wapentake of Holderness, liberties of Hedon and St. Peter; 8 miles from Hull, 10 from Pattrington, 15 from Hornsea, 45 from York, 182 from London.—*Market*, Saturday.—*Fairs*, January 15, August 2, September 22, for Horses, &c. November 7, December 6, for Horned Cattle, Drapery, &c. and every other Monday for Horned Cattle and

EAST-RIDING

Sheep.—Sends two Members to Parliament—*Principal Inns*, Sun, and Running-Horses.—Population 592.

HELPERTHORPE, in the parish of Helperthorpe, wapentake of Buckrose; 4 miles from Sledmere, 9 from Driffield.—Population 72.

HEMINGBROUGH, in the parish of Hemingbrough, wapentake of Ouse and Derwent; 4 miles from Selby, 6 from Howden, 16 from Pocklington.—Population 387.

HEMPHOLME, in the parish of Leven, north-division of the wapentake and liberty of Holderness; 8¼ miles from Driffield, 9¼ from Beverley, 15 from Bridlington, 17 from Hull.—Population 57.

HESLERTON, EAST, in the parish of West-Heslerton, wapentake of Buckrose; 8 miles from Sledmere, 10 from Malton.—Population 139.

HESLERTON, WEST, in the parish of West-Heslerton, wapentake of Buckrose; *(the seat of John Robinson Foulis, Esq.)* 9 miles from Malton, 9 from Sledmere.—Population 129.

HESLINGTON, in the parish of St. Lawrence, York, wapentake of Ouse and Derwent, a part in the liberty of St. Peter; *(the seat of Henry Yarburgh, Esq.)* 2 miles from York, 11¼ from Pocklington, 15 from Selby.—Pop. 416.

HESSLE, in the parish of Hessle, County of the Town of Kingston-upon-Hull; 5 miles from Hull, 7½ from South-Cave, 9 from Beverley.—Population 681.

HESSLE-WOOD-HOUSE, in the parish of Hessle, County of the Town of Kingston-upon-Hull; *(the seat of John Robinson Pease, Esq.)* 5 miles from South-Cave, 7 from Hull, 9¼ from Beverley.

HILDERTHORPE, in the parish of Bridlington, wapentake of Dickering; 1¼ mile from Bridlington, 10 from Driffield, 22 from Beverley.—Population 40.

HILSTON, in the parish of Hilston, middle-division of the wapentake and liberty of Holderness; 9 miles from Hedon, 11¼ from Hornsea, 14 from Hull, 22 from Beverley.—Population 37.

HIVE, in the parish of Eastrington, wapentake and liberty of Howdenshire; 4 miles from Howden, 11¼ from South-Cave.

HOLLYM, in the parish of Hollym, south-division of the wapentake and liberty of Holderness; 2 miles from Pattrington, 11 from Hedon, 19 from Hull.—Population 223.

HOLME-HOUSE, in the the parish of Holme-on-Spalding-Moor, Holme-Beacon division of the wapentake of Harthill; 6¼ miles foom Market-Weighton, 8 from Howden, 9 from Pocklington.

EAST-RIDING.

HOLME-ON-SPALDING-MOOR, *(which gives name to the division)* in the parish of Holme-on-Spalding-Moor, Holme-Beacon division of the wapentake of Harthill, liberty of St. Peter ; *(the seat Lord Stourton)* 4¼ miles from Market-Weighton, 7 from Howden, 8 from Pocklington, 13¼ from Selby.—Population 1,024.

HOLME-ON-THE-WOLDS, in the parish of Holme-on-the-Wolds, Bainton-Beacon division of the wapentake of Harthill ; 6 miles from Beverley, 7½ from Market-Weighton.—Population 127.

HOLMPTON, in the parish of Holmpton, south division of the wapentake and liberty of Holderness ; 4 miles from Pattrington, 14 from Hedon, 22 from Hull.—Population 165.

HORNSEA, in the parish of Hornsea, north-division of the wapentake and liberty of Holderness; *(the seat of Peter Acklam, Esq.)* 14 miles from Beverley, 15 from Hedon, 15 from Driffield, 16 from Bridlington, 16 from Hull, 20 from Pattrington, 33 from York, 196 from London.—*Market*, Monday.—*Fairs*, August 12, and December 17, for Horses, Horned Cattle, &c.—*Principal Inns*, Hotel, and Blacksmiths' Arms.—Population 533.

HOTHAM, in the parish of Hotham, Hunsley-Beacon division of the wapentake of Harthill ; *(the seat of Robert Christie Burton, Esq.)* 3 miles from South-Cave, 5 from Market-Weighton, 9 from Beverley.—Pop. 256.

HOUGHTON, in the parish of Sancton, Hunsley-Beacon division of the wapentake of Harthill ; *(the seat of Philip Langdale, Esq.)* 6 miles from South-Cave, 8 from Market-Weighton.

HOWDEN, in the parish of Howden, wapentake and liberty of Howdenshire ; 10 miles from Selby, 10 from Snaith, 12 from South-Cave, 12 from Market-Weighton, 13¼ from Thorne, 16½ from Pocklington, 20 from Beverley, 20 from York, 25 from Hull, from London *by Thorne* 181, *by Lincoln* 199.—*Market*, Saturday.—*Fairs*, second Tuesday in January, second Tuesday after July 11, for Horned Cattle and Line ; October 2, and the six preceding Days, for Horses.—*Principal Inn*, Half-Moon.—Population 1,552.

HOWDEN-DYKE, in the parish of Howden, wapentake and liberty of Howdenshire ; 1¼ mile from Howden, 11 from Selby.

HOWDEN-PRICE, in the parish of Cottingham, Hunsley-Beacon division of the wapentake of Harthill ; 6 miles from Hull, 8 from South-Cave, 8 from Beverley.

HOWSHAM, in the parish of Scrayingham, wapentake of Buckrose ; *(the seat of Henry Cholmley, Esq.)* 8 miles from Malton, 12 from York.—Population 203.

HUGGATE, in the parish of Huggate, Wilton-Beacon division of the wapentake of Harthill; 7 miles from Pocklington, 8 from Driffield, 12 from Malton.—Pop. 302.

HUGGATE-WOLD-HOUSE, in the parish of Huggate, Wilton-Beacon division of the wapentake of Harthill; 7 miles from Pocklington, 10 from Driffield, 11 from Malton.

HULL, KINGSTON-UPON, a distinct County, under 3d. Geo. I. Chap. 5. called the Town and County of Kingston-upon-Hull, in the parishes of St. Mary and the Holy-Trinity, Hull; 8 miles from Hedon, 9 from Beverley, 12¼ from South-Cave, 16 from Hornsea, 18 from Pattrington, 25 from Howden, 39 from York, from London by Lincoln 174, by York, 236.—*Markets*, Tuesday and Friday, *Fair*, October 10, for Horned Cattle, Horses, Woollen-Cloth, Toys. &c.—*Bankers*, Old-Bank, Messrs. J. R. Pease, Knowsley, Wray and Liddle draw on Messrs. Boldero, Lushington, and Co. 30, Cornhill; Commercial-Bank, Messrs. Moxons draw on Messrs. Masterman, Peters, and Co. 2, White-Hart Court, Grace-Church Street; East-Riding-Bank, Messrs. Raikes, and Co. draw on Messrs. Denison and Co. St. Mary-Axe; Custom-House-Bank, Messrs. Smith and Thompson draw on Messrs. Smith, Payne, and Smiths, George-Street, by the Mansion-House; New-Bank, Messrs. R. C. Pease, Harrison and Co. draw on Messrs. Harrison, Price, and Co. 1, Mansion-house-street. —Sends two Members to Parliament.—*Principal Inns*, Cross-Keys, Neptune, and George.—Population 22,161.

HULL-BANK, in the parish of Cottingham, Hunsley-Beacon division of the wapentake of Harthill; *(the seat of John Wray, Esq.)* 3 miles from Hull, 6 from Beverley.

HUMBER, LITTLE, in the parish of Paul, south-division of the wapentake and liberty of Holderness; 3 miles from Hedon, 7 from Pattrington, 11 from Hull.

HUMBER-SIDE, in the parish of Pattrington, south-division of the wapentake and liberty of Holderness; 1 mile from Pattrington, 11 from Hedon.

HUMBLETON, in the parish of Humbleton, middle division of the wapentake and liberty of Holderness, 5 miles from Hedon, 10 from Hull, 17 from Beverley.—Population 89.

HUNMANBY, in the parish of Hunmanby, wapentake of Dickering; *(the seat of H. B. Osbaldeston, Esq.)* 10¼ miles from Bridlington, from Scarborough, *by Gristhorpe and Muston* 8½, *by Seamor and Flixton* 11¼, 38 from York, 210 from London.—*No Market.*—*Fairs*, May 6, and October 29, for Horned Cattle and Sheep.—*Principal Inn*, Swan.—Population 757.

HUNSLEY-HIGH, *(which gives name to the division)* in the parish of Rowley, Hunsley-Beacon division of the wapentake of Harthill ; 5 miles from South-Cave, 5 from Beverley.

HUNSLEY-LOW, in the parish of Rowley, Hunsley-Beacon division of the wapentake of Harthill ; 5 miles from South-Cave, 5¼ from Beverley.

HUTTON-CRANSWICK, in the parish of Hutton-Cranswick, Bainton-Beacon division of the wapentake of Harthill ; 3¾ miles from Driffield, 10 from Beverley.—Pop. 602.

HYTHE, in the parish of Eastrington, wapentake and liberty of Howdenshire ; 5 miles from Howden, 8 from South-Cave.

K.

KAYINGHAM, in the parish of Kayingham, south-division of the wapentake and liberty of Holderness ; 5 miles from Pattrington, 5 from Hedon, 13 from Hull.—Pop. 399.

KALLINGWOLD-GROVE, in the parish of Bishop-Burton, Hunsley-Beacon division of the wapentake of Harthill ; 3 miles from Beverley, 7½ from Market-Weighton.

KAYINGHAM-MARSH, in the parish of Kayingham, south-division of the wapentake and liberty of Holderness ; 6 miles from Hedon, 6½ from Pattrington, 14 from Hull.

KELFIELD, in the parish of Stillingfleet, wapentake of Ouse and Derwent ; 7 miles from Selby, 9 from York, 15 from Pocklington.—Population 175.

KELK, GREAT, in the parish of Foston, wapentake of Dickering ; 6 miles from Driffield, 10 from Bridlington.— Population 61.

KELK, LITTLE, (extraparochial) wapentake of Dickering ; 6 miles from Driffield, 9 from Bridlington.—Pop. 21.

KELLEYTHORPE, in the parish of Great-Driffield, Bainton-Beacon division of the wapentake of Harthill ; 2 miles from Driffield, 12 from Beverley, 14¼ from Bridlington.

KENDALL, in the parish of Great-Driffield, Bainton-Beacon division of the wapentake of Harthill ; 2 miles from Driffield, 9 from Sledmere, 13 from Bridlington, 15 from Beverley.

KENNYTHORPE, in the parish of Langton, wapentake of Buckrose ; 3¼ miles from Malton, 10 from Sledmere.— Population 50.

KEXBY, in the parish of Low-Catton, wapentake of Ouse and Derwent ; 5¼ miles from York, 7 from Pocklington, 12¼ from Market-Weighton.—Population 129.

KILDWICK-PERCY, in the parish of Kildwick-Percy, Wilton-Beacon division of the wapentake of Harthill; *(the seat of Robert Denison, Esq.)* 2 miles from Pocklington, 9 from Market-Weighton, 15 from York.—Pop. 43.

KILHAM, in the parish of Kilham, wapentake of Dickering, a part in the liberty of St. Peter; 6 miles from Driffield, 7 from Sledmere, 8 from Bridlington, 12 from Scarborough, 31¼ from York, 231 from London.—*Market*, Thursday. —*Fairs*, August 21, and November 12, for Horses, Horned Cattle, and Sheep.—*Principal Inn*, Hare and Hounds. —Population 588.

KILNSEA, in the parish of Kilnsea, south-division of the wapentake and liberty of Holderness; 8 miles from Pattrington, 18 from Hedon.—Population 98.

KILNWICK-ON-THE-WOLDS, in the parish of Kilnwick-on-the-Wolds, Bainton-Beacon division of the wapentake of Harthill; *(the seat of Thomas Grimston, Esq.)* 7½ miles from Driffield, 8 from Beverley.—Population 199.

KILPIN, in the parish of Howden, wapentake and liberty of Howdenshire; 2 miles from Howden, 11½ from Selby, 12¼ from South-Cave.—Population 183.

KILPIN-PIKE, in the parish of Howden, wapentake and liberty of Howdenshire; 1¼ mile from Howden, 11 from Selby.

KINGSFIELD, NORTH, in the parish of Carnaby, wapentake of Dickering; 4 miles from Bridlington, 10 from Driffield.

KIPLIN-COATES-HOUSE, in the parish of Middleton, Bainton-Beacon division of the wapentake of Harthill; 5 miles from Market-Weighton, 6½ from Pocklington, 10 from Beverley.

KIRBY-GRINDALYTH, in the parish of Kirby-Grindalyth, wapentake of Buckrose; 2 miles from Sledmere, 9 from Malton.—Population 144.

KIRBY-UNDERDALE, in the parish of Kirby-Underdale, wapentake of Buckrose; 7 miles from Pocklington, 9 from Sledmere.—Population 230.

KIRKBURN, in the parish of Kirkburn, Bainton-Beacon division of the wapentake of Harthill; 4 miles from Driffield, 11 from Beverley.—Population 92.

KIRKHAM, in the parish of Kirkham, wapentake of Buckrose; 6 miles from Malton, 12¼ from York.—Pop. 29.

KNAPTON, in the parish of Winteringham, wapentake of Buckrose; 7 miles from Malton, 9 from Sledmere.—Pop. 139.

KNEDLINGTON, in the parish of Howden, wapentake and liberty of Howdenshire; 1 mile from Howden, 9½ from Selby.—Population 90.

EAST-RIDING.

L.

LANGTHORPE, in the parish of Swine, middle division of the wapentake and liberty of Holderness ; 9 miles from Hedon, 9 from Hull, 10 from Beverley.

LANGTOFT, in the parish of Langtoft, wapentake of Dickering, liberty of St. Peter ; 6 miles from Driffield, 6 from Sledmere, 12 from Bridlington, 15¼ from Scarborough.—Population 276.

LANGTON, in the parish of Langton, wapentake of Buckrose; *(the seat of Thomas Norcliffe, Esq.)* 3¼ miles from Malton, 9 from Sledmere, 14¼ from Pocklington.—Pop. 216

LANGWITH, in the parish of Wheldrake, wapentake of Ouse and Derwent ; 2 miles from York, 12 from Pocklington, 17 from Selby.—Population 29.

LAXTON, in the parish of Howden, wapentake and liberty of Howdenshire; 3 miles from Howden, 12 from Selby, 13¼ from South-Cave.—Population 219.

LAYTHAM, in the parish of Aughton, Holme-Beacon division of the wapentake of Harthill ; 8 miles from Howden, 8 from Pocklington.—Population 92.

LEAVENING, in the parish of Acklam, wapentake of Buckrose, liberty of St. Peter ; 5 miles from Malton, 9¼ from Pocklington, 11 from Sledmere.—Population 176.

LECKONFIELD, in the parish of Leckonfield, Hunsley-Beacon division of the wapentake of Harthill ; 2¼ miles from Beverley, 10 from Market-Weighton, 10¼ from Driffield.—Population 316.

LELLAY, in the parish of Preston, middle-division of the wapentake and liberty of Holderness ; 4 miles from Hedon, 8 from Hull, 17 from Beverley.—Population 107.

LEPPINGTON, in the parish of Scrayingham, wapentake of Buckrose ; 8 miles from Malton, 8¼ from Pocklington. —Population 118.

LEVEN, in the parish of Leven, north-division of the wapentake and liberty of Holderness ; 6¼ miles from Hornsea, 6¼ from Beverley, 14 from Hull, 17 from Bridlington.—Population 411.

LINCOLN-FLATTS, in the parish of Seaton-Ross, Holme-Beacon division of the wapentake of Harthill ; 7 miles from Market-Weighton, 11 from Selby.

LINGCROFT, in the parish of St. Dennis, York, wapentake of Ouse and Derwent ; 3 miles from York, 12 from Selby, 13¼ from Pocklington.

LINTON, in the parish of Winteringham, wapentake of Buckrose ; 4 miles from Sledmere, 10 from Malton, 12 from Driffield.

LINTON, EAST, in the parish of Howden, wapentake and liberty of Howdenshire; 3 miles from Howden, 10 from South-Cave, 13 from Selby.

LINTON-GRANGE, in the parish of Winteringham, wapentake of Buckrose; 3 miles from Sledmere, 11 from Malton, 11 from Driffield.

LINTON, WEST, in the parish of Howden, wapentake and liberty of Howdenshire; 2¼ miles from Howden, 12¼ from Selby, 18 from Beverley.

LISSETT, in the parish of Beeford, north-division of the wapentake and liberty of Holderness; 7 miles from Bridlington, 10 from Driffield, 16 from Beverley.—Population 122.

LOCKINGTON, in the parishes of Lockington and Kilnwick, Bainton-Beacon division of the wapentake of Harthill; *(the seat of the Rev. Francis Lundy)* 6½ miles from Beverley, 8¼ from Driffield.—Population 379.

LOFTSOME and LOFTSOME-BRIDGE, in the parish of Wressle, Holme-Beacon division of the wapentake of Harthill; 4 miles from Howden, 6 from Selby.

LONDESBROUGH, in the parish of Londesbrough, Holme-Beacon division of the wapentake of Harthill; *(the seat of the Duke of Devonshire)* 2½ miles from Market-Weighton, 5 from Pocklington.—Population 166.

LONGBROUGH-LANE-HOUSE, in the parish of Humbleton, middle-division of the wapentake and liberty of Holderness; 8 miles from Hedon, 15 from Hull, 21 from Beverley.

LOWTHORPE, in the parish of Lowthorpe, wapentake of Dickering; 5 miles from Driffield, 9 from Bridlington.— Population 159.

LUND, in the parish of Lund, Bainton-Beacon division of the wapentake of Harthill; 7 miles from Beverley, 7 from Market-Weighton, 9 from Driffield.—*Market* every Wednesday, in *Lent only.*—Population 310.

LUND, in the parish of Hemingbrough, wapentake of Ouse and Derwent; 4¼ miles from Selby, 7½ from Howden, 14 from York.

LUTTON, EAST, in the parish of Weaverthorpe, wapentake of Buckrose, liberty of St. Peter; 4 miles from Sledmere, 10 from Malton.

LUTTON, WEST, in the parish of Weaverthorpe, wapentake of Buckrose liberty, of St. Peter; 4 miles from Sledmere, 10 from Malton.—Population 207.

M.

MAPPLETON, in the parish of Mappleton, north-division of the wapentake of Holderness, liberties of St. Peter and Holderness; 3 miles from Hornsea, 14¼ from Beverley, 15 from Hull, 16¼ from Driffield.—Population 159.

MARFLEET, in the parish of Marfleet, middle-division of the wapentake and liberty of Holderness; 3 miles from Hedon, 5¼ from Hull, 14½ from Beverley.—Population 116.

MARTON, in the parish of Swine, middle-division of the wapentake and liberty of Holderness; 7 miles from Hedon, 7 from Hull, 12 from Beverley.—Population 127.

MARTON, in the parish of Bridlington, wapentake of Dickering; *(the seat of Ralph Creyke, Esq.)* 1¼ mile from Bridlington, 11¼ from Driffield.

MELBURN, in the parish of Thornton, Holme-Beacon division of the wapentake of Harthill; *(the seat of Sir Henry Vavasour, Bart.)* 5 miles from Pocklington, 9 from Market-Weighton, 12 from York.—Population 308.

MELTON, in the parish of Welton, wapentake and liberty of Howdenshire; *(the seat of B. Blaydes, Esq.)* 5 miles from South-Cave, 9 from Beverley, 9 from Hull.—Pop. 98.

MELTON-HILL, in the parish of Welton, wapentake and liberty of Howdenshire; *(the seat of J.S. Williamson, Esq.)* 5¼ miles from South-Cave, 9½ from Hull, 9½ from Beverley.

MELTONBY, in the parish of Pocklington, Wilton-Beacon division of the wapentake of Harthill; 2 miles from Pocklington, 9 from Market-Weighton, 15 from York.—Pop. 41.

MENNYTHORP, in the parish of Westow, wapentake of Buckrose; 3 miles from Malton, 12 from Sledmere.—Population 104.

MENTHORPE, in the parish of Hemingbrough, wapentake of Ouse and Derwent, liberty of Howdenshire; 5 miles from Selby, 5 from Howden, 14 from York.—Population 61.

METTHAM, in the parish of Howden, wapentake and liberty of Howdenshire; 4¼ miles from Howden, 11 from South-Cave, 14¼ from Selby.—Population 38.

MEUX, or MELSA, in the parish of Waghen, middle-division of the wapentake and liberty of Holderness; 6 miles from Hull, 6 from Beverley, 13 from Hedon.—Pop. 49.

MIDDLETON, in the parish of Middleton, Bainton-Beacon division of the wapentake of Harthill; 8¼ miles from Beverley, 8¼ from Driffield, 9¼ from Pocklington.—Pop. 286.

MILL-HOUSES, in the parish of Kirby-Underdale, wapentake of Buckrose; 9 miles from Sledmere, 9 from Pocklington, 10 from Malton.

EAST-RIDING.

MILLINGTON, in the parish of Great-Givendale, Wilton-Beacon division of the wapentake of Harthill; a part in the liberty of St. Peter; 3 miles from Pocklington, 8 from Market-Weighton, 15 from York.—Population 183.

MOLESCROFT, in the parish of St. John, Beverley, liberty of Beverley; Hunsley-Beacon division of the wapentake of Harthill; 1 mile from Beverley, 10 from Hull, 12¼ from Driffield.—Population 67.

MOORBY, in the parish of Stillingfleet, wapentake of Ouse and Derwent; *(the seat of the Rev. Thomas Preston)* 5½ miles from York, 9 from Selby, 13¼ from Pocklington.

MOOR-GRANGE, in the parish of Nunkilling, north-division of the wapentake and liberty of Holderness; 6¼ miles from Hornsea, 10 from Driffield, 13 from Beverley.

MOOR-HOUSE, in the parish of Burton-Agnes, wapentake of Dickering; 7 miles from Bridlington, 7 from Driffield.

MOOR-HOUSE, in the parish of Humbleton, middle-division of the wapentake and liberty of Holderness; 5 miles from Hedon, 9 from Hull, 14 from Beverley.

MOOR-TOWN, in the parish of Brandesburton, north-division of the wapentake and liberty of Holderness; 7 miles from Hornsea, 10 from Beverley, 13 from Bridlington, 15 from Hull.—Population 32.

MOUNT-FARRAN, in the parish of Birdsall, wapentake of Buckrose; 4½ miles from Malton, 9 from Sledmere, 12 from Pocklington.

MOWTHORPE, in the parish of Kirby-Grindalyth, wapentake of Buckrose; 3 miles from Sledmere, 11 from Malton, 11 from Driffield.

MUSTON, in the parish of Muston, wapentake of Dickering; 2 miles from Hunmanby, 10 from Bridlington, 10 from Scarborough.—Population 236.

N.

NABURN, in the parishes of Acaster Malbis, and St. Dennis, York, wapentake of Ouse and Derwent, *(the seat of George Palmes, Esq.)* 4 miles from York, 11 from Selby, 15 from Pocklington.—Population 363.

NAFFERTON, in the parish of Nafferton, wapentake of Dickering; 2¼ miles from Driffield, 9 from Bridlington, 15 from Beverley.—Population 721.

NEVILLE-GRANGE, in the parish of Leven, north-division of the wapentake and liberty of Holderness; 5 miles from Beverley, 11 from Hull, 11 from Hedon.

NESWICK, in the parish of Bainton, Bainton-Beacon division of the wapentake of Harthill; *(the seat of John Grimstone, Esq.)* 6 miles from Driffield, 19 from Beverley, 10 from Malton, 22 from York.—Population 54.

NEWBALD, NORTH, in the parish of North-Newbald, Hunsley-Beacon division of the wapentake of Harthill, liberty of St. Peter; 3¼ miles from South Cave, 4¼ from Market Weighton, 8 from Beverley.—Population 517.

NEWBALD, SOUTH, in the parish of North-Newbald, Hunsley-Beacon division of the wapentake of Harthill, liberty of St. Peter; 3 miles from South-Cave, 4 from Market-Weighton, 8 from Beverley.—Population 144.

NEW-FIELDS, in the parish of Howden, wapentake and liberty of Howdenshire; 1 mile from Howden, 11 from Selby, 12 from South Cave.

NEWLAND, in the parishes of Howden and Eastrington, wapentake and liberty of Howdenshire; 3 miles from Howden, 10 from South-Cave, 13 from Selby.

NEWLAND, in the parish of Cottingham, Hunsley-Beacon division of the wapentake of Harthill; *(the seat of B. B. Haworth, Esq.)* 2 miles from Hull, 7 from Beverley.

NEWPORT, in the parish of Eastrington, wapentake and liberty of Howdenshire; 4½ miles from South-Cave, 7½ from Howden.—Population 169.

NEWSAM, or NEWSHOLME, in the parish of Wressel, Holme-Beacon division of the wapentake of Harthill; 3 miles from Howden, 7 from Selby.—Population 192.

NEWTON, in the parish of Wintringham, wapentake of Buckrose; *(the seat of Sir William Strickland, Bart.)* 8 miles from Malton, 8 from Sledmere.

NEWTON, in the parish of Eastrington, wapentake and liberty of Howdenshire; 4 miles from Howden, 9¼ from South-Cave.

NEWTON, EAST, in the parish of Aldbrough, middle-division of the wapentake and liberty of Holderness; 8 miles from Hornsea, 9 from Hedon, 14 from Hull, 18 from Beverley.—Population 24.

NEWTON, OUT, in the parish of Easington, south-division of the wapentake and liberty of Holderness; 4 miles from Pattrington, 14 from Hedon, 22 from Hull.—Pop. 35.

NEWTON-UPON-DERWENT, in the parish of Wilberfoss, Wilton-Beacon, division of the wapentake of Harthill; 5 miles from Pocklington, 8 from York, 13 from Selby.—Population 188.

NEWTON, WEST, in the parish of Aldbrough, middle-division of the wapentake and liberty of Holderness; 5 miles

EAST-RIDING.

from Hedon, 9 from Hull, 13 from Beverley.—Pop. 172.

NEW-VILLAGE, (extraparochial) Hunsley-Beacon division of the wapentake of Harthill; 4¼ miles from South-Cave, 7¼ from Market-Weighton, 7½ from Howden.—Population 108.

NORTON, in the parish of Norton, wapentake of Buckrose; (*the seat of Thomas Norcliffe, Esq.*) ½ a mile from Malton, 12 from Sledmere, 19 from York.—Population 615.

NUNBURNHOLME, in the parish of Nunburnholme, Wilton-Beacon division of the wapentake of Harthill; 3 miles from Pocklington, 5 from Market-Weighton, 15 from York.—Population 125.

NUNKILLING, or NUNKEELING, in the parish of Nunkilling, north-division of the wapentake and liberty of Holderness; 6 miles from Hornsea, 9½ from Driffield, 10 from Beverley, 14 from Bridlington, 16 from Hull.—Population 173.

NUTHILL, in the parish of Skeckling, south-division of the wapentake and liberty of Holderness; 3 miles from Hedon, 8 from Hull, 13 from Pattrington.

NUTTLES, in the parish of Skeckling, south-division of the wapentake and liberty of Holderness; 4 miles from Hedon, 8 from Hull, 17 from Beverley.

O.

OCTON, in the parish of Thwing, wapentake of Dickering; 8 miles from Bridlington, 13 from Scarborough.

OCTON-GRANGE, in the parish of Thwing, wapentake of Dickering; 9 miles from Bridlington, 13 from Scarborough.

OSGODBY, in the parish of Hemingbrough, wapentake of Ouse and Derwent, liberty of Howdenshire; 3 miles from Selby, 5 from Howden, 13 from York.—Population 146.

OTTRINGHAM, in the parish of Ottringham, south-division of the wapentake and liberty of Holderness; 3½ miles from Pattrington, 6½ from Hedon, 15 from Hull.—Pop. 622.

OTTRINGHAM-MARSH, in the parish of Ottringham, south-division of the wapentake and liberty of Holderness; 4 miles from Pattrington, 7¼ from Hedon, 16 from Hull.

OWBROUGH, in the parish of Swine, middle-division of the wapentake and liberty of Holderness; 6 miles from Hedon, 7 from Hull, 9 from Beverley.

OWSTHILL, in the parish of Aldbrough, middle-division of the wapentake and liberty of Holderness; 8 miles from Hedon, 14 from Hull, 13 from Beverley.

OWSTHORPE, in the parish of Pocklington, Wilton-Beacon division of the wapentake of Harthill; 1¼ mile from Pocklington, 8 from Market-Weighton, 13 from York.—Population 15.

OWSTROP, in the parish of Eastrington, wapentake and liberty of Howdenshire; 3¼ miles from Howden, 8¼ from South-Cave.

OWSTWICK, in the parishes of Garton and Rooss, middle-division of the wapentake and liberty of Holderness; 8 miles from Hedon, 13 from Hull, 22 from Beverley.—Pop. 109.

OWTHORN, in the parish of Owthorn, south-division of the wapentake and liberty of Holderness; 5 miles from Pattrington, 10 from Hedon, 18 from Hull.—Pop. 89.

P.

PAINSTHORPE, in the parish of Kirby-Underdale, wapentake of Buckrose; 7 miles from Pocklington, 9 from Sledmere.

PARKHOUSE, in the parish of Thornton, Holme-Beacon division of the wapentake of Harthill; 7 miles from Pocklington, 11 from York.

PATTRINGTON, in the parish of Pattrington, south division of the wapentake and liberty of Holderness; 10 miles from Hedon, 18 from Hull, 20 from Hornsea, 56 from York, 192 from London.—*Market*, Saturday.—*Fairs*, March 28, July 18, and December 6, for Drapery, Millinery, Shoes, &c.—*Principal Inns*, Three Tuns, and Simpson's Inn.—Population 894.

PAUL, or PAGHILL, in the parish of Paul, south-division of the wapentake and liberty of Holderness; 3 miles from Hedon, 7 from Pattrington, 10 from Hull.—Pop. 212.

PAUL, HIGH, in the parish of Paul, south-division of the wapentake and liberty of Holderness; *(the seat of Hugh Blaydes, Esq.)* 3½ miles from Hedon, 6¼ from Pattrington, 10¼ from Hull.

PAUL-HOLMES, in the parish of Paul, south-division of the wapentake and liberty of Holderness; 3½ miles from Hedon, 7 from Pattrington, 11 from Hull.

PENSTHORPE, in the parish of Welwick, south-division of the wapentake and liberty of Holderness; 1 mile from Pattrington, 11 from Hedon, 19 from Hull.

PLOUGHLANG, in the parish of Welwick, south-division of the wapentake and liberty of Holderness; 1 mile from Pattrington, 11 from Hedon, 19 from Hull.

PLUCKHAM, in the parish of Wharram-Percy, wapentake of Buckrose; 5 miles from Pocklington, 6 from Sledmere, 10 from Driffield.

POCKLINGTON, in the parish of Pocklington, Wilton-Beacon division of the wapentake of Karthill; a part in the liberty of St. Peter, 6¼ miles from Market-Weighton, 12¼ from York, 13 from Sledmere, 15 from Driffield, 16 from Malton, 16½ from Howden, 212 from London.—*Market*, Saturday.—*Fairs*, March 7, May 6, August 5, and November 8, for Horned Cattle, Horses, Sheep, Cloth, &c. —*Principal Inns*, Feathers, Buck, Black-Bull.—Population 1,502.

POCKLINGTON-NEW-INN, in the parish of Pocklington, Wilton-Beacon division of the wapentake of Harthill; 1½ mile from Pocklington, 5¼ from Market-Weighton, 13 from York.

POCKTHORPE, in the parish of Nafferton, wapentake of Dickering; *(Pockthorpe-House, the seat of the Rev. John Watts)* 4 miles from Driffield, 10 from Bridlington.

PORTINGTON, in the parish of Eastrington, wapentake and liberty of Howdenshire; 3 miles from Howden, 11 from South-Cave.—Population 100.

PRESTON, in the parish of Preston, middle-division of the wapentake of Holderness, liberties of St. Peter and Holderness; 1 mile from Hedon, 8 from Hull.—Pop. 681.

PRICKETT-HILL, in the parish of Wressle, Holme-Beacon division of the wapentake of Harthill; 2 miles from Howden, 9 from Selby, 12 from Market-Weighton.

R.

RAGWELL, in the parish of Cottingham, Hunsley-Beacon, division of the wapentake of Harthill; *(the seat of Daniel Sykes Esq.)* 4 miles from Beverley, 5 from Hull, 30 from York.

RAISTHORPE, in the parish of Wharram, wapentake of Buckrose; 6 miles from Sledmere, 6 from Malton, 9 from Pocklington.—Population 35.

REIGHTON, in the parish of Reighton, wapentake of Dickering; 2¼ miles from Hunmanby, 7 from Bridlington, Population 149.

RICCALL, in the parish of Riccall, wapentake of Ouse and Derwent, liberties of St. Peter and Howdenshire; *(the seat of Toft Richardson, Esq.)* 5¼ miles from Selby, 9¼ from York, 12 from Howden.—Population 517.

RIDGEMONT, in the parishes of Skeckling and Burton-Pidsea, south-division of the wapentake and liberty of Holderness; 5 miles from Hedon, 9 from Pattrington, 12 from Hull.

RILLINGTON, in the parish of Rillington, wapentake of Buckrose; 4¼ miles from Malton, 8 from Sledmere.—Population 380.

RILLINGTON-MOORS, in the parish of Rillington, wapentake of Buckrose; 7 miles from Malton, 10 from Sledmere.

RIMSWELL, in the parish of Owthorn, south-division of the wapentake and liberty of Holderness; 5 miles from Pattrington, 11 from Hedon, 19 from Hull.—Pop. 107.

RINGBROUGH, in the parish of Aldbrough, middle-division of the wapentake and liberty of Holderness; 8 miles from Hornsea, 10 from Pattrington, 14 from Hull.

RIPLINGHAM, in the parish of Rowley, Hunsley-Beacon division of the wapentake of Harthill; 4 miles from Beverley, 8 from Hull, 28 from York.

RISBY, in the parish of Rowley, Hunsley-Beacon division of the wapentake of Harthill; 4 miles from Beverley, 6 from South-Cave, 8 from Hull.

RISE, in the parish of Rise, north-division of the wapentake and liberty of Holderness; *(the seat of Mrs. Betholl)* 6¼ miles from Hornsea, 9¼ from Hull, 14 from Driffield, 20 from Bridlington.—Population 155.

RISOME-GARTH, in the parish of Hollym, south-division of the wapentake and liberty of Holderness; *(the seat of George Sherwood, Esq.)* 4 miles from Pattrington, 13 from Hedon, 21 from Hull.

RISTON, LONG, in the parish of Long-Riston, north-division of the wapentake and liberty of Holderness; 6½ miles from Beverley, 14 from Driffield, 18 from Bridlington.—Population 259.

ROOSS, or ROOSE, in the parish of Rooss, middle-division of the wapentake and liberty of Holderness; 7 miles from Hedon, 14 from Hull, 20 from Beverley.—Population 272.

ROTSEA, in the parish of Hutton-Cranswick, Bainton-Beacon division of the wapentake of Harthill; 6 miles from Driffield, 12 from Beverley.—Population 13.

ROUTH, in the parish of Routh, north-division of the wapentake and liberty of Holderness; 4¼ miles from Beverley, 10 from Hornsea, 13 from Hull, 20 from Bridlington.—Population 115.

ROUTON, in the parish of Swine, middle-division of the wapentake and liberty of Holderness; 7¼ miles from Beverley, 11 from Hull, 15 from Driffield.

EAST-RIDING.

ROWLEY, in the parish of Rowley, Hunsley-Beacon division of the wapentake of Harthill; 2½ miles from South-Cave, 5 from Beverley, 8½ from Hull.—Population 347.

ROWLSTON, in the parish of Mappleton, north-division of the wapentake and liberty of Holderness; 2 miles from Hornsea, 14 from Beverley, 16 from Driffield.

RUDDINGS, see *Aughton-Ruddings*.

RUDSTON, in the parish of Rudston, wapentake of Dickering; 5 miles from Bridlington, 6 from Hunmanby, 7 from Driffield.—Population 296.

RUSTON-PARVA, in the parish of Lowthorpe, wapentake of Dickering; 4 miles from Driffield, 9 from Bridlington.—Population 94.

RYALL, or **RYEHILL**, in the parish of Skeckling, south-division of the wapentake and liberty of Holderness; 3½ miles from Hedon, 7¼ from Pattrington.—Population 214.

RYTHAM-GATE, in the parish of Seaton-Ross, Holme-Beacon division of the wapentake of Harthill; 5 miles from Pocklington, 6 from Market-Weighton.

S.

SALTAGH, in the parish Ottringham, south-division of the wapentake and liberty of Holderness; 6 miles from Pattrington, 6 from Hedon, 14 from Hull.

SALTMARSH, in the parish of Howden, wapentake and liberty of Howdenshire; *(the seat of Philip Saltmarsh, Esq.)* 4 miles from Howden, 14 from South-Cave, 14 from Selby.—Population 160.

SANCTON, in the parish of Sancton, Hunsley-Beacon division of the wapentake of Harthill; 2½ miles from Market-Weighton, 6 from South-Cave, 9 from Beverley.—Pop. 282.

SAND-HALL, in the parish of Howden, wapentake and liberty of Howdenshire; 3½ miles from Howden, 13 from Selby, 14 from South-Cave.

SANDHOLME, in the parish of Eastrington, wapentake and liberty of Howdenshire; 4¼ miles from Howden, 12 from South-Cave.

SAND-HOLME, in the parish of St. John, Beverley, Huns-Beacon division of the wapentake of Harthill, liberty of Beverley; 1¼ mile from Beverley, 10 from Hull, 15 from Driffield.

SCAGGLETHORPE, in the parish of Settrington, wapentake of Buckrose ; 3 miles from Malton, 10 from Sledmere.—Population 200.

SCALBY, in the parish of Eastrington, wapentake and liberty of Howdenshire ; 5¼ miles from South-Cave, 6¼ from Howden.—Population 66.

SCAMPSTON, in the parish of Rillington, wapentake of Buckrose ; *(the seat of Sir William St. Quintin, Bart.)* 6 miles from Malton, 9 from Sledmere.—Population 201.

SCEFF, or SKEFF, in the parish of Holme-on-Spalding-Moor, Hunsley-Beacon division of the wapentake Harthill; 5¼ miles from Market-Weighton, 8 from Howden.

SCORBROUGH, in the parish of Scorbrough, Bainton Beacon division of the wapentake of Harthill ; 4¼ miles from Beverley, 9 from Driffield.—Population 61.

SCOREBY, in the parish of Low-Catton, wapentake of Ouse and Derwent; 6 miles from York, 8 from Pocklington.

SCRAYINGHAM, in the parish of Scrayingham, wapentake of Buckrose ; 9 miles from Pocklington, 11 from York.—Population 140.

SCULCOATES, in the parish of Sculcoates, Hunsley-Beacon division of the wapentake of Harthill ; adjoins Hull, 9 miles from Beverley, 14 from South-Cave.—Population 5,448.

SEATON, in the parish of Sigglesthorne, north-division of the wapentake and liberty of Holderness; 2¼ miles from Hornsea, 10¼ from Beverley, 12¼ from Driffield, 13¼ from Hull.—Population 178.

SEATON-HALL, in the parish of Seaton-Ross, Holme-Beacon division of the wapentake of Harthill ; 6¼ miles from Market-Weighton, 7 from Pocklington, 9¼ from Howden.

SEATON-ROSS, in the parish of Seaton-Ross, Holme-Beacon division of the wapentake of Harthill ; 5¼ miles from Pocklington, 7 from Market-Weighton, 10 from Howden.—Population 385.

SETTRINGTON, in the parish of Settrington, wapentake of Buckrose ; *(the seat of Sir Mark Masterman Sykes, Bart.)* 4 miles from Malton, 8 from Sledmere—Pop. 414.

SEWERBY, in the parish of Bridlington, wapentake of Dickering; *(the seat of John Greame, Esq.)* 1½ mile from Bridlington, 11¼ from Driffield.—Population 279.

SHERBURN, in the parish of Sherburn, wapentake of Buckrose ; 8 miles from Sledmere, 12 from Malton.—Pop. 288.

SHIPTON, in the parish of Market-Weighton, Holme-Beacon division of the wapentake of Harthill, a part in the liberty of St. Peter ; 2 miles from Market-Weighton 4¼ from Pocklington.—Population 325.

SIGGLESTHORNE, in the parish of Sigglesthorne north-division of the wapentake and liberty of Holderness; 3¼ miles from Hornsea, 9¼ from Beverley, 14 from Driffield, 12¼ from Hull, 16 from Bridlington.—Population 185.

SKECKLING, in the parish of Skeckling, south-division of of the wapentake and liberty of Holderness; 3 miles from Hedon, 7 from Pattrington, 11 from Hull.

SKEFFLING, in the parish of Skeffling, south-division of the wapentake and liberty of Holderness; 3¼ miles from Pattrington, 13¼ from Hedon, 22 from Hull.—Pop. 155.

SKELTON, in the parish of Howden, wapentake and liberty of Howdenshire; 2 miles from Howden, 12 from Selby, 13¼ from South-Cave.—Population 146.

SKERNE, or SKYREN, in the parish of Skerne, Bainton-Beacon division of the wapentake of Harthill; 2¼ miles from Driffield, 12 from Beverley.—Population 184.

SKIDBY, in the parish of Cottingham, Hunsley-Beacon division of the wapentake of Harthill; 4 miles from Beverley, 7 from Hull, 7 from South-Cave.—Population 243.

SKIPSEA, in the parish of Skipsea, north-division of the wapentake and liberty of Holderness; 9 miles from Bridlington, 10¼ from Driffield, 15 from Beverley.—Pop. 220.

SKIPSEA-BROUGH, in the parish of Skipsea, north-division of the wapentake and liberty of Holderness; 9 miles from Bridlington, 10¼ from Driffield, 15 from Beverley.

SKIPWITH, in the parish of Skipwith, wapentake of Ouse and Derwent, liberty of Howdenshire; *(the seat of Robert Hudson, Esq.)* 5¼ miles from Selby, 7½ from Howden, 9¼ from York.—Population 247.

SKIRLAUGH, NORTH, in the parish of Swine, north-division of the wapentake and liberty of Holderness; 7¼ miles from Hornsea, 8¼ from Hull, 15 from Driffield.

SKIRLAUGH, SOUTH, in the parish of of Swine, middle-division of the wapentake and liberty of Holderness; 8 miles from Hedon, 6 from Hull, 9 from Beverley.—Population 123.

SKIRLINGTON, in the parish of Atwicke, north-division of the wapentake and liberty of Holderness; 2¼ miles from Hornsea, 11¼ from Bridlington, 12 from Driffield, 13 from Beverley.

SKIRPENBECK, in the parish of Skirpenbeck, wapentake of Buckrose; a part in the liberty of St. Peter; 6 miles from Pocklington, 10 from York.—Population 167.

SLEDMERE, in the parish of Sledmere, wapentake of Buckrose; *(the seat of Sir Mark Masterman Sykes, Bart.)* 8 miles from Driffield, 11¼ from Malton, 12 from Pocklington, 17 from Bridlington, 18 from Beverley, 18 from Scarborough, 24 from York, 223 from London.—*Principal Inn*, Triton-Inn.—Population 335.

SMITHY-BRIGG, in the parish of Swine, middle-division of the wapentake and liberty of Holderness; 7 miles from Hedon, 9 from Hull, 12 from Beverley.

SOUTHBURN, in the parish of Kirkburn, Bainton-Beacon division of the wapentake of Harthill; 4½ miles from Driffield, 10½ from Beverley.—Population 75.

SOUTHCOATES, in the parish of Drypool, middle-division of the wapentake and liberty of Holderness; 2 miles from Hull, 8 from Hedon, 11 from Beverley.—Population 235.

SPALDINGTON, in the parishes of Bubwith and Aughton, Holme-Beacon division of the wapentake of Harthill; 4½ miles from Howden, 10 from Selby, 10 from Market-Weighton.—Population 331.

SPEETON, in the parish of Bridlington, wapentake of Dickering; 4 miles from Hunmanby, 5¼ from Bridlington.—Population 104.

SPITTAL, in the parish of Barmby-on-the-Moor, Wilton-Beacon division of the wapentake of Harthill; 3½ miles from Pocklington, 9½ from York, 10½ from Market-Weighton, 16 from Malton.

SPITTAL-HOUSE, in the parish of Willerby, wapentake of Dickering; 8 miles from Scarborough, 11 from Bridlington, 13 from Driffield.

SPRINGHEAD, in the parish of Cottingham, Hunsley-Beacon division of the wapentake of Harthill; 3 miles from Hull, 8 from Beverley.

SPROATLEY, in the parish of Sproatley, middle-division of the wapentake and liberty of Holderness; 5 miles from Hedon, 8 from Hull, 15 from Beverley.—Population 232.

SPURNHEAD, in the parish of Kilnsea, south-division of the wapentake and liberty of Holderness; 11¼ miles from Pattrington, 21¼ from Hedon, 29¼ from Hull.

STADDLETHORPE, in the parish of Howden, wapentake and liberty of Howdenshire; 7 miles from Howden, 8 from South-Cave.

STAMFORD-BRIDGE, in the parishes of Low-Catton, and Gate-Helmsley, wapentake of Ouse and Derwent, and Wilton-Beacon division of the wapentake of Harthill, a part in the liberty of St. Peter; 7½ miles from York, 7½ from Pocklington, 16½ from Sledmere, 18 from Selby, 23 from Driffield.—*No Market.*—*Fair*, December 1, for Horses, Horned Cattle, Sheep, Boots, Shoes, &c.—Pop. 293.

STANINGHOLME, in the parish of Watton, Bainton-Beacon division of the wapentake of Harthill; 8 miles from

Driffield, 10 from Beverley, 17 from Pocklington.

STAXTON, in the parish of Willerby, wapentake of Dickering; 6 miles from Hunmanby, 7 from Scarborough, 12 from Bridlington, 14¼ from Driffield.—Population 125.

STEPNEY, in the parish of Sculcoates, Hunsley-Beacon division of the wapentake of Harthill; 1 mile from Hull, 8 from Beverley.

STILLINGFLEET, in the parish of Stillingfleet, wapentake of Ouse and Derwent, a part in the liberty of St. Peter; 7 miles from York, 8 from Selby, 8 from Tadcaster, 15 from Pocklington.—Population 304.

STONE-FERRY, in the parish of Sutton, middle-division of the wapentake and liberty of Holderness; 2 miles from Hull, 9 from Hedon, 13 from Beverley.

STORK-HILL, in the parish of St. John, Beverley, Hunsley-Beacon division of the wapentake of Harthill, liberty of Beverley; 1¼ mile from Beverley, 10 from Hull.

STORTHWAITE, or STORTHWOOD, in the parish of Thornton, Holme-Beacon division of the wapentake of Harthill; 7 miles from Pocklington, 10 from Market-Weighton, 10 from York.—Population 86.

SUNDERLANDWICK, in the parish of Hutton-Cranswick, Bainton-Beacon division of the wapentake of Harthill; *(the seat of Simon Horner, Esq.)* 2 miles from Driffield, 11 from Beverley.—Population 19.

SUNK-ISLAND, *(extraparochial)* middle-division of the wapentake and liberty of Holderness; 8 miles from Pattrington, 8 from Hedon, 16 from Hull.

SUTTON, in the parish of Sutton, middle-division of the wapentake and liberty of Holderness; 4 miles from Hull, 9 from Hedon, 13 from Beverley.—Population 1,569.

SUTTON, in the parish of Norton, wapentake of Buckrose; 1 mile from Malton, 11 from Sledmere.

SUTTON, FULL, in the parish of Full-Sutton, Wilton-Beacon division of the wapentake of Harthill, a part in the liberty of St. Peter; 5 miles from Pocklington, 10 from York, 12 from Malton.—Population 100.

SUTTON-UPON-DERWENT, in the parish of Sutton-upon-Derwent, Wilton-Beacon division of the wapentake of Harthill; 6 miles from York, 7 from Pocklington, 12 from Selby.—Population 274.

SWANLAND, in the parish of Ferriby, County of the Town of Kingston-upon-Hull; *(the seat of Mrs. Pater)* 6 miles from South-Cave, 7 from Hull.

SWINE, in the parish of Swine, middle-division of the wapentake and liberty of Holderness; 7 miles from Hedon, 8 from Hull, 8 from Beverley.—Population 204.

SWINKELL, in the parish of Watton, Bainton-Beacon division of the wapentake of Harthill; 5 miles from Driffield, 9 from Beverley, 13 from Market-Weighton.

T.

TANSTON, or TANSTERNE, in the parish of Aldbrough, middle-division of the wapentake and liberty of Holderness; 7 miles from Hedon, 12 from Hull, 16 from Beverley.

THEARNE, in the parish of St. John, Beverley, Hunsley-Beacon division of the wapentake of Harthill; liberty of Beverley; 3 miles from Beverley, 7 from Hull.—Pop. 74.

THICKETT, in the parish of Wheldrake, wapentake of Ouse and Derwent; 9 miles from York, 9 from Pocklington, 12 from Selby.

THIRKLEBY, in the parish of Kirby-Grindalyth, wapentake of Buckrose; 3 miles from Sledmere, 10 from Malton. —Population 39.

THIXENDALE, in the parish of Wharram-Percy, wapentake of Buckrose; 8 miles from Sledmere, 9 from Pocklington.—Population 137.

THORGANBY, in the parish of Thorganby, wapentake of Ouse and Derwent; 8 miles from Selby, 10 from Howden, 12 from York.—Population 294.

THORNGUMBALD, in the parish of Paul, south-division of the wapentake and liberty of Holderness; 2¼ miles from Hedon, 7¼ from Pattrington, 10¼ from Hull.—Pop. 190.

THORNHOLME, in the parish of Burton-Agnes, wapentake of Dickering; 4¼ miles from Bridlington, 7¼ from Driffield.—Population 81.

THORNTON, in the parish of Thornton, Wilton-Beacon division of the wapentake of Harthill; 4 miles from Pocklington, 7 from Market-Weighton, 9 from York.—Pop. 217.

THORPE, EAST, see *Easthorpe*.

THORPE, in the parish of Howden, wapentake and liberty of Howdenshire; 1 mile from Howden, 11 from Selby, 12 from South-Cave.—Population 54.

THORPE, in the parish of Rudston, wapentake of Dickering; (*Thorpe-Hall, the seat of William Bosville, Esq.*) 4 miles from Bridlington, 8 from Driffield, 8 from Hunmanby.

THORPE-BASSETT, in the parish of Thorpe-Bassett, wapentake of Buckrose; 5 miles from Malton, 16 from Driffield, 17 from Scarborough, 22 from York.—Pop. 145.

THORPE-BRANTINGHAM, in the parish of Brantingham Hunsley-Beacon division of the wapentake of Harthill; 2 miles from South-Cave, 9 from Hull, 12 from Beverley.

THORPE-LE-STREET, in the parish of Nunburnholme, Holme-Beacon division of the wapentake of Harthill; 2¼ miles from Market-Weighton, 4 from Pocklington, 12 from Beverley.—Population 15.

THORTLEBY, or THIRKLEBY, in the parish of Swine, middle-division of the wapentake and liberty of Holderness; 5 miles from Hedon, 7 from Hull, 10 from Beverley.

THWING, in the parish of Thwing, wapentake of Dickering; 8 miles from Bridlington, 10 from Driffield, 13 from Scarborough.—Population 217.

TIBTHORPE, in the parish of Kirkburn, Bainton-Beacon division of the wapentake of Harthill, 6¾ miles from Driffield, 12 from Beverley, 16¼ from Malton.—Population 132.

TICKTON, in the parish of St. John, Beverley, Hunsley-Beacon division of the wapentake of Harthill, liberty of Beverley; *(Tickton-Bridge, the seat of Major Coates)* 2¼ miles from Beverley, 11 from Hull, 11 from Hornsea.—Population 134.

TORMOND-HALL, in the parish of Hemingbrough, wapentake of Ouse and Derwent; *(the seat of John Burton, Esq.)* 2¼ miles from Selby, 7¼ from Howden, 14 from York.

TOWTHORPE, in the parish of Wharram-Percy, wapentake of Buckrose; 2 miles from Sledmere, 9 from Driffield, 9 from Malton.—Population 45.

TRESWICK, in the parish of Hayton, Holme-Beacon division of the wapentake of Harthill; 3¼ miles from Market-Weighton, 3¼ from Pocklington.

TUNSTALL, in the parish of Tunstall, middle division of the wapentake of Holderness, liberty of St. Peter; 8 miles from Hedon, 8 from Hornsea, 15 from Hull.—Pop. 145.

TURMER-HALL, in the parish of Swine, middle-division of the wapentake and liberty of Holderness; 4 miles from Hedon, 6 from Hull, 12 from Beverley.

U.

ULROME, or ULRAM, in the parish of Ulrome, north-division of the wapentake and liberty of Holderness; 6¾ miles from Hornsea, 9 from Bridlington, 12 from Driffield. 16 from Beverley.—Population 143.

UNCLEBY, in the parish of Kirby-Underdale, wapentake of Buckrose; 8 miles from Pocklington, 9 from Sledmere.

UPTON, in the parish of Skipsea, north-division of the wapentake and liberty of Holderness; 9½ miles from Bridlington, 11¼ from Driffield, 15 from Beverley.

W.

WAGHEN, in the parish of Waghen, middle-division of the wapentake of Holderness, liberty of St. Peter; 5 miles from Hull, 8 from Beverley, 12 from Hedon.—Population 299.

WALDBY, in the parish of Elloughton, Hunsley-Beacon division of the wapentake of Harthill; 5 miles from South-Cave, 8 from Beverley, 9 from Hull.—Population 29.

WALKINGTON, in the parish of Walkington, Hunsley-Beacon division of the wapentake of Harthill; 2¼ miles from Beverley, 7 from South-Cave, 11 from Hull.—Pop. 403.

WANSFORD, in the parish of Nafferton, wapentake of Dickering; 4 miles from Driffield, 10¼ from Bridlington.—Population 378.

WAPLINGTON, in the parish of Pocklington, Wilton-Beacon division of the wapentake of Harthill; *(the seat of Thomas Chatterton, Esq.)* 2¼ miles from Pocklington, 7 from Market-Weighton, 11 from York.—Population 11.

WARTER, in the parish of Warter, Bainton-Beacon division of the wapentake of Harthill; 5 miles from Pocklington, 11 from Driffield, 12 from Beverley.—Population 355.

WARTER-HALL, in the parish of Warter, Bainton-Beacon division of the wapentake of Harthill; *(the seat of Mrs Pennington)* 4 miles from Pocklington, 6¼ from Market-Weighton, 14 from Beverley.

WASSAND, in the parish of Sigglesthorne, north-division of the wapentake and liberty of Holderness; *(the seat of Marmaduke Constable, Esq.)* 11 miles from Beverley, 13 from Driffield, 14 from Hull, 16 from Bridlington.

WATTON, in the parish of Watton, Bainton-Beacon division of the wapentake of Harthill; *(Watton-Abbey, the seat of Mrs. Bethell)* 6 miles from Driffield, 7¼ from Beverley, 12 from Market-Weighton.—Population 197.

WAXHOLME, in the parish of Owthorn, middle-division of the wapentake and liberty of Holderness; 6 miles from Pattrington; 10 from Hedon, 12¼ from Hull.—Pop. 61.

WEADLAND, in the parish of Brandesburton, north-division of the wapentake and liberty of Holderness; 5 miles from Driffield, 10 from Beverley, 18 from Hull.

WEAVERTHORPE, in the parish of Weaverthorpe, wapentake of Buckrose; 4 miles from Sledmere, 12 from Malton.—Population 182.

WEEDLEY, in the parish of South-Cave, Hunsley-Beacon division of the wapentake of Harthill; 3 miles from South-Cave, 6 from Beverley.

WEEL, in the parish of St. John, Beverley, Hunsley-Beacon division of the wapentake of Harthill, liberty of Beverley; 1¼ mile from Beverley, 8 from Hull, 15 from Hedon.—Population 96.

WEETON, in the parish of Welwick, south-division of the wapentake and liberty of Holderness; 2¼ miles from Pattrington, 12¼ from Hedon.

WEIGHTON, MARKET, in the parish of Market-Weighton, Holme-Beacon division of the wapentake of Harthill, a part in the liberty of St. Peter; 6¼ miles from Pocklington, 8 from South-Cave, 10 from Beverley, 12 from Howden, 18 from Selby, 19 from York, from London, *by Howden* 193¾, *by York* 217¼.—*Market*, Wednesday.—*Fairs*, May 14, September 25, for Horses, Horned Cattle, Sheep, &c.—*Principal Inns*, Briggs' New-Inn, King's Arms, Half-Moon.—Population 1,183.

WEIGHTON, LITTLE, in the parish of Rowley, Hunsley-Beacon division of the wapentake of Harthill; 4 miles from South-Cave, 5 from Beverley, 9 from Hull.

WELHAM, in the parish of Norton, wapentake of Buckrose; *(the seat of Robert Bower, Esq.)* 1 mile from Malton, 11 from Sledmere.

WELHAM-BRIDGE, in the parish of Holme-on-Spadling-Moor, Holme-Beacon division of the wapentake of Harthill; 5 miles from Howden, 7 from Market-Weighton.

WELTON, in the parish of Welton, wapentake and liberty of Howdenshire; *(the seat of T. Williamson, Esq.)* 4 miles from South-Cave, 9 from Beverley, 10 from Hull.—Population 449.

WELWICK, in the parish of Welwick, south-division of the wapentake and liberty of Holderness; 2 miles from Pattrington, 12 from Hedon.—Population 312.

WELWICKTHORPE, in the parish of Welwick, south-division of the wapentake and liberty of Holderness; 1 mile from Pattrington, 11 from Hedon.

WESTALL, in the parish of Aldbrough, middle division of the wapentake and liberty of Holderness; 9 miles from Hedon, 14 from Hull, 15 from Beverley.

WESTOW, in the parish of Westow, wapentake of Buckrose; *(the seat of Joseph Field, Esq.)* 6 miles from Malton, 12 from Sledmere, 14 from York.—Population 274.

WETWANG, in the parish of Wetwang, wapentake of Buckrose, liberty of St. Peter; 4 miles from Sledmere, 6 from Driffield, 13 from Malton.—Population 193.

WHARRAM-GRANGE, in the parish of Wharram-le-Street, wapentake of Buckrose; 5 miles from Malton, 5 from Sledmere, 12 from Driffield.

WHARRAM-LE-STREET, in the parish of Wharram-le-Street, wapentake of Buckrose; 5 miles from Sledmere, 7 from Malton, 21¼ from Beverley.—Population 112.

WHARRAM-PERCY, in the parish of Wharram-Percy, wapentake of Buckrose; 4¼ miles from Sledmere, 7 from Malton.—Population 38.

WHELDRAKE, in the parish of Wheldrake, wapentake of Ouse and Derwent; 8 miles from York, 10 from Pocklington, 12 from Selby.—Population 493.

WHOLESEA, in the parish of Holme-on-Spalding-Moor, Holme-Beacon division of the wapentake of Harthill; 6 miles from Market-Weighton, 8 from Howden.

WILBERFOSS, in the parish of Wilberfoss, Wilton-Beacon division of the wapentake of Harthill; *(the seat of Robert Wright, Esq.)* 5¼ miles from Pocklington, 7¼ from York, 10¼ from Market-Weighton.—Population 289.

WILFEHOLME, in the parish of Beswick, Bainton-Beacon division of the wapentake of Harthill; 9 miles from Driffield, 10 from Beverley, 17 from Pocklington.

WILLERBY, in the parish of Willerby, wapentake of Dickering; 6 miles from Hunmanby, 6¼ from Scarborough, 12 from Bridlington.—Population 29.

WILLERBY, in the parishes of Cottingham and Kirk-Ella, Hunsley-Beacon division of the wapentake of Harthill, and County of the Town of Kingston-upon-Hull; *(the seat of Thomas Osborne, Esq.)* 6 miles from Hull, 7 from South-Cave, 8 from Beverley.—Population 138.

WILLYTOFT, in the parish of Bubwith, Holme-Beacon division of the wapentake of Harthill; 5 miles from Howden, 10 from Selby.

WILSTHORPE, in the parish of Bridlington, wapentake of Dickering; 2¼ miles from Bridlington, 10 from Driffield.

WILTON, BISHOP, *(which gives name to the division)* in the parish of Bishop-Wilton, Wilton-Beacon division of the wapentake of Harthill, liberty of St. Peter; 4 miles from Pocklington, 18 from York, 14 from Malton.—Population 398.

WINBRY-HILL, in the parish of Wilberfoss, Wilton-Beacon division of the wapentake of Harthill; 6 miles from Pocklington, 9 from York.

WINESTEAD, in the parish of Winestead, south-division of the wapentake and liberty of Holderness; *(the seat of Henry Maisters, Esq. Winestead-Hall, the seat of Sir Robert D'Arcy Hilyard, Bart.)* 1¼ mile from Pattrington, 8¼ from Hedon, 17 from Hull.—Population 103.

WINKTON, in the parish of Barmston, north-division of the wapentake and liberty of Holderness; 6 miles from Bridlington, 10 from Hornsea.

WINTRINGHAM, in the parish of Wintringham, wapentake of Buckrose; 7 miles from Malton, 7 from Sledmere. —Population 229.

WITHERNSEA, in the parish of Hollym, south-division of the wapentake and liberty of Holderness; 4 miles from Pattrington, 12 from Hedon.—Population 76.

WITHERNWICK, in the parish of Withernwick, north-division of the wapentake of Holderness, liberty of St. Peter; 6 miles from Hedon, 13½ from Beverley, 14 from Hull, 17 from Driffield.—Population 292.

WOLD-COTTAGE, in the parish of Thwing, wapentake of Dickering; *(the seat of Edward Topham, Esq.)* 8 miles from Bridlington, 10 from Driffield, 13 from Scarborough.

WOLD-HOUSE, in the parish of Great-Driffield, Bainten-Beacon division of the wapentake of Harthill; 3 miles from Driffield, 11 from Bridlington, 16 from Beverley.

WOLD-NEWTON, in the parish of Wold-Newton, wapentake of Dickering; 8 miles from Bridlington, 13 from Scarborough.—Population 106.

WOODALL, in the parish of Hemingbrough, wapentake of Ouse and Derwent; 6 miles from Selby, 7 from Howden, 14 from York.

WOOD-HOUSE, in the parish of Pocklington, Wilton-Beacon division of the wapentake of Harthill; *(the seat of Robert Denison, Esq.)* 1 mile from Pocklington, 8 from Market-Weighton, 14 from York.

WOOD-HOUSE, in the parish of Sutton-on-Derwent, Wilton-Beacon division of the wapentake of Harthill; 5 miles Pocklington, 8 from York, 13 from Selby.

WOODLEY, in the parish of Kirby-Underdale, wapentake

of Buckrose; 9 miles from Malton, 9 from Sledmere, 14 from York.

WOODMANSEA, in the parish of St. John, Beverley, Hunsley-Beacon division of the wapentake of Harthill, liberty of Beverley; 2 miles from Beverley, 7 from Hull.—Population 229.

WRESSLE, in the parish of Wressle, Holme-Beacon division of the wapentake of Harthill; *(the seat of the Earl of Egremont)* 4 miles from Howden, 6½ from Selby, 13 from Market-Weighton.—Population 191.

WYTON, in the parish of Swine, middle-division of the wapentake and liberty of Holderness; 4 miles from Hedon, 6 from Hull, 14 from Beverley.—Population 86.

Y.

YAPHAM, in the parish of Pocklington, Wilton-Beacon division of the wapentake of Harthill; 3 miles from Pocklington, 10 from York, 10 from Market-Weighton.—Population 107.

YEDDINGHAM, and YEDDINGHAM-BRIDGE, in the parish of Yeddingham, wapentake of Buckrose; 9 miles from Malton, 10 from Sledmere, 13 from Scarborough.—Population 115.

YOKEFLEET, or YOAKFLEET, in the parish of Howden, wapentake and liberty of Howdenshire; 5 miles from Howden, 12 from South-Cave, 15 from Selby.—Pop. 165.

YOULTHORPE, in the parish of Bishop-Wilton, Wilton-Beacon division of the wapentake of Harthill, liberty of St. Peter; 5 miles from Pocklington, 9 from York, 13 from Malton.—Population 130.

EAST-RIDING. 137

LORD LIEUTENANT.

THE RIGHT HON. LORD MULGRAVE,
Mulgrave-Castle.

NAMES OF ACTING MAGISTRATES.

BARNARD, H. BOLDERO,	Esq.	*Cave-Castle.*
BETHELL, RICHARD,	Esq.	*Catfoss.*
BEVERLEY, WILLIAM,	Esq.	*Beverley.*
BROWN, JONAS,	Esq.	*Sculcoates.*
CONSTABLE, MARMADUKE,	Esq.	*Wassand.*
CONSTABLE, CHARLES,	Clerk,	*Beverley.*
CREYKE, RALPH,	Esq.	*Marton.*
CREYKE, RALPH, Jun.	Esq.	*Beverley.*
DENISON, ROBERT,	Esq.	*Kildwick-Percy.*
EGLIN, THOMAS,	Clerk,	*Stillingfleet.*
ELLIOT, ROBERT,	Clerk,	*Huggate.*
FOULIS, JOHN ROBINSON,	Esq.	*West-Heslerton.*
GILBY, JOHN,	Clerk,	*Beverley.*
GRIMSTON, THOMAS,	Esq.	*Grimston.*
GRIMSTON, HENRY,	Esq.	*Etton.*
KIPLING, THOMAS, Dean of Peterborough,	D. D.	*Holme.*
KNOWSLEY, GEORGE,	Esq.	*Cottingham.*
LUNDY, FRANCIS,	Clerk,	*Lockington.*
OSBALDESTON, H. B.	Esq.	*Hunmanby.*
PRESTON, THOMAS,	Clerk,	*Moreby.*
READ, T. CUTLER RUDSTON,	Clerk,	*Sandhutton.*
SIMPSON, JOHN,	Clerk,	*Rooss.*
SYKES, SIR M. M.	Bart.	*Sledmere.*
SYKES, CHRISTOPHER.	Clerk,	*Westow.*
SYKES, RICHARD,	Clerk,	*West-Ella.*
TOPHAM, EDWARD,	Esq.	*Wold-Cottage.*
TORRE, NICHOLAS,	Clerk,	*Rise.*
VAVASOUR, SIR HENRY,	Bart.	*Melburn.*

LORDS AND CHIEF BAILIFFS.

THE RIGHT REV. THE LORD BISHOP OF DURHAM, } HOWDENSHIRE.
FRANCIS CONSTABLE, Esq. *Burton-Constable,* } THE SEIGNIORY OF HOLDERNESS.

EAST-RIDING.

CLERK OF THE PEACE.

RICHARD WILLIAM JOHNSTON, Esq. *Darlington*.
JOHN LOCKWOOD, Esq. *Beverley*, his Deputy.

TREASURER.

HENRY JOHN SHEPHERD, Esq. *Beverley*.

CORONERS.

GEORGE CONYERS, ... *Driffield*.
THOMAS SHEPLEY, ... *Selby*.
WILLIAM IVESON, ... *Hedon*.
JAMES IVESON, ... *Ditto*.
ROBERT SPOFFORTH, Jun. .. *Howden*.

CHIEF CONSTABLES.

R. SMELT, *Beverley*, } HUNSLEY-BEACON, }
R. ROBINSON, *Lockington*, } BAINTON-BEACON, } HARTHILL.
B. CLARKSON, *Holme-House*, } HOLME-BEACON, }
G. BAGLEY, *Pocklington*, } WILTON-BEACON, }
R. POWLEY, *Hornsea*, } NORTH, ... }
J. ROGERSON, *Hilston*, } MIDDLE, ... } HOLDERNESS.
R. SIMPSON, *Pattrington*, } SOUTH, ... }
W. JOHNSON, *Fulford*, ... OUSE & DERWENT
JOHN HUDSON, *Howsam*, ... BUCKROSE.
C. LAYBORN, *Nafferton*, ... DICKERING.
E. SPOFFORTH, *Howden*, ... HOWDENSHIRE.

CLERK OF GENERAL MEETINGS OF LIEUTENANTCY.

JOHN LOCKWOOD, Esq. *Beverley*.

EAST-RIDING.

CLERKS OF SUBDIVISION MEETINGS OF LIEUTENANTCY.

J. BRAMWELL, *Hull.* .... Hull & County.

J. LOCKWOOD, *Beverley.*
- Hunsley-Beacon, Holme-Beacon, Wilton-Beacon, } Harthill.
- North, Middle, South, } Holderness.
- .... Howdenshire.
- .... Ouse & Derwent.
- .... Beverley.

W. WARDELL, *Beverley.* } Bainton-Beacon, Harthill.
M. PRICKETT, *Bridlington.* } .... Dickering.
G. BRITTON, *Sledmere,* } .... Buckrose.

BAILIFFS.

THOMAS MASTERMAN, *Malton,* Buckrose.
EDMUND MALTBY, *Driffield,* ... Dickering.
JOHN GROVES, *Pocklington,* .... Harthill.
WILLIAM BROOM, *Howden,* .... Ouse & Derwent.

BAILIFFS AT LARGE, WHO RESIDE IN THIS RIDING.

TIMOTHY MASON, ... *Hull.*
GEORGE SIMMONS, ... *Ditto.*
JOHN DAY, ... *Beverley.*
CHARLES TATE, ... *Bridlington.*

DEPUTY BAILIFFS.

JOHN JARUM, *Hedon,* .... Holderness.
WILLIAM BROOM, *Howden,* .... Howdenshire.
JOHN DAY, *Beverley* .... Beverley.
TIMOTHY MASON, *Hull,* .... Hull.

DIRECTIONS FOR WARRANTS, ON WRITS, TO LIBERTIES.

BEVERLEY. .... To the Mayor of the Town of Beverley, and his Serjeants at Mace.
HEDON. .... To the Mayor of the Town of Hedon, and his Serjeants at Mace.
HOLDERNESS. ..... To the Chief Bailiff of the Liberty of Holderness, and his Deputies.
HOWDENSHIRE. ... To the Chief Bailiff of the Liberty of Howden and Howdenshire, and his Deputies.

SESSIONS.

The *Christmas* General Quarter Sessions of the Peace, are held at Beverley, on Tuesday in the first whole week after the Epiphany;—*Easter Sessions*, on Tuesday in the first whole week after Easter;—*Midsummer Sessions*, on Tuesday in the first whole week after St. Thomas the Martyr;—and *Michaelmas Sessions*, on Tuesday in the first whole week after St. Michael.

WEST-RIDING.

ABBERFORD, in the parishes of Abberford and Sherburn, wapentakes of Skirack (lower division) and Barkston-Ash, liberties of the Honour of Pontefract and St. Peter; *(the seat of Sir Charles Turner, Bart.)* 4¼ miles from Tadcaster, 7½ from Wetherby, 9¼ from Ferrybridge, 11¼ from Leeds, 14¼ from Selby, 13¼ from York, 186 from London.—*Market*, Wednesday.—*Fairs*, last Mondays in April and May, first Monday in October, first Monday after St. Luke, first Monday after All Saints, for Horses, Horned Cattle, Sheep, &c. If either of the two last days fall on a Monday, the Fair will be held on that day.—*Principal Inn*, Swan.—Population 650.

ABDY, in the parish of Wath, north-division of the wapentake of Strafforth and Tickhill, liberty of Tickhill; 5 miles from Rotherham, 7 from Barnsley, 10 from Doncaster.

ACKWORTH, HIGH, in the parish of High-Ackworth, wapentake of Osgoldcross, liberty of the Honour of Pontefract; *(the seat of Col. Baldwin)* 3 miles from Pontefract, 6 from Ferrybridge, 8 from Wakefield.—Population 1,432.

ACKWORTH-LOW, in the parish of High-Ackworth, wapentake of Osgoldcross, liberty of the Honour of Pontefract; *(Ackworth-Villa, the seat of Charles Mortimer, Esq.)* 3 miles from Pontefract, 9 from Wakefield, 13 from Doncaster.

ACKWORTH-MOOR-TOP, in the parish of High-Ackworth, wapentake of Osgoldcross, liberty of the Honour of Pontefract; *(the seat of the Earl of Darlington)* 4 miles from Pontefract, 7 from Wakefield.

ACKWORTH-PARK, in the parish of High-Ackworth, wapentake of Osgoldcross, liberty of the Honour of Pontefract; *(the seat of John Harwood Jessop, Esq.)* 2¼ miles from Pontefract, 9¼ from Wakefield.

DDINGHAM, in the parish of Addingham, east-division of the wapentake of Staincliffe, liberty of Clifford's Fee; 6 miles from Skipton, 7 from Keighley, 9 from Otley.——Population 1,157.

T

ADDLE, in the parish of Addle, upper-division of the wapentake of Skirack; 4 miles from Harewood, 4 from Leeds, 8 from Otley.—Population 606.

ADDLETHORPE, in the parish of Spofforth, upper-division of the wapentake of Claro; 2¼ miles from Wetherby, 5 from Knaresborough.

ADLINGFLEET, in the parish of Adlingfleet, wapentake of Osgoldcross, liberty of the Honour of Pontefract; 8 miles from Howden, 8 from Crowle, *(Linc.)* 17 from Snaith.—Population 203.

ADWALTON, in the parish of Birstall, Morley-division of the wapentake of Agbrigg and Morley, liberty of the Honour of Pontefract; 5¼ miles from Bradford, 6¾ from Leeds, 8¼ from Wakefield.—*No Market.—Fairs*, Thursdays in Easter and Whitsun-weeks, for Horses and Horned Cattle; and every other Thursday, for Lean Cattle.

ADWICKE-IN-THE-STREET, in the parish of Adwicke-in-the-Street, north-division of the wapentake of Strafforth and Tickhill, liberty of Tickhill; *(Adwicke-Hall, the seat of George Wroughton, Esq.)* 4 miles from Doncaster, 6 from Rotherham, 10 from Pontefract, 12 from Barnsley.—Population 284.

ADWICKE-UPON-DEARN, in the parish of Adwicke-upon-Dearn, north-division of the wapentake of Strafforth and Tickhill, liberty of Tickhill; 6 miles from Rotherham, 8 from Doncaster.—Population 142.

AGBRIGG, *(which gives name to the division)* in the parish of Warmfield, Agbrigg-division of the wapentake of Agbrigg and Morley, liberty of the Honour of Pontefract; 1¼ mile from Wakefield, 8 from Pontefract, 9¼ from Barnsley.

AGDEN, in the parish of Mitton, west-division of the wapentake and liberty of Staincliffe; 5 miles from Clitheroe, *(Lanc.)* 11 from Blackburn, *(ditto)* 12 from Gisburn.

AIKTON, in the parish of Fetherston, Agbrigg-division of the wapentake of Agbrigg and Morley, liberty of the Honour of Pontefract; 3 miles from Pontefract, 5¼ from Wakefield.—Population 86.

AIRMYN, in the parish of Snaith, wapentake of Osgoldcross, liberty of the Honour of Pontefract; 3¼ miles from Howden, 6¼ from Snaith, 8 from Thorne.—Population 391.

AIRMYN, LITTLE, in the parish of Drax, wapentake of Barkston-Ash; 3¼ miles from Howden, 6¼ from Snaith.

AIRTON, in the parish of Kirkby-Malhamdale, west-division of the wapentake of Staincliffe, liberty of Clifford's Fee; 6 miles from Settle, 8 from Skipton, 12 from Kettlewell.—Population 139.

AISMUNDERBY, in the parish of Ripon, lower-division of the wapentake of Claro, liberty of Ripon.; ¼ of a mile from Ripon, 6 from Boroughbridge.—Population 496.

AKEHOLME, or ALKHOLME, in the parish of Finningly, *(Notts.)* south-division of the wapentake of Strafforth and Tickhill; 6¼ miles from Bawtry, 7 from Thorne.

ALDBOROUGH, in the parish of Aldborough, lower-division of the wapentake of Claro, a part in the liberty of St. Peter; 2 miles from Boroughbridge, 7 from Knaresborough, 7 from Ripon, 16 from York.—Sends two Members to Parliament.—Population 445.

ALDERMANSHEAD, in the parish of Penistone, wapentake of Staincross, liberty of the Honour of Pontefract; 2¼ miles from Penistone, 9¼ from Barnsley, 13 from Sheffield.

ALDFIELD, *(Aldfield-Spa, a Mineral Water)* in the parish of Ripon, lower-division of the wapentake of Claro, liberty of Ripon; 4 miles from Ripon, 8 from Pateleybridge, 10 from Boroughbridge.—Population 122.

ALDWARKE, in the parish of Ecclesfield, north-division of the wapentake of Strafforth and Tickhill; *(the seat of J. S. Foljambe, Esq.)* 2 miles from Rotherham, 10 from Doncaster.

ALECOMDEN, in the parish of Halifax, Morley-division of the wapentake of Agbrigg and Morley, liberty of the Honour of Pontefract; 9 miles from Colne, *(Lanc.)* 11 from Halifax.

ALLERTON, in the parish of Bradford, Morley-division of the wapentake of Agbrigg and Morley, liberty of the Honour of Pontefract; 4 miles from Bradford, 7 from Halifax.—Population 809.

ALLERTON-BYWATER, in the parish of Kippax, lower-division of the wapentake of Skirack, liberty of the Honour of Pontefract; 5 miles from Pontefract, 8 from Leeds, 8 from Wakefield.—Population. 331.

ALLERTON, CHAPEL, in the parish of Leeds, lower-division of the wapentake of Skirack, liberty of the Honour of Pontefract; *(the seat of William Bingley, Esq.)* 2¼ miles from Leeds, 5½ from Harewood, 9 from Wetherby, 11 from Otley.—Population 1,054.

ALLERTON-LEE, in the parish of Bradford, Morley-division of the wapentake of Agbrigg and Morley, liberty of the Honour of Pontefract; 3½ miles from Bradford, 6½ from Halifax.

ALLERTON-MAULEVERER, in the parish of Allerton-Mauleverer, upper-division of the wapentake of Claro; 4½ miles from Knaresborough, 5 from Wetherby, 7 from Boroughbridge.—Population 182.

ALMHOLME, in the parish of Arksey, north-division of the wapentake of Strafforth and Tickhill, liberty of Tickhill; 5¼ miles from Doncaster, 8 from Thorne.

ALMONDBURY, in the parish of Almondbury, Agbrigg-division of the wapentake of Agbrigg and Morley, liberty of the Honour of Pontefract; 2 miles from Huddersfield, 10 from Halifax, 10¼ from Penistone, 11 from Wakefield.—Population 3,751.

ALTOFTS, and ALTOFTS-HALL, in the parish of Normanton, Agbrigg-division of the wapentake of Agbrigg and Morley, liberty of the Honour of Pontefract; 4 miles from Wakefield, 5¼ from Pontefract.—Population 334.

ALVERLEY-GRANGE, in the parish of Warmsworth, south-division of the wapentake of Strafforth and Tickhill; *(the seat of Bryan Derwent Cook, Esq.)* 3 miles from Doncaster, 10 from Rotherham.

ALVERTHORPE, in the parish of Wakefield, Agbrigg-division of the wapentake of Agbrigg and Morley, liberty of the Manor of Wakefield; 1 mile from Wakefield, 4 from Dewsbury.—Population 3,105.

ALWOODLEY, in the parish of Harewood, upper-division of the wapentake of Skirack; 3 miles from Harewood, 5¼ from Leeds, 11 from Otley, 14 from Tadcaster.—Pop. 143.

AMPHER-BRIDGE, in the parish of Pannal, lower-division of the wapentake of Claro, liberty of Knaresborough; 4 miles from Knaresborough, 7 from Ripley.

ANGRAM, in the parish of Kirkby-Malzeard, lower-division of the wapentake of Claro; 4 miles from Kettlewell, 10 from Middleham, 13 from Pateleybridge.

ANSTON, NORTH, or CHAPEL, in the parish of South-Anston, south-division of the wapentake of Strafforth and Tickhill, liberties of St. Peter and Tickhill; 6 miles from Worksop, *(Notts.)* 8 from Rotherham, 9 from Tickhill.

ANSTON, SOUTH, or CHURCH, in the parish of South-Anston, south-division of the wapentake of Strafforth and Tickhill, liberties of St. Peter and Tickhill; 6 miles from Worksop, *(Notts.)* 8 from Rotherham, 9 from Tickhill, 12 from Sheffield.—Population 625.

APPERLEY-BRIDGE, in the parish of Calverley, Morley division of the wapentake of Agbrigg and Morley; 3 miles from Bradford, 5 from Otley, 10¼ from Leeds.

APPLEDAY, in the parish of Royston, wapentake of Staincross, liberty of the Honour of Pontefract; 4¼ miles from Barnsley, 6¼ from Wakefield, 10 from Pontefract.

APPLETREWICK, in the parish of Burnsall, east-division of the wapentake of Staincliffe, liberty of Clifford's Fee;

WEST-RIDING. 145

8 miles from Skipton, 8 from Pateleybridge, 10 from Kettlewell.—*No Market.*—*Fair*, October 25 for Horses and Horned Cattle.—Population 244.

ARDSLEY, in the parish of Darfield, wapentake of Staincross, liberty of the Honour of Pontefract; *(the seats of John Micklethwaite, and Richard Taylor, Esqrs.)* 2½ miles from Barnsley, 9 from Rotherham, 9½ from Wakefield, 13 from Doncaster.—Population 461.

ARDSLEY-CARR, in the parish of East-Ardsley, Agbrigg division of the wapentake of Agbrigg and Morley, liberty of the Honour of Pontefract; 2½ miles from Wakefield, 7 from Leeds, 11¼ from Bradford.

ARDSLEY-EAST, in the parish of East-Ardsley, Agbrigg division of the wapentake of Agbrigg and Morley, liberties of the Honour of Pontefract; 3½ miles from Wakefield, 8 from Leeds, 11¼ from Bradford.—Population 686.

ARDSLEY-WEST, or WESTERTON, in the parish of Woodchurch, Agbrigg-division of the wapentake of Agbrigg and Morley, liberty of the Manor of Wakefield; 4¼ miles from Wakefield, 5 from Dewsbury, 9¼ from Bradford.—Population 1,032.

ARKENDALE, in the parish of Knaresborough, lower-division of the wapentake of Claro, liberty of Knaresborough; 4 miles from Knaresborough, 4 from Boroughbridge.—Population 218.

ARKSEY, in the parish of Arksey, north-division of the wapentake of Strafforth and Tickhill, liberty of Tickhill; *(the seat of Thomas Foster, Esq.)* 3¼ miles from Doncaster, 9 from Thorne.—Population 980.

ARMENTHWAITE, in the parish of Kirby-Malzeard, lower-division of the wapentake of Claro; 7 miles from Kettlewell, 10 from Pateleybridge.

ARMITAGEFOLD, in the parish of Almondbury, Agbrigg-division of the wapentake of Agbrigg and Morley; 2¼ miles from Huddersfield, 10 from Halifax.

ARMLEY, in the parish of Leeds, Morley-division of the wapentake of Agbrigg and Morley, liberty of the Honour of of Pontefract; 3 miles from Leeds, 9 from Bradford.—Population 2,695.

ARMLEY-HOUSE, in the parish of Leeds, Morley-division of the wapentake of Agbrigg and Morley, liberty of the Honour of Pontefract; *(the seat of Benjamin Gott, Esq.)* 3¼ miles from Leeds 9 from Bradford.

ARMTHORPE, in the parish of Armthorpe, south-division of the wapentake of Strafforth and Tickhill; 4 miles from Doncaster, 7¼ from Bawtry, 7½ from Thorne.—Pop. 272.

ARNECLIFFE, in the parish of Arnecliffe, west-division of the wapentake and liberty of Staincliffe; 5 miles from Kettlewell, 11 from Settle, 16 from Skipton.—Population 241.

ARNECLIFFE-COTE, in the parish of Arnecliffe, west-division of the wapentake and liberty of Staincliffe; 4 miles from Kettlewell, 11 from Settle, 15 from Skipton.

ARNFORTH, in the parish of Long-Preston, west-division of the wapentake and liberty of Staincliffe; 6¼ miles from Settle, 10 from Skipton.

ARNOLD-BIGGIN, in the parish of Gisburn, west-division of the wapentake and liberty of Staincliffe; 11 miles from Settle, 11 from Skipton, 11 from Burnley, *(Lanc.)*

ARTHINGTON, in the parish of Addle, upper-division of the wapentake of Skirack; *(Arthington-Hall, the seat of Mrs. Caruthers)* 3 miles from Harewood, 5 from Otley, 6 from Leeds.—Population 360.

ARTHINGTON-NUNNERY, in the parish of Addle, upper division of the wapentake of Skirack; 2 miles from Harewood, 6 from Otley, 6 from Leeds.

ASHFORD, or ASHFORTH-SIDE, in the parish of Kirby-Malzeard, lower-division of the wapentake of Claro; 3 miles from Pateleybridge, 13 from Skipton.

ASKRON, or ASKERNE, in the parish of Campsall, wapentake of Osgoldcross, liberty of the Honour of Pontefract; 7 miles from Doncaster, 11 from Ferrybridge.

ASKWITH, in the parish of Weston, upper-division of the wapentake of Claro; 3 miles from Otley, 13 from Leeds, 13 from Skipton.—Population 317.

ASSON-THORPE, in the parish of Fishlake, north-division of the wapentake of Strafforth and Tickhill; 4 miles from Thorne, 7¼ from Snaith.

ASTLEY, in the parish of Swillington, lower-division of the wapentake of Skirack, liberty of the Honour of Pontefract; 6 miles from Leeds, 8 from Wakefield, 8 from Pontefract.

ASTON, in the parish of Aston, south-division of the wapentake of Strafforth and Tickhill; *(the seats of Mrs. Verelst and the Rev. Christopher Alderson,)* 6 miles from Rotherham, 8¼ from Sheffield, 9¼ from Worksop, *(Notts.)* —Population 586.

ATTERCLIFFE, in the parish of Sheffield, south-division of the wapentake of Strafforth and Tickhill, liberty of Hallamshire; *(the seat of Gamelial Milner, Esq. and New-Hall, the seat of Richard Swallow, Esq.)* 1½ mile from Sheffield, 4¼ from Rotherham, 13 from Chesterfield, *(Derby.)*—Population 2.281.

AUDZUS, in the parish of South-Anston, south-division of

the wapentake of Strafforth and Tickhill; 5 miles from Worksop, *(Notts.)* 6¼ from Tickhill, 9¼ from Rotherham.

AUGHTON, in the parish of Aston, south-division of the wapentake of Strafforth and Tickhill; 4 miles from Rotherham, 9¼ from Worksop,*(Notts.)* 18 from Mansfield,*(ditto.)*

AUKLEY, in the parish of Finningley, *(Notts.)* south-division of the wapentake of Strafforth and Tickhill, a part in the soke of Doncaster; 6 miles from Doncaster, 6¼ from Bawtry.—Population 406.

AUSBY, in the parish of Ilkley, upper-division of the wapentake of Claro; 7 miles from Otley, 9 from Skipton.

AUSTERFIELD, in the parish of Blythe, *(Notts.)* south-division of the wapentake of Strafforth and Tickhill; 3 miles from Bawtry, 8 from Doncaster.—Population 232.

AUSTERLANDS, in the parish of Rochdale, *(Lanc.)* Agbrigg-division of the wapentake of Agbrigg and Morley; 9 miles from Rochdale, *(Lanc.)* 10 from Manchester, *(ditto)* 15 from Huddersfield.

AUSTONLEY, or HORSTENLY, in the parish of Almondbury, Agbrigg-division of the wapentake of Agbrigg and Morley, liberty of the Manor of Wakefield; 7 miles from Huddersfield, 15 from Halifax.—Population 674.

AUSTHORPE, in the parish of Whitchurch, lower-division of the wapentake of Skirack; 4 miles from Pontefract, 9 from Wakefield, 10 from Wetherby, 11 from Ferrybridge. —Population 103.

AUSTWICK, in the parish of Clapham, wapentake of Ewcross, *(the seats of C. and T. Inglebys, Esqrs.)* 5 miles from Settle, 12 from Kirby-Lonsdale, *(Westm.)* 21 from Skipton.—*No Market.*—*Fair*, Thursday before Whitsuntide, for Horned Cattle, &c.—Population 478.

AZERLEY, in the parish of Kirby-Malzeard, lower-division of the wapentake of Claro; *(the seat of Major Hall)* 5 miles from Ripon, 5¼ from Masham, 15 from Knaresborough.—Population 521.

B.

BADSWORTH, in the parish of Badsworth, wapentake of Osgoldcross, liberty of the Honour of Pontefract; *(Badsworth-Hall, the seat of J. P. Neville, Esq.)* 4 miles from Pontefract 6 from Ferrybridge, 10 from Wakefield.— Population 182.

BAGDEN, LOWER, in the parish of Penistone, wapentake of Staincross, liberty of the Honour of Pontefract; 4¼ miles from Penistone, 6 from Barnsley, 10¼ from Wakefield.

BAGDEN, UPPER, in the parish of Penistone, wapentake of Staincross, liberty of the Honour of Pontefract; 4 miles from Penistone, 6 from Barnsley, 11 from Wakefield.

BAGLEY, in the parish of Tickhill, south-division of the wapentake of Strafforth and Tickhill, liberty of Tickhill; 1 mile from Tickhill, 8 from Worksop, *(Notts.)* 8 from Doncaster.

BAILDON, in the parish of Otley, lower-division of the wapentake of Skirack, liberty of Ripon; 3 miles from Otley, 4 from Bradford, 15 from Leeds.—Population 1,719.

BAITINGS, in the parish of Halifax, Morley-division of the wapentake of Agbrigg and Morley; 8 miles from Rochdale, *(Lanc.)* 8¼ from Halifax, 12 from Huddersfield.

BALK, in the parish of Darfield, wapentake of Staincross, liberty of the Honour of Pontefract; 8 miles from Barnsley, 9 from Rotherham, 11 from Sheffield.

BALLIFIELD, in the parish of Hansworth, south-division of the wapentake of Strafforth and Tickhill; *(the seat of John Jubb, Esq.)* 4 miles from Sheffield, 5 from Rotherham, 13¼ from Worksop, *(Notts.)*

BALNE, in the parish of Snaith, wapentake of Osgoldcross, liberty of the Honour of Pontefract; 4 miles from Snaith, 9 from Pontefract.—Population 312.

BALNE-CROFT, and BALNE-HOUSE, in the parish of Snaith, wapentake of Osgoldcross, liberty of the Honour of Pontefract; 4 miles from Snaith, 9 from Pontefract.

BANKS, in the parish of Silkston, wapentake of Staincross, liberty of the Honour of Pontefract; *(the seat of Samuel Thorp, Esq.)* 3 miles from Penistone, 4¼ from Barnsley, 10 from Wakefield.

BANKSIDE, in the parish of Thorne, north-division of the wapentake of Strafforth and Tickhill; 4 miles from Snaith 4 from Thorne, 14 from Howden.

BANKSIDE-HOUSES, in the parish of Snaith, wapentake of Osgoldcross liberty of the Honour of Pontefract; 4 miles from Thorne, 4 from Snaith, 14 from Howden.

BANK-TOP, in the parish of Halifax, Morley-division of the wapentake of Agbrigg and Morley; 1 mile from Halifax 6¼ from Bradford, 9 from Huddersfield.

BANK-TOP, and BANK-TOP-INN, in the parish of Darfield, wapentake of Staincross, liberty of the Honour of Pontefract; 1¼ mile from Barnsley, 11 from Wakefield, 12¼ from Sheffield.

BANNER-CROSS, in the parish of Sheffield, south-division

WEST-RIDING. 149

– of the wapentake of Strafforth and Tickhill; *(the seat of Brigadier General Murray)* 2 miles from Sheffield, 8 from Rotherham, 12 from Chesterfield, *(Derby.)*

BARAUGH, in the parish of Darton, wapentake of Staincross, liberty of the Honour of Pontefract; 3 miles from Barnsley, 5 from Penistone, 9¼ from Wakefield.—Pop. 362.

BARBOT-HALL, in the parish of Rotherham, south-division of the wapentake of Strafforth and Tickhill, liberty of Tickhill; 1 mile from Rotherham, 11 from Barnsley, 13 from Doncaster.

BARCROFT, in the parish of Bingley, upper-division of the wapentake of Skirack; 4 miles from Bradford, 8 from Halifax, 15 from Leeds.

BARDEN, in the parish of Skipton, east-division of the wapentake and liberty, of Staincliffe; *(Barden-Tower, the seat of the Duke of Devonshire)* 5 miles from Skipton, 10 from Pateleybridge, 11 from Kettlewell.—Population 191.

BARKISLAND, in the parish of Halifax, Morley-division of the wapentake of Agbrigg and Morley, liberty of the Manor of Wakefield; *(Barkisland-Hall, the seat of David Dyson, Esq.)* 5¼ miles from Halifax, 6 from Huddersfield, 12 from Rochdale, *(Lanc.)*—Population 1,799.

BARKSTON, *(which gives name to the wapentake)* in the parishes of Sherburn and Saxton, wapentake of Barkston-Ash, liberty of the Honour of Pontefract; 4 miles from Abberford, 5 from Tadcaster, 11 from Pontefract.—Pop. 264.

BARLEY, in the parish of Brayton, wapentake of Barkston-Ash, liberty of the Honour of Pontefract; 3 miles from Selby, 5 from Snaith, 13 from Pontefract.—Population 173.

BARMBROUGH, in the parish of Barmbrough, north-division of the wapentake of Strafforth and Tickhill, liberty of Tickhill; 6 miles from Doncaster, 9 from Barnsley.—Population 446.

BARMBROUGH-GRANGE, in the parish of Barmbrough, north-division of the wapentake of Strafforth and Tickhill, liberty of Tickhill; *(the seat of Francis Fawkes, Esq.)* 5¼ miles from Doncaster, 9¼ from Barnsley.

BARNAWICK, or BARNHOLMSWICK, in the parish of Thornton-in-Lonsdale, wapentake of Ewcross; 6 miles from Kirby-Lonsdale, *(Westm.)* 11 from Settle, 17 from Lancaster, *(Lanc.)*

BARNBOW, in the parish of Barwick-in-Elmet, wapentake of Skirack; 6 miles from Leeds, 8 from Wetherby.

BARNBY-FURNACE, in the parish of Silkston, wapentake of Staincross, liberty of the Honour of Pontefract; 3¼ miles from Barnsley, 5¼ from Penistone, 9 from Wakefield.

BARNBY-HALL, in the parish of Silkston, wapentake of Staincross, liberty of the Honour of Pontefract; 3¼ miles from Barnsley, 5 from Penistone, 9 from Wakefield.

BARNBY-UPON-DON, in the parish of Barnby-upon-Don, south-division of the wapentake of Strafforth and Tickhill, liberty of Tickhill; 5¼ miles from Doncaster, 5½ from Thorne, 7¼ from Bawtry.—Population 369.

BARNFIELD-SMITHY, in the parish of Low-Bentham, wapentake of Ewcross; 10¼ miles from Kirby-Lonsdale, (*Westm.*) 12¼ from Settle.

BARNOLDSWICK, in the parish of Barnoldswick, east-division of the wapentake and liberty of Staincliffe; 4 miles from Colne, (*Lanc.*) 8 from Skipton, 10 from Burnley, (*Lanc.*)

BARNSDALE-HOUSE, in the parish of Kirk-Smeaton, wapentake of Osgoldcross, liberty of the Honour of Pontefract; 6 miles from Pontefract, 6 from Ferrybridge.

BARNSDALE-LODGE, in the parish of Burghwallis, wapentake of Osgoldcross, liberty of the Honour of Pontefract; (*the seat of Bacon Frank, Esq.*) 7¼ miles from Pontefract, 7¼ from Doncaster.

BARNSGREEN, in the parish of Ecclesfield, north-division of the wapentake of Strafforth and Tickhill; 5 miles from Sheffield, 8 from Rotherham, 10 from Barnsley.

BARNSHALL, in the parish of Ecclesfield, north-division of the wapentake of Strafforth and Tickhill; 4¼ miles from Sheffield, 8 from Rotherham, 10 from Barnsley.

BARNSIDE-WOOD, in the parish of Kirk-Burton, Agbrigg-division of the wapentake of Agbrigg and Morley; 6 miles from Penistone, 8 from Huddersfield.

BARNSLEY, in the parish of Silkston, wapentake of Staincross, liberty of the Honour of Pontefract; 8 miles from Penistone, 10 from Wakefield, 12 from Rotherham, 14 from Sheffield, 14 from Pontefract, 15 from Doncaster, 19 from Huddersfield, 32 from York, 176¼ from London.—*Market*, Wednesday.—*Fairs*, the Wednesday before February 28, May 13, and October 11, for Horses, Horned Cattle, Pigs, &c.—*Bankers*, Messrs. Beckett and Clark draw on Messrs. Sir R. C. Glyn, Mills, Hallifax, and Co. 12, Birchin-Lane. —*Principal Inns*, White-Bear, King's Head.—Population 3,606.

BARNSLEY, OLD, in the parish of Silkston, wapentake of Staincross, liberty of the Honour of Pontefract; 1 mile from Barnsley, 7 from Penistone, 10 from Wakefield.

BARROW, in the parish of Wath, north-division of the wapentake of Strafforth and Tickhill; 5 miles from Rotherham, 13½ from Doncaster.

BARROWBY-GRANGE, in the parish of Kirby-Overblow, upper-division of the wapentake of Claro; 5 miles from Otley, 8 from Ripley.

BARROWBY-HALL, in the parish of Garforth, lower-division of the wapentake of Skirack, liberty of the Honour of Pontefract; *(the seat of Charles Smith, Esq.)* 6 miles from Leeds, 9 from Pontefract, 11 from Wetherby.

BARWICK-IN-ELMET, in the parish of Barwick-in-Elmet, lower-division of the wapentake of Skirack, liberty of the Honour of Pontefract; 6 miles from Wetherby, 8 from Leeds.—Population 1,370.

BASHALL, in the parish of Mitton, west-division of the wapentake of Staincliffe, liberty of Bolland; 4 miles from Clitheroe, *(Lanc.)* 11 from Blackburn, *(ditto)* 11 from Burnley, *(ditto)* 18 from Skipton.

BASHALLEAVES, in the parish of Mitton, west-division of the wapentake and liberty of Staincliffe; 4 miles from Clitheroe, *(Lanc.)* 9 from Gisburn, 11 from Blackburn, *(ditto.)*

BASHALL-LODGE, in the parish of Witton, west-division of the wapentake and liberty of Staincliffe; 4 miles from Clitheroe, *(Lanc.)* 10 from Gisburn.

BASINGTHORPE, in the parish of Rotherham, south-division of the wapentake of Strafforth and Tickhill; 1¼ mile from Rotherham, 10½ from Barnsley.

BATLEY, in the parish of Batley, Agbrigg-division of the wapentake of Agbrigg and Morley, liberty of the Honour of Pontefract; 2¼ miles from Dewsbury, 6¼ from Bradford, 8 from Leeds.—Population 2,574.

BATLEY-CARR, in the parish of Batley, Agbrigg-division of the wapentake of Agbrigg and Morley, liberty of the Honour of Pontefract; 1 mile from Dewsbury, 6 from Wakefield.

BATLEY, UPPER, in the parish of Batley, Agbrigg-division of the wapentake of Agbrigg and Morley, liberty of the Honour of Pontefract; 3¼ miles from Dewsbury, 6 from Bradford.

BATTERAX, in the parish of Slaidburn, west-division of the wapentake of Staincliffe, liberty of Bolland; 8 miles from Clitheroe, *(Lanc.)* 13 from Settle.

BAWTRY, in the parish of Bawtry, *Nottinghamshire* and the south-division of the wapentake of Strafforth and Tickhill; *(the seat of Lady Galloway)* 5¼ miles from Barnby-Moor-Inn, 9 from Doncaster, 9 from Retford, *(Notts.)* 12 from Gainsborough, *(Linc.)* 14 from Thorne, 20 from Sheffield, 46 from York, 153 from London.—*Market,** Wed-

* When this Sheet was put to Press, some propositions were made to alter this Market to THURSDAY.

nesday.—*Fairs*, Thursday in Whitsun-week, and Old Martinmas-Day, for Horses, Horned Cattle, Sheep, Merchandise, &c.—*Principal Inns*, Crown, and Swan.—Pop. 798.

BEACON-HILL, in the parish of Halifax, Morley-division of the wapentake of Agbrigg and Morley; 1 mile from Halifax, 7 from Bradford.

BEAGHALL, in the parish of Kellington, wapentake of Osgoldcross, liberty of the Honour of Pontefract; 6 miles from Pontefract, 8 from Snaith.—Population 384.

BEAMSLEY, or BETHMESLEY, in the parishes of Addingham and Skipton, upper-division of the wapentake of Claro; *(the seat of Josiah Norley, Esq.)* 6 miles from Skipton, 8¼ from Otley, 17 from Knaresborough.—Population 276.

BEARCROFTS-HALL, in the parish of Horton, wapentake of Ewcross; 8 miles from Settle, 14 from Kirby-Lonsdale, *(Westm.)*

BEARWOOD-GREEN, in the parish of Hatfield, south-division of the wapentake of Strafforth and Tickhill; 1¼ mile from Thorne, 8 from Doncaster.

BEASDEN, in the parish of Burnsall, east-division of the wapentake and liberty of Staincliffe; 8 miles from Skipton, 10 from Pateleybridge, 11 from Kettlewell.

BECKA-HALL, in the parish of Abberford, lower-division of the wapentake of Skirack, liberty of the Honour of Pontefract; *(the seat of William Martcham, Esq.)* 5 miles from Wetherby, 8 from Leeds, 8 from Tadcaster.

BECK-BOTTOM, in the parish of Kirby-Overblow, upper-division of the wapentake of Claro; 4¼ miles from Otley, 7¼ from Knaresborough.

BECK-FOOT and MILL, in the parish of Bingley, upper-division of the wapentake of Skirack; 4 miles from Bradford, 8 from Halifax, 15 from Leeds.

BECK-MEETING, in the parish of Kirby-Malzeard, lower-division of the wapentake of Claro; 5¼ miles from Masham, 8 from Ripon.

BECKWITH, in the parish of Pannall, lower-division of the wapentake of Claro, liberty of Knaresborough; 4 miles from Knaresborough, 4 from Ripley.

BECKWITH-GREEN, in the parish of Pannall, lower-division of the wapentake of Claro, liberty of Knaresborough; 4 miles from Ripley, 5 from Knaresborough.

BECKWITH-SHAW, in the parish of Pannall, lower-division of the wapentake of Claro, liberty of Knaresborough; 4¼ miles from Ripon, 5¼ from Knaresborough, 7¼ from Otley.

BECKURMONDS, in the parish of Arncliffe, east-division of the wapentake and liberty of Staincliffe; 8 miles from Kettlewell, 14 from Settle, 17 from Leyburn.

BEESTON, in the parish of Leeds, Morley-division of the wapentake of Agbrigg and Morley; 2¼ miles from Leeds, 10¼ from Wakefield, 13 from Bradford, 13¼ from Huddersfield.—Population 1,427.

BEGGERINGTON, in the parish of Bradford, Morley-division of the wapentake of Agbrigg and Morley; 3 miles from Halifax, 5¼ from Bradford.

BELL-BUSK, in the parish of Gargrave, east-division of the wapentake and liberty of Staincliffe; 8 miles from Skipton, 10 from Settle, 13 from Colne, *(Lanc.)*

BELL-FLASK-HOUSE, in the parish of Ripon, lower-division of the wapentake of Claro; 3 miles from Ripley, 4 from Ripon, 8¼ from Knaresborough.

BELL-HAGG, in the parish of Sheffield, south-division of the wapentake of Strafforth and Tickhill; 3 miles from Sheffield, 9 from Rotherham, 15 from Chesterfield, *(Derby.)*

BELLE-VUE, in the parish of Sandall, Agbrigg-division of the wapentake of Agbrigg and Morley; *(the seat of Dowager Lady Pilkington)* 1 mile from Wakefield, 9 from Pontefract.

BELL-WOOD, in the parish of Ripon, lower-division of the wapentake of Claro, liberty of Ripon; 1½ mile from Ripon, 6 from Ripley, 9 from Knaresborough.

BELLY-BRIDGE, in the parish of Dewsbury, Agbrigg-division of the wapentake of Agbrigg and Morley, 4 miles from Halifax, 5 from Bradford, 6¼ from Huddersfield.

BENTHAM-HIGH, in the parish of Low-Bentham, wapentake of Ewcross; 10 miles from Kirby-Lonsdale, *(Westm.)* 12 from Settle, 15 from Lancaster, *(Lanc.)*—*No Market.*—*Fairs*, January 25, Saturday in Easter-week, June 22, and October 25, for Horned Cattle, &c.

BENTHAM, LOW, in the parish of Low-Bentham, wapentake of Ewcross; 9 miles from Kirby-Lonsdale, *(Westm.)* 13 from Settle, 14 from Lancaster, *(Lanc.)*—Pop. 1,487.

BENTLEY, in the parish of Arksey, north-division of the wapentake of Strafforth and Tickhill, liberty of Tickhill; 1½ mile from Doncaster, 10 from Thorne.

BENTLEY-GRANGE, in the parish of Elmley, Agbrigg-division of the wapentake of Agbrigg and Morley, liberty of the Manor of Wakefield; 7 miles from Wakefield, 8 from Barnsley, 10 from Huddersfield.

BENT'S GREEN, in the parish of Sheffield, south-division of the wapentake of Strafforth and Tickhill; 3¼ miles from Sheffield, 9¼ from Rotherham, 12 from Chesterfield, *(Derby.)*

BERKBY, in the parish of Thorner, lower-division of the wapentake of Skirack, liberty of the Honour of Pontefract; 4 miles from Leeds, 6 from Wetherby, 12 from Tadcaster.

BERRY-MOOR, in the parish of Silkston, wapentake of Staincross, liberty of the Honour of Pontefract; 3¼ miles from Penistone, 4 from Barnsley, 11 from Wakefield.

BERWICK, in the parish of Skipton, east-division of the wapentake of Staincliffe, liberty of Clifford's Fee; 4 miles from Skipton, 9 from Keighley, 12 from Otley.—Population 173.

BESSACAR, in the parish of Cantley, south-division of the wapentake of Strafforth and Tickhill; 4 miles from Doncaster, 5 from Bawtry.

BEWERLEY, in the parish of Ripon, lower-division of the wapentake of Claro; (Bewerley-Hall, the seat of John Yorke, Esq.) ¼ of a mile from Pateleybridge, 6 from Ripley, 13 from Ripon.—Population 1,075.

BIERLEY, EAST, in the parish of Birstall, Morley-division of the wapentake of Agbrigg and Morley, liberty of the Honour of Pontefract; 4 miles from Bradford, 7 from Halifax, 10¼ from Wakefield.

BIERLEY, NORTH, in the parish of Bradford, Morley-division of the wapentake of Agbrigg and Morley, liberty of the Honour of Pontefract; 2 miles from Bradford, 8 from Halifax, 12 from Wakefield.—Population 3,820.

BIERLEY, SOUTH, in the parish of Bradford, Morley-division of the wapentake of Agbrigg and Morley, liberty of the Honour of Pontefract; 2¼ miles from Bradford, 8¼ from Halifax, 12 from Wakefield.

BIERLEY, WEST, in the parish of Bradford, Morley-division of the wapentake of Agbrigg and Morley; (the seat of J. Cranshaw, Esq.) 3 miles from Bradford, 6 from Halifax, 12 from Wakefield.

BIGGIN, in the parish of Kirby-Malzeard, lower-division of the wapentake of Claro; (the seat of the Rev. J. Geldart) 5 miles from Masham, 8 from Ripon, 11 from Ripley.

BIGGIN, in the parish of Church-Fenton, wapentake of Barkston-Ash, liberties of St. Peter and the Honour of Pontefract; 6 miles from Tadcaster, 3 from Selby, 10 from Pontefract.

BIGGIN-HILL, in the parish of Church-Fenton, wapentake of Barkston-Ash; 6 miles from Tadcaster, 3 from Selby, 10 from Pontefract.

BILCLIFFE, in the parish of Penistone, wapentake of Staincross, liberty of the Honour of Pontefract; 2 miles from Penistone, 9 from Barnsley, 12 from Sheffield.

BILHAM, in the parishes of Hutton-Pagnall and Barnbrough, north-division of the wapentake of Strafforth and Tickhill, liberty of Tickhill; (*Bilham-House, the seat of W. N. W. Hewett, Esq.*) 6 miles from Doncaster, 10 from Barnsley. —Population 45.

BILHAM-GRANGE, in the parish of High-Hoyland, wapentake of Staincross, liberty of the Honour of Pontefract; 7 miles from Barnsley, 7 from Penistone, 7½ from Wakefield.

BILHAM-ROW, in the parish of Hutton-Pagnall, north-division of the wapentake of Strafforth and Tickhill; 6 miles from Doncaster, 10¼ from Barnsley.

BILLINGLEY, in the parish of Darfield, north-division of the wapentake of Strafforth and Tickhill, liberty of Tickhill; 6 miles from Barnsley, 8 from Doncaster.—Population 172.

BILLINGLEY-GREEN, in the parish of Darfield, north-division of the wapentake of Strafforth and Tickhill; 6½ miles from Barnsley, 8½ from Doncaster.

BILTON, in the parish of Knaresborough, lower-division of the wapentake of Claro, liberty of Knaresborough; (*Bilton-Hall, the seat of John Watson, Esq.*) 1 mile from Knaresborough, 8 from Wetherby.

BINGLEY, in the parish of Bingley, upper-division of the wapentake of Skirack; (*Myrtle-Grove, the seat of —— Birch, Esq.*) 4¼ miles from Keighley, 6 from Bradford, 10 from Otley, 11 from Halifax.—*Market*, Tuesday.—*Fairs*, January 25, for Horned Cattle, August 25, 26, and 27, for Horned Cattle, Sheep, and Linen.—*Principal Inns*, Brown Cow, and King's Head.—Population 4,100.

BIRCHAM-CLIFFE, in the parish of Huddersfield, Agbrigg-division of the wapentake of Agbrigg and Morley; 2 miles from Huddersfield, 6 from Halifax.

BIRDWELL, in the parish of Tankersley, north-division of the wapentake of Strafforth and Tickhill; 3½ miles from Barnsley, 10¼ from Sheffield.

BIRDWELL-FLATT, in the parish of Wath-upon-Dearn, north-division of the wapentake of Strafforth and Tickhill; 4¼ miles from Rotherham, 9 from Doncaster.

BIRFITT, in the parish of Ripley, upper-division of the wapentake of Claro; 1½ mile from Ripley, 7 from Ripon.

BIRK-HOUSES, in the parish of Sedberg, wapentake of Eweross; 3¼ miles from Sedberg, 9½ from Kirby-Stephen, (*Westm.*)

BIRKIN, in the parish of Birkin, wapentake of Barkston-Ash, liberty of the Honour of Pontefract; (*the seats of William Towtill, Esq. and the Rev. George Alderson*) 4 miles from Ferrybridge, 7 from Pontefract, 8 from Selby.—Population 139.

BIRKINSHAW, in the parish of Birstall, Morley-division of the wapentake of Agbrigg and Morley, liberty of the Honour of Pontefract ; 5 miles from Bradford, 8 from Leeds 9 from Halifax.

BIRKLEY, in the parish of Huddersfield, Agbrigg-division of the wapentake of Agbrigg and Morley ; 2 miles from Huddersfield, 9 from Halifax, 9¼ from Dewsbury.

BIRKLEY-NAB, in the parish of Ripon, lower-division of the wapentake of Claro, liberty of Ripon ; 2 miles from Ripon, 8 from Boroughbridge.

BIRKWITH, in the parish of Horton, wapentake of Ewcross, 8 miles from Settle, 15 from Askrigg.

BIRLEY-CARR, in the parish of Ecclesfield, north-division of the wapentake of Strafforth and Tickhill ; 3 miles from Sheffield, 9 from Rotherham, 9¼ from Penistone.

BIRSTALL, in the parish of Birstall, Morley-division of the wapentake of Agbrigg and Morley, liberty of the Honour of Pontefract ; 7 miles from Leeds, 7 from Bradford, 7¼ from Halifax, 8¼ from Huddersfield.

BIRSTWITH, in the parish of Hampsthwaite, lower-division of the wapentake of Claro, liberty of Knaresborough ; *(the seat of William Day, Esq.)* 3 miles from Ripley, 8 from Knaresborough.—Population 630.

BISHOPSIDE-HIGH, in the parish of Ripon, lower-division of the wapentake of Claro, liberty of Ripon ; 1 mile from Pateleybridge, 9 from Knaresborough, 11 from Ripon. —Population 1,487.

BISHOPSIDE, LOW, in the parish of Ripon, lower-division of the wapentake of Claro ; 1¼ mile from Pateleybridge, 7¼ from Ripley, 11 from Ripon.

BISHOPTON, in the parish of Ripon, lower-division of the wapentake of Claro, liberty of Ripon ; *(the seat of George Coates, Esq.)* 1 mile from Ripon, 8 from Ripley, 10¼ from Pateleybridge.—Population 106.

BLACK-BANK, in the parish of Leeds, lower-division of the wapentake of Skirack ; 1 mile from Leeds, 8 from Harewood, 14 from Ferrybridge.

BLACKBURNE-COMMON, in the parish of Rotherham, south-division of the wapentake of Strafforth and Tickhill ; 3 miles from Rotherham, 8 from Sheffield.

BLACKER, LOW, in the parish of Wath-upon-Dearn, north-division of the wapentake of Strafforth and Tickhill ; 5 miles from Barnsley, 10¼ from Rotherham.

BLACKER, MIDDLE, in the parish of Wath-upon-Dearn, north-division of the wapentake of Strafforth and Tickhill ; 5¼ miles from Barnsley, 10¼ from Rotherham.

BLACKER, OVER, in the parish of Wath-upon-Dearn, north-division of the wapentake of Strafforth and Tickhill; 5¼ miles from Barnsley, 10 from Rotherham.

BLACK-MOOR, in the parish of Penistone, wapentake of Staincross, liberty of the Honour of Pontefract; 2¼ miles from Penistone, 6 from Barnsley, 10¼ from Sheffield.

BLACK-MOOR-FOOT, in the parish of Almondbury, Agbrigg division of the wapentake of Agbrigg and Morley; 3¼ miles from Huddersfield, 11¼ from Halifax, 21¼ from Manchester, *(Lanc.)*

BLACKSHAW-HEAD, in the parish of Halifax, Morley division of the wapentake of Agbrigg and Morley; 10 miles from Halifax, 18 from Bradford, 18 from Huddersfield.

BLACKSTONE, in the parish of Spofforth, upper-division of the wapentake of Claro; 3 miles from Wetherby, 4 from Knaresborough.

BLACKSTONE-EDGE, in the parish of Halifax, Morley division of the wapentake of Agbrigg and Morley; 6 miles from Rochdale, *(Lanc.)* 9 from Halifax, 17 from Bradford.

BLAKE-HALL, in the parish of Mirfield, Agbrigg-division of the wapentake of Agbrigg and Morley; 3 miles from Dewsbury, 6¼ from Huddersfield.

BLAKESTONE, in the parish of Finningley, *(Notts.)* south-division of the wapentake of Strafforth and Tickhill, a part in the soke of Doncaster; 5 miles of Bawtry, 7¼ from Doncaster.

BLAND-CANDLEY or CAUTLEY, in the parish of Sedbergh, wapentake of Ewcross; 1½ mile from Sedbergh, 6½ from Dent, 8¼ from Kendall, *(Westm.)*

BLEAK-ROYD, in the parish of Penistone, wapentake of Staincross, liberty of the Honour of Pontefract; 2 miles from Penistone, 9 from Barnsley, 11 from Sheffield.

BLUBBER-HOUSES, in the parish of Fewston, lower-division of the wapentake of Claro, liberty of Knaresborough; 11 miles from Skipton, 12 from Knaresborough, 19 from Ripon.—Population 120.

BLYTH-GARTH, or ELDROTH-CHAPEL, *see Eldroth-Chapel.*

BOARD-HILL, in the parish of Penistone, wapentake of Staincross, liberty of the Honour of Pontefract; 5 miles from Penistone, 12 from Barnsley, 16 from Sheffield.

BOARHURST, in the parish of Rochdale, *(Lanc.)* Agbrigg division of the wapentake of Agbrigg and Morley; 10 miles from Rochdale, *(Lanc.)* 13 from Manchester, *(ditto)* 14 from Huddersfield.

BOGG-HALL, in the parish of Kirkheaton, Agbrigg-division of the wapentake of Agbrigg and Morley; 4 miles from Huddersfield, 10 from Wakefield.

BOLSTERSTONE, in the parish of Ecclesfield, north-division of the wapentake of Strafforth and Tickhill; 9 miles from Penistone, 9¼ from Barnsley, 12 from Rotherham.

BOLTON, in the parish of Calverley, Morléy-division of the wapentake of Agbrigg and Morley, liberty of the Honour of Pontefract; 2 miles from Bradford, 8 from Otley.—Population 474.

BOLTON, juxta BOWLAND, or WEST-BOLTON, in the parish of Bolton, west-division of the wapentake and liberty of Staincliffe; *(Bolton-Hall, the seat of —— Bolton, Esq.)* 10 miles from Settle, 12 from Colne, *(Lanc.)* 14 from Skipton.—*No Market.*—*Fairs*, June 28, 29, and 30, for Horned Cattle, Pedlary, &c.—Population 996.

BOLTON-ABBEY, in the parish of Skipton, east-division of the wapentake and liberty of Staincliffe; 5¼ miles from Skipton, 10 from Keighley, 11½ from Pateleybridge, 12 from Otley.—Population 120.

BOLTON-BRIDGE, in the parish of Skipton, east-division of the wapentake and liberty of Staincliffe; 6 miles from Skipton, 12 from Pateleybridge.

BOLTON-UPON-DEARN, in the parish of Bolton-upon-Dearn, north-division of the wapentake of Strafforth and Tickhill, liberty of Tickhill; 7¼ miles from Rotherham, 7½ from Barnsley, 7¼ from Doncaster.—Population 547.

BONDGATE, in the parish and a part of Ripon.

BOOLTCLIFFE, in the parish of Sandall, Agbrigg-division of the wapentake of Agbrigg and Morley; 5 miles from Wakefield, 7 from Barnsley.

BOOTH-FERRY, in the parish of Snaith, wapentake of Osgoldcross, liberty of the Honour of Pontefract; 1¼ miles from Howden, 7¼ from from Snaith, 10 from Selby, 12 from Thorne, 20 from York, 183 from London.—Wells' Inn.

BOOTHROYD, in the parish of Dewsbury, Agbrigg division of the wapentake of Agbrigg and Morley, liberty of the Manor of Wakefield; 1 mile from Dewsbury, 6 from Wakefield.

BOOTHS-TOWN, in the parish of Halifax, Morley-division of the wapentake of Agbrigg and Morley; 1 mile from Halifax, 7 from Bradford.

BORDLEY, in the parish of Burnsall, east-division of the wapentake of Staincliffe, liberty of Clifford's Fee; 7 miles from Kettlewell, 10 from Skipton, 10 from Settle.

BORHOLME, and BORHOLME-BRIDGE, in the parish of Bolland, *(Lanc.)* wapentake and liberty of Staincliffe;

8 miles from Clitheroe, *(Lanc.)* 16 from Lancaster, *(ditto.)*

BOROUGHBRIDGE, in the parish of Aldborough, lower-division of the wapentake of Claro; *(the seat of the Rev. M. Lawson)* 6 miles from Ripon, 7 from Knaresborough, 11 from Thirsk, 12 from Wetherby, 17 from York, 17 from Bedale, 19 from Northallerton, 22 from Catterick, 206 from London.—*Market*, Saturday.—*Fairs*, April 27 and 28, for Horned Cattle and Sheep, June 22, for Horned Cattle, Horses &c. 23 for Sheep, and the Week preceding for Hardware, Woollen-Cloth, Pedlary-Ware, &c. October 25, and 26, for Horned Cattle and Sheep.—Sends two Members to Parliament.—*Principal Inns*, Crown, and Three Greyhounds.—Population 680.

BOTANY-BAY-INN, in the parish of Brayton, wapentake of Barkston-Ash; 1¼ mile from Selby 6¼ from Snaith.

BOUSDEN, in the parish of Slaidburn, west-division of the wapentake and liberty of Staincliffe; 9 miles from Clitheroe, *(Lanc.)* 17 from Lancaster, *(ditto.)*

BOWER-HILL, in the parish of Penistone, wapentake of Staincross, liberty of the Honour of Pontefract; 2 miles from Penistone, 5 from Barnsley, 11 from Sheffield.

BOWLAND-FOREST, in the parish of Slaidburn, west-division of the wapentake and liberty of Staincliffe; 5 miles from Clitheroe, *(Lanc.)* 18 from Lancaster, *(ditto.)* 18 from Preston, *(ditto.)*

BOWLING, in the parish of Bradford, Morley-division of the wapentake of Agbrigg and Morley; 1 mile from Bradford, 9 from Halifax.—Population 2,055.

BOWLING-HALL, in the parish of Bradford, Morley-division of the wapentake of Agbrigg and Morley; *(the seat of John Sturges, Esq.)* 1 mile from Bradford, 9 from Halifax.

BOWTHWAITE, in the parish of Kirby-Malzeard, lower-division of the wapentake of Claro; 5 miles from Pateley-bridge, 8 from Masham, 14 from Ripon.

BOYN-HILL, in the parish of Sandall, Agbrigg-division, of the wapentake of Agbrigg and Morley, liberty of the Manor of Wakefield; 4 miles from Wakefield, 5 from Barnsley.

BRACEWELL, in the parish of Bracewell, east-division of the wapentake of Staincliffe, liberty of Clifford's Fee; 5 miles from Colne, *(Lanc.)* 9 from Skipton, 11 from Burnley, *(Lanc.)*—Population 173.

BRACKEN-BOTTOM, in the parish of Horton, wapentake of Ewcross; 6 miles from Sedbergh, 10 from Kirby-Lonsdale, *(Westm.)* 18 from Hawes.

BRACKEN-FOOT, in the parish of Kirby-Overblow, upper-division of the wapentake of Claro ; 6 miles from Otley, 7 from Knaresborough, 7 from Ripley.

BRACKENTHWAITE, in the parish of Pannall, lower-division of the wapentake of Claro; 5¼ miles from Ripley, 6 from Knaresborough, 6¼ from Otley.

BRADAPHOUSE, in the parish of Mitton, west-division of the wapentake and liberty of Staincliffe ; 4 miles from Clitheroe, (Lanc.) 12 from Blackburn, (ditto) 12 from Gisburn.

BRADFIELD, in the parish of Ecclesfield, north-division of the wapentake of Strafforth and Tickhill, liberty of Hallamshire ; 6 miles from Rotherham, 9 from Penistone.—*No Market.*—*Fairs*, Friday Fortnight before Good-Friday, and second Friday after Old Michaelmas-day, for Horned Cattle, Swine, &c.—Population 4,102.

BRADFIELD, NETHER, in the parish of Ecclesfield, wapentake of Strafforth and Tickhill, liberty of Hallamshire ; 6¼ miles from Rotherham, 9½ from Penistone.

BRADFORD, in the parish of Bradford, Morley-division of the wapentake of Agbrigg and Morley, liberty of the Honour of Pontefract ; 5¼ miles from Bingley, 8 from Halifax, 10 from Leeds, 10 from Keighley, 10 from Otley, 14 from Huddersfield, 14 from Wakefield, 33¼ from York, 196 from London.—*Market*, Thursday.—*Fairs*, June 17 and 18, December 9 and 10, for Horned Cattle, Horses, Pigs, &c. *Bankers*, Messrs. Peckover, Harrison, and Co. draw on Messrs. Sir. James Esdaile, and Co. 21 Lombard Street, —*Principal Inns*, Sun, and Talbot.—Population 6,393.

BRADFORD-BRIDGE, in the parish of Mitton, west-division of the wapentake of Staincliffe, liberty of Bolland ; 2¼ miles from Clitheroe, (Lanc.) 8 from Gisburn.

BRADFORD, WEST, in the parish of Waddington, wapentake of Staincliffe, liberty of Bolland ; 15 miles from Blackburn, (Lanc.) 15 from Burnley, (ditto.)

BRADGATE, in the parish of Rotherham, south-division of the wapentake of Strafforth and Tickhill, liberty of Tickhill ; 2 miles from Rotherham, 10 from Barnsley.

BRADHOLME, in the parish of Thorne, south-division of the wapentake of Strafforth and Tickhill, liberty of Tickhill ; 1¼ mile from Thorne, 10 from Doncaster.

BRADLEY, in the parish of Huddersfield, Agbrigg-division of the wapentake of Agbrigg and Morley, liberty of the Honour of Pontefract ; 3 miles from Huddersfield, 7 from Halifax, 12¼ from Leeds.

BRADLEY, or BRIDLEY-BROOK, in the parish of Almondbury, Agbrigg-divison of the wapentake of Agbrigg

WEST-RIDING. 161

and Morley; 5 miles from Huddersfield, 13 from Halifax, 20 from Manchester. *(Lanc.)*

BRADLEY-HALL, in the parish of Huddersfield, Agbrigg-division of the wapentake of Agbrigg and Morley; 4 miles from Huddersfield, 8 from Halifax.

BRADLEY-HALL, in the parish of Halifax, Morley-division of the wapentake of Agbrigg and Morley; 4 miles from Halifax, 6 from Doncaster, 6¼ from Huddersfield.

BRADLEY, LOWER, in the parish of Kildwick, east-division of the wapentake of Staincliffe, liberty of Clifford's Fee; 3½ miles from Skipton, 6¼ from Keighley, 12 from Colne, *(Lanc.)*—Population 385.

BRADLEY, UPPER, in the parish of Kildwick, east-division of the wapentake of Staincliffe, liberty of Clifford's Fee; 3 miles from Skipton, 7 from Keighley, 12 from Colne, *(Lanc.)*

BRADSEY, in the parish of Bradsey, lower-division of the wapentake of Skirack; 4 miles from Wetherby, 8 from Otley, 8¼ from Leeds.—Population 364.

BRADSHAW, in the parish of Penistone, wapentake of Staincross, liberty of the Honour of Pontefract; 2¼ miles from Penistone, 9¼ from Barnsley, 14 from Sheffield.

BRAIM-HALL, in the parish of Spofforth, upper-division of the wapentake of Claro; 3 miles from Knaresborough, 4 from Wetherby.

BRAITHWAITE, in the parish of Kirk-Bramwith, wapentake of Osgoldcross, liberty of the Honour of Pontefract; 6 miles from Doncaster, 8 from Thorne.

BRAITHWAITE-HALL, in the parish of Darton, wapentake of Staincross, liberty of the Honour of Pontefract; *(the seat of John Perkins, Esq.)* 4 miles from Barnsley, 5 from Penistone, 8 from Wakefield.

BRAITHWAITE-HALL, in the parish of Ripon, lower-division of the wapentake of Claro; 4 miles from Ripon, 11 from Knaresborough.

BRAITHWELL, in the parish of Braithwell, south-division of the wapentake of Strafforth and Tickhill; 6 miles from Rotherham, 8 from Doncaster.—Population 331.

BRAMHAM, in the parish of Bramham, wapentake of Barkston-Ash, liberty of St. Peter; 3½ miles from Abberford, 4 from Tadcaster, 4 from Wetherby, 12 from Pontefract.—Population 792.

BRAMHAM-BIGGIN, in the parish of Bramham, wapentake of Barkston-Ash; *(the seat of Lord Headley)* 3¼ miles from Abberford, 4 from Wetherby, 4 from Tadcaster, 12 from Pontefract.

BRAMHAM-PARK, in the parish of Bramham, wapentake of Barkston-Ash; *(the seat of James Lane Fox, Esq.)* 4 miles from Tadcaster, 4 from Wetherby, 12 from Pontefract.

BRAMHOPE, in the parish of Otley, lower-division of the wapentake of Skirack; *(Bramhope-Hall, the seat of C. Smith, Esq.)* 3 miles from Otley, 7 from Leeds, 8 from Wetherby.—Population 261.

BRAMLEY, in the parish of Leeds, Morley-division of the wapentake of Agbrigg and Morley, liberty of the Honour of Pontefract; 4 miles from Leeds, 9 from Bradford.—Population 2,562.

BRAMLEY and GRANGE, in the parish of Braithwell, south-division of the wapentake of Strafforth and Tickhill; 4 miles from Rotherham, 10 from Doncaster.—Pop. 238.

BRAMLEY-HALL, in the parish of Hansworth, south-division of the wapentake of Strafforth and Tickhill; *(the seat of Thomas Weldon, Esq.)* 4 miles from Sheffield, 6 from Rotherham.

BRAMPTON, in the parish of Cantley, south-division of the wapentake of Strafforth and Tickhill; 4¼ miles from Doncaster, 6½ from Bawtry.

BRAMPTON, in the parish of Treton, south-division of the wapentake of Strafforth and Tickhill; 4½ miles from Rotherham, 9 from Sheffield.—Population 120.

BRAMPTON-BIERLOW, in the parish of Wath, north-division of the wapentake of Strafforth and Tickhill, liberty of Tickhill; 6 miles from Rotherham, 6 from Barnsley, 12 from Sheffield.—Population 860.

BRAMPTON-ULLEY, *see Ulley.*

BRAMWITH, KIRK, in the parish of Kirk-Bramwith, wapentake of Osgoldcross, liberty of the Honour of Pontefract; 6 miles from Doncaster, 8 from Thorne.—Population 214.

BRAMWITH, SAND, in the parishes of Barnby-upon-Don and Hatfield, south-division of the wapentake of Strafforth and Tickhill; 5 miles from Thorne, 7 from Doncaster, 8¼ from Bawtry.

BRANDFIELD-HOUSE, in the parish of Sprotbrough, north-division of the wapentake of Strafforth and Tickhill; 3½ miles from Doncaster, 11¼ from Barnsley.

BRANDON, in the parish of Harewood, upper-division of the wapentake of Skirack; 4 miles from Leeds, 6¼ from Wetherby, 12¼ from Tadcaster.

BRANIER, in the parish of Low-Bentham, wapentake of Ewcross; 14 miles from Settle, 22 from Lancaster, *(Lanc.)* 10 from Kirby-Lonsdale, *(Westm.)*

BRANTON GREEN, in the parish of Aldborough, upper-

WEST-RIDING. 163

division of the wapentake of Claro ; 4 miles from Boroughbridge, 9 from Ripon, 11 from Knaresborough.

BRATHWAITE, in the parish of Keighley, east-division of the wapentake and liberty of Staincliffe ; 1¼ mile from Keighley, 11¼ from Skipton.

BRAYSTAY-HALL, in the parish of Kirkby-Malhamdale, east-division of the wapentake and liberty of Staincliffe ; 7 miles from Skipton, 9 from Settle, 11 from Kettlewell.

BRAYTON, in the parish of Brayton, wapentake of Barkston-Ash, liberty of the Honour of Pontefract, 1 mile from Selby, 7 from Snaith, 11 from Pontefract.—Population 227.

BREARLEY-HALL, in the parish of Halifax, Morley-division of the wapentake of Agbrigg and Morley, liberty of the Honour of Pontefract ; 6 miles from Halifax, 14 from Bradford, 14 from Huddersfield.

BREARTON, in the parish of Knaresborough, lower-division of the wapentake of Claro, liberty of Knaresborough ; 4 miles from Knaresborough, 5 from Boroughbridge, 6 from Ripon.—Population 146.

BREARY, in the parish of Addle, upper-division of the wapentake of Skirack, 5 miles from Leeds, 5 from Otley, 8 from Wetherby.

BRECKA-MOOR-HOUSE, in the parish of Ripon, lower-division of the wapentake of Claro ; *(the seat of Marmaduke Hodgson, Esq.)* 2 miles from Ripon, 8 from Boroughbridge, 14 from Knaresborough.

BRECKS, in the parish of Birstall, Morley-division of the wapentake of Agbrigg and Morley ; 4 miles from Bradford, 7¼ from Leeds.

BRENNARD, in the parish of Slaidburn, west-division of the wapentake and liberty of Staincliffe ; 12 miles from Clitheroe, *(Lanc.)* 12 from Lancaster, *(ditto.)*

BRETTON, in the parishes of Sandall-Magna and Silkston, wapentakes of Agbrigg and Morley ('Agbrigg-division) and Staincross, liberties of the Honour of Pontefract and Manor of Wakefield ; 6 miles from Wakefield, 6½ from Barnsley, 8 from Penistone, 10¼ from Huddersfield.—Population 491.

BRETTON-DYKES, in the parish of Silkston, wapentake of Staincross, liberty of the Honour of Pontefract ; 6 miles from Barnsley, 6 from Wakefield, 7 from Penistone.

BRETTON, MONK, or BURTON, in the parish of Royston, wapentake of Staincross, liberty of the Honour of Pontefract ; 2 miles from Barnsley, 8½ from Wakefield, 10 from Rotherham.—Population 480.

BRETTON-MONK-PRIORY, in the parish of Royston, wapentake of Staincross, liberty of the Honour of Pontefract; 2¼ miles from Barnsley, 9 from Wakefield, 9¼ from Rotherham.

BRETTON-PARK, in the parish of Silkston, wapentake of Staincross, liberty of the Honour of Pontefract; *(the seat of Thomas Richard Beaumont, Esq.)* 6½ miles from Barnsley, 6¼ from Wakefield, 7¼ from Penistone.

BRIAR-FLATTS, in the parish of Ackworth, wapentake of Osgoldcross, liberty of the Honour of Pontefract; 2¼ miles from Pontefract, 9¼ from Wakefield.

BRIDGE-END-HOUSES, or BRIDGE-HOUSE-GATE, in the parish of Ripon, lower-division of the wapentake of Claro; ¼ of a mile from Pateleybridge, 9¼ from Ripley, 11¼ from Ripon.

BRIDGE-HOUSES, in the parish of Sheffield, north-division of the wapentake of Strafforth and Tickhill; 1 mile from Sheffield, 7 from Rotherham.

BRIERLEY, in the parish of Felkirk, wapentake of Staincross, liberty of the Honour of Pontefract; *(the seat of John Hoyland, Esq.)* 5 miles from Barnsley, 7½ from Wakefield, 8½ from Pontefract.—Population 415.

BRIERLEY-MANOR, in the parish of Felkirk, wapentake of Staincross, liberty of the Honour of Pontefract; *(the seat of William Elmsall, Esq.)* 5 miles from Barnsley, 8 from Wakefield, 8½ from Pontefract.

BRIERY-BUSK, in the parish of Penistone, wapentake of Staincross, liberty of the Honour of Pontefract; 3½ miles from Penistone, 7 from Barnsley, 10½ from Sheffield.

BRIESTWHISTLE, in the parish of Thornhill, Agbrigg-division of the wapentake of Agbrigg and Morley; 6¼ miles from Huddersfield, 8¼ from Wakefield.

BRIGG-FLATT, in the parish of Sedbergh, wapentake of Ewcross; 1½ mile from Sedbergh, 6½ from Dent.

BRIGHOUSE, in the parish of Halifax, Morley-division of the wapentake of Agbrigg and Morley, liberty of the Manor of Wakefield; 4 miles from Halifax, 4 from Huddersfield. —*No Market.*—*Fair,* the Day after Martinmas-Day, for Horned Cattle, Sheep, and Pigs.

BRIGHTSIDE-BIERLOW, in the parish of Sheffield, south-division of the wapentake of Strafforth and Tickhill, liberty of Hallamshire; ¼ of a mile from Sheffield, 5½ from Rotherham, 12½ from Chesterfield, *(Derby.)*— Pop. 4,030.

BRIGHTOLMLEY, in the parish of Ecclesfield, north-division of the wapentake of Strafforth and Tickhill; 8 miles from Sheffield, 10 from Rotherham.

BRIMHAM, in the parish of Kirby-Malzeard, lower-division of the wapentake of Claro; 5 miles from Pateleybridge, 9 from Ripon, 10 from Knaresborough.

WEST-RIDING.

BRIMHAM-CRAGGS, in the parish of Kirby-Malzeard; lower-division of the wapentake of Claro; 4¼ miles from Pateleybridge, 9 from Ripon, 10 from Knaresborough.

BRINDSWORTH, in the parish of Rotherham, south-division of the wapentake of Strafforth and Tickhill, liberty of Hallamshire; 2 miles from Rotherham, 4 from Sheffield.—Population 183.

BROADLANE-HOUSE, in the parish of South-Kirkby, wapentake of Osgoldcross, liberty of the Honour of Pontefract; 7¼ miles from Doncaster, 9 from Pontefract.

BROADROAD-HEAD, in the parish of Darton, wapentake of Staintross, liberty of the Honour of Pontefract; 3 miles from Barnsley, 8 from Wakefield, 8¼ from Penistone.

BROCKDEN, in the parish of Barnoldswick, east-division of the wapentake and liberty of Staincliffe; 5 miles from Colne, *(Lanc.)* 9 from Skipton, 11 from Burnley, *(Lanc.)*—Population 189.

BROCKHOLE, in the parish of Cantley, south-division of the wapentake of Strafforth and Tickhill; 4¼ miles from Doncaster, 7 from Bawtry.

BROCKHOLES, in the parish of Drax, wapentake of Barkston-Ash; 4 miles from Snaith, 7 from Selby.

BRODSWORTH, in the parish of Brodsworth, north-division of the wapentake of Strafforth and Tickhill, liberty of Tickhill; *(Brodsworth-Hall, the seat of the late Peter Thelluson, Esq.)* 4 miles from Doncaster, 11 from Barnsley, 16 from Wakefield.—Population 302.

BROOK-BOTTOM, in the parish of Rochdale, *(Lanc.)* Agbrigg-division of the wapentake of Agbrigg and Morley; 9 miles from Manchester, *(Lanc.)* 10 from Rochdale, *(ditto)* 15 from Huddersfield.

BROOK-FOOT, in the parish of Halifax, Morley-division of the wapentake of Agbrigg and Morley; 3¼ miles from Halifax, 5 from Huddersfield.

BROOK-HOUSE, in the parish of Penistone, wapentake of Staincross, liberty of the Honour of Pontefract; 4¼ miles from Penistone, 11¼ from Barnsley, 13 from Sheffield.

BROOK-HOUSE, in the parish of Maltby, south-division of the wapentake of Strafforth and Tickhill, liberty of St. Peter; 5 miles from Tickhill, 7 from Rotherham.

BROOM-HALL, in the parish of Sheffield, south-division of the wapentake of Strafforth and Tickhill; *(the seat of Philip Gill, Esq.)* 1 mile from Sheffield, 7 from Rotherham.

BROOM-HEAD-HALL, in the parish of Ecclesfield, north-division of the wapentake of Strafforth and Tickhill; *(the seat of William Wilson, Esq.*) 7 miles from Penistone, 10 from Sheffield, 11 from Hope, *(Derb.)*

BROOM-HOUSE, in the parish of Rotherham, south-division of the wapentake of Strafforth and Tickhill; 1 mile from Rotherham, 6¼ from Sheffield, 12 from Doncaster.

BROOM-RIDDINS, in the parish of Rotherham, south-division of the wapentake of Strafforth and Tickhill; 1 mile from Rotherham, 6¼ from Sheffield, 12 from Doncaster.

BROTHERTON, in the parish of Brotherton, wapentake of Barkston-Ash, liberties of St. Peter and the Honour of Pontefract; *(the seat of John Crowder, Esq.)* 1 mile from Ferrybridge, 3 from Pontefract, 8¼ from Abberford, 11 from Selby, 12 from Tadcaster.—Population 994.

BROUGHTON, in the parish of Broughton, east-division of the wapentake of Staincliffe, liberty of Clifford's Fee; *(Broughton-Hall, the seat of Stephen Tempest, Esq.)* 3 miles from Skipton, 9 from Colne, *(Lanc.)* 12 from Keighley, 15¼ from Clitheroe, *(Lanc.)*—Population 200.

BROWN-EDGE, in the parish of Rochdale, *(Lanc.)* Agbrigg-divison of the wapentake of Agbrigg and Morley; 9 miles from Rochdale, *(Lanc.)* 13 from Manchester, *(ditto)* 13 from Huddersfield.

BROWN-HILLS, in the parish of Slaidburn, west division of the wapentake and liberty of Staincliffe; 8 miles from Clitheroe, *(Lanc.)* 13 from Settle.

BROWSHOLME, in the parish of Mitton, west-division of the wapentake of Staincliffe, liberty of Bolland; *(the seat of Thomas Lister Parker, Esq.)* 5 miles from Clitheroe, *(Lanc.)* 12 from Blackburn, *(ditto)* 13 from Gisburn.

BRUMLEY, in the parish of Tankersley, wapentake of Staincross, liberty of the Honour of Pontefract; 5 miles from Barnsley, 7 from Rotherham, 7 from Sheffield.

BRUMTHWAITE, in the parish of Kildwick, east-division of the wapentake and liberty of Staincliffe; 5 miles from Keighley, 8 from Skipton, 12 from Otley.

BRUNCLIFFE, in the parish of Batley, Morley-division of the wapentake of Agbrigg and Morley, liberty of the Honour of Pontefract; 4 miles from Dewsbury, 5¼ from Leeds, 6¼ from Bradford, 7¼ from Wakefield.

BRUSH-HOUSE, in the parish of Ecclesfield, north-division of the wapentake of Strafforth and Tickhill; *(the seat of Dr. Booth)* 3 miles from Sheffield, 5 from Rotherham, 10 from Barnsley.

BUCKDEN, in the parish of Arncliffe, east-division of the wapentake and liberty of Staincliffe; 4 miles from Kettlewell, 10 from Settle, 16 from Leyburn.—Population 280.

BULL-HOUSE, in the parish of Penistone, wapentake of Staincross, liberty of the Honour of Pontefract; 2¼ miles from Penistone, 9¼ from Barnsley, 13 from Sheffield.

BURGHWALLIS, in the parish of Burghwallis, wapentake of Osgoldcross, liberty of the Honour of Pontefract; 6 miles from Doncaster, 9 from Pontefract.—Population 182.

BURLEY, in the parish of Leeds, lower-division of the wapentake of Skirack, *(the seat of Sir Richard Johnson, Bart.)* 1¼ mile from Leeds, 8 from Bradford, 9 from Otley.

BURLEY, in the parsh of Otley, upper-division of the wapentake of Skirack, liberty of Cawood, Wistow and Otley; *(the seat of John Lee, Esq,)* 2 miles from Otley, 12 from Leeds, 13 from Skipton.—Population 842.

BURN, in the parish of Brayton, wapentake of Barkston-Ash; 3 miles from Selby, 7 from Snaith, 8 from Pontefract.—Population 189.

BURNHOUSE, in the parish of Slaidburn, west-division of the wapentake and liberty of Staincliffe; 9 miles from Colne, *(Lanc.)* 13 from Settle.

BURNSALL, in the parish of Burnsall, east-division of the wapentake of Staincliffe, liberty of Clifford's Fee; 9¼ miles Skipton, 10 from Kettlewell, 10 from Pateleybridge.—Population 142.

BURNTWOOD-LODGE, or NOOK, in the parish of Darfield, north-division of the wapentake of Strafforth and Tickhill; *(the seat of —— Masden, Esq.)* 7 miles from Barnsley, 8 from Doncaster.

BURNT, or BRAINT-GATES, in the parish of Kirby-Malzeard, lower-division of the wapentake of Claro; 2¼ miles from Ripley, 6¼ from Pateleybridge.

BURROW-LEE, in the parish of Sheffield, south-division of of the wapentake of Strafforth and Tickhill; 2 miles from Sheffield, 7 from Rotherham, 12 from Penistone.

BURTON, or MONK-BRETTON, *see Bretton, Monk.*

BURTON, in the parish of Thornton-in-Lonsdale, wapentake of Ewcross; 6 miles from Kirby-Lonsdale, *(Westm.)* 13 from Settle, 15 from Lancaster, *(Lanc.)*

BURTON-HALL, in the parish of Brayton, wapentake of Barkston-Ash; 3 miles from Selby, 7 from Ferrybridge, 9 from Pontefract.

BURTON, HIGH, in the parish of Kirk-Burton, Agbrigg-division of the wapentake of Agbrigg and Morley, liberty of the Manor of Wakefield; 4¼ miles Huddersfield, 11 from Wakefield, 12½ from Halifax.

BURTON, KIRK, in the parish of Kirk-Burton, Agbrigg-division of the wapentake of Agbrigg and Morley, liberty of the Manor of Wakefield; 5 miles from Huddersfield, 9 from Penistone, 11 from Wakefield.—Population 1,405.

BURTON-LEONARD, in the parish of Burton-Leonard, lower-division of the wapentake of Claro, liberties of St. Peter and Knaresborough; 5 miles from Knaresborough, 5 from Ripon, 5 from Boroughbridge.—Population 352.

BURTON-SALMON, in the parish of Monk-Fryston, wapentake of Barkston-Ash; *(the seat of Mrs. Middleton)* 5 miles from Pontefract, 9 from Selby, 9 from Tadcaster. —Population 114.

BUSLINGTHORPE, in the parish of Leeds, lower-division of the wapentake of Skirack, liberty of the Honour of Pontefract; 1 mile from Leeds, 12 from Ferrybridge, 12 from Pontefract.

BUTTERBUSK, in the parish of Warmsworth, south-division of the wapentake of Strafforth and Tickhill; 3¼ miles from Doncaster, 9¼ from Rotherham.

BUTTERTHWAITE, in the parish of Ecclesfield, north-division of the wapentake of Strafforth and Tickhill; 4¼ miles from Sheffield, 6 from Rotherham, 9 from Barnsley.

BUTTON-HILL, in the parish of Sheffield, south-division of the wapentake of Strafforth and Tickhill; *(the seat of John Crawshaw, Esq.)* 3 miles from Sheffield, 9 from Rotherham, 11 from Chesterfield, *(Derb.)*

BYRAM, in the parish of Brotherton, wapentake of Barkston-Ash, liberties of St. Peter and the Honor of Pontefract; *(the seat of Sir John Ramsden, Bart.)* 2 miles from Ferrybridge, 4 from Pontefract, 11 from Selby.—Pop. 69.

C.

CADEBY, in the parish of Sprotbrough, north-division of the wapentake of Strafforth and Tickhill, liberty of Tickhill; 4¼ miles from Doncaster, 8¼ from Rotherham.—Pop. 155.

CALCOATES, in the parish of Leeds, lower-division of the wapentake of Skirack; 3 miles from Leeds, 8¼ from Abberford, 13 from Bradford.

CALICO-HALL, in the parish of Halifax, Morley-division of the wapentake of Agbrigg and Morley; *(the seat of the Rev. William Prescot)* ¼ of a mile from Halifax, 8 from Huddersfield.

CALSHAWS, or CALFHAW, in the parish of Kirby-Malzeard, lower-division of the wapentake of Claro; 9 miles from Kettlewell, 9 from Pateleybridge.

CALTON, in the parish of Kirby-Malhamdale, east-division of the wapentake of Staincliffe, liberty of Clifford's Fee; 7 miles from Skipton, 7 from Settle, 12 from Kettlewell.—Population 98.

CALVEL-HOUSES, in the parish of Kirby-Malzeard, lower-division of the wapentake of Claro; 4 miles from Pateley-bridge, 10 from Masham.

CALVERLEY, in the parish of Calverley, Morley-division of the wapentake of Agbrigg and Morley, liberty of the Honour of Pontefract; 3 miles from Bradford, 7 from Leeds, 7 from Otley.—Population 1,127.

CALVERLEY-BRIDGE, in the parish of Calverley, Morley-division of the wapentake of Agbrigg and Morley; 3¼ miles from Bradford, 6½ from Leeds.

CAMBLESFORTH, in the parish of Drax, wapentake of Barkston-Ash; *(the seat of S. W. Waude, Esq.)* 3¼ miles from Snaith, 4¼ from Selby, 14 from Pontefract.—Pop. 190.

CAM-HOUSES, in the parish of Horton, wapentake of Ewcross; 9¼ miles from Askrigg, 14 from Settle.

CAMPSALL, in the parish of Campsall, wapentake of Osgoldcross, liberty of the Honour of Pontefract; *(the seat of Bacon Frank, Esq.)* 8 miles from Doncaster, 8 from Pontefract, 9 from Ferrybridge, 15 from Wakefield.—Population 317.

CAMPS-MOUNT, in the parish of Campsall, wapentake of Osgoldcross, liberty of the Honour of Pontefract; *(the seat of John Cooke, Esq.)* 8 miles from Doncaster, 9 from Ferrybridge, 15 from Wakefield.

CANKLOW, in the parish of Rotherham, south-division of the wapentake of Strafforth and Tickhill; 1¼ mile from Rotherham, 6 from Sheffield, 13 from Doncaster.

CANNON-HALL, in the parish of Silkston, wapentake of Staincross, liberty of the Honour of Pontefract; *(the seat of W. Spencer Stanhope, Esq.)* 4 miles from Penistone, 5 from Barnsley, 9 from Wakefield.

CANTLEY, in the parish of Cantley, south-division of the wapentake of Strafforth and Tickhill; *(Cantley-Lodge, the seat of John Walbank Childers, Esq.)* 3½ miles from Doncaster, 6½ from Bawtry.—Population 500.

CAR, in the parish of Maltby, south-division of the wapentake of Strafforth and Tickhill, liberty of Tickhill; 5 miles from Tickhill, 6 from Rotherham.

CARBROOK, in the parish of Rotherham, south-division of the wapentake of Strafforth and Tickhill; 2¼ miles from Sheffield, 3¾ from Rotherham.

CARCROFT, in the parish of Owston, wapentake of Osgoldcross, liberty of the Honour of Pontefract; 6 miles from Doncaster, 10 from Pontefract.

CAR-GREEN, LOWER, in the parish of Darton, wapentake of Staincross, liberty of the Honour of Pontefract; 2¼ miles from Barnsley, 8¼ from Wakefield, 8¼ from Penistone.

CAR-GREEN, UPPER, in the parish of Darton, wapentake of Staincross, liberty of the Honour of Pontefract; 3 miles from Barnsley, 8 from Wakefield, 8¼ from Penistone.

CAR-HEAD, in the parish of Kildwick, east-division of the wapentake and liberty of Staincliffe; *(the seat of William Wainman, Esq.)* 5 miles from Colne, *(Lanc.)* 5 from Skipton, 8 from Keighley.

CAR-HOUSE, in the parish of Rotherham, south-division of the wapentake of Strafforth and Tickhill; ¼ a mile from Rotherham, 5¼ from Sheffield, 11¼ from Barnsley.

CAR-HOUSE, in the parish of Doncaster, south-division of the wapentake of Strafforth and Tickhill, liberty of St. Peter; *(the seat of ―――― Bacon, Esq)* 1½ mile from Doncaster, 8¼ from Bawtry.

CARLCOTES, in the parish of Penistone, wapentake of Staincross, liberty of the Honour of Pontefract; 5 miles from Penistone, 12 from Barnsley, 13 from Huddersfield.

CARLESMOOR, in the parish of Kirby-Malzeard, lower-division of the wapentake of Claro; 6¼ miles from Masham, 9 from Ripon.

CARLETON, in the parish of Pontefract, wapentake of Osgoldcross, liberty of the Honour of Pontefract; 1¼ mile from Pontefract, 3¼ from Ferrybridge, 14 from Doncaster. —Population 112.

CARLETON, in the parish of Snaith, wapentake of Barkston-Ash; *(Carleton-Hall, the seat of Thomas Stapleton, Esq.)* 2 miles from Snaith, 6 from Selby, 15 from Pontefract.—Population 536.

CARLINGHOW, in the parish of Batley, Abbrigg-division of the wapentake of Agbrigg and Morley, liberty of the Honour of Pontefract; 3 miles from Dewsbury, 9 from Leeds.

CARLTON, in the parish of Guiseley, upper-division of the wapentake of Skirack; 2 miles from Otley, 9 from Leeds, 8 from Bradford.—Population 115.

CARLTON, in the parish of Rothwell, Agbrigg-division of the wapentake of Agbrigg and Morley, liberty of the Honour of Pontefract; 4 miles from Wakefield 5 from Leeds. Population 978.

CARLTON, in the parish of Royston, wapentake of Staincross, liberty of the Honour of Pontefract; 3 miles from Barnsley, 8 from Wakefield, 9 from Penistone.—Pop. 291.

CARLTON, in the parish of Carlton, east division of the wapentake and liberty of Staincliffe; 2 miles from Skipton, 10 from Keighley, 10 from Colne, (Lanc.)—Pop. 845.

CARLTON-NEWBIGGIN, in the parish of Carlton, east division of the wapentake and liberty of Staincliffe; 2½ miles from Skipton, 9¼ from Keighley.

CARR, in the parish of Kirk-Heaton, Agbrigg division of the wapentake of Agbrigg and Morley; 7 miles from Wakefield, 7½ from Huddersfield.

CARRIS, or CARHOUSE, in the parish of Tickhill, south division of the wapentake of Strafforth and Tickhill, liberty of Tickhill; 1¼ mile from Tickhill, 8 from Doncaster, 10 from Rotherham.

CARTWORTH, in the parish of Kirk-Burton, Agbrigg division of the wapentake of Agbrigg and Morley; 6 miles from Huddersfield, 14 from Halifax, 17 from Wakefield.—Population 907.

CASTLEFORD, in the parish of Castleford, wapentake of Osgoldcross, liberty of the Honour of Pontefract; 3¼ miles from Pontefract, 3 from Ferrybridge.—Pop. 793.

CASTLESHAW, in the parish of Rochdale, (Lanc.) Agbrigg division of the wapentake of Agbrigg and Morley; 9 miles from Rochdale, (Lanc.) 11 from Huddersfield.

CASTLEY, in the parish of Leathley, upper division of the wapentake of Claro; 5 miles from Otley, 10 from Knaresborough.—Population 82.

CATCLIFFE, in the parish of Rotherham, south division of the wapentake of Strafforth and Tickhill, liberty of Tickhill; 2 miles from Rotherham, 6 from Sheffield.—Pop. 135.

CATHERINE-HOUSE, in the parish of Halifax, Morley division of the wapentake of Agbrigg and Morley, (the seat of Michael Stocks, Esq.) 2 miles from Halifax, 6½ from Bradford.

CATHERINE-SLACK, in the parish of Halifax, Morley division of the wapentake of Agbrigg and Morley; 3¼ miles from Halifax, 5 from Bradford.

CATHILL, in the parish of Silkston, wapentake of Staincross, liberty of the Honour of Pontefract; 1 mile from Penistone, 6¼ from Barnsley, 13 from Huddersfield.

CATTAL MAGNA, in the parish of Hunsingore, upper division of the wapentake of Claro; 4¼ miles from Wetherby, 7 from Knaresborough.—Population 152.

CASTERELL-HALL, in the parish of Giggleswick, west division of the wapentake and liberty of Staincliffe; 2 miles from Settle, 17 from Kirby-Lonsdale, (Westm.)

CATTLE-LAITHE, in the parish of Pontefract, wapentake of Osgoldcross, liberty of the Honour of Pontefract; 2 miles from Ferrybridge, 3 from Pontefract, 13 from Doncaster.

CAUD, or COLD-HILL, in the parish of Almondbury, Agbrigg-division of the wapentake of Agbrigg and Morley; 2 miles from Huddersfield, 11 from Wakefield, 14 from Barnsley.

CAUSEYSETT, in the parish of Rochdale, *(Lanc.)* Agbrigg-division of the wapentake of Agbrigg and Morley; 8 miles from Rochdale, *(Lanc.)* 11 from Huddersfield.

CAUTLEY, in the parish of Sedbergh, wapentake of Ewcross; 1¼ mile from Sedbergh, 6¼ from Dent, 11¼ from Kendal, *(Westm.)*

CAWELL, in the parish of Almondbury, Agbrigg-division of the wapentake of Agbrigg and Morley; 7¼ miles from Huddersfield, 17 from Wakefield.

CAWOOD, in the parish of Cawood, wapentake of Barkston-Ash, liberties of St. Peter, and Cawood, Wistow, and Otley; 5 miles from Selby, 7¼ from Tadcaster, 10 from York, 12 from Pontefract, 186 from London.—*Market*, Wednesday.—*Fairs*, Old May-day and September 23, for Horned Cattle, &c.—*Principal Inn*, the Ferry-House.—Population 1,025.

CAWTHORNE, in the parish of Silkston, wapentake of Staincross, liberty of the Honour of Pontefract; *(the seat of Thomas West, Esq.)* 4 miles from Barnsley, 4¼ from Penistone, 9¼ from Wakefield.—Population 1,055.

CAYTON, in the parish of South-Stainley, lower-division of the wapentake of Claro; *(the seat of Mrs. Messenger)* 5 miles from Ripon, 6 from Knaresborough.

CHAMPNEY-HILL, in the parish of Silkston, wapentake of Staincross, liberty of the Honour of Pontefract; 3 miles from Barnsley, 4 from Penistone, 9¼ from Wakefield.

CHAPEL-HOUSE, in the parish of Burnsall, east-division of the wapentake and liberty of Staincliffe; 4 miles from Kettlewell, 11 from Skipton, 12 from Settle.

CHAPEL-LE-DALE, in the parish of Low-Bentham, wapentake of Ewcross; 10 miles from Kirby-Lonsdale, *(Westm.)* 13 from Settle, 21 from Lancaster, *(Lanc.)*

CHAPEL-LE-GROVE, in the parish of Halifax, Morley-division of the wapentake of Agbrigg and Morley; 3¼ miles from Halifax, 7 from Huddersfield.

CHAPEL-THORPE, in the parish of Sandall, Agbrigg-division of the wapentake of Agbrigg and Morley, liberty of the Manor of Wakefield; 5 miles from Wakefield, 5 from Barnsley.

CHAPEL-TOWN, in the parish of Ecclesfield, north-division of the wapentake of Strafforth and Tickhill; 6 miles from Rotherham, 6 from Sheffield, 7¼ from Barnsley.
CHARLSTON, see Sharlestone.
CHELOW-HEIGHT, in the parish of Bradford, Morley-division of the wapentake of Agbrigg and Morley; 2¼ miles from Bradford, 3 from Bingley.
CHERRY-TREE-HILL, in the parish of Sheffield, north-division of the wapentake of Strafforth and Tickhill; 2 miles from Sheffield, 8 from Rotherham.
CHESTER-COTES, in the parish of Drax, wapentake of Barkston-Ash; 4 miles from Selby, 4 from Snaith, 10 from Pontefract.
CHEVET, in the parish of Royston, wapentake of Staincross, liberty of the Honour of Pontefract; *(the seat of Sir Thomas Pilkington, Bart.)* 5 miles from Wakefield, 6 from Barnsley, 9 from Pontefract.—Population 75.
CHICKENLEY, in the parish of Dewsbury, Agbrigg-division of the wapentake of Agbrigg and Morley, liberty of the Manor of Wakefield; 1¼ mile from Dewsbury, 4¼ from Wakefield.
CHIDSALL, in the parish of Dewsbury, Agbrigg division of the wapentake of Agbrigg and Morley, liberty of the Manor of Wakefield, 3 miles from Dewsbury, 5¼ from Wakefield.
CHURWELL, in the parish of Batley, Morley-division of the wapentake of Agbrigg and Morley, liberty of the Honour of Pontefract; 3¼ miles from Leeds, 9 from Bradford, 12¼ from Huddersfield.—Population 502.
CISSETT, in the parish of High-Hoyland, Agbrigg-division of the wapentake of Agbrigg and Morley; 8 miles from Huddersfield, 8 from Wakefield.
CLACK-HEATON, in the parish of Birstall, Morley-division of the wapentake of Agbrigg and Morley, liberty of the Honour of Pontefract; 5¼ miles from Bradford, 7 from Halifax, 9 from Leeds.—Population 1,637.
CLAPDALE, in the parish of Clapham, wapentake of Ew-cross; 9 miles from Settle, 11½ from Kirby-Lonsdale, *(Westm.)*
CLAPHAM, in the parish of Clapham, wapentake of Ew-cross; 8¼ miles from Settle, 11 from Kirby-Lonsdale, *(Westm.)* 22 from Skipton.—Population 847.
CLARETON, in the parish of Allerton-Mauliverer, upper-division of the wapentake of Claro; 4 miles from Knaresborough, 5 from Boroughbridge, 7 from Wetherby.
CLAY-CLIFFE, in the parish of Darton, wapentake of

Staincross, liberty of the of Honour Pontefract, ; 2 miles from Barnsley, 5¼ from Penistone, 9¼ from Wakefield.

CLAY-HILL, in the parish of Ilkley, upper-division of the wapentake of Claro ; 8 miles from Otley, 8 from Skipton.

CLAY-MOOR, in the parish of Huddersfield, Agbrigg-division of the wapentake of Agbrigg and Morley ; 4 miles from Huddersfield, 9¼ from Halifax.

CLAYTON, in the parish of Bradford, Morley-division of the wapentake of Agbrigg and Morley, liberty of the Honour of Pontefract ; 3 miles from Bradford, 4¼ from Halifax.—Population 2,040.

CLAYTON, in the parish of Clayton, north-division of the wapentake of Strafforth and Tickhill ; *(the seat of William Bruckenbury, Esq.)* 8 miles from Barnsley, 8 from Doncaster, 13 from Wakefield.—Population 302.

CLAYTON-HEIGHTS, in the parish of Bradford, Morley-division of the wapentake of Agbrigg and Morley ; 4 miles from Bradford, 4 from Halifax.

CLAYTON, WEST, in the parish of High-Hoyland, wapentake of Staincross, liberty of the Honour of Pontefract ; 7 miles from Barnsley, 7 from Penistone, 9 from Wakefield.—Population 668.

CLIFFE-HILL, in the parish of Halifax, Morley-division of the wapentake of Agbrigg and Morley ; *(the seat of John Walker, Esq.)* 3 miles from Halifax, 6 from Huddersfield, 6¼ from Bradford.

CLIFFE-HILL, in the parish of Halifax, Morley-division of the wapentake of Agbrigg and Morley ; *(the seat of Thomas Milne, Esq.)* 3 miles from Halifax, 10 from Huddersfield, 11 from Bradford.

CLIFFE-HOUSE, in the parish of South-Anston, south-division of the wapentake of Strafforth and Tickhill ; 4¼ miles from Worksop, *(Notts.)* 10 from Sheffield.

CLIFFORD, in the parish of Bramham, wapentake of Barkston-Ash ; 2 miles from Wetherby, 4 from Tadcaster, 13 from Ferrybridge.—Population 660.

CLIFTON, in the parish of Rotherham, south-division of the wapentake of Strafforth and Tickhill ; *(the seat of Joseph Walker, Esq.)* ½ a mile from Rotherham, 6¼ from Sheffield, 11¼ from Doncaster.

CLIFTON, in the parish of Dewsbury, Morley-division of the wapentake of Agbrigg and Morley, liberty of the Manor of Wakefield ; 5 miles from Halifax, 5 from Huddersfield, 10 from Wakefield.—Population 1,108.

CLIFTON, in the parish of Conisbrough, south-division of the wapentake of Strafforth and Tickhill ; 6½ miles from Rotherham, 6¼ from Doncaster.

CLIFTON, in the parish of Otley, lower-division of the wapentake of Claro, liberty of Knaresborough; 2¼ miles from Otley, 13 from Knaresborough, 13½ from Skipton.—Population 403.

CLINT, in the parish of Ripley, lower-division of the wapentake of Claro, liberty of Knaresborough; 2 miles from Ripley, 7 from Knaresborough, 8 from Ripon.—Pop. 480.

CLOCK-HOUSE, in the parish of Bradford, Morley-division of the wapentake of Agbrigg and Morley; *(the seat of Nathaniel Jowitt, Esq.)* 1½ mile from Bradford, 8 from Otley, 9 from Halifax.

CLOTHERHAM, in the parish of Ripon, lower-division of the wapentake of Claro, liberty of Ripon; 1¼ mile from Ripon, 7½ from Boroughbridge, 12 from Knaresborough. —Population 11.

CLOUGH, in the parish of Rotherham, south-division of the wapentake of Strafforth and Tickhill; *(the seat of Mrs Westby)* 1 mile from Rotherham, 7 from Sheffield.

COALEY-LANE, in the parish of Wath-upon-Dearn, north-division of the wapentake of Strafforth and Tickhill; 5 miles from Rotherham, 6 from Barnsley.

COATES, in the parish of Barnoldswick, east-division of the wapentake and liberty of Staincliffe; *(Coates-Hall, the seat of —— Bagshaw, Esq.)* 6 miles from Colne, *(Lanc.)* 7 from Skipton, 11 from Burnley, *(Lanc.)*—Pop. 45.

COCKBRIDGE, in the parish of Saxton, wapentake of Barkston-Ash; 2 miles from Tadcaster, 9 from Ferrybridge, 11 from Pontefract.

COCKCROFT-MILL, in the parish of Bingley, upper-division of the wapentake of Skirack; 1 mile from Bingley, 5 from Bradford, 6 from Halifax.

COCKHILL-HOUSE, in the parish of Edlington, south-division of the wapentake of Strafforth and Tickhill; 6 miles from Doncaster, 7 from Rotherham.

COCKLETT, in the parish of Giggleswick, west-division of the wapentake and liberty of Staincliffe; 7 miles from Settle, 18¼ from Skipton.

COCKLEY-HILL, in the parish of Kirk-Heaton, Agbrigg-division of the wapentake of Agbrigg and Morley; 3 miles from Huddersfield, 10 from Wakefield.

COGHILL-HALL, in the parish of Knaresborough, lower-division of the wapentake of Claro; *(the seat of Lady Conyngham)* ½ a mile from Knaresborough, 7½ from Boroughbridge, 12 from Ripon.

COIT-HILL, in the parish of Silkston, wapentake of Staincross, liberty of the Honour of Pontefract; 2 miles from

Penistone, 5¼ from Barnsley, 11 from Sheffield.

COLCOTE, in the parish of Low-Bentham, wapentake of Ewcross; 8 miles from Settle, 9 from Kirby-Lonsdale, (*Westm.*) 20 from Lancaster, (*Lanc.*)

COLEY, in the parish of Halifax, Morley-division of the wapentake of Agbrigg and Morley, liberty of the Manor of Wakefield; 3 miles from Halifax, 6 from Bradford.

COLLING, in the parish of Kildwick, east-division of the wapentake of Staincliffe, liberty of Clifford's Fee; 5 miles from Colne, (*Lanc.*) 6 from Skipton, 8 from Keighley.— Population 1,140.

COLLINGHAM, in the parish of Collingham, lower-division of the wapentake of Skirack; 1 mile from Wetherby, 6¼ from Tadcaster, 9 from Leeds, 12¼ from Otley.—Population 287.

COLN-BRIDGE, in the parish of Kirk-Heaton, Agbrigg-division of the wapentake of Agbrigg and Morley; *(the seat of General Barnard)* 4 miles from Huddersfield, 6 from Halifax, 10¼ from Wakefield.

COLTHOUSE, in the parish of Kirby-Malzeard, lower-division of the wapentake of Claro; 7 miles from Ripon, 9 from Knaresborough.

COLTON, in the parish of Whitchurch, lower-division of the wapentake of Skirack; 5 miles from Leeds, 9 from Wakefield, 10 from Pontefract.

COMBES, FAR and NEAR, in the parish of Ecclesfield, north-division of the wapentake of Strafforth and Tickhill; 4 miles from Rotherham, 5 from Sheffield, 7 from Barnsley.

CONDUIT-HILL, in the parish of Aston, south-division of the wapentake of Strafforth and Tickhill; 6¼ miles from Rotherham, 8¼ from Worksop, (*Notts.*) 9½ from Sheffield.

CONDUIT-HOUSE, in the parish of Tankersley, wapentake of Staincross, liberty of the Honour of Pontefract; 5¼ miles from Penistone, 6 from Barnsley, 7 from Sheffield.

CONEYSTHORPE, in the parish of Goldsbrough, lower-division of the wapentake of Claro; 4 miles from Knaresborough, 5 from Boroughbridge, 7 from Wetherby.—Population 99.

CONISBROUGH, in the parish of Conisbrough, south-division of the wapentake of Strafforth and Tickhill; *(the seat of John Tudor, Esq.)* 5 miles from Doncaster, 7 from Rotherham.—Population 843.

CONISTON, in the parish of Burnsall, east-division of the wapentake of Staincliffe, liberty of Clifford's Fee; 3 miles from Kettlewell, 12 from Skipton, 12 from Settle.—Population 182.

CONISTON, COLD, in the parish of Gargrave, east-division of the wapentake of Staincliffe, liberty of Clifford's Fee; 6¼ miles from Skipton, 9½ from Settle, 12 from Colne, *(Lanc.)*—Population 274.

CONONLEY, in the parish of Kildwick, east-division of the wapentake of Staincliffe, liberty of Clifford's Fee; *(Cononly-Hall, the seat of John Atkinson Busfield, Esq.)* 3 miles from Skipton, 6 from Keighley, 10 from Colne, *(Lanc.)*

COOKRIDGE, in the parish of Addle, upper-division of the wapentake of Skirack; *(Cookridge-Hall, the seat of Sir John Sheffield, Bart.)* 4½ miles from Otley, 5¼ from Leeds.

COPGROVE, in the parish of Copgrove, lower-division of the wapentake of Claro; *(the seat of Henry Duncombe, Esq.)* 4 miles from Knaresborough, 4 from Boroughbridge, 6 from Ripon.—Population 105.

COPLEY-HALL, in the parish of Halifax, Morley-division of the wapentake of Agbrigg and Morley; 2½ miles from Halifax, 7 from Huddersfield.

CORN-CLOSE, in the parish of Kirby-Malzeard, lower-division of the wapentake of Claro; 7 miles from Ripon, 9 from Knaresborough.

CORNSHAW, in the parish of Kildwick, east-division of the wapentake and liberty of Staincliffe; 4 miles from Colne, *(Lanc.)* 7 from Skipton, 8 from Keighley.

CORTWORTH-COLLIERY, in the parish of Wath, north-division of the wapentake of Strafforth and Tickhill; 4 miles from Doncaster, 8 from Barnsley, 10 from Sheffield.

COTTINGLEY, in the parish of Bingley, upper-division of the wapentake of Skirack; *(the seat of Mrs Ferrand)* 3¼ miles from Bradford, 6¼ from Keighley, 15 from Leeds.

COTTINGLEY-BRIDGE, in the parish of Bingley, upper-division of the wapentake of Skirack; 4¼ miles from Bradford, 5¼ from Keighley, 16 from Leeds.

COW-GILL, in the parish of Gisburn, west-division of the wapentake and liberty of Staincliffe; 3 miles from Gisburn, 6¼ from Clitheroe, *(Lanc.)* 14 from Skipton.

COW-HOUSE, in the parish of Bingley, upper-division of the wapentake of Skirack; 6 miles from Bradford, 8 from Halifax, 9 from Otley.

COWICK, in the parish of Snaith, wapentake of Osgoldcross, liberty of the Honour of Pontefract; *(Cowick-Hall, the seat of Lord Downe)* 1¼ mile from Snaith, 8¼ from Howden.—Population 709.

COW-ROYD-HILL, in the parish of Kirk-Heaton, Agbrigg-division of the wapentake of Agbrigg and Morley; 2

miles from Huddersfield, 11 from Wakefield.

COWTHORPE, or COLTHORPE, in the parish of Cowthorpe, upper-division of the wapentake of Claro; 4 miles from Wetherby, 7 from Knaresborough.—Population 148.

CRACOW, in the parish of Burnsall, east-division of the wapentake of Staincliffe, liberty of Clifford's Fee; 6 miles from Skipton, 10 from Kettlewell, 15 from Colne, *(Lanc.)* —Population 191.

CRACOW-HILL, in the parish of Gisburn, west-division of the wapentake and liberty of Staincliffe; 8 miles from Settle, 16 from Skipton.

CRAGG-HALL, in the parish of Fewston, lower-division of the wapentake of Claro; *(the seat of Thomas Parkinson, Esq.)* 7 miles from Otley, 11 from Knaresborough.

CRANE-MOOR, in the parish of Silkston, wapentake of Staincross, liberty of the Honour of Pontefract; 4 miles from Penistone, 4¼ from Barnsley, 9 from Sheffield.

CRAVEN-CROSS-BAR, in the parish of Burnsall, east-division of the wapentake and liberty of Staincliffe; 4 miles from Pateleybridge, 11 from Skipton, 12 from Kettlewell.

CRAY, in the parish of Arncliffe, east-division of the wapentake and liberty of Staincliffe; 5¼ miles from Kettlewell, 8¼ from Askrigg.

CRIDDLING-PARK, in the parish of Darrington, wapentake of Osgoldcross, liberty of the Honour of Pontefract; 2¼ miles from Ferrybridge, 4¼ from Pontefract.

CRIDDLING-STUBBS, in the parish of Womersley, wapentake of Osgoldcross, liberty of the Honour of Pontefract; 2¼ miles from Ferrybridge, 4¼ from Pontefract.—Pop. 83.

CRIGGLESTON, in the parish of Sandall, Agbrigg-division of the wapentake of Agbrigg and Morley, liberty of the Manor of Wakefield; 4¼ miles from Wakefield, 6 from Barnsley.—Population 1,216.

CRIMESWORTH-DEAN, in the parish of Halifax, Morley-division of the wapentake of Agbrigg and Morley; 8½ miles from Halifax, 11¼ from Colne, *(Lanc.)* 14¼ from Rochdale. *(ditto.)*

CRIMESWORTH-HALL, in the parish of Halifax, Morley-division of the wapentake of Agbrigg and Morley; 8 miles from Halifax, 12 from Colne, *(Lanc.)* 14 from Rochdale, *(ditto.)*

CRINGLES, in the parish of Kildwick, east-division of the wapentake and liberty of Staincliffe; 5 miles from Skipton, 5 from Keighley, 12 from Otley.

CROFTON, in the parish Crofton, Agbrigg-division of the wapentake of Agbrigg and Morley, liberty of the Honour of Pontefract; *(the seat of Sir Henry Wilson, Bart.)* 3½ miles from Wakefield, 6 from Pontefract.—Pop. 535.

CROMWELL-BOTTOM, in the parish of Halifax, Morley-division of the wapentake of Agbrigg and Morley, liberty of the Honour of Pontefract; 3 miles from Halifax, 5 from Huddersfield.

CROOK, or CROOK'S HOUSE, in the parish of Bracewell, west-division of the wapentake and liberty of Staincliffe; 10 miles from Skipton, 11 from Settle, 11 from Burnley, *(Lanc.)*

CROOK-HILL, in the parish of Edlington, south-division of the wapentake of Strafforth and Tickhill; *(Crook-hill-Hall, the seat of John Woodyear, Esq.)* 5 miles from Doncaster, 8 from Rotherham.

CROOK-OF-LUNE, in the parish of Sedbergh, wapentake Ewcross; 3¼ miles from Sedbergh, 8 from Kendal, *(Westm.)*

CROOKS, in the parish of Sheffield, south-divison of the wapentake of Strafforth and Tickhill; 1¼ mile from Sheffield, 7¼ from Rotherham, 13 from Chesterfield, *(Derb.)*

CROOKS-MOOR, in the parish of Sheffield, south-division of the wapentake of Strafforth and Tickhill; *(Tapton-Grove, the seat of William Shore, Esq.)* 1 mile from Sheffield, 7 from Rotherham, 13 from Chesterfield, *(Derb.)*

CROSLAND-HILL, in the parish of Almondbury, Agbrigg-division of the wapentake of Agbrigg and Morley, liberty of the Manor of Wakefield; 2 miles from Huddersfield, 10 from Halifax.

CROSLAND, NORTH, in the parish of Almondbury, Agbrigg-division of the wapentake of Agbrigg and Morley, liberty of the Manor of Wakefield; 3½ miles from Huddersfield, 11¼ from Halifax, 13¼ from Penistone.

CROSLAND, SOUTH, in the parish of Almondbury, Agbrigg-division of the wapentake of Agbrigg and Morley, liberty of the Honour of Pontefract; 4 miles from Huddersfield, 12 from Halifax, 13 from Penistone.—Pop 1,221.

CROSS-FLATTS, in the parish of Bingley, upper-division of the wapentake of Skirack; 1 mile from Bingley, 7 from Bradford, 9 from Halifax.

CROSS-GATES, in the parish of Whitchurch, lower-division of the wapentake of Skirack; 4 miles from Leeds, 9 from Wetherby, 10 from Wakefield.

CROSS-HILL, in the parish of Kildwick, east-division of the wapentake and liberty of Staincliffe; 5 miles from Keighley, 5 from Skipton, 8 from Colne, *(Lanc.)*

CROSS-ROYD, in the parish of Penistone, wapentake of Staincross, liberty of the Honour of Pontefract; 1 mile from Penistone, 8 from Barnsley, 13 from Huddersfield.

CROSS-STONE, in the parish of Halifax, Morley-division of the wapentake of Agbrigg and Morley; 8 miles from Rochdale, (*Lanc.*) 11 from Halifax.

CROW-NEST, in the parish of Halifax, Morley-division of the wapentake of Agbrigg and Morley; *(the seat of William Walker, Esq.)* 3 miles from Halifax, 6 from Huddersfield, 13 from Wakefield.

CROW-NEST, in the parish of Dewsbury, Agbrigg-division of the wapentake of Agbrigg and Morley; *(the seat of J. Hague, Esq.)* ½ a mile from Dewsbury, 5¼ from Wakefield.

CUBLEY, in the parish of Penistone, wapentake of Staincross, liberty of the Honour of Pontefract; 1 mile from Penistone, 8 from Barnsley, 13 from Sheffield.

CUCKOLDS-HAVEN, in the parish of Firbeck, south-division of the wapentake of Strafforth and Tickhill; 4 miles from Tickhill, 5 from Worksop, (*Notts.*) 11¼ from Rotherham.

CUCKHOW-NEST, in the parish of Bingley, upper-division of the wapentake of Skirack; 1 mile from Bingley, 7 from Keighley, 14 from Otley.

CUDWORTH, NETHER, in the parish of Royston, wapentake of Staincross, liberty of the Honour of Pontefract; 3¼ miles from Barnsley, 8½ from Wakefield, 10½ from Pontefract.

CUDWORTH, OVER, in the parish of Royston, wapentake of Staincross, liberty of the Honour of Pontefract; 3¼ miles from Barnsley, 8 from Wakefield, 10½ from Pontefract.—Population 396.

CULLINGWORTH, in the parish of Bingley, upper-division of the wapentake of Skirack; 3½ miles from Keighley, 7 from Bradford, 8½ from Halifax.

CUMBERWORTH, in the parishes of Kirk-Burton and Silkston, wapentakes of Agbrigg and Morley (Agbrigg-division) and Staincross, liberties of the Manor of Wakefield, and the Honour of Pontefract; 5½ miles from Penistone, 8 from Huddersfield, 10 from Barnsley.—Pop. 450.

CUMBERWORTH, NETHER, in the parish of Silkston, wapentake of Staincross, liberty of the Honour of Pontefract; 6 miles from Penistone, 8 from Huddersfield, 10 from Barnsley.—Population 854.

CLUMPTON, in the parish of Collingham, lower-division of the wapentake of Skirack; 1 mile from Wetherby, 5 from Tadcaster, 6 from Otley.

CUSWORTH, in the parish of Sprotbrough, north-division of the wapentake of Strafforth and Tickhill, liberty of Tick-

WEST-RIDING. 181

hill; *(the seat of William Wrightson, Esq.)* 2 miles from Doncaster, 13 from Barnsley.

CUTLER-HEIGHT, in the parish of Bradford, Morley-division of the wapentake of Agbrigg and Morley; 1¼ mile from Bradford, 9 from Halifax, 9 from Leeds.

D.

DACRE, in the parish of Ripon, lower-division of the wapentake of Claro; 4 miles from Pateleybridge, 6 from Ripley, 12 from Ripon.—Population 592.

DACRE-BANKS, in the parish of Ripon, lower-division, of the wapentake of Claro; 3¼ miles from Pateleybridge, 6¼ from Ripley.

DALE-END, in the parish of Carlton, east-division of the wapentake and liberty of Staincliffe; 6 miles from Skipton, 9 from Keighley.

DALLA, HIGH, or HOLE, in the parish of Kirby-Malzeard, lower-division of the wapentake of Claro; 8 miles from Masham, 10 from Ripon.

DALTON, in the parish of Kirk-Heaton, Agbrigg-division of the wapentake of Agbrigg and Morley, liberty of the Manor of Wakefield; 1 mile from Huddersfield, 9 from Halifax, 13 from Wakefield.—Population 1,222.

DALTON, NETHER, in the parishes of Thribergh and Rotherham, south-divison of the wapentake of Strafforth and Tickhill; 2 miles from Rotherham, 8 from Sheffield, 10 from Doncaster.—Population 225.

DALTON, OVER, in the parishes of Thribergh and Rotherham, south-division of the wapentake of Strafforth and Tickhill; 3 miles from Rotherham, 9 from Sheffield, 10 from Doncaster.

DANDER-MIRE, in the parish of Sedbergh, wapentake of Ewcross; 9 miles from Sedbergh, 10 from Askrigg.

DARFIELD, in the parish of Darfield, north-division of the wapentake of Strafforth and Tickhill; 5¼ miles from Barnsley, 10 from Doncaster.—Population 447.

DARLANDS, in the parish of Ecclesfield, north-division of the wapentake of Strafforth and Tickhill; 4 miles from Sheffield, 6 from Rotherham, 9 from Barnsley.

DARLEY, in the parish of Hampsthwaite, lower-division of the wapentake of Claro, liberty of Knaresborough; 4 miles from Ripley, 8 from Ripon, 9 from Knaresborough.

DARNALL, in the parish of Sheffield, south-division of the

wapentake of Strafforth and Tickhill, liberty of Hallamshire; *(the seat of Samuel Staniforth, Esq.)* 2¼ miles from Sheffield, 5 from Rotherham, 14 from Chesterfield, *(Derb.)*

DARRINGTON, in the parish of Darrington, wapentake of Osgoldcross, liberty of the Honour of Pontefract; *(the seat of —— Sotheran, Esq.)* 3 miles from Ferrybridge, 3 from Pontefract, 12¼ from Doncaster, 14¼ from Barnsley. —Population 379.

DARTON, in the parish of Darton, wapentake of Staincross, liberty of the Honour of Pontefract; 3¼ miles from Barnsley, 6 from Penistone, 8¼ from Wakefield.—Pop. 936.

DARTON-HALL, in the parish of Darton, wapentake of Staincross, liberty of the Honour of Pontefract; 4 miles from Barnsley, 6 from Penistone, 8¼ from Wakefield.

DAW-GREEN, in the parish of Dewsbury, Agbrigg-division of the wapentake of Agbrigg and Morley, liberty of the Manor of Wakefield; ½ a mile from Dewsbury, 5¼ from Wakefield.

DAY-HOUSE, in the parish of Darton, wapentake of Staincross, liberty of the Honour of Pontefract; 2 miles from Barnsley, 6 from Penistone, 9¼ from Wakefield.

DEAN-HEAD, in the parish of Penistone, wapentake of Staincross, liberty of the Honour of Pontefract; 3 miles from Penistone, 6¼ from Barnsley, 10¼ from Sheffield.

DEAN-HEAD, or SCAMMONDEN, in the parish of Huddersfield, Agbrigg-division of the wapentake of Agbrigg and Morley, liberty of the Manor of Wakefield; 6¼ miles from Huddersfield, 9 from Halifax.—Population 626.

DEAN-HOUSE, in the parish of Huddersfield, Agbrigg-division of the wapentake of Agbrigg and Morley; 5¼ miles from Huddersfield, 8 from Halifax.

DEANSHAW, in the parish of Rochdale, *(Lanc.)* Agbrigg-division of the wapentake of Agbrigg and Morley; 6 miles from Rochdale, *(Lanc.)* 12 from Manchester, *(ditto)* 12 from Huddersfield.

DEEP-CARR, in the parish of Ecclesfield, north-division of the wapentake of Strafforth and Tickhill; 5 miles from Sheffield, 9 from Penistone, 10 from Rotherham.

DEEP-DALE, in the parish of Arncliffe, east-division of the wapentake and liberty of Staincliffe; 6 miles from Kettlewell, 15 from Settle, 17 from Leyburn.

DEEP-DALE, in the parish of Sedbergh, wapentake of Ewcross; 1¼ mile from Dent, 6¼ from Sedbergh, 10 from Hawes.

DEEP-DALE-HEAD, in the parish of Long-Preston, west-division of the wapentake and liberty of Staincliffe; 6¼ miles from Settle, 5 from Gisburn.

DEIGHTON, in the parish of Huddersfield, Agbrigg-division of the wapentake of Agbrigg and Morley, liberty of the Honour of Pontefract; 2¼ miles from Huddersfield, 6 from Dewsbury, 7 from Halifax.

DEIGHTON, KIRK, in the parish of Kirk-Deighton, upper-division of the wapentake of Claro; *(the seat of the Rev. James Geldart)* 1¼ mile from Wetherby, 5½ from Knaresborough.—Population 320.

DEIGHTON, NORTH, in the parish of Kirk-Deighton, upper-division of the wapentake of Claro; *(the seat of Sir William Ingleby, Bart.)* 2¼ miles from Wetherby, 4½ from Knaresborough.—Population 163.

DELFE, or DELPH, in the parish of Rochdale, *(Lanc.)* Agbrigg-division of the wapentake of Agbrigg and Morley; 8 miles from Rochdale, *(Lanc.)* 11¼ from Huddersfield, 13½ from Manchester, *(Lanc.)*

DENABY, in the parish of Mexbrough, south-division of the wapentake of Strafforth and Tickhill; 6 miles from Rotherham, 6 from Doncaster.—Population 128.

DENBY-DIKE-SIDE, in the parish of Penistone, wapentake of Staincross, liberty of the Honour of Pontefract; 4½ miles from Penistone, 8 from Barnsley, 9 from Huddersfield.

DENBY-GRANGE, in the parish of Kirk-Heaton, Agbrigg-division of the wapentake of Agbrigg and Morley, liberty of the Honour of Pontefract; 6¼ miles from Wakefield, 7 from Huddersfield.

DENBY, HIGH, in the parish of Penistone, wapentake of Staincross, liberty of the Honour of Pontefract; 3 miles from Penistone, 6½ from Barnsley, 9 from Huddersfield.—Population 1,061.

DENBY, LOW, in the parish of Penistone, wapentake of Staincross, liberty of the Honour of Pontefract; 3½ miles from Penistone, 7¼ from Barnsley, 9½ from Huddersfield.

DENHOLME-CAR, in the parish of Bradford, Morley-division of the wapentake of Agbrigg and Morley; 6 miles from Halifax, 6 from Keighley, 6¼ from Bradford.

DENT, in the parish of Sedbergh, wapentake of Ewcross; 5 miles from Sedbergh, 8 from Kirby-Lonsdale, *(Westm.)* 11¼ from Hawes, 16¼ from Askrigg, 21 from Settle, 59 from York, 266 from London.—*Market*, Friday.—*Fairs*, first Friday after February 13, and every Fortnight until May 12, for Horned Cattle.—Population 1,773.

DENTON, in the parish of Otley, upper-division of the wapentake of Claro; *(Denton-Park, the seat of Sir Henry Carr Ibbotson, Bart.)* 5¼ miles from Otley, 8 from Keighley, 10½ from Skipton.—Population 192.

DENTON, UPPER, in the parish of Otley, upper-division of the wapentake of Claro; 6 miles from Otley, 10 from Skipton.

DEWSBURY, in the parish of Dewsbury, Agbrigg-division of the wapentake of Agbrigg and Morley, liberty of the Manor of Wakefield; 5 miles from Wakefield, 8 from Huddersfield, 9 from Bradford, 10 from Leeds, 11 from Halifax, 33 from York, 187 from London.—*Market*, Wednesday.—*Fairs*, Wednesday before New Michaelmas-day, October 5, and Wednesday before Old May-day, for Horses, Horned Cattle, Sheep, Cloth, &c.—*Principal Inns*, Man and Saddle, George and Dragon, and Commercial Coffee-House. —Population 4,566.

DEWSBURY-MOORSIDE, in the parish of Dewsbury, Agbrigg-division of the wapentake of Agbrigg and Morley, liberty of the Manor of Wakefield; 1 mile from Dewsbury, 6 from Wakefield.

DEYKIN-BROOK, in the parish of Silkston, wapentake of Staincross, liberty of the Honour of Pontefract; 3 miles from Penistone, 5¼ from Barnsley, 11 from Wakefield.

DICK-ROYD-HOUSE, in the parish of Penistone; wapentake of Staincross, liberty of the Honour of Pontefract; 5 miles from Penistone, 12 from Barnsley, 13 from Huddersfield.

DIGGLE, in the parish of Rochdale, *(Lanc.)* Agbrigg-division of the wapentake of Agbrigg and Morley; 11 miles from Huddersfield, 11 from Rochdale, *(Lanc.)* 14 from Manchester, *(ditto.)*

DIGLEY-ROYD, in the parish of Almondbury, Agbrigg-division of the wapentake of Agbrigg and Morley; 8 miles from Huddersfield, 10 from Penistone, 17 from Halifax.

DIKES-MARSH, in the parish of Thorne, south-division of the wapentake of Strafforth and Tickhill; 2 miles from Thorne, 8 from Snaith.

DINNINGTON, in the parish of Dinnington, south-division of the wapentake of Strafforth and Tickhill, liberty of Tickhill; *(the seat of Thomas Athorpe, Esq.)* 8 miles from Tickhill, 8 from Worksop, *(Notts.)* 8½ from Rotherham.— Population 162.

DIRTCAR, in the parish of Sandall, Agbrigg-division of the wapentake of Agbrigg and Morley, liberty of the Manor of Wakefield; 4 miles from Wakefield, 7 from Barnsley.

DOBCROSS, in the parish of Rochdale, *(Lanc.)* Agbrigg-division of the wapentake of Agbrigg and Morley; 9 miles from Rochdale, *(Lanc.)* 12 from Manchester, *(ditto)* 13 from Huddersfield.

DODWORTH, in the parish of Silkston, wapentake of Staincross, liberty of the Honour of Pontefract; *(the seats of William Garlick, and Richard Parkins, Esqrs.)* 2 miles from Barnsley, 5¼ from Penistone, 10 from Wakefield.—Population 403.

DODWORTH-BOTTOMS, in the parish of Silkston, wapentake of Staincross, liberty of the Honour of Pontefract; 2 miles from Barnsley, 6½ from Penistone, 10½ from Wakefield.

DOG-PARK, in the parish of Weston, upper-division of the wapentake of Claro; 5 miles from Otley, 12 from Knaresborough, 15 from Leeds.

DONCASTER, in the parish and soke of Doncaster, south-division of the wapentake of Strafforth and Tickhill; 7 miles from Tickhill, 9 from Bawtry, 12 from Thorne, 12 from Rotherham, 12 from Blythe, *(Notts.)* 15 from Ferrybridge, 15 from Pontefract, 17 from Worksop, *(Notts.)* 20 from Wakefield, 36 from York, 162 from London.—*Market*, Saturday.—*Fairs*, April 5, and August 5, for Horses, and Horned Cattle.—*Bankers*, Old-Bank, Messrs. Ellison, Yarborough, Cook, Childers, and Co. draw on Messrs. Goslings and Sharp, 19, Fleet-Street; New-Bank, Messrs. Leatham, Jackson, Few, and Trueman, draw on Messrs. Harrisons, Price, Kay, and Chapman, 1, Mansion-house-Street.—*Principal Inns*, Angel, Red-Lion, Rein-Deer, Black-Boy, and Green-Dragon.—Population 5,697.

DOUGHBIGGIN, in the parish of Sedbergh, wapentake of Ewcross; 1¼ mile from Sedbergh, 6½ from Dent, 11½ from Kendal, *(Westm.)*

DOUK-COVE, in the parish of Thornton-in-Lonsdale, wapentake of Ewcross; 9½ miles from Kirby-Lonsdale, *(Westm.)* 15¼ from Askrigg.

DOWEY, in the parish of Rochdale, *(Lanc.)* Agbrigg-division of the wapentake of Agbrigg and Morley; 7 miles from Rochdale, *(Lanc.)* 11 from Huddersfield.

DOWGILL-HALL, in the parish of Kirby-Malzeard, lower-division of the wapentake of Claro; 4 miles from Ripley, 9 from Knaresborough.

DRANFIELD-HILL, in the parish of Kirk-Heaton, Agbrigg-division of the wapentake of Agbrigg and Morley; 3¼ miles from Huddersfield, 9 from Wakefield.

DRAUGHTON, or DRAIGHTON, in the parish of Skipton, east-division of the wapentake of Staincliffe, liberty of Clifford's Fee; 3 miles from Skipton, 8 from Keighley, 13 from Otley.

DRAX, in the parish of Drax, wapentake of Barkston-Ash

4 miles from Snaith, 8 from Selby, 14 from Pontefract.—Population 221.

DRAX-ABBEY, in the parish of Drax, wapentake of Barkston-Ash; 5 miles from Snaith, 8 from Selby.

DRAX, LONG, in the parish of Drax, wapentake of Barkston-Ash; 5 miles from Snaith, 8 from Selby, 14½ from Pontefract.—Population 170.

DREBLEY, in the parish of Skipton, east-division of the wapentake and liberty of Staincliffe; 5 miles from Skipton, 10 from Pateleybridge.

DRIGHLINGTON, in the parish of Birstall, Morley-division of the wapentake of Agbrigg and Morley, liberty of the Honour of Pontefract; 5 miles from Bradford, 7 from Leeds.—Population 1,232.

DUBSYKE, in the parish of Horton, wapentake of Ewcross; 9 miles from Settle, 16 from Kirby-Lonsdale, *(Westm.)*

DUDLEY-HILL, in the parish of Bradford, Morley-division of the wapentake of Agbrigg and Morley; 2 miles from Bradford, 8 from Halifax, 10 from Otley.

DUNGWORTH, in the parish of Ecclesfield, north-division of the wapentake of Strafforth and Tickhill; 6 miles from Sheffield, 9 from Rotherham, 10 from Penistone.

DUN-KESWICK, *see Keswick, Dun.*

DUNKIRK, in the parish of Penistone, wapentake of Staincross, liberty of the Honour of Pontefract; 4 miles from Penistone, 7¼ from Barnsley, 10¼ from Huddersfield.

DUNNAH, in the parish of Slaidburn, west-division of the wapentake and liberty of Staincliffe; 8¼ miles from Clitheroe, *(Lanc.)* 12 from Settle.

DUNNINGLEY, in the parish of Woodchurch, Agbrigg-division of the wapentake of Agbrigg and Morley, liberty of the Manor of Wakefield; 6 miles from Wakefield, 6 from Dewsbury.

DUNSCROFT, in the parish of Hatfield, south-division of the wapentake of Strafforth and Tickhill; 3 miles from Thorne, 8 from Doncaster.

DUNSFORTH, HIGH, in the parish of Aldborough, upper-division of the wapentake of Claro; 3 miles from Boroughbridge, 7 from Knaresborough.—Population 110.

DUNSFORTH, LOW, in the parish of Aldborough, upper-division of the wapentake of Claro; 3 miles from Boroughbridge, 8 from Knaresborough.—Population 118.

DUNSOP, in the parish of Slaidburn, west-division of the wapentake and liberty of Staincliffe; 10 miles from Clitheroe, *(Lanc.)* 12 from Settle.

DYSON-COIT, in the parish of Penistone, wapentake of

Staincross, liberty of the Honour of Pontefract; 2 miles from Penistone, 7 from Barnsley, 12 from Sheffield.

DYSON-HOLME, in the parish of Ecclesfield, north-division of the wapentake of Strafforth and Tickhill; 6 miles from Sheffield, 10 from Rotherham, 10 from Penistone.

E.

EADSFORD-BRIDGE, in the parish of Mitton, west-division of the wapentake and liberty of Staincliffe; 1¼ mile from Clitheroe, *(Lanc.)* 9¼ from Gisburn, 11 from Blackburn, *(Lanc.)*

EALAND-EDGE, in the parish of Halifax, Morley-division of the wapentake of Agbrigg and Morley, liberty of the Honour of Pontefract; 4¼ miles from Huddersfield, 5 from Halifax.

EAREBY, in the parish of Thornton, east-division of the wapentake and liberty of Staincliffe; 5 miles from Colne, *(Lanc.)* 7 from Skipton, 11 from Burnley, *Lanc.)*

EASINGTON, in the parish of Slaidburn, west-divison of the wapentake of Staincliffe, liberty of Bolland; 9 miles from Settle, 16 from Skipton, 16 from Colne, *(Lanc.)*— Population 376.

EASTBURN, in the parish of Kildwick, east-division of the wapentake of Staincliffe, liberty of Clifford's Fee; 4¼ miles from Keighley, 5¼ from Skipton, 10 from Colne, *(Lanc.)*

EASTBY, in the parish of Skipton, east-division of the wapentake of Staincliffe, liberty of Clifford's Fee; 2¼ miles from Skipton, 12¼ from Keighley, 14¼ from Colne, *(Lanc.)*

EASTFIELD, in the parish of Silkston, wapentake of Staincross, liberty of the Honour of Pontefract; 3 miles from Penistone, 4¼ from Barnsley, 12 from Wakefield.

EASTFIELD, or EASTWOOD, in the parish of Tickhill, south-division of the wapentake of Strafforth and Tickhill; *(the seat of Edward Eastfield Laughton, Esq.)* ½ a mile from Tickhill; 6½ from Doncaster, 11¼ from Rotherham.

EASTOFT, *(a part in Lincolnshire)* in the parish of Adlingfleet, wapentake of Osgoldcross, liberty of the Honour of Pontefract; 7¼ miles from Crule, *(Linc.)* 9 from Howden, 16¼ from Snaith.

EASTWOOD, in the parish of Rotherham, south-division of the wapentake of Strafforth and Tickhill; *(the seat of Joseph Walker, Esq.)* 1 mile from Rotherham, 11 from Doncaster.

EASTWOOD, in the parish of Halifax, Morley-division of the wapentake of Agbrigg and Morley; 7½ miles from Rochdale, *(Lanc.)* 10 from Halifax.

ECCLESALL-BIERLEY, in the parish of Sheffield, south-division of the wapentake of Strafforth and Tickhill, liberty of Hallamshire; ¼ of a mile from Sheffield, 6¼ from Rotherham, 11 from Chesterfield, *(Derb.)*—Population 5,362.

ECCLESFIELD, in the parish of Ecclesfield, north-division of the wapentake of Strafforth and Tickhill, liberty of Hallamshire; 4 miles from Sheffield, 7 from Rotherham, 10 from Barnsley.—Population 5,114.

ECCLESHILL, in the parish of Bradford, Morley-division of the wapentake of Agbrigg and Morley, liberty of the Manor of Wakefield; 2½ miles from Bradford, 7 from Otley, 10¼ from Halifax.—Population 1,351.

ECCUP, in the parish of Addle, upper-division of the wapentake of Skirack; 3 miles from Harewoood, 5 from Leeds, 8 from Otley.

ECKLANDS, in the parish of Penistone, wapentake of Staincross, liberty of the Honour of Pontefract; 2 miles from Penistone, 9 from Barnsley, 12 from Sheffield.

EDDERCLIFFE, in the parish of Birstall, Morley-division of the wapentake of Agbrigg and Morley; 7 miles from Bradford, 10 from Wakefield.

EDEN, in the parish of Kildwick, east-division of the wapentake and liberty of Staincliffe; 4 miles from Keighley, 6 from Skipton, 10 from Colne, *(Lanc.)*

EDGE, in the parish of Sheffield, south-division of the wapentake of Strafforth and Tickhill; 3¼ miles from Sheffield, 9¼ from Rotherham, 11 from Chesterfield, *(Derb.)*

EDGERTON, in the parish of Huddersfield, Agbrigg-division of the wapentake of Agbrigg and Morley, liberty of the Honour of Pontefract; 6½ miles from Huddersfield, 9¼ from Halifax.

EDLINGTON, in the parish of Edlington, south-division of the wapentake of Strafforth and Tickhill; 4½ miles from Doncaster, 8¼ from Rotherham.—Population 127.

EGBROUGH, HIGH, in the parish of Kellington, wapentake of Osgoldcross, liberty of the Honour of Pontefract; 4¼ miles from Snaith, 9 from Pontefract.—Population 186.

EGBROUGH, LOW, in the parish of Kellington, wapen. of Osgoldcross, liberty of the Honour of Pontefract; 4 miles from Snaith, 9 from Pontefract.

ELLAND, in the parish of Halifax, Morley-division of the wapentake of Agbrigg and Morley, liberty of the Honour of Pontefract; 3 miles from Halifax, 5 from Huddersfield, 15 from Leeds.—Population 3,385.

WEST-RIDING.

ELLENTHORPE, in the parish of Gisburn, west-division of the wapentake and liberty of Staincliffe; 1¾ mile from Gisburn, 11 from Settle.

ELLERKER, in the parish of Fewston, lower-division of the wapentake of Claro; 6 miles from Otley, 11¼ from Skipton.

ELLANGTHORPE, in the parish of Aldborough, wapentake of Halikeld; (*North-Riding*) 5 miles from Boroughbridge, 7 from Ripon, 10 from Easingwold.

ELM-GREEN, in the parish of Ecclesfield, north-division of the wapentake of Strafforth and Tickhill; 3 miles from Sheffield, 7¼ from Rotherham, 10 from Barnsley.

ELM-HURST, in the parish of Silkston, wapentake of Staincross, liberty of the Honour of Pontefract; 2 miles from Penistone, 5½ from Barnsley, 12 from Wakefield.

ELMLEY, in the parish of Elmley, Agbrigg-division of the wapentake of Agbrigg and Morley, liberty of the Manor of Wakefield; 7 miles from Huddersfield, 8½ from Wakefield, 9 from Barnsley.—Population 1,120.

ELMSALL-LODGE, in the parish of South-Kirkby, wapentake of Osgoldcross, liberty of the Honour of Pontefract; (*the seat of Christopher Wilson, Esq.*) 7¼ miles from Pontefract, 9¾ from Doncaster, 11 from Wakefield.

ELMSALL, NORTH, in the parish of South-Kirkby, wapentake of Osgoldcross, liberty of the Honour of Pontefract; 7 miles from Pontefract, 9 from Doncaster, 9 from Barnsley, 11 from Wakefield.—Population 223.

ELMSALL, SOUTH, in the parish of South-Kirkby, wapentake of Osgoldcross, liberty of the Honour of Pontefract; 8 miles from Doncaster, 8 from Barnsley, 8 from Pontefract, 11¼ from Wakefield.—Population 348.

ELPHABROUGH-HALL, in the parish of Halifax, Morley-division of the wapentake of Agbrigg and Morley; 6 miles from Halifax, 13 from Colne, (*Lanc.*) 15 from Rochdale, (*ditto.*)

ELSEKER, in the parish of Wath-upon-Dearn, north-division of the wapentake of Strafforth and Tickhill; 5¼ miles from Barnsley, 6¼ from Rotherham, 10 from Sheffield.

ELSLACK, in the parish of Broughton, east-division of the wapentake of Staincliffe, liberty of Clifford's Fee; 4 miles from Skipton, 8 from Colne, (*Lanc.*) 12 from Keighley.—Population 180.

EMBSEY, in the parish of Skipton, east-division of the wapentake of Staincliffe, liberty of Clifford's Fee; 1¼ mile from Skipton, 11¼ from Keighley, 16 from Settle.—Population 623.

Bb

EMBSEY, KIRK, in the parish of Skipton, east-division of the wapentake of Staincliffe, liberty of Clifford's Fee; *(the seat of William Baynes, Esq.)* 2 miles from Skipton, 12 from Keighley, 16 from Settle.

ERRINGDEN, in the parish of Halifax, Morley-division of the wapentake of Agbrigg and Morley, liberty of the Manor of Wakefield; 6¼ miles from Halifax, 10 from Rochdale, *(Lanc.)* 14 from Huddersfield.—Pop. 1,313.

ESHOLT, in the parish of Guiseley, upper-division of the wapentake of Skirack, liberty of Cawood, Wistow, and Otley; *(Esholt-Hall, the seat of Joshua Crompton, Esq.)* 5 miles from Bradford, 5 from Otley, 9 from Leeds.—Population 268.

ESHTON, in the parish of Gargrave, east-division of the wapentake of Staincliffe, liberty of Clifford's Fee; *(Eshton-Hall, the seat of Matthew Wilson, Esq.)* 5 miles from Skipton, 12 from Kettlewell, 12 from Colne, *(Lanc.)*—Population 84.

ESSINGTON, in the parish of Slaidburn, west-division of the wapentake and liberty of Staincliffe; 7 miles from Clitheroe, *(Lanc.)* 9 from Gisburn.

ETHERTHORPE, in the parish of Darfield, north-division of the wapentake of Strafforth and Tickhill; 4¼ miles from Barnsley, 11 from Doncaster.

EAVESTONE, in the parish of Ripon, lower-division of the wapentake of Claro, liberty of Ripon; 6 miles from Ripon, 9 from Knaresborough.—Population 57.

EWOOD-HALL, in the parish of Halifax, Morley-division of the wapentake of Agbrigg and Morley; 6½ miles from Halifax, 13 from Keighley, 14¼ from Huddersfield.

EXA, in the parish of Mitton, west-division of the wapentake and liberty of Staincliffe; 5 miles from Clitheroe, *(Lanc.)* 12 from Blackburn, *(ditto)* 13 from Gisburn.

EXLEY, in the parish of Halifax, Morley-division of the wapentake of Agbrigg and Morley; 2½ miles from Halifax, 5¼ from Huddersfield.

EXLEY-GATE, in the parish of Penistone, wapentake of Staincross, liberty of the Honour of Pontefract; 4 miles from Penistone, 7 from Barnsley, 11 from Wakefield.

EXLEY-HEAD, in the parish of Keighley, east-division of the wapentake and liberty of Staincliffe; 1 mile from Keighley, 10 from Skipton, 10¼ from Colne, *(Lanc.)*

WEST-RIDING.

F.

FAIRBURN, in the parish of Ledsam, wapentake of Barkston-Ash, liberty of the Honour of Pontefract; *(the seat of Thomas Jackson, Esq.)* 2¼ miles from Ferrybridge, 4 from Pontefract, 6¼ from Abberford, 11 from Selby, 12¼ from Leeds.—Population 339.

FAIRWEATHER-GREEN, in the parish of Bradford, Morley-division of the wapentake of Agbrigg and Morley; 1¼ mile from Bradford, 7 from Halifax.

FALDRING, in the parish of Ecclesfield, north-division of the wapentake of Strafforth and Tickhill; 3¼ miles from Sheffield, 7 from Rotherham, 10 from Barnsley.

FALL-HOUSE, in the parishes of Thornton and Kirk-Heaton, Agbrigg-division of the wapentake of Agbrigg and Morley; 3 miles from Dewsbury, 7 from Wakefield.

FARFIELD, in the parish of Addingham, east-division of the wapentake and liberty of Staincliffe; *(the seat of John Traverse, Esq.)* 5 miles from Skipton, 7 from Keighley, 10 from Otley.

FARFIELD, in the parish of Sheffield, south-division of the wapentake of Strafforth and Tickhill; 1 mile from Sheffield, 7 from Rotherham, 11 from Chesterfield, *(Derb.)*

FARM, in the parish of Sheffield, south-division of the wapentake of Strafforth and Tickhill; *(the seat of Thomas Eyre, Esq.)* 1 mile from Sheffield, 7 from Rotherham, 12 from Chesterfield, *(Derb.)*

FARN, or BURN-CROSS, in the parish of Ecclesfield, north-division of the wapentake of Strafforth and Tickhill; 7 miles from Sheffield, 7 from Barnsley, 8 from Rotherham.

FARNHAM, in the parish of Farnham, lower-division of the wapentake of Claro, liberty of Knaresborough; *(the seat of Robert Harvey, Esq.)* 2 miles from Knaresborough, 5 from Boroughbridge, 8 from Ripon.—Population 125.

FARNHILL, in the parish of Kildwick, east-division of the wapentake of Staincliffe, liberty of Clifford's Fee; 4¼ miles from Skipton, 5½ from Keighley, 10 from Colne, *(Lanc.)* —Population 876.

FARNLEY, in the parish of Leeds, Morley-division of the wapentake of Agbrigg and Morley, liberty of the Honour of Pontefract; *(the seat of Edward Armitage, Esq.)* 6 miles from Leeds, 7 from Bradford.—Population 943.

FARNLEY, in the parish of Otley, upper-division of the wapentake of Claro, liberty of Cawood, Wistow, and Otley; 2 miles from Otley, 10 from Ripley, 11 from Knaresborough.—Population 194.

FARNLEY-HALL, in the parish of Otley, upper division of the wapentake of Claro, liberty of Cawood, Wistow, and Otley; *(the seat of Walter Fawkes, Esq.)* 2¼ miles from Otley, 10 from Ripley, 11 from Knaresborough.

FARNLEY, HIGH, in the parish of Birstall, Morley division of the wapentake of Agbrigg and Morley, liberty of the Honour of Pontefract; 4½ miles from Bradford, 6 from Halifax.

FARNLEY-TYAS, in the parish of Almondbury, Agbrigg division of the wapentake of Agbrigg and Morley, liberty of the Honour of Pontefract; 4 miles from Huddersfield, 9¼ from Penistone, 12 from Halifax, 13 from Wakefield.—Population 730.

FARSLEY, in the parish of Calverley, Morley division of the wapentake of Agbrigg and Morley, liberty of the Honour of Pontefract; 3 miles from Bradford, 6¼ from Leeds.—Population 954.

FAUCATHER, in the parish of Bingley, upper division of the wapentake of Skirack; 3 miles from Bingley, 5 from Bradford.

FAULFITT, in the parish of Silkston, wapentake of Staincross, liberty of the Honour of Pontefract; 3 miles from Penistone, 4¼ from Barnsley, 12 from Wakefield.

FEARNE-LEE, in the parish of Rochdale, *(Lanc.)* Agbrigg division of the wapentake of Agbrigg and Morley; 10 miles from Rochdale, *(Lanc.)* 13 from Manchester, *(ditto)* 14 from Huddersfield.

*FEIZER, in the parish of Clapham, wapentake of Ewcross; 4 miles from Settle, 13 from Kirby-Lonsdale, *(Westm.)* 20 from Skipton.

FELKIRK, in the parish of Felkirk, wapentake of Staincross, liberty of the Honour of Pontefract; 5 miles from Barnsley, 6¼ from Wakefield, 9 from Pontefract.—Population 33.

FELL-BECK, in the parish of Ripon, lower division of the wapentake of Claro, liberty of Ripon; 3 miles from Pateleybridge, 9 from Ripon, 10 from Knaresborough.

FELLISCLIFFE, in the parish of Hampsthwaite, lower division of the wapentake of Claro, liberty of Knaresborough; 4 miles from Ripley, 7 from Knaresborough.—Pop. 424.

* One circumstance with respect to the Village of Feizer deserves to be mentioned.—Of ten houses in this place, seven are always in the township of Lawkland and parish of Clapham; one is always in the parish of Giggleswick; and the remaining two, one year within Clapham and the next within Giggleswick.—The inhabitants have seats in both churches, and resort to them alternately, and pay corn-tythe to the Rectors, and Easter-dues to the Vicars of the two churches alternately also; but all pay their assessed taxes to Stainforth.—WHITAKER'S HIST. OF CRAVEN.

FELL-LANE, in the parish of Keighley, east-division of the wapentake of Staincliffe; 1 mile from Keighley, 10 from Skipton, 10¼ from Colne, *(Lanc.)*

FENTON, CHURCH or KIRK, in the parish of Church-Fenton, wapentake of Barkston-Ash, liberties of St. Peter and the Honour of Pontefract; 6 miles from Tadcaster, 7 from Selby, 10 from Pontefract.—Population 291.

FENTON, LITTLE, in the parish of Church-Fenton, wapentake of Barkston-Ash, liberties of St. Peter and the Honour of Pontefract; 6 miles from Tadcaster, 7 from Selby, 10 from Pontefract.

FENTON, SOUTH, in the parish of Church-Fenton, wapentake of Barkston Ash, liberties of St. Peter and the Honour of Pontefract; 6 miles from Tadcaster, 7 from Selby, 10 from Pontefract.—Population 223.

FENWICK, in the parish of Campsall, wapentake of Osgoldcross, liberty of the Honour of Pontefract; 8 miles from Doncaster, 11 from Pontefract.—Population 240.

FERHAM, in the parish of Rotherham, south-division of the wapentake of Strafforth and Tickhill; *(the seat of Jonathan Walker, Esq.)* 1 mile from Rotherham, 6 from Sheffield, 13 from Doncaster.

FERRENSBY, in the parish of Farnham, lower-division of the wapentake of Claro; *(the seat of Sir Thomas Turner Slingsby, Bart.)* 2¼ miles from Knaresborough, 4¼ from Boroughbridge.—Population 86.

FERRYBRIDGE, in the parishes of Ferry-Fryston and Pontefract, wapentake of Barkston Ash, liberty of the Honour of Pontefract; 2 miles from Pontefract, 9¼ from Abberford, 11 from Snaith, 11 from Selby, 12 from Tadcaster, 15 from Doncaster, 15 from Leeds, 21 from York, 177 from London.—*Principal Inns*, Angel, Greyhound, and Swan.

FERRY-HOUSE, in the parish of Snaith, wapentake of Osgoldcross, liberty of the Honour of Pontefract; 3¼ miles from Snaith, 6¼ from Howden.

FERRY-MOOR, in the parish of Felkirk, wapentake of Staincross, liberty of the Honour of Pontefract; 5 miles Barnsley, 7 from Wakefield, 10 from Pontefract.

FETHERSTONE, in the parish of Fetherstone, wapentake of Osgoldcross, liberty of the Honour of Pontefract; 2 miles Pontefract, 4 from Ferrybridge, 6¼ from Wakefield.—Population 305.

FEWSTON, in the parish of Fewston, lower-division of the wapentake of Claro; 7 miles from Otley, 11 from Knaresborough, 14¼ from Skipton.—Population 526.

FIELD-HEAD, *see High-Field*.

FIELD-HOUSE, in the parish of Halifax, Morley-division of the wapentake of Agbrigg and Morley; *(the seat of Robert Stansfield, Esq.)* 4 miles from Halifax, 7¼ from Huddersfield.

FINKLEY-STEET, in the parish of Tankersley, wapentake of Staincross, liberty of the Honour of Pontefract; 5 miles from Penistone, 6 from Barnsley, 8 from Sheffield.

FINNAY, in the parish Almondbury, Agbrigg-division of the wapentake of Agbrigg and Morley; 2¼ miles from Huddersfield, 10½ from Halifax, 10¼ from Wakefield.

FINTHORPE, in the parish of Almondbury, Agbrigg-division of the wapentake of Agbrigg and Morley; *(the seat of John Woolley, Esq.)* 2¼ miles from Huddersfield, 10¼ from Halifax, 10¼ from Wakefield.

FIRBECK, in the parish of Firbeck, south-division of the wapentake of Strafforth and Tickhill, liberties of St Peter and Tickhill; *(Firbeck-Hall, the seat of Mrs. Knight)* 4 miles from Tickhill, 6 from Worksop, *(Notts.)* 7¼ from Bawtry, 11 from Rotherham.—Population 161.

FISHLAKE, in the parish of Fishlake, north-division of the wapentake of Strafforth and Tickhill; 2 miles from Thorne, 8 from Snaith, 8 from Doncaster.—Population 691.

FIXBY, in the parish of Halifax, Morley-division of the wapentake of Agbrigg and Morley, liberty of the Manor of Wakefield; *(the seat of Thomas Thornhill, Esq.)* 2¼ miles from Huddersfield, 6 from Halifax, 16 from Leeds.—Population 346.

FLASBY, in the parish of Gargrave, east-division of the wapentake and liberty of Staincliffe; *(Flasby-Hall, the seat of the Rev. John Preston)* 6 miles from Skipton, 11 from Kettlewell, 13 from Colne, *(Lanc.)*—Population 120.

FLASH-HOUSE, in the parish of Penistone, wapentake of Staincross, liberty of the Honour of Pontefract; 3 miles from Penistone, 10 from Barnsley, 11 from Huddersfield.

FLAXBY, in the parish of Goldsbrough, upper-division of wapentake of Claro; 3 miles from Knaresborough, 6 from Boroughbridge, 6¾ from Wetherby.—Population 66.

FLOCKTON, NETHER, in the parish of Thornhill, Agbrigg-division of the wapentake of Agbrigg and Morley, liberty of the Manor of Wakefield; 6½ miles from Huddersfield, 7¼ from Wakefield, 10½ from Barnsley.—Pop. 800.

FLOCKTON, OVER, in the parish of Thornhill, Agbrigg-division of the wapentake of Agbrigg and Morley, liberty of the Manor of Wakefield; 6½ miles from Wakefield, 7 7 from Huddersfield.

WEST-RIDING. 195

FOCCARBY, in the parish of Adlingfleet, wapentake of Osgoldcross, liberty of the Honour of Pontefract; 7 miles from Crowle, *(Linc.)* 9 from Howden, 16¼ from Snaith.—Population 84.

FOLDBY, in the parish of Wragby, Agbrigg-division of the wapentake of Agbrigg and Morley, liberty of the Honour of Pontefract; 5 miles from Wakefield, 5 from Pontefract, 13 from Barnsley, 15 from Doncaster.

FOLDS, in the parish of Tickhill, south-division of the wapentake of Strafforth and Tickhill, liberty of Tickhill; 1½ mile from Tickhill, 7½ from Worksop, *(Notts.)* 8¾ from Doncaster.

FOLLYFOOT, in the parish of Spofforth, upper-division of the wapentake of Claro; 3 miles from Knaresborough, 4 from Wetherby.—Population 273.

FOLLYFOOT-LODGE, in the parish of Spofforth, upper-division of the wapentake of Claro; *(the seat of the Hon. W. Gordon)* 3 miles from Knaresborough, 5 from Wetherby.

FOREST BECKS, in the parish of Gisburn, west-division of the wapentake and liberty of Staincliffe; 6 miles from Gisburn, 6 from Clitheroe, *(Lanc.)*

FOSTER-HOUSES, in the parish of Fishlake, north-division of the wapentake of Strafforth and Tickhill; 2½ miles from Thorne, 7 from Snaith, 8½ from Doncaster.

FOWGILL, in the parish of Low Bentham, wapentake of Ewcross; 11 miles from Settle, 11 from Kirby Lonsdale, *(Westm.)*

FOULSTONE, in the parish of Kirk-Burton, Agbrigg-division of the wapentake of Agbrigg and Morley, liberty of the Manor of Wakefield; 6 miles from Huddersfield, 8¼ from Penistone, 14 from Halifax.—Population 1,128.

FOUNTAINS-ABBEY, *in Studley-Park*, in the parish of Kirby-Malzeard, lower-division of the wapentake of Claro; 3¼ miles from Ripon, 5 from Ripley, 9 from Pateleybridge.

FOUNTAINS-EARTH, in the parish of Kirby-Malzeard, lower-division of the wapentake of Claro; 3 miles from Pateleybridge, 12 from Ripley, 14 from Ripon.—Pop. 329.

FOUNTAINS HALL, *in Studley-Park*, in the parish of Kirby Malzeard, lower division of the wapentake of Claro; *(the seat of Miss Lawrence)* 3¼ miles from Ripon, 5 from Ripley, 9 from Pateleybridge.

FOX HALL, in the parish of Darton, wapentake of Staincross, liberty of the Honour of Pontefract; 4½ miles from Barnsley, 5 from Penistone, 8 from Wakefield.

FOXUP, in the parish of Arncliffe, west-division of the wapentake and liberty of Staincliffe; 10 miles from Settle, 19 from Kettlewell, 21 from Skipton.

FRICKLEY, in the parish of Clayton, north-division of the wapentake of Strafforth and Tickhill, liberty of the Honour of Pontefract; (*the seat of William Payne, Esq.*) 7 miles from Doncaster, 9 from Barnsley, 13¼ from Wakefield.

FRIERHEAD, in the parish of Gargrave, east-division of the wapentake and liberty of Staincliffe; 6¼ miles from Skipton, 9 from Settle.

FRIZING-HALL, in the parish of Bradford, Morley-division of the wapentake of Agbrigg and Morley; (*the seat of Richard Fox Lister, Esq.*) 2 miles from Bradford, 8 from Keighley, 9 from Halifax.

FROSTRAW, in the parish of Sedbergh, wapentake of Ewcross, 1¼ mile from Sedbergh, 6 from Dent, 9½ from Kendal, (*Westm.*)

FRYSTON-FERRY, or WATER FRYSTON, in the parish of Ferry-Fryston, wapentake of Osgoldcross, liberties of St. Peter and the Honour of Pontefract; (*the seat of Richard Rodes Milnes, Esq.*) 1 mile from Ferrybridge, 2 from Pontefract, 11 from Wakefield, 13 from Doncaster, 16 from Wetherby.—Population 705.

FRYSTON, MONK, in the parish of Monk-Fryston, wapentake of Barkston-Ash, a part in the liberty of St. Peter; 4 miles from Ferrybridge, 6 from Pontefract, 7½ from Selby, 13¼ from Leeds.—Population 277.

FULHAM-LANES, in the parish of Womersley, wapentake of Osgoldcross, liberty of the Honour of Pontefract; 7 miles from Pontefract, 7 from Snaith, 7 from Ferrybridge.

FULNECK, in the parish of Calverley, Morley-division of the wapentake of Agbrigg and Morley; 5¼ miles from Bradford, 7 from Leeds.

FULWOOD, in the parish of Sheffield, south-division of the wapentake of Strafforth and Tickhill; 5 miles from Sheffield, 11 from Rotherham, 10 from Chesterfield, (*Derb.*)

FULWOOD-BOOTH, and FULWOOD-HEAD, in the parish of Sheffield, south-division of the wapentake of Strafforth and Tickhill; 6 miles from Sheffield, 10 from Chesterfield, (*Derb.*) 12 from Rotherham.

FURTOWN, in the parish of Huddersfield, Agbrigg-division of the wapentake of Agbrigg and Morley, liberty of the Honour of Pontefract; (*Flash House, the seat of John Brook, Esq.*) 1½ mile from Huddersfield, 7½ from Halifax.

G.

GAISGILL, in the parish of Gisburn, west-division of the wapentake and liberty of Staincliffe; 3 miles from Gisburn, 7 from Clitheroe, (*Lanc.*) 12½ from Skipton.

GALFAY, in the parish of Kirby-Malzeard, lower-division of the wapentake of Claro; 4 miles from Ripon, 10 from Knaresborough, 10 from Pateleybridge.

GARFORTH, in the parish of Garforth, lower-division of the wapentake of Skirack, liberty of the Honour of Pontefract; 3 miles from Abberford, 7 from Leeds, 9 from Wetherby, 9 from Wakefield.—Population 234.

GARFORTH-MOOR, in the parish of Garforth, lower-division of the wapentake of Skirack, liberty of the Honour of Pontefract; 2¼ miles from Abberford, 7¼ from Leeds.

GARFORTH, WEST, in the parish of Garforth, lower-division of the wapentake of Skirack, liberty of the Honour of Pontefract; 6¼ miles from Leeds, 8 from Wakefield, 8¼ from Ferrybridge.

GARGRAVE, in the parish of Gargrave, east-division of the wapentake of Staincliffe, liberty of Clifford's Fee; (*Gargrave-House, the seat of John Coulthurst, Esq.*) 4¼ miles from Skipton, 11 from Colne, (*Lanc.*) 11¼ from Kettlewell, 15¼ from Settle.—*No Market.*—*Fairs,* December 12, for Horned Cattle, Woollen Cloth, &c.—Pop. 728.

GARSDALE, in the parish of Sedbergh, wapentake of Ewcross; 3¼ miles from Sedbergh, 5 from Dent, 13 from Hawes. —Population 571.

GARSTONES, in the parish of Horton, wapentake of Ewcross; 8 miles from Hawes, 11½ from Askrigg, 12 from Settle.

GATEFORTH, in the parish of Brayton, wapentake of Barkston-Ash; 5 miles from Selby, 6 from Ferrybridge, 8 from Pontefract.—Population 178.

GATEHAM, or YATEHOLME, in the parish of Almondbury, Agbrigg-division of the wapentake of Agbrigg and Morley; 10 miles from Huddersfield, 12 from Penistone.

GATEHEAD, in the parish of Almondbury, Agbrigg-division of the wapentake of Agbrigg and Morley; 6 miles from Huddersfield, 13 from Halifax, 19 from Manchester,(*Lanc.*)

GATEUP, in the parish of Burnsall, east-division of the wapentake and liberty of Staincliffe; 8 miles from Pateleybridge, 10 from Kettlewell.

GATEWOOD-END, in the parish of Cantley, south-division of the wapentake of Strafforth and Tickhill; 6 miles from Doncaster, 6 from Thorne.

GAWBER-HALL, in the parish Darton, wapentake of Staincross, liberty of the Honour of Pontefract; 1¼ mile from Barnsley, 6 from Penistone, 9¼ from Wakefield.

GAWTHORPE, in the parish of Dewsbury, Agbrigg-division of the wapentake of Agbrigg and Morley, liberty of the Manor of Wakefield; 2 miles from Dewsbury, 3¼ from Wakefield, 8 from Leeds.

GAWTHORPE, in the parish of Kirk-Heaton, Agbrigg-division of the wapentake of Agbrigg and Morley, liberty of the Honour of Pontefract; 5 miles from Huddersfield, 8 from Wakefield.

GAWTHORPE, in the parish of Sedbergh, wapentake of Ewcross; 1 mile from Dent, 4 from Sedbergh, 7 from Kirby-Lonsdale, *(Westm.)*

GAWTHORPE-HALL, in the parish of Bingley, upper-division of the wapentake of Skirack, liberty of the Honour of Pontefract; *(the seat of Joseph Heaton, Esq.)* 1 mile from Bingley, 6 from Bradford, 9 from Otley.

GELLEY-ROYD, in the parish of Huddersfield, Agbrigg-division of the wapentake of Agbrigg and Morley; 3 from Huddersfield, 5¼ from Halifax.

GETTINGLEY, in the parish of Thornhill, Agbrigg-division of the wapentake of Agbrigg and Morley; 3¼ miles from Dewsbury, 5 from Huddersfield.

GIGGLESWICK, in the parish of Giggleswick, west-division of the wapentake and liberty of Staincliffe; *(Bell-Hill, the seat of Anthony Lister, Esq.)* 1 mile from Settle, 7 from Kirby-Lonsdale, *(Westm.)* 17 from Skipton.—Population 556.

GILDINGWELLS, or GILDENWELLS, in the parish of Laughton-le-Morthen, south-division of the wapentake of Strafforth and Tickhill, liberties of St. Peter and Tickhill; *(the seat of Sir Thomas White, Bart.)* 4¼ miles from Worksop, *(Notts.)* 6 from Tickhill, 9¼ from Bawtry, 12 from Rotherham.

GILDERSBAR, in the parish of Addingham, east-division of the wapentake and liberty of Staincliffe; 6 miles from Skipton, 7½ from Keighley, 8 from Otley.

GILDERSOME, in the parish of Batley, Morley-division of the wapentake of Agbrigg and Morley, liberty of the Honour of Pontefract; 5 miles from Leeds, 7 from Bradford.—Population 1,232.

GILKIRK, or BARNOLDSWICK, *see Barnoldswick*, which was formerly called Gilkirk.—Population 769.

GILL-BOTTOM, in the parish of Fewston, lower division

of the wapentake of Claro; 6¼ miles from Otley, 11 from Knaresborough.

GILSTEAD, in the parish of Bingley, upper-division of the wapentake of Skirack; 1 mile from Bingley, 6 from Bradford, 9 from Otley.

GILTHWAITE-HALL, in the parishes of Whiston, and Rotherham, south-division of the wapentake of Strafforth and Tickhill; *(the seat of —— Westby, Esq.)* 2 miles from Rotherham, 6 from Sheffield, 12 from Worksop, *(Notts.)*

GINGLE-POT, in the parish of Thornton-in-Lonsdale, wapentake of Ewcross; 10 miles from Hawes, 13 from Settle.

GINHOUSE, in the parish of Rotherham, south-division of the wapentake of Strafforth and Tickhill; 1 mile from Rotherham, 6¼ from Sheffield.

GIPTON, in the parish of Leeds, lower-division of the wapentake of Skirack; 2¼ miles from Leeds, 4 from Harewood, 6 from Wetherby.

GISBURN, in the parish of Gisburn, west-division of the wapentake and liberty of Staincliffe; *(Gisburn-Park, the seat of Lord Ribblesdale)* 7 miles from Clitheroe, *(Lanc.)* 9 from Colne, *(ditto)* 11½ from Skipton, 12 from Settle, 52¼ from York, 224 from London.—Market, Monday.—Fairs, Easter-Monday, that day fortnight, and that day month, and Saturday after that day month, for Horned Cattle, Monday five weeks after Easter, for Pedlary-Ware, &c. September 18, for Calves, and every other Monday, for Fat Cattle, &c.——Population 485.

GISBURN-COTES, in the parish of Gisburn, west-division of the wapentake and liberty of Staincliffe, 3 miles from Gisburn, 12 from Skipton, 12 from Settle.

GISBURN-FOREST, in the parish of Gisburn, west-division of the wapentake and liberty of Staincliffe; 8 miles from Settle, 15 from Colne, *(Lanc.)* 17 from Skipton.—Population 396.

GIVENDALE, in the parish of Ripon, lower-division of the wapentake of Claro, 2 miles from Ripon, 4 from Boroughbridge, 11 from Knaresborough.—Population 19.

GLEADLESS, in the parish of Handsworth, south-division of the wapentake of Strafforth and Tickhill, 3¼ miles from Sheffield, 7½ from Rotherham, 8½ from Chesterfield, *(Derb.)*

GLEDHOW, in the parish of Leeds, lower-division of the wapentake of Skirack, liberty of the Honour of Pontefract; *(the seat of John Dixon, Esq.)* 3 miles from Leeds, 10 from Otley, 10 from Wetherby.

GLEDSTON-HOUSE, in the parish of Marton, east-division of the wapentake and liberty of Staincliffe; *(the seat of the Rev. William Roundell)* 5 miles from Skipton, 7¾ from Colne, *(Lanc.)* 11 from Settle.

GLUSBOURN, in the parish of Kildwick, east-division of the wapentake of Staincliffe, liberty of Clifford's Fee; 5 miles from Skipton, 5¼ from Keighley, 8 from Colne, *(Lanc.)*—Population 533.

GOLCAR, in the parish of Huddersfield, Agbrigg-division of the wapentake of Agbrigg and Morley, liberty of the Manor of Wakefield; *(the seat of Joseph Haigh, Esq.)* 2¼ miles from Huddersfield, 7 from Halifax, 23 from Manchester, *(Lanc.)*—Population 1,846.

GOLDSBOROUGH, in the parish of Goldsborough, upper-division of the wapentake of Claro; *(the seat of James Starkey, Esq.)* 2¼ miles from Knaresborough, 5 from Wetherby, 7¼ from Boroughbridge.—Population 177.

GOLDTHORPE, in the parish of Bolton-upon-Dearn, north-division of the wapentake of Strafforth and Tickhill, liberty of Tickhill; 7 miles from Barnsley, 7¼ from Doncaster.

GOMERSALL, GREAT, in the parish of Birstall, Morley-division of the wapentake of Agbrigg and Morley, liberty of the Honour of Pontefract; 5¼ miles from Bradford, 7 from Leeds.—Population 4,303.

GOMERSALL, LITTLE, in the parish of Birstall, Morley-division of the wapentake of Agbrigg and Morley, liberty of the Honour of Pontefract; 5¼ miles from Bradford, 7 from Leeds.

GOOLE, in the parish of Snaith, wapentake of Osgoldcross, liberty of the Honour of Pontefract; 4¼ miles from Howden, 7 from Snaith.—Population 294.

GOOLE-FIELD-HOUSES, in the parish of Snaith, wapentake of Osgoldcross, liberty of the Honour of Pontefract; 4 miles from Howden, 7½ from Snaith,

GOOSNER-HEIGHT, in the parish of Long-Preston, west-division of the wapentake and liberty of Staincliffe; 7 miles from Skipton, 10 from Settle.

GOTHER-BOTTOM, in the parish of Silkston, wapentake of Staincross, liberty of the Honour of Pontefract; 1¼ mile from Penistone, 6 from Barnsley, 12¼ from Wakefield.

GOWBUSK, in the parish of Ripon, lower-division of the wapentake of Claro; 5½ miles from Pateleybridge, 6 from Ripon.

GOWDALL, in the parish of Snaith, wapentake of Osgoldcross, liberty of the Honour of Pontefract; 1 mile from Snaith, 10 from Ferrybridge, 12 from Pontefract.—Pop. 218.

GOWTHWAITE-HALL, in the parish of Kirby-Malzeard,

lower-division of the wapentake of Claro; 3 miles from Pateleybridge, 11 from Masham.

GOYDEN-POT-HOLE, in the parish of Kirby-Malzeard, lower-division of the wapentake of Claro; 10 miles from Pateleybridge, 10 from Masham.

GRAFTON, in the parish of Marton, upper-division of the wapentake of Claro, a part in the liberty of St. Peter; 2¾ miles from Boroughbridge, 6¼ from Knaresborough.

GRANGE, in the parish of Rochdale, *(Lanc.)* Agbrigg-division of the wapentake of Agbrigg and Morley; 8 miles from Rochdale, *(Lanc.)* 12 from Huddersfield.

GRANGE, in the parish of Bingley, upper-division of the wapentake of Skirack; *(the seat of Walker Farrand, Esq.)* 1 mile from Bingley, 6 from Bradford, 10 from Halifax.

GRANGE-ASH, in the parish of Kirk-Heaton, Agbrigg-division of the wapentake of Agbrigg and Morley; *(the seat of John Lister Kaye, Esq.)* 6½ miles from Huddersfield, 6½ from Wakefield, 7 from Dewsbury.

GRANTLEY, in the parish of Ripon, lower-division of the wapentake of Claro, liberty of Ripon; 5 miles from Ripley, 6 from Ripon, 6¼ from Pateleybridge.—Pop. 195.

GRANTLEY-HALL, in the parish of Ripon, lower-division of the wapentake of Claro, liberty of Ripon, *(the seat of Lord Grantley)* 5 miles from Ripley, 5½ from Ripon, 6¼ from Pateleybridge.

GRASS-CROFT, in the parish of Rochdale, *(Lanc.)* Agbrigg-division of the wapentake of Agbrigg and Morley; 9 miles from Rochdale, *(Lanc.)* 12 from Manchester, *(ditto)* 14 from Huddersfield.

GRASS-GARTH, in the parish of Weston, upper-division of the wapentake of Claro; 2¼ miles from Otley, 12¼ from Leeds, 16¼ from Knaresborough.

GRASSINGTON, in the parish of Linton, east-division of the wapentake and liberty of Staincliffe; *(the seat of —— Brown, Esq.)* 6 miles from Kettlewell, 10 from Skipton, 10 from Pateleybridge, 14 from Settle.—*No Market.*—Fairs, March 4, for Horned Cattle, April 24, June 29, for Sheep, September 26, for Horned Cattle.—Pop. 763.

GREASBROUGH, in the parish of Rotherham, north-division of the wapentake of Strafforth and Tickhill, liberty of Tickhill; 1¼ miles from Rotherham, 7¼ from Sheffield, 10¼ from Barnsley.—Population 1,166.

GREEN-CLOSE, in the parish of Clapham, wapentake of Ewcross; 8½ miles from Settle, 10 from Kirby-Lonsdale, *(Westm.)*

GREENFIELD, in the parish of Arnecliffe, west-division of the wapentake and liberty of Staincliffe; 13 miles from Settle, 10¼ from Kettlewell.

GREEN-GATES, in the parish of Calverley, Morley-division of the wapentake of Agbrigg and Morley; 2¼ miles from Bradford, 6 from Otley, 11¼ from Leeds.

GREEN-HAMMERTON, in the parish of Whixley, upper-division of the wapentake of Claro; 7 miles from Boroughbridge, 7 from Wetherby, 8 from Knaresborough, 10 from York.—*Principal Inn*, George.—Population 259.

GREENHEAD, in the parish of Huddersfield, Agbrigg-division of the wapentake of Agbrigg and Morley, liberty of the Honour of Pontefract; *(the seat of Thomas Allen, Esq.)* ¼ a mile from Huddersfield, 8 from Halifax, 16 from Leeds.

GREEN-HILL, in the parish of Bingley, upper-division of the wapentake of Skirack; 1 mile from Bingley, 6 from Bradford, 9 from Otley.

GREENHOUSE, in the parish and soke of Doncaster, south-division of the wapentake of Strafforth and Tickhill, 1¼ mile from Doncaster, 9¼ from Thorne.

GREENHOW-HILL, in the parish of Ripon, lower-division of the wapentake of Claro; 3 miles from Pateleybridge, 11 from Kettlewell, 12 from Ripley, 14 from Ripon.

GREENLAND, in the parish of Snaith, wapentake of Osgoldcross, liberty of the Honour of Pontefract; 4 miles from Snaith, 6¼ from Pontefract, 14 from Howden.

GREENSIDE, in the parish of Kirk-Burton, Agbrigg-division of the wapentake of Agbrigg and Morley; 5 miles from Huddersfield, 14 from Wakefield.

GREENWOOD, in the parish of Halifax, Morley-division of the wapentake of Agbrigg and Morley; 9¼ miles from Halifax, 12¼ from Rochdale, *(Lanc.)*

GREETLAND, in the parish of Halifax, Morley-division of the wapentake of Agbrigg and Morley, liberty of the Honour of Pontefract, 4 miles from Halifax, 4 from Huddersfield,

GRENOSIDE, in the parish of Ecclesfield, north-division of the wapentake of Strafforth and Tickhill; 4¼ miles from Sheffield, 5 from Rotherham, 8 from Penistone.

GREWELTHORPE, in the parish of Kirby-Malzeard, lower-division of the wapentake of Claro; 3 miles from Masham, 8 from Ripon.—Population 479.

GREYSTONES, in the parish of Sheffield, south-division of the wapentake of Strafforth and Tickhill; *(the seats of Samuel Greaves, and Thomas Hawkesley, Esqrs.)* 2¼ miles from Sheffield, 8½ from Rotherham, 11 from Chesterfield, *(Derb.)*

GRIMESTHORPE, in the parish of Sheffield, north-division of the wapentake of Strafforth and Tickhill; 2¼ miles from Sheffield, 3¼ from Rotherham.

GRIMETHORPE, in the parish of Felkirk, wapentake of Staincross, liberty of the Honour of Pontefract; 5 miles from Barnsley, 7 from Wakefield, 10 from Pontefract.

GRIMSTONE, in the parish of Kirby-Wharfe, wapentake of Barkston-Ash, liberty of the Honour of Pontefract; *(Grimstone-Hall, the seat of George Townend, Esq.)* 1¼ mile from Tadcaster, 11½ from Ferrybridge, 13 from Pontefract.—Population 71.

GRINDLETON, in the parish of Mitton, west-division of the wapentake of Staincliffe, liberty of Bolland; 14 miles from Skipton, 14 from Colne, *(Lanc.)* 14 from Burnley, *(ditto.)* —Population 927.

GRISEDALE, in the parish of Sedbergh, wapentake of Ewcross; 8 miles from Sedbergh, 8 from Dent, 8 from Hawes.

GROVE-HALL, in the parish of Darrington, wapentake of Osgoldcross, liberty of the Honour of Pontefract; *(the seat William Lee, Esq.)* 2 miles from Ferrybridge, 3 from Pontefract, 13 from Doncaster.

GUISELEY, in the parish of Guiseley, upper-division of the wapentake of Skirack, liberty of Cawood, Wistow, and Otley; *(the seat of F. Ridsdale, Esq.)* 1½ mile from Otley, 9 from Bradford, 10 from Leeds.—Population 825.

GUNTHWAITE, in the parish of Penistone, wapentake of Staincross, liberty of the Honour of Pontefract; *(Gunthwaite-Hall, the seat of William Bosville, Esq.)* 2 miles from Penistone, 7 from Barnsley, 11 from Huddersfield.—Population 111.

H.

HACKFALL, in the parish of Kirby-Malzeard, lower-division of the wapentake of Claro; 3 miles from Masham, 8 from Ripon, 9 from Bedale.

HADDINGLEY, in the parish of Kirk-Burton, Agbrigg-division of the wapentake of Agbrigg and Morley; 9 miles from Huddersfield, 9 from Penistone.

HADDLESEY, CHAPEL, in the parish of Birkin, wapentake of Barkston-Ash, liberty of the Honour of Pontefract; 5 miles from Selby, 5 from Snaith, 7 from Ferrybridge.

HADDLESEY, EAST, in the parish of Birkin, wapentake of Barkston-Ash, liberty of the Honour of Pontefract ; 5 miles from Selby, 5 from Snaith, 7 from Ferrybridge.—Pop. 152.

HADDLESEY, WEST, in the parish of Birkin, wapentake of Barkston-Ash, liberty of the Honour of Pontefract ; 5 miles from Selby, 6 from Ferrybridge, 8 from Pontefract.

HAGEND, in the parish of South-Kirkby, wapentake of Osgoldcross, liberty of the Honour of Pontefract ; 6 miles from Pontefract, 9 from Wakefield, 10 from Doncaster.

HAG, NETHER, and HAG, OVER, in the parish of Almondbury, Agbrigg-division of the wapentake of Agbrigg and Morley ; 4¼ miles from Huddersfield, 10 from Penistone, 15¼ from Wakefield.

HAGGSIDE, *see Spofforth-Haggs.*

HAGUE, in the parish of Thornton, east-division of the wapentake and liberty of Staincliffe ; 3 miles from Colne, *(Lanc.)* 9½ from Skipton.

HAGUE-HALL, in the parish of South-Kirkby, wapentake of Osgoldcross, liberty of the Honour of Pontefract ; *(the seat of James Allott, Esq.)* 7 miles from Pontefract, 8 from Barnsley.

HAIGH, in the parish of Darton, wapentake of Staincross, liberty of the Honour of Pontefract ; *(Haigh-Hall, the seat of Mrs. Cotton)* 6 miles from Barnsley, 7 from Penistone, 7 from Wakefield.—Population 798.

HAINWORTH, in the parish of Bingley, upper-division of the wapentake of Skirack ; 2 miles from Bingley, 7 from Bradford, 8 from Halifax.

HALDENBY, in the parish of Adlingfleet, wapentake of Osgoldcross, liberty of the Honour of Pontefract ; *(the seat of John Gee, Esq.)* 6 miles from Crowle, *(Linc.)* 10 from Howden.—Population 150.

HALDWORTH, in the parish of Bradford, Morley-division of the wapentake of Agbrigg and Morley ; 4 miles from Halifax, 6 from Bradford, 8 from Keighley.

HALES, in the parish of Drax, wapentake of Barkston-Ash, 3 miles from Snaith, 6 from Selby.

HALIFAX, in the parish of Halifax, Morley-division of the wapentake of Agbrigg and Morley, liberty of the Manor of Wakefield ; 8 miles from Bradford, 8 from Huddersfield, 11 from Dewsbury, 12 from Keighley, 12 from Todmorden, 16¼ from Rochdale, *(Lanc.)* 18 from Leeds, 36 from York, 197 from London.—*Market*, Saturday, for Woollen-Cloths, Provisions, &c.—*Fairs*, June 24, and first Saturday in November, for Horses, Horned Cattle, &c.—*Bankers*, Messrs. John Rawson, William Rawson, John

wapentake of Strafforth and Tickhill; 4 miles from Rotherham, 8 from Sheffield.

HARDWICK, BLIND or SPITAL, in the parish of Pontefract, wapentake of Osgoldcross, liberty of the Honour of Pontefract; 1 mile from Pontefract, 2 from Ferrybridge.—Population 110.

HARDWICK, EAST, in the parish of Pontefract, wapentake of Osgoldcross, liberty of the Honour of Pontefract; 2 miles from Pontefract, 9¼ from Wakefield.

HARDWICK, WEST, in the parish of Wragby, wapentake of Osgoldcross, liberty of the Honour of Pontefract; 3 miles from Pontefract, 7 from Wakefield.—Population 108.

HARE-HILLS, in the parish of Keighley, east-division of the wapentake and liberty of Staincliffe; 3 miles from Keighley, 9 from Colne, (Lanc.)

HARENDEN, in the parish of Kirk-Burton, Agbrigg-division of the wapentake of Agbrigg and Morley; 9 miles from Huddersfield, 9 from Penistone.

HAREWOOD, in the parish of Harewood, upper-division of the wapentake of Skirack; 6 miles from Leeds, 6 from Wetherby, 8 from Otley, 10 from Knaresborough, 11 from Tadcaster, 12 from Bradford, 12 from Ripley, 20 from York, 197 from London.—*Market*, Monday.—*Principal Inn*, Harewood's Arms.—Population 707.

HAREWOOD-HOUSE, in the parish of Harewood, upper-division of the wapentake of Skirack; *(the seat of Lord Harewood)* 6 miles from Leeds, 6 from Wetherby, 8 from Otley.

HARKER, in the parish of Slaidburn, west-division of the wapentake and liberty of Staincliffe; 11 miles from Settle, 11 from Clitheroe, (Lanc.)

HARLINGTON, in the parish of Barmbrough, north-division of the wapentake of Strafforth and Tickhill, liberty of Tickhill; 6 miles from Doncaster, 9¼ from Barnsley.

HARLOW, in the parish of Wath-upon-Dearn, north-division of the wapentake of Strafforth and Tickhill; 7 miles from Rotherham, 8 from Barnsley.

HARROGATE, HIGH, in the parish of Knaresborough, lower-division of the wapentake of Claro, liberty of Knaresborough; 3 miles from Knaresborough, 4 from Ripley, 8 from Wetherby, 9 from Hopper-Lane-Inn, 9 from Otley, 10 from Boroughbridge, 11 from Ripon, 15¼ from Leeds, 20 from York, 211 from London.—*Principal Inns*, Dragon, Granby, Queen's Head, and Hope-Tavern.—Pop. 1,195.

HARROGATE, LOW, in the parish of Knaresborough, lower-division of the wapentake of Claro, liberty of Knares-

division of the wapentake of Strafforth and Tickhill; 6¼ miles from Doncaster, 9 from Pontefract, 13½ from Wakefield.—Population 91,

HAMPSTHWAITE, in the parish of Hampsthwaite, lower-division of the wapentake of Claro, liberty of Knaresborough; 2 miles from Ripley, 7 from Knaresborough, 8 from Ripon.—Population 439.

HAND-BANK, in the parish of Penistone, wapentake of Staincross, liberty of the Honour of Pontefract; 3 miles from Penistone, 9 from Barnsley, 12¼ from Sheffield.

HANDSWORTH, in the parish of Handsworth, south-division of the wapentake of Strafforth and Tickhill, liberties of St. Peter and Hallamshire; *(the seat of the Rev. Wilfred Huddlestone)* 4¼ miles from Sheffield, 7 from Rotherham, 12¼ from Chesterfield, *(Derb.)*—Population 1,424.

HANDSWORTH-WOOD-HOUSE, in the parish of Handsworth, south-division of the wapentake of Strafforth and Tickhill, liberty of St. Peter; 5 miles from Sheffield, 6¼ from Rotherham, 12¼ from Chesterfield, *(Derb.)*

HANGING-STONES, in the parish of Ilkley, upper-division of the wapentake of Skirack; 4 miles from Otley, 8 from Bradford.

HANLITH, in the parish of Kirkby-Malhamdale, west-division of the wapentake of Staincliffe, liberty of Clifford's Fee; *(Hanlith Hall, the seat of —— Sarginson, Esq.)* 6¼ miles from Settle, 10½ from Skipton, 10½ from Kettlewell.—Population 31.

HARDCASTLE, FAR and NEAR, in the parish of Ripon, lower-division of the wapentake of Claro; 4 miles from Pateleybridge, 14 from Kettlewell, 15 from Ripon.

HARDEN, in the parish of Slaidburn, east-division of the wapentake and liberty of Staincliffe; 5 miles from Colne, *(Lanc.)* 7 from Skipton, 11 from Burnley, *(Lanc.)*

HARDEN, in the parish of Bingley, upper-division of the wapentake of Skirack; 2 miles from Bingley, 5 from Bradford, 8 from Halifax.

HARD-GATE, in the parish of Ripon, lower-division of the wapentake of Claro; 3 miles from Ripley, 7 from Pateleybridge.

HARDINGLEY, in the parish of Kirk-Burton, Agbrigg-division of the wapentake of Agbrigg and Morley; 9 miles from Huddersfield, 9 from Penistone.

HARDISTY-HILL, in the parish of Fewston, lower-division of the wapentake of Claro; 8¼ miles from Otley, 9½ from Ripley, 11½ from Knaresborough.

HARDWICK, in the parish of Aston, south-division of the

wapentake of Strafforth and Tickhill ; 4 miles from Rotherham, 8 from Sheffield.

HARDWICK, BLIND or SPITAL, in the parish of Pontefract, wapentake of Osgoldcross, liberty of the Honour of Pontefract ; 1 mile from Pontefract, 2 from Ferrybridge.—Population 110.

HARDWICK, EAST, in the parish of Pontefract, wapentake of Osgoldcross, liberty of the Honour of Pontefract ; 2 miles from Pontefract, 9¼ from Wakefield.

HARDWICK, WEST, in the parish of Wragby, wapentake of Osgoldcross, liberty of the Honour of Pontefract ; 3 miles from Pontefract, 7 from Wakefield.—Population 108.

HARE-HILLS, in the parish of Keighley, east-division of the wapentake and liberty of Staincliffe ; 3 miles from Keighley, 9 from Colne, (Lanc.)

HARENDEN, in the parish of Kirk-Burton, Agbrigg-division of the wapentake of Agbrigg and Morley ; 9 miles from Huddersfield, 9 from Penistone.

HAREWOOD, in the parish of Harewood, upper-division of the wapentake of Skirack ; 6 miles from Leeds, 6 from Wetherby, 8 from Otley, 10 from Knaresborough, 11 from Tadcaster, 12 from Bradford, 12 from Ripley, 20 from York, 197 from London.—*Market*, Monday.—*Principal Inn*, Harewood's Arms.—Population 707.

HAREWOOD-HOUSE, in the parish of Harewood, upper-division of the wapentake of Skirack ; *(the seat of Lord Harewood)* 6 miles from Leeds, 6 from Wetherby, 8 from Otley.

HARKER, in the parish of Slaidburn, west-division of the wapentake and liberty of Staincliffe ; 11 miles from Settle, 11 from Clitheroe, (Lanc.)

HARLINGTON, in the parish of Barmbrough, north-division of the wapentake of Strafforth and Tickhill, liberty of Tickhill ; 6 miles from Doncaster, 9½ from Barnsley.

HARLOW, in the parish of Wath-upon-Dearn, north-division of the wapentake of Strafforth and Tickhill ; 7 miles from Rotherham, 8 from Barnsley.

HARROGATE, HIGH, in the parish of Knaresborough, lower-division of the wapentake of Claro, liberty of Knaresborough ; 3 miles from Knaresborough, 4 from Ripley, 8 from Wetherby, 9 from Hopper-Lane-Inn, 9 from Otley, 10 from Boroughbridge, 11 from Ripon, 15¼ from Leeds, 20 from York, 211 from London.—*Principal Inns*, Dragon, Granby, Queen's Head, and Hope-Tavern.—Pop. 1,195.

HARROGATE, LOW, in the parish of Knaresborough, lower-division of the wapentake of Claro, liberty of Knaresborough; 3¼ miles from Knaresborough, 4 from Ripley, 8 from Wetherby, 9 from Hopper-Lane-Inn, 9 from Otley, 11 from Ripon, 10¼ from Boroughbridge, 15¼ from Leeds.— *Principal Inns*, Crown, White-Hart, Crescent, and Bell.

HARRUP, FAR, and HARRUP, NEAR, in the parish of Slaidburn, west-division of the wapentake and liberty of Staincliffe; 6¼ miles from Gisburn, 7 from Clitheroe, *(Lanc.)*

HARTHILL, in the parish of Harthill, south-division of the wapentake of Strafforth and Tickhill; 7 miles from Worksop, *(Notts.)* 8 from Rotherham, 11¼ from Tickhill.—Population 660.

HARTISHEAD, in the parish of Dewsbury, Morley-division of the wapentake of Agbrigg and Morley, liberty of the Manor of Wakefield; 5 miles from Huddersfield, 5 from Dewsbury, 6 from Halifax.—Population 520.

HARTLINGTON, in the parish of Burnsall, east-division of the wapentake of Staincliffe, liberty of Clifford's Fee; 9 miles from Skipton, 9 from Pateleybridge, 11 from Kettlewell.—Population 105.

HARTWITH, in the parish of Kirby-Malzeard, lower-division of the wapentake of Claro; 4 miles from Pateleybridge, 10 from Ripon, 10 from Knaresborough.—Population 449.

HARWOOD-WELL, in the parish of Halifax, Morley-division of the wapentake of Agbrigg and Morley; 2 miles from Halifax, 8½ from Huddersfield.

HASLE, in the parish of Wragby, wapentake of Osgoldcross, liberty of the Honour of Pontefract; 4 miles from Pontefract, 7 from Wakefield.

HASLEWOOD-HALL, (extraparochial) wapentake of Barkston-Ash; *(the seat of Sir Thomas Vavasour, Bart.)* 3 miles from Tadcaster, 7 from Wetherby, 12 from Pontefract.

HATFIELD, in the parish of Hatfield, south-division of the wapentake of Strafforth and Tickhill; *(the seats of William Gossip and St. Andrew Warde, Jun. Esqrs.)* 4 miles from Thorne, 8 from Doncaster, 11 from Bawtry.—Population 1,301.

HATFIELD-HALL, in the parish of Wakefield, Agbrigg-division of the wapentake of Agbrigg and Morley; *(the seat of Mrs. Hayes)* 2 miles from Wakefield, 8 from Leeds.

HATFIELD-HOUSE, in the parish of Ecclesfield, north-division of the wapentake of Strafforth and Tickhill; 4 miles from Sheffield, 5 from Rotherham, 9 from Penistone.

HATFIELD-WOOD-HOUSE, in the parish of Hatfield, south-division of the wapentake of Strafforth and Tickhill; 2 miles from Thorne, 8½ from Doncaster.

HAUGH-END, in the parish of Halifax, Morley-division of

the wapentake of Agbrigg and Morley; 3½ miles from Halifax, 8½ from Huddersfield.

HAUGH, NETHER, in the parish of Rotherham, north-division of the wapentake of Strafforth and Tickhill, liberty of Tickhill; 2¾ miles from Rotherham, 8¾ from Sheffield, 9¼ from Barnsley.

HAUGH, UPPER, in the parish of Rawmarsh, north-division of the wapentake of Strafforth and Tickhill; 3 miles from Rotherham, 9 from Sheffield, 9 from Barnsley.

HAVERAH-PARK, (extraparochial) lower-division of the wapentake of Claro; 7 miles from Knaresborough, 8 from Otley.—Population 71.

HAVERCROFT in the parish of Felkirk, wapentake of Staincross, liberty of the Honour of Pontefract; 5 miles Barnsley, 6½ from Wakefield, 9 from Pontefract.—Population 160.

HAVERCROFT, in the parish of Batley, Agbrigg-division of the wapentake of Agbrigg and Morley; 2½ miles from Dewsbury, 6¼ from Bradford.

HAWKESTONE-SLACK, in the parish of Halifax, Morley-division of the wapentake of Agbrigg and Morley; 10 miles from Burnley, (Lanc.) 12 from Halifax.

HAWKESWORTH, in the parish of Otley, upper-division of the wapentake of Skirack, liberty of Cawood, Wistow, and Otley; *(the seat of —— Wilkinson, Esq.)* 4 miles from Otley, 6 from Bradford, 10 from Leeds.—Population 227.

HAWKSWICK, in the parish of Arncliffe, west-division of the wapentake of Staincliffe, liberty of Clifford's Fee; 4 miles from Kettlewell, 11 from Settle, 15 from Skipton.—Population 69.

HAWORTH, in the parish of Bradford, Morley-division of the wapentake of Agbrigg and Morley, liberty of the Honour of Pontefract; 5 miles from Keighley, 7 from Bradfrod, 8 from Halifax, 9½ from Colne, (Lanc.)—*No Market.*—*Fairs*, July 22, for Pedlary-Ware, and October 14, for Horned Cattle, Pedlary-Ware, &c.

HAWSHAW, in the parish of Thornton, east-division of the wapentake and liberty of Staincliffe; 4½ miles from Colne, (Lanc.) 9 from Skipton, 12 from Keighley.

HAYFIELDS, in the parish of Finningley, (Notts.) south-division of the wapentake of Strafforth and Tickhill, liberty of Tickhill; *(the seat of James Smith, Esq.)* 5 miles from Doncaster, 5½ from Bawtry.

HAYLEY-HILL, in the parish of Halifax, Morley-division of the wapentake of Agbrigg and Morley; ½ a mile from Halifax, 7½ from Bradford.

HAY-PARK-FARMS, in the parish of Knaresborough, lower-division of the wapentake of Claro; 1 mile from Knaresborough, 7 from Wetherby.

HAYWOOD, in the parish of Campsall, wapentake of Osgoldcross, liberty of the Honour of Pontefract; 7 miles from Doncaster, 7 from Thorne.

HAZLE-HEAD, in the parish of Penistone, wapentake of Staincross, liberty of the Honour of Pontefract; 3 miles from Penistone, 10 from Barnsley, 13 from Huddersfield.

HAZLE-WOOD, in the parish of Skipton, lower-division of the wapentake of Claro; 7¼ miles from Skipton, 13 from Pateleybridge, 16¼ from Knaresborough.—Population 181.

HEADLEY-HALL, in the parishes of Bramham and Tadcaster, wapentake of Barkston-Ash; 3 miles from Tadcaster, 5 from Wetherby.

HEALEY, in the parish of Batley, Agbrigg-division of the wapentake of Agbrigg and Morley; 2 miles from Leeds, 6 from Wakefield.

HEALEY, in the parish of Sheffield, south-division of the wapentake of Strafforth and Tickhill; 1½ mile from Sheffield, 7¼ from Rotherham, 10½ from Chesterfield, *(Derb.)*

HEALEY, UPPER, in the parish of Sheffield, south-division of the wapentake of Strafforth and Tickhill; 2 miles from Sheffield, 6 from Rotherham, 10½ from Chesterfield, *(Derb.)*

HEANING, in the parish of Slaidburn, west-division of the wapentake and liberty of Staincliffe; 8 miles from Clitheroe, *(Lanc.)* 13 from Settle.

HEATH, in the parish of Warmfield, Agbrigg-division of the wapentake of Agbrigg and Morley, liberty of the Honour of Pontefract, *(the seat of the Rt. Hon. John Smyth, and Heath-Hall, the seat of W. Farquier, Esq.)* 2 miles from Wakefield, 10 from Barnsley.

HEATHEN-CARR, in the parish of Kirby-Malzeard, lower-division of the wapentake of Claro; 5 miles from Kettlewell, 12 from Pateleybridge.

HEATH-FIELD, in the parish of Kirby-Malzeard, lower-division of the wapentake of Claro; 2 miles from Pateleybridge, 11 from Ripley, 12 from Ripon.

HEATH-HOUSE, in the parish of Huddersfield, Agbrigg-division of the wapentake of Agbrigg and Morley; 3 miles from Huddersfield, 7½ from Halifax.

HEATON, in the parish of Bradford, Morley-division of the wapentake of Agbrigg and Morley, liberty of the Honour of Pontefract; 2 miles from Bradford, 4¼ from Bingley, 10 from Halifax.—Population 951.

WEST-RIDING. 211

HEATON, CLACK, commonly called White Chapel in the North, see *Clack-Heaton*.

HEATON-EARLS, in the parish of Dewsbury, Agbrigg-division of the wapentake of Agbrigg and Morley, liberty of the Manor of Wakefield; 1 mile from Dewsbury, 4 from Wakefield.

HEATON-HANGING, in the parish of Dewsbury, Agbrigg-division of the wapentake of Agbrigg and Morley, liberty of the Manor of Wakefield; 1 mile from Dewsbury, 5 from Wakefield.

HEATON-HILL, in the parish of Dewsbury, Agbrigg-division of the wapentake of Agbrigg and Morley, liberty of the Manor of Wakefield; ½ a mile from Dewsbury, 4½ from Wakefield.

HEATON, KIRK, in the parish of Kirk-Heaton, Agbrigg-division of the wapentake of Agbrigg and Morley, liberty of the Honour of Pontefract; 2 miles from Huddersfield, 10 from Halifax, 11 from Wakefield.—Population 1,469.

HEATON-ROYDS, in the parish of Bradford, Morley-division of the wapentake of Agbrigg and Morley, liberty of the Honour of Pontefract; 2¼ miles from Bradford, 4 from Bingley, 10 from Halifax.

HEATON, UPPER, in the parish of Kirk-Heaton, Agbrigg-division of the wapentake of Agbrigg and Morley, liberty of the Honour of Pontefract; 2½ miles from Huddersfield, 11 from Wakefield.

HEBDEN, in the parish of Halifax, Morley-division of the wapentake of Agbrigg and Morley; 8 miles from Halifax, 10 from Rochdale, *(Lanc.)*

HEBDEN, in the parish of Linton, east-division of the wapentake and liberty of Staincliffe; 8 miles from Kettlewell, 8¼ from Pateleybridge, 12 from Skipton.—Pop. 341.

HEBDEN-BANK, in the parish of Linton, east-division of the wapentake and liberty of Staincliffe; 6 miles from Kettlewell, 8¼ from Pateleybridge.

HEBDEN-MOORSIDE, in the parish of Linton, east-division of the wapentake and liberty of Staincliffe; 7¼ miles from Pateleybridge, 9 from Kettlewell.

HECK, GREAT, in the parish of Snaith, wapentake of Osgoldcross, liberty of the Honour of Pontefract; 2 miles from Snaith, 8 from Ferrybridge, 9 from Thorne.—Pop. 194.

HECK, LITTLE, in the parish of Snaith, wapentake of Osgoldcross, liberty of the Honour of Pontefract; 2¼ miles from Snaith, 7¼ from Ferrybridge, 8¼ from Thorne.

HECKMONDWICK, in the parish of Birstall, Morley-division of the wapentake of Agbrigg and Morley, liberty of

WEST-RIDING.

Honour of Pontefract; 2 miles from Dewsbury, 7 from efield, 9 from Halifax.—Population 1,742.

BINGLEY, in the parish of Leeds, lower-division of wapentake of Skirack, liberty of the Honour of Pontefract; 2 miles from Leeds, 8 from Bradford, 8 from Otley. Population 1,313.

EIGHT, in the parish of Almondbury, Agbrigg-division of the wapentake of Agbrigg and Morley; 3¼ miles from Huddersfield, 11¼ from Halifax.

EIGHT, in the parish of Rochdale, (Lanc.) Agbrigg-division of the wapentake of Agbrigg and Morley; 8 miles from Rochdale, (Lanc.) 12 from Manchester, (ditto) 12 from Huddersfield.

HELABY-HALL, in the parish of Wath-upon-Dearn, south-division of the wapentake of Strafforth and Tickhill; 5¼ miles from Tickhill, 5¼ from Rotherham.

HELABY-HALL, in the parish of Stainton, south-division of the wapentake of Strafforth and Tickhill; 5 miles from Rotherham, 6 from Tickhill, 10 from Bawtry.

HELEN'S WELL, ST. in the parish of Royston, wapentake of Staincross, liberty of the Honour of Pontefract; 2 miles from Barnsley, 8¼ from Wakefield, 9¼ from Penistone.

HELLIFIELD-COCHINS, in the parish of Long-Preston, west-division of the wapentake and liberty of Staincliffe; 6¼ miles from Settle, 9¼ from Skipton, 12¼ from Colne, (Lanc.)—Population 237.

HELLIFIELD-PEEL, in the parish of Long-Preston, west-division of the wapentake of Staincliffe, liberty of Clifford's Fee; (the seat of James Hammerton, Esq.) 6 miles from Settle, 10 from Skipton, 13 from Colne, (Lanc.)

HELWICK, in the parish of Bingley, upper-division of the wapentake of Skirack; 4 miles from Keighley, 6 from Otley, 7 from Bradford.

HELWICK-HALL, in the parish of Bingley, upper-division of the wapentake of Skirack; 4 miles from Keighley, 6¼ from Otley, 6¼ from Bradford.

HEMINGFIELD, in the parish of Darfield, north-division of the wapentake of Strafforth and Tickhill, liberty of Tickhill; 5 miles from Barnsley, 7¼ from Rotherham.

HEMSWORTH, in the parish of Hemsworth, wapentake of Staincross, liberty of the Honour of Pontefract; (the seat of Sir Francis Lindley Wood, Bart.) 5½ miles from Pontefract, 7 from Wakefield, 9 from Barnsley.—Pop. 803

HEMSWORTH-LANE-END, in the parish of Hemsworth, wapentake of Staincross, liberty of the Honour of Pontefract; (the seat of John Vincent, Esq.) 5¼ miles from Pontefract, 6¼ from Wakefield, 9 from Barnsley.

HEMSWORTH-LODGE, in the parish of Hemsworth, wapentake of Osgoldcross, liberty of the Honour of Pontefract; 6 miles from Pontefract, 9 from Barnsley.

HEMSWORTH-MARSH, in the parish of Hemsworth, wapentake of Staincross, liberty of the Honour of Pontefract; 5 miles from Pontefract, 7 from Wakefield.

HENSALL, in the parish of Snaith, wapentake of Osgoldcross, liberty of the Honour of Pontefract; 3 miles from Snaith, 7 from Ferrybridge.—Population 213.

HEPTONSTALL, in the parish of Halifax, Morley-division of the wapentake of Agbrigg and Morley, liberty of the Manor of Wakefield; 9 miles from Halifax, 12 from Rochdale, (Lanc.)—Population 2,983.

HEPTONSTALL-LANES, in the parish of Halifax, Morley-division of the wapentake of Agbrigg and Morley, liberty of the Manor of Wakefield; 9 miles from Halifax, 12 from Rochdale, (Lanc.)

HEPTONSTALL-PARK, in the parish of Halifax, Morley-division of the wapentake of Agbrigg and Morley, liberty of the Manor of Wakefield; 8¼ miles from Halifax, 13 from Rochdale, (Lanc.)

HEPTONSTALL-SLACK, in the parish of Halifax, Morley-division of the wapentake of Agbrigg and Morley, liberty of the Manor of Wakefield; 9 miles from Halifax, 12¼ from Rochdale, (Lanc.)

HEPWORTH, in the parish of Kirk-Burton, Agbrigg-division of the wapentake of Agbrigg and Morley, liberty of the Manor of Wakefield; 6 miles from Huddersfield, 7 from Penistone.—Population 804.

HERMIT-HILL, in the parish of Tankersley, wapentake of Staincross, liberty of the Honour of Pontefract; 5 miles from Barnsley, 6 from Penistone, 8 from Sheffield.

HERRINTHORPE, in the parish of Rotherham, south-division of the wapentake of Strafforth and Tickhill; 2 miles from Rotherham, 6 from Sheffield.

HESLEY, in the parish of Rossington, south-division of the wapentake of Strafforth and Tickhill; (Hesley-Hall, the seat of George Bustard Greaves, Esq.) 3¼ miles from Bawtry, 6¼ from Doncaster.

HESSLEDEN, NETHER, in the parish of Arnecliffe, west-division of the wapentake and liberty of Staincliffe; 9 miles Kettlewell, 11¼ from Settle.

HESSLEDEN, OVER, in the parish of Arnecliffe, west-division of the wapentake and liberty of Staincliffe; 9½ miles from Kettlewell, 12 from Settle.

HETTON, in the parish of Burnsall, east-division of the wa-

Ee

pentake of Staincliffe, liberty of Clifford's Fee; 5 miles from Skipton, 10 from Kettlewell, 13 from Settle.—Population 172.

HEWBY, in the parish of Harewood, upper-division of the wapentake of Claro; 5 miles from Otley, 8 from Wetherby, 9 from Leeds.

HEWICK-BRIDGE, in the parish of Ripon, lower-division of the wapentake of Claro, liberty of Ripon; 1½ mile from Ripon, 4¼ from Boroughbridge.

HEWICK, COPT, in the parish of Ripon, lower-division of the wapentake of Claro, liberties of St. Peter and Ripon; 2 miles from Ripon, 5 from Boroughbridge.—Pop. 183.

HEXTHORPE, in the parish and soke of Doncaster, south-division of the wapentake of Strafforth and Tickhill; 1¼ mile from Doncaster, 10¼ from Rotherham.

HICKLETON, in the parish of Doncaster, north-division of the wapentake of Strafforth and Tickhill; *(the seat of Godfrey Wentworth Wentworth, Esq.)* 6 miles from Doncaster, 9¼ from Barnsley, 10 from Rotherham.—Pop. 174.

HIENDLEY, COLD, or NORTH, in the parish of Felkirk, wapentake of Staincross, liberty of the Honour of Pontefract; 7 miles from Wakefield, 8 from Huddersfield, 9 from Barnsley.

HIENDLEY, SOUTH, in the parish of Felkirk, wapentake of Staincross, liberty of the Honour of Pontefract; 6 miles from Barnsley, 6 from Wakefield, 10 from Pontefract.— Population 265.

HIGHAM, in the parish of Darton, wapentake of Staincross, liberty of the Honour of Pontefract; 2¼ miles from Barnsley 5 from Penistone, 10 from Wakefield.

HIGH-ELLERS, in the parish of Cantley, south-division of the wapentake of Strafforth and Tickhill; 3 miles from Doncaster, 6 from Bawtry.

HIGH-FIELD, in the parish of Sheffield, south-division of the wapentake of Strafforth and Tickhill; *(the seat of George Woodhead, Esq.)* 1 mile from Sheffield, 7 from Rotherham.

HIGH-FIELD, or FIELD-HEAD, in the parish of Silkston, wapentake of Staincross, liberty of the Honour of Pontefract; *(the seat of William Parker, Esq.)* 3 miles from Barnsley, 4¼ from Penistone, 8¼ from Wakefield.

HIGH-FLATTS, in the parish of Penistone, wapentake of Staincross, liberty of the Honour of Pontefract; 3¼ miles from Penistone, 8 from Barnsley, 9¼ from Huddersfield.

HIGH-GREEN, in the parish of Ecclesfield, north-division of the wapentake of Strafforth and Tickhill; 7 miles from Sheffield, 7 from Barnsley, 8 from Rotherham.

WEST-RIDING. 215

HIGH-HOUSE, in the parish of Sheffield, south-division of the wapentake of Strafforth and Tickhill; *(the seat of Christopher Oates, Esq.)* 1¼ mile from Sheffield, 7½ from Rotherham.

HIGH-TOWN, in the parish of Birstall, Morley-division of the wapentake of Agbrigg and Morley; 4 miles from Dewsbury, 6 from Halifax, 9 from Wakefield.

HIGH-WOOD, in the parish of Ripon, lower-division of the wapentake of Claro; 1 mile from Pateleybridge, 9 from Knaresborough, 13 from Ripon.

HILLAM, in the parish of Monk-Fryston, wapentake of Barkston-Ash; 4 miles from Ferrybridge, 6 from Pontefract, 7 from Selby.—Population 190.

HILL-FOOT, in the parish of Sheffield, south-division of the wapentake of Strafforth and Tickhill; 1 mile from Sheffield, 7 from Rotherham, 14 from Chesterfield, *(Derb.)*

HILLS, in the parish of Sheffield, south-division of the wapentake of Strafforth and Tickhill; 2 miles from Sheffield, 4¼ from Rotherham, 11½ from Barnsley.

HILL-TOP, in the parish of Sandall, Agbrigg-division of the wapentake of Agbrigg and Morley; 4 miles from Wakefield, 6 from Barnsley.

HILL-TOP, in the parish of Thornhill, Agbrigg-division of the wapentake of Agbrigg and Morley; 7 miles from Wakefield, 8 from Huddersfield, 9½ from Barnsley.

HILL-TOP, in the parish of Kirk-Burton, Agbrigg-division of the wapentake of Agbrigg and Morley; 5¼ miles from Huddersfield, 6 from Penistone.

HILL-TOP, in the parish of Rotherham, south-division of the wapentake of Strafforth and Tickhill; 2 miles from Rotherham, 8 from Sheffield, 10 from Doncaster.

HIPPERHOLME, in the parish of Halifax, Morley-division of the wapentake of Agbrigg and Morley, liberty of the Manor of Wakefield; 2¼ miles from Halifax, 6¼ from Bradford, 7 from Huddersfield, 13¼ from Wakefield.—Population 2,879.

HOBBERLEY-HOUSE, in the parishes of Thorne and Barwick-in-Elmet, lower-division of the wapentake of Skirack; 4½ miles from Leeds, 6 from Harewood, 6 from Wetherby.

HOGLEY, in the parish of Almondbury, Agbrigg-division of the wapentake of Agbrigg and Morley; 6 miles from Huddersfield, 10 from Penistone.

HOLBECK, in the parish of Leeds, Morley-division of the wapentake of Agbrigg and Morley, liberty of the Honour of Pontefract; 1 mile from Leeds, 11 from Otley, 13 from Bradford.—Population 4,196.

HOLDEN-CLOUGH, in the parish of Batley, Agbrigg-division of the wapentake of Agbrigg and Morley; 4 miles from Dewsbury, 6 from Leeds.

HOLDEN-HOUSE, in the parish of Ecclesfield, north-division of the wapentake of Strafforth and Tickhill; 8 miles from Penistone, 10 from Sheffield.

HOLDSWORTH, in the parish of Halifax, Morley-division of the wapentake of Agbrigg and Morley; 4 miles from Halifax, 6¼ from Bradford, 7¼ from Keighley.

HOLDSWORTH, in the parish of Ecclesfield, north-division of the wapentake of Strafforth and Tickhill; 6 miles from Sheffield, 10 from Penistone.

HOLLEY-HALL, in the parish of Penistone, wapentake of Staincross, liberty of the Honour of Pontefract; 4 miles from Penistone, 7 from Barnsley, 9½ from Sheffield.

HOLLIN-GROVE, in the parish of Rochdale, *(Lanc.)* Agbrigg-division of the wapentake of Agbrigg and Morley; 9 miles from Rochdale, *(Lanc.)* 12 from Manchester, *(ditto)* 14 from Huddersfield.

HOLLIN-HALL, in the parish of Ripon, lower-division of the wapentake of Claro; *(the seat of Richard Wood, Esq.)* 2¼ miles from Ripon, 5 from Ripley.

HOLLINGS-HALL, in the parish of Ilkley, upper-division of the wapentake of Skirack; *(the seat of John Dearden, Esq.)* 8 miles from Skipton, 8 from Bradford, 9 from Keighley.

HOLLINS, in the parish of Keighley, east-division of the wapentake and liberty of Staincliffe; 2 miles from Keighley, 8 from Skipton.

HOLLINTHORPE, in the parish of Sandall, Agbrigg-division of the wapentake of Agbrigg and Morley; 4¼ miles from Wakefield, 6 from Barnsley.

HOLME, in the parish of Hampsthwaite, lower-division of the wapentake of Claro; 4 miles from Ripley, 8 from Knaresborough.

HOLME, in the parish of Almondbury, Agbrigg-division of the wapentake of Agbrigg and Morley, liberty of the Manor of Wakefield; 9 miles from Huddersfield, 11 from Penistone.—Population 302.

HOLME-BRIDGE, in the parish of Skipton, east-division of the wapentake and liberty of Staincliffe; 3¼ miles from Skipton 12¼ from Settle.

HOLMEFIRTH, in the parish of Kirk-Burton, Agbrigg-division of the wapentake of Agbrigg and Morley, liberty of the Manor of Wakefield; 7 miles from Huddersfield, 8 from Penistone.

HOLME-HOUSE, in the parish of Keighley, east-division of the wapentake and liberty of Staincliffe; *(the seat of the Rev. Thomas Dunham Whittaker)* 2 miles from Keighley, 8 from Skipton, 10 from Colne, *(Lanc.)*

HOLME-HOUSES, in the parish of Kirby-Malzeard, lower-division of the wapentake of Claro; 3 miles from Pateley-bridge, 10 from Masham.

HOLMES, in the parish of Rotherham, south-division of the wapentake of Strafforth and Tickhill, liberty of Tickhill; 1 mile from Rotherham, 5 from Sheffield.

HONLEY, in the parish of Almondbury, Agbrigg-division of the wapentake of Agbrigg and Morley, liberty of the Honour of Pontefract; 3 miles from Huddersfield, 12 from Penistone, 13¼ from Wakefield.—Population 2,529.

HOOBER-STAND, in the parish of Wath-upon-Dearn, north-division of the wapentake of Strafforth and Tickhill; 4 miles from Doncaster, 8 from Barnsley.

HOOBROM, in the parish of Almondbury, Agbrigg-division of the wapentake of Agbrigg and Morley; 8 miles from Huddersfield, 11 from Penistone.

HOOD-GREEN, in the parish of Silkston, wapentake of Staincross, liberty of the Honour of Pontefract; 3 miles from Barnsley, 4 from Penistone, 11 from Sheffield.

HOOD, or HUT-GREEN, in the parish of Kellington, wapentake of Osgoldcross, liberty of the Honour of Pontefract; 5 miles from Snaith, 7 from Pontefract.

HOOD-LAND, in the parish of Penistone, wapentake of Staincross, liberty of the Honour of Pontefract; 2¼ miles from Penistone, 9¼ from Barnsley, 14 from Sheffield.

HOOK, in the parish of Snaith, wapentake of Osgoldcross, liberty of the Honour of Pontefract; 2 miles from Howden, 8½ from Thorne, 9 from Snaith.—Population 248.

HOOTON-LEVETT, in the parish of Maltby, south-division of the wapentake of Strafforth and Tickhill; 4¼ miles from Tickhill, 6 from Rotherham, 9¼ from Bawtry.—Population 73.

HOOTON, HIGH, in the parish of Maltby, south-division of the wapentake of Strafforth and Tickhill; *(the seat of —— Hoyle, Esq.)* 4¼ miles from Tickhill 6 from Rotherham.

HOOTON-PAGNELL, or HUTTON-PAGNALL, in the parish of Hooton-Pagnell, north-division of the wapentake of Strafforth and Tickhill; 5¼ miles from Doncaster, 10 from Barnsley.

HOOTON-ROBERTS, in the parish of Hooton-Roberts, south-division of the wapentake of Strafforth and Tickhill, liberty of Tickhill; 4¼ miles from Rotherham, 7¼ from Doncaster.—Population 158

HOOTON-SLADE, in the parish of Maltby, south-division of the wapentake of Strafforth and Tickhill, liberty of St. Peter; 5 miles from Tickhill, 7 from Rotherham.

HOPPER-LANE-INN, in the parish of Fewston, lower-division of the wapentake of Claro; 9 miles from Otley, 9 from Pateleybridge, 11 from Knaresborough, 13 from Skipton, 17 from Ripon.—Smiths' Arms.

HOPPERTON, in the parish of Allerton-Mauleverer, upper-division of the wapentake of Claro; 5 miles from Wetherby, 6 from Knaresborough.

HOPTON, in the parish of Mirfield, Agbrigg-division of the wapentake of Agbrigg and Morley; 3½ miles from Huddersfield, 4 from Dewsbury.

HORBURY, in the parish of Wakefield, Agbrigg-division of the wapentake of Agbrigg and Morley, liberty of the Manor of Wakefield; 2¼ miles from Wakefield, 11 from Huddersfield.—Population 2,101.

HORDRON, NETHER, in the parish of Penistone, wapentake of Staincross, liberty of the Honour of Pontefract; 5 miles from Penistone, 12 from Barnsley, 14 from Sheffield.

HORDRON, OVER, in the parish of Penistone, wapentake of Staincross, liberty of the Honour of Pontefract; 5 miles from Penistone, 12 from Barnsley, 14 from Sheffield.

HORLEY, or HOLYWELL GREEN, in the parish of Halifax, Morley-division of the wapentake of Agbrigg and Morley; 5 miles from Halifax, 5 from Huddersfield.

HORNTHWAITE, in the parish of Penistone, wapentake of Staincross, liberty of the Honour of Pontefract; 1 mile from Penistone, 8 from Barnsley, 14 from Huddersfield.

HORSEFORTH, in the parish of Guiseley, upper-division of the wapentake of Skirack; *(the seat of Peter Rhodes, Esq.)* 6 miles from Leeds, 6 from Otley.—Pop. 2,099.

HORSHOLD, in the parish of Halifax, Morley-division of the wapentake of Agbrigg and Morley; 8 miles from Halifax, 13 from Rochdale, *(Lanc.)*

HORSTENLEY, see *Austonley*.

HORTON, in the parish of Horton, wapentake of Ewcross; 5½ miles from Settle, 16 from Kirby-Lonsdale, *(Westm.)* 19¼ from Askrigg.—Population 570.

HORTON, in the parish of Gisburn, west-division of the wapentake and liberty of Staincliffe; 8 miles from Colne, *(Lanc.)* 9 from Skipton, 10 from Settle.—Population 109.

HORTON, GREAT, in the parish of Bradford, Morley-division of the wapentake of Agbrigg and Morley, liberty of the Honour of Pontefract; 2 miles from Bradford, 6½ from Halifax.—Population 3,459.

HORTON, LITTLE, in the parish of Bradford, Morley-division of the wapentake of Agbrigg and Morley, liberty of the Honour of Pontefract; *(the seat of —— Sharpe, Esq.)* 1 mile from Bradford, 7 from Halifax.

HOTHEROYD, in the parish of Felkirk, wapentake of Staincross, liberty of the Honour of Pontefract; 5 miles from Barnsley, 6½ from Wakefield, 9 from Pontefract.

HOUDEN, in the parish of Bolton, west-division of the wapentake and liberty of Staincliffe; *(Houden-Clough, the seat of Robert Tipping, Esq.)* 10 miles from Settle, 13 from Skipton, 15 from Kettlewell.

HOUGHTON, GLASS, in the parish of Castleford, wapentake of Osgoldcross, liberty of the Honour of Pontefract; 2 miles from Pontefract, 3 from Ferrybridge, 9 from Wakefield.—Population 382.

HOUGHTON, GREAT or LONG, in the parish of Darfield, north-division of the wapentake of Strafforth and Tickhill; 7½ miles from Doncaster, 8 from Barnsley.—Population 257.

HOUGHTON, LITTLE, in the parish of Darfield, north-division of the wapentake of Strafforth and Tickhill; 7 miles from Barnsley, 8 from Doncaster.—Population 128.

HOUNDHILL, in the parish of Ackworth, wapentake of Osgoldcross, liberty of the Honour of Pontefract; *(the seat of the Rev. Thomas Horton)* 2 miles from Pontefract, 4 from Ferrybridge, 9½ from Wakefield.

HOUSLEY-HALL, in the parish of Ecclesfield, north-division of the wapentake of Strafforth and Tickhill; 6½ miles from Sheffield, 6½ from Barnsley, 7½ from Rotherham.

HOW-BROOK, in the parish of Tankersley, wapentake of Staincross, liberty of the Honour of Pontefract; 5 miles from Barnsley, 7 from Rotherham, 8 from Sheffield.

HOWGILL, in the parish of Sedbergh, wapentake of Ewcross; *(the seat of the Rev. Daniel Peacock)* 1½ mile from Sedbergh, 6½ from Dent, 8½ from Kendal, *(Westm.)*

HOWGILL, in the parish of Gisburn, west-division of the wapentake and liberty of Staincliffe; 3 miles from Gisburn, 7 from Clitheroe, *(Lanc.)* 12½ from Skipton.

HOWGILL, in the parish of Skipton, lower-division of the wapentake of Claro; 7½ miles from Skipton, 18 from Pateleybridge, 16½ from Knaresborough.

HOWORTH-HALL, in the parish of Rotherham, south-division of the wapentake of Strafforth and Tickhill; *(the seat of Mrs. Westby)* 2 miles from Rotherham, 6 from Sheffield, 12 from Worksop, *(Notts.)*

HOWROYD, or HOLROYD, in the parish of Halifax, Morley-division of the wapentake of Agbrigg and Morley; *(the seat of Thomas Horton, Esq.)* 6 miles from Halifax, 6 from Huddersfield.

HOYLAND, HIGH, in the parish of High-Hoyland, wapentake of Staincross, liberty of the Honour of Pontefract; 6 miles from Penistone, 6¼ from Barnsley, 9 from Wakefield.—Population 270.

HOYLAND, NETHER, in the parish of Wath-upon-Dearn, north-division of the wapentake of Strafforth and Tickhill, liberty of Tickhill; 5¾ miles from Barnsley, 6½ from Rotherham, 9½ from Sheffield.

HOYLAND-SWAINE, in the parish of Silkston, wapentake of Staincross, liberty of the Honour of Pontefract; 2 miles from Penistone, 6¼ from Barnsley, 14 from Huddersfield.—Population 562.

HOYLAND, UPPER, in the parish of Wath-upon-Dearn, north-division of the wapentake of Strafforth and Tickhill, liberty of Tickhill; 5 miles from Barnsley, 7 from Rotherham, 10 from Sheffield.—Population 823.

HUBBERHOLME, or HUBBORAM, in the parish of Arncliffe, east-division of the wapentake and liberty of Staincliffe; 5 miles from Kettlewell, 15 from Settle, 17 from Leyburn.

HUDDERSFIELD, in the parish of Huddersfield, Agbrigg-division of the wapentake of Agbrigg and Morley, liberty of the Honour of Pontefract; 8 miles from Halifax, 8 from Dewsbury, 12¼ from Penistone, 13 from Wakefield, 16 from Leeds, 18 from Barnsley, 24 from Manchester, *(Lanc.)* 39 from York, 189 from London.—*Market*, Tuesday, for Woollen-Cloth, Provisions, &c.—*Fairs*, May 14 and 15, for Pedlary-Ware, &c.—*Bankers*, Old-Bank, Messrs. Dobson and Son, draw on Messrs. Dickinson, Goodall, and Dickinson, 33, Poultry; Huddersfield-Bank, Messrs. Perfect, Seaton, Brooke, and Co. draw on Messrs. Kensington, Styan, and Adams, 20, Lombard-Street; Commercial-Bank, Messrs. B. and J. Inghams, draw on Messrs. Were, Bruce, Simpson, and Taylor, 2, Bartholomew-Lane.—*Principal Inns*, Rose and Crown, George, Swan, Pack-Horse, and Ramsden's Arms.—Population 7,268.

HUDDLESTON, in the parish of Sherburn, wapentake of Barkston-Ash; 4 miles from Ferrybridge, 6 from Pontefract, 7 from Tadcaster.—Population 108.

HUD-HOLLINGS, in the parish of Wath-upon-Dearn, north-division of the wapentake of Strafforth and Tickhill; 5 miles from Barnsley, 7 from Rotherham, 9 from Sheffield.

WEST-RIDING. 221

HUGH-GREEN, in the parish of Hampsthwaite, lower-division of the wapentake of Claro; 3¼ miles from Ripley, 8¼ from Knaresborough.

HUMBURTON, in the parish of Aldborough, lower-division of the wapentake of Claro; 3 miles from Boroughbridge, 8 from Ripon, 10 from Knaresborough.—Population 28.

HUNDGATE, in the parish of Ripon, lower-division of the wapentake of Claro; 5 miles from Ripon, 7 from Pateley-bridge.

HUNGER-HILL, in the parish of Bolton, west-division of the wapentake and liberty of Staincliffe; *(the seat of E. King, Esq.)* 10 miles from Settle, 12 from Colne, *(Lanc.)* 14 from Skipton.

HUNGER-HILL, in the parish of Thornhill, Agbrigg-division of the wapentake of Agbrigg and Morley; 7 miles from Huddersfield, 9 from Wakefield.

HUNGER-HILL, in the parish of Ecclesfield, north-division of the wapentake of Strafforth and Tickhill; 5 miles from Sheffield, 8 from Barnsley, 11 from Rotherham.

HUNSHELF, in the parish of Penistone, wapentake of Staincross, liberty of the Honour of Pontefract; 3 miles from Penistone, 7 from Barnsley, 10 from Sheffield.—Population 327.

HUNSHELF-BANK, in the parish of Penistone, wapentake of Staincross, liberty of the Honour of Pontefract; 3 miles from Penistone, 7 from Barnsley, 10 from Sheffield.

HUNSINGORE, in the parish of Hunsingore, upper-division of the wapentake of Claro; 4 miles from Wetherby, 6¼ from Knaresborough.—Population 192.

HUNSLETT, in the parish of Leeds, Morley-division of the wapentake of Agbrigg and Morley, liberty of the Honour of Pontefract; 1¼ mile from Leeds, 7¼ from Wakefield, 12 from Bradford.—Population 5,799.

HUNSLETT-LANE, in the parish of Leeds, Morley-division of the wapentake of Agbrigg and Morley; extends from Leeds to Hunslett.

HUNSWORTH, in the parish of Birstall, Morley-division of the wapentake of Agbrigg and Morley, liberty of the Honour of Pontefract; 3 miles form Halifax, 5 from Bradford.—Population 585.

HUNTWICK, or HUNTIC, in the parish of Wragby, wapentake of Osgoldcross, liberty of the Honour of Pontefract; 4¼ miles from Pontefract, 6¼ from Ferrybridge, 13¼ from Doncaster.

HURLEFIELD, in the parish of Handsworth, south-division

Ff

WEST-RIDING.

of the wapentake of Strafforth and Tickhill; 3¼ miles from Sheffield, 10 from Chesterfield, (*Derb.*)

HURST-COURTNEY, in the parish of Birkin, wapentake of Barkston-Ash, liberty of the Honour of Pontefract; 4 miles from Selby, 4 from Snaith, 9 from Pontefract.—Pop 132.

HURST-GREEN, in the parish of Ecclesfield, north-division of the wapentake of Strafforth and Tickhill; 4 miles from Sheffield, 5 from Penistone, 7 from Rotherham.

HURST, TEMPLE, in the parish of Birkin, wapentake of Barkston-Ash, liberty of the Honour of Pontefract; 4 miles from Snaith, 5 from Selby, 7 from Ferrybridge.—Population 119.

HURTLEPOT, in the parish of Thornton-in-Lonsdale, wapentake of Ewcross; 10 miles from Kirby-Lonsdale, (*Westm.*) 13 from Settle.

HUSTHWAITE, in the parish of Silkston, wapentake of Staincross, liberty of the Honour of Pontefract; *(the seat of James Cockshut, Esq.)* 3 miles from Penistone, 5 from Barnsley, 10 from Sheffield.

HUTTON-PAGNALL, *see Hooton-Pagnell.*

I.

ICKLES, in the parish of Rotherham, south-division of the wapentake of Strafforth and Tickhill; 1 mile from Rotherham, 5 from Sheffield, 13 from Doncaster.

IDLE, in the parish of Calverley, Morley-division of the wapentake of Agbrigg and Morley, liberty of the Honour of Pontefract; 3¼ miles from Bradford, 6 from Otley, 9 from Leeds.—Population 3,398.

ILKLEY, in the parish of Ilkley, upper-division of the wapentake of Skirack; 6 miles from Otley, 7 from Keighley, 9 from Skipton.—Population 426.

ILLINGWORTH, in the parish of Halifax, Morley-division of the wapentake of Agbrigg and Morley; 2¼ miles from Halifax, 6 from Bradford,

ILLIONS, in the parish of Penistone, wapentake of Staincross, liberty of the Honour of Pontefract; 3 miles from Penistone, 10 from Barnsley, 11 from Huddersfield.

INGBIRCHWORTH, in the parish of Penistone, wapentake of Staincross, liberty of the Honour of Pontefract; 2¾ miles from Penistone, 8 from Barnsley, 11 from Huddersfield.—Population 170.

INGERTHORPE, in the parish of Ripon, lower-division of

WEST-RIDING.

the wapentake of Claro, liberty of Ripon; 4 miles from Ripon, 7 from Knaresborough.—Population 46.

INGLETON, in the parish of Low-Bentham, wapentake of Ewcross; *(the seat of Mrs. Alice Redmayne)* 7 miles from Kirby-Lonsdale, *(Westm.)* 10¾ from Settle, 18¼ from Lancaster, *(Lanc.)* 20 from Askrigg.—*No Market.—Fair*, November 17, for Horned Cattle.—Pop. 1,106.

INGMAN-LODGE, in the parish of Horton, wapentake of Ewcross; 11 miles from Settle, 13 from Askrigg.

INGMANTHORPE, in the parish of Kirk-Deighton, upper-division of the wapentake of Claro; *(the seat of Richard Yorke, Esq.)* 3 miles from Wetherby, 7 from Knaresborough, 12½ from York.

INGMIRE-HALL, in the parish of Sedbergh, wapentake of Ewcross; *(the seat of John Upton, Esq.)* 1¼ mile from Sedbergh, 8¼ from Kendal, *(Westm.)*

INGROW, in the parish of Keighley, east-division of the wapentake and liberty of Staincliffe; 1 mile from Keighley, 11 from Skipton, 11 from Halifax.

INTACK-END, in the parish of Handsworth, south-division of the wapentake of Strafforth and Tickhill; 3 miles from Sheffield, 7 from Rotherham.

INTACK-HEAD, in the parish of Huddersfield, Agbrigg-division of the wapentake of Agbrigg and Morley; 2 miles from Huddersfield, 7 from Halifax.

IVES, ST. in the parish of Bingley, upper-division of the wapentake of Skirack; *(the seat of Edward Ferrand, Esq.)* 8 miles from Skipton, 12 from Otley.

JACK-HILL, in the parish of Fewston, lower-division of the wapentake of Claro; 6 miles from Otley, 11 from Knaresborough.

JENNETT'S-CAVE, in the parish of Kirkby-Malhamdale, west-division of the wapentake and liberty of Staincliffe; 6 miles from Settle, 9 from Kettlewell, 12 from Skipton.

JOHNNY-MOOR-LONG, in the parish of Thorne, south-division of the wapentake of Strafforth and Tickhill; 3 miles from Thorne, 11 from Howden.

JOHN, ST. in the parish of Laughton-le-Morthen, south-division of the wapentake of Strafforth and Tickhill; liberty of Tickhill; 5¼ miles from Tickhill, 5½ from Rotherham.

K.

KAYLEY-HALL, in the parish of Otley, upper-division of the wapentake of Skirack; *(the seat of John Raistrick, Esq.)* 3 miles from Otley, 9 from Skipton, 10 from Bradford.

KEARBY, in the parish of Kirkby-Overblow, upper-division of the wapentake of Claro; 5 miles from Wetherby, 8 from Knaresborough.—Population 220.

KEB-ROYD, in the parish of Halifax, Morley-division of the wapentake of Agbrigg and Morley; *(the seat of Robert Holroyd, Esq.)* 5 miles from Halifax, 12 from Rochdale, *(Lanc.)*

KEIGHLEY, in the parish of Keighley, east-division of the wapentake of Staincliffe, liberty of Clifford's Fee; 4 miles from Bingley, 10 from Bradford, 10 from Skipton, 11 from Colne, *(Lanc.)* 12 from Otley, 12 from Halifax, 40 from York, 209 from London.—*Market*, Wednesday.—*Fairs*, May 8, for Horned Cattle and Horses, 9, and 10, for Pedlary-ware, November 7, for Horned Cattle, Horses and Sheep, and 8, and 9, for Pedlary-ware.—*Principal Inns*, Devonshire's Arms, and King's Arms.—Pop. 5,745.

KELLBROOK, in the parish of Thornton, east-division of the wapentake and liberty of Staincliffe; 4 miles from Colne, *(Lanc.)* 8 from Skipton, 10 from Burnley, *(Lanc.)*

KELLINGLEY, in the parish of Kellington, wapentake of Osgoldcross, liberty of the Honour of Pontefract; 4 miles from Pontefract, 8½ from Snaith.

KELLINGTON, in the parish of Kellington, wapentake of Osgoldcross, liberty of the Honour of Pontefract; 5¼ miles from Pontefract, 8 from Snaith.—Population 253.

KENDALL-GREEN, in the parish of Silkston, wapentake of Staincross, liberty of the Honour of Pontefract; 2 miles from Barnsley, 7 from Penistone, 9½ from Rotherham.

KERESFORTH-HILL, in the parish of Silkston, wapentake of Staincross, liberty of the Honour of Pontefract; 1 mile from Barnsley, 6 from Penistone, 11 from Wakefield.

KERSHALL, in the parish of Addle, upper-division of the wapentake of Skirack; 4 miles from Harewood, 5 from Otley, 6 from Leeds.

KESWICK, EAST, in the parish of Harewood, lower-division of the wapentake of Skirack; 6 miles from Leeds, 10 from Skipton, 14 from Bradford.—Population 535.

KESWICK, DUN, in the parish of Harewood, upper-division of the wapentake of Claro; 7 miles from Wetherby, 8¼ from Knaresborough, 10 from Leeds.—Population 218.

KETSMOOR, in the parish of Kirby-Malzeard, lower-division of the wapentake of Claro; 6 miles from Masham, 9 from Ripon.

KETTLESING-HEAD, in the parish of Hampsthwaite, lower-division of the wapentake of Claro; 6 miles from Ripley, 8¼ from Knaresborough.

KETTLETHORPE, in the parish of Sandall, Agbrigg-division of the wapentake of Agbrigg and Morley, liberty of the Manor of Wakefield; *(the seat of J. Armitage, Esq.)* 2¼ miles from Wakefield, 7½ from Barnsley.—Pop. 141.

KETTLEWELL, in the parish of Kettlewell, east-division of the wapentake and liberty of Staincliffe; 14¼ miles from Askrigg, 15 from Middleham, 15 from Settle, 16 from Skipton, 16 from Pateleybridge, 17 from Leyburn, 48 from York, 233 from London.—*Market*, Thursday.—*Fairs*, July 6, for Pedlary-ware, September 2, and October 23, for Sheep.—*Principal Inn*, Spread Eagle.—Pop. 437.

KEVETON, in the parish of Harthill, south-division of the wapentake of Strafforth and Tickhill; *(the seat of the Duke of Leeds)* 7 miles from Worksop, *(Notts.)* 8 from Rotherham, 11 from Tickhill.

KEXBROUGH, in the parish of Darton, wapentake of Staincross, liberty of the Honour of Pontefract; 4 miles from Barnsley, 5¼ from Penistone, 8½ from Wakefield.—Population 401.

KIDHALL-INN, in the parish of Barwick-in-Elmet, lower-division of the wapentake of Skirack, liberty of the Honour of Pontefract; 4 miles from Abberford, 6¼ from Tadcaster, 8 from Leeds.

KILDWICK, in the parish of Kildwick, east-division of the wapentake of Staincliffe, liberty of Clifford's Fee; *(Kildwick-Hall, the seat of Miss Currer)* 4¼ miles from Skipton, 5¼ from Keighley, 9 from Colne, *(Lanc.)*—Pop. 209.

KILDWICK-GRANGE, in the parish of Kildwick, east-division of the wapentake and liberty of Staincliffe; 5 miles from Keighley, 5½ from Skipton, 9¼ from Colne, *(Lanc.)*

KILHILL, in the parish of Ripon, lower-division of the wapentake of Claro; 1 mile from Pateleybridge, 10¼ from Ripon.

KILHOLME, in the parish of Cantley, south-division of the wapentake of Strafforth and Tickhill; 6 miles from Doncaster, 6 from Bawtry.

KILLINGBECK, in the parish of Whitchurch, lower-division of the wapentake of Skirack, liberty of the Honour of Pontefract; *(the seat of —— Walker, Esq.)* 3 miles from Leeds, 13 from Bradford, 13 from Otley.

KILLINGHALL, in the parish of Ripley, lower-division of the wapentake of Claro, liberties of Knaresborough and Ripon; 1¼ mile from Ripley, 5 from Knaresborough, 7 from Ripon.—Population 462.

KILNHURST, in the parish of Rawmarsh, north-division of the wapentake of Strafforth and Tickhill; 5 miles from Rotherham, 8 from Barnsley.

KILNSEY, in the parish of Burnsall, east-division of the wapentake of Staincliffe, liberty of Clifford's Fee; 3 miles from Kettlewell, 12 from Skipton, 12 from Settle.

KIMBERWORTH, in the parish of Rotherham, north-division of the wapentake of Strafforth and Tickhill, liberty of Tickhill; 2 miles from Rotherham, 7 from Sheffield, 13 from Penistone.—Population 3,326.

KINSLEY, in the parish of Hemsworth, wapentake of Staincross; liberty of the Honour of Pontefract; *(the seat of John Stocks, Esq.)* 7 miles from Pontefract, 7 from Wakefield, 10 from Barnsley.

KIPPAX, in the parish of Kippax, lower-division of the wapentake of Skirack, liberty of the Honour of Pontefract; 8 miles from Leeds, 8 from Pontefract.—Pop. 779.

KIPPAX-PARK, in the parish of Kippax, lower-division of the wapentake of Skirack, liberty of the Honour of Pontefract; *(the seat of Thomas Bland Davison Bland, Esq.)* 7 miles from Pontefract, 9 from Leeds.

KIRBY, in the parish of Little-Ouseburn, upper-division of the wapentake of Claro; 5 miles from Boroughbridge, 8 from Knaresborough, 8 from Wetherby.

KIRBY-COT, in the parish of Halifax, Morley-division of the wapentake of Agbrigg and Morley; 4¼ miles from Halifax, 8 from Todmorden.

KIRBY-HALL, in the parish of Little-Ouseburn, upper-division of the wapentake of Claro; *(the seat of Henry Thompson, Esq.)* 5 miles from Boroughbridge, 9 from Knaresborough, 9 from Wetherby.

KIRBY-MALZEARD, in the parish of Kirby-Malzeard, lower-division of the wapentake of Claro, liberty of St. Peter; *(the seat of Tomyns Dickins, Esq.)* 4 miles from Masham, 7 from Ripon, 10 from Pateleybridge.—Pop. 524.

KIRBY-WHARFE, in the parish of Kirby-Wharfe, wapentake of Barkston-Ash, liberties of St. Peter and the Honour of Pontefract; 2 miles from Tadcaster, 12 from Selby, 13 from Pontefract.—Population 79.

KIRKBY-MALHAMDALE, or MALGHDALE, in the parish of Kirkby-Malhamdale, west-division of the wapentake and liberty of Staincliffe; 6 miles from Settle, 10 from Skipton, 10 from Kettlewell.—Population 167.

KIRKBY-OVERBLOW, in the parish of Kirkby-Overblow, upper-division of the wapentake of Claro; *(the seat of the Hon. and Rev. — Marsham, D. D.)* 5½ miles from Wetherby, 6¼ from Knaresborough.—Population 294.

KIRKBY, SOUTH, in the parish of South-Kirkby, wapentake of Osgoldcross, liberty of the Honour of Pontefract; 7 miles from Barnsley, 10 from Wakefield, 10 from Doncaster.—Population 509.

KIRK-GILL, in the parish of Arnecliffe, west-division of the wapentake and liberty of Staincliffe; 5 miles from Kettlewell, 16¼ from Settle.

KIRK-HOUSE-GREEN, in the parish of Kirk-Bramwith, wapentake of Osgoldcross, liberty of the Honour of Pontefract; 4 miles from Thorne, 7 from Doncaster, 8 from Snaith.

KIRKLEES-HALL, in the parish of Dewsbury, Agbrigg-division of the wapentake of Agbrigg and Morley, liberty of the Manor of Wakefield; *(the seat of Sir George Armitage, Bart.)* 4½ miles from Huddersfield, 6 from Halifax, 12 from Leeds.

KIRKSTALL, and ABBEY, in the parish of Leeds, lower-division of the wapentake of Skirack, liberty of the Honour of Pontefract; 3¼ miles from Leeds, 7 from Bradford.

KIRKTHORPE, or CAYTHORPE, in the parish of Warmfield, Agbrigg-division of the wapentake of Agbrigg and Morley, liberty of the Honour of Pontefract; 3 miles Wakefield, 11 from Barnsley.

KNARESBOROUGH, or KNARESBROUGH, in the parish of Knaresborough, lower-division of the wapentake of Claro, liberties of St. Peter and Knaresborough; 5 miles from Ripley, 7 from Boroughbridge, 7 from Wetherby, 10 from Ripon, 11 from Hopper-Lane-Inn, 13 from Otley, 18 from Leeds, 18 from York, 201 from London.—*Market*, Wednesday.—*Fairs*, first Wenesday after January 13, for Horned Cattle, and the day preceding, for Sheep; first Wednesday after March 12, May 6, unless it falls on a Sunday, then the day following, first Monday after August 12, first Tuesday after October 11, first Wednesday after December 10, for Horned Cattle, and the day following the five last mentioned Fairs, for Sheep; Statute-day, Wednesday before November 23, and on no other day.—*Bankers*, Messrs. Harrison and Terry, draw on Messrs. Willis, Wood, Percival, and Co. 76, Lombard-Street; Messrs. Coates and Fairbank, draw on Messrs. Robarts, Curtis, and Co. 15, Lombard-Street.—Sends two Members to Parliament.—*Principal Inns*, Elephant and Castle, Crown and Bell, and Bay Horse.—Population 3,388.

KNOTTINGLEY, in the parish of Pontefract, wapentake of Osgoldcross liberty of the Honour of Pontefract; 1 mile from Ferrybridge, 3 from Pontefract, 9½ from Snaith, 15¾ from Doncaster.—Population 2,602.

KOW-BANK, in the parish of Burnsall, east-division of the wapentake and liberty of Staincliffe; 9 miles from Settle, 10 from Skipton.

KNOWLES, *see Raven's-Knowles*.

L.

LAMBCOTE-GRANGE, in the parish of Braithwell, south division of the wapentake of Strafforth and Tickhill, liberty of Tickhill; 5 miles from Tickhill, 6 from Rotherham.

LANE-ENDS, in the parish of Keighley, east-division of the wapentake and liberty of Staincliffe; 3 miles from Keighley, 9 from Colne, (*Lanc.*) 10 from Skipton.

LANE-HEAD, in the parish of Kirk-Burton, Agbrigg-division of the wapentake of Agbrigg and Morley; 5 miles from Penistone, 7¼ from Huddersfield.

LANE-HEAD, in the parish of Darton, wapentake of Staincross, liberty of the Honour of Pontefract; 3½ miles from Barnsley, 6¼ from Penistone, 8 from Wakefield.

LANE-HEAD, in the parish of Rawmarsh, north-division of the wapentake of Strafforth and Tickhill; 3 miles from Rotherham, 9 from Sheffield.

LANE-HEAD, or LANE-HOUSES, in the parish of Weston, upper-division of the wapentake of Claro; 3 miles from Otley, 13 from Leeds, 13 from Skipton.

LANGBER, in the parish of Ilkley, lower-division of the wapentake of Claro; 7¼ miles from Skipton, 8¼ from Otley.

LANGCLIFFE, in the parish of Giggleswick, west-division of the wapentake and liberty of Staincliffe; (*Langcliffe-Hall*, the seat of Pudsey Dawson, Esq. *Langcliffe-Place*, the seat of Edward Clayton. Esq.) 1 mile from Settle, 17 from Skipton.—Population 260.

LANGER-HOUSE, in the parish of Burnsall, east-division of the wapentake and liberty of Staincliffe; 9 miles from Settle, 11 from Skipton.

LANGFIELD, in the parish of Halifax, Morley-division of the wapentake of Agbrigg and Morley, liberty of the Manor of Wakefield; 11 miles from Halifax, 11 from Rochdale, (*Lanc.*)—Population 1170.

WEST-RIDING.

LANGHILL-HOUSE, in the parish of Burnsall, east-division of the wapentake and liberty of Staincliffe; 8 miles from Skipton, 9 from Settle.

LANGILL, in the parish of Giggleswick, west-division of the wapentake and liberty of Staincliffe; 5 miles from Settle, 16¼ from Skipton.

LANGLEY-BROOK, in the parish of Ecclesfield, north-division of the wapentake of Strafforth and Tickhill; 3 miles from Sheffield, 5 from Rotherham, 10 from Barnsley.

LANGLEY-HALL, in the parish of Almondbury, Agbrigg-division of the wapentake of Agbrigg and Morley; *(the seat of Sir John Ramsden, Bart.)* 1 mile from Huddersfield, 9 from Halifax.

LANGOLD, in the parish of Laughton-le Morthen, south-division of the wapentake of Strafforth and Tickhill, liberty of Tickhill; *(the seat of Henry Galleyknight, Esq.)* 4 miles from Worksop, *(Notts.)* 5 from Tickhill, 12 from Rotherham.

LANGRICK, in the parish of Drax, wapentake of Barkston-Ash; 5 miles from Selby, 6 from Snaith, 15 from Ferrybridge.

LANGSETT, in the parish of Penistone, wapentake of Staincross, liberty of the Honour of Pontefract; 3 miles from Penistone, 10 from Barnsley, 12 from Sheffield.—Pop. 204.

LANGTHWAITE, in the parish of Doncaster, north-division of the wapentake of Strafforth and Tickhill, liberty of Tickhill; 4 miles from Doncaster, 9 from Thorne.—Population 34.

LAPWATER, in the parish of Rotherham, north-division of the wapentake of Strafforth and Tickhill; 1½ mile from Rotherham, 10¼ from Barnsley.

LASINGCROFT, in the parish of Barwick-in-Elmet, lower-division of the wapentake of Skirack, liberty of the Honour of Pontefract; 5 miles from Leeds, 9 from Pontefract, 9½ from Wakefield.

LASSIL'S-HALL, in the parish of Kirk-Heaton, Agbrigg-division of the wapentake of Agbrigg and Morley; *(the seat of Samuel Walker, Esq.)* 2½ miles from Huddersfield, 11 from Wakefield.

LAUGHTON-LE-MORTHEN, in the parish of Laughton-le-Morthen, south-division of the wapentake of Strafforth and Tickhill, liberty of St. Peter; 5¼ miles from Rotherham, 5½ from Tickhill, 8 from Worksop, *(Notts.)* 10 from Bawtry.—Population 465.

LAUND-HOUSE, in the parish of Bingley, upper-division

of the wapentake of Skirack; 5 miles from Bradford, 10 from Otley.

LAVERICK-HALL, in the parish of Keighley, east-division of the wapentake and liberty of Staincliffe; 3 miles from Keighley, 10 from Colne, *(Lanc.)*

LAVERTON, in the parish of Kirby-Malzeard, lower-division of the wapentake of Claro; 5 miles from Masham, 8 from Ripon.—Population 368.

LAWKLAND, in the parish of Clapham, wapentake of Ewcross; *(Lawkland-Hall, the seat of John Ingleby, Esq.)* 4 miles from Settle, 13 from Kirby-Lonsdale, *(Westm.)*—Population 368.

LAYCOCK, in the parish of Keighley, east-division of the wapentake and liberty of Staincliffe; 2 miles from Keighley, 8 from Skipton, 10½ from Colne, *(Lanc.)*

LAYS, in the parish of Monk-Fryston, wapentake of Barkston-Ash; *(the seat of David Himsworth, Esq.)* 4 miles from Ferrybridge, 6 from Pontefract, 10 from Tadcaster.

LEADHALL, in the parish of Saxton, wapentake of Barkston-Ash; 5 miles from Tadcaster, 8 from Wetherby, 10 from Pontefract.

LEATHLEY, in the parish of Leathley, upper-division of the wapentake of Claro; 2 miles from Otley, 11 from Leeds, 12 from Knaresborough.—Population 284.

LEDSAM, in the parish of Ledsam, wapentake of Barkston-Ash, liberty of the Honour of Pontefract; 5 miles from Pontefract, 10 from Tadcaster, 10 from Selby.—Pop. 220.

LEDSTON, in the parish of Ledsam, wapentake of Barkston-Ash, liberty of the Honour of Pontefract; 5 miles from Pontefract, 10 from Leeds, 10 from Tadcaster.—Population 238.

LEDSTON-LODGE, in the parish of Ledsam, wapentake of Barkston-Ash, liberty of the Honour of Pontefract; *(the seat of Michael Angelo Taylor, Esq.)* 6 miles from Pontefract, 10 from Tadcaster, 10 from Leeds.

LEEDS, in the parish of Leeds, lower-division of the wapentake of Skirack, liberty of the Honour of Pontefract; 9 miles from Wakefield, 10 from Bradford, 10 from Dewsbury, 10 from Otley, 11¼ from Abberford, 15 from Tadcaster, 15 from Pontefract, 15 from Ferrybridge, 15¼ from Harrogate, 16 from Wetherby, 16 from Huddersfield, 18 from Knaresborough, 20 from Selby, 23 from York, 191 from London.—*Markets*, Tuesday and Saturday, for Woollen-Cloth, Provisions, &c.—*Fairs*, July 10 and 11, for Horses, and Pedlary-Ware, November 8 and 9, for Horned Cattle, &c.—*Bankers*, Commercial-Bank, Messrs. Fenton, Scott,

Nicholson, and Smith, draw on Messrs. Boldero, Lushington, and Co. 30 Cornhill; New-Bank, Messrs. Fields, Cleaver, and Greenwood, draw on Messrs. Robarts, Curtis, and Co. 15 Lombard Street; Old-Bank, Messrs. Beckett, Calverley, and Co. draw on Sir Richard Carr Glyn, Mills, and Co. 12 Birchin Lane.—*Principal Inns,* Hotel, Bull and Mouth, Golden Lion, Rose and Crown, and King's Arms.—Population 53,162.

LEE-GREEN, or GAP, *(a Common)* in the parish of Mirfield, Morley-division of the wapentake of Agbrigg and field; 2 miles from Dewsbury, 7 from Huddersfield.—*No Market.*—*Fairs,* August 24, and September 17, for Horses, Horned Cattle, &c.

LEES-HALL, in the parish of Thornhill, Agbrigg-division of the wapentake of Agbrigg and Morley; 2 miles from Dewsbury, 7 from Wakefield.

LENERTON, in the parish of Sherburn, wapentake of Barkston-Ash; 5 miles from Pontefract, 7 from Tadcaster, 12 from Wetherby.

LENIKER, in the parish of Sedbergh, wapentake of Ewcross; 4½ miles from Sedbergh, 9 from Kirby-Lonsdale, *(Westm.)*

LEPTON, GREAT, in the parish of Kirk-Heaton, Agbrigg-division of the wapentake of Agbrigg and Morley, liberty of the Honour of Pontefract; 4½ miles from Huddersfield, 9 from Wakefield, 10½ from Penistone, 12½ from Barnsley.

LEPTON, LITTLE, in the parish of Kirk-Heaton, Agbrigg-division of the wapentake of Agbrigg and Morley, liberty of the Honour of Pontefract; 4¼ miles from Huddersfield, 9 from Wakefield.

LETWELL, in the parish of Laughton-le-Morthen, south-division of the wapentake of Strafforth and Tickhill, liberties of St. Peter and Tickhill; 5 miles from Tickhill, 5¼ from Worksop, *(Notts.)* 9 from Rotherham.—Pop. 216.

LEVELS, HIGH, in the parish of Thorne, south-division of the wapentake of Strafforth and Tickhill; 4½ miles from Thorne, 6 from Crowle, *(Linc.)* 13½ from Doncaster.

LEVELS, LOW, in the parish of Thorne, south-division of the wapentake of Strafforth and Tickhill; 3¼ miles from Thorne, 6 from Crowle, *(Linc.)* 13 from Doncaster.

LEVENTHORPE, in the parish of Swillington, lower-division of the wapentake of Skirack; *(the seat of —— Green, Esq.)* 6 miles from Leeds, 7 from Wakefield, 9 from Pontefract.

LEWDEN, in the parish of Darfield, wapentake of Staincross,

liberty of the Honour of Pontefract; 2¼ miles from Barnsley, 8 from Penistone, 9 from Rotherham.

LEYS, in the parish of Bingley, upper-division of the wapentake of Skirack; 6 miles from Bingley, 8 from Bradford.

LIDGATE, in the parish of Rochdale, (*Lanc.*) Agbrigg-division of the wapentake of Agbrigg and Morley; 8 miles from Rochdale, (*Lanc.*) 11 from Manchester, (*ditto.*) 14 from Huddersfield.—Population 323.

LIDGET, in the parish of Kirk-Heaton, Agbrigg-division of the wapentake of Agbrigg and Morley; 4¼ miles from Huddersfield, 8¼ from Wakefield.

LIDGET-HOUSE, in the parish of Sheffield, south-division of the wapentake of Strafforth and Tickhill; 3 miles from Sheffield, 9 from Rotherham, 13 from Chesterfield, (*Derb.*).

LIGHTCLIFFE, in the parish of Halifax, Morley-division of the wapentake of Agbrigg and Morley, (*the seat of William Walker, Esq.*) 3¼ miles from Halifax, 6 from Bradford, 7 from Huddersfield.

LIGHT-RIDGE, in the parish of Huddersfield, Agbrigg-division of the wapentake of Agbrigg and Morley; 2¼ from Huddersfield, 6 from Halifax.

LILEY, or LILLEY, in the parish of Kirk-Heaton, Agbrigg-division of the wapentake of Agbrigg and Morley; 5 miles from Huddersfield, 8 from Wakefield.—Pop. 315.

LIMLEY, in the parish of Kirby-Malzeard, lower-division of the wapentake of Claro; 10 miles from Masham, 10 from Pateleybridge, 10 from Kettlewell.

LINDERICK, (extraparochial) lower-division of the wapentake of Claro; 2 miles from Ripon, 8 from Boroughbridge, 12 from Knaresborough.—Population 26.

LINDLEY, in the parish of Otley, upper-division of the wapentake of Claro, liberty of Cawood, Wistow, and Otley; 4 miles from Otley, 11 from Knaresborough.—Pop. 164.

LINDLEY, in the parish of Huddersfield, Agbrigg-division of the wapentake of Agbrigg and Morley, liberty of the Manor of Wakefield; 3 miles from Huddersfield, 6 from Halifax.

LINDLEY-OLD, in the parish of Huddersfield, Agbrigg-division of the wapentake of Agbrigg and Morley, liberty of the Manor of Wakefield; 3 miles from Huddersfield, 6 from Halifax.

LINFITS, in the parish of Rochdale, (*Lanc.*) Agbrigg-division of the wapentake of Agbrigg and Morley; 8 miles from Rochdale, (*Lanc.*) 12 from Manchester, (*ditto*) 12 from Huddersfield.

LINFIT-HALL, in the parish of Huddersfield, Agbrigg-division of the wapentake of Agbrigg and Morley, liberty of the Honour of Pontefract; *(the seat of George Roberts, Esq.)* 3 miles from Huddersfield, 11 from Halifax.

LINFIT-LANES, in the parish of Kirk-Heaton, Agbrigg-division of the wapentake of Agbrigg and Morley; 4¼ miles from Huddersfield, 8 from Wakefield, 10 from Halifax.

LINGARDS, or LINGARTHS, in the parish of Almondbury, Agbrigg-division of the wapentake of Agbrigg and Morley; 5¼ miles from Huddersfield, 12 from Halifax.—Population 642.

LINGBOB, in the parish of Bradford, Morley-division of the wapentake of Agbrigg and Morley; 3 miles from Bradford, 8 from Halifax, 13½ from Colne, *(Lanc.)*

LINGERDALE, in the parish of Firbeck, south-division of the wapentake of Strafforth and Tickhill; 5 miles from Tickhill, 5 from Worksop, *(Notts.)* 9 from Rotherham.

LINGILL-BRIDGE, in the parish of Horton, wapentake of Ewcross; 11 miles from Settle, 13 from Askrigg.

LINGWELL-GATE, in the parish of Rothwell, Agbrigg-division of the wapentake of Agbrigg and Morley; 3¼ miles from Wakefield, 6¼ from Leeds.

LINTHWAITE, in the parish of Almondbury, Agbrigg-division of the wapentake of Agbrigg and Morley; 3 miles from Huddersfield, 11 from Halifax.—Population 1,381.

LINTON, in the parish of Linton, east-division of the wapentake and liberty of Staincliffe; 7 miles from Kettlewell, 9 from Skipton, 10 from Pateleybridge.—Population 186.

LINTON, in the parish of Spofforth, upper-division of the wapentake of Claro; 1¼ mile from Wetherby, 7 from Knaresborough.—Population 155.

LINTON-SPRING, in the parish of Spofforth, upper-division of the wapentake of Claro; *(the seat of Thomas Wybergh, Esq.)* 2 miles from Wetherby, 6½ from Knaresborough.

LITTLE-COMMON, in the parish of Sheffield, south-division of the wapentake of Strafforth and Tickhill; 4 miles from Sheffield, 10 from Rotherham.

LITTLE-THORPE, in the parish of Ripon, lower-division of the wapentake of Claro, liberty of Ripon; *(the seat of Major Brooke)* 1 mile from Ripon, 6 from Boroughbridge, 10 from Knaresborough.

LITTLE-TOWN, in the parish of Birstall, Morley-division of the wapentake of Agbrigg and Morley; 8 miles from Halifax, 8 from Wakefield, 8 from Leeds.

LITTLE-TOWN, in the parish of Sedbergh, wapentake of Ewcross; 3 miles from Dent, 6¼ from Sedbergh, 11 from Kirby-Lonsdale, *(Westm.)* 13½ from Askrigg.

LITTLEWORTH, in the parish of Royston, wapentake of Staincross, liberty of the Honour of Pontefract; 2 miles from Barnsley, 8¼ from Wakefield, 10 from Rotherham.

LITTON, in the parish of Arncliffe, west-division of the wapentake and liberty of Staincliffe; 7 miles from Kettlewell, 11 from Settle, 18 from Skipton.—Population 114.

LIVERSEDGE, in the parish of Birstall, Morley-division of the wapentake of Agbrigg and Morley, liberty of the Honour of Pontefract; 7½ miles from Halifax, 8½ from Wakefield.—Population 2,837.

LOCKWOOD, in the parish of Almondbury, Agbrigg-division of the wapentake of Agbrigg and Morley; *(the seat of Joseph Armitage, Esq.)* 1¼ mile from Huddersfield, 9¼ from Halifax, 14 from Wakefield.—Population 1,253.

LODGE, in the parish of Kirby-Malzeard, lower-division of the wapentake of Claro; 5¼ miles from Kettlewell, 10 from Middleham, 12 from Pateleybridge.

LODGE, in the parish of Giggleswick, west-division of the wapentake and liberty of Staincliffe; 1¼ mile from Settle, 14¼ from Skipton.

LOFTHOUSE, in the parish of Rothwell, Agbrigg-division of the wapentake of Agbrigg and Morley, liberty of the Honour of Pontefract; *(the seat of Benjamin Dealtry, Esq.)* 3¼ miles from Wakefield, 6 from Leeds.

LOFTHOUSE, in the parish of Harewood, upper-division of the wapentake of Skirack; 2 miles from Harewood, 4 from Leeds.

LOFTHOUSE-HILL, in the parish of Staveley, lower-division of the wapentake of Claro; *(the seat of Charles Slingsby, Esq.)* 3 miles from Knaresborough, 4 from Boroughbridge.

LOFTHOUSES, in the parish of Kirby-Malzeard, lower-division of the wapentake of Claro; 8 miles from Pateleybridge, 9 from Masham.

LONGLEY, in the parish of Ecclesfield, north-division of the wapentake of Strafforth and Tickhill; 2½ miles from Sheffield, 5 from Rotherham 10 from Barnsley.

LONG-PRESTON, in the parish of Long-Preston, west-division of the wapentake and liberty of Staincliffe; 4 miles from Settle, 12 from Skipton, 15 from Colne, *(Lanc.)*—No Market.—*Fairs*, March 1, and September 4, for Horned Cattle, &c.

LONGROYD-BRIDGE, in the parish of Huddersfield, Agbrigg-division of the wapentake of Agbrigg and Morley, liberty of the Manor of Wakefield; *(the seat of John Fisher, Esq.)* 1 mile from Huddersfield, 8 from Halifax;

WEST-RIDING.

LONGSIDE, in the parish of Kirby-Malzeard, lower-division of the wapentake of Claro; 6 miles from Pateleybridge, 9 from Masham.

LONGWOOD, in the parish of Huddersfield, Agbrigg-division of the wapentake of Agbrigg and Morley; $3\frac{1}{2}$ miles from Huddersfield, 8 from Halifax.—Pop. 1,276.

LONGWOOD-HOUSE, in the parish of Huddersfield, Agbrigg division of the wapentake of Agbrigg and Morley; *(the seat of John Roberts, Esq.)* 2 miles from Huddersfield, 6 from Halifax.

LORDLAND, NORTH, in the parish of Sedbergh, wapentake of Ewcross; 1 mile from Dent, 4 from Sedbergh, 10 from Kirby-Lonsdale, *(Westm.)*

LORDLAND, SOUTH, in the parish of Sedbergh, wapentake of Ewcross; 1 mile from Dent, 4 from Sedbergh, 10 from Kirby-Lonsdale, *(Westm.)*

LOSCOE-GRANGE, in the parish of Fetherstone, Agbrigg-division of the wapentake of Agbrigg and Morley; 3 miles from Pontefract, $6\frac{1}{2}$ from Wakefield.

LOTHERSDEN, in the parish of Carlton, east-division of the wapentake and liberty of Staincliffe; 4 miles from Skipton, 6 from Colne, *(Lanc.)* 8 from Keighley.

LOTHERTON, in the parish of Sherburn, wapentake of Barkston-Ash; *(the seat of John Raper, Esq.)* 5 miles from Tadcaster, 8 from Wetherby, 10 from Pontefract,— Population 323.

LOVERSALL, in the parish and soke of Doncaster, south-division of the wapentake of Strafforth and Tickhill; *(the seat of —— Dawson, Esq.)* $3\frac{1}{2}$ miles from Doncaster, 4 from Tickhill, 10 from Rotherham.—Population 133.

LUDDINGDEN, in the parish of Halifax, Morley-division of the wapentake of Agbrigg and Morley, liberty of the Manor of Wakefield; 5 miles from Halifax, 11 from Keighley, 13 from Huddersfield.

LUDDINGDEN-FOOT, in the parish of Halifax, Morley-division of the wapentake of Agbrigg and Morley; $4\frac{1}{2}$ miles from Halifax, $7\frac{1}{2}$ from Todmorden.

LUMLEY, in the parish of Sherburn, wapentake of Barkston-Ash; 7 miles from Pontefract, 8 from Tadcaster, 12 from Selby.

LUND, in the parish of Brayton, wapentake of Barkston-Ash; 4 miles from Selby, 7 from Ferrybridge, 9 from Pontefract.

LUNDLEY'S-GREEN, in the parish of Pannall, lower-division of the wapentake of Claro; $5\frac{1}{2}$ miles from Knaresborough, $6\frac{1}{2}$ from Ripley.

LUPSETT-HALL, in the parish of Wakefield, Agbrigg-division of the wapentake of Agbrigg and Morley ; *(the seat of Daniel Gaskill, Esq.)* 1 mile from Wakefield, 4 from Dewsbury, 13 from Huddersfield.

M.

MACHON-BANK, in the parish of Sheffield, south-division of the wapentake of Strafforth and Tickhill; *(the seat of Peter Wigfall, Esq.)* 2¼ miles from Sheffield, 8¼ from Rotherham, 11 from Chesterfield, *(Derb.)*

MALHAM, in the parish of Kirkby-Malhamdale, west-division of the wapentake and liberty of Staincliffe; *(Malham-Water-House, the seat of Lord Ribblesdale)* 6 miles from Settle, 9 from Kettlewell, 12 from Skipton.—No Market.—Fairs, July 1, and October 15, for Sheep.—Pop. 262.

MALHAM-MOOR, in the parish of Kirkby-Malhamdale, west-division of the wapentake and liberty of Staincliffe; 5¼ miles from Settle, 8¼ from Kettlewell, 13¼ from Skipton. —Population 98.

MALHAM-WATER, in the parish of Kirkby-Malhamdale, west-division of the wapentake and liberty of Staincliffe; 5¼ miles from Settle, 8¼ from Kettlewell, 13¼ from Skipton.

MALON-BRIDGE, in the parish of Ecclesfield, north-division of the wapentake of Strafforth and Tickhill; 3 miles from Sheffield, 9 from Rotherham, 10 from Penistone.

MALTBY, in the parish of Maltby, south-division of the wapentake of Strafforth and Tickhill, liberty of Tickhill; *(the seat of —— Cook, Esq.)* 4 miles from Tickhill, 7 from Rotherham, 10 from Doncaster, 13 from Sheffield.—Population 527.

MANINGHAM, in the parish of Bradford, Morley-division of the wapentake of Agbrigg and Morley, liberty of the Honour of Pontefract ; 1¼ mile from Bradford, 8¼ from Halifax, 8¼ from Keighley.—Population 1,357.

MANIWELL-HEIGHTS, in the parish of Bradford, Morley-division of the wapentake of Agbrigg and Morley; liberty of the Honour of Pontefract ; 4 miles from Keighley, 4 from Bingley, 7½ from Halifax.

MANKIN-HOLES, in the parish of Halifax, Morley-division of the wapentake of Agbrigg and Morley ; 10 miles from Halifax, 12 from Rochdale, *(Lanc.)*

MANTLE-YATE, or GATE, in the parish of Rochdale, *(Lanc.)* Agbrigg division of the wapentake of Agbrigg and

Morley; 6 miles from Rochdale, *(Lanc.)* 11 from Manchester, *(ditto)* 14 from Huddersfield.

MAPPLEWELL, in the parish of Darton, wapentake of Staincross, liberty of the Honour of Pontefract, 3 miles from Barnsley, 8 from Penistone, 8 from Wakefield.

MARKENFIELD-HALL, in the parish of Ripon, lower-division of the wapentake of Claro; 3 miles from Ripon, 4 from Ripley, 8 from Knaresborough.

MARKINGTON, in the parish of Ripon, lower division of the wapentake of Claro, liberty of Ripon; 4 miles from Ripley, 4¼ from Ripon.—Population 389.

MARR, in the parish of Marr, north-division of the wapentake of Strafforth and Tickhill, liberty of Tickhill; 4 miles from Doncaster, 11 from Barnsley.—Population 165.

MARR-GRANGE, in the parish of Marr, north-division of the wapentake of Strafforth and Tickhill, liberty of Tickhill; 3¼ miles from Doncaster, 11¼ from Barnsley.

MARSDEN, in the parishes of Almondbury and Huddersfield, Agbrigg-division of the wapentake of Agbrigg and Morley, liberty of the Honour of Pontefract; 7 miles from Huddersfield, 15 from Halifax, 18 from Manchester.—Population 1,958.

MARSH, in the parish of Huddersfield, Agbrigg-division of the wapentake of Agbrigg and Morley, liberty of the Honour of Pontefract; 2 miles from Huddersfield, 8 from Halifax, 16 from Rochdale *(Lanc.)*

MARSH-FIELD, in the parish of Giggleswick, west-division of the wapentake and liberty of Staincliffe; *(the seat of Mrs. Parker.)* ½ a mile frm Settle, 15¼ from Skipton.

MARSHALL-HALL, in the parish of Halifax, Morley-division of the wapentake of Agbrigg and Morley; 3 miles from Halifax, 5 from Huddersfield.

MARTHWAITE, in the parish of Sedbergh, wapentake of Ewcross; ¼ a mile from Sedbergh, 6 from Dent, 9½ from Kendal, *(Westm.)*

MARTON, in the parish of Marton, upper-division of the wapentake of Claro, liberty of St. Peter; 3 miles from Boroughbridge, 6 from Knaresborough.—Population 393.

MARTON, CHURCH, in the parish of East-Marton, east-division of the wapentake and liberty of Staincliffe; 5¼ miles from Skipton, 7¼ from Colne, *(Lanc.)* 11 from Settle.

MARTON, EAST, in the parish of East-Marton, east-division of the wapentake and liberty of Staincliffe; 5 miles from Skipton, 7¼ from Colne, *(Lanc.)* 11 from Settle.—Population 322.

MARTON-SCAR, in the parish of East-Marton, east-divi-

Hh

sion of the wapentake and liberty of Staincliffe; 7½ miles from Skipton, 8 from Colne, (*Lanc.*)

MARTON-TOP, in the parish of Gisburn, west-division of the wapentake and liberty of Staincliffe; 3 miles from Gisburn, 9 from Colne (*Lanc.*)

MARTON, WEST, in the parish of East-Marton, east-division of the wapentake and liberty of Staincliffe; (*Marton-Hall, the seat of Richard Heber, Esq.*) 6¼ miles from Skipton, 7¼ from Colne, (*Lanc.*) 11 from Settle.

MASONGILL, in the parish of Thornton-in-Lonsdale, wapentake of Ewcross; 5 miles from Kirby-Lonsdale, (*Westm.*) 12 from Settle.

MASBROUGH, in the parish of Rotherham, north-division of the wapentake of Strafforth and Tickhill; ¼ a mile from Rotherham, 6½ from Sheffield, 12¼ from Barnsley.

MAY, or BAY-HALL, in the parish of Huddersfield, Agbrigg-division of the wapentake of Agbrigg and Morley; ¼ a mile from Huddersfield, 7¼ from Halifax.

MAY-ROYD, in the parish of Halifax, Morley-division of the wapentake of Agbrigg and Morley; 7 miles from Halifax, 14 from Keighley.

MAY-THORNE, in the parish of Kirk-Heaton, Agbrigg-division of the wapentake of Agbrigg and Morley; 6 miles from Penistone, 8½ from Huddersfield.

MEAN-WOOD, in the parish of Leeds, lower-division of the wapentake of Skirack; (*the seat of John Beckitt, Esq.*) 3 miles from Leeds, 8 from Otley, 8 from Bradford.

MEER-BECK, or MEER-SYKES, in the parish of Giggleswick, west-division of the wapentake and liberty of Staincliffe; 2 miles from Settle, 14 from Skipton.

MELTHAM, in the parish of Almondbury, Agbrigg-division of the wapentake of Agbrigg and Morley, liberty of the Honour of Pontefract; (*Thick-Hollins, the seat of Joseph Armitage, Esq.*) 5 miles from Huddersfield, 13 from Halifax, 20 from Manchester, (*Lanc.*)—Population 1,278.

MELTON-ON-THE-HILL, in the parish of Melton-on-the-Hill, north-division of the wapentake of Strafforth and Tickhill, liberty of Tickhill; (*the seat of Richard Fountayne Wilson, Esq.*) 4¾ miles from Doncaster, 10¼ from Barnsley.—Population 165.

MELTON, WEST, in the parish of Wath-upon-Dearn, north-division of the wapentake of Strafforth and Tickhill, liberty of Tickhill; 5 miles from Rotherham, 6 from Barnsley, 11 from Doncaster.

MENSTHORPE, in the parish of South-Kirkby, wapentake of Osgoldcross, liberty of the Honour of Pontefract; 5 miles from Pontefract, 9 from Doncaster.

WEST-RIDING. 239

MENSTON, in the parish of Otley, upper-division of the wapentake of Claro, liberty of Cawood, Wistow, and Otley; 3 miles from Otley, 9 from Keighley, 10 from Leeds.—Population 193.

MENWITH, in the parish of Hampsthwaite, lower-division of the wapentake of Claro, liberty of Knaresborough; *(the seat of John Day, Esq.)* 5 miles from Pateleybridge, 6¼ from Ripley, 11¼ from Knaresborough.—Population 554.

METHLEY, in the parish of Methley, Agbrigg-division of the wapentake of Agbrigg and Morley, liberty of the Honour of Pontefract; 6 miles from Wakefield, 6¾ from Leeds, 6¾ from Pontefract.—Population 1,234.

METHLEY-PARK, in the parish of Methley, Agbrigg-division of the wapentake of Agbrigg and Morley, liberty of the Honour of Pontefract; *(the seat of the Earl of Mexborough)* 6¾ miles from Leeds, 6¾ from Wakefield, 6¾ from Pontefract.

MEWITH, in the parish of Low-Bentham, wapentake of Ewcross; 11 miles from Kirby-Lonsdale, *(Westm.)* 13 from Settle, 14 from Lancaster *(Lanc.)*

MEXBROUGH, in the parish of Mexbrough, north-division of the wapentake of Strafforth and Tickhill, liberties of St. Peter and Tickhill; 5½ miles from Rotherham, 8 from Doncaster.—Population 417.

MICKLEBRIG, in the parish of Braithwell, south-division of the wapentake of Strafforth and Tickhill; 5½ miles from Rotherham, 9 from Doncaster.

MICKLEFIELD, in the parish of Sherburn, wapentake of Barkston-Ash; 2¾ miles from Abberford, 6½ from Ferrybridge, 14½ from Selby.—Population 135.

MICKLEHOW-HILL, or MICHAEL-HOW-HILL, in the parish of Ripon, lower-division of the wapentake of Claro; 5 miles from Ripon, 9 from Knaresborough.

MICKLETHWAITE, in the parish of Bingley, upper-division of the wapentake of Skirack; 3½ miles from Keighley, 9 from Otley.

MICKLETHWAITE-GRANGE, *(extraparochial)* wapentake of Barkston-Ash; 2 miles from Wetherby, 6 from Tadcaster.

MICKLEY, in the parish of Kirby-Malzeard, lower-division of the wapentake of Claro; 5 miles from Masham, 6 from Ripon.

MIDDLESMOOR, in the parish of Kirby-Malzeard, lower-division of the wapentake of Claro; 10 miles from Masham, 10 from Pateleybridge.

MIDDLETON, in the parish of Ilkley, upper-division of the wapentake of Claro; *(Middleton-Lodge, the seat of*

William Middleton, Esq.) 6¼ miles from Otley, 9 from Skipton.—Population 201.

MIDDLETON, in the parish of Rothwell, Agbrigg-division of the wapentake of Agbrigg and Morley, liberties of the Manor of Wakefield, and Honour of Pontefract; 4¼ miles from Leeds, 5 from Wakefield.—Population 831.

MIDDLETON-GREEN, in the parish of Ecclesfield, north-division of the wapentake of Strafforth and Tickhill; 4¼ miles from Sheffield, 8 from Penistone, 10¼ from Rotherham.

MIDDLETON-MOOR-HOUSES, in the parish of Ilkley, upper-division of the wapentake of Claro; 8 miles from Otley, 9 from Skipton.

MIDDLEWOOD-HALL, in the parish of Darfield, north-division of the wapentake of Strafforth and Tickhill; (*the seat of the Hon. Lumley Savile, Esq.*) 5¼ miles from Barnsley, 10 from Doncaster.

MIDGLEY, in the parish of Halifax, Morley-division of the wapentake of Agbrigg and Morley, liberty of the Manor of Wakefield; 4¼ miles from Halifax, 12 from Keighley, 12 from Bradford.—Population 1,209.

MIDGLEY, NETHER, in the parish of Thornhill, Agbrigg-division of the wapentake of Agbrigg and Morley, liberty of the Honour of Pontefract; 6 miles from Wakefield, 9 from Huddersfield.

MIDGLEY, OVER, in the parish of Thornhill, Agbrigg-division of the wapentake of Agbrigg and Morley, liberty of the Honour of Pontefract; 6¼ miles from Wakefield, 10¼ from Huddersfield.

MIDHOPE, in the parish of Gisburn, west-division of the wapentake and liberty of Staincliffe; 9 miles from Colne, (*Lanc.*) 11 from Burnley, (*ditto,*) 12 from Skipton.—Population 87.

MIDHOPE, in the parish of Ecclesfield, north-division of the wapentake of Strafforth and Tickhill; 8 miles from Penistone, 10 from Sheffield, 16 from Rotherham.

MIDHOPE, LITTLE, in the parish of Gisburn, west-division of the wapentake and liberty of Staincliffe; 3 miles from Gisburn, 8¼ from Colne, (*Lanc.*)

MIDHOPE, OVER, in the parish of Ecclesfield, north-division of the wapentake of Strafforth and Tickhill; 8 miles from Penistone, 10¼ from Sheffield, 16¼ from Rotherham.

MILBANK, in the parish of Halifax, Morley-division of the wapentake of Agbrigg and Morley; 5 miles from Halifax, 8 from Huddersfield.

MILFORTH, NORTH, in the parish of Kirby-Wharfe, wapentake of Barkston-Ash, liberty of the Honour of Pontefract; 3 miles from Tadcaster, 11 from Selby, 12 from Pontefract.

MILFORTH, SOUTH, in the parish of Sherburn, wapentake of Barkston-Ash, liberties of St. Peter and the Honour of Pontefract; 6 miles from Pontefract, 8 from Selby, 8¼ from Tadcaster.—Population 457.

MILLER-DAM, NEW, in the parish of Sandall, Agbrigg-division of the wapentake of Agbrigg and Morley; 3¼ miles from Wakefield, 6¼ from Barnsley.

MILLSHAW, in the parish of Leeds, Morley-division of the wapentake of Agbrigg and Morley; 3 miles from Leeds, 9 from Bradford.

MILLTHORPE, in the parish of Sandall, Agbrigg-division of the wapentake of Agbrigg and Morley, liberty of the Manor of Wakefield; 2¼ miles from Wakefield, 7¼ from Barnsley.

MILL-WOOD, in the parish of Halifax, Morley-division of the wapentake of Agbrigg and Morley; 10 miles from Halifax, 12 from Rochdale, *(Lanc.)*

MILN-HOUSES, in the parish of Sheffield, south-division of the wapentake of Strafforth and Tickhill; 3¼ miles from Sheffield, 9¼ from Rotherham, 10 from Chesterfield, *(Derb.)*

MILNSBRIDGE-HOUSE, in the parish of Huddersfield, Agbrigg-division of the wapentake of Agbrigg and Morley, liberty of the Manor of Wakefield; *(the seat of Joseph Radcliffe, Esq.)* 2 miles from Huddersfield, 6 from Halifax.

MILTHORPE, in the parish of Sedbergh, wapentake of Ewcross; 1 mile from Sedbergh, 4 from Dent.

MILTON-FURNACE, in the parish of Wath-upon-Dearn, north-division of the wapentake of Strafforth and Tickhill; 6¼ miles from Barnsley, 8¼ from Sheffield.

MINSKIP, in the parish of Aldborough, lower-division of the wapentake of Claro, liberty of St. Peter; 1½ mile from Boroughbridge, 5¼ from Knaresborough, 7 from Ripon.—Population 204.

MIRFIELD, in the parish of Mirfield, Agbrigg-division of the wapentake of Agbrigg and Morley, liberty of the Honour of Pontefract; 3 miles from Dewsbury, 4¼ from Huddersfield, 8 from Wakefield.—Population 3,724.

MYRTLE-GROVE, *see Bingley.*

MITTON, in the parish of Mitton, west-division of the wapentake of Staincliffe, liberty of Bolland; *(Mitton-Hall, the seat of Richard Henry Beaumont, Esq.)* 8 miles from Clitheroe, *(Lanc.)* 10 from Blackburn, *(ditto,)* 12 from Gisburn.—Population 552.

MYTHOLME-ROYD-BRIDGE, in the parish of Halifax,

Morley-division of the wapentake of Agbrigg and Morley; 6 miles from Halifax, 14 from Huddersfield.

MOAT, in the parish of Wickersley, south-division of the wapentake of Strafforth and Tickhill; 5 miles from Rotherham, 7½ from Tickhill.

MOLE, or MOLD-GREEN, in the parish of Kirk-Heaton, Agbrigg-division of the wapentake of Agbrigg and Morley; *(the seat of Thomas and Law Atkinson, Esqrs.)* 1 mile from Huddersfield, 9 from Halifax.

MONK-HILL, in the parish of Pontefract, wapentake of Osgoldcross, liberty of the Honour of Pontefract; adjoins Pontefract.

MONKTON, BISHOP, in the parish of Ripon, lower-division of the wapentake of Claro, liberty of Ripon; *(the seat of John Charnock, Esq.)* 4 miles from Boroughbridge, 4 from Ripon, 6 from Knaresborough.—Population 363.

MONKTON, NUN, in the parish of Nun-Monkton, upper-division of the wapentake of Claro; 8 miles from York, 10 from Knaresborough, 11 from Boroughbridge.—Pop. 308.

MONYBENT, in the parish of Gisburn, west-division of the wapentake and liberty of Staincliffe; 6 miles from Gisburn, 9 from Settle.

MONYBENT-HILL, in the parish of Slaidburn, west-division of the wapentake and liberty of Staincliffe; 10 miles from Settle, 12 from Clitheroe, *(Lanc.)*

MOOR-ENDS, in the parish of Thorne, south-division of the wapentake of Strafforth and Tickhill; 1¼ mile from Thorne, 13 from Howden.

MOOR-GATE, in the parish of Rotherham, south-division of the wapentake of Strafforth and Tickhill; *(the seat of Richard Holden, Esq.)* ½ a mile from Rotherham, 6½ from Sheffield.

MOOR-GRANGE, in the parish of Leeds, lower-division of the wapentake of Skirack; 3 miles from Leeds, 6 from Wetherby, 10 from Wakefield.

MOOR-HALLOWS, in the parish of Penistone, wapentake of Staincross, liberty of the Honour of Pontefract; 2 miles from Penistone, 9 from Barnsley, 12¼ from Huddersfield.

MOOR-HEAD, in the parish of Kirby-Malzeard, lower-division of the wapentake of Claro; 5 miles from Masham, 11 from Bedale, 15 from Ripon.

MOORHOUSE, in the parish of Hooton-Pagnell, north-division of the wapentake of Strafforth and Tickhill; 6 miles from Doncaster, 9 from Barnsley.

MOOR-HOUSE, in the parish of Ackworth, wapentake of Osgoldcross, liberty of the Honour of Pontefract; 4¼ mile from Pontefract, 9 from Wakefield.

MOOR-HOUSE, in the parish of Tickhill, south-division of the wapentake of Strafforth and Tickhill; 1 mile from Tickhill, 3 from Bawtry, 7 from Doncaster.

MOORSIDE, in the parish of Halifax, Morley-division of the wapentake of Agbrigg and Morley; 2 miles from Halifax, 6¼ from Bradford.

MOORTHWAITE-BRIDGE, in the parish of Sedbergh, wapentake of Ewcross; 3¼ miles from Sedbergh, 9 from Kendal, *(Westm.)* 16½ from Askrigg.

MORLEY, in the parish of Batley, Agbrigg-division of the wapentake of Agbrigg and Morley, liberty of the Honour of Pontefract; 4 miles from Dewsbury, 4¼ from Leeds, 11 from Wakefield.—Population 2,108.

MORRETTS, in the parish of Skipton, east-division of the wapentake and liberty of Staincliffe; 2 miles from Skipton, 16 from Settle.

MORTHEN, in the parishes of Whiston and Rotherham, south-division of the wapentake of Strafforth and Tickhill; *(the seat of Carver Middleton, Esq.)* 4 miles from Rotherham, 10 from Sheffield, 11 from Tickhill.

MORTOMLEY, in the parish of Ecclesfield, north-division of the wapentake of Strafforth and Tickhill; 6 miles from Barnsley, 6 from Rotherham, 7 from Sheffield.

MORTON, EAST, in the parish of Bingley, upper-division of the wapentake of Skirack, liberty of Clifford's Fee; 3 miles from Keighley, 4 from Bingley, 12 from Otley.— Population 838.

MORTON, WEST, in the parish of Bingley, upper-division of the wapentake of Skirack; 3 miles from Keighley, 4 from Bingley, 12 from Otley.

MORWICK, in the parish of Barwick-in Elmet, lower-division of the wapentake of Skirack; 6 miles from Leeds, 6 from Wetherby, 9 from Tadcaster.

MOSELEY, in the parish of Guiseley, upper-division of the wapentake of Skirack; 4 miles from Bradford, 4 from Otley, 9 from Leeds.

MOSS, or MOSELEY, in the parish of Campsall, wapentake of Osgoldcross, liberty of the Honour of Pontefract; 6 miles from Thorne, 9 from Doncaster, 13 from Pontefract. —Population 226.

MOSSON-GREEN, in the parish of Fishlake, north-division of the wapentake of Strafforth and Tickhill; 4 miles from Thorne, 8 from Snaith.

MOSS-WOOD-HOUSES, in the parish of Kirby-Malzeard, lower-division of the wapentake of Claro; 3 miles from Pateleybridge, 8½ from Masham.

MOTHORP, in the parish of South-Kirkby, wapentake of Osgoldcross, liberty of the Honour of Pontefract; 8 miles from Pontefract, 11 from Wakefield, 12 from Doncaster.

MOUNT-PLEASANT, in the parish of Sheffield, south-division of the wapentake of Strafforth and Tickhill; *(the seat of Broomhead Ward, Esq.)* 1 mile from Sheffield, 7 from Rotherham.

MULWITH, in the parish of Ripon, lower-division of the wapentake of Claro, liberty of Ripon; 3 miles from Boroughbridge, 4 from Ripon.

N.

NAPPA, in the parish of Gisburn, west-division of the wapentake and liberty of Staincliffe; 9 miles from Settle, 11 from Colne, *(Lanc.)* 11 from Skipton.—Population 32.

NAPPA-FLATTS, in the parish of Gisburn, west-division of the wapentake and liberty of Staincliffe; 9 miles from Skipton, 9 from Settle.

NEEPSEND, in the parish of Sheffield, north-division of the wapentake of Strafforth and Tickhill; 1 mile from Sheffield, 7 from Rotherham, 13 from Chesterfield, *(Derb.)*

NESFIELD, in the parish of Ilkley, upper-division of the wapentake of Claro; 7 miles from Otley, 8 from Skipton. —Population 101.

NETHER-BANK, in the parish of Ecclesfield, north-division of the wapentake of Strafforth and Tickhill; 4 miles from Sheffield, 5 from Rotherham, 6 from Barnsley.

NETHERBY, in the parish of Kirkby-Overblow, upper-division of the wapentake of Claro; 4¼ miles from Wetherby, 8 from Knaresborough.

NETHER-GREEN, in the parish of Sheffield, south-division of the wapentake of Strafforth and Tickhill; 3 miles from Sheffield, 9 from Rotherham, 11 from Chesterfield, *(Derb.)*

NETHER-HALL, in the parish of Doncaster, south-division of the wapentake of Strafforth and Tickhill; *(the seat of Thomas Copley, Esq.)* ¼ of a mile from Doncaster, 9 from Bawtry.

NETHERTHORPE, in the parish of Aston, south-division of the wapentake of Strafforth and Tickhill; 6 miles from Rotherham, 8½ from Worksop, *(Notts.)*.

NETHER-LODGE, in the parish of Horton, wapentake of Ewcross; 10 miles from Settle, 13 from Askrigg.

NETHER-SHIRE, in the parish of Ecclesfield, north-division of the wapentake of Strafforth and Tickhill; *(the seat of Hugh Miller, Esq.*) 4 miles from Sheffield, 5 from Rotherham, 9 from Barnsley.

NETHERTON, in the parish of Sandall, Agbrigg division of the wapentake of Agbrigg and Morley, liberty of the Honour of Pontefract; 5 miles from Wakefield, 9¼ from Huddersfield.

NETHERTON, in the parish of Almondbury, Agbrigg division of the wapentake of Agbrigg and Morley, liberty of the Honour of Pontefract; 3 miles from Huddersfield, 11 from Halifax.

NEWAP, in the parish of Drax, wapentake of Barkston-Ash; 5 miles from Selby, 7 from Howden, 7 from Snaith.

NEWBRIDGE, in the parish of Kirby-Malzeard, lower-division of the wapentake of Claro; 2 miles from Pateleybridge, 10 from Masham.

NEWBY, in the parish of Gisburn, west-division of the wapentake and liberty of Staincliffe; 5¼ miles from Clitheroe, (*Lanc.*) 2 miles from Gisburn, 12 from Skipton.

NEWBY, in the parish of Harewood, upper-division of the wapentake of Claro; 4¼ miles from Otley, 8½ from Wetherby, 10 from Knaresborough.

NEWBY, in the parish of Clapham, wapentake of Ewcross; 7 miles from Settle 10 from Kirby-Lonsdale, (*Westm.*).

NEWBY-COTE, in the parish of Clapham, wapentake of Ewcross; 7 miles from Settle, 10 from Kirby-Lonsdale, (*Westm.*)

NEWBY-HALL, in the parish of Ripon, lower-division of the wapentake of Claro, liberty of Ripon; (*the seat of Lord Grantham*) 3 miles from Boroughbridge, 4 from Ripon, 10 from Knaresborough.

NEWFIELD, in the parish of Sheffield, south-division of the wapentake of Strafforth and Tickhill; ½ a mile from Sheffield, 6¼ from Rotherham.

NEW-GRANGE, in the parish of Leeds, lower-division of the wapentake of Skirack; 3 miles from Leeds, 4 from Harewood, 7 from Wetherby.

NEWHALL, in the parish of Otley, upper-division of the wapentake of Claro, liberty of Cawood, Wistow, and Otley; (*the seat of Thomas Clifton, Esq.*) 1 mile from Otley, 11 from Leeds, 14 from Knaresborough.—Population 203.

NEW-HALL, in the parish of Pontefract, wapentake of Osgoldcross, liberty of the Honour of Pontefract; ½ a mile from Pontefract, 1½ from Ferrybridge.

NEW-HALL, in the parish of Rothwell, Morley-division of the wapentake of Agbrigg and Morley; 3 miles from Leeds, 5¼ from Wakefield.

NEW-HALL, in the parish of Thornhill, Agbrigg-division

of the wapentake of Agbrigg and Morley; 4 miles from Dewsbury, 5 from Wakefield.

NEW-HOUSE, in the parish of Mitton, west-division of the wapentake and liberty of Staincliffe; 4 miles from Clitheroe, (Lanc.) 12 from Blackburn, (ditto) 12 from Gisburn.

NEW-HOUSE, in the parish of Horton wapentake of Ewcross; 6½ miles from Settle, 15 from Kirby-Lonsdale, (Westm.)

NEW-HOUSES, in the parish of Kirby-Malzeard, lower-division of the wapentake of Claro; 10 miles from Pateley-bridge, 10 from Masham.

NEWHILL, in the parish of Wath-upon-Dearn, north-division of the wapentake of Strafforth and Tickhill, liberty of Tickhill; (the seat of John Payne, Esq.) 5 miles from Rotherham, 7 from Barnsley.

NEWLAND, in the parish of Halifax, Morley-division of the wapentake of Agbrigg and Morley; 2½ miles from Halifax, 10¼ from Huddersfield, 11 from Keighley.

NEWLAND, in the parish of Drax, wapentake of Barkston-Ash; 5 miles from Snaith, 9 from Selby, 16 from Pontefract.—Population 179.

NEWLAND-HALL, in the parish of Normanton, Agbrigg-division of the wapentake of Agbrigg and Morley; (the seat of Sir Edward Smith, Bart.) 4½ miles from Wakefield, 6¼ from Pontefract.

NEW-LAITH, in the parish of Ferry-Fryston, wapentake of Osgoldcross, liberty of the Honour of Pontefract; 1¼ mile from Ferrybridge, 3 from Pontefract.

NEW-LAITHES, in the parish of Royston, wapentake of Staincross, liberty of the Honour of Pontefract; 2 miles from Barnsley, 7½ from Penistone, 8 from Wakefield.

NEW-LAITHES, in the parish of Guiseley, upper-division of the wapentake of Skirack; 6 miles from Bradford, 6½ from Otley, 7 from Leeds.

NEWSHAM, in the parish of Almondbury, Agbrigg-division of the wapentake of Agbrigg and Morley, liberty of the Honour of Pontefract; 1½ mile from Huddersfield, 9¼ from Halifax.

NEWSHOLME, in the parish of Keighley, east-division of the wapentake and liberty of Staincliffe; 2½ miles from Keighley, 8 from Skipton, 10 from Colne, (Lanc.)

NEWSOME-GREEN, see Temple-Newsome.

NEWSOME, in the parish of Gisburn, west-division of the wapentake and liberty of Staincliffe; 10 miles from Settle, 10 from Skipton, 10 from Colne, (Lanc.)—Pop. 78.

NEWSTEAD-HALL, in the parish of Hemsworth, wapen-

MENSTON, in the parish of Otley, upper-division of the wapentake of Claro, liberty of Cawood, Wistow, and Otley; 3 miles from Otley, 9 from Keighley, 10 from Leeds.—Population 193.

MENWITH, in the parish of Hampsthwaite, lower-division of the wapentake of Claro, liberty of Knaresborough; *(the seat of John Day, Esq.)* 5 miles from Pateleybridge, 6½ from Ripley, 11¼ from Knaresborough.—Population 554.

METHLEY, in the parish of Methley, Agbrigg-division of the wapentake of Agbrigg and Morley, liberty of the Honour of Pontefract; 6 miles from Wakefield, 6¼ from Leeds, 6¾ from Pontefract.—Population 1,234.

METHLEY-PARK, in the parish of Methley, Agbrigg-division of the wapentake of Agbrigg and Morley, liberty of the Honour of Pontefract; *(the seat of the Earl of Mexborough)* 6¼ miles from Leeds, 6¼ from Wakefield, 6¾ from Pontefract.

MEWITH, in the parish of Low-Bentham, wapentake of Ewcross; 11 miles from Kirby-Lonsdale, *(Westm.)* 13 from Settle, 14 from Lancaster *(Lanc.)*

MEXBROUGH, in the parish of Mexbrough, north-division of the wapentake of Strafforth and Tickhill, liberties of St. Peter and Tickhill; 5½ miles from Rotherham, 8 from Doncaster.—Population 417.

MICKLEBRIG, in the parish of Braithwell, south-division of the wapentake of Strafforth and Tickhill; 5½ miles from Rotherham, 9 from Doncaster.

MICKLEFIELD, in the parish of Sherburn, wapentake of Barkston-Ash; 2¼ miles from Abberford, 6½ from Ferrybridge, 14¼ from Selby.—Population 135.

MICKLEHOW-HILL, or MICHAEL-HOW-HILL, in the parish of Ripon, lower-division of the wapentake of Claro; 5 miles from Ripon, 9 from Knaresborough.

MICKLETHWAITE, in the parish of Bingley, upper-division of the wapentake of Skirack; 3½ miles from Keighley, 9 from Otley.

MICKLETHWAITE-GRANGE, *(extraparochial)* wapentake of Barkston-Ash; 2 miles from Wetherby, 6 from Tadcaster.

MICKLEY, in the parish of Kirby-Malzeard, lower-division of the wapentake of Claro; 5 miles from Masham, 6 from Ripon.

MIDDLESMOOR, in the parish of Kirby-Malzeard, lower-division of the wapentake of Claro; 10 miles from Masham, 10 from Pateleybridge.

MIDDLETON, in the parish of Ilkley, upper-division of the wapentake of Claro; *(Middleton-Lodge, the seat of*

vision of the wapentake of Agbrigg and Morley, liberty of the Manor of Wakefield; 4 miles from Wakefield, 5 from Pontefract.—Population 276.

NORTH-COTE, in the parish of Burnsall, east-division of the wapentake and liberty of Staincliffe; 2¼ miles from Kettlewell, 18 from Skipton, 13 from Settle.

NORTH-CROFTS, in the parish of Silkston, wapentake of Staincross, liberty of the Honour of Pontefract; 3½ miles from Penistone, 3¼ from Barnsley, 13 from Sheffield.

NORTH LANE HOUSE, in the parish of Drax, wapentake of Barkston-Ash; 5 miles from Snaith, 9 from Selby.

NORTH-LEAS, or LEYS, in the parish of Ripon, lower-division of the wapentake of Claro, liberty of Ripon; 1½ mile from Ripon, 7½ from Boroughbridge, 11¼ from Knaresborough.

NORTHORPE, in the parish of Mirfield, Agbrigg-division of the wapentake of Agbrigg and Morley; *(the seat of George Webster, Esq.)* 2¼ miles from Dewsbury, 5 from Wakefield, 6 from Huddersfield.

NORTH-OWRAM, *see Owram, North*.

NORTH-PASTURE, in the parish of Ripon, lower-division of the wapentake of Claro; 3 miles from Pateleybridge, 9 from Ripon.

NORTH-SIDE-HEAD, in the parish of Kirby-Malzeard, lower-division of the wapentake of Claro; 9 miles from Pateleybridge, 10 from Masham.

NORTH-THORPE, in the parish of Tankersley, wapentake of Staincross, liberty of the Honour of Pontefract; 4 miles from Penistone, 5 from Barnsley, 9 from Sheffield.

NORTON-PRIORY, in the parish of Campsall, wapentake of Osgoldcross, liberty of the Honour of Pontefract; 8 miles from Doncaster, 7½ from Pontefract, 8½ from Ferrybridge.—Population 479.

NORWOOD, in the parish of Fewston, lower-division of the wapentake of Claro; 6 miles from Otley, 11 from Knaresborough.

NORWOOD-HALL, in the parish of Sheffield, south-division of the wapentake of Strafforth and Tickhill; *(the seat of James Wheat, Esq.)* 2¼ miles from Sheffield, 8¾ from from Rotherham, 11¼ from Barnsley.

NOSTAL, in the parish of Wragby, wapentake of Osgoldcross, liberty of the Honour of Pontefract; *(the seat of —— Williamson, Esq.)* 5 miles from Pontefract, 7 from Ferrybridge, 15 from Doncaster.

NOSTROP, in the parish of Leeds, lower-division of the wapentake of Skirack, *(the seat of —— Dade, Esq.)*

mile from Leeds, 10 from Bradford, 10 from Wakefield.

NOTTON, in the parish of Royston, wapentake of Staincross, liberty of the Honour of Pontefract; 4 miles from Barnsley, 6¼ from Wakefield, 10 from Pontefract.—Population 323.

NUNBROOK, in the parish of Mirfield, Agbrigg-division of the wapentake of Agbrigg and Morley, liberty of the Honour of Pontefract; *(the seat of Charles rook, Esq.)* 4½ miles from Huddersfield, 8½ from Wakefield, 11 from Leeds.

NUNWICK, in the parish of Wath, lower-division of the wapentake of Claro, liberty of Ripon; 1¼ mile from Ripon, 7¼ from Boroughbridge, 10 from Bedale.—Population 27.

O.

OAKENSHAW, in the parish of Crofton, Agbrigg-division of the wapentake of Agbrigg and Morley, liberty of the Honour of Pontefract; 1¼ mile from Wakefield, 7 from Pontefract.

OAKS, in the parish of Darton, wapentake of Staincross, liberty of the Honour of Pontefract; 3 miles from Barnsley, 7¼ from Penistone, 8¼ from Wakefield.

OAKS-GREEN, in the parish of Halifax, Morley-division of the wapentake of Agbrigg and Morley; 4 miles from Huddersfield, 6 from Halifax.

OAKTON, in the parish of Spofforth, upper-division of the wapentake of Claro; 3½ miles from Knaresborough, 4 from Wetherby.

OAKWELL-HALL, in the parish of Birstall, Morley-division of the wapentake of Agbrigg and Morley, *(the seat of Benjamin Fernley Esq.)* 6 miles from Bradford, 8 from Halifax, 8 from Leeds.

OAKWORTH, in the parish of Keighley, east-division of the wapentake and liberty of Staincliffe; 3 miles from Keighley, 10 from Skipton, 10 from Colne, *(Lanc.)*

OCKENY, OAKNANEY, or OCCANEY, in the parish of Knaresborough, lower-division of the wapentake of Claro; 3½ miles from Knaresborough, 5 from Ripley.—Pop. 14.

OGLETHORPE, in the parish of Bramham, wapentake of Barkston-Ash; 4 miles from Tadcaster, 4 from Wetherby.

OKENSHAW, in the parish of Birstall, Morley division of the wapentake of Agbrigg and Morley, liberty of the Honour of Pontefract; 6 miles from Bradford, 6 from Halifax.

OLD-BOOTH, in the parish of Ecclesfield, north-division

Morley-division of the wapentake of Agbrigg and Morley; 6 miles from Halifax, 14 from Huddersfield.

MOAT, in the parish of Wickersley, south-division of the wapentake of Strafforth and Tickhill; 5 miles from Rotherham, 7½ from Tickhill.

MOLE, or MOLD-GREEN, in the parish of Kirk-Heaton, Agbrigg-division of the wapentake of Agbrigg and Morley; *(the seat of Thomas and Law Atkinson, Esqrs.)* 1 mile from Huddersfield, 9 from Halifax.

MONK-HILL, in the parish of Pontefract, wapentake of Osgoldcross, liberty of the Honour of Pontefract; adjoins Pontefract.

MONKTON, BISHOP, in the parish of Ripon, lower-division of the wapentake of Claro, liberty of Ripon; *(the seat of John Charnock, Esq.)* 4 miles from Boroughbridge, 4 from Ripon, 6 from Knaresborough.—Population 363.

MONKTON, NUN, in the parish of Nun-Monkton, upper-division of the wapentake of Claro; 8 miles from York, 10 from Knaresborough, 11 from Boroughbridge.—Pop. 308.

MONYBENT, in the parish of Gisburn, west-division of the wapentake and liberty of Staincliffe; 6 miles from Gisburn, 9 from Settle.

MONYBENT-HILL, in the parish of Slaidburn, west-division of the wapentake and liberty of Staincliffe; 10 miles from Settle, 12 from Clitheroe, *(Lanc.)*

MOOR-ENDS, in the parish of Thorne, south-division of the wapentake of Strafforth and Tickhill; 1¼ mile from Thorne, 13 from Howden.

MOOR-GATE, in the parish of Rotherham, south-division of the wapentake of Strafforth and Tickhill; *(the seat of Richard Holden, Esq.)* ¼ a mile from Rotherham, 6¼ from Sheffield.

MOOR-GRANGE, in the parish of Leeds, lower-division of the wapentake of Skirack; 3 miles from Leeds, 6 from Wetherby, 10 from Wakefield.

MOOR-HALLOWS, in the parish of Penistone, wapentake of Staincross, liberty of the Honour of Pontefract; 2 miles from Penistone, 9 from Barnsley, 12¼ from Huddersfield.

MOOR-HEAD, in the parish of Kirby-Malzeard, lower-division of the wapentake of Claro; 5 miles from Masham, 11 from Bedale, 15 from Ripon.

MOORHOUSE, in the parish of Hooton-Pagnell, north-division of the wapentake of Strafforth and Tickhill; 6 miles from Doncaster, 9 from Barnsley.

MOOR-HOUSE, in the parish of Ackworth, wapentake of Osgoldcross, liberty of the Honour of Pontefract; 4¼ mile from Pontefract, 9 from Wakefield.

MOOR-HOUSE, in the parish of Tickhill, south-division of the wapentake of Strafforth and Tickhill; 1 mile from Tickhill, 3 from Bawtry, 7 from Doncaster.

MOORSIDE, in the parish of Halifax, Morley-division of the wapentake of Agbrigg and Morley; 2 miles from Halifax, 6½ from Bradford.

MOORTHWAITE-BRIDGE, in the parish of Sedbergh, wapentake of Ewcross; 3½ miles from Sedbergh, 9 from Kendal, *(Westm.)* 16½ from Askrigg.

MORLEY, in the parish of Batley, Agbrigg-division of the wapentake of Agbrigg and Morley, liberty of the Honour of Pontefract; 4 miles from Dewsbury, 4¼ from Leeds, 11 from Wakefield.—Population 2,108.

MORRETTS, in the parish of Skipton, east-division of the wapentake and liberty of Staincliffe; 2 miles from Skipton, 16 from Settle.

MORTHEN, in the parishes of Whiston and Rotherham, south-division of the wapentake of Strafforth and Tickhill; *(the seat of Carver Middleton, Esq.)* 4 miles from Rotherham, 10 from Sheffield, 11 from Tickhill.

MORTOMLEY, in the parish of Ecclesfield, north-division of the wapentake of Strafforth and Tickhill; 6 miles from Barnsley, 6 from Rotherham, 7 from Sheffield.

MORTON, EAST, in the parish of Bingley, upper-division of the wapentake of Skirack, liberty of Clifford's Fee; 3 miles from Keighley, 4 from Bingley, 12 from Otley.—Population 838.

MORTON, WEST, in the parish of Bingley, upper-division of the wapentake of Skirack; 3 miles from Keighley, 4 from Bingley, 12 from Otley.

MORWICK, in the parish of Barwick-in Elmet, lower-division of the wapentake of Skirack; 6 miles from Leeds, 6 from Wetherby, 9 from Tadcaster.

MOSELEY, in the parish of Guiseley, upper-division of the wapentake of Skirack; 4 miles from Bradford, 4 from Otley, 9 from Leeds.

MOSS, or MOSELEY, in the parish of Campsall, wapentake of Osgoldcross, liberty of the Honour of Pontefract; 6 miles from Thorne, 9 from Doncaster, 13 from Pontefract.—Population 226.

MOSSON-GREEN, in the parish of Fishlake, north-division of the wapentake of Strafforth and Tickhill; 4 miles from Thorne, 8 from Snaith.

MOSS-WOOD-HOUSES, in the parish of Kirby-Malzeard, lower-division of the wapentake of Claro; 3 miles from Pateleybridge, 8½ from Masham.

MOTHORP, in the parish of South-Kirkby, wapentake of Osgoldcross, liberty of the Honour of Pontefract; 8 miles from Pontefract, 11 from Wakefield, 12 from Doncaster.

MOUNT-PLEASANT, in the parish of Sheffield, south-division of the wapentake of Strafforth and Tickhill; *(the seat of Broomhead Ward, Esq.)* 1 mile from Sheffield, 7 from Rotherham.

NULWITH, in the parish of Ripon, lower-division of the wapentake of Claro, liberty of Ripon; 3 miles from Boroughbridge, 4 from Ripon.

N.

NAPPA, in the parish of Gisburn, west-division of the wapentake and liberty of Staincliffe; 9 miles from Settle, 11 from Colne, *(Lanc.)* 11 from Skipton.—Population 32.

NAPPA-FLATTS, in the parish of Gisburn, west-division of the wapentake and liberty of Staincliffe; 9 miles from Skipton, 9 from Settle.

NEEPSEND, in the parish of Sheffield, north-division of the wapentake of Strafforth and Tickhill; 1 mile from Sheffield, 7 from Rotherham, 13 from Chesterfield, *(Derb.)*

NESFIELD, in the parish of Ilkley, upper-division of the wapentake of Claro; 7 miles from Otley, 8 from Skipton.—Population 101.

NETHER-BANK, in the parish of Ecclesfield, north-division of the wapentake of Strafforth and Tickhill; 4 miles from Sheffield, 5 from Rotherham, 6 from Barnsley.

NETHERBY, in the parish of Kirkby-Overblow, upper-division of the wapentake of Claro; 4¼ miles from Wetherby, 8 from Knaresborough.

NETHER-GREEN, in the parish of Sheffield, south-division of the wapentake of Strafforth and Tickhill; 3 miles from Sheffield, 9 from Rotherham, 11 from Chesterfield, *(Derb.)*

NETHER-HALL, in the parish of Doncaster, south-division of the wapentake of Strafforth and Tickhill; *(the seat of Thomas Copley, Esq.)* ¼ of a mile from Doncaster, 9 from Bawtry.

NETHERTHORPE, in the parish of Aston, south-division of the wapentake of Strafforth and Tickhill; 6 miles from Rotherham, 8½ from Worksop, *(Notts.).*

NETHER-LODGE, in the parish of Horton, wapentake of Ewcross; 10 miles from Settle, 13 from Askrigg.

NETHER-SHIRE, in the parish of Ecclesfield, north-division of the wapentake of Strafforth and Tickhill; *(the seat of Hugh Miller, Esq.*) 4 miles from Sheffield, 5 from Rotherham, 9 from Barnsley.

NETHERTON, in the parish of Sandall, Agbrigg-division of the wapentake of Agbrigg and Morley, liberty of the Honour of Pontefract; 5 miles from Wakefield, 9¼ from Huddersfield.

NETHERTON, in the parish of Almondbury, Agbrigg division of the wapentake of Agbrigg and Morley, liberty of the Honour of Pontefract; 3 miles from Huddersfield, 11 from Halifax.

NEWAP, in the parish of Drax, wapentake of Barksten-Ash; 5 miles from Selby, 7 from Howden, 7 from Snaith.

NEWBRIDGE, in the parish of Kirby-Malzeard, lower-division of the wapentake of Claro; 2 miles from Pateley-bridge, 10 from Masham.

NEWBY, in the parish of Gisburn, west-division of the wapentake and liberty of Staincliffe; 5¼ miles from Clitheroe, (*Lanc.*) 2 miles from Gisburn, 12 from Skipton.

NEWBY, in the parish of Harewood, upper-division of the wapentake of Claro; 4¼ miles from Otley, 8¼ from Wetherby, 10 from Knaresborough.

NEWBY, in the parish of Clapham, wapentake of Ewcross; 7 miles from Settle 10 from Kirby-Lonsdale, (*Westm.*)

NEWBY-COTE, in the parish of Clapham, wapentake of Ewcross; 7 miles from Settle, 10 from Kirby-Lonsdale, (*Westm.*)

NEWBY-HALL, in the parish of Ripon, lower-division of the wapentake of Claro, liberty of Ripon; (*the seat of Lord Grantham*) 3 miles from Boroughbridge, 4 from Ripon, 10 from Knaresborough.

NEWFIELD, in the parish of Sheffield, south-division of the wapentake of Strafforth and Tickhill; ¼ a mile from Sheffield, 6¼ from Rotherham.

NEW-GRANGE, in the parish of Leeds, lower-division of the wapentake of Skirack; 3 miles from Leeds, 4 from Harewood, 7 from Wetherby.

NEWHALL, in the parish of Otley, upper-division of the wapentake of Claro, liberty of Cawood, Wistow, and Otley; (*the seat of Thomas Clifton, Esq.*) 1 mile from Otley, 11 from Leeds, 14 from Knaresborough.—Population 203.

NEW-HALL, in the parish of Pontefract, wapentake of Osgoldcross, liberty of the Honour of Pontefract; ¼ a mile from Pontefract, 1¼ from Ferrybridge.

NEW-HALL, in the parish of Rothwell, Morley-division of the wapentake of Agbrigg and Morley; 3 miles from Leeds, 5¼ from Wakefield.

NEW-HALL, in the parish of Thornhill, Agbrigg-division

of the wapentake of Agbrigg and Morley; 4 miles from Dewsbury, 5 from Wakefield.

NEW-HOUSE, in the parish of Mitton, west-division of the wapentake and liberty of Staincliffe; 4 miles from Clitheroe, *(Lanc.)* 12 from Blackburn, *(ditto)* 12 from Gisburn.

NEW-HOUSE, in the parish of Horton wapentake of Ewcross; 6½ miles from Settle, 15 from Kirby-Lonsdale, *(Westm.)*

NEW-HOUSES, in the parish of Kirby-Malzeard, lower-division of the wapentake of Claro; 10 miles from Pateley-Bridge, 10 from Masham.

NEWHILL, in the parish of Wath-upon-Dearn, north-division of the wapentake of Strafforth and Tickhill, liberty of Tickhill; *(the seat of John Payne, Esq.)* 5 miles from Rotherham, 7 from Barnsley.

NEWLAND, in the parish of Halifax, Morley-division of the wapentake of Agbrigg and Morley; 2½ miles from Halifax, 10½ from Huddersfield, 11 from Keighley.

NEWLAND, in the parish of Drax, wapentake of Barkston-Ash; 5 miles from Snaith, 9 from Selby, 16 from Pontefract.—Population 179.

NEWLAND-HALL, in the parish of Normanton, Agbrigg-division of the wapentake of Agbrigg and Morley; *(the seat of Sir Edward Smith, Bart.)* 4¼ miles from Wakefield, 5¼ from Pontefract.

NEW-LAITH, in the parish of Ferry-Fryston, wapentake of Osgoldcross, liberty of the Honour of Pontefract; 1¼ mile from Ferrybridge, 3 from Pontefract.

NEW-LAITHES, in the parish of Royston, wapentake of Staincross, liberty of the Honour of Pontefract; 2 miles from Barnsley, 7½ from Penistone, 8 from Wakefield.

NEW-LAITHES, in the parish of Guiseley, upper-division of the wapentake of Skirack; 6 miles from Bradford, 6½ from Otley, 7 from Leeds.

NEWSHAM, in the parish of Almondbury, Agbrigg-division of the wapentake of Agbrigg and Morley, liberty of the Honour of Pontefract; 1½ mile from Huddersfield, 9½ from Halifax.

NEWSHOLME, in the parish of Keighley, east-division of the wapentake and liberty of Staincliffe; 2½ miles from Keighley, 8 from Skipton, 10 from Colne, *(Lanc.)*

NEWSOME-GREEN, see Temple-Newsome.

NEWSOME, in the parish of Gisburn, west-division of the wapentake and liberty of Staincliffe; 10 miles from Settle, 10 from Skipton, 10 from Colne, *(Lanc.)*—Pop. 78.

NEWSTEAD-HALL, in the parish of Hemsworth, wapentake of Staincross, liberty of the Honour of Pontefract; *(the seat of John Naylor, Esq.)* 5 miles from Pontefract, 6 from Wakefield, 9 from Barnsley.

NEWTHORPE, in the parish of Sherburn, wapentake of Barkston-Ash, liberty of St. Peter; 3 miles from Abberford, 7 from Ferrybridge, 11 from Selby.—*Pop.* 46.

NEWTON, in the parish of Slaidburn, west-division of the wapentake of Staincliffe, liberty of Bolland; *(Newton-House, the seat of Thomas Parker, Esq.)* 7 miles from Clitheroe, *(Lanc.)* 13 from Settle, 18 from Lancaster, *(Lanc.)* 20 from Skipton.—*No Market.*—*Fair,* March 14, for Horned Cattle.—Population 378.

NEWTON, in the parish of Sprotbrough, north-division of the wapentake of Strafforth and Tickhill, liberty of Tickhill; 1½ mile from Doncaster, 11 from Rotherham, 14 from Pontefract.

NEWTON, in the parish of Wakefield, Agbrigg-division of the wapentake of Agbrigg and Morley, liberty of the Manor of Wakefield; 1 mile from Wakefield, 8 from Leeds.

NEWTON, BANK, in the parish of Gargrave, east-division of the wapentake and liberty of Staincliffe; 5 miles from Skipton, 9 from Colne, *(Lanc.)* 11 from Settle.— Population 68.

NEWTON-KYME, or KINE, in the parish of Newton-Kyme, wapentake of Barkston-Ash; *(Newton-Hall, the seat of — Fairfax, Esq.)* 1½ mile from Tadcaster, 5 from Wetherby, 13 from Ferrybridge.—Population 149.

NEWTON, LITTLE, in the parish of Long-Preston, west-division of the wapentake and liberty of Staincliffe; 5 miles from Settle, 11 from Skipton.

NEWTON, POTTER, *see Potter-Newton.*

NEWTON-WILLOWS, in the parish of Ledsam, wapentake of Barkston-Ash; 5 miles from Pontefract, 10 from Tadcaster, 10 from Selby.

NIDD, in the parish of Nidd, lower-division of the wapentake of Claro, liberty of Ripon; *(Nidd-Hall, the seat of Francis Trapps, Esq.)* 2 miles from Ripley, 3½ from Knaresborough.—Population 114.

NOBLETHORPE, in the parish of Silkston, wapentake of Staincross, liberty of the Honour of Pontefract; 2¼ miles from Penistone, 4¼ from Barnsley, 12 from Sheffield.

NORLAND, in the parish of Halifax, Morley-division of the wapentake of Agbrigg and Morley, liberty of the Manor of Wakefield; 4 miles from Halifax, 7 from Huddersfield.—Population 1,181.

NORMANTON, in the parish of Normanton, Agbrigg-division of the wapentake of Agbrigg and Morley, liberty of the Manor of Wakefield; 4 miles from Wakefield, 5 from Pontefract.—Population 276.

NORTH-COTE, in the parish of Burnsall, east-division of the wapentake and liberty of Staincliffe; 2¼ miles from Kettlewell, 18 from Skipton, 13 from Settle.

NORTH-CROFTS, in the parish of Silkston, wapentake of Staincross, liberty of the Honour of Pontefract; 8½ miles from Penistone, 3¼ from Barnsley, 13 from Sheffield.

NORTH LANE HOUSE, in the parish of Drax, wapentake of Barkston-Ash; 5 miles from Snaith, 9 from Selby.

NORTH-LEAS, or LEYS, in the parish of Ripon, lower-division of the wapentake of Claro, liberty of Ripon; 1¼ mile from Ripon, 7½ from Boroughbridge, 11¼ from Knaresborough.

NORTHORPE, in the parish of Mirfield, Agbrigg-division of the wapentake of Agbrigg and Morley; *(the seat of George Webster, Esq.)* 2¼ miles from Dewsbury, 5 from Wakefield, 6 from Huddersfield.

NORTH-OWRAM, *see Owram, North.*

NORTH-PASTURE, in the parish of Ripon, lower-division of the wapentake of Claro; 3 miles from Pateleybridge, 9 from Ripon.

NORTH-SIDE-HEAD, in the parish of Kirby-Malzeard, lower-division of the wapentake of Claro; 9 miles from Pateleybridge, 10 from Masham.

NORTH-THORPE, in the parish of Tankersley, wapentake of Staincross, liberty of the Honour of Pontefract; 4 miles from Penistone, 5 from Barnsley, 9 from Sheffield.

NORTON-PRIORY, in the parish of Campsall, wapentake of Osgoldcross, liberty of the Honour of Pontefract; 8 miles from Doncaster, 7½ from Pontefract, 8½ from Ferrybridge.—Population 479.

NORWOOD, in the parish of Fewston, lower-division of the wapentake of Claro; 6 miles from Otley, 11 from Knaresborough.

NORWOOD-HALL, in the parish of Sheffield, south-division of the wapentake of Strafforth and Tickhill; *(the seat of James Wheat, Esq.)* 2¼ miles from Sheffield, 8¼ from from Rotherham, 11¼ from Barnsley.

NOSTAL, in the parish of Wragby, wapentake of Osgoldcross, liberty of the Honour of Pontefract; *(the seat of —— Williamson, Esq.)* 5 miles from Pontefract, 7 from Ferrybridge, 15 from Doncaster.

NOSTROP, in the parish of Leeds, lower-division of the wapentake of Skirack, *(the seat of —— Dade, Esq.)*

mile from Leeds, 10 from Bradford, 10 from Wakefield.

NOTTON, in the parish of Royston, wapentake of Staincross, liberty of the Honour of Pontefract; 4 miles from Barnsley, 6¼ from Wakefield, 10 from Pontefract.—Population 323.

NUNBROOK, in the parish of Mirfield, Agbrigg-division of the wapentake of Agbrigg and Morley, liberty of the Honour of Pontefract; *(the seat of Charles rook, Esq.)* 4½ miles from Huddersfield, 8¼ from Wakefield, 11 from Leeds.

NUNWICK, in the parish of Wath, lower-division of the wapentake of Claro, liberty of Ripon; 1¼ mile from Ripon, 7¼ from Boroughbridge, 10 from Bedale.—Population 27.

O.

OAKENSHAW, in the parish of Crofton, Agbrigg-division of the wapentake of Agbrigg and Morley, liberty of the Honour of Pontefract; 1¼ mile from Wakefield, 7 from Pontefract.

OAKS, in the parish of Darton, wapentake of Staincross, liberty of the Honour of Pontefract; 3 miles from Barnsley, 7¼ from Penistone, 8¼ from Wakefield.

OAKS-GREEN, in the parish of Halifax, Morley-division of the wapentake of Agbrigg and Morley; 4 miles from Huddersfield, 6 from Halifax.

OAKTON, in the parish of Spofforth, upper-division of the wapentake of Claro; 3½ miles from Knaresborough, 4 from Wetherby.

OAKWELL-HALL, in the parish of Birstall, Morley-division of the wapentake of Agbrigg and Morley, *(the seat of Benjamin Fernley Esq.)* 6 miles from Bradford, 8 from Halifax, 8 from Leeds.

OAKWORTH, in the parish of Keighley, east-division of the wapentake and liberty of Staincliffe; 3 miles from Keighley, 10 from Skipton, 10 from Colne, *(Lanc.)*

OCKENY, OAKNANEY, or OCCANEY, in the parish of Knaresborough, lower-division of the wapentake of Claro; 3¼ miles from Knaresborough, 5 from Ripley.—Pop. 14.

OGLETHORPE, in the parish of Bramham, wapentake of Barkston-Ash; 4 miles from Tadcaster, 4 from Wetherby.

OKENSHAW, in the parish of Birstall, Morley division of the wapentake of Agbrigg and Morley, liberty of the Honour of Pontefract; 6 miles from Bradford, 6 from Halifax.

OLD-BOOTH, in the parish of Ecclesfield, north-division

of the wapentake of Strafforth and Tickhill; 6 miles from Penistone, 12 from Barnsley, 12 from Sheffield,

OLDCOTES, in the parish of Calverley, Morley-division of the wapentake of Agbrigg and Morley; 3 miles from Bradford, 7¼ from Leeds.

OLDCOTES, in the parish of Arncliffe, west-division of the wapentake of Staincliffe, liberty of Clifford's Fee; 5 miles from Kettlewell, 11½ from Settle.

OLDHAM-MILL, in the parish of Darfield, north-division of the wapentake of Strafforth and Tickhill; 3 miles from Barnsley, 7¼ from Rotherham, 10 from Penistone.

OLERS, in the parish of Huddersfield, Agbrigg-division of the wapentake of Agbrigg and Morley; 8 miles from Huddersfield, 17 from Manchester, *(Lanc.)*

OLERS, NETHER, in the parish of Huddersfield, Agbrigg-division of the wapentake of Agbrigg and Morley; 8¼ miles from Huddersfield, 18 from Manchester, *(Lanc.)*

ORGRAVE, in the parish of Hansworth, south-division of the wapentake of Strafforth and Tickhill, liberty of Tickhill; 4 miles from Rotherham, 5 from Sheffield.—Population 45.

OSSENDIKE, in the parish of Rither, wapentake of Barkston-Ash, liberty of the Honour of Pontefract; 3 miles from Tadcaster, 7 from Selby, 13 from Pontefract.

OSSETT, in the parish of Dewsbury, Agbrigg-division of the wapentake of Agbrigg and Morley, liberty of the Manor of Wakefield; 2¼ miles from Wakefield, 3 from Dewsbury.—Population 3,424.

OSWINTHORPE, or OSMONDTHORPE, in the parish of Leeds, lower-division of the wapentake of Skirack; *(the seat of —— Motley, Esq.)* 3 miles from Leeds, 10 from Ferrybridge, 10 from Tadcaster.

OTLEY, in the parish of Otley, upper-division of the wapentake of Skirack, liberty of Cawood, Wistow, and Otley; *(the seat of Matthew, Wilson, Esq.)* 8 miles from Harewood, 10 from Leeds, 10 from Wetherby, 10 from Bingley, 10 from Bradford, 12 from Keighley, 12 from Ripley, 13 from Knaresborough, 15 from Skipton, 28 from York, 205 from London.—*Market*, Friday.—*Fairs*, First Monday after August 2, for Horses and Horned Cattle; Friday between new and old Martinmas-day, for hiring Servants; Fortnight Fairs, on Mondays, for Horned Cattle, and Sheep. —*Principal Inns*, White Horse, Black Horse, and New-Inn.—Population 2,332.

OTTERBURN, in the parish of Kirkby-Malhamdale, west-division of the wapentake of Staincliffe, liberty of Clifford's Fee; 8 miles from Settle, 9 from Skipton, 11 from Colne, *(Lanc.)*—Population 26.

OUGHTHERSHAW, in the parish of Arncliffe, west division of the wapentake and liberty of Staincliffe; 8¼ miles from Kettlewell, 14 from Settle.

OUGHTY-BRIDGE, in the parish of Ecclesfield, north division of the wapentake of Strafforth and Tickhill; 3 miles from Sheffield, 8 from Penistone, 9 from Rotherham.

OULTON, in the parish of Rothwell, Agbrigg-division of the wapentake of Agbrigg and Morley, liberty of the Honour of Pontefract; 5 miles from Wakefield, 5 from Leeds.—Population 1,223.

OUSEBURN, GREAT, in the parish of Great-Ouseburn, lower-division of the wapentake of Claro, liberty of Knaresborough; 4 miles from Boroughbridge, 7 from Knaresborough, 14 from York.—Population 415.

OUSEBURN, LITTLE, in the parish of Little-Ouseburn, upper-division of the wapentake of Claro, liberty of St. Peter; 5 miles from Boroughbridge, 8 from Knaresborough, 12 from York.—Population 182.

OUSEFLEET, in the parish of Whitgift, wapentake of Osgoldcross, liberty of the Honour of Pontefract; 7 miles from Howden, 8 from Crowle, (*Linc.*) 14 from Snaith.—Population 207.

OUSEFLEET-GRANGE, in the parish of Whitgift, wapentake of Osgoldcross, liberty of the Honour of Pontefract; 7 miles from Howden, 7 from Crowle, (*Linc.*) 14 from Snaith.

OUSE-HEAD, in the parish of Great-Ouseburn, lower-division of the wapentake of Claro; 3½ miles from Boroughbridge, 7¼ from Knaresborough, 14¼ from York.

OUSLETHWAITE, in the parish of Darfield, wapentake of Staincross, liberty of the Honour of Pontefract; (*the seat of William Elmhirst, Esq.*). 1½ mile from Barnsley, 6¼ from Penistone, 9 from Rotherham.

OVENDEN, in the parish of Halifax, Morley-division of the wapentake of Agbrigg and Morley, liberty of the Manor of Wakefield; 1½ mile from Halifax, 9 from Bradford, 10¼ from Keighley.—Population 4,513.

OWLERTON, in the parish of Sheffield, south-division of the wapentake of Strafforth and Tickhill; 1½ mile from Sheffield, 7¼ from Rotherham, 11 from Penistone.

OWLSHAW, in the parish of Giggleswick, west-division of the wapentake and liberty of Staincliffe; 4 miles from Settle, 16 from Skipton.

OWNS-ACRE, in the parish of Ecclesfield, north-division of the wapentake of Strafforth and Tickhill; 4½ miles from Sheffield, 8 from Penistone,

OWRAM, NORTH, in the parish of Halifax, Morley-division of the wapentake of Agbrigg and Morley, liberties of the Manor of Wakefield and Honour of Pontefract; (*Owram Hall,* the seat of *John Edwards, Esq.*) 2 miles from Halifax, 5¼ from Bradford.—Population 4,887.

OWRAM, SOUTH, in the parish of Halifax, Morley-division of the wapentake of Agbrigg and Morley, liberties of the Manor of Wakefield and Honour of Pontefract; 2¼ miles from Halifax, 5¼ from Bradford.—Pop. 3,148.

OWSTON, in the parish of Owston, wapentake of Osgoldcross, liberty of the Honour of Pontefract; *(the seat of Bryan Cooke, Esq.)* 6 miles from Doncaster, 10 from Pontefract.—Population 250.

OXNOP, FAR, in the parish of Bradford, Morley-division of the wapentake of Agbrigg and Morley; 5 miles from Keighley, 6 from Bingley.

OXNOP, NEAR, in the parish of Bradford, Morley-division of the wapentake of Agbrigg and Morley; 5½ miles from Keighley, 6 from Bingley.

OXSPRING, in the parish of Penistone, wapentake of Staincross, liberty of the Honour of Pontefract; 1 mile from Penistone, 6 from Barnsley, 11 from Sheffield.—Pop. 219.

P.

PAA, in the parish of Gisburn, west-division of the wapentake and liberty of Staincliffe; 9 miles from Settle, 11 from Skipton.

PACEYATE, in the parish of Skipton, lower-division of the wapentake of Claro; 8 miles from Skipton, 15 from Knaresborough.

PADDOCK, in the parish of Huddersfield, Agbrigg-division of the wapentake of Agbrigg and Morley, liberty of the Honour of Pontefract; 1 mile from Huddersfield, 8 from Halifax.

PADDOCK-FOOT, in the parish of Huddersfield, Agbrigg-division of the wapentake of Agbrigg and Morley, liberty of the Honour of Pontefract; 1 mile from Huddersfield, 8¼ from Halifax.

PADSIDE, in the parish of Hampsthwaite, lower-division of the wapentake of Claro; 4¼ miles from Pateleybridge, 9 from Ripley.

PAGE-FOLD, in the parish of Mitton, east-division of the wapentake and liberty of Staincliffe; 4 miles from Clitheroe,

(Lanc.) 12 from Blackburn, *(ditto)* 12 from Gisburn.

PAGE-HALL, in the parish of Ecclesfield, north-division of the wapentake of Strafforth and Tickhill; *(the seat of George Burton Greaves, Esq.)* 3 miles from Sheffield, 4¾ from Rotherham, 10 from Barnsley.

PAINLEY, in the parish of Gisburn, west-division of the wapentake and liberty of Staincliffe; 1¼ mile from Gisburn, 10¼ from Skipton.

PAINTHORPE, in the parish of Sandall, Agbrigg-division of the wapentake of Agbrigg and Morley, liberty of the Manor of Wakefield; 4 miles from Wakefield, 5 from Barnsley.

PANNALL, in the parish of Pannall, lower-division of the wapentake of Claro; 5½ miles from Knaresborough, 7 from Ripley, 8 from Otley.—Population 789.

PARK-GATE, in the parish of Almondbury, Agbrigg-division of the wapentake of Agbrigg and Morley; 2 miles from Huddersfield, 10 from Halifax, 13 from Wakefield.

PARK-GATE-HALL, in the parish of Guiseley, upper-division of the wapentake of Skirack; *(the seat of Francis Ridsdale, Esq.)* 2½ miles from Otley, 10 from Leeds, 12 from Wetherby.

PARK-GATE, in the parish of Rotherham, north-division of the wapentake of Strafforth and Tickhill; 4 miles from Rotherham, 8 from Barnsley, 10 from Doncaster.

PARK-GATE, in the parish of High-Hoyland, Agbrigg-division of the wapentake of Agbrigg and Morley; 9 miles from Huddersfield, 8 from Wakefield.

PARK-HILL, in the parish of Firbeck, south-division of the wapentake of Strafforth and Tickhill; *(the seat of James Fenton, Esq.)* 4 miles from Tickhill, 6 from Worksop, *(Notts.)* 11 from Rotherham.

PARK-HOUSE, in the parish of Elmley, Agbrigg-division of the wapentake of Agbrigg and Morley; 8 miles from Huddersfield, 8 from Wakefield.

PARK-LANE, in the parish of Hatfield, south-division of the wapentake of Strafforth and Tickhill; 5¼ miles from Doncaster, 6¼ from Thorne.

PARLINGTON, in the parish of Abberford, lower-division of the wapentake of Skirack, liberty of the Honour of Pontefract; *(the seat of Sir Thomas Gascoigne, Bart.)* 1 mile from Abberford, 7 from Wetherby, 10 from Leeds, 10 from Pontefract.—Population 180.

PATELEYBRIDGE, in the parish of Ripon, lower-division of the wapentake of Claro, liberty of Ripon; 9 miles from Ripley, 10 from Grassington, 11¼ from Ripon, 14 from

Knaresborough, 14 from Harrogate, 15 from Skipton, 15 from Masham, 15 from Otley, 16 from Kettlewell, 32 from York, 224 from London.—*Market*, Saturday.—*Fairs*, Easter and Whitsun-eve; September 17, if on a Saturday, or the first Saturday after September 17, and Christmas-eve, for Woollen-Cloth, Pedlary-Ware, &c.—*Principal Inns*, Crown, and George.

PAW-HILL, in the parish of Penistone, wapentake of Staincross, liberty of the Honour of Pontefract; 3 miles from Penistone, 10 from Barnsley, 12 from Sheffield.

PAYLEY-GREEN, HIGH and LOW, in the parish of Giggleswick, west-division of the wapentake and liberty of Staincliffe; 2 miles from Settle, 17 from Kirby-Lonsdale, (*Westm.*)

PAYTHORNE, in the parish of Gisburn, west-division of the wapentake and liberty of Staincliffe; 9 miles from Settle, 11 from Skipton, 11 from Colne, (*Lanc.*)—Population 198.

PECKFIELD-HOUSE, in the parish of Church-Garforth, wapentake of Barkston-Ash; 5 miles from Ferrybridge, 6 from Pontefract, 10 from Leeds.

PENISTONE, in the parish of Penistone, wapentake of Staincross, liberty of the Honour of Pontefract; 7 miles from Barnsley, 12¼ from Huddersfield, 13¼ from Sheffield, 15 from Rotherham, 26 from Stockport, (*Chesh.*) 45 from York, 175 from London.—*Market*, Thursday.—*Fairs*, last Thursin February, last Thursday in March, first Thursday in May, and Thursday after old Michaelmas-day, for Horses and Horned Cattle.—*Principal Inn*, Rose and Crown.—Population 493.

PIGBURN, in the parish of Brodsworth, north-division of the wapentake of Strafforth and Tickhill, liberty of Tickhill; 4 miles from Doncaster, 11 from Barnsley.

PILLEY, in the parish of Tankersley, wapentake of Staincross, liberty of the Honour of Pontefract; 4 miles from Barnsley, 7 from Penistone, 7 from Rotherham.

PITTS-MOOR, in the parish of Sheffield, north-division of the wapentake of Strafforth and Tickhill; 1¼ mile from Sheffield, 7¼ from Rotherham, 12¼ from Barnsley.

PLEADWICK, in the parish of Sandall, Agbrigg-division of the wapentake of Agbrigg and Morley, liberty of the Manor of Wakefield; 2½ miles from Wakefield, 7¼ from Barnsley.

PLUMPTON, or PLOMPTON, in the parish of Spofforth, upper-division of the wapentake of Claro; 3 miles from Knaresborough, 4 from Wetherby.—Population 191.

POG-MOOR, in the parish of Silkston, wapentake of

WEST-RIDING. 255

Staincross, liberty of the Honour of Pontefract; 1½ mile from Barnsley, 6½ from Penistone, 9¼ from Wakefield.

POLLINGTON, in the parish of Snaith, wapentake of Osgoldcross, liberty of the Honour of Pontefract; 2 miles from Snaith, 7 from Thorne, 8½ from Ferrybridge.—Pop. 378.

POND, in the parish of Penistone, wapentake of Staincross, liberty of the Honour of Pontefract; 8 miles from Penistone, 7 from Barnsley, 10½ from Sheffield.

PONTEFRACT, in the parish of Pontefract, wapentake of Osgoldcross, liberty of the Honour of Pontefract; 2 miles from Ferrybridge, 9 from Wakefield, 13 from Snaith, 14 from Barnsley, 15 from Doncaster, 15 from Wetherby, 15 from Leeds, 23 from York, 177 from London.—*Market*, Saturday.—*Fairs*, first Saturday after January 13, first Saturday before February 2, first Saturday after February 13, Saturday before Palm-Sunday, Low-Sunday, and Trinity-Sunday, Saturday after September 12, and the first Saturday in December, for Horses, Horned Cattle, and Sheep; the Fortnight-Fairs are on Saturday next after the York Fortnight-Fairs.—*Bankers*, Old-Bank, Messrs. Perfect, Seaton, and Co. draw on Messrs Robarts, Curtis, and Co. 15, Lombard-Street; New-Bank, Messrs. Leathams, Jackson, Tew, and Trueman, draw on Messrs. Harrison, Price, Kay, and Chapman, 1, Mansion-House-Street.—Sends two Members to Parliament.—*Principal Inns*, Red-Lion, New-Elephant, and Star.—Population 3,097.

PONTEFRACT-PARK, District, (extraparochial) wapentake of Osgoldcross, liberty of the Honour of Pontefract; 1½ mile from Pontefract, 7¼ from Wakefield.—Pop. 47.

POOL, in the parish of Otley, upper-division of the wapentake of Skirack, liberty of Cawood, Wistow, and Otley; 3 miles from Otley, 5 from Harewood, 10 from Leeds.—Population 182.

POOLE, in the parish of Brotherton, wapentake of Barkston-Ash, liberties of St. Peter, and the Honour of Pontefract; 3 miles from Ferrybridge, 5 from Pontefract.

PORTO-BELLO, in the parish of Sheffield, south-division of the wapentake of Strafforth and Tickhill; ¼ a mile from Sheffield, 6¼ from Rotherham.

POTTER-NEWTON, in the parish of Leeds, lower-division of the wapentake of Skirack, liberty of the Honour of Pontefract; 2 miles from Leeds, 9 from Otley, 14 from Bradford.—Population 509.

POTTERTON, in the parish of Barwick-in-Elmet, lower-division of the wapentake of Skirack, liberty of the Honour of Pontefract; *(the seat of E. Wilkinson, Esq.)* 6 miles from Wetherby, 6 from Tadcaster, 8 from Leeds.

POTGATE-HOUSE, in the parish of Ripon, lower-division of the wapentake of Claro; 4 miles from Ripon, 10 from Boroughbridge.

PRESTON, GREAT, in the parish of Kippax, lower-division of the wapentake of Skirack, liberty of the Honour of Pontefract; 7 miles from Pontefract, 8 from Wakefield, 8 from Leeds.—Population 413.

PRESTON, LITTLE, in the parish of Kippax, lower-division of the wapentake of Skirack, liberty of the Honour of Pontefract; 7 miles from Leeds, 8 from Pontefract, 8 from Wakefield.

PRESTON, LONG, *see Long-Preston.*—Pop. 573.

PRIESTHORPE, in the parish of Bingley, upper-division of the wapentake of Skirack; 6 miles from Keighley, 6 from Bradford, 9¼ from Otley.

PUDDING-HOLE, in the parish of Kirby-Malzeard, lower-division of the wapentake of Claro; 9 miles from Pateley-bridge, 9 from Masham.

PUDSEY, in the parish of Calverley, Morley-division of the wapentake of Agbrigg and Morley, liberty of the Honour of Pontefract; 4 miles from Bradford, 6 from Leeds.—Population 4,422.

PURSTON-JACKLING, in the parish of Fetherstone, wapentake of Osgoldcross, liberty of the Honour of Pontefract; 2¼ miles from Pontefract, 7 from Wakefield, 11 from Barnsley.—Population 177.

PURWELL, in the parish of Batley, Agbrigg-division of the wapentake of Agbrigg and Morley; *(the seat of John Taylor, Esq.)* 1¼ mile from Dewsbury, 6 from Wakefield.

PYE-NEST, in the parish of Halifax, Morley-division of the wapentake of Agbrigg and Morley; *(the seat of John Edwards, Esq.)* 1½ mile from Halifax, 9 from Huddersfield, 10 from Bradford.

Q.

QUARMBY, in the parish of Huddersfield, Agbrigg-division of the wapentake of Agbrigg and Morley, liberty of the Manor of Wakefield; 2 miles from Huddersfield, 8 from Halifax.

QUARRY-HILL, in the parish of Mirfield, Agbrigg-division of the wapentake of Agbrigg and Morley; 2¼ miles from Dewsbury, 5½ from Huddersfield.

QUARRY-HILL, in the parish of Almondbury, Agbrigg-division of the wapentake of Agbrigg and Morley; 2 miles from Huddersfield, 10 from Halifax, 11 from Wakefield.

QUARRY-HOUSE, in the parish of Halifax, Morley-division of the wapentake of Agbrigg and Morley; 2 miles from Halifax, 6 from Bradford.

QUEEN'S-HEAD, in the parish of Halifax, Morley-division of the wapentake of Agbrigg and Morley; 3¼ miles from Halifax, 5¼ from Bradford.

QUICK, in the parish of Rochdale, (Lanc.) Agbrigg-division of the wapentake of Agbrigg and Morley, liberty of the Honour of Pontefract; 9 miles from Rochdale, (Lanc.) 11 from Manchester, (ditto) 15 from Huddersfield.

R.

RAISGILL, in the parish of Arnecliffe, east-division of the wapentake and liberty of Staincliffe; 6 miles from Kettlewell, 15 from Settle, 17 from Leyburn.

RAINBER-PARK, in the parish of Wath-upon-Dearn, north-division of the wapentake of Strafforth and Tickhill; 5 miles from Rotherham, 7 from Barnsley.

RAMSGILL, in the parish of Kirby-Malzeard, lower-division of the wapentake of Claro; 6 miles from Pateleybridge, 10 from Masham, 15 from Ripon.

RAMSGILL, in the parish of Ilkley, upper-division of the wapentake of Skirack; 5 miles from Otley, 7 from Bingley.

RAND-MOOR, in the parish of Sheffield, south-division of the wapentake of Strafforth and Tickhill; 3 miles from Sheffield, 9 from Rotherham, 12 from Chesterfield, (Derb.)

RASTRICK, in the parish of Halifax, Morley-division of the wapentake of Agbrigg and Morley, liberty of the Manor of Wakefield; 4 miles from Halifax, 5 from Huddersfield.—Population 2,053.

RATHMELL, in the parish of Giggleswick, west-division of the wapentake and liberty of Staincliffe; 3¼ miles from Settle, 15 from Skipton, 16 from Colne, (Lanc.)—Pop. 306.

RATTINSTALL, ROTTONSTALL, or RAWTONSTONE-BANK, in the parish of Halifax, Morley-division of the wapentake of Agbrigg and Morley, liberty of the Manor of Wakefield; 9 miles from Halifax, 9 from Rochdale, (Lanc.)

RAVENFIELD, in the parish of Mexbrough, south-division of the wapentake of Strafforth and Tickhill; (the seat of William Perkin Bosville, Esq.) 3 miles from Rotherham, 8 from Tickhill, 9 from Sheffield.—Population 172.

RAVENTOFTS-HALL, in the parish of Ripon, lower-division of the wapentake of Claro; 4 miles from Ripley, 6 from Ripon, 8 from Knaresborough.

RAVENS-KNOWLES, or KNOWLES, in the parish of Kirk-Heaton, Agbrigg-division of the wapentake of Agbrigg and Morley; 1 mile from Huddersfield, 9 from Halifax.

RAW, in the parish of Horton, wapentake of Ewcross; 6¼ miles from Settle, 15½ from Kirby-Lonsdale, *(Westm.)*

RAWCLIFFE, in the parish of Snaith, wapentake of Osgoldcross, liberty of the Honour of Pontefract; *(the seat of Ralph Creyke, Esq.)* 2¼ miles from Snaith, 6¼ from Howden, 7 from Thorne.—Population 920.

RAWCLIFFE-BRIDGE, in the parish of Snaith, wapentake of Osgoldcross, liberty of the Honour of Pontefract; 4¼ miles from Snaith, 5 from Thorne, 8¼ from Howden.

RAWDEN, in the parish of Guiseley, upper-division of the wapentake of Skirack; 5 miles from Otley, 5 from Bradford, 7 from Leeds.—Population 1,115.

RAWMARSH, in the parish of Rawmarsh, north-division of the wapentake of Strafforth and Tickhill; 2 miles from Rotherham, 8 from Sheffield, 10 from Barnsley.—Pop. 1,014.

RAWTHORPE-HALL, in the parish of Kirk-Heaton, Agbrigg-division of the wapentake of Agbrigg and Morley; 1¼ mile from Huddersfield, 9½ from Halifax.

REDDING-HOUSE, in the parish of Fewston, lower-division of the wapentake of Claro; 6 miles from Otley, 7¼ from Ripley, 11 from Knaresborough.

RED-HALL, in the parishes of Thorner, and Barwick-in-Elmet, lower-division of the wapentake of Skirack; 5 miles from Leeds, 10 from Otley, 14 from Bradford.

RED-HOUSE, in the parish of Adwicke-in-the-Street, north-division of the wapentake of Strafforth and Tickhill; 5 miles from Doncaster, 10 from Pontefract, 15¼ from Wakefield.

RED-MIRES, in the parish of Ripon, lower-division of the wapentake of Claro; 5 miles from Ripon, 7 from Pateley-bridge.

REEDHOLME, in the parish of Arksey, north-division of the wapentake of Strafforth and Tickhill; 4½ miles from Doncaster, 9 from Thorne.

REEDNESS, in the parish of Whitgift, wapentake of Osgoldcross, liberty of the Honour of Pontefract; 6½ miles from Howden, 7½ from Crowle, *(Linc.)*—Population 520.

REGILL-HOUSE, in the parish of Kirby-Malzeard, lower-division of the wapentake of Claro; 5 miles from Pateley-bridge, 10 from Kettlewell.

WEST-RIDING.

RENHOLL, in the parish of Drax, wapentake of Barkston-Ash; 4 miles from Snaith, 7 from Selby.

REYNALL, in the parish of Penistone, wapentake of Staincross, liberty of the Honour of Pontefract; 3 miles from Penistone, 10 from Barnsley, 13 from Huddersfield.

RHODES-GREEN, in the parish of Rothwell, Agbrigg-division of the wapentake of Agbrigg and Morley, liberty of the Honour of Pontefract; 4¼ miles from Wakefield, 7 from Leeds.

RIBSTON, GREAT, in the parish of Hunsingore, upper-division of the wapentake of Claro; *(Ribston-Hall, the seat of Lady Goodrick)* 4 miles from Knaresborough, 4 from Wetherby.—Population 121.

RIBSTON, LITTLE, in the parish of Spofforth, upper-division of the wapentake of Claro; 3¼ miles from Knaresborough, 3¼ from Wetherby.—Population 181.

RICHMOND, in the parish of Handsworth, south-division of the wapentake of Strafforth and Tickhill; 4 miles from Sheffield, 5 from Rotherham, 12 from Chesterfield, *(Derb.)*

RIDDLESDEN, EAST, and WEST, in the parish of Bingley, upper-division of the wapentake of Skirack, liberty of Clifford's Fee; 2 miles from Keighley, 12 from Otley.

RIDGE-CROSS, in the parish of Halifax, Morley-division of the wapentake of Agbrigg and Morley; 9 miles from Colne, *(Lanc.)* 10 from Halifax.

RIGGE, and RIGGE-COTE, in the parish of Leeds, Morley-division of the wapentake of Agbrigg and Morley; 3 miles from Leeds, 9 from Bradford.

RIGTON, in the parish of Kirkby-Overblow, upper-division of the wapentake of Claro; 6¼ miles from Otley, 8 from Knaresborough.—Population 414.

RIGTON, in the parish of Bardsey, lower-division of the wapentake of Skirack; 8 miles from Leeds, 8 from Wetherby.

RILSTON, in the parish of Burnsall, east-division of the wapentake of Staincliffe, liberty of Clifford's Fee; 5 miles from Skipton, 11 from Kettlewell, 14 from Settle.—Population 177.

RIMINGTON, in the parish of Gisburn, west-division of the wapentake and liberty of Staincliffe; 5 miles from Clitheroe, *(Lanc.)* 10 from Colne, *(ditto,)* 12 from Skipton.—Population 487.

RING-BECK, in the parish of Kirby-Malzeard, lower-division of the wapentake of Claro; 6 miles from Masham, 8 from Ripon.

RINGSTON-HILL, in the parish of Felkirk, wapentake of Staincross, liberty of the Honour of Pontefract; 5¼ miles from Barnsley, 8 from Wakefield, 9 from Pontefract.

RIPLEY, in the parish of Ripley, upper-division of the wapentake of Claro; *(the seat of Sir John Ingleby, Bart.)* 4 miles from Harrogate, 5 from Knaresborough, 7 from Ripon, 9 from Pateleybridge, 12 from Otley, 23 from York, 206 from London.—*Market*, Monday.—*Fairs*, Easter-Monday, for Horned Cattle and Sheep, August 25, for Sheep, and 26, for Horses and Horned Cattle.—*Principal Inns*, Star, and Boars's-Head.—Population 270.

RIPON, in the parish of Ripon, lower-division of the wapentake of Claro, liberty of Ripon; 6 miles from Boroughbridge, 7 from Ripley, 10 from Masham, 10 from Oak-Tree-Inn, *Leeming-Lane*, 11 from Harrogate, 11 from Thirsk, 12 from Knaresborough, 13 from Bedale, 17 from Northallerton, 17 from Hopper-Lane-Inn, 20 from Otley, 23 from York, from London *by Boroughbridge* 212, *by Leeds* 223.—*Market*, Thursday.—*Fairs*, Thursday after January 13, for Horned Cattle, Leather, Woollen-Cloth, &c. May 13 and 14, for Horses, Horned-Cattle, Sheep, Woollen-Cloth, &c. first Thursday and Friday in June, for Horned Cattle, Sheep, Woollen-Cloth, &c. first Thursday after August 2, first Thursday in November, and November 23, for Horned Cattle, &c.—*Bankers*, Old-Bank, Messrs. Harrison and Terry, draw on Messrs. Willis, Wood, Percival, and Co. 76, Lombard-Street; Ripon and Nidderdale-Bank, Messrs. Coates, Pearson, and Coates, draw on Sir James Esdaile and Co. 21, Lombard-Street; Ripon-Bank, Messrs. Horseman, Brittain, and Co. draw on Messrs. Were, Bruce, Simson, and Taylor, 2, Bartholomew-Lane.—Sends two Members to Parliament.—*Principal Inns*, Unicorn, Crown and Anchor, and Norfolk's Arms.—Population 3,211.

RIPONDEN, in the parish of Halifax, Morley-divison of the wapentake of Agbrigg and Morley, liberty of the Manor of Wakefield; 5¼ miles from Halifax, 9 from Huddersfield, 10¾ from Rochdale, *(Lanc.)*

RISHFORTH-HALL, in the parish of Bingley, upper-division of the wapentake of Skirack; 4 miles from Keighley, 12 from Skipton, 14 from Leeds.

RISHWORTH, in the parish of Halifax, Morley-division of the wapentake of Agbrigg and Morley; 4 miles from Halifax, 5 from Huddersfield, 12 from Bradford.—Pop. 960.

RISPLITH, in the parish of Ripon, lower-division of the wapentake of Claro; 6 miles from Ripon, 9 from Knaresborough.

RITHER, in the parish of Rither, wapentake of Barkston-Ash, liberty of the Honour of Pontefract; 3 miles from Tadcaster, 9 from Selby, 13 from Pontefract.—Pop. 299.

ROACH, in the parish of Kippax, lower-division of the wapentake of Skirack; 5 miles from Abberford, 7 from Ferrybridge, 8 from Leeds.

ROADS-MOOR-HOUSE, in the parish of Rotherham, south-division of the wapentake of Strafforth and Tickhill 3 miles from Rotherham, 15 from Doncaster.

ROBERT-TOWN, in the parish of Birstall, Morley-division of the wapentake of Agbrigg and Morley; 8 miles from Halifax, 8 from Wakefield, 8 from Leeds.

ROBIN HOOD'S WELL, in the parish of Adwicke-in-the Street, wapentake of Osgoldcross, liberty of the Honour of Pontefract; 7 miles from Doncaster, 7¼ from Pontefract.

ROCARR, in the parish of Selby, wapentake of Barkston-Ash; 2 miles from Selby, 9 from Snaith, 15 from Pontefract.

ROCHE-ABBEY, in the parish of Maltby, south-division of the wapentake of Strafforth and Tickhill; 3 miles from Tickhill, 6 from Bawtry, 8 from Rotherham.

ROCKING-STONE-HALL, in the parish of Fewston, lower-division of the wapentake of Claro; 11 miles from Skipton, 12 from Otley.

ROCKLEY, in the parish of Tankersley, wapentake of Staincross, liberty of the Honour of Pontefract; 3 miles from Barnsley, 6½ from Penistone, 7 from Rotherham.

RODLEY, in the parish of Calverley, Morley-division of the wapentake of Agbrigg and Morley; 3¾ miles from Bradford, 6¼ from Leeds.

ROECLIFFE, in the parish of Aldborough, lower-division of the wapentake of Claro; 1¼ mile from Boroughbridge, 8 from Knaresborough.—Population 208.

ROGERTHORPE-HALL, in the parish of Badsworth, wapentake of Osgoldcross, liberty of the Honour of Pontefract; 4 miles from Pontefract, 6 from Ferrybridge, 9¼ from Wakefield.

ROME, in the parish of Giggleswick, west-division of the wapentake and liberty of Staincliffe; 2 miles from Settle, 17 from Kirby-Lonsdale, *(Westm.)*

ROSSINGTON, in the parish of Rossington, south-division of the wapentake of Strafforth and Tickhill, soke of Doncaster; *(the seat of the Rev. James Stoven)* 5 miles from Bawtry, 5 from Doncaster.—Population 247.

ROSSINGTON-BRIDGE, in the parish of Rossington, south-division of the wapentake of Strafforth and Tickhill, soke of Doncaster; 4½ miles from Doncaster, 4¼ from Bawtry.

ROTHERHAM in the parish of Rotherham, south-division of the wapentake of Strafforth and Tickhill, liberty of

Hallamshire; 6 miles from Sheffield, 11 from Tickhill, 12 from Doncaster, 12 from Barnsley, 15 from Penistone, 15 from Worksop, (*Notts.*) 48 from York, 160 from London.—*Market*, Monday, for Horned Cattle, Provisions, &c.—*Fairs*, Whit-Monday, December 1, for Horses, Horned Cattle, Sheep, &c. and Fortnight-Fairs on Monday, for Horned Cattle, &c.—*Bankers*, Messrs. Walker, Eyre, and Stanley, draw on Messrs. Downe, Thornton, Free and Downe, 1, Bartholomew-Lane.—*Principal Inns*, Crown, and Red-Lion.—Population 3,070.

ROTHWELL, in the parish of Rothwell, Agbrigg-division of the wapentake of Agbrigg and Morley, liberty of the Honour of Pontefract; 4 miles from Leeds, 5¼ from Wakefield.—Population 1,689.

ROTHWELL-HAIGH, in the parish of Rothwell, Agbrigg-division of the wapentake of Agbrigg and Morley, liberty of the Honour of Pontefract; 4 miles from Leeds, 5¼ from Wakefield.

ROUGH-BIRCHWORTH, in the parish of Penistone, wapentake of Staincross, liberty of the Honour of Pontefract; 2 miles from Penistone, 7 from Barnsley, 11 from Sheffield.

ROUNDHAY, in the parish of Barwick-in-Elmet, lower-division of the wapentake of Skirack, liberty of the Honour of Pontefract; 3 miles from Leeds, 8 from Wetherby.—Population 84.

ROUNDHAY-GRANGE, in the parish of Thorner, lower-division of the wapentake of Skirack, liberty of the Honour of Pontefract; 3 miles from Leeds, 8 from Wetherby.

ROUND-GREEN, in the parish of Darfield, wapentake of Staincross, liberty of the Honour of Pontefract; 2¼ miles from Barnsley, 6¼ from Penistone, 9 from Rotherham.

ROUND-WOOD, in the parish of Rawmarsh, north-division of the wapentake of Strafforth and Tickhill; 2¼ miles from Rotherham, 8¼ from Sheffield, 10 from Barnsley.

ROW, in the parish of Horton, wapentake of Ewcross; 6¼ miles from Settle, 18¼ from Askrigg.

ROWLE-HALL, in the parish of Kellington, wapentake of Osgoldcross, liberty of the Honour of Pontefract; 5 miles from Snaith, 7 from Pontefract.

ROWLEY, in the parish of Kirk-Heaton, Agbrigg-division of the wapentake of Agbrigg and Morley, liberty of the Honour of Pontefract; 3 miles from Huddersfield, 10 from Wakefield.

ROYD-BANK, in the parish of Almondbury, Agbrigg-division of the wapentake of Agbrigg and Morley; 4 miles from Huddersfield, 12 from Halifax, 12 from Wakefield.

ROYD-BRIDGE, in the parish of Halifax, Morley-division of the wapentake of Agbrigg and Morley; 8 miles from Halifax, 9 from Rochdale, *(Lanc.)*

ROYD-FIELDS, in the parish of Penistone, wapentake of Staincross, liberty of the Honour of Pontefract; 1 mile from Penistone, 8 from Barnsley, 12½ from Sheffield.

ROYD, HIGH, in the parish of Almondbury, Agbrigg-division of the wapentake of Agbrigg and Morley; *(the seat of George Armitage, Esq.)* 3 miles from Huddersfield, 11 from Halifax, 13 from Wakefield.

ROYD-HOUSE, in the parish of Kirk-Burton, Agbrigg-division of the wapentake of Agbrigg and Morley, liberty of the Manor of Wakefield; 7¼ miles from Huddersfield, 8 from Penistone.

ROYD-MOOR, in the parish of Penistone, wapentake of Staincross, liberty of the Honour of Pontefract; 8 miles from Barnsley, 11¼ from Huddersfield, 14 from Sheffield.

ROYD-MOOR, in the parish of Hemsworth, wapentake of Staincross, liberty of the Honour of Pontefract; 5 miles from Pontefract, 7 from Wakefield, 9½ from Barnsley.

ROYDS, in the parish of Ecclesfield, north-division of the wapentake of Strafforth and Tickhill; 5 miles from Sheffield, 6 from Rotherham, 7 from Barnsley.

ROYDS, in the parish of Wath-upon-Dearn, north-division of the wapentake of Strafforth and Tickhill; 6 miles from Rotherham, 6 from Barnsley, 10 from Sheffield.

ROYDS-HALL, in the parish of Bradford, Morley-division of the wapentake of Agbrigg and Morley; *(the seat of Joseph Dawson, Esq.)* 4 miles from Bradford, 5 from Halifax.

ROYSTON, in the parish of Royston, wapentake of Staincross, liberty of the Honour of Pontefract; 4¼ miles from Barnsley, 6 from Wakefield, 9½ from Pontefract.—Population 360.

RUFF-HOLME, in the parish of Drax, wapentake of Barkston-Ash; 3 miles from Howden, 6 from Snaith, 9 from Selby.

RUSH-PARK, in the parish of Sherburn, wapentake of Barkston-Ash; 7 miles from Tadcaster, 7 from Ferrybridge, 9 from Pontefract.

RUSHWORTH-HALL, in the parish of Halifax, Morley-division of the wapentake of Agbrigg and Morley, liberty of the Manor of Wakefield; 4 miles from Halifax, 5 from Huddersfield, 12 from Bradford.

RYE-CROFT, in the parish of Rawmarsh, north-division of the wapentake of Strafforth and Tickhill; 3 miles from

Rotherham, 9 from Sheffield, 9 from Barnsley.

RYHILL, in the parish of Wragby, wapentake of Staincross, liberty of the Honour of Pontefract; 6 miles from Wakefield, 6¼ from Barnsley, 9 from Pontefract.—Pop. 142.

S.

SADDLEWORTH, in the parish of Rochdale, *(Lanc.)* Agbrigg-division of the wapentake of Agbrigg and Morley, liberty of the Honour of Pontefract; 9 miles from Rochdale, *(Lanc.)* 12 from Manchester, *(ditto)* 12 from Huddersfield.—Population 10,665.

SAIL-HILL, in the parish of Drax, wapentake of Barkston-Ash; 4 miles from Selby, 4 from Snaith, 6 from Howden.

SAINT ANNS, *in the Grove*, in the parish of Halifax, Morley-division of the wapentake of Agbrigg and Morley; 3 miles from Halifax, 8 from Huddersfield.

SALLAY-ABBEY, in the parish of Gisburn, west-division of the wapentake and liberty of Staincliffe; 3 miles from Clitheroe, *(Lanc.)* 12 from Colne, *(ditto)* 15¼ from Skipton.—Population 552.

SALTERFORTH, in the parish of Barnoldswick, east-division of the wapentake and liberty of Staincliffe; 4 miles from Colne, *(Lanc.)* 8 from Skipton, 10 from Burnley, *(Lanc.)*—Population 398.

SALTERHEBBLE, in the parish of Halifax, Morley-division of the wapentake of Agbrigg and Morley; 1¼ mile from Halifax, 6¼ from Huddersfield.

SALTERSBROOK, in the parish of Penistone, wapentake of Staincross, liberty of the Honour of Pontefract; 7¼ miles from Penistone, 14 from Barnsley, 17¼ from Stockport, *(Chesh.)*

SANDALL, in the parish of Sandall, Agbrigg-division of the wapentake of Agbrigg and Morley, liberties of the Manor of Wakefield and Honour of Pontefract; *(the seat of the Rev. Thomas Zouch, D. D.)* 2 miles from Wakefield, 8½ from Barnsley, 9 from Pontefract.—Population 765.

SANDALL, KIRK, in the parish of Kirk-Sandall, south-division of the wapentake of Strafforth and Tickhill; *(the seat of George Martin, Esq.)* 4½ miles from Doncaster, 6½ from Thorne.—Population 156.

SANDALL, PARVA, or LONG-SANDALL, in the parishes of Doncaster and Kirk-Sandall, south-division of the wapentake of Strafforth and Tickhill, soke of Doncaster; 3

miles from Doncaster, 8¼ from Thorne.—Population 107.

SANDALL-THREE-HOUSES, in the parish of Sandall, Agbrigg-division of the wapentake of Agbrigg and Morley, liberties of the Manor of Wakefield and Honour of Pontefract; 2½ miles from Wakefield, 7¼ from Barnsley.

SAND-BECK, in the parish of Spofforth, upper-division of the wapentake of Claro; 1 mile from Wetherby, 6¼ from Knaresborough.

SANDBECK, in the parish of Maltby, south-division of the wapentake of Strafforth and Tickhill, liberty of Tickhill; *(the seat of the Earl of Scarborough)* 2½ miles from Tickhill, 6 from Bawtry, 9 from Rotherham.

SAND-GATE, in the parish of Sheffield, south-division of the wapentake of Strafforth and Tickhill, liberty of Hallamshire; 3 miles from Sheffield, 9 from Rotherham, 13 from Bakewell, *(Derb.)*

SANTINLEY, in the parish of Wragby, wapentake of Staincross, liberty of the Honour of Pontefract; 5 miles from Wakefield, 7 from Barnsley, 8 from Pontefract.

SAVILE-HOUSE, in the parish of Penistone, wapentake of Staincross, liberty of the Honour of Pontefract; 4 miles from Penistone, 11 from Barnsley, 12 from Huddersfield.

SAWLEY, in the parish of Ripon, lower-division of the wapentake of Claro, liberty of Ripon; *(Sawley-Hall, the seat of Conyers Norton, Esq.)* 6 miles from Ripon, 6 from Pateleybridge.—Population 438.

SAW-WOOD, in the parish of Halifax, Morley-division of the wapentake of Agbrigg and Morley; 5 miles from Huddersfield, 5¼ from Halifax.

SAXTON, in the parish of Saxton, wapentake of Barkston-Ash, liberty of the Honour of Pontefract; 4 miles from Tadcaster, 9 from Ferrybridge, 11 from Pontefract.—Population 362.

SCALES, in the parish of Weston, upper-division of the wapentake of Claro; 5 miles from Otley, 12 from Knaresborough, 15 from Leeds.

SCALES, in the parish of Long-Preston, west-division of the wapentake and liberty of Staincliffe; 6¼ miles from Settle, 12 from Skipton.

SCAMMONDEN, *see Dean-Head.*

SCARCROFT, in the parish of Thorner, lower-division of the wapentake of Skirack; 4 miles from Leeds, 7 from Wetherby, 14 from Otley.—Population 659.

SCARO, in the parish of Ripley, lower-division of the wapentake of Claro; ½ a mile from Ripley, 6¼ from Ripon, 8¼ from Pateleybridge.

SCARTHINGWELL, in the parish of Saxton, wapentake of Barkston-Ash, liberty of the Honour of Pontefract; *(Scarthingwell-Hall, the seat of Lord Hawke)* 5 miles from Tadcaster, 8 from Ferrybridge, 10 from Pontefract.

SCHOLES, in the parish of Barwick-in-Elmet, lower-division of the wapentake of Skirack; 5 miles from Leeds, 7 from Wetherby, 14 from Otley.

SCHOLES, in the parish of Birstall, Morley-division of the wapentake of Agbrigg and Morley; 5 miles from Halifax, 11 from Wakefield, 11 from Leeds.

SCHOLES, in the parish of Halifax, Morley-division of the wapentake of Agbrigg and Morley, liberty of the Honour of Pontefract; 4¼ miles from Halifax, 5¼ from Bradford.

SCHOLES, in the parish of Rotherham, north-division of the wapentake of Strafforth and Tickhill, liberty of Tickhill; 3 miles from Rotherham, 9½ from Barnsley.

SCHOLES-CARR, in the parish of Kirk-Burton, Agbrigg-division of the wapentake of Agbrigg and Morley, liberty of the Manor of Wakefield; 6 miles from Huddersfield, 8 from Penistone.

SCHOLES-PLAIN, in the parish of Barwick-in-Elmet, lower-division of the wapentake of Skirack; 5 miles from Leeds, 7¼ from Wetherby.

SCHOLES-MOOR, in the parish of Bradford, Morley-division of the wapentake of Agbrigg and Morley; 2 miles from Bradford, 6 from Halifax.

SCOLE-HILL, in the parish of Penistone, wapentake of Staincross, liberty of the Honour of Pontefract; ¼ a mile from Penistone, 7¼ from Barnsley, 13 from Huddersfield.

SCORESBY-HALL, in the parish of Brodsworth, north-division of the wapentake of Strafforth and Tickhill; 3 miles from Doncaster, 12 from Barnsley.

SCOSTROP, in the parish of Kirkby-Malhamdale, west-division of the wapentake of Staincliffe, liberty of Clifford's Fee; 6 miles from Settle, 8½ from Skipton, 11½ from Kettlewell.—Population 90.

SCOTLAND, in the parish of Guiseley, upper-division of the wapentake of Skirack; 4 miles from Otley, 6 from Leeds, 7 from Bradford.

SCOTTON, in the parish of Farnham, lower-division of the wapentake of Claro, liberty of Knaresborough; 2 miles from Knaresborough, 3 from Ripley, 8 from Ripon.—Population 220.

SCRIVEN, in the parish of Knaresborough, lower-division of the wapentake of Claro, liberty of Knaresborough; *(the seat of Sir Thomas Turner Slingsby, Bart.)* 1 mile from

WEST-RIDING.

Knaresborough, 6 from Boroughbridge, 11 from Ripon.—Population 814.

SCURFF, in the parish of Drax, wapentake of Barkston-Ash; 5 miles from Snaith, 8 from Selby.

SEACROFT, in the parish of Whitchurch, lower-division of the wapentake of Skirack, liberty of the Honour of Pontefract; *(the seat of —— Micklethwaite, Esq.)* 4¼ miles from Leeds, 8 from Wetherby, 10 from Tadcaster.—Population 70.

SEDBERGH, in the parish of Sedbergh, wapentake of Ewcross; 5 miles from Dent, 10 from Kendal, *(Westm.)* 13 from Kirby-Stephen, *(ditto)* 19 from Askrigg, 25 from Lancaster, *(Lanc.)* 77 from York, 265 from London.—*Market*, Wednesday.—*Fairs*, March 20, October 29, for Horned Cattle, &c.—*Principal Inn*, King's Arms.—Population 1,639.

SEGSWORTH, in the parish of Kirby-Malzeard, lower-division of the wapentake of Claro; 2½ miles from Pateley-bridge, 10 from Masham.

SELBY, in the parish of Selby, wapentake of Barkston-Ash, a part in the liberty of St. Peter; 8 miles from Snaith, 10 from Howden, 11 from Ferrybridge, 12½ from Tadcaster, 13 from Pontefract, 15 from York, 18 from Market-Weighton, 20 from Leeds, 183 from London.—*Market*, Monday.—*Fairs*, Easter Tuesday, the Monday after Boroughbridge Barnabas Fair, and old Michaelmas-day, for Horses, Horned Cattle, Sheep, &c. the Horse Show commences September 20, and ends on the 26th; Line Fairs are on Thursday every Six Weeks, from Michaelmas to St. Peter's-day, old Style.—*Bankers*, Messrs. Seatons and Fosters, draw on Messrs. Kensington, Styan, and Adams, 20, Lombard Street.—*Principal Inns*, George, and King's Head.—Population 2,861.

SELSIDE, in the parish of Horton, wapentake of Ewcross; 9 miles from Settle, 13 from Kirby-Lonsdale, *(Westm.)*

SETTLE, in the parish of Giggleswick, west-division of the wapentake and liberty of Staincliffe; 12 miles from Gisburn, 16 from Skipton, 15 from Kettlewell, 17¼ from Kirby-Lonsdale, *(Westm.)* 21 from Dent, 24 from Askrigg, 57 from York, 235 from London.—*Market*, Tuesday.—*Fairs*, April 26, Whit-Tuesday, August 18, 19, and 20, Tuesday after October 27, and every other Friday from Easter to Whitsuntide, for Lean Cattle, and every other Monday through the year for Fat Cattle, &c.—*Bankers*, Craven Bank, Messrs. Birkbecks, Alcock, Peart, and Smith, draw on Messrs. Dimsdale, Barnard, and Co. 50 Cornhill.—

Principal Inns, Golden Lion, and Spread Eagle.—Population 1,136.

SHACKLETON, in the parish of Halifax, Morley-division of the wapentake of Agbrigg and Morley, liberty of the Manor of Wakefield; 8 miles from Halifax, 12 from Rochdale, (*Lanc.*)

SHADWELL, in the parish of Thorner, lower-division of the wapentake of Skirack, liberty of the Honour of Pontefract; 4 miles from Leeds, 8 from Wetherby, 14 from Otley.—Population 141.

SHAFTHOLME, in the parish of Arksey, north-division of the wapentake of Strafforth and Tickhill, liberty of Tickhill; 5 miles from Doncaster, 8 from Thorne.

SHAFTON, in the parish of Felkirk, wapentake of Staincross, liberty of the Honour of Pontefract; 5 miles from Barnsley, 7 from Wakefield, 9 from Pontefract.—Pop. 174.

SHARLESTONE, or CHARLSTON, in the parish of Warmfield, Agbrigg-division of the wapentake of Agbrigg and Morley, liberty of the Honour of Pontefract; (*the seat of the Earl of Westmoreland*) 4¼ miles from Wakefield, 5¼ from Pontefract.—Population 179.

SHAROW, in the parish of Ripon, lower-division of the wapentake of Claro, liberty of Ripon; 1 mile from Ripon, 6 from Boroughbridge.—Population 106.

SHARROWHEAD, in the parish of Sheffield, south-division of the wapentake of Strafforth and Tickhill; (*the seat of the Rev. Alex. Mackenzie*) 1¾ mile from Sheffield, 7¼ from Rotherham, 11 from Chesterfield, (*Derb.*)

SHAW-CROSS, in the parish of Dewsbury, Agbrigg-division of the wapentake of Agbrigg and Morley; 2 miles from Dewsbury, 3 from Wakefield.

SHAW-HALL, in the parish of Rochdale, (*Lanc.*) Agbrigg-division of the wapentake of Agbrigg and Morley; 9 miles from Rochdale, (*Lanc.*) 12 from Manchester, (*ditto*) 14 from Huddersfield.

SHEEP-HOUSE, in the parish of Penistone, wapentake of Staincross, liberty of the Honour of Pontefract; 2 miles from Penistone, 8 from Barnsley, 12 from Sheffield.

SHEEP-WASH, in the parish of Giggleswick, west-division of the wapentake and liberty of Staincliffe; 3 miles from Settle, 16 from Skipton.

SHEFFIELD, in the parish of Sheffield, south-division of the wapentake of Strafforth and Tickhill, liberty of Hallamshire; 6 miles from Rotherham, 12 from Chesterfield, (*Derb.*) 13¼ from Penistone, 14 from Barnsley, 18 from Worksop, (*Notts.*) 21 from Mansfield, (*ditto*) 24 from

Buxton, *(Derb.)* 54 from York, 162 from London.—*Markets*, Tuesday and Saturday.—*Fairs*, Monday after Whit-sun Week, and November 28, for Horses, Horned Cattle, &c.—*Bankers*, Sheffield Bank, Messrs. I. and W. Shore, and Co. draw on Messrs. Ransom, Morland, and Co. 56, Pall Mall; Sheffield and Rotherham Bank, Messrs. Walker, Eyre, and Stanley, draw on Messrs. Downe, Thornton, and Co. 1, Bartholomew Lane.—*Principal Inns*, Tontine, Angel, Commercial, King's Head, and Hotel.— Population 31,314.

SHEFFIELD, LITTLE, in the parish of Sheffield, south-division of the wapentake of Strafforth and Tickhill, liberty of Hallamshire; 1¼ mile from Sheffield, 7 from Rotherham.

SHEFFIELD-MANOR, in the parish of Sheffield, south-division of the wapentake of Strafforth and Tickhill, liberty of Hallamshire; *(the seat of the Duke of Norfolk)* 2 miles from Sheffield, 8 from Rotherham.

SHELFE, in the parish of Halifax, Morley-division of the wapentake of Agbrigg and Morley, liberty of the Manor of Wakefield; 3¾ miles from Halifax, 4¼ from Bradford, 12¼ from Leeds.—Population 1,306.

SHELLEY, in the parish of Kirk-Burton, Agbrigg-division of the wapentake of Agbrigg and Morley, liberty of the Manor of Wakefield; 6 miles from Huddersfield, 7½ from Penistone.—Population 416.

SHEPLEY, in the parish of Bradford, Morley-division of the wapentake of Agbrigg and Morley, liberties of the Honour of Pontefract and Manor of Wakefield; *(the seats of William Wainman, Esq. and the Rev. John Shepley)* 3 miles from Bradford, 11 from Leeds.—Population 1,008.

SHEPLEY, NETHER, in the parish of Kirk-Burton, Agbrigg-division of the wapentake of Agbrigg and Morley; 6¼ miles from Penistone, 6½ from Huddersfield.—Pop. 619.

SHEPLEY, OVER, in the parish of Kirk-Burton, Agbrigg-division of the wapentake of Agbrigg and Morley, liberty of the Manor of Wakefield; 5 miles from Penistone, 7¼ from Huddersfield.—Population 610.

SHERBURN, in the parish of Sherburn, wapentake of Barkston-Ash, a part in the liberty of St. Peter; 3¼ miles from Abberford, 6 from Ferrybridge, 7 from Tadcaster, 7 from Pontefract, 8 from Selby, 12¼ from Leeds, 15 from York, 183 from London.—*Market*, Friday.—*Fair*, September 25, for Horses, Line, &c.—*Principal Inn*, Red-Bear.—Population 953.

SHERWOOD-HALL, in the parish of Kellington, wapentake of Osgoldcross, liberty of the Honour of Pontefract; 6 miles from Snaith, 7 from Pontefract.

SHIPSCARR, in the parish of Leeds, lower-division of the wapentake of Skirack; 1 mile from Leeds, 5 from Harewood.

SHIRE-GREEN, in the parish of Ecclesfield, north-division of the wapentake of Strafforth and Tickhill; 3 miles from Sheffield, 4 from Rotherham, 11 from Barnsley.

SHIRTCLIFFE-HALL, in the parish of Ecclesfield, north-division of the wapentake of Strafforth and Tickhill; 2 miles from Sheffield, 8 from Rotherham, 12½ from Barnsley.

SHITLINGTON-MIDDLE, in the parish of Thornhill, Agbrigg-division of the wapentake of Agbrigg and Morley, liberty of the Manor of Wakefield; 3 miles from Dewsbury, 4 from Wakefield.—Population 1,166.

SHITLINGTON, NETHER, in the parish of Thornhill, Agbrigg-division of the wapentake of Agbrigg and Morley, liberty of the Honour of Pontefract; 4 miles from Dewsbury, 4 from Wakefield.

SHITLINGTON, OVER, in the parish of Thornhill, Agbrigg-division of the wapentake of Agbrigg and Morley, liberty of the Honour of Pontefract; 4 miles from Dewsbury, 4¼ from Wakefield, 8¼ from Huddersfield.

SHOOTER'S-HILL, in the parish of Rossington, south-division of the wapentake of Strafforth and Tickhill, soke of Doncaster; *(the seat of Michael Humble, Esq.)* 3¾ miles from Bawtry, 6 from Doncaster.

SICKLINGHALL, in the parish of Kirkby-Overblow, upper-division of the wapentake of Claro; 3 miles from Wetherby, 5 from Harewood, 6 from Knaresborough.—Population 230.

SIGSWORTH, in the parish of Ecclesfield, north-division of the wapentake of Strafforth and Tickhill; 3 miles from Sheffield, 5 from Rotherham, 11 from Barnsley.

SILKSTON, in the parish of Silkston, wapentake of Staincross, liberty of the Honour of Pontefract; 4 miles from Barnsley, 4½ from Penistone, 10½ from Wakefield.—Population 542.

SILSDEN, in the parish of Kildwick, east-division of the wapentake and liberty of Staincliffe; 4 miles from Keighley, 7 from Skipton, 12 from Colne, *(Lanc.)*—Pop. 1,323.

SILSDEN-MOOR, in the parish of Kildwick, east-division of the wapentake and liberty of Staincliffe; 4 miles from Skipton, 6 from Keighley.

SKELBROOK, in the parish of South-Kirkby, wapentake of Osgoldcross, liberty of the Honour of Pontefract; *(the seat of Dawson Humble, Esq,)* 7 miles from Ferrybridge,

7¼ from Pontefract, 8 from Doncaster, 12 from Barnsley.
—Population 91.

SKELDA, in the parish of Gisburn, west-division of the wapentake and liberty of Staincliffe; 8 miles from Skipton, 8¼ from Colne, *(Lanc.)* 11½ from Clitheroe, *(ditto.)*

SKELDEN, in the parish of Kirby-Malzeard, lower-division of the wapentake of Claro; 5 miles from Ripon, 8 from Masham.

SKELDERSLOW, in the parish of Rochdale, *(Lanc.)* Agbrigg-division of the wapentake of Agbrigg and Morley; 8 miles from Rochdale, *(Lanc.)* 10 from Manchester, *(ditto)* 15 from Huddersfield.

SKELLANDS, or SKELLINS, in the parish of Kirkby-Malhamdale, west-division of the wapentake and liberty of Staincliffe; 7 miles from Settle, 9 from Skipton, 11 from Kettlewell.

SKELLOW, in the parish of Owston, wapentake of Osgoldcross, liberty of the Honour of Pontefract; 5 miles from Doncaster, 10 from Pontefract.—Population 105.

SKELLOW-GRANGE, in the parish of Owston, wapentake of Osgoldcross, liberty of the Honour of Pontefract; *(the seat of Godfrey Higgins, Esq.)* 6 miles from Doncaster, 9 from Pontefract

SKELMANTHORPE, in the parishes of High-Hoyland and Elmley, Agbrigg-division of the wapentake of Agbrigg and Morley; 8 miles from Huddersfield, 8 from Wakefield. —Population 309.

SKELTON, in the parish of Ripon, lower-division of the wapentake of Claro, liberty of Ripon; 2½ miles from Boroughbridge, 3¼ from Ripon.—Population 240.

SKELTON, in the parish of Leeds, lower-division of the wawapentake of Skirack; 1 mile from Leeds, 9 from Wakefield, 12 from Ferrybridge.

SKIBEDEN, in the parish of Skipton, east-division of the wapentake and liberty of Staincliffe; 2½ miles from Skipton, 13½ from Otley.

SKIERS-HALL, in the parish of Wath-upon-Dearn, north-division of the wapentake of Strafforth and Tickhill; 6 miles from Rotherham, 6 from Barnsley, 6 from Sheffield.

SKIERS-MOOR, in the parish of Darton, wapentake of Staincross, liberty of the Honour of Pontefract; 1¼ mile from Barnsley, 9 from Wakefield.

SKIP-BRIDGE, in the parish of Kirk-Hammerton, lower-division of the wapentake of Claro, and Ainsty; 8¼ miles from Boroughbridge, 8¼ from York.

SKIPTON, in the parish of Skipton, east-division of the wapentake of Staincliffe, liberty of Clifford's Fee; *(Skipton-Castle, the seat of the Earl of Thanet)* 10 miles from Keighley, 11¼ from Gisburn, 12 from Colne, *(Lanc.)* 13 from Hopper-Lane-Inn, 15 from Otley, 16 from Settle, 16 from Kettlewell, 41 from York, 220 from London.—*Market*, Saturday.—*Fairs*, first Saturday after the Old-twelfth-day, called Black-Saturday, March 13, Saturday before Palm-Sunday, Tuesday in Easter-week, and every other Tuesday until Whitsuntide, for Lean-Cattle; Saturday before Whitsun-eve, Saturday before Trinity-Sunday, Old St. James's day, and Martinmas-day, viz. Nov. 21 and 23, and every other Tuesday through the year, for Fat-Cattle, &c.—*Bankers*, Messrs. Chippendale, Netherwood, and Carr, draw on Messrs. Masterman, Peters, Walker, and Co. 2, White-hart-Court, Gracechurch-Street.—*Principal Inns*, New-Inn and Black-Horse.—Population 2,305.

SKIERAM, or SKIREHOLME, in the parish of Burnsall, east-division of the wapentake and liberty of Staincliffe; 7 miles from Pateleybridge, 8 from Skipton.

SKIRCOTE, in the parish of Halifax, Morley-division of the wapentake of Agbrigg and Morley, liberty of the Manor of Wakefield; 1½ mile from Halifax, 7¼ from Huddersfield, 9¼ from Bradford.—Population 2,338.

SKIRDEN-HALL, in the parish of Bolton, west-division of the wapentake and liberty of Staincliffe; 9 miles from Settle, 14 from Skipton.

SKYRETHORNES, in the parish Linton, east-division of the wapentake and liberty of Staincliffe; 6 miles from Kettlewell, 10 from Skipton, 11¼ from Pateleybridge.

SLADES, in the parish of Rochdale, *(Lanc.)* Agbrigg-division of the wapentake of Agbrigg and Morley; 9 miles from from Rochdale, *(Lanc.)* 12 from Manchester, *(ditto)* 12 from Huddersfield.

SLAIDBURN, or SLATEBURN, in the parish of Slaidburn, west-division of the wapentake of Staincliffe, liberty of Bolland; 9 miles from Clitheroe, *(Lanc.)* 12 from Settle, 19 from Lancaster, *(Lanc.)* 20 from Skipton,—Pop. 631.

SLATENBERG, in the parish of Low-Bentham, wapentake of Ewcross; 8½ miles from Kirby-Lonsdale, *(Westm.)* 9¼ from Settle.

SLAUGHWAITE, in the parish of Huddersfield, Agbrigg-division of the wapentake of Agbrigg and Morley, liberty of the Honour of Pontefract; 4 miles from Huddersfield, 12 from Halifax, 20 from Manchester, *(Lanc.)*—Pop. 2,007.

SLENINGFORD, in the parish of Ripon, lower-division of the wapentake of Claro, liberty of Ripon; *(the seat of John*

WEST-RIDING. 273

Dalton, Esq.) 4 miles from Ripon, 5½ from Masham.

SMALL-FIELD, in the parish of Ecclesfield, north-division of the wapentake of Strafforth and Tickhill; 4 miles from Sheffield, 10 from Barnsley, 10 from Rotherham.

SMALL-SHAW, in the parish of Penistone, wapentake of Staincross, liberty of the Honour of Pontefract; 3 miles from Penistone, 10 from Barnsley, 11 from Huddersfield.

SMAWS-HALL, in the parish of Tadcaster, wapentake of Barkston-Ash; 1 mile from Tadcaster, 7 from Wetherby.

SMEATON, KIRK, in the parish of Kirk-Smeaton, wapentake of Osgoldcross, liberty of the Honour of Pontefract; 6 miles from Pontefract, 6 from Ferrybridge, 10 from Doncaster, 14 from Wakefield.—Population 248.

SMEATON, LITTLE, in the parish of Womersley, wapentake of Osgoldcross, liberty of the Honour of Pontefract; 6 miles from Ferrybridge, 6½ from Pontefract, 10 from Doncaster.—Population 179.

SMIDLEY, in the parish of Darfield, north-division of the wapentake of Strafforth and Tickhill; 3 miles from Barnsley, 9 from Rotherham.

SMITHY-BROOK, in the parish of Thornhill, Agbrigg-division of the wapentake of Agbrigg and Morley; 3 miles from Dewsbury, 5 from Wakefield.

SMITHY-MILL, in the parish of Royston, wapentake of Staincross, liberty of the Honour of Pontefract; 2 miles from Barnsley, 8 from Wakefield, 8½ from Penistone.

SMITHYS, in the parish of Kirk-Heaton, Agbrigg-division of the wapentake of Agbrigg and Morley; 3 miles from Huddersfield, 10¼ from Wakefield.

SMOLLIDGE, in the parish of Fishlake, north-division of the wapentake of Strafforth and Tickhill; 4 miles from Thorne, 9 from Snaith.

SNAITH, in the parish of Snaith, wapentake of Osgoldcross, liberty of the Honour of Pontefract; 7 miles from Thorne, 8 from Selby, 10 from Howden, 11 from Ferrybridge, 13 from Pontefract, 23 from York, 175 from London.—*Market*, Thursday.—*Fairs*, Last Thursday in April for Horned Cattle, Sheep, and Woollen-Cloth; August 10, for Horned Cattle, Woollen-Cloth, Line, Cheese, and Quills; last Thursday in September is Chartered, but not now attended.—*Principal-Inns*, Blue Bell, Black Lion, Bell and Crown, and Green Dragon.—Population 688.

SNAYGILL, in the parish of Skipton, east-division of the wapentake and liberty of Staincliffe; 1 mile from Skipton, 9 from Keighley.

SNIDALL, in the parish of Normanton, Agbrigg-division of

the wapentake of Agbrigg and Morley, liberty of the Honour of Pontefract; *(the seat of James Torre, Esq.)* 3½ miles from Pontefract, 6 from Wakefield.—Pop. 127.

SNOWDON-HILL, in the parish of Penistone, wapentake of Staincross, liberty of the Honour of Pontefract; 2 miles from Penistone, 7 from Barnsley, 11 from Sheffield.

SNOWDON, LOWER, in the parish of Weston, upper-division of the wapentake of Claro; 5 miles from Otley, 12 from Knaresborough.

SNOWDON, UPPER, in the parish of Weston, upper-division of the wapentake of Claro; 5½ miles from Otley, 12 from Knaresborough.

SOFTLEY, in the parish of Penistone, wapentake of Staincross, liberty of the Honour of Pontefract; 4 miles from Penistone, 11 from Barnsley, 12 from Huddersfield.

SOOLBANK, in the parish of Sedbergh, wapentake of Ewcross; 5 miles from Dent, 11 from Kirby-Lonsdale, *(Westm.)* 11 from Kendal, *(ditto.)*

SOOTHILL, UPPER, and NETHER, in the parish of Dewsbury, Agbrigg-division of the wapentake of Agbrigg and Morley, liberty of the Manor of Wakefield; 2 miles from Dewsbury, 4 from Wakefield, 12 from Halifax, 12 from Leeds.—Population 2,134.

SOUTHEY-GREEN, in the parish of Ecclesfield, north-division of the wapentake of Strafforth and Tickhill; 3 miles from Sheffield, 5 from Rotherham, 11 from Barnsley.

SOUTHOWRAM, *see Owram, South.*

SOUTH-WANG, in the parish of Tickhill, south-division of the wapentake of Strafforth and Tickhill; 1¼ mile from Tickhill, 7¼ from Worksop, *(Notts.)* 8¼ from Doncaster.

SOWERBY, in the parish of Halifax, Morley-division of the wapentake of Agbrigg and Morley, liberties of the Honour of Pontefract and Manor of Wakefield; 3 miles from Halifax, 11 from Bradford.—Population 4,275.

SOWERBY-BRIDGE, in the parish of Halifax, Morley-division of the wapentake of Agbrigg and Morley; 2¼ miles from Halifax, 8 from Huddersfield, 13¼ from Rochdale, *(Lanc.)*

SOYLAND, in the parish of Halifax, Morley-division of the wapentake of Agbrigg and Morley, liberty of the Manor of Wakefield; 4¼ miles from Halifax, 10½ from Huddersfield, 11¼ from Rochdale, *(Lanc.)*—Population 1,888.

SOYLAND-MILL, in the parish of Halifax, Morley-division of the wapentake of Agbrigg and Morley, liberty of the Manor of Wakefield; 4 miles from Halifax, 12 from Rochdale, *(Lanc.)*

SPACEY-HOUSE, in the parish of Pannall, lower-division of the wapentake of Claro; 5 miles from Knaresborough, 7¼ from Ripley, 13 from Leeds.

SPARK-HAGG, in the parish of Selby, wapentake of Barkston-Ash; 1¼ mile from Selby, 12 from Tadcaster.

SPEN-HALL, in the parish of Birstall, Morley-division of the wapentake of Agbrigg and Morley; 7½ miles from Halifax, 8¼ from Leeds.

SPICER-HILL, in the parish of Penistone, wapentake of Staincross, liberty of the Honour of Pontefract; 3 miles from Penistone, 10 from Barnsley, 11 from Huddersfield.

SPINK-WELL, in the parish of Dewsbury, Morley-division of the wapentake of Agbrigg and Morley; 6½ miles from Wakefield, 10 from Halifax, 10 from Bradford.

SPITTAL, in the parish of Wath-upon-Dearn, north-division of the wapentake of Strafforth and Tickhill; 5 miles from Rotherham, 7 from Barnsley.

SPITTAL-CROFT, in the parish of Arnecliffe, west-division of the wapentake and liberty of Staincliffe; 8½ miles from Kettlewell, 12 from Settle.

SPITTAL-HILL, in the parish of Tickhill, south-division of the wapentake of Strafforth and Tickhill; 1 mile from Tickhill, 3 from Bawtry, 7 from Doncaster.

SPOFFORTH, in the parish of Spofforth, upper-division of the wapentake of Claro; *(the seat of the Rev. John Trip, L.L.D.)* 3 miles from Wetherby, 4 from Knaresborough.—Population 859.

SPOFFORTH-HAGGS, or HAGSIDE, in the parish of Spofforth, upper-division of the wapentake of Claro; 4 miles from Knaresborough, 4¼ from Wetherby.

SPRING-HOUSE, in the parish of Kirby-Malzeard, lower-division of the wapentake of Claro; 3¼ miles from Ripley, 5¼ from Pateleybridge.

SPROTBROUGH, in the parish of Sprotbrough, north-division of the wapentake of Strafforth and Tickhill, liberty of Tickhill; *(the seat of Sir James Copley, Bart.)* 3¼ miles from Doncaster, 12 from Barnsley.—Population 250.

STACK-HOUSE, in the parish of Giggleswick, west-division of the wapentake and liberty of Staincliffe; 1 mile from Settle, 17 from Skipton, 17 from Kirby-Lonsdale, *(Westm.)*

STAINBROUGH, in the parish of Silkston, wapentake of Staincross, liberty of the Honour of Pontefract; 2¼ miles from Barnsley, 5½ from Penistone, 7½ from Wakefield.—Population 227.

STAINBURN, in the parish of Kirkby-Overblow, upper-division of the wapentake of Claro; 4¼ miles from Otley, 9 from Knaresborough.—Population 311.

STAINBURN-MOOR-SIDE, in the parish of Kirkby-Overblow, upper-division of the wapentake of Claro; 4¼ miles from Otley, 9 from Knaresborough.

STAINCROSS, *(which gives name to the wapentake)* in the parish of Darton, wapentake of Staincross, liberty of the Honour of Pontefract; 3¼ miles from Barnsley, 7 from Penistone, 7 from Wakefield.

STAINFORTH, in the parish of Hatfield, south-division of the wapentake of Strafforth and Tickhill, a part in the liberty of St. Peter; 3½ miles from Thorne, 7½ from Doncaster.—Population 472.

STAINFORTH, GREAT, in the parish of Giggleswick, west-division of the wapentake and liberty of Staincliffe; 2¼ miles from Settle, 14 from Kettlewell, 18 from Skipton, 21¼ from Askrigg.—Population 203.

STAINFORTH, LITTLE, or KNIGHT-STAINFORTH, in the parish of Giggleswick, west-division of the wapentake and liberty of Staincliffe; 2 miles from Settle, 14¼ from Kettlewell, 17½ from Skipton.

STAINLAND, in the parish of Halifax, Morley-division of the wapentake of Agbrigg and Morley, liberty of the Manor of Wakefield; 5 miles from Halifax, 5 from Huddersfield.—Population 1,800.

STAINLEY, NORTH, in the parish of Ripon, lower-division of the wapentake of Claro, liberty of Ripon; 3¼ miles from Ripon, 6 from Masham, 10 from Bedale.—Pop. 315.

STAINLEY, SOUTH, in the parish of South-Stainley, lower-division of the wapentake of Claro, liberty of Knaresborough; 2¼ miles from Ripley, 5 from Ripon, 6 from Knaresborough.—Population 217.

STAINSCLIFFE-MOOR, in the parish of Batley, Agbrigg-division of the wapentake of Agbrigg and Morley; 2 miles from Dewsbury, 8 from Wakefield, 8 from Halifax.

STAINSCROFT, or TAMECROFT, in the parish of Rochdale, *(Lanc.)* Agbrigg-division of the wapentake of Agbrigg and Morley; 7 miles from Rochdale, *(Lanc.)* 12 from Manchester, *(ditto)* 13 from Huddersfield.

STAINTON, in the parish of Stainton, south-division of the wapentake of Strafforth and Tickhill; 2 miles from Tickhill, 6 from Bawtry, 9 from Rotherham.—Population 151.

STAINTON-COTES, in the parish of Gargrave, east-division of the wapentake and liberty of Staincliffe; 7 miles from Skipton, 10 from Settle.

STAIRFOOT, in the parish of Darfield, wapentake of Staincross, liberty of the Honour of Pontefract; 2 miles from Barnsley, 8 from Penistone, 9 from Rotherham.

WEST-RIDING.

STANBURY, in the parish of Bradford, Morley-division of the wapentake of Agbrigg and Morley; 7 miles from Keighley, 8¼ from Bradford, 8¼ from Colne, *(Lanc.)*

STAND-BRIDGE, in the parish of Sandall, Agbrigg-division of the wapentake of Agbrigg and Morley; 3 miles from Wakefield, 7 from Barnsley.

STANDSFIELD, in the parish of Halifax, Morley-division of the wapentake of Agbrigg and Morley, liberty of the Manor of Wakefield; 4 miles from Halifax, 7 from Huddersfield.—Population 4,768.

STANNINGLEY, in the parish of Calverley, Morley division of the wapentake of Agbrigg and Morley; 3¼ miles from Bradford, 6 from Leeds.

STANNINGTON, in the parish of Ecclesfield, north-division of the wapentake of Strafforth and Tickhill; 4 miles from Sheffield, 10 from Rotherham, 12 from Penistone.

STANK-HOUSE, in the parish of Barwick-in-Elmet, lower-division of the wapentake of Skirack; 3 miles from Abberford, 7 from Leeds, 10 from Tadcaster.

STANLEY, in the parish of Wakefield, Agbrigg-division of the wapentake of Agbrigg and Morley, liberty of the Manor of Wakefield; 1 mile from Wakefield, 8 from Leeds, 14 from Huddersfield.—Population 3,260.

STANLEY-HALL, in the parish of Wakefield, Agbrigg-division of the wapentake of Agbrigg and Morley, liberty of the Manor of Wakefield, *(the seat of Benjamin Haywood, Esq.)* 1½ mile from Wakefield, 6¼ from Leeds.

STANSILL, in the parish of Tickhill, south-division of the wapentake of Strafforth and Tickhill, liberty of Tickhill; 2 miles from Tickhill, 7 from Doncaster, 10 from Rotherham. —Population 46.

STAPLETON, in the parish of Darrington, wapentake of Osgoldcross, liberty of the Honour of Pontefract; *(the seat of Ellis Leckonby Hodgson, Esq.)* 4 miles from Ferrybridge, 4½ from Pontefract, 12 from Doncaster.— Population 101.

STARBOTTOM, in the parsh of Kettlewell, east division of the wapentake and liberty of Staincliffe; 2 miles from Kettlewell, 15 from Leyburn, 17 from Settle.—Pop. 197.

STARTH, in the parish of Slaidburn, west-division of the wapentake and liberty of Staincliffe; 6¼ miles from Clitheroe, *(Lanc.)* 10 from Gisburn.

STAVELEY, in the parish of Staveley, lower-division of the wapentake of Claro, liberty of Knaresborough; 3 miles from Boroughbridge, 4 from Knaresborough.—Pop. 255.

STEAD, in the parish of Wath-upon Dearn, north-division

of the wapentake of Strafforth and Tickhill ; 5¼ miles from Barnsley, 8¼ from Rotherham.

STEAN, in the parish of Kirby-Malzeard, lower-division of the wapentake of Claro ; 9 miles from Pateleybridge, 10 from Kettlewell, 10 from Masham.

STEEL-BANK, in the parish of Sheffield, south-division of the wapentake of Strafforth and Tickhill ; 1¼ mile from Sheffield, 7½ from Rotherham, 13¼ from Chesterfield, *(Derb.)*

STEETON, in the parish of Kildwick, east-division of the wapentake and liberty of Staincliffe; *(Steeton-Hall, the seat of Thomas Garforth, Esq.)* 3 miles from Keighley, 7 from Skipton, 11 from Colne, *(Lanc.)*—Pop. 510.

STEETON-HALL, in the parish of Sherburn, wapentake of Barkston-Ash ; 8 miles from Pontefract, 8 from Tadcaster.

STEPHEN-PARK, in the parish of Slaidburn, west-division of the wapentake and liberty of Staincliffe ; 10 miles from Settle, 18 from Skipton.

STIRK-HOUSE, in the parish of Gisburn, west-division of the wapentake and liberty of Staincliffe ; 12 miles from Skipton, 12 from Settle, 13 from Burnley, *(Lanc.)*

STIRTON, or STRETTON, in the parish of Skipton, east-division of the wapentake and liberty of Staincliffe ; 1¼ mile from Skipton, 12 from Colne, *(Lanc.)* 14½ from Settle.— Population 134.

STOCK, in the parish of Bracewell, east-division of the wapentake of Staincliffe, liberty of Clifford's Fee ; 5¼ miles from Colne, *(Lanc.)* 9¼ from Skipton.

STOCKBRIDGE, in the parish of Arksey, north-division of the wapentake of Strafforth and Tickhill, liberty of Tickhill; 2¼ miles from Doncaster, 10 from Thorne.

STOCKELD, in the parish of Spofforth, upper-division of the wapentake of Claro ; *(Stockeld-Park, the seat of William Middleton, Esq.)* 2 miles from Wetherby, 6 from Knaresborough.

STOCKHILL, in the parish of Ilkley, upper-division of the wapentake of Claro, 6¼ miles from Otley, 9 from Skipton.

STOCKS, in the parish of Slaidburn, west-division of the wapentake and liberty of Staincliffe ; 9 miles from Settle, 12 from Clitheroe, *(Lanc.)*

STOCKWELL-GREEN, in the parish of Sheffield, south-division of the wapentake of Strafforth and Tickhill ; 3 miles from Sheffield, 9 from Rotherham.

STONE, in the parish of Maltby, south-division of the wapentake of Strafforth and Tickhill ; 3 miles from Tickhill, 6 from Bawtry, 8 from Rotherham.

STONE-BECK, DOWN, or NETHER-STAINBECK, in

the parish of Kirby-Malzeard, lower-division of the wapentake of Claro; 5 miles from Pateleybridge, 12 from Ripley, 14 from Ripon.—Population 434.

STONE-BECK, UPPER, in the parish of Kirby-Malzeard, lower-division of the wapentake of Claro; 6 miles from Pateleybridge, 13 from Ripley, 16 from Ripon.—Pop. 304.

STONE-BREAKS, in the parish of Rochdale, *(Lanc.)* Agbrigg-division of the wapentake of Agbrigg and Morley; 8 miles from Rochdale, *(Lanc.)* 10 from Manchester, *(ditto)* 15 from Huddersfield.

STONE-GAP, in the parish of Carlton, east-division of the wapentake and liberty of Staincliffe; *(the seat of William Sedgwick, Esq.)* 4½ miles from Skipton, 7 from Keighley.

STONER-HALL, in the parish of Selby, wapentake of Barkston-Ash; 1¼ mile from Selby, 7¼ from Snaith.

STONE-ROYD, in the parish of Kirk-Heaton, Agbrigg-division of the wapentake of Agbrigg and Morley; 5 miles from Huddersfield, 9 from Wakefield.

STONEY-BANK, in the parish of Slaidburn, west-division of the wapentake and liberty of Staincliffe; 9 miles from Settle, 16 from Skipton.

STORRS, in the parish of Ecclesfield, north-division of the wapentake of Strafforth and Tickhill; 7 miles from Sheffield, 11 from Penistone.

STORRS, in the parish of Silkston, wapentake of Staincross, liberty of the Honour of Pontefract; 3 miles from Penistone, 4 from Barnsley, 11 from Wakefield.

STORRS-HALL, in the parish of Kirk-Heaton, Agbrigg-division of the wapentake of Agbrigg and Morley; 5½ miles from Huddersfield, 12 from Wakefield.

STOTFOLD, or STOTFIELD, in the parish of Hooton-Pagnall, north-division of the wapentake of Strafforth and Tickhill, liberty of Tickhill; 7 miles from Doncaster, 8½ from Barnsley.—Population 8.

STOTT-HILL, in the parish of Kildwick, east-division of the wapentake and liberty of Staincliffe; 5 miles from Colne, *(Lanc.)* 7 from Skipton, 7 from Keighley.

STRAINDS, in the parish of Penistone, wapentake of Staincross, liberty of the Honour of Pontefract; 4 miles from Penistone, 8¼ from Huddersfield.

STRAWHOUSES, in the parish of Ripon, lower-division of the wapentake of Claro; 1¼ mile from Ripon, 8 from Ripley.

STREETHOUSE, in the parish of Normanton, Agbrigg-division of the wapentake of Agbrigg and Morley; 4 miles from Pontefract, 5 from Wakefield.

STREET-FARM, in the parish of Wath-upon-Dearn, north-division of the wapentake of Strafforth and Tickhill; 6 miles from Rotherham, 6 from Barnsley.

STREETSIDE, in the parish of Dewsbury, Agbrigg-division of the wapentake of Agbrigg and Morley; 1¼ mile from Dewsbury, 3¼ from Wakefield.

STREET-THORPE, in the parish of Kirk-Sandall, south-division of the wapentake of Strafforth and Tickhill; 3½ miles from Doncaster, 8¼ from Thorne.

STRINDS, in the parish of Ecclesfield, north-division of the wapentake of Strafforth and Tickhill; 6 miles from Sheffield, 11 from Penistone.

STUBBING, in the parish of Rawmarsh, north-division of the wapentake of Strafforth and Tickhill; 3 miles from Rotherham, 9 from Barnsley.

STUBBING-LANE, in the parish of Rawmarsh, north-division of the wapentake of Strafforth and Tickhill; 3 miles from Rotherham, 10 from Barnsley.

STUBBS, in the parish of Adwick-in-the-Street, north-division of the wapentake of Strafforth and Tickhill; 7 miles from Doncaster, 9¼ from Pontefract, 12¼ from Wakefield.

STUBHAM-LODGE, in the parish of Ilkley, lower-division of the wapentake of Claro; 7 miles from Otley, 9 from Skipton.

STUDFIELD, in the parish of Horton, wapentake of Ewcross; 5 miles from Settle, 18 from Askrigg.

STUDFOLD, in the parish of Kirby-Malzeard, lower-division of the wapentake of Claro; 8 miles from Pateleybridge, 9 from Masham, 11 from Kettlewell.

STUDLEY, in the parish of Ripon, lower-division of the wapentake of Claro, liberty of Ripon; 1¼ mile from Ripon, 7¼ from Boroughbridge, 8 from Ripley.—Pop. 143.

STUDLEY-ROYAL, in the parish of Ripon, lower-division of the wapentake of Claro, liberty of Ripon; *(the seat of Miss Lawrence)* 2 miles from Ripon, 8 from Boroughbridge, 8 from Ripley.

STUMP-CROSS, in the parish of Dewsbury, Agbrigg-division of the wapentake of Agbrigg and Morley; 3¼ miles from Dewsbury, 4 from Wakefield.

STUMPER LOW-HALL, in the parish of Sheffield, south-division of the wapentake of Strafforth and Tickhill; *(the seat of John Oats, Esq.)* 3 miles from Sheffield, 9 from Rotherham, 12 from Chesterfield, *(Derb.)*

STURTON-GRANGE, in the parish of Abberford, lower-division of the wapentake of Skirack; 3 miles from Abberford, 8 from Leeds, 11 from Tadcaster.—Pop. 64.

STUTTON, in the parish of Tadcaster, wapentake of Barkston-Ash, liberty of the Honour of Pontefract; 1 mile from Tadcaster, 11 from Ferrybridge, 13 from Pontefract.—Population 252.

STUTTON-HILL, in the parish of Tadcaster, wapentake of Barkston-Ash, liberty of the Honour of Pontefract; 1 mile from Tadcaster, 11 from Ferrybridge, 13 from Pontefract.

SUMMER-SCALES, in the parish of Skipton, lower-division of the wapentake of Claro; 7 miles from Skipton, 16 from Knaresborough.

SUNLEY-RAINS, in the parish of Ripon, lower-division of the wapentake of Claro; 1¼ mile from Ripon, 9 from Ripley.

SUTTON, in the parish of Ripon, lower-division of the wapentake of Claro, liberty of Ripon; 2 miles from Ripon, 8 from Masham.—Population 103.

SUTTON, in the parish of Brotherton, wapentake of Barkston-Ash, liberty of St. Peter; 1 mile from Ferrybridge, 3 from Pontefract, 12 from Tadcaster.—Pop. 52.

SUTTON, in the parish of Kildwick, east-division of the wapentake of Staincliffe, liberty of Clifford's Fee; 5 miles from Keighley, 5 from Skipton, 9 from Colne, *(Lanc.)*—Population 809.

SUTTON, in the parishes of Campsall and Burghwallis, wapentake of Osgoldcross, liberty of the Honour of Pontefract; 7 miles from Doncaster, 11 from Ferrybridge.—Pop. 179.

SUTTON-GRANGE, in the parish of Ripon, lower-division of the wapentake of Claro; 2 miles from Ripon, 8 from Masham.

SWALLOW-HILL, in the parish of Darton, wapentake of Staincross, liberty of the Honour of Pontefract; 2¼ miles from Barnsley, 5¼ from Penistone, 9 from Wakefield.

SWARTHE-HALL, in the parish of Darfield, wapentake of Staincross, liberty of the Honour of Pontefract; *(the seat of Mrs. Elmhirst)* 2 miles from Barnsley, 9 from Rotherham, 11 from Wakefield.

SWARTHEY, in the parish of Kildwick, east-division of the wapentake and liberty of Staincliffe; 4¼ miles from Keighley, 7¼ from Skipton.

SWETTON, in the parish of Kirby-Malzeard, lower-division of the wapentake of Claro; 7 miles from Masham, 10 from Ripon.

SWIFT-PLACE, in the parish of Halifax, Morley-division of the wapentake of Agbrigg and Morley; 6 miles from Halifax, 8 from Huddersfield.

SWILLINGTON, in the parish of Swillington, lower-division of the wapentake of Skirack, liberty of the Honour of Pontefract; 6 miles from Leeds, 8 from Pontefract, 8 from Wakefield.—Population 491.

SWILLINGTON-HOUSE, in the parish of Swillington, lower-division of the wapentake of Skirack, liberty of the Honour of Pontefract; *(the seat of John Lowther, Esq.)* 6 miles from Leeds, 8 from Pontefract, 8 from Wakefield.

SWINDEN, in the parish of Gisburn, west-division of the wapentake and liberty of Staincliffe; 6¼ miles from Skipton, 11 from Settle, 17 from Colne, *(Lanc.)*—Population 52.

SWINDON, in the parish of Penistone, wapentake of Staincross, liberty of the Honour of Pontefract; 4¼ miles from Penistone, 11¼ from Barnsley, 14 from Sheffield.

SWINDON, in the parish of Kirkby-Overblow, upper-division of the wapentake of Claro; 7 miles from Wetherby, 7 from Knaresborough, 9 from Otley.

SWINDON-HALL, in the parish of Kirkby-Overblow, upper-division of the wapentake of Claro; 7 miles from Wetherby, 7 from Knaresborough, 9 from Otley.

SWINDON-WALLS, in the parish of Penistone, wapentake of Staincross, liberty of the Honour of Pontefract; 4 miles from Penistone, 11 from Barnsley, 14 from Sheffield.

SWINE-LANE, in the parish of Fetherstone, wapentake of Osgoldcross, liberty of the Honour of Pontefract; 1¼ mile from Pontefract; 7½ from Wakefield.

SWINFLEET, in the parish of Whitgift, wapentake of Osgoldcross, liberty of the Honour of Pontefract; 4¼ miles from Howden, 10 from Snaith, 10 from Crowle, *(Linc.)*—Population 632.

SWINNO, in the parish of Spofforth, upper-division of the wapentake of Claro; *(the seat of —— Walker, Esq.)* 1¼ mile from Wetherby, 7 from Tadcaster, 7¼ from Knaresborough.

SWINSTEY-HALL, in the parish of Otley, lower-division of the wapentake of Claro; 6 miles from Otley, 11 from Knaresborough.

SWINTON, in the of parishes of Wath-upon-Dearn and Mexbrough, *alternately*, north-division of the wapentake of Strafforth and Tickhill, liberty of Tickhill; 4 miles from Rotherham, 8 from Doncaster.—Population 437.

SWITHINGS, in the parish of Darton, wapentake of Staincross, liberty of the Honour of Pontefract; 5 miles from Barnsley, 6¼ from Penistone, 7¼ from Wakefield.

SYKEHOUSES, in the parish of Fishlake, north-division of the wapentake of Strafforth and Tickhill; 3 miles from Thorne, 7 from Snaith, 11 from Doncaster.—Pop. 497.

SYKES, in the parish of Slaidburn, west-division of the wapentake and liberty of Staincliffe; 10 miles from Clithroe, *(Lanc.)* 13 from Lancaster, *(ditto.)*

SYKES, in the parish of Kirby-Malzeard, lower-division of the wapentake of Claro; 7 miles from Pateleybridge, 9 from from Masham.

SYM-HILL, in the parish of Silkston, wapentake of Staincross, liberty of the Honour of Pontefract; 3 miles from Penistone, 4¼ from Barnsley, 10 from Sheffield.

T.

TADCASTER, in the parish of Tadcaster, wapentake of Barkston-Ash, and Ainsty, a part in the liberty of St. Peter; 4¼ miles from Abberford, 7 from Wetherby, 9 from York, 12 from Ferrybridge, 12½ from Selby, 14 from Pontefract, 15 from Leeds, 190 from London.—*Market*, Wednesday.—*Fairs*, last Wednesday in April, May, September, and October, for Horned Cattle, Sheep, Pigs, &c.—*Principal Inns*, White-Horse, Rose and Crown, and the Angel.—Population 1,411.

TAME, NEW, in the parish of Rochdale, *(Lanc.)* Agbrigg-division of the wapentake of Agbrigg and Morley; 7 miles from Rochdale, *(Lanc.)* 12 from Manchester, *(ditto)* 13 from Huddersfield.

TAME, OLD, in the parish of Rochdale, *(Lanc.)* Agbrigg-division of the wapentake of Agbrigg and Morley; 6 miles from Rochdale, *(Lanc.)* 11 from Manchester, *(ditto)* 13 from Huddersfield.

TANKERSLEY, in the parish of Tankersley, wapentake of Staincross, liberty of the Honour of Pontefract; 4¼ miles from Barnsley, 6½ from Rotherham, 7 from Penistone.—Population 382.

TANSHELF, in the parish of Pontefract, wapentake of Osgoldcross, liberty of the Honour of Pontefract; adjoins Pontefract.—Population 378.

TAPTON-GROVE, *see Crookes-Moor*.

TEMPLE-NEWSOME, in the parish of Whitchurch, lower-division of the wapentake of Skirack; *(the seat of Viscountess Irvine)* 4¼ miles from Leeds, 8 from Wakefield, 9 from Pontefract.

THACKLEY, in the parish of Calverley, Morley-division of the wapentake of Agbrigg and Morley; 3¼ miles from Bradford, 6 from Otley, 9 from Leeds.

the wapentake of Agbrigg and Morley, liberty of the Honour of Pontefract ; *(the seat of James Torre, Esq.)* 3¼ miles from Pontefract, 6 from Wakefield.—Pop. 127.

SNOWDON-HILL, in the parish of Penistone, wapentake of Staincross, liberty of the Honour of Pontefract ; 2 miles from Penistone, 7 from Barnsley, 11 from Sheffield.

SNOWDON, LOWER, in the parish of Weston, upper-division of the wapentake of Claro ; 5 miles from Otley, 12 from Knaresborough.

SNOWDON, UPPER, in the parish of Weston, upper-division of the wapentake of Claro ; 5½ miles from Otley, 12 from Knaresborough.

SOFTLEY, in the parish of Penistone, wapentake of Staincross, liberty of the Honour of Pontefract ; 4 miles from Penistone, 11 from Barnsley, 12 from Huddersfield.

SOOLBANK, in the parish of Sedbergh, wapentake of Ewcross; 5 miles from Dent, 11 from Kirby-Lonsdale, *(Westm.)* 11 from Kendal, *(ditto.)*

SOOTHILL, UPPER, and NETHER, in the parish of Dewsbury, Agbrigg-division of the wapentake of Agbrigg and Morley, liberty of the Manor of Wakefield ; 2 miles from Dewsbury, 4 from Wakefield, 12 from Halifax, 12 from Leeds.—Population 2,134.

SOUTHEY-GREEN, in the parish of Ecclesfield, north-division of the wapentake of Strafforth and Tickhill ; 3 miles from Sheffield, 5 from Rotherham, 11 from Barnsley.

SOUTHOWRAM, *see Owram, South.*

SOUTH-WANG, in the parish of Tickhill, south-division of the wapentake of Strafforth and Tickhill ; 1¼ mile from Tickhill, 7¼ from Worksop, *(Notts.)* 8¼ from Doncaster.

SOWERBY, in the parish of Halifax, Morley-division of the wapentake of Agbrigg and Morley, liberties of the Honour of Pontefract and Manor of Wakefield ; 3 miles from Halifax, 11 from Bradford.—Population 4,275.

SOWERBY-BRIDGE, in the parish of Halifax, Morley-division of the wapentake of Agbrigg and Morley ; 2¼ miles from Halifax, 8 from Huddersfield, 13¼ from Rochdale, *(Lanc.)*

SOYLAND, in the parish of Halifax, Morley-division of the wapentake of Agbrigg and Morley, liberty of the Manor of Wakefield ; 4¼ miles from Halifax, 10½ from Huddersfield, 11½ from Rochdale, *(Lanc.)*—Population 1,888.

SOYLAND-MILL, in the parish of Halifax, Morley-division of the wapentake of Agbrigg and Morley, liberty of the Manor of Wakefield ; 4 miles from Halifax, 12 from Rochdale, *(Lanc.)*

SPACEY-HOUSE, in the parish of Pannall, lower-division of the wapentake of Claro; 5 miles from Knaresborough, 7½ from Ripley, 13 from Leeds.

SPARK-HAGG, in the parish of Selby, wapentake of Barkston-Ash; 1¼ mile from Selby, 12 from Tadcaster.

SPEN-HALL, in the parish of Birstall, Morley-division of the wapentake of Agbrigg and Morley; 7½ miles from Halifax, 8¼ from Leeds.

SPICER-HILL, in the parish of Penistone, wapentake of Staincross, liberty of the Honour of Pontefract; 3 miles from Penistone, 10 from Barnsley, 11 from Huddersfield.

SPINK-WELL, in the parish of Dewsbury, Morley-division of the wapentake of Agbrigg and Morley; 6¼ miles from Wakefield, 10 from Halifax, 10 from Bradford.

SPITTAL, in the parish of Wath-upon-Dearn, north-division of the wapentake of Strafforth and Tickhill; 5 miles from Rotherham, 7 from Barnsley.

SPITTAL-CROFT, in the parish of Arnecliffe, west-division of the wapentake and liberty of Staincliffe; 8¼ miles from Kettlewell, 12 from Settle.

SPITTAL-HILL, in the parish of Tickhill, south-division of the wapentake of Strafforth and Tickhill; 1 mile from Tickhill, 3 from Bawtry, 7 from Doncaster.

SPOFFORTH, in the parish of Spofforth, upper-division of the wapentake of Claro; *(the seat of the Rev. John Trip, L.L.D.)* 3 miles from Wetherby, 4 from Knaresborough. —Population 859.

SPOFFORTH-HAGGS, or HAGSIDE, in the parish of Spofforth, upper-division of the wapentake of Claro; 4 miles from Knaresborough, 4¼ from Wetherby.

SPRING-HOUSE, in the parish of Kirby-Malzeard, lower-division of the wapentake of Claro; 3¼ miles from Ripley, 5¼ from Pateleybridge.

SPROTBROUGH, in the parish of Sprotbrough, north-division of the wapentake of Strafforth and Tickhill, liberty of Tickhill; *(the seat of Sir James Copley, Bart.)* 3¼ miles from Doncaster, 12 from Barnsley.—Population 250.

STACK-HOUSE, in the parish of Giggleswick, west-division of the wapentake and liberty of Staincliffe; 1 mile from Settle, 17 from Skipton, 17 from Kirby-Lonsdale, *(Westm.)*

STAINBROUGH, in the parish of Silkston, wapentake of Staincross, liberty of the Honour of Pontefract; 2¼ miles from Barnsley, 5¼ from Penistone, 7¼ from Wakefield.— Population 227.

STAINBURN, in the parish of Kirkby-Overblow, upper-division of the wapentake of Claro; 4¼ miles from Otley, 9 from Knaresborough.—Population 311.

STAINBURN-MOOR-SIDE, in the parish of Kirkby-Overblow, upper-division of the wapentake of Claro; 4¼ miles from Otley, 9 from Knaresborough.

STAINCROSS, *(which gives name to the wapentake)* in the parish of Darton, wapentake of Staincross, liberty of the Honour of Pontefract ; 3¼ miles from Barnsley, 7 from Penistone, 7 from Wakefield.

STAINFORTH, in the parish of Hatfield, south-division of the wapentake of Strafforth and Tickhill, a part in the liberty of St. Peter; 3½ miles from Thorne, 7½ from Doncaster. —Population 472.

STAINFORTH, GREAT, in the parish of Giggleswick, west-division of the wapentake and liberty of Staincliffe ; 2¼ miles from Settle, 14 from Kettlewell, 18 from Skipton, 21¼ from Askrigg.—Population 203.

STAINFORTH, LITTLE, or KNIGHT-STAINFORTH, in the parish of Giggleswick, west-division of the wapentake and liberty of Staincliffe ; 2 miles from Settle, 14¼ from Kettlewell, 17½ from Skipton.

STAINLAND, in the parish of Halifax, Morley-division of the wapentake of Agbrigg and Morley, liberty of the Manor of Wakefield ; 5 miles from Halifax, 5 from Huddersfield. —Population 1,800.

STAINLEY, NORTH, in the parish of Ripon, lower-division of the wapentake of Claro, liberty of Ripon ; 3¼ miles from Ripon, 6 from Masham, 10 from Bedale.—Pop. 315.

STAINLEY, SOUTH, in the parish of South-Stainley, lower-division of the wapentake of Claro, liberty of Knaresborough ; 2¼ miles from Ripley, 5 from Ripon, 6 from Knaresborough.—Population 217.

STAINSCLIFFE-MOOR, in the parish of Batley, Agbrigg-division of the wapentake of Agbrigg and Morley ; 2 miles from Dewsbury, 8 from Wakefield, 8 from Halifax.

STAINSCROFT, or TAMECROFT, in the parish of Rochdale, *(Lanc.)* Agbrigg-division of the wapentake of Agbrigg and Morley ; 7 miles from Rochdale, *(Lanc.)* 12 from Manchester, *(ditto)* 13 from Huddersfield.

STAINTON, in the parish of Stainton, south-division of the wapentake of Strafforth and Tickhill ; 2 miles from Tickhill, 6 from Bawtry, 9 from Rotherham.—Population 151.

STAINTON-COTES, in the parish of Gargrave, east-division of the wapentake and liberty of Staincliffe ; 7 miles from Skipton, 10 from Settle.

STAIRFOOT, in the parish of Darfield, wapentake of Staincross, liberty of the Honour of Pontefract; 2 miles from Barnsley, 8 from Penistone, 9 from Rotherham.

STANBURY, in the parish of Bradford, Morley-division of the wapentake of Agbrigg and Morley; 7 miles from Keighley, 8¼ from Bradford, 8¼ from Colne, (*Lanc.*)

STAND-BRIDGE, in the parish of Sandall, Agbrigg-division of the wapentake of Agbrigg and Morley; 3 miles from Wakefield, 7 from Barnsley.

STANDSFIELD, in the parish of Halifax, Morley-division of the wapentake of Agbrigg and Morley, liberty of the Manor of Wakefield; 4 miles from Halifax, 7 from Huddersfield.—Population 4,768.

STANNINGLEY, in the parish of Calverley, Morley division of the wapentake of Agbrigg and Morley; 3¼ miles from Bradford, 6 from Leeds.

STANNINGTON, in the parish of Ecclesfield, north-division of the wapentake of Strafforth and Tickhill; 4 miles from Sheffield, 10 from Rotherham, 12 from Penistone.

STANK-HOUSE, in the parish of Barwick-in-Elmet, lower-division of the wapentake of Skirack; 3 miles from Abberford, 7 from Leeds, 10 from Tadcaster.

STANLEY, in the parish of Wakefield, Agbrigg-division of the wapentake of Agbrigg and Morley, liberty of the Manor of Wakefield; 1 mile from Wakefield, 8 from Leeds, 14 from Huddersfield.—Population 3,260.

STANLEY-HALL, in the parish of Wakefield, Agbrigg-division of the wapentake of Agbrigg and Morley, liberty of the Manor of Wakefield, (*the seat of Benjamin Haywood, Esq.*) 1½ mile from Wakefield, 6¼ from Leeds.

STANSILL, in the parish of Tickhill, south-division of the wapentake of Strafforth and Tickhill, liberty of Tickhill; 2 miles from Tickhill, 7 from Doncaster, 10 from Rotherham.—Population 46.

STAPLETON, in the parish of Darrington, wapentake of Osgoldcross, liberty of the Honour of Pontefract; (*the seat of Ellis Leckonby Hodgson, Esq.*) 4 miles from Ferrybridge, 4½ from Pontefract, 12 from Doncaster.—Population 101.

STARBOTTOM, in the parsh of Kettlewell, east division of the wapentake and liberty of Staincliffe; 2 miles from Kettlewell, 15 from Leyburn, 17 from Settle.—Pop. 197.

STARTH, in the parish of Slaidburn, west-division of the wapentake and liberty of Staincliffe; 6¼ miles from Clitheroe, (*Lanc.*) 10 from Gisburn.

STAVELEY, in the parish of Staveley, lower-division of the wapentake of Claro, liberty of Knaresborough; 3 miles from Boroughbridge, 4 from Knaresborough.—Pop. 255.

STEAD, in the parish of Wath-upon Dearn, north-division

of the wapentake of Strafforth and Tickhill; 5¼ miles from Barnsley, 8¼ from Rotherham.

STEAN, in the parish of Kirby-Malzeard, lower-division of the wapentake of Claro; 9 miles from Pateleybridge, 10 from Kettlewell, 10 from Masham.

STEEL-BANK, in the parish of Sheffield, south-division of the wapentake of Strafforth and Tickhill; 1¼ mile from Sheffield, 7¼ from Rotherham, 13¼ from Chesterfield, (Derb.)

STEETON, in the parish of Kildwick, east-division of the wapentake and liberty of Staincliffe; (Steeton-Hall, the seat of Thomas Garforth, Esq.) 3 miles from Keighley, 7 from Skipton, 11 from Colne, (Lanc.)—Pop. 510.

STEETON-HALL, in the parish of Sherburn, wapentake of Barkston-Ash; 8 miles from Pontefract, 8 from Tadcaster.

STEPHEN-PARK, in the parish of Slaidburn, west-division of the wapentake and liberty of Staincliffe; 10 miles from Settle, 18 from Skipton.

STIRK-HOUSE, in the parish of Gisburn, west-division of the wapentake and liberty of Staincliffe; 12 miles from Skipton, 12 from Settle, 13 from Burnley, (Lanc.)

STIRTON, or STRETTON, in the parish of Skipton, east-division of the wapentake and liberty of Staincliffe; 1¼ mile from Skipton, 12 from Colne, (Lanc.) 14¼ from Settle.—Population 134.

STOCK, in the parish of Bracewell, east-division of the wapentake of Staincliffe, liberty of Clifford's Fee; 5¼ miles from Colne, (Lanc.) 9¼ from Skipton.

STOCKBRIDGE, in the parish of Arksey, north-division of the wapentake of Strafforth and Tickhill, liberty of Tickhill; 2¼ miles from Doncaster, 10 from Thorne.

STOCKELD, in the parish of Spofforth, upper-division of the wapentake of Claro; (Stockeld-Park, the seat of William Middleton, Esq.) 2 miles from Wetherby, 6 from Knaresborough.

STOCKHILL, in the parish of Ilkley, upper-division of the wapentake of Claro, 6¼ miles from Otley, 9 from Skipton.

STOCKS, in the parish of Slaidburn, west-division of the wapentake and liberty of Staincliffe; 9 miles from Settle, 12 from Clitheroe, (Lanc.)

STOCKWELL-GREEN, in the parish of Sheffield, south-division of the wapentake of Strafforth and Tickhill; 3 miles from Sheffield, 9 from Rotherham.

STONE, in the parish of Maltby, south-division of the wapentake of Strafforth and Tickhill; 3 miles from Tickhill, 6 from Bawtry, 8 from Rotherham.

STONE-BECK, DOWN, or NETHER-STAINBECK, in

the parish of Kirby-Malzeard, lower-division of the wapentake of Claro ; 5 miles from Pateleybridge, 12 from Ripley, 14 from Ripon.—Population 434.

STONE-BECK, UPPER, in the parish of Kirby-Malzeard, lower-division of the wapentake of Claro ; 6 miles from Pateleybridge, 13 from Ripley, 16 from Ripon.—Pop. 304.

STONE-BREAKS, in the parish of Rochdale, *(Lanc.)* Agbrigg-division of the wapentake of Agbrigg and Morley ; 8 miles from Rochdale, *(Lanc.)* 10 from Manchester, *(ditto)* 15 from Huddersfield.

STONE-GAP, in the parish of Carlton, east-division of the wapentake and liberty of Staincliffe ; *(the seat of William Sedgwick, Esq.)* 4¼ miles from Skipton, 7 from Keighley.

STONER-HALL, in the parish of Selby, wapentake of Barkston-Ash ; 1¼ mile from Selby, 7¼ from Snaith.

STONE-ROYD, in the parish of Kirk-Heaton, Agbrigg-division of the wapentake of Agbrigg and Morley ; 5 miles from Huddersfield, 9 from Wakefield.

STONEY-BANK, in the parish of Slaidburn, west-division of the wapentake and liberty of Staincliffe ; 9 miles from Settle, 16 from Skipton.

STORRS, in the parish of Ecclesfield, north-division of the wapentake of Strafforth and Tickhill ; 7 miles from Sheffield, 11 from Penistone.

STORRS, in the parish of Silkston, wapentake of Staincross, liberty of the Honour of Pontefract ; 3 miles from Penistone, 4 from Barnsley, 11 from Wakefield.

STORRS-HALL, in the parish of Kirk-Heaton, Agbrigg-division of the wapentake of Agbrigg and Morley ; 5¼ miles from Huddersfield, 12 from Wakefield.

STOTFOLD, or STOTFIELD, in the parish of Hooton-Pagnall, north-division of the wapentake of Strafforth and Tickhill, liberty of Tickhill ; 7 miles from Doncaster, 8½ from Barnsley.—Population 8.

STOTT-HILL, in the parish of Kildwick, east-division of the wapentake and liberty of Staincliffe ; 5 miles from Colne, *(Lanc.)* 7 from Skipton, 7 from Keighley.

STRAINDS, in the parish of Penistone, wapentake of Staincross, liberty of the Honour of Pontefract ; 4 miles from Penistone, 8¼ from Huddersfield.

STRAWHOUSES, in the parish of Ripon, lower-division of the wapentake of Claro ; 1¼ mile from Ripon, 8 from Ripley.

STREETHOUSE, in the parish of Normanton, Agbrigg-division of the wapentake of Agbrigg and Morley ; 4 miles from Pontefract, 5 from Wakefield.

STREET-FARM, in the parish of Wath-upon-Dearn, north-division of the wapentake of Strafforth and Tickhill; 6 miles from Rotherham, 6 from Barnsley.

STREETSIDE, in the parish of Dewsbury, Agbrigg-division of the wapentake of Agbrigg and Morley; 1¼ mile from Dewsbury, 3¼ from Wakefield.

STREET-THORPE, in the parish of Kirk-Sandall, south-division of the wapentake of Strafforth and Tickhill; 3½ miles from Doncaster, 8¼ from Thorne.

STRINDS, in the parish of Ecclesfield, north-division of the wapentake of Strafforth and Tickhill; 6 miles from Sheffield, 11 from Penistone.

STUBBING, in the parish of Rawmarsh, north-division of the wapentake of Strafforth and Tickhill; 3 miles from Rotherham, 9 from Barnsley.

STUBBING-LANE, in the parish of Rawmarsh, north-division of the wapentake of Strafforth and Tickhill; 3 miles from Rotherham, 10 from Barnsley.

STUBBS, in the parish of Adwick-in-the-Street, north-division of the wapentake of Strafforth and Tickhill; 7 miles from Doncaster, 9¼ from Pontefract, 12¼ from Wakefield.

STUBHAM-LODGE, in the parish of Ilkley, lower-division of the wapentake of Claro; 7 miles from Otley, 9 from Skipton.

STUDFIELD, in the parish of Horton, wapentake of Ewcross; 5 miles from Settle, 18 from Askrigg.

STUDFOLD, in the parish of Kirby-Malzeard, lower-division of the wapentake of Claro; 8 miles from Pateleybridge, 9 from Masham, 11 from Kettlewell.

STUDLEY, in the parish of Ripon, lower-division of the wapentake of Claro, liberty of Ripon; 1½ mile from Ripon, 7¼ from Boroughbridge, 8 from Ripley.—Pop. 143.

STUDLEY-ROYAL, in the parish of Ripon, lower-division of the wapentake of Claro, liberty of Ripon; *(the seat of Miss Lawrence)* 2 miles from Ripon, 8 from Boroughbridge, 8 from Ripley.

STUMP-CROSS, in the parish of Dewsbury, Agbrigg-division of the wapentake of Agbrigg and Morley; 3¼ miles from Dewsbury, 4 from Wakefield.

STUMPER LOW-HALL, in the parish of Sheffield, south-division of the wapentake of Strafforth and Tickhill; *(the seat of John Oats, Esq.)* 3 miles from Sheffield, 9 from Rotherham, 12 from Chesterfield, *(Derb.)*

STURTON-GRANGE, in the parish of Abberford, lower-division of the wapentake of Skirack; 3 miles from Abberford, 8 from Leeds, 11 from Tadcaster.—Pop. 64.

STUTTON, in the parish of Tadcaster, wapentake of Barkston-Ash, liberty of the Honour of Pontefract ; 1 mile from Tadcaster, 11 from Ferrybridge, 13 from Pontefract.—Population 252.

STUTTON-HILL, in the parish of Tadcaster, wapentake of Barkston-Ash, liberty of the Honour of Pontefract ; 1 mile from Tadcaster, 11 from Ferrybridge, 13 from Pontefract.

SUMMER-SCALES, in the parish of Skipton, lower-division of the wapentake of Claro ; 7 miles from Skipton, 16 from Knaresborough.

SUNLEY-RAINS, in the parish of Ripon, lower-division of the wapentake of Claro ; 1¼ mile from Ripon, 9 from Ripley.

SUTTON, in the parish of Ripon, lower-division of the wapentake of Claro, liberty of Ripon ; 2 miles from Ripon, 8 from Masham.—Population 103.

SUTTON, in the parish of Brotherton, wapentake of Barkston-Ash, liberty of St. Peter ; 1 mile from Ferrybridge, 3 from Pontefract, 12 from Tadcaster.—Pop. 52.

SUTTON, in the parish of Kildwick, east-division of the wapentake of Staincliffe, liberty of Clifford's Fee ; 5 miles from Keighley, 5 from Skipton, 9 from Colne, *(Lanc.)*—Population 809.

SUTTON, in the parishes of Campsall and Burghwallis, wapentake of Osgoldcross, liberty of the Honour of Pontefract ; 7 miles from Doncaster, 11 from Ferrybridge.—Pop. 179.

SUTTON-GRANGE, in the parish of Ripon, lower-division of the wapentake of Claro ; 2 miles from Ripon, 8 from Masham.

SWALLOW-HILL, in the parish of Darton, wapentake of Staincross, liberty of the Honour of Pontefract ; 2¼ miles from Barnsley, 5¼ from Penistone, 9 from Wakefield.

SWARTHE-HALL, in the parish of Darfield, wapentake of Staincross, liberty of the Honour of Pontefract ; *(the seat of Mrs. Elmhirst)* 2 miles from Barnsley, 9 from Rotherham, 11 from Wakefield.

SWARTHEY, in the parish of Kildwick, east-division of the wapentake and liberty of Staincliffe ; 4¼ miles from Keighley, 7¼ from Skipton.

SWETTON, in the parish of Kirby-Malzeard, lower-division of the wapentake of Claro ; 7 miles from Masham, 10 from Ripon.

SWIFT-PLACE, in the parish of Halifax, Morley-division of the wapentake of Agbrigg and Morley ; 6 miles from Halifax, 8 from Huddersfield.

SWILLINGTON, in the parish of Swillington, lower-divi-

UNDER-BANK, in the parish of Penistone, wapentake of Staincross, liberty of the Honour of Pontefract; *(the seat of William Fenton, Esq.)* 3 miles from Penistone, 8 from Barnsley, 10 from Sheffield.

UNDER-BANK, in the parish of Halifax, Morley-division of the wapentake of Agbrigg and Morley; *(the seat of Christopher Rawdon, Esq.)* 9 miles from Halifax, 12 from Rochdale, *Lanc.)*

UNDERCLIFFE, in the parish of Bradford, Morley-division of the wapentake of Agbrigg and Morley; ¼ of a mile from Bradford, 8¼ from Halifax, 9 from Otley.

UNSHRIVEN-BRIDGE, in the parish of Penistone, wapentake of Staincross, liberty of the Honour of Pontefract; 3 miles from Penistone, 8 from Barnsley, 11 from Sheffield.

UPPER-MILL, in the parish of Rochdale, *Lanc.)* Agbrigg-division of the wapentake of Agbrigg and Morley; 9 miles from Rochdale, *(Lanc.)* 13 from Huddersfield.

UPPER-THORPE, in the parish of Sheffield, south-division of the wapentake of Strafforth and Tickhill; 1 mile from Sheffield, 7 from Rotherham, 13 from Chesterfield, *(Derb.)*

UPTON, in the parish of Badsworth, wapentake of Osgoldcross, liberty of the Honour of Pontefract; 6 miles from Pontefract, 10 from Doncaster, 10 from Wakefield, 12 from Barnsley.—Population 162.

USKELFE, or ULLESKELFE, in the parish of Kirby-Wharfe, wapentake of Barkston-Ash, liberty of St. Peter; *(the seat of John Shillito, Esq.)* 2 miles from Tadcaster, 9 from Selby, 14 from Pontefract.—Population 355.

UTLEY, in the parish of Keighley, east-division of the wapentake and liberty of Staincliffe; 1 mile from Keighley, 9 from Skipton, 11 from Bradford.

VIEWS, in the parish of Darfield, wapentake of Staincross, liberty of the Honour of Pontefract; 1¼ mile from Barnsley, 7 from Penistone, 9½ from Rotherham.

VIZITT, in the parish of Hemsworth, wapentake of Staincross, liberty of the Honour of Pontefract; 6 miles from Pontefract, 7 from Wakefield, 8½ from Barnsley.

W.

WADDINGTON, in the parish of Mitton, west-division of the wapentake of Staincliffe, liberty of Bolland; 8¼ miles from Gisburn, 14 from Blackburn, *(Lanc.)* 16 from Burnley, *(ditto)* 20 from Skipton.—Pop. 481.

WEST-RIDING.

WADDOW-HALL, in the parish of Mitton, west-division of the wapentake and liberty of Staincliffe; *(the seat of Thomas Clarke, Esq.)* 2 miles from Clitheroe, *(Lanc.)* 12 from Blackburn, *(ditto)* 12 from Gisburn.

WADSLEY, in the parish of Ecclesfield, north-division of the wapentake of Strafforth and Tickhill; 2¼ miles from Sheffield, 8½ from Rotherham, 10¼ from Penistone.

WADSLEY-BRIDGE, in the parish of Ecclesfield, north-division of the wapentake of Strafforth and Tickhill; 2¼ miles from Sheffield, 8½ from Rotherham, 10 from Penistone.

WADSWORTH, in the parish of Halifax, Morley-division of the wapentake of Agbrigg and Morley, liberty of the Manor of Wakefield; 8 miles from Halifax, 12 from Rochdale, *(Lanc.)*—Population 2,801.

WADSWORTH-LANES, in the parish of Halifax, Morley-division of the wapentake of Agbrigg and Morley, liberty of the Manor of Wakefield; 8 miles from Halifax, 12 from Rochdale, *(Lanc.)*

WADWORTH, in the parish of Wadworth, south-division of the wapentake of Strafforth and Tickhill, liberty of Tickhill; *(the seat of Mrs. Wordsworth)* 3 miles from Tickhill, 4 from Doncaster, 8½ from Rotherham.—Pop. 446.

WAKEFIELD, in the parish of Wakefield, Agbrigg-division of the wapentake of Agbrigg and Morley, liberty of the Manor of Wakefield; 5 miles from Dewsbury, 9 from Leeds, 9 from Pontefract, 10 from Barnsley, 13 from Huddersfield, 13 from Abberford, 14 from Bradford, 20 from Doncaster, 28 from York, 182 from London.—*Market*, Friday.—*Fairs*, July 4 and 5, for Pedlary-Ware, November 11 and 12, for Horses, Horned Cattle, &c.; and every other Wednesday for Horned Cattle.—*Bankers*, New-Bank, Messrs. Townend and Rishforth, draw on Messrs. Boldero, Lushington, and Co. 30 Cornhill.—*Principal Inns*, White-Hart, Strafford-Arms, George, and Black-Bull.—Population 8,131.

WAKEFIELD-LODGE, in the parish of Wakefield, Agbrigg-division of the wapentake of Agbrigg and Morley, liberty of the Manor of Wakefield; *(the seat of Joseph Armitage, Esq.)* 1 mile from Wakefield, 9 from Barnsley.

WALDEN-STUBBS, in the parish of Womersley, wapentake of Osgoldcross, liberty of the Honour of Pontefract; 7 miles from Pontefract, 7 from Ferrybridge.—Population 127.

WALES, in the parish of Laughton-le-Morthen, south-division of the wapentake of Strafforth and Tickhill, liberty of St. Peter; 7 miles from Worksop, *(Notts.)* 8 from Rotherham, 10 from Sheffield.—Population 229.

WEST-RIDING.

WALES-WOOD, in the parishes of Treton and Laughton-le-Morthen, south-division of the wapentake of Strafforth and Tickhill; 5¼ miles from Rotherham, 9 from Sheffield, 9 from Worksop, *(Notts.)*

WALKINGHAM, in the parish of Knaresborough, lower-division of the wapentake of Claro; 4 miles from Knaresborough, 4 from Boroughbridge, 5 from Ripley.

WALKLEY, in the parish of Sheffield, south-division of the wapentake of Strafforth and Tickhill; 2 miles from Sheffield, 8 from Rotherham, 11½ from Penistone.

WALLERTHWAITE, in the parish of Ripon, lower-division of the wapentake of Claro, liberty of Ripon; 4 miles from Ripon, 7 from Knaresborough.

WALL-HILL, in the parish of Rochdale, *(Lanc.)* Agbrigg-division of the wapentake of Agbrigg and Morley; 9 miles from Rochdale, *(Lanc.)* 11 from Manchester, *(ditto)* 14 from Huddersfield.

WALSHFORD-BRIDGE, in the parish of Hunsingore, upper-division of the wapentake of Claro; 3 miles from Wetherby, 5 from Knaresborough, 9 from Boroughbridge.

WALTON-HALL, in the parish of Sandall, Agbrigg-division of the wapentake of Agbrigg and Morley, liberty of the Manor of Wakefield; *(the seat of Thomas Waterton, Esq.)* 4 miles from Wakefield, 8 from Barnsley.

WALTON-HEAD, in the parish of Kirkby-Overblow, upper-division of the wapentake of Claro; 6 miles from Knaresborough, 6¼ from Wetherby.

WALTON, MIDDLE, in the parish of Sandall, Agbrigg-division of the wapentake of Agbrigg and Morley, liberty of the Manor of Wakefield; 3 miles from Wakefield, 8 from Barnsley.—Population 315.

WALTON, OVER, in the parish of Sandall, Agbrigg-division of the wapentake of Agbrigg and Morley, liberty of the Manor of Wakefield; 3 miles from Wakefield, 8 from Barnsley.

WALTON-WOOD, in the parish of Badsworth, wapentake of Osgoldcross, liberty of the Honour of Pontefract; 4¼ miles from Pontefract, 8 from Wakefield.

WARDSEND, in the parish of Ecclesfield, north-division of the wapentake of Strafforth and Tickhill; *(the seat of Thomas Rawson, Esq.)* 2½ miles from Sheffield, 8½ from Rotherham, 10 from Penistone.

WARLEY, in the parish of Halifax, Morley-division of the wapentake of Agbrigg and Morley, liberty of the Manor of Wakefield; 2½ miles from Halifax, 8 from Huddersfield.—Population 3,546.

WARMFIELD, in the parish of Warmfield, Agbrigg-division of the wapentake of Agbrigg and Morley, liberty of the Honour of Pontefract; 4 miles from Wakefield, 5 from Pontefract.—Population 625.

WARMSWORTH, in the parishes of Warmsworth and Doncaster, south-division of the wapentake of Strafforth and Tickhill; *(the seat of Mrs. Buck)* 3 miles from Doncaster, 9 from Rotherham.—Population 254.

WARREN-LANE, in the parish of Kirby-Malzeard, lower-division of the wapentake of Claro; 5 miles from Masham, 7 from Ripon.

WARSELL, in the parish of Ripon, lower-division of the wapentake of Claro, liberty of Ripon; 5 miles from Ripon, 7 from Ripley, 7 from Knaresborough.

WASS-LANE-HEAD, in the parish of Darfield, wapentake of Staincross, liberty of the Honour of Pontefract; 1 mile from Barnsley, 7¼ from Penistone, 11 from Rotherham.

WATERTON, in the parish of Armthorpe, south-division of the wapentake of Strafforth and Tickhill; 5 miles from Doncaster, 9 from Bawtry.

WATH-UPON-DEARN, in the parish of Wath-upon-Dearn, north-division of the wapentake of Strafforth and Tickhill, liberty of Tickhill; 5 miles from Rotherham, 9 from Doncaster, 11 from Sheffield.—Population 662.

WEARDLEY, in the parish of Harewood, upper-division of the wapentake of Skirack; 1 mile from Harewood, 5 from Leeds, 6¼ from Otley.—Population 139.

WEELAND, in the parish of Snaith, wapentake of Osgoldcross, liberty of the Honour of Pontefract; 2 miles from Snaith, 7¼ from Selby.

WEETON, in the parish of Harewood, upper-division of the wapentake of Claro; 5 miles from Otley, 7 from Wetherby, 9½ from Leeds.—Population 237.

WEETWOOD-HALL, in the parish of Leeds, lower-division of the wapentake of Skirack; *(the seat of ——Brown, Esq.)* 3 miles from Leeds, 8 from Bradford.

WELDON-HALL, in the parish of Water-Fryston, wapentake of Osgoldcross, liberty of the Honour of Pontefract; 2 miles from Pontefract, 2¼ from Ferrybridge.

WELLIHOLE, in the parish of Rochdale, *(Lanc.)* Agbrigg-division of the wapentake of Agbrigg and Morley; 9 miles from Rochdale, *(Lanc.)* 12 from Manchester, *(ditto)* 14 from Huddersfield.

WELLINGLEY, in the parish of Tickhill, south-division of the wapentake of Strafforth and Tickhill; 2 miles from Tickhill, 7 from Doncaster, 10 from Rotherham.

WENTBRIDGE, in the parishes of Kirk-Smeaton, Bads-worth, and Darrington, wapentake of Osgoldcross, liberty of the Honour of Pontefract; 4¼ miles from Pontefract, 4¼ from Ferrybridge, 10¼ from Doncaster.

WENTWORTH, in the parish of Wath-upon-Dearn, north-division of the wapentake of Strafforth and Tickhill, liberty of Tickhill; *(the seat of the Rev. John Lowe)* 6 miles from Rotherham, 8 from Barnsley, 13½ from Doncaster.—Population 978.

WENTWORTH-CASTLE, in the parish of Silkston, wapentake of Staincross, liberty of the Honour of Pontefract; *(the seat of Henry Vernon, Esq.)* 2 miles from Barnsley, 5½ from Penistone, 8 from Rotherham.

WENTWORTH-HOUSE, in the parish of Wath-upon-Dearn, north-division of the wapentake of Strafforth and Tickhill, liberty of Tickhill; *(the seat of Earl Fitzwilliam)* 4 miles from Rotherham, 9½ from Sheffield, 13 from Doncaster.

WESKETT, or WESTGATE-HILL, in the parish of Birstall, Morley-division of the wapentake of Agbrigg and Morley; 3½ miles from Bradford, 8 from Halifax, 10¼ from Wakefield.

WESTBY, in the parish of Gisburn, west-division of the wapentake and liberty of Staincliffe; 1 mile from Gisburn, 8 from Clitheroe, *(Lanc.)* 12½ from Skipton.

WEST-END, in the parish of Fewston, lower-division of the wapentake of Claro; 10¼ miles from Otley, 11½ from Skipton, 14 from Knaresborough.

WEST-END, in the parish of Kirkby-Overblow, upper-division of the wapentake of Claro; 3¼ miles from Otley, 8 from Ripley.

WESTERTON, *see Ardsley, West*.

WESTERTON-HALL, in the parish of Woodchurch, Agbrigg-division of the wapentake of Agbrigg and Morley, liberty of the Manor of Wakefield; *(the seat of the Rev. —— Wood)* 4 miles from Wakefield, 10 from Bradford.

WEST-FIELD, in the parish of Kirby-Malzeard, lower-division of the wapentake of Claro; 6 miles from Ripon, 6 from Masham.

WEST-FIELD, in the parish of Fishlake, north-division of the wapentake of Strafforth and Tickhill; 4 miles from Thorne, 7½ from Snaith.

WEST-GILL, in the parish of Sedbergh, wapentake of Ewcross; 5 miles from Sedbergh, 14¼ from Askrigg.

WEST-HALL, in the parish of Wakefield, Agbrigg-division of the wapentake of Agbrigg and Morley; 3 miles from Wakefield, 9 from Leeds.

WEST-HOUSES, in the parish of Fewston, lower-division of the wapentake of Claro; 8 miles from Otley, 12 rom Skipton, 12 from Knaresborough.

WEST-HOUSES, in the parish of Kirby-Malzeard, lower-division of the wapentake of Claro; 4 miles from Kettlewell, 10 from Middleham, 13 from Pateleybridge.

WEST-HOUSES, in the parish of Thornton-in-Lonsdale, wapentake of Ewcross; 5 miles from Kirby-Lonsdale, *(Westm.)* 12 from Settle.

WESTKEY-HILL, in the parish of Harewood, upper-division of the wapentake of Claro; 5 miles from Otley, 5 from Harewood.

WESTON, in the parish of Weston, upper-division of the wapentake of Claro; *(Weston-Hall, the seat of William Vavasour, Esq.)* 2 miles from Otley, 12 from Leeds, 16 from Knaresborough.—Population 120.

WEST-SCHOLES, in the parish of Bradford, Morley-division of the wapentake of Agbrigg and Morley; 3¼ miles from Bradford, 5¼ from Halifax.

WEST-THORPE, in the parish of Silkston, wapentake of Staincross, liberty of the Honour of Pontefract; 1½ mile from Penistone, 7 from Barnsley, 11¼ from Huddersfield.

WESTWICK, in the parish of Ripon, lower-division of the wapentake of Claro, liberty of Ripon; 2 miles from Boroughbridge, 4 from Ripon, 7 from Knaresborough.—Pop. 20.

WEST-WOOD, in the parish of Huddersfield, Agbrigg-division of the wapentake of Agbrigg and Morley; 3 miles from Huddersfield, 8 from Halifax.

WETHERBY, in the parish of Spofforth, upper-division of the wapentake of Claro; 6 miles from Harewood, 7 from Knaresborough, 7 from Tadcaster, 7¼ from Abberford, 10 from Otley, 12 from Boroughbridge, 15¼ from York, 16 from Leeds, 194 from London.—*Market*, Thursday.—*Fairs*, Holy-Thursday, and August 5, for Sheep and Pigs. *Principal Inns*, Angel, and Dog and Swan.—Pop. 1,144.

WETHERBY-GRANGE, in the parish of Collingham, wapentake of Barkston-Ash; *(the seat of Richard Thompson, Esq.)* 1 mile from Wetherby, 6 from Tadcaster, 7 from Abberford.

WHAITBER, in the parish of Thornton-in-Lonsdale, wapentake of Ewcross; 4½ miles from Kirby-Lonsdale, *(Westm.)* 14 from Settle.

WHARNCLIFFE-LODGE, in the parish of Tankersley, wapentake of Staincross, liberty of the Honour of Pontefract; *(the seat of the Hon. James Archibald Stuart Wortley)* 6 miles from Sheffield, 8½ from Penistone, 9 from Rotherham.

WEST-RIDING.

WHEAT-CROFT, in the parish of Rawmarsh, north-division of the wapentake of Strafforth and Tickhill; 2 miles from Rotherham, 8 from Sheffield, 12 from Barnsley.

WHEAT-HOUSE, in the parish of Firbeck, south-division of the wapentake of Strafforth and Tickhill; 5 miles from Tickhill, 5 from Workson, (*Notts.*) 9 from Rotherham.

WHEATLEY, in the parish and Soke of Doncaster, south-division of the wapentake of Strafforth and Tickhill; *(the seat of Sir George Cooke, Bart.)* $2\frac{1}{4}$ miles from Doncaster, 9 from Thorne.

WHEATLEY, in the parish of Ilkley, upper-division of the wapentake of Skirack; 5 miles from Otley, 8 from Bradford, 9 from Skipton.

WHELPSTONE'S-HEAD, in the parish of Giggleswick, west-division of the wapentake and liberty of Staincliffe; 4 miles from Settle, 16 from Skipton.

WHIRLOW, in the parish of Sheffield, south-division of the wapentake of Strafforth and Tickhill; 4 miles from Sheffield, 10 from Rotherham, 10 from Chesterfield, *(Derb.)*

WHISTON, in the parish of Whiston, south-division of the wapentake of Strafforth and Tickhill, liberty of Hallamshire; 2 miles from Rotherham, $7\frac{1}{4}$ from Sheffield, 11 from Tickhill.—Population 672.

WHISTON, UPPER, in the parish of Whiston, south-division of the wapentake of Strafforth and Tickhill; $2\frac{1}{4}$ miles from Rotherham, 8 from Sheffield.

WHITCHURCH, or WHITKIRK, in the parish of Whitchurch, lower-division of the wapentake of Skirack; $4\frac{1}{4}$ miles from Leeds, 8 from Wakefield, $10\frac{1}{4}$ from Ferrybridge, —Population 1,033.

WHITCLIFFE, in the parish of Ripon, lower-division of the wapentake of Claro, liberty of Ripon; $1\frac{1}{4}$ mile from Ripon, $7\frac{1}{4}$ from Boroughbridge.—Population 136.

WHITCROSS, in the parish of Elmley, Agbrigg-division of the wapentake of Agbrigg and Morley; 7 miles from Huddersfield, 7 from Wakefield.

WHITE-CHAPEL-IN-THE-NORTH, see *Heaton, Clack.*

WHITE-HILL, in the parish of Rotherham, south-division of the wapentake of Strafforth and Tickhill; 2 miles from Rotherham, 5 from Sheffield.

WHITE-HOUSES, in the parish of Ripon, lower-division of the wapentake of Claro; 1 mile from Pateleybridge, 7 from Ripley, 11 from Ripon.

WHITELEE, in the parish of Rochdale, *(Lanc.)* Agbrigg-division of the wapentake of Agbrigg and Morley; 10 miles from Rochdale, *(Lanc.)* 13 from Manchester, *(ditto)* 15 from Huddersfield.

WHITE-LEES, in the parish of Huddersfield, Agbrigg-division of the wapentake of Agbrigg and Morley ; 6¼ miles from Huddersfield, 9½ from Halifax.

WHITELEY-WOOD-HALL, in the parish of Sheffield, south-division of the wapentake of Strafforth and Tickhill ; *(the seat of William Hutton, Esq.)* 4 miles from Sheffield, 10 from Rotherham, 12 from Bakewell, *(Derb.)*

WHITE-WELL, in the parishes of Slaidburn and Clitheroe, *(Lanc.)* west-division of the wapentake and liberty of Staincliffe ; 6¼ miles from Clitheroe, *(Lanc.)* 13½ from Gisburn, 17 from Lancaster, *(Lanc.)*

WHITE-WINDOWS, in the parish of Halifax, Morley-division of the wapentake of Agbrigg and Morley ; *(the seat of Joseph Priestley, Esq.)* 3¼ miles from Halifax, 8 from Huddersfield, 13 from Rochdale, *(Lanc.)*

WHITGIFT, in the parish of Whitgift, wapentake of Osgoldcross, liberty of the Honour of Pontefract ; 6 miles from Howden, 8 from Crowle, *(Linc.)* 13 from Snaith.—Population 263.

WHITLEY, in the parishes of Kellington and Snaith, wapentake of Osgoldcross, liberty of the Honour of Pontefract; 6¾ miles from Snaith, 6¼ from Pontefract.—Pop. 225.

WHITLEY, in the parish of Ecclesfield, north-division of the wapentake of Strafforth and Tickhill ; 5 miles from Sheffield, 7 from Barnsley, 7 from Rotherham.

WHITLEY-HALL, in the parish of Kirk-Heaton, Agbrigg-division of the wapentake of Agbrigg and Morley, liberty of the Honour of Pontefract ; *(the seat of Richard Henry Beaumont, Esq.)* 5¼ miles from Huddersfield, 7½ from Wakefield.

WHITLEY, LOWER, in the parish of Thornhill, Agbrigg-division of the wapentake of Agbrigg and Morley, liberty of the Honour of Pontefract ; 6¼ miles from Huddersfield, 8½ from Wakefield.—Population 819.

WHITLEY-THORPE, in the parish of Kellington, wapentake of Osgoldcross, liberty of the Honour of Pontefract; 7 miles from Pontefract, 7 from Snaith.

WHITLEY, UPPER, in the parish of Kirk-Heaton, Agbrigg-division of the wapentake of Agbrigg and Morley, liberty of the Honour of Pontefract ; 5½ miles from Huddersfield, 7½ from Wakefield.

WHITWELL, in the parish of Ecclesfield, north-division of the wapentake of Strafforth and Tickhill ; 4¼ miles from Sheffield, 7 from Rotherham, 8 from Barnsley.

WHITWELL-PLACE, in the parish of Halifax, Morley-division of the wapentake of Agbrigg and Morley ; 5½ miles from Halifax, 12¾ from Rochdale, *(Lanc.)*

sion of the wapentake of Agbrigg and Morley, liberty of the Manor of Wakefield; 6 miles from Wakefield, 6 from Dewsbury.

TOPITH, in the parish of High-Hoyland, wapentake of Staincross, liberty of the Honour of Pontefract; 6 miles from Penistone, 7 from Barnsley, 10 from Wakefield.

TOSSIDE, in the parish of Gisburn, west-division of the wapentake and liberty of Staincliffe; 7½ miles from Settle, 15 from Clitheroe, (*Lanc.*) 16 from Skipton.

TOSSIDE-ROW, (extraparochial) west-division of the wapentake and liberty of Staincliffe; 8 miles from Settle, 14½ Clitheroe, (*Lanc.*) 15 from Skipton.

TOTTIS, in the parish of Kirk-Burton, Agbrigg-division of the wapentake of Agbrigg and Morley; 7 miles from Huddersfield, 8¼ from Penistone.

TOWLSTON, in the parish of Newton-Kine, wapentake of Barkston-Ash; 3 miles from Tadcaster, 5 from Wetherby, 12 from Ferrybridge.

TOWLSTON-LODGE, in the parish of Newton-Kine, wapentake of Barkston-Ash; (*the seat of Peregrine Wentworth, Esq.*) 3 miles from Tadcaster, 6 from Wetherby, 12 from Ferrybridge.

TOWN-END, in the parish of Kirk-Burton, Agbrigg-division of the wapentake of Agbrigg and Morley; 6 miles from Huddersfield, 9 from Penistone.

TOWN-GATE, in the parish of Mirfield, Agbrigg-division of the wapentake of Agbrigg and Morley; 2½ miles from Dewsbury, 6 from Wakefield, 6 from Huddersfield.

TOWN-HEAD, in the parish of Slaidburn, west-division of of the wapentake of Staincliffe, liberty of Bolland; (*the seat of James Wigglesworth, Esq.*) 12 miles from Settle, 19 from Skipton, 19 from Lancaster, (*Lanc.*)

TOWN-HILL, in the parish of Bradford, Morley-division of the wapentake of Agbrigg and Morley; (*the seat of Francis Duffield, Esq.*) ¼ a mile from Bradford, 8½ from Halifax, 14 from Wakefield.

TOWTON, in the parish of Saxton, wapentake of Barkston-Ash, liberty of the Honour of Pontefract; (*Towton-Hall, the seat of the Hon. Martin Bladin Hawke*) 3 miles from Tadcaster, 10 from Ferrybridge, 12 from Pontefract.—Pop. 96.

TRANMORE, in the parish of Kellington, wapentake of Osgoldcross, liberty of the Honour of Pontefract; 6 miles from Snaith, 7 from Pontefract.

TRETON, in the parish of Treton, south-division of the wapentake of Strafforth and Tickhill, liberty of Hallamshire; 3 miles from Rotherham, 7 from Sheffield.—Population 312.

of the wapentake and liberty of Staincliffe ; 10 miles from Skipton, 12 from Settle, 12 from Burnley, *(Lanc.)*

WILLOW-EDGE, in the parish of Halifax, Morley-division of the wapentake of Agbrigg and Morley; *(the seat of Thomas Dyson, Esq.)* 2 miles from Halifax, 9 from Huddersfield.

WILLOW-HALL, in the parish of Halifax, Morley-division of the wapentake of Agbrigg and Morley; *(the seat of Thomas Lodge, Esq.)* 2 miles from Halifax, 9 from Huddersfield.

WILSDEN, in the parish of Bradford, Morley-division of the wapentake of Agbrigg and Morley, liberty of the Honour of Pontefract; 4 miles from Bradford, 5 from Keighley, 8 from Halifax.—Population 913.

WILSELL, in the parish of Ripon, lower-division of the wapentake of Claro, liberty of Ripon; 1 mile from Pateleybridge, 7 from Ripley, 11 from Ripon.

WILSICK, in the parish of Tickhill, south-division of the wapentake of Strafforth and Tickhill, liberty of Tickhill; *(the seat of John Brewin, Esq.)* 2 miles from Tickhill, 5 from Doncaster, 6 from Bawtry, 9 from Rotherham.

WINCO-BANK, in the parish of Ecclesfield, north-division of the wapentake of Strafforth and Tickhill; 4 miles from Sheffield, 4 from Rotherham, 10 from Barnsley.

WINDFIELD, in the parish of Rotherham, south-division of the wapentake of Strafforth and Tickhill; 2 miles from Rotherham, 10 from Barnsley.

WINDHILL, in the parish of Calverley, Morley-division of the wapentake of Agbrigg and Morley, liberty of the Honour of Pontefract; 3 miles from Bradford, 7½ from Otley.

WINDHILL-GATE, in the parish of Darton, wapentake of Staincross, liberty of the Honour of Pontefract; 5 miles from Barnsley, 5 from Wakefield, 9 from Penistone.

WINDLEDEN, in the parish of Penistone, wapentake of Staincross, liberty of the Honour of Pontefract; 6 miles from Penistone, 13 from Barnsley, 13 from Huddersfield.

WIND-MILL-HOUSE, in the parish of Crofton, Agbrigg-division of the wapentake of Agbrigg and Morley; 4 miles from Wakefield, 5 from Pontefract.

WINKSLEY, in the parish of Ripon, lower-division of the wapentake of Claro; 5 miles from Ripon, 6 from Masham.—Population 144.

WINSLEY, or WINSLOW, in the parish of Ripon, lower-division of the wapentake of Claro; 3 miles from Ripley, 6 from Pateleybridge, 7 from Ripon.

WINSKILL, in the parish of Giggleswick, west-division of

UNDER-BANK, in the parish of Penistone, wapentake of Staincross, liberty of the Honour of Pontefract; *(the seat of William Fenton, Esq.)* 3 miles from Penistone, 8 from Barnsley, 10 from Sheffield.

UNDER-BANK, in the parish of Halifax, Morley-division of the wapentake of Agbrigg and Morley; *(the seat of Christopher Rawdon, Esq.)* 9 miles from Halifax, 12 from Rochdale, *Lanc.)*

UNDERCLIFFE, in the parish of Bradford, Morley-division of the wapentake of Agbrigg and Morley; ¼ of a mile from Bradford, 8¼ from Halifax, 9 from Otley.

UNSHRIVEN-BRIDGE, in the parish of Penistone, wapentake of Staincross, liberty of the Honour of Pontefract; 3 miles from Penistone, 8 from Barnsley, 11 from Sheffield.

UPPER-MILL, in the parish of Rochdale, *Lanc.)* Agbrigg-division of the wapentake of Agbrigg and Morley; 9 miles from Rochdale, *(Lanc.)* 13 from Huddersfield.

UPPER-THORPE, in the parish of Sheffield, south-division of the wapentake of Strafforth and Tickhill; 1 mile from Sheffield, 7 from Rotherham, 13 from Chesterfield, *(Derb.)*

UPTON, in the parish of Badsworth, wapentake of Osgoldcross, liberty of the Honour of Pontefract; 6 miles from Pontefract, 10 from Doncaster, 10 from Wakefield, 12 from Barnsley.—Population 162.

USKELFE, or ULLESKELFE, in the parish of Kirby-Wharfe, wapentake of Barkston-Ash, liberty of St. Peter; *(the seat of John Shillito, Esq.)* 2 miles from Tadcaster, 9 from Selby, 14 from Pontefract.—Population 355.

UTLEY, in the parish of Keighley, east-division of the wapentake and liberty of Staincliffe; 1 mile from Keighley, 9 from Skipton, 11 from Bradford.

VIEWS, in the parish of Darfield, wapentake of Staincross, liberty of the Honour of Pontefract; 1¼ mile from Barnsley, 7 from Penistone, 9½ from Rotherham.

VIZITT, in the parish of Hemsworth, wapentake of Staincross, liberty of the Honour of Pontefract; 6 miles from Pontefract, 7 from Wakefield, 8½ from Barnsley.

W.

WADDINGTON, in the parish of Mitton, west-division of the wapentake of Staincliffe, liberty of Bolland; 8½ miles from Gisburn, 14 from Blackburn, *(Lanc.)* 16 from Burnley, *(ditto)* 20 from Skipton.—Pop. 481.

WEST-RIDING.

WADDOW-HALL, in the parish of Mitton, west-division of the wapentake and liberty of Staincliffe; *(the seat of Thomas Clarke, Esq.)* 2 miles from Clitheroe, *(Lanc.)* 12 from Blackburn, *(ditto)* 12 from Gisburn.

WADSLEY, in the parish of Ecclesfield, north-division of the wapentake of Strafforth and Tickhill; 2¼ miles from Sheffield, 8½ from Rotherham, 10¼ from Penistone.

WADSLEY-BRIDGE, in the parish of Ecclesfield, north-division of the wapentake of Strafforth and Tickhill; 2¼ miles from Sheffield, 8½ from Rotherham, 10 from Penistone.

WADSWORTH, in the parish of Halifax, Morley-division of the wapentake of Agbrigg and Morley, liberty of the Manor of Wakefield; 8 miles from Halifax, 12 from Rochdale, *(Lanc.)*—Population 2,801.

WADSWORTH-LANES, in the parish of Halifax, Morley-division of the wapentake of Agbrigg and Morley, liberty of the Manor of Wakefield; 8 miles from Halifax, 12 from Rochdale, *(Lanc.)*

WADWORTH, in the parish of Wadworth, south-division of the wapentake of Strafforth and Tickhill, liberty of Tickhill; *(the seat of Mrs. Wordsworth)* 3 miles from Tickhill, 4 from Doncaster, 8½ from Rotherham.—Pop. 446.

WAKEFIELD, in the parish of Wakefield, Agbrigg-division of the wapentake of Agbrigg and Morley, liberty of the Manor of Wakefield; 5 miles from Dewsbury, 9 from Leeds, 9 from Pontefract, 10 from Barnsley, 13 from Huddersfield, 13 from Abberford, 14 from Bradford, 20 from Doncaster, 28 from York, 182 from London.—*Market*, Friday.—*Fairs*, July 4 and 5, for Pedlary-Ware, November 11 and 12, for Horses, Horned Cattle, &c.; and every other Wednesday for Horned Cattle.—*Bankers*, New-Bank, Messrs. Townend and Rishforth, draw on Messrs. Boldero, Lushington, and Co. 30 Cornhill.—*Principal Inns*, White-Hart, Strafford-Arms, George, and Black-Bull.—Population 8,131.

WAKEFIELD-LODGE, in the parish of Wakefield, Agbrigg-division of the wapentake of Agbrigg and Morley, liberty of the Manor of Wakefield; *(the seat of Joseph Armitage, Esq.)* 1 mile from Wakefield, 9 from Barnsley.

WALDEN-STUBBS, in the parish of Womersley, wapentake of Osgoldcross, liberty of the Honour of Pontefract; 7 miles from Pontefract, 7 from Ferrybridge.—Population 127.

WALES, in the parish of Laughton-le-Morthen, south-division of the wapentake of Strafforth and Tickhill, liberty of St. Peter; 7 miles from Worksop, *(Notts.)* 8 from Rotherham, 10 from Sheffield.—Population 229.

Pp

WALES-WOOD, in the parishes of Treton and Laughton-le-Morthen, south-division of the wapentake of Strafforth and Tickhill ; 5¼ miles from Rotherham, 9 from Sheffield, 9 from Worksop, *(Notts.)*

WALKINGHAM, in the parish of Knaresborough, lower-division of the wapentake of Claro ; 4 miles from Knaresborough, 4 from Boroughbridge, 5 from Ripley.

WALKLEY, in the parish of Sheffield, south-division of the wapentake of Strafforth and Tickhill ; 2 miles from Sheffield, 8 from Rotherham, 11½ from Penistone.

WALLERTHWAITE, in the parish of Ripon, lower-division of the wapentake of Claro, liberty of Ripon ; 4 miles from Ripon, 7 from Knaresborough.

WALL-HILL, in the parish of Rochdale, *(Lanc.)* Agbrigg-division of the wapentake of Agbrigg and Morley ; 9 miles from Rochdale, *(Lanc.)* 11 from Manchester, *(ditto)* 14 from Huddersfield.

WALSHFORD-BRIDGE, in the parish of Hunsingore, upper-division of the wapentake of Claro ; 3 miles from Wetherby, 5 from Knaresborough, 9 from Boroughbridge.

WALTON-HALL, in the parish of Sandall, Agbrigg-division of the wapentake of Agbrigg and Morley, liberty of the Manor of Wakefield; *(the seat of Thomas Waterton, Esq.)* 4 miles from Wakefield, 8 from Barnsley.

WALTON-HEAD, in the parish of Kirkby-Overblow, upper-division of the wapentake of Claro ; 6 miles from Knaresborough, 6¼ from Wetherby.

WALTON, MIDDLE, in the parish of Sandall, Agbrigg-division of the wapentake of Agbrigg and Morley, liberty of the Manor of Wakefield ; 3 miles from Wakefield, 8 from Barnsley.—Population 315.

WALTON, OVER, in the parish of Sandall, Agbrigg-division of the wapentake of Agbrigg and Morley, liberty of the Manor of Wakefield ; 3 miles from Wakefield, 8 from Barnsley.

WALTON-WOOD, in the parish of Badsworth, wapentake of Osgoldcross, liberty of the Honour of Pontefract ; 4¼ miles from Pontefract, 8 from Wakefield.

WARDSEND, in the parish of Ecclesfield, north-division of the wapentake of Strafforth and Tickhill ; *(the seat of Thomas Rawson, Esq.)* 2¼ miles from Sheffield, 8½ from Rotherham, 10 from Penistone.

WARLEY, in the parish of Halifax, Morley-division of the wapentake of Agbrigg and Morley, liberty of the Manor of Wakefield ; 2¼ miles from Halifax, 8 from Huddersfield.—Population 3,546.

WARMFIELD, in the parish of Warmfield, Agbrigg-division of the wapentake of Agbrigg and Morley, liberty of the Honour of Pontefract; 4 miles from Wakefield, 5 from Pontefract.—Population 625.

WARMSWORTH, in the parishes of Warmsworth and Doncaster, south-division of the wapentake of Strafforth and Tickhill; *(the seat of Mrs. Buck)* 3 miles from Doncaster, 9 from Rotherham.—Population 254.

WARREN-LANE, in the parish of Kirby-Malzeard, lower-division of the wapentake of Claro; 5 miles from Masham, 7 from Ripon.

WARSELL, in the parish of Ripon, lower-division of the wapentake of Claro, liberty of Ripon; 5 miles from Ripon, 7 from Ripley, 7 from Knaresborough.

WASS-LANE-HEAD, in the parish of Darfield, wapentake of Staincross, liberty of the Honour of Pontefract; 1 mile from Barnsley, 7¼ from Penistone, 11 from Rotherham.

WATERTON, in the parish of Armthorpe, south-division of the wapentake of Strafforth and Tickhill; 5 miles from Doncaster, 9 from Bawtry.

WATH-UPON-DEARN, in the parish of Wath-upon-Dearn, north-division of the wapentake of Strafforth and Tickhill, liberty of Tickhill; 5 miles from Rotherham, 9 from Doncaster, 11 from Sheffield.—Population 662.

WEARDLEY, in the parish of Harewood, upper-division of the wapentake of Skirack; 1 mile from Harewood, 5 from Leeds, 6½ from Otley.—Population 139.

WEELAND, in the parish of Snaith, wapentake of Osgoldcross, liberty of the Honour of Pontefract; 2 miles from Snaith, 7½ from Selby.

WEETON, in the parish of Harewood, upper-division of the wapentake of Claro; 5 miles from Otley, 7 from Wetherby, 9¼ from Leeds.—Population 237.

WEETWOOD-HALL, in the parish of Leeds, lower-division of the wapentake of Skirack; *(the seat of ——Brown, Esq.)* 3 miles from Leeds, 8 from Bradford.

WELDON-HALL, in the parish of Water-Fryston, wapentake of Osgoldcross, liberty of the Honour of Pontefract; 2 miles from Pontefract, 2¼ from Ferrybridge.

WELLIHOLE, in the parish of Rochdale, *(Lanc.)* Agbrigg-division of the wapentake of Agbrigg and Morley; 9 miles from Rochdale, *(Lanc.)* 12 from Manchester, *(ditto)* 14 from Huddersfield.

WELLINGLEY, in the parish of Tickhill, south-division of the wapentake of Strafforth and Tickhill; 2 miles from Tickhill, 7 from Doncaster, 10 from Rotherham.

WENTBRIDGE, in the parishes of Kirk-Smeaton, Bads-worth, and Darrington, wapentake of Osgoldcross, liberty of the Honour of Pontefract; 4¼ miles from Pontefract, 4¼ from Ferrybridge, 10½ from Doncaster.

WENTWORTH, in the parish of Wath-upon-Dearn, north-division of the wapentake of Strafforth and Tickhill, liberty of Tickhill; *(the seat of the Rev. John Lowe)* 6 miles from Rotherham, 8 from Barnsley, 13½ from Doncaster.—Population 978.

WENTWORTH-CASTLE, in the parish of Silkston, wapentake of Staincross, liberty of the Honour of Pontefract; *(the seat of Henry Vernon, Esq.)* 2 miles from Barnsley, 5½ from Penistone, 8 from Rotherham.

WENTWORTH-HOUSE, in the parish of Wath-upon-Dearn, north-division of the wapentake of Strafforth and Tickhill, liberty of Tickhill; *(the seat of Earl Fitzwilliam)* 4 miles from Rotherham, 9½ from Sheffield, 13 from Doncaster.

WESKETT, or WESTGATE-HILL, in the parish of Birstall, Morley-division of the wapentake of Agbrigg and Morley; 3¼ miles from Bradford, 8 from Halifax, 10¼ from Wakefield.

WESTBY, in the parish of Gisburn, west-division of the wapentake and liberty of Staincliffe; 1 mile from Gisburn, 8 from Clitheroe, *(Lanc.)* 12½ from Skipton.

WEST-END, in the parish of Fewston, lower-division of the wapentake of Claro; 10¼ miles from Otley, 11½ from Skipton, 14 from Knaresborough.

WEST-END, in the parish of Kirkby-Overblow, upper-division of the wapentake of Claro; 3¼ miles from Otley, 8 from Ripley.

WESTERTON, *see Ardsley, West.*

WESTERTON-HALL, in the parish of Woodchurch, Agbrigg-division of the wapentake of Agbrigg and Morley, liberty of the Manor of Wakefield; *(the seat of the Rev. —— Wood)* 4 miles from Wakefield, 10 from Bradford.

WEST-FIELD, in the parish of Kirby-Malzeard, lower-division of the wapentake of Claro; 6 miles from Ripon, 6 from Masham.

WEST-FIELD, in the parish of Fishlake, north-division of the wapentake of Strafforth and Tickhill; 4 miles from Thorne, 7½ from Snaith.

WEST-GILL, in the parish of Sedbergh, wapentake of Ewcross; 5 miles from Sedbergh, 14¼ from Askrigg.

WEST-HALL, in the parish of Wakefield, Agbrigg-division of the wapentake of Agbrigg and Morley; 3 miles from Wakefield, 9 from Leeds.

WEST-HOUSES, in the parish of Fewston, lower-division of the wapentake of Claro; 8 miles from Otley, 12 rom Skipton, 12 from Knaresborough.

WEST-HOUSES, in the parish of Kirby-Malzeard, lower-division of the wapentake of Claro; 4 miles from Kettlewell, 10 from Middleham, 13 from Pateleybridge.

WEST-HOUSES, in the parish of Thornton-in-Lonsdale, wapentake of Ewcross; 5 miles from Kirby-Lonsdale, (*Westm.*) 12 from Settle.

WESTKEY-HILL, in the parish of Harewood, upper-division of the wapentake of Claro; 5 miles from Otley, 5 from Harewood.

WESTON, in the parish of Weston, upper-division of the wapentake of Claro; (*Weston-Hall, the seat of William Vavasour, Esq.*) 2 miles from Otley, 12 from Leeds, 16 from Knaresborough.—Population 120.

WEST-SCHOLES, in the parish of Bradford, Morley-division of the wapentake of Agbrigg and Morley; 3¼ miles from Bradford, 5¼ from Halifax.

WEST-THORPE, in the parish of Silkston, wapentake of Staincross, liberty of the Honour of Pontefract; 1¼ mile from Penistone, 7 from Barnsley, 11½ from Huddersfield.

WESTWICK, in the parish of Ripon, lower-division of the wapentake of Claro, liberty of Ripon; 2 miles from Boroughbridge, 4 from Ripon, 7 from Knaresborough.—Pop. 20.

WEST-WOOD, in the parish of Huddersfield, Agbrigg-division of the wapentake of Agbrigg and Morley; 3 miles from Huddersfield, 8 from Halifax.

WETHERBY, in the parish of Spofforth, upper-division of the wapentake of Claro; 6 miles from Harewood, 7 from Knaresborough, 7 from Tadcaster, 7½ from Abberford, 10 from Otley, 12 from Boroughbridge, 15¼ from York, 16 from Leeds, 194 from London.—*Market*, Thursday.—*Fairs*, Holy-Thursday, and August 5, for Sheep and Pigs. *Principal Inns*, Angel, and Dog and Swan.—Pop. 1,144.

WETHERBY-GRANGE, in the parish of Collingham, wapentake of Barkston-Ash; (*the seat of Richard Thompson, Esq.*) 1 mile from Wetherby, 6 from Tadcaster, 7 from Abberford.

WHAITBER, in the parish of Thornton-in-Lonsdale, wapentake of Ewcross; 4½ miles from Kirby-Lonsdale, (*Westm.*) 14 from Settle.

WHARNCLIFFE-LODGE, in the parish of Tankersley, wapentake of Staincross, liberty of the Honour of Pontefract; (*the seat of the Hon. James Archibald Stuart Wortley*) 6 miles from Sheffield, 8½ from Penistone, 9 from Rotherham.

WHEAT-CROFT, in the parish of Rawmarsh, north-division of the wapentake of Strafforth and Tickhill; 2 miles from Rotherham, 8 from Sheffield, 12 from Barnsley.

WHEAT-HOUSE, in the parish of Firbeck, south-division of the wapentake of Strafforth and Tickhill; 5 miles from Tickhill, 5 from Workson, *(Notts.)* 9 from Rotherham.

WHEATLEY, in the parish and Soke of Doncaster, south-division of the wapentake of Strafforth and Tickhill; *(the seat of Sir George Cooke, Bart.)* $2\frac{1}{4}$ miles from Doncaster, 9 from Thorne.

WHEATLEY, in the parish of Ilkley, upper-division of the wapentake of Skirack; 5 miles from Otley, 8 from Bradford, 9 from Skipton.

WHELPSTONE'S-HEAD, in the parish of Giggleswick, west-division of the wapentake and liberty of Staincliffe; 4 miles from Settle, 16 from Skipton.

WHIRLOW, in the parish of Sheffield, south-division of the wapentake of Strafforth and Tickhill; 4 miles from Sheffield, 10 from Rotherham, 10 from Chesterfield, *(Derb.)*

WHISTON, in the parish of Whiston, south-division of the wapentake of Strafforth and Tickhill, liberty of Hallamshire; 2 miles from Rotherham, $7\frac{1}{4}$ from Sheffield, 11 from Tickhill.—Population 672.

WHISTON, UPPER, in the parish of Whiston, south-division of the wapentake of Strafforth and Tickhill; $2\frac{1}{4}$ miles from Rotherham, 8 from Sheffield.

WHITCHURCH, or WHITKIRK, in the parish of Whitchurch, lower-division of the wapentake of Skirack; $4\frac{1}{4}$ miles from Leeds, 8 from Wakefield, $10\frac{1}{4}$ from Ferrybridge,—Population 1,033.

WHITCLIFFE, in the parish of Ripon, lower-division of the wapentake of Claro, liberty of Ripon; $1\frac{1}{4}$ mile from Ripon, $7\frac{1}{4}$ from Boroughbridge.—Population 136.

WHITCROSS, in the parish of Elmley, Agbrigg-division of the wapentake of Agbrigg and Morley; 7 miles from Huddersfield, 7 from Wakefield.

WHITE-CHAPEL-IN-THE-NORTH, *see Heaton, Clack.*

WHITE-HILL, in the parish of Rotherham, south-division of the wapentake of Strafforth and Tickhill; 2 miles from Rotherham, 5 from Sheffield.

WHITE-HOUSES, in the parish of Ripon, lower-division of the wapentake of Claro; 1 mile from Pateleybridge, 7 from Ripley, 11 from Ripon.

WHITELEE, in the parish of Rochdale, *(Lanc.)* Agbrigg-division of the wapentake of Agbrigg and Morley; 10 miles from Rochdale, *(Lanc.)* 13 from Manchester, *(ditto)* 15 from Huddersfield.

WHITE-LEES, in the parish of Huddersfield, Agbrigg-division of the wapentake of Agbrigg and Morley; 6¼ miles from Huddersfield, 9½ from Halifax.

WHITELEY-WOOD-HALL, in the parish of Sheffield, south-division of the wapentake of Strafforth and Tickhill; *(the seat of William Hutton, Esq.)* 4 miles from Sheffield, 10 from Rotherham, 12 from Bakewell, *(Derb.)*

WHITE-WELL, in the parishes of Slaidburn and Clitheroe, *(Lanc.)* west-division of the wapentake and liberty of Staincliffe; 6¼ miles from Clitheroe, *(Lanc.)* 13½ from Gisburn, 17 from Lancaster, *(Lanc.)*

WHITE-WINDOWS, in the parish of Halifax, Morley-division of the wapentake of Agbrigg and Morley; *(the seat of Joseph Priestley, Esq.)* 3¾ miles from Halifax, 8 from Huddersfield, 13 from Rochdale, *(Lanc.)*

WHITGIFT, in the parish of Whitgift, wapentake of Osgoldcross, liberty of the Honour of Pontefract; 6 miles from Howden, 8 from Crowle, *(Linc.)* 13 from Snaith.—Population 263.

WHITLEY, in the parishes of Kellington and Snaith, wapentake of Osgoldcross, liberty of the Honour of Pontefract; 6¼ miles from Snaith, 6¾ from Pontefract.—Pop. 225.

WHITLEY, in the parish of Ecclesfield, north-division of the wapentake of Strafforth and Tickhill; 5 miles from Sheffield, 7 from Barnsley, 7 from Rotherham.

WHITLEY-HALL, in the parish of Kirk-Heaton, Agbrigg-division of the wapentake of Agbrigg and Morley, liberty of the Honour of Pontefract; *(the seat of Richard Henry Beaumont, Esq.)* 5¼ miles from Huddersfield, 7¼ from Wakefield.

WHITLEY, LOWER, in the parish of Thornhill, Agbrigg-division of the wapentake of Agbrigg and Morley, liberty of the Honour of Pontefract; 6¼ miles from Huddersfield, 8¼ from Wakefield.—Population 819.

WHITLEY-THORPE, in the parish of Kellington, wapentake of Osgoldcross, liberty of the Honour of Pontefract; 7 miles from Pontefract, 7 from Snaith.

WHITLEY, UPPER, in the parish of Kirk-Heaton, Agbrigg-division of the wapentake of Agbrigg and Morley, liberty of the Honour of Pontefract; 5½ miles from Huddersfield, 7½ from Wakefield.

WHITWELL, in the parish of Ecclesfield, north-division of the wapentake of Strafforth and Tickhill; 4¼ miles from Sheffield, 7 from Rotherham, 8 from Barnsley.

WHITWELL-PLACE, in the parish of Halifax, Morley-division of the wapentake of Agbrigg and Morley; 5¼ miles from Halifax, 12¾ from Rochdale, *(Lanc.)*

WHITWOOD, in the parish of Fetherstone, Agbrigg-division of the wapentake of Agbrigg and Morley, liberty of the Honour of Pontefract; 4 miles from Pontefract, 6 from Wakefield.—Population 233.

WHITWOOD-MERE, in the parish of Fetherstone, Agbrigg-division of the wapentake of Agbrigg and Morley, liberty of the Honour of Pontefract; 3¼ miles from Pontefract, 6¼ from Wakefield, 10 from Leeds.

WHIXLEY, in the parish of Whixley, upper-division of the wapentake of Claro; 6 miles from Boroughbridge, 7½ from Wetherby, 8 from Knaresborough.—Population 378.

WIBSEY, in the parish of Bradford, Morley-division of the wapentake of Agbrigg and Morley, liberty of the Honour of Pontefract; 3 miles from Bradford, 5 from Halifax.

WIBSEY-LOW-MOOR, in the parish of Bradford, Morley-division of the wapentake of Agbrigg and Morley, liberty of the Honour of Pontefract; 3½ miles from Bradford, 5 from Halifax.

WICKERSLEY, in the parish of Wickersley, south-division of the wapentake of Strafforth and Tickhill, liberty of Tickhill; 4 miles from Rotherham, 7 from Tickhill, 9 from Sheffield.—Population 270.

WIDDINGTON, in the parish of Little-Ouseburn, upper-division of the wapentake of Claro; 8 miles from Boroughbridge, 11 from Knaresborough.

WIGGLESWORTH, in the parish of Long-Preston, west-division of the wapentake and liberty of Staincliffe; 5 miles Settle, 13 from Skipton, 13½ from Colne, (Lanc.)—Population 371.

WIGTON, in the parish of Harewood, upper-division of the wapentake of Skirack; 3 miles from Leeds, 8 from Wetherby, 10 from Otley.—Population 134.

WIGTWIZLE, in the parish of Ecclesfield, north-division of the wapentake of Strafforth and Tickhill; 6 miles from Penistone, 12 from Sheffield, 12 from Barnsley.

WIKE, in the parishes of Harewood and Bardsey, upper-division of the wapentake of Skirack; 1¼ mile from Harewood, 4¼ from Leeds, 8 from Wetherby.—Population 59.

WIKE, in the parish of Birstall, Morley-division of the wapentake of Agbrigg and Morley, liberty of the Honour of Pontefract; 4¼ miles from Bradford, 5 from Halifax, 8 from Huddersfield.—Population 985.

WILBY, in the parish of Cantley, south-division of the wapentake of Strafforth and Tickhill; 2½ miles from Doncaster, 7 from Bawtry.

WILCROSS-BROW, in the parish of Gisburn, west-division

of the wapentake and liberty of Staincliffe ; 10 miles from Skipton, 12 from Settle, 12 from Burnley, *(Lanc.)*

WILLOW-EDGE, in the parish of Halifax, Morley-division of the wapentake of Agbrigg and Morley; *(the seat of Thomas Dyson, Esq.)* 2 miles from Halifax, 9 from Huddersfield.

WILLOW-HALL, in the parish of Halifax, Morley-division of the wapentake of Agbrigg and Morley; *(the seat of Thomas Lodge, Esq.)* 2 miles from Halifax, 9 from Huddersfield.

WILSDEN, in the parish of Bradford, Morley-division of the wapentake of Agbrigg and Morley, liberty of the Honour of Pontefract ; 4 miles from Bradford, 5 from Keighley, 8 from Halifax.—Population 913.

WILSELL, in the parish of Ripon, lower-division of the wapentake of Claro, liberty of Ripon ; 1 mile from Pateleybridge, 7 from Ripley, 11 from Ripon.

WILSICK, in the parish of Tickhill, south-division of the wapentake of Strafforth and Tickhill, liberty of Tickhill; *(the seat of John Brewin, Esq)* 2 miles from Tickhill, 5 from Doncaster, 6 from Bawtry, 9 from Rotherham.

WINCO-BANK, in the parish of Ecclesfield, north-division of the wapentake of Strafforth and Tickhill ; 4 miles from Sheffield, 4 from Rotherham, 10 from Barnsley.

WINDFIELD, in the parish of Rotherham, south-division of the wapentake of Strafforth and Tickhill ; 2 miles from Rotherham, 10 from Barnsley.

WINDHILL, in the parish of Calverley, Morley-division of the wapentake of Agbrigg and Morley, liberty of the Honour of Pontefract ; 3 miles from Bradford, 7½ from Otley.

WINDHILL-GATE, in the parish of Darton, wapentake of Staincross, liberty of the Honour of Pontefract ; 5 miles from Barnsley, 5 from Wakefield, 9 from Penistone.

WINDLEDEN, in the parish of Penistone, wapentake of Staincross, liberty of the Honour of Pontefract ; 6 miles from Penistone, 13 from Barnsley, 13 from Huddersfield.

WIND-MILL-HOUSE, in the parish of Crofton, Agbrigg-division of the wapentake of Agbrigg and Morley; 4 miles from Wakefield, 5 from Pontefract.

WINKSLEY, in the parish of Ripon, lower-division of the wapentake of Claro ; 5 miles from Ripon, 6 from Masham. —Population 144.

WINSLEY, or WINSLOW, in the parish of Ripon, lower-division of the wapentake of Claro ; 3 miles from Ripley, 6 from Pateleybridge, 7 from Ripon.

WINSKILL, in the parish of Giggleswick, west-division of

the wapentake and liberty of Staincliffe; 1 mile from Settle, 17 from Skipton.

WINTERBURNE, in the parish of Gargrave, east-division of the wapentake and liberty of Staincliffe; 7 miles from Skipton, 9 from Settle, 11 from Kettlewell.

WINTERSCALE, in the parish of Sedbergh, wapentake of Ewcross; 4 miles from Sedbergh, 15¼ from Askrigg.

WINTERSETT, in the parish of Wragby, wapentake of Staincross, liberty of the Honour of Pontefract; 6 miles from Wakefield, 6½ from Barnsley, 9½ from Pontefract.—Population 133.

WISTOW, in the parish of Wistow, wapentake of Barkston-Ash, liberties of St. Peter, and Cawood, Wistow, and Otley; 2 miles from Selby, 8 from Tadcaster, 15 from Pontefract.—Population 647.

WITHENS, in the parish of Halifax, Morley-division of the wapentake of Agbrigg and Morley; 2¼ miles from Halifax, 10¼ from Huddersfield.

WITHER, in the parish of Leeds, Morley-division of the wapentake of Agbrigg and Morley; 3¼ miles from Leeds, 9 from Bradford.

WOLFORD, in the parish of Tickhill, south-division of the wapentake of Strafforth and Tickhill; 2 miles from Tickhill, 9 from Doncaster, 10¼ from Rotherham.

WOMBWELL, in the parish of Darfield, north-division of the wapentake of Strafforth and Tickhill, liberty of Tickhill; 4¼ miles from Barnsley, 7¼ from Rotherham, 10 from Sheffield.—Population 614.

WOMBWELL-WOOD-HEAD, in the parish of Darfield, north-division of the wapentake of Strafforth and Tickhill, liberty of Tickhill; *(the seat of —— Verells, Esq.)* 4 miles from Barnsley, 8 from Rotherham.

WOMERSLEY, in the parish of Womersley, wapentake of Osgoldcross, liberty of the Honour of Pontefract; *(the seat of Lord Hawke)* 5 miles from Pontefract, 5 from Ferrybridge.—Population 351.

WOODALE, HIGH, and LOW, in the parish of Kirby-Malzeard, lower-division of the wapentake of Claro; 7 miles from Kettlewell, 11 from Pateleybridge.

WOOD-CHURCH, or WOOD-KIRK, in the parish of Woodchurch, Agbrigg-division of the wapentake of Agbrigg and Morley, liberty of the Manor of Wakefield; 6 miles from Wakefield, 6 from Dewsbury.

WOOD-FOOT, in the parish of Rotherham, south-division of the wapentake of Strafforth and Tickhill; 2 miles from Rotherham, 8 from Sheffield, 10 from Doncaster.

WOOD-HALL, or HILLS, in the parish of Calverley, Morley-division of the wapentake of Agbrigg and Morley, liberty of the Honour of Pontefract; 3 miles from Bradford, 7 from Leeds.

WOOD-HALL, in the parish of Kirkby-Overblow, upper-division of the wapentake of Claro; *(the seat of William Fenton Scott, Esq.)* 2 miles from Wetherby, 7 from Knaresborough, 13 from Otley.

WOOD-HALL, in the parish of Womersley, wapentake of Osgoldcross, liberty of the Honour of Pontefract; 5 miles from Pontefract, 5 from Ferrybridge.

WOOD-HALL, in the parish of Harthill, south-division of the wapentake of Strafforth and Tickhill; 5 miles from Worksop, *(Notts.)* 10 from Rotherham, 14 from Sheffield.

WOOD-HALL, MIDDLE, in the parish of Darfield, north-division of the wapentake of Strafforth and Tickhill; $3\frac{1}{4}$ miles from Barnsley, 8 from Rotherham.

WOOD-HALL, NETHER, in the parish of Darfield, north-division of the wapentake of Strafforth and Tickhill; $3\frac{1}{4}$ miles from Barnsley, 8 from Rotherham.

WOOD-HALL, OVER, in the parish of Darfield, north-division of the wapentake of Strafforth and Tickhill; $3\frac{1}{2}$ miles from Barnsley, 8 from Rotherham.

WOOD-HOUSE, in the parish of Halifax, Morley-division of the wapentake of Agbrigg and Morley; 2 miles from Halifax, 6 from Huddersfield.

WOOD-HOUSE, in the parish of Handsworth, south-division of the wapentake of Strafforth and Tickhill; $4\frac{1}{4}$ miles from Sheffield, 6 from Rotherham.

WOOD-HOUSE, in the parish of Normanton, Agbrigg-division of the wapentake of Agbrigg and Morley, liberty of the Manor of Wakefield; 4 miles from Pontefract, $5\frac{1}{4}$ from Wakefield.

WOOD-HOUSE, in the parish of Huddersfield, Agbrigg-division of the wapentake of Agbrigg and Morley; *(the seat of John Whitacre, Esq.)* 1 mile from Huddersfield, 8 from Halifax, 15 from Leeds.

WOOD-HOUSE, in the parish of Leeds, lower-division of the wapentake of Skirack, liberty of the Honour of Pontefract; $1\frac{1}{4}$ mile from Leeds, 9 from Otley.

WOOD-HOUSE-CARR, in the parish of Leeds, lower-division of the wapentake of Skirack, liberty of the Honour of Pontefract; 1 mile from Leeds, 10 from Otley, 10 from Bradford.

WOOD-HOUSE, LITTLE, in the parish of Leeds, lower-division of the wapentake of Skirack, liberty of the Honour of Pontefract; 1 mile from Leeds, 9 from Otley, 9 from Bradford.

WOOD-HOUSE-YATE, in the parish of Slaidburn, west-division of the wapentake and liberty of Staincliffe; 10 miles from Clitheroe, *(Lanc.)* 11 from Settle.

WOODLANDS, in the parish of Adwick-in-the-Street, north-division of the wapentake of Strafforth and Tickhill; *(the seat of Edward Waterton, Esq)* 3½ miles from Doncaster, 11¼ from Pontefract, 16¼ from Wakefield.

WOOD-LANE-HALL, in the parish of Halifax, Morley-division of the wapentake of Agbrigg and Morley; 4 miles from Halifax, 10 from Huddersfield, 12 from Bradford.

WOOD-LEE-MILL, in the parish of Maltby, south-division of the wapentake of Strafforth and Tickhill; 5¼ miles from Tickhill, 5¼ from Bawtry, 7¼ from Worksop, *(Notts.)*

WOODLESFORD, in the parish of Rothwell, Agbrigg-division of the wapentake of Agbrigg and Morley; 4½ miles from Leeds, 5 from Wakefield.

WOOD-NOOK, in the parish of Almondbury, Agbrigg-division of the wapentake of Agbrigg and Morley; 4¼ miles from Huddersfield, 12¼ from Halifax.

WOOD-ROW, in the parish of Kirk-Burton, Agbrigg-division of the wapentake of Agbrigg and Morley; 6 miles from Huddersfield, 7 from Dewsbury.

WOOD-SEAT, in the parish of Ecclesfield, north-division of the wapentake of Strafforth and Tickhill; 5 miles from Sheffield, 7 from Rotherham, 7 from Barnsley.

WOOD-SEAT, in the parish of Ecclesfield, south-division of the wapentake of Strafforth and Tickhill; 7 miles from Penistone, 8¼ from Hope, *(Derb.)* 10 from Sheffield.

WOODSETT, in the parish of South-Anston, south-division of the wapentake of Strafforth and Tickhill, liberty of St. Peter; 4½ miles from Worksop, *(Notts.)* 6½ from Tickhill, 9½ from Rotherham.—Population 123.

WOODSHAM, or WOODSOME, in the parish of Almondbury, Agbrigg-division of the wapentake of Agbrigg and Morley, liberty of the Honour of Pontefract; *(Woodsham-Hall, the seat of the Earl of Dartmouth)* 3 miles from Huddersfield, 11 from Wakefield, 11 from Halifax.

WOODSIDE, in the parish of Kildwick, east-division of the wapentake and liberty of Staincliffe; 4½ miles from Keighley, 6 from Skipton.

WOODTHORPE, in the parish of Sandall, Agbrigg-division of the wapentake of Agbrigg and Morley, liberty of the Manor of Wakefield; *(the seat of the Rev. William Wood)* 3 miles from Wakefield, 7 from Barnsley.

WOODTHORPE, in the parish of Handsworth, south division of the wapentake of Strafforth and Tickhill *(the seat of Hugh Parker, Esq.)* 3 miles from Sheffield, 6 from Rotherham, 11½ from Chesterfield, *(Derb.)*

WOOLDALE, or WOLFSDALE, in the parish of Kirk-Burton, Agbrigg-division of the wapentake of Agbrigg and Morley, liberty of the Manor of Wakefield; 6¼ miles from Huddersfield, 8 from Penistone.—Population 2,620.

WOOLLEY, in the parish of Royston, wapentake of Staincross, liberty of the Honour of Pontefract; 5 miles from Barnsley, 5 from Wakefield, 10 from Penistone.—Pop. 565.

WOOLLEY-EDGE, in the parish of Royston, wapentake of Staincross, liberty of the Honour of Pontefract; 6 miles from Barnsley, 6 from Wakefield, 8½ from Penistone.

WOOLLEY-PARK, in the parish of Royston, wapentake of Staincross, liberty of the Honour of Pontefract; *(the seat of Godfrey Wentworth Wentworth, Esq.)* 5 miles from Barnsley, 5 from Wakefield, 10¼ from Penistone.

WORMLEY-HILL, in the parish of Fishlake, north-division of the wapentake of Strafforth and Tickhill; 4 miles from Thorne, 7½ from Snaith.

WORRALL, in the parish of Ecclesfield, north-division of the wapentake of Strafforth and Tickhill; 4 miles from Sheffield, 10 from Rotherham, 11 from Barnsley.

WORSBROUGH, in the parish of Darfield, wapentake of Staincross, liberty of the Honour of Pontefract; *(the seat of Francis Edmunds, Esq.)* 2½ miles from Barnsley, 7 from Penistone, 11 from Sheffield.—Population 879.

WORTLEY, in the parish of Leeds, Morley-division of the wapentake of Agbrigg and Morley, liberty of the Honour of Pontefract; 3 miles from Leeds, 8 from Bradford.—Population 1,925.

WORTLEY, in the parish of Tankersley, wapentake of Staincross, liberty of the Honour of Pontefract; *(Wortley Hall, the seat of James Archibald Stuart Wortley, Esq)* 5 miles from Barnsley, 5¼ from Penistone, 8 from Sheffield, 10 from Rotherham.—Population 846.

WOTHERSOME, in the parish of Bardsey, lower-division of the wapentake of Skirack; 5 miles from Wetherby, 5½ from Tadcaster.—Pop. 15.

WRAGBY, in the parish of Wragby, wapentake of Osgoldcross, liberty of the Honour of Pontefract; 5¼ miles from Pontefract, 6 from Wakefield, 14 from Doncaster.

WRANGBROOK, in the parish of South-Kirkby, wapentake of Osgoldcross, liberty of the Honour of Pontefract; 6 miles from Pontefract, 9 from Doncaster.

WRENTHORPE, in the parish of Wakefield, Agbrigg-division of the wapentake of Agbrigg and Morley, liberty of the Manor of Wakefield; 1 mile from Wakefield, 8 from Leeds.

WRETH-HOUSE, in the parish of Penistone, wapentake of Staincross, liberty of the Honour of Pontefract; 2 miles from Penistone, 5½ from Barnsley, 11 from Sheffield.

WROSE, in the parish of Calverley, Morley-division of the wapentake of Agbrigg and Morley, liberty of the Honour of Pontefract; 3 miles from Bradford, 7 from Otley, 10 from Leeds.

Y.

YARLSBER, in the parish of Ingleton, wapentake of Ewcross; 8 miles from Kirby-Lonsdale, (*Westm.*) 10½ from Settle.

YEADON, NETHER, in the parish of Guiseley, upper-division of the wapentake of Skirack; 4¼ miles from Otley, 5¼ from Bradford, 9 from Leeds.

YEADON, UPPER, in the parish of Guiseley, upper-division of the wapentake of Skirack; 3¼ miles from Otley, 6¼ from Bradford, 8 from Leeds.—Population 1,695.

YEWS, in the parish of Maltby, south-division of the wapentake of Strafforth and Tickhill; 4 miles from Tickhill; 5¼ from Worksop, (*Notts.*)

YEWS, in the parish of Ecclesfield, north-division of the wapentake of Strafforth and Tickhill; 4¼ miles from Sheffield, 10¼ from Rotherham, 11 from Barnsley.

YOKENTHWAITE, in the parish of Arncliffe, east-division of the wapentake and liberty of Staincliffe; 5 miles from Kettlewell, 15 from Settle, 17 from Leyburn.

WEST-RIDING.

LORD LIEUTENANT.

THE RIGHT HON. EARL FITZWILLIAM,
Wentworth-House.

NAMES OF ACTING MAGISTRATES.

ALDERSON, C.	Clerk,	*Aston.*
ARMITSTEAD, JOHN,	Clerk,	*Bawtry.*
ARMITAGE, GEORGE,	Esq.	*Highroyd.*
ATHORPE, THOMAS,	Esq.	*Dinnington, near Worksop.*
BAGSHAW, SIR W. C.	Knt.	*The Oaks, (Derb.)*
BEAUMONT, R. H.	Esq.	*Whitley-Hall.*
BECKETT, JOHN,	Esq.	*Leeds.*
BLOIS, CHARLES,	Esq.	
BROOKSBANK, B.	Esq.	*Healaugh-Hall.*
BUSFIELD, J. A.	Esq.	*Cononley-Hall.*
CHILDERS, J. W.	Esq.	*Cantley.*
COCKSHUTT, JAMES,	Esq.	*Husthwaite,*
COLLINS, THOMAS,	D. D.	*Gisburn.*
CONSTABLE, CHARLES,	Clerk,	*Maltby.*
COOKE, BRYAN,	Esq.	*Owston.*
CORBETT, STUART,	Clerk,	*Wortley.*
COULTHURST, H. W.	D. D.	*Halifax.*
DAWSON, WILLIAM,	Esq.	*Wakefield.*
DEALTRY, BENJAMIN,	Esq.	*Lofthouse-Hall.*
DEARDEN, JOHN,	Esq.	*Hollins-Hall.*
DIXON, JOHN,	Esq.	*Gledhow.*
DIXON, JEREMIAH,	Clerk,	*Woolley.*
DRAKE, THOMAS,	D. D.	*Rochdale, (Lanc.)*
EDMUNDS, FRANCIS,	Esq.	*Worsbrough.*
ELLISON, RICHARD,	Esq.	*Sudbrook, near Lincoln.*
ENTWISLE, JOHN,	Esq.	*Foxholes, near Rochdale.*
FAWKES, WALTER,	Esq.	*Farnley-Hall.*
FERRAND, EDWARD,	Esq.	*St. Ives.*
FOLJAMBE, F. F.	Esq.	*Osberton, Retford.*
FOSTER, JOHN,	Clerk,	*Ryther.*
FRANK, BACON,	Esq.	*Campsall.*
GALWAY, RT. HON. VISC.		*Searlby, (Notts.)*
GARFORTH, THOMAS,	Esq.	*Steeton-Hall.*

WEST-RIDING.

GELDART, JAMES,	Clerk,	Kirk-Deighton.
HAWKE, RT. HON. LORD		Womersley.
HAY, WILLIAM ROBERT,	Clerk,	Ackworth.
HIRD, LAMPLUGH,	Esq.	Bradford.
HODGSON, JAMES,	Clerk,	Barwick.
HORTON, SIR WATTS,	Bart.	Chatterton, Oldham
HORTON, THOMAS,	Esq.	Howroyd.
INGILBY, SIR JOHN,	Bart.	Ripley.
KNOWLTON, CHARLES,	Clerk,	Keighley.
LEAF, JOHN,	Esq.	Manchester.
LODGE, THOMAS,	Esq.	Willow-Hall.
LONG, RICHARD,	Clerk,	Whiston.
LOWE, JOHN,	Clerk,	Wentworth.
LUMLEY, HON. F.		Tickhill-Castle.
MILNER, SIR W. M.	Bart.	Nun-Appleton.
MYERS, JOHN,	Clerk,	Shepley.
MILTON, RT. HON. LORD	VISC.	Wentworth-House.
NEVILE, CHRISTOPHER,	Esq.	Scaftworth, (Notts)
PARKER, HUGH,	Esq.	Woodthorpe.
PLUMER, HALL,	Esq.	Bilton Hall.
PRIESTLEY, JOSEPH,	Esq.	White-Windows.
RADCLIFFE, JOSEPH,	Esq.	Milnsbridge-House.
SITWELL, SIR SITWELL,	Bart.	Renishaw, (Derb.)
SMYTH, RIGHT HON. JOHN,		Heath.
STAPYLTON, HON. G. A. C.		Wighill-Park.
STOCKS, MICHAEL,	Esq.	Catherine-House.
STOVEN, JAMES,	D. D.	Rossington.
TAYLOR, M. A.	Esq.	Ledstone-Lodge.
TAYLOR, JOHN,	Clerk,	Horbury.
THORNTON, THOMAS,	Esq.	Falconer's Hall.
TRIPP, JOHN,	L.L.D.	Spofforth.
WADDILOVE, R. D.	D. D.	Ripon.
WALKER, RICHARD,	Esq.	Ridings.
WATSON, JOHN,	Esq.	Bilton-Park.
WAUD, SAMUEL WILKES,	Esq.	Camblesforth.
WENTWORTH, G. W.	Esq.	Woolley-Park.
WHITAKER, T. D.	Clerk,	Holme.
WILSON, MATTHEW,	Esq.	Eshton-Hall.
WOOD, WILLIAM,	Clerk,	Wood-Thorpe.
WORTLEY, J. A. S.	Esq.	Wortley Hall.
WRIGHTSON, WILLIAM,	Esq.	Cusworth.

LORDS AND CHIEF BAILIFFS.

HIS GRACE THE LORD ARCHBISHOP OF YORK, *Bishopthorpe*,	LIBERTY OF RIPON.
HIS GRACE THE DUKE OF DEVONSHIRE, *Barden-Tower*,	STAINCLIFFE AND LIBERTY OF KNARESBOROUGH.
HIS GRACE THE DUKE OF BUCCLEUGH,	LIBERTY OF BOLLAND.
HIS GRACE THE DUKE OF LEEDS, *Hornby-Castle*,	MANOR OF WAKEFIELD.
THE RIGHT HON. EARL OF SCARBOROUGH, *Sandbeck*,	LIBERTY OF TICKHILL.
WILLIAM CARR, Esq. *Rothwell-Haigh*,	HONOUR OF PONTEFRACT.
HIS GRACE THE DUKE OF NORFOLK, *Sheffield-Manor*,	HALLAMSHIRE.
HIS GRACE THE DUKE OF DEVONSHIRE, *Barden-Tower*,	CLIFFORD'S FEE.

CLERK OF THE PEACE.

THOMAS WYBERGH, Esq. *Linton-Spring.*
JOHN FOLJAMBE, Esq. *Wakefield*, his Deputy.

TREASURER.

JOHN SEATON, Esq. *Pontefract.*

CORONERS.

HENRY BREARY,	*York.*
WILLIAM TINDAL,	*Skipton.*
JOHN FOSTER,	*High-Green.*
RICHARD DUNHILL,	*Newton.*
JAMES WIGLESWORTH,	*Halifax*
THOMAS SHEPLEY,	*Selby.*
EDWARD BROOK,	*Wakefield.*
WILLIAM CARRET,	*Rothwell,*

For the HONOUR OF PONTEFRACT.

JOHN CARTMAN, ... *Ripon,*

For the LIBERTY OF RIPON.

WEST-RIDING.

CHIEF CONSTABLES.

Name	Division	Wapentake
R. BEATSON, Sandall,	Agbrigg-Division	Agbrigg and Morley.
T. SELBY, Bingley,	Morley-ditto,	
E. TRUEMAN, Pontefract,	....	Barkston-Ash.
R. WILEY, Selby,	....	
H. FLETCHER, Boroughbridge,	Lower-Division,	Claro.
J. GILBERTSON, Westwick,	Upper-ditto, ...	
R. WILKINSON, Ackworth,	....	Osgoldcross.
W. EARNSHAW, Rowle,	....	
R. PARR, Oulton,	Lower-Division,	Skirack.
R. LUMB, Swillington,	Upper-ditto,	
J. SYKES, Worsbrough,	....	Staincross.
C. STRINGER, High-Hoyland.	....	
J. WILDMAN, Threshfield,	East-Division,	Staincliffe & Ewcross.
J. BOOTH, Settle,	West-ditto,	
W. MASON, Doncaster,	North-Division,	Strafforth & Tickhill.*
J. FOSTER, High-Green,	South-ditto,	
J. GILBERTSON, Westwick,	....	Liberty of Ripon.

CLERK OF GENERAL MEETINGS OF LIEUTENANTCY.†

THOMAS BOLLAND, Esq. *Leeds.*

---

*Strafforth and Tickhill is divided into two Divisions, by the River Don, denominated North and South, now usually called Upper and Lower, the former of which we have made use of.

†In all matters relating to LIEUTENANTCY, the City of York, and County of the said City, and Liberty of St. Peter, are included in the West-Riding.

WEST-RIDING.

CLERKS OF SUBDIVISION MEETINGS OF LIEUTENANTCY.

B. CLARKSON, Wakefield.	AGBRIGG-DIVISION	AGBRIGG AND MORLEY.
C. F. BUSFIELD, Cottingley-Bridge.	MORLEY DITTO	
E. TRUEMAN, Pontefract.	....	BARKSTON-ASH.
S. POWELL, Knaresborough.	....	CLARO.
R. WILKINSON, Ackworth.	....	OSGOLDCROSS.
T. BOLLAND, Leeds.	....	SKIRACK AND BORO' OF LEEDS.
G. KEIR, Barnsley.	....	STAINCROSS.
R. DANSER, Doncaster.	NORTH-DIVISION	STRAFFORTH AND TICKHILL.
J. FISHER, Masbrough.	SOUTH DITTO	
J. HARTLEY, Settle.	....	STAINCLIFFE EAST AND WEST AND EWCROSS.
R. TOWNEND, York.	....	AINSTY AND LIBERTY OF ST. PETER.

BAILIFFS.

JOHN LISTER, ... Halifax, AGBRIGG AND MORLEY.
THOMAS HAMPSHIRE, Leeds, SKIRACK.
GEORGE FOSTER, Otley, ... CLARO.
THOMAS COULTER, Doncaster, OSGOLDCROSS.
THOMAS HARRAP, Dewsbury, ... BARKSTON-ASH.
JOHN CLEGG, West-Clayton, ... STAINCROSS.
JOHN HUDSON, Rotherham, ... STRAFFORTH AND TICKHILL.
WILLIAM SHACKLETON, Skipton, EWCROSS.

BAILIFFS AT LARGE, WHO RESIDE IN THIS RIDING.

JOSHUA CRAVEN,	Bradford.
WILLIAM LYAL,	Ripon.
JAMES POLLARD,	Halifax.
JOSEPH FOSTER,	Pontefract.
SAMUEL LANCASTER,	Huddersfield.
WILLIAM LEE,	Leeds.
WILLIAM NEEDHAM,	Sheffield.
GEORGE SMITH,	Ditto.
ANTHONY BRANSON,	Ditto.
JAMES GREEN,	Worsbrough.
JOHN SENIOR,	Wakefield.

DIRECTIONS FOR WARRANTS, ON WRITS, TO LIBERTIES

BOLLAND.	To the Chief Bailiff of the Liberty of the Forest of Bolland and his Deputies.
CLIFFORD'S FEE.	To the Chief Bailiff of Clifford's Fee, and his Deputies.
DONCASTER.	To the Mayor of Doncaster, and his Serjeants at Mace.
HALLAMSHIRE.	To the Chief Bailiff of the Liberty of Hallamshire, and his Deputies.
KNARESBOROUGH.	To the Chief Bailiff of the Liberty of Knaresborough, and his Deputies.
LEEDS.	To the Mayor of Leeds, and his Serjeants at Mace.
PONTEFRACT.	To the Chief Bailiff of the Liberty of the Honour of Pontefract, and his Deputies.
PONTEFRACT TOWN.	To the Mayor of Pontefract, and his Serjeants at Mace.
RIPON.	To the Chief Bailiff of the Liberty of Ripon, and his Deputies.
STAINCLIFFE.	To the Chief Bailiff of the Liberty of Staincliffe, and his Deputies.
TICKHILL.	To the Chief Bailiff of the Liberty of Tickhill, and his Deputies.
WAKEFIELD.	To the Lord of the Manor of Wakefield, and his Deputies.

WEST-RIDING.

SESSIONS.

The *Easter* Quarter Sessions are held at Pontefract only, and always begin on Monday after Low-Sunday, or the first Sunday after Easter.—The *Midsummer* Quarter Sessions always begin at Skipton on Tuesday in the first whole week after the 7th of July; Bradford, Thursday after; and Rotherham, on the Wednesday following.—The *Michaelmas* Quarter Sessions always begin at Knaresborough, on Tuesday in the first whole week after the 29th of September; Leeds, on Thursday after; and Sheffield and Rotherham, alternately, on the Wednesday following.—The *Christmas* Quarter Sessions always begin at Wetherby, on Tuesday in the first whole week after the Epiphany; Wakefield on Thursday after; and Doncaster on the Wednesday following.

If any of the Days by which the Sessions are regulated, happen to fall upon a Sunday, the Sessions will not be held until the Tuesday week following.

After each of the above mentioned Quarter Sessions, there is an adjournment to Wakefield, for the purpose of inspecting the Prison, &c. which is generally held within a Month or Six weeks from the last adjournment.

AINSTY AND CITY OF YORK.

ACASTER-MALBIS, in the parish of Acaster-Malbis; 4¾ miles from York, 7 from Tadcaster.—Population 265.

ACASTER-SELBY, or SAILBY, in the parish of Stillingfleet; 6 miles from Tadcaster, 6 from York, 8 from Selby.—Population 178.

ACOMB, in the parish of Acomb, liberty of St. Peter; *(the seat of the Rev. Henry Percival)* 2¼ miles from York, 8 from Tadcaster, 12¼ from Wetherby.—Population 587.

ANGRAM, in the parish of Long-Marston; 4 miles from Tadcaster, 7 from York, 8½ from Wetherby.

APPLETON, NUN, in the parish of Bolton-Percy; *(the seat of Sir William Mordaunt Milner, Bart.)* 6 miles from Tadcaster, 9 from York.

APPLETON-ROEBUCK, in the parish of Bolton-Percy; 5 miles from Tadcaster, 8 from York.—Population 406.

ASKAM-BRYAN, or GREAT, in the parish of Askam-Bryan; 4 miles from York, 6 from Tadcaster.—Pop 295.

ASKAM-RICHARD, or LITTLE, in the parish of Askam-Richard; *(the seat of William Carr, Esq.)* 4¼ miles from Tadcaster, 5 from York.—Population 170.

BICKERTON, in the parish of Bilton; 4 miles from Wetherby, 7 from Tadcaster, 10 from York.—Population 127.

BILBROUGH, in the parish of Bilbrough; *(the seat of —— Agar, Esq)* 4½ miles from Tadcaster, 5¼ from York.—Population 185.

BILTON, in the parish of Bilton, liberty of St. Peter; *(Bilton-Hall, the seat of Hall Plumer, Esq.)* 4¼ miles from Wetherby, 5½ from Tadcaster, 9½ from Knaresborough, 10¾ from York.—Population 220.

AINSTY.

BISHOPTHORPE, in the parish of Bishopthorpe ; *Bishopthorpe-Palace, the seat of the Archbishop of York*) 2¼ miles from York, 8 from Tadcaster.—Population 218.

BOLTON-PERCY, in the parish of Bolton-Percy ; *(the seat of the Rev. Robert Markham)* 3 miles from Tadcaster, 9 from York.—Population 189.

CATTERTON, in the parish of Tadcaster ; 2 miles from Tadcaster, 7 from York 8 from Wetherby.—Population 68.

COLTON, in the parish of Bolton-Percy ; *(the seat of Christopher Morritt, Esq.)* 4 miles from Tadcaster, 6 from York.—Population 155.

COPMANTHORPE, in the parish of St. Mary, Bishop-Hill, the Younger, York, a part in the liberty of St. Peter ; 4 miles from York, 5¼ from Tadcaster.—Population 184.

CUMBERLAND-ROW, or NEW-STREET, and part of DAVYGATE, York, *(extraparochial)*

DRINGHOUSES, in the parishes of St. Mary, Bishop-Hill, the Elder, Holy Trinity, Micklegate, York, and Acomb, liberty of St. Peter ; 1¼ mile from York, 7¼ from Tadcaster, 15 from Wetherby.—Population 124.

EASDIKE, in the parish of Wighill ; 1 mile from Tadcaster, 7 from Wetherby, 8 from York.

HEALAUGH, in the parish of Healaugh, 3 miles from Tadcaster, 7 from Wetherby, 8 from York.—Population 233.

HEALAUGH-HALL, in the parish of Healaugh ; *(the seat of Benjamin Brookshank, Esq.)* 1 mile from Tadcaster, 6 from Wetherby, 10 from York.

HEALAUGH-MANOR, in the parish of Healaugh ; 2 miles from Tadcaster, 7 from Wetherby, 8 from York.

HESSAY, in the parish of Moor-Monkton ; 6 miles from York, 9 from Wetherby.—Population 114.

HOLDGATE, or HOLEGATE, in the parish of Acomb, liberty of St. Peter ; *(the seat of Lindley Murray, Esq.)* 1¼ mile from York, 8¼ from Tadcaster, 12¼ from Wetherby. —Population 55.

HORNINGTON, in the parish of Bolton-Percy ; 3 miles from Tadcaster, 9¼ from York.

HUTTON, in the parish of Long-Marston ; 7 miles from Tadcaster, 8 from Wetherby, 8 from York.

KNAPTON, in the parish of Acomb ; 3½ miles from York, 8½ from Tadcaster.—Population 120.

MARSTON, LONG, in the parish of Long-Marston ; 6¼ miles from Wetherby, 7 from York, 8 from Tadcaster.—Population 399.

MIDDLETHORPE, in the parish of Bishophill, the Elder, York ; *(the seat of John Barlow, Esq.)* 1¼ mile from York, 8 from Tadcaster —Population 47.

AINSTY.

MOATHOUSE, in the parish of Wighill; 3 miles from Tadcaster, 4 from Wetherby, 12 from York.

MOOR-MONKTON, in the parish of Moor-Monkton; 8 miles from York, 9 from Knaresborough, 10 from Wetherby.—Population 256.

OXTON, in the parish of Tadcaster; *(the seat of John William Clough, Esq.)* 1 mile from Tadcaster, 9½ from York.—Population 49.

POPPLETON, LAND, in the parish of Bishop-Hill, Jun. York, liberty of St. Peter; 4 miles from York, 12 from Wetherby, 12 from Easingwold.—Population 210.

POPPLETON, WATER, in the parish of Water-Poppleton, 4 miles from York, 11 from Easingwold, 13 from Wetherby.—Population 250.

RUFFORTH, in the parish of Rufforth; 5½ miles from York, 9¼ from Wetherby.—Population 273.

SADDLETHORP, in the parish of Moor-Monkton, 6 miles from York, 8 from Boroughbridge.

SKEWKIRK, in the parish of Kirk-Hammerton; 7 miles from Wetherby, 9 from York, 10 from Knaresborough.

SKIPBRIDGE, *see Skipbridge in the West-Riding*

STEETON, in the parish of Bolton-Percy; 3 miles from Tadcaster, 7 from York.—Population 77.

STREETHOUSES, in the parishes of Bolton-Percy and Bilbrough; 3¼ miles from Tadcaster, 5¼ from York.

SYNINGTHWAITE, in the parish of Bilton; 4 miles from Wetherby, 5 from Tadcaster, 10 from York.

TADCASTER, *see Tadcaster in the West-Riding.*

THORP-ARCH, in the parish of Thorp-Arch; *(the seat of Wilmer Gossip, Esq.)* 3 miles from Wetherby, 4 from Tadcaster, 13 from York.—*Principal Inn*, Red Lion.—Population 314.

TOCKWITH, in the parish of Bilton; 7½ miles from Tadcaster, 8⅞ from York.

WALTON, in the parish of Walton; 2 miles from Wetherby, 5 from Tadcaster, 13 from York.—Population 205.

WIGHILL, in the parish of Wighill; 2½ miles from Tadcaster, 6 from Wetherby, 8½ from York —Population 216.

WIGHILL-PARK, in the parish of Wighill; *(the seat of the Hon. Granville Anson Chetwynd Stapylton)* 4 miles from Tadcaster, 4 from Wetherby, 9 from York.

WILSTROP, or WILSTHORP, in the parish of Kirk-Hammerton; 8½ miles from York, 10 from Knaresborough.

YORK, in the parishes of All Saints, Pavement, and North-Street; Bishophill the Elder, and Younger; Christ Church; St. Crux; St. Cuthbert; St. Dennis; St. Helen; St John;

St. Lawrence; St. Michael-le-Belfrey; St. Martin, Coney-street; St. Mary, Castlegate; St. Michael, Spurriergate; St, Martin, Micklegate; St. Maurice; St. Margaret; St Olave; St. Saviour; St. Sampson; Holy-Trinity, Goodramgate; Holy-Trinity, Micklegate; St. Andrew; St. Giles; and St. Peter; 9 miles from Tadcaster, 13 from Easingwold, 13 from Pocklington, 14¼ from Wetherby, 15 from Selby, 17 from Boroughbridge, 18 from Malton, 18 from Knaresborough, 19 from Market-Weighton, 20 from Howden, 23 from Helmsley, 29 from Great-Driffield, 199 from London.—*Markets*, Tuesday, Thursday, and Saturday. —*Fairs*, Candlemas-Fair is held on Thursday and Friday before old Candlemas-day; Palmsun-Fair, on Thursday before Palm-Sunday; All-Souls'-Fair, on November 13, and Martinmas-Fair on November 22, for Horned Cattle, Sheep, Horses, &c. in the Streets of Walmgate, Fossgate, Colliergate, and Pavement; the Statutes for hiring servants, are held also in Pavement on November 22. St. Luke's Fair, commonly called Dish-Fair, is held in Micklegate, on old St. Luke's-day, for all sorts of Dishes, small Wares, &c. The Horse-Shows are held without-Micklegate-Bar, on Monday in the August Race-week; the last week in September, called Michaelmas-show; and the first whole week before Christmas. There are likewise Fairs held in Walmgate, every other Thursday, for Horned Cattle and Sheep. Three Fairs are held on the north-side of the city, called the Horse-fair, for all sorts of Cattle, viz. on Whit-Monday, old St. Peter's-day, and old Lammas-day. At the latter Fair, from three o'Clock on the 11th of August, to the same hour on the 13th, the Sheriff's authority of arresting any person within the city and suburbs is suspended, the Archbishop's Bailiff or Substitute having the only power of executing any judicial process at that time. Line Fairs, Saturday before old Candlemas-day, Saturday before old Lady-day, Whit-Monday, old St. Peter's-day, old Lammas-day, Saturday before old Michaelmas, Saturday before old Martinmas, and Saturday before old Christmas-day.—*Bankers*, Messrs. Raper, Swanns, Clough, and Co. in New-Street, draw on Messrs. Boldero, Lushington, and Co. 30 Cornhill; and Messrs. Wilson, Smith, and Co. in High-Ousegate, draw on Messrs. Robarts, Curtis, and Co. 15 Lombard Street.—Sends two Members to Parliament.—*Principal Inns*, Etridge's Hotel, in Blake Street; Tavern, in St. Helen's Square; George, and Black Swan, in Coney Street; White Horse, in Coppergate; Old George, and White Swan, in Pavement.—Population 16,846.

CITY AND AINSTY.

NAMES OF THE MAGISTRATES.

THE RIGHT HON. THE LORD MAYOR,
For the Time being.

RECORDER.
ROBERT SINCLAIR, ... Esq. *York.*

CITY COUNSEL.
J. P. HEYWOOD, ... Esq. *Wakefield.*
SAMUEL WILLIAM NICOL, .. Esq. *York.*

ALDERMEN.
THOMAS SMITH, ... Esq. *York.*
SIR W. M. MILNER, ... Bart. *Nun-Appleton.*
THOMAS WILSON, ... Esq. *York and Fulford.*
WILLIAM HOTHAM, ... Esq. *York.*
WILLIAM ELLIS, ... Esq. *York and Fulford-Field.*
JOHN KILBY, ... Esq. *York.*
ROBERT STOCKTON, ... Esq. *York.*
ROBERT RHODES, ... Esq. *York.*
SAMUEL WORMALD, ... Esq. *York.*
  LORD MAYOR, 1809.
GEORGE PEACOCK, ... Esq. *York.*
THE HON. LAWRENCE DUNDAS, *Marske-Hall.*
WILLIAM BAYLDON, ... Esq. *York.*
GEORGE TOWNEND, ... Esq. *York.*

CLERK OF THE PEACE.
RICHARD TOWNEND, Esq, *York.*

TREASURER.
WILLIAM ELLIS, Esq. *York.*

CORONERS.
THOMAS HUNT, ... *York.*
HENRY BREARY, ... *York.*

CITY AND AINSTY.

CHIEF CONSTABLES.

JOSEPH KIRK, ... *Acomb.*
THOMAS BEAL, ... *Dringhouses.*
WILLIAM BAYNES, ... *York,*
For the CITY OF YORK.

SERJEANTS AT MACE, AND BAILIFFS.

JOSEPH CLAYTON,   *York.*
GEORGE RYLAH,   *York.*

BAILIFF AT LARGE, WHO RESIDES IN THE AINSTY.

WILLIAM WALKER, ... *York,*

SESSIONS

Are held on the Friday in the same Week, as the Sessions in the three Ridings.

ASSIZES

Commence on Saturday three-weeks, after Hilary-Term ends; and on Saturday before the seventh Sunday after Trinity.

LIBERTY OF ST. PETER.

NAMES OF THE MAGISTRATES.

BARNARD, H. BOLDERO, .. Clerk, *Cave-Castle.*
BROOKSBANK, B. .... Esq. *Healaugh-Hall.*
CROFT, ROBERT, ... Clerk, *Rowley.*
DICKENS, HENRY JOHN ... Esq. *York.*
DEALTRY, WILLIAM, ... Clerk, *Wigginton.*
EGLIN THOMAS, ... Clerk, *Stillingfleet.*
ELLIOT, ROBERT, ... Clerk, *Wheldrake.*
ELLIS, JOHN, ... Clerk, *Strensall.*
EYRE, JOHN, ... Clerk,
KELLY, GEORGE D. .... Clerk,
MARKHAM, GEORGE, ... D. D. *York.*
MARKHAM, ROBERT, ... Clerk, *Bolton-Percy.*
PLUMER, HALL, ... Esq. *Bilton-Hall.*
READ, T. C. R. .... Clerk, *Sandhutton.*
SEDGWICK, LEONARD, ... Clerk, *Brafferton.*
RICE, HON. EDWARD, ... Clerk, *Sutton-Forest.*
WADDILOVE, R. D. .... D. D. *Ripon.*

CHIEF BAILIFF.

THOMAS PLUMMER, Esq. .... *York.*

CLERK OF THE PEACE.

CHRISTOPHER NEWSTEAD, Esq. *York.*

STEWARD OF THE COURT OF PLEAS, &c.

HENRY JOHN DICKINS, Esq. ..... *York.*
CHRISTOPHER NEWSTEAD Esq. ..... *York.*
UNDER STEWARD.

CORONERS.

HENRY BREARY, ... *York.*
WILLIAM UMPLEBY, ... *Heslington.*
GEORGE CONYERS, ... *Great-Driffield.*

LIBERTY OF ST. PETER.

CHIEF CONSTABLES.

WILLIAM UMPLEBY, ... Heslington.
WILLIAM SUTCLIFFE, ... Brotherton.
WILLIAM COOKE, ... Pocklington.
THOMAS HESSAY, ... Bishop-Wilton.
WILLIAM TAYLOR, ... Husthwaite.

DEPULY BAILIFF.

THOMAS HARRISON, ... York.

DIRECTIONS FOR WARRANTS, ON WRITS.

To the Chief Bailiff of the liberty of St. Peter, York, and his Deputies.

SESSIONS

Are held on the Saturday in the same Week, as the City and Ainsty.

RIVERS.

The AIR, or ARE has its source from above Malham, about 5½ miles N. E. of Settle, which runs south by Kirkby, Airton, Calton, Conistone, Gargrave, and passes by Skipton, where it runs by the side of the Leeds and Liverpool Canal, by Keighley and Bingley to Leeds, passing through which place, and running to Castleford, about 3 miles N. W. of Ferrybridge, it receives the Calder, then passes by Brotherton, Ferrybridge, Snaith, Rawcliffe, and collecting, during its course, many tributary streams, joins the Ouse below Airmyn, 3 miles S. W. of Howden.

The CALDER flows on the borders of this County and Lancashire, and enters the former at Todmorden, 12 miles west of Halifax, passes by Elland, Kirklees, Dewsbury, Sandall, Wakefield, and runs into the Air at Castleford.

The DEARN rises N. W. of Barnsley, a little above Bretton-Dikes, and passes by Darton, Barnsley, Darfield, Bolton, Adwicke, and joins the Don, near Conisbrough.

The DERWENT takes its rise in the North-Riding, a little north of Harwood-Dale, about 4 miles distant from the east-coast, and takes a southerly direction parallel to the coast, until it comes near Ganton, there it takes a west and afterwards a south-west direction, and passes by the town of Malton, to which it is navigable from the Humber, for vessels of 25 tons burthen.—It is the boundary between the North and East-Ridings, from its junction with the little river Hertford, until it arrives near Stamford-Bridge, where it enters the East-Riding, and passing by Elvington, Bubwith, Wressle, joins the Ouse at Barmby.

The DON takes its rise west of Penistone, on the borders of Cheshire, and passes by Wortley, Sheffield, Rotherham, Conisbrough, Doncaster, Barnby and Fishlake, leaving Thorne, about 1 mile on the East; after which it runs north towards Cowick, near to which place it divides into two streams, both of which are soon lost; one in the Air, near Rawcliffe, and the other in the Ouse, near Goole.—It is navigable nearly to Sheffield.—Over this River, between Snaith and Thorne, there is a wooden bridge which turns upon a pivot, and affords a passage for the numerous Shipping employed in the inland trade.

The FOSS, a small stream which rises near the western end of the Howardian-Hills, in the North-Riding, passes by Stillington, Haxby, and joins the Ouse at York.—It was made navigable, by a subscription of £25,000, in 1793.

The HULL takes its rise in the Wolds, not far from Driffield, E. R. pursues a southern course, and passing the town of Beverley, to which it is united by a Canal, falls into the Humber at Hull, contributing to form the Port.—A canal from Great-Driffield communicates with this river.

The HUMBER is formed by the junction of the Ouse and Trent; the former having first received the Nidd, Wharfe, Derwent, and Air. It divides Yorkshire from Lincolnshire, and falls into the German Ocean at Spurn-Head.—It has a canal communication with the Mersey, Dee, Ribble, Severn, Thames, and Avon.

The NIDD has its rise at the upper-end of Nidderdale, about 3 miles N. E. of Kettlewell; after running a considerable distance from its fountain, enters the earth, by a wide and rocky cavern, called Goydon-Pot-Hole; then taking a subterraneous course of some miles, again emerges to the light by two issues, whose waters are soon united, a little below Middlesmoor, and passing by Ramsgill, Pateleybridge, Hampsthwaite, Killinghall, Ripley, Knaresborough, Ribston, Walshford, Cowthorpe, and Nun-Monkton, where it empties itself into the Ouse.

The OUSE, a name given to the river Ure, after its junction with the river Swale, about 3 miles below Boroughbridge, whence it proceeds by Nun-Monkton, to York; and passing by Naburn, Nun-Appleton, Cawood, Selby, Barnby, Airmyn, Hooke, Goole, and Whitgift, receives the Trent, where it forms the Humber, having, during its course, received the rivers Nidd, Foss, Wharfe, Derwent, Air, and many other tributary streams.

The RIBBLE rises in the wapentake of Ewcross, about 11 miles north of Settle; it runs south by Horton, Settle, Gisburn-Park, Clitheroe, Mitton, crosses Lancashire, and falls into the Irish Sea, below Preston.

The RYE rises in Snilesworth, N. R. passes through Bilsdale, by Rivaulx-Abbey, Helmsley, Butterwick, Wycomb, below which place it runs into the Derwent, having previously received the Dove, and Costa.—It gives name to the wapentake of Rydale.

The SKELL rises a few miles north of Pateleybridge; it passes by Grantley, Fountain's-Abbey, through that part of Ripon called Skelgate, below which it empties itself into the Ure.—It is a small river, but of great utility to the inhabitants of Ripon, they being well supplied with excellent water, by means of an engine erected by W. Askwith, Esq. by which water is conveyed into every house, at a small annual rent.

The TEES rises between the counties of Westmoreland and Durham, beyond the north-west extremity of the North-Riding, and taking an easterly direction near Cronkley, divides it from the county of Durham through its whole extent, and falls into the German Ocean below Stockton; it is navigable for vessels of large burthen from the Ocean to Yarm, where the spring tide rises 7 feet.

The SWALE rises near Wild-Boar-Fell, on the Borders of Westmoreland, after which it passes through a vale from thence, called Swale-Dale, by Richmond, Catterick, Ellerton, Langton, Morton, Maunby, at which place there is a ferry, Skipton-Bridge, Topcliffe, Helperby, and runs into the Ure at Myton.

The Swale, the Esk, and the Rye, rise and flow, for their whole course, within the North-Riding; though considerable streams, they are scarce capable of navigation, for having their sources in very mountainous countries, they are shallow, rapid, and, as well as other streams in this Riding except the Wisk alone, subject to sudden, violent and frequent floods.—An Act was some years since obtained for rendering the Swale navigable to Morton, with a branch up Cotbeck* to Thirsk, and another up Bedale-beck to Bedale; but the navigation was never completed.—The benefits arising from, and the necessity of such a Canal, or one up the Wiske, which was surveyed some very few years ago, must be evident to the most careless observer.

The URE rises on the borders of Westmoreland; passes by Askrigg, Middleham, Masham, Tanfield, Ripon, and Boroughbridge; where after being joined by the Swale at Myton, passes by Ouseburn, where it changes its name from Ure to Ouse, and proceeds to York.—It is navigable with the aid of a short Canal for Vessels of Thirty Tons as far as Ripon, W. R. where, on account of the rapidity of the stream, all prospect of navigation ceases

The WHARFE rises above Oughtershaw, and runs by Becknrmonds, Deepdale, Yokenthwaite, Hubberholme, Buckden, Starbottom, Kettlewell, Conistone, Burnsall, Appletrewick, Barden-Tower, Bolton Abbey, Ilkley, Otley, Arthington, Harewood, crosses the great north-road at Wetherby, passes by Thorp-Arch, Tadcaster, and joins the Ouse from York at Nun-Appleton.

The WISK rises on the breast of the Hills near Osmotherley, taking a southerly and afterwards a northerly direction as far as Staddlebridge, leaving the Monastery of Mount-Grace on the right, where it changes its course westerly,

* This Brook is generally called Codbeck, and even so long since as 1612, by Drayton, in his Polyolbion; but it evidently derives its name from the British word, Couæ, signifying Woody; so Cottæ Alpes, to distinguish them from Græ or Craggy Alpes.

passes by West-Rounton, Appleton, and Smeaton, then veering to the south, passes by Danby, Yafforth, Otterington, and Kirby, a mile below which it empties itself into the Swale.

CANALS.

The RIVER FOSS NAVIGATION proceeds from the junction of the river Foss, with the Ouse at York. Its course is the river Foss as far as Farlington-Common; thence, by a new cut, to Marton-Lordship, and the river Foss to Stillington-Mill; the total length is about 13 miles.

The LEEDS and LIVERPOOL CANAL begins out of the River Mersey, at low water, just at the lower extremity of the town of Liverpool, by Bank-hall, and goes over the River Alt to Mill-house, it then takes a large half circle round the town of Ormskirk, and crosses Toadbrook, near Newborough, whence it proceeds by the Douglas Navigation to Wigan; from which place goods are forwarded by land to Blackburn about 20 miles, the Canal at present being cut no further; it then proceeds in a circular course to Burnley and Colne to Foulbridge, where a bason is cut to supply the Canal, of which it is the head. The Canal here begins to fall to Leeds, and goes from Foulbridge, by Salterford, East-Marton, and crosses the River Air, near Gargrave, by Thoralby, Stirton, and the town of Skipton, by Bradley, Kildwick, near the town of Keighley, and by Bingley; a little below which it crosses the River Air again, passes Shepley, and takes a semi-circular course round the Idle, near Apperleybridge, Kirkstall Abbey, by Burley and Holbeck, to the town of Leeds, making in the whole, a course of 130 miles, with 838 feet fall. There is also a collateral cut from near Shepley to Bradford.

The HUDDERSFIELD CANAL joins Sir John Ramsden's Canal on the south-side of Huddersfield, and taking a westerly course, runs parallel with the River Colne, which it passes twice, passing Longwood, Slaithwaite, and Marsden; from Marsden, under Pule-moss and Brunn-Top, there is a tunnel of nearly three miles and a half long, which brings the Canal to Rasp-Mill, on the Digglewater, and within about two miles of Dubcross; passing which, it takes the rout of the River Tame, the windings of which it frequently intersects, and passes within one mile of Lidgate, by Mossley, Steyleybridge, and there joins the Ashton and Oldham Canal on the south-side of Ashton, being a course of nineteen miles and five furlongs, with 770 feet lockage.

The BARNSLEY CANAL joins the River Calder, below the town of Wakefield, and passes Crofton, Felkirk, Royston, and Barnsley, whence it takes a circular course to Barnbybridge, near the town of Cawthorn, the length about 14 miles. There are several rail-ways to the Canal from Barnsley, and others from Barnby-bridge. The fall from the junction with the Dearn and Dove canal, is 120 feet to the River Calder.

The DEARN and DOVE CANAL commences from the cut which has been made for the accommodation of the River Don navigation, between Swinton, and Mexbrough, and proceeds by Wath, Wombwell, and Ardsley, to near Barnsley Canal, which joins the River Calder. There are two small branches, one parallel with Knolbeck-brook, at the Iron-Work at Cob-car-Ing; the other along the head stream of the River Don, to Worsbrough-bridge; with a proposed extension of this Branch, near one mile and a half, to Rockcliffe-bridge, adjoining the grounds of Earl Stratford, at Wentworth-Castle.

The branch to Cob-car-Ing is one mile and three quarters, and is level, by means of some deep cutting at the extremity. The branch to Worsbrough-bridge, is one mile five furlongs in length.

The STAINFORTH and KEADBY CANAL commences at the River Don, about a mile to the west of Fishlake, and runs parallel with the River opposite to Thorne; whence in a line due east, it passes Crowle, and Keadby, where it joins the River Trent. There is a branch about a mile across Thorn's Common, to a place called Hangman-hill, which joins the River Don. The total length of this Canal is between fourteen and fifteen miles, and running through a part of the fenny country has little elevation, and no lockage, except out of the Rivers at the extremities.

The CALDER NAVIGATION commences at the junction of the Air and Calder at Castleford, passes by Wakefield, to Horbury-Bridge, Dewsbury, Cooper-Bridge, Brighouse, Elland, and Salterhebble, where goods are left for Halifax, Sowerby-bridge, and then joins the Rochdale and Manchester canal; and passes by Hebden-Bridge, to Rochdale and Manchester.—There is a branch from Cooper-Bridge, to Huddersfield of 3 miles, called Sir John Ramsden's canal, which joins the Huddersfield and Ashton canal.

The AIR and CALDER NAVIGATION, commences at Selby from the river Ouse, and proceeds by Haddlesey, Knottingley, Ferrybridge, Brotherton, and joins the Air at Castleford, and whence it proceeds up the Air to Leeds, where it joins the Leeds and Liverpool Canal.

Errata et Addenda.

Fallsgrave, *see* Wallsgrave—At Manfield, *add* the seat of the Hon. and Rev. James Arthur Cochrane—at Tanfield-Hall, *add* the seat of William Fendall, Esq.—at Redmire, *add* Elm-House, the seat of Thomas Other, Esq.—at Summer Lodge *for* ¼ miles, *read* ½ a mile—at Warthill, *read* parishes of Warthill and Holtby—at Burton, Hum, *add* Population 102.—at Mickleby, *add* Pop 176—at Seamor, *add* Pop. 515—at Thornton-on-the-Hill, *add* Pop. 71—*omit* the Pop. at Ingleby 253, Limber-Hill 345, Newton-Dale 151, and Fremington 879—at Bedale, *for* 12 from Middleham, *read* 10.

At Catfoss, *for* Mrs. Bethell, *read* Richard Bethell, Esq. —at Etton, *for* Lady Legard, *read* Sir Thomas Legard, Bart. —at Thortleby, *add* the Population 44—at Beverley, amongst the Principal Inns, *add* the Tiger.

BRADLEY-MILLS, in the parish of Huddersfield, Agbrigg-division of the wapentake of Agbrigg and Morley, liberty of the Honour of Pontefract ; *(the seat of Thomas Atkinson, Esq.)* 1 mile from Huddersfield, 9 from Halifax.

FARSIDE-MOOR, in the parish of Mirfield, Agbrigg-division of the wapentake of Agbrigg and Morley; *(the seat of George Webster, Esq.)* 3 miles from Dewsbury, 5 from Huddersfield, 5 from Wakefield.

HEBDEN-BRIDGE, in the parish of Halifax, Morley-division of the wapentake of Agbrigg and Morley; 8 miles from Halifax, 10 from Rochdale, *(Lanc.) Fairs*, Whit-Monday, and September 25, for Horned Cattle, Horses, Sheep, &c.

SPRING-GROVE, in the parish of Huddersfield, Agbrigg-division of the wapentake of Agbrigg and Morley ; *(the seat of William Fenton, Esq.)* 1 mile from Huddersfield, 8 from Halifax.

For Burn-Cross, *see* Farn-Cross—for Bay-Hall, *see* May-Hall—at Blake-Hall, *add* seat of Joshua Ingham, Esq. and *read* 4 miles from Huddersfield—Heaton-Lodge, the seat of General Barnard, *see* Coln-Bridge—At Clapham, *add* No Market, Fairs, Ash Wednesday, May 2, July 31, and October 2, for Horned Cattle, Sheep, &c.—at Burton, *add* Fair, Whit-Monday, for Cattle, &c.—at Buckden, *add* Fair October 12, for Cattle, &c.—for Birkley, *read* Birkby, the seat of Thomas Holroyd, Esq.—at Dean-head, *read* 5 miles from Huddersfield, 5 from Halifax—at Doncaster, amongst Bankers Names, for Few, *read* Tew—for Burnt or Braint Gates, *read* Bond-Gates-School—at Bradfield, and Bradfield Nether, *for* Rotherham, *read* Sheffield—at Egerton, *read* 1 mile from Huddersfield, 7 from Halifax—at Bradley-Hall *read* 6¼ miles from Halifax—for Follyfoot-Lodge, *read* Rudding-Hall—at Giggleswick, *read* 17 from Kirby-Lonsdale—for Bradsey, *read* Bardsey.

Lightning Source UK Ltd.
Milton Keynes UK
UKHW02f1807190718
326001UK00007B/159/P